Research T
for
Social Scie

UNIVERSITY OF
GLOUCESTERSHIRE
at Cheltenham and Gloucester

# Research Training for Social Scientists

## A Handbook for Postgraduate Researchers

edited by
DAWN BURTON

SAGE Publications
London • Thousand Oaks • New Delhi

First published 2000

SAGE Publications Ltd
6 Bonhill Street
London EC2A 4PU

SAGE Publications Inc.
2455 Teller Road
Thousand Oaks, California 91320

SAGE Publications India Pvt Ltd
32, M-Block Market
Greater Kailash – I
New Delhi 110 048

**British Library Cataloguing in Publication data**

A catalogue record for this book is available from the British Library

ISBN 0 7619 6350 2
ISBN 0 7619 6351 0 (pbk)

**Library of Congress catalog record available**

Typeset by Mayhew Typesetting, Rhayader, Powys
Printed in Great Britain by The Cromwell Press Ltd, Trowbridge, Wiltshire

# CONTENTS

Notes on contributors        viii

Acknowledgements        xii

Foreword by Robert G. Burgess        xiii

Introduction        xiv

**Part I    Philosophy of the Social Sciences**        1

1    Philosophy of Science and its Relevance for the
Social Sciences        5
*Peter K. Smith*

2    Questions of Hermeneutics: Beyond Empiricism and
Post-modernism        21
*Nick Stevenson*

3    Feminist Methodologies for Social Researching        33
*Sue Webb*

4    Race and Racism        49
*Peter Jackson*

**Part II    Ethical and Legal Issues in Social Science
Research**        59

5    Ethical Principles        61
*Gerry Kent*

6    The Power of Research        68
*Iain Crow*

7    Informed Consent        81
*Gerry Kent*

8   Can the Law Prescribe an Ethical Framework for Social
Science Research?   88
*D.M.R. Townend*

9   Ethics in the Field   97
*Anne Celnick*

10   How does Substantive Law Currently Regulate Social
Science Research?   109
*D.M.R. Townend*

**Part III   Getting Started**   135

11   Using Literature to Support Research   137
*Dawn Burton*

**Part IV   Qualitative Methods: Design, Data Collection and
Analysis**   153

12   Theory and Method in Qualitative Research   156
*Simon Holdaway*

13   Participatory Research as Emancipatory Method:
Challenges and Opportunities   167
*Wanda Thomas Bernard*

14   The Use of Focus Groups in Social Science Research   186
*Caroline Oates*

15   Qualitative Interviewing   196
*Matt Stroh*

16   The Use of Case Studies in Social Science Research   215
*Dawn Burton*

17   Computers and Qualitative Data Analysis: To Use or
Not to Use . . .?   226
*Matt Stroh*

18   Writing up Qualitative Data   244
*Peter Jackson*

**Part V   Using Computers for Qualitative Data Analysis**   253

19   Using NUD•IST Version 4: A Hands-on Lesson   257
*Matt Stroh*

**Part VI    Survey Research in the Social Sciences: Design
             and Data Collection**                          289

20   Design Issues in Survey Research                        292
     *Dawn Burton*

21   Sampling Strategies in Survey Research                  307
     *Dawn Burton*

22   Data Collection Issues in Survey Research               320
     *Dawn Burton*

23   Questionnaire Design                                    335
     *Dawn Burton*

24   Secondary Data Analysis                                 347
     *Dawn Burton*

**Part VII   Quantitative Data Analysis**                    361

25   Descriptive Statistics                                  363
     *Vernon Gayle*

26   Inferential Statistics                                  385
     *Vernon Gayle*

27   Getting Started                                         414
     *Vernon Gayle*

**Part VIII   Finishing Off: Writing, Presenting and
              Publishing**                                   421

28   Writing a Thesis                                        423
     *Dawn Burton*

29   Presentation Skills                                     437
     *H. Doug Watts and Paul White*

30   Getting Published                                       456
     *H. Doug Watts and Paul White*

References                                                   477

Index                                                        499

# NOTES ON CONTRIBUTORS

**Dawn Burton** was Director of Social Sciences Research Training at the University of Sheffield during the period 1994–1997. She has taught research methods to undergraduate and postgraduate students from a wide range of social science backgrounds in Britain and overseas. Dr Burton currently teaches marketing and research methods at the Business School, at the University of Leeds. Her research interests include critical perspectives on marketing theory, ethnicity and marketing and consumer financial behaviour. She is author of *Financial Services and the Consumer* (Routledge, 1994) and founding editor of a new journal published by Sage, *Marketing Theory*, which is committed to developing critical and alternative theoretical perspectives in marketing.

**Anne Celnick** began working for the probation service as a member of South Yorkshire Probation Service's research unit, but then qualified as a probation officer. She returned to research when she was seconded to evaluate a special probation project. That led to a doctorate, and in 1985 she became a research officer for South Yorkshire Probation Service. Anne was also a research advisor to the Association of Chief Officers of Probation before she retired in 1999.

**Iain Crow** is Lecturer in Research Methods in the Department of Law, University of Sheffield. He is a criminologist. He was formerly head of research for NACRO, a non-statutory organization working with offenders and actively engaged in the development of criminal justice policy. His research has often involved working with a range of community-based organizations concerned with offenders, drug users, the unemployed and the homeless.

**Vernon Gayle** is a lecturer in Sociology at Stirling University. He teaches research methods to undergraduates and postgraduates and has research interests in statistical modelling and the sociology of youth.

**Simon Holdaway** is Professor of Sociology in the Department of Sociological Studies, Sheffield University. Before appointment to Sheffield University he was a police officer for eleven years. His publications have mostly been about policing, especially police race relations, equal opportunities and the probation service. Among his publications are *The Radicalisation of British*

*Policing* (Macmillan, 1996) and *Resigners?: The Experience of Black and Asian Police Officers* (Macmillan, 1997).

**Peter Jackson** is Professor of Human Geography and co-Director of the Migration and Ethnicity Research Centre at Sheffield University. His research interests centre on the relationship between consumption and identity and the cultural politics of 'race' and racism. He teaches various aspects of social and cultural geography. Recent publications include *Maps of Meaning* (Routledge, 1992) and *Constructions of Race, Place, and Nation*, co-edited with Jan Penrose (UCL Press, 1993). He is co-editor of *Environment and Planning D: Society and Space*.

**Gerry Kent** is Lecturer in Clinical Psychology in the Department of Psychology at Sheffield University. His main teaching commitments are to clinical psychology trainees in the Clinical Psychology Unit, where he covers various aspects of research skills. His research interests concern the effects of health-care interventions on psychological well-being and ethical aspects of care and treatment, especially informed consent.

**Caroline Oates** joined the University of Sheffield's Management School as a lecturer in marketing in 1997. She holds a first degree in sociology and social policy from the University of Sheffield and a PhD from the Department of Sociological Studies, also at Sheffield. Her teaching and research interests include: marketing promotions and communication, consumer behaviour, research methods, children and advertising, recycling behaviour and the consumption of popular culture. Her publications include articles on the role of market information in the design process and women's magazines.

**Peter K. Smith** is Professor of Psychology at Goldsmiths College, University of London, having earlier been Professor at the University of Sheffield. Besides interests in the philosophy of science, he has researched extensively in the area of children's development and co-authored *Understanding Children's Behaviour* with Helen Cowie (Blackwells, 1988, 1991). His work on school bullying resulted in two books edited with Sonia Sharp, *School Bullying: Insights and Perspectives* and *Tackling Bullying in Your School* (both Routledge, 1994). He co-edited *Theories of Theories of the Mind* with Peter Carruthers (CUP, 1996).

**Nick Stevenson** is a lecturer in sociological studies at the University of Sheffield. His books include *Culture, Ideology and Socialism* (1995, Avebury), *Understanding Media Cultures* (1995, Sage) and *The Transformation of the Media* (Longman, 1999).

**Matt Stroh** is a lecturer in the School of Geography at the University of Leeds. His PhD entitled 'The Social Constructions of Green: Accessing

Popular Attitudes Towards the Environment' was undertaken in the Department of Geography at Sheffield University. The project was based on qualitative research methods and the computer package NUD•IST was used to assist in the analysis of the data.

**Wanda Thomas Bernard** is an associate professor at the Maritime School of Social Work, Dalhousie University, in Halifax, Canada. She is a graduate of the University of Sheffield and used a participatory research methodology for her PhD research. Wanda is particularly interested in community-based research and research in social work practice. A social work practitioner and educator, she is committed to engaging in research for empowerment and bridging the gap between academia and the communities.

**David Townend** is a lecturer in the department of Law at Sheffield University. His research interests are in the areas of Welfare Law – Housing, Family and Social Security Law – and Intellectual Property. He is also involved in the department's Free Legal Information Project. His research includes work on how children's best interests are determined in parental separation disputes. His present work is on the way in which intellectual property rights are and could be further used as security interests in loan financing.

**Doug Watts** is Reader in Geography and Director of the Human Geography postgraduate training programme at Sheffield University. He has supervised a number of successful PhD candidates over the last five years and has acted as external examiner of PhD theses in several UK universities. His research interests are in the economic restructuring of large manufacturing organizations and the impact of restructuring on the geography of industrial activity. Recently published papers include studies of the local economic and political environment in plant closure decisions. He is also the author of a standard text in the field, *Industrial Geography* (Longman, 1997).

**Sue Webb** is the Director of Part-time Women's Studies in the Division of Adult Continuing Education at Sheffield University where she teaches a number of courses on research methods and feminism. Her research interests include women, education and work and she has published various articles in these areas including 'Counter-arguments: an ethnographic look at "women and class"', in *Feminist Praxis* (L. Stanley ed., Routledge, 1990). More recently, she has been involved both as a practitioner and researcher in developments in widening access to higher education. Aspects of this research are discussed in her recent book, with J. Williams (eds), *Negotiating Access to Higher Education: The Discourse of Selectivity and Equity* (Open University Press).

**Paul White** is Professor of Geography at Sheffield University having taught there since 1974. He has also held temporary appointments at the universities of Oxford, Paris-Sorbonne, Zaragoza (Spain) and Cagliari (Italy). His research interests are in international migration and ethnicity, particularly relating to urban areas in Europe. He has supervised over fifteen successful PhD students, and has wide experience as an external examiner for doctorates in both the UK and France.

# ACKNOWLEDGEMENTS

When I was appointed as Director of Social Science Research Training at the University of Sheffield in 1994, it was my first full-time academic appointment. It was a considerable task for me to take on the responsibility for reorganizing, developing and managing a programme which involved significant numbers of research students drawn from sixteen different departments and research centres. The task would not have been possible without the help and support of a considerable number of my social science colleagues, some of whom have contributed to this book and from whom I learned a great deal. It is a testament to their supportive attitude towards research training and the view that experienced researchers should pass on their experiences, both good and bad, that this book was developed. It has taken an enormous amount of effort to get the text written and edited and I hope that everyone concerned thinks it has all been worthwhile. I sincerely wish to thank them all for their help, kindness and good humour. A special thanks must go to Katherine Steele who is still the administrator and secretary in the Social Sciences Research Training Office and who worked so diligently to keep the Office in order.

# FOREWORD

Research training has become a hallmark of doctoral work in the social sciences during the 1990s. In the early part of the decade attention was given to filling a gap in understanding and using research methodologies. The emphasis was on bringing all social scientists who held a research studentship from the Economic and Social Research Council (ESRC) up to a minimum standard whereby they became acquainted with a range of methodologies.

Such was the success of this form of doctoral training that many social scientists argued that these courses were an essential part of doctoral work for all students. The programmes on offer covered philosophy of the social sciences, quantitative and qualitative research strategies and methods, ethical issues of social research, strategies of data analysis and sessions on writing and dissemination.

Much of this material has been taught in the first year of doctoral training (for full-time students) or the first two years (for part-time students). The challenge for those who teach these courses has been to find an approach that covers the field while providing relevant material for the doctoral student. A further problem that looms large is whether the training courses provided are *postgraduate in level*.

In addressing these issues doctoral students and their teachers demand a range of suitable material. It is rare to find a comprehensive range of material on social research methodology brought together in one volume. Yet Dawn Burton has assembled a collection that provides a comprehensive discussion on a range of issues together with detailed bibliographies that will assist students to develop their knowledge in depth.

Overall, this volume provides a starting point for doctoral students who wish to embark on research training that is relevant for postgraduate study.

**Robert G. Burgess**
Vice-Chancellor, University of Leicester

Chairman, Postgraduate Training Board,
Economic & Social Research Council

# INTRODUCTION

This text is based on the Social Science Research Training Programme which was developed for first-year research students at the University of Sheffield. The chapters are based on distance learning units which were originally designed to fulfil the research training needs of part-time research students who were unable to attend the taught courses. The book provides guidance on research training which the Economic and Social Research Council (ESRC) believes is appropriate for first-year research students in all social science disciplines. Although it is clearly not the case that all students in British universities studying for a PhD are funded by the ESRC, or any other sponsor for that matter, the guidelines are considered to be the kitemark of quality and are therefore widely adhered to. Since the ESRC guidelines are extensively used in Britain as a benchmark for research training, the text is representative of research training practices in most British universities. The organization of the book reflects the knowledge and skills that are required of social scientists in order to become competent and effective researchers.

The text is written in an accessible style to meet the needs of students from a wide variety of social science backgrounds who often have highly varying degrees of research experience and expertise. The book is deliberately wide ranging in its coverage and specifically designed as a one-stop text. The range of training issues covered makes it distinctive and hopefully good value for money. The book is constructed so that it parallels the research process. It begins with some discussion of ethical and philosophical issues as they relate to social science research. Following this, students are taken through the process of using relevant literature to develop social research projects. Quantitative and qualitative data collection and analysis techniques are discussed in considerable depth. The final section includes material about how to write up and present research projects. The book therefore reflects the life cycle of the research project and will hopefully help students to develop their own research projects in addition to providing advice on particular aspects of researching for a PhD.

The extensive range of issues covered by the book make it distinctive, but this was not the reason behind the development of the text. It was the concern of many academics involved in the research training programme that there was not an appropriate text available to meet the needs of research students. Many of the existing texts provide a very prescriptive analysis of the process of undertaking research. This approach is not particularly useful for research students because it can often give the impression that research is a relatively unproblematic activity. This is clearly an unrealistic view and one which needs counteracting. The purpose of this text is to provide readers with a realistic view of how social science research is conducted. This includes owning up to mistakes so that others can learn from them in addition to documenting good practice. In summary we all hope that the book will go some way to making the research process more transparent. While the text is specifically designed for research students, we anticipate that the book will be useful for all students who are trying to get to grips with the exciting and demanding task of undertaking research in the social sciences.

# PART I

# PHILOSOPHY OF THE SOCIAL SCIENCES

Research students often question why they are required to have an understanding of the philosophy of the social sciences literature as part of their research training. Training is often associated with the acquisition of research skills that will help students collect, process and analyse data, and not to study philosophical issues which are often regarded as marginal and rather a waste of time. According to this interpretation, social science research skills should be acquired and then applied as though they were the skills of a craft. What this view fails to acknowledge is that philosophical assumptions about human nature and how society is conceptualized are directly related to issues about social research, whether that be the nature and status of data that is collected and the validity of the methods by which data is analysed, interpreted and understood. To quote Hughes (1993: 11) 'Whether they may be treated as such or not, research instruments and methods cannot be divorced from theory; as research tools they operate only within a given set of assumptions about the nature of society, the nature of human beings, the relationship between the two and how they may be known.'

Methodological debates in the social sciences cannot be understood without reference to the wider cultural setting in which those discussions take place. It is also arguably the case that the social sciences have not been as successful in their ability to produce analyses of the social world as the natural sciences have of the natural world. It is therefore not surprising that a significant amount of energy has been devoted to comparing the methodology of the 'natural' and the social sciences. Whether the social sciences are in fact 'sciences' is a controversial issue. Peter Smith addresses this debate in the first chapter by assessing the philosophy of science literature and exploring its relevance for the social sciences. A number of features are discussed, specifically: what is meant by philosophy of science; whether social scientists can productively apply methods used by scientists, whether they can be modified in some way, or if they should be rejected outright.

The focus of Chapter 2 by Nick Stevenson is hermeneutics. Although rather a grand word, hermeneutics is simply another way of referring to the process of interpretation. Interpretavist or 'humanistic' views of social behaviour are in direct opposition to positivistic, 'scientific' notions of human behaviour which reduce social life to the interaction of variables. The negative consequences of the positivistic view of human behaviour are that it provides only a partial account of social life and distorts the nature of human interaction in profound ways. Nick discusses the ways in which understanding and interpretation are bound up with linguistic practices; the impact of symbolic culture on the nature of interpretation; and ways in which hermeneutics are likely to become more rather than less important in the future.

In Chapter 3 Sue Webb evaluates some of the main issues associated with feminist methodologies for social researching. Some of the main philosophical issues raised by feminists about social research and why feminist discussions should be perceived as an important contribution to contemporary debates are considered. How feminists have distinguished their research activities from others and reasons why they have taken this turn are also evaluated, along with feminist debates about quantitative and qualitative methods and the issue of methodological pluralism.

Peter Jackson's chapter on race and racism provides a welcome contribution to the philosophy of the social sciences debate, since it is an area which is very often neglected. A focal point of the discussion involves evaluating essentialist versus social constructionist approaches to 'race'. He argues against an essentialist view of 'race' which is highly biologically deterministic, in favour of understanding 'race' as being socially constructed across time and space. He suggests that the concepts of race and racism cannot be divorced from the wider politics of 'race' in society which in turn raises questions about the neutrality of social science researchers and the need for more committed approaches while simultaneously retaining intellectual integrity. This should be read in conjunction with Chapter 13 by Wanda Thomas Bernard, who deliberately chose participative research methods because of their emancipatory potential in her research with black men in Britain and Canada.

## SUPPLEMENTARY READING

Anderson, R.J., Hughes, J.A. and Sharrock, W.W. (1986) *Philosophy and the Human Sciences*. London: Croom Helm.
Bauman, Z. (1978) *Hermeneutics and Social Science*. London: Hutchinson.
Hammersley, M. (1992) *Social Research Philosophy, Politics and Practice*. London: Sage.
Harding, S. (1987) *Feminism and Methodolgy*. Milton Keynes: Open University Press.
Hughes, J. (1993) *The Philosophy of Social Research*. London: Longman.
Miles, R. (1993) *Racism After 'Race Relations'*. London: Routledge.

Norris, C. (1990) *What's Wrong with Post-modernism*. London: Harvester.

Solomos, J. (1993) *Race and Racism in Contemporary Britain*. London: Macmillan.

Stanley, L. (1990) *Feminist Praxis*. London: Routledge.

Stanley, L. and Wise, S. (1993) *Breaking Out Again: Feminist Ontology and Epistemology*. London: Routledge.

# PHILOSOPHY OF SCIENCE AND ITS RELEVANCE FOR THE SOCIAL SCIENCES

*Peter K. Smith*

Are the social sciences really sciences, or is this a misnomer? In the UK, the Social Science Research Council (SSRC) had to change its name to the Economic and Social Research Council (ESRC), in part because of a belief in government at the time that the social sciences were not sciences. And academics also debate these issues. This is not just a matter of a name – it affects how we carry out our research and what we think is the status of 'facts', 'evidence' and 'theories'. These are issues which confront all researchers. At times, we may get by unthinkingly, doing as colleagues have done previously; but we may also be challenged – by new ideas or by other disciplines – and these issues will come to the forefront.

As part of such considerations, it is important for social scientists to understand something of the 'philosophy of science' even as it applies to the traditional 'hard' sciences, the physical sciences especially, and the biological and earth sciences. After all, a significant part of the debate about procedures in the social sciences is whether we can profitably apply – or whether instead we routinely misapply – methods and procedures from the physical sciences. Often, too, the procedures of the physical sciences are misunderstood. So, it is very relevant to know how the traditional sciences work, or are thought to work, whether we as social scientists then imitate these methods, modify them, or reject them.

In this chapter I will define what is meant by Philosophy of Science and give a brief historical survey of the main issues. I will review the traditional 'inductivist' view of science, the hypothetico-deductive view of Popper, and the alternative views of Kuhn and Lakatos, including more recent critiques and ideas (see also Chalmers, 1982; Hacking, 1981; Losee, 1980).

## WHAT IS MEANT BY PHILOSOPHY OF SCIENCE?

The philosophy of science is concerned with questions such as:

1   What characteristics distinguish science from non-science?
2   What procedures should scientists follow?

3    What conditions must be satisfied for a scientific explanation to be correct?
4    What is the cognitive status of scientific laws and principles? (See Losee, 1980: 2.)

These are fundamental questions: (1) and (2) are definitional for the scientific method; (3) and (4) may seem more abstract, but they too are fundamental.

Question (4) was a matter of life and death in the case of Galileo. Traditionally (and following obvious perceptual information) people believed that the sun revolved round the earth. Following the work of Copernicus, Galileo (1564–1642) argued that in fact the earth revolved round the sun. This brought him into conflict with the Catholic Church at the time. In 1615 Cardinal Bellarmine corresponded with Galileo about this. It is permissible, he said to Galileo, for you to argue that the earth revolving around the sun is a possible mathematical model; in fact, it is even permissible for you to argue that it is the best model at the moment; but you must not say that it is actually, physically, true. Despite this warning, Galileo continued to assert that it was true. In 1633 the Inquisition condemned Galileo's views, which he subsequently recanted. Only in 1992, after 359 years, did the Catholic Church admit it was wrong to condemn him. This was a debate about the status of a scientific law. Interestingly, most modern philosophers of science would accept the 'best model' compromise without qualms, rather than insisting on an actual physical truth which, ultimately, is provisional rather than certain.

As a discipline, the philosophy of science is related to other areas, notably:

- *the history of science* – how science has actually developed, whatever the 'ideal' science might do;
- *the sociology of knowledge* – how social structures and institutions, scientific societies and journals and the social networks of individual scientists affect the growth of science;
- *the psychology of research* – how individual scientists develop ways of thinking about and interpreting the world; pressures for conformity and bursts of creativity.

Of twentieth-century philosophers of science, Kuhn has reached out to the history of science and the sociology of knowledge. However, the origins of the philosophy of science go back long before the twentieth century.

## HISTORICAL ORIGINS OF THE PHILOSOPHY OF SCIENCE

Systematic writing about the philosophy of science can be dated back to the ancient Greeks. Aristotle (384–322 BC) provided a foundation for speculating about 'the nature of things' which had an enduring influence. In particular, he had an 'inductive-deductive' view of how we obtained systematic knowledge. According to this, we first 'induce' certain regularities in the world around us. For example, we might notice the regularity of flowering plants in springtime; we 'deduce' that next spring the plants will flower again. This very simple example could be made more sophisticated by induced explanatory principles such as the effects of rain and sun on plants. We could then deduce that a drought or lack of sunshine will prevent or delay plant growth in the spring.

Aristotle also started the consideration of what is meant by causality. Looking at the regularities or 'correlations' in observed phenomena, he clearly distinguished between accidental correlations and causal correlations. As an example of an accidental correlation, at the time of year when plants start blossoming, birds start singing (plant blossom does not cause birds to sing; bird song does not cause plants to blossom; both are caused by the increase in temperature and hours of daylight during spring). As an example of a causal correlation, when we feel the wind blowing strongly, we see clouds scudding across the sky (the same wind which blows on us also causes the clouds to move). However, Aristotle was not an experimentalist. As we shall see, the role of experiments was a gradual, later development in the philosophy of science, linked to the greater importance given to deductivism.

The works of Aristotle and other Greek philosophers from the classical period were translated from Greek into Latin and Arabic (since Arab philosophers kept these works alive during the European 'dark ages'). Latin translations of Aristotle's writings on science became available to European philosophers as learning revived during the twelfth and thirteenth centuries.

Roger Bacon (1214–1292), for example, affirmed Aristotle's 'inductive-deductive' pattern of scientific inquiry, but took it one stage further. Bacon argued that the factual base available for induction to operate on could be augmented by active experimentation on the world. At the time there was much interest in magnetism (and its possible uses in compasses and for navigation). What happens if you break a magnetic bar or needle? You get two magnets, each with its own N and S poles. These simple kinds of 'experimentation' would be useful, Bacon argued. Note, however, that Bacon was not testing any theory here; rather, this was experimentation to 'see what happens'. Bacon and a few other philosophers at the time did begin to point to the need to test exploratory principles arrived at by induction, but this did not proceed very far.

In fact, another tradition from classical Greek writings laid the foundation for hypothesis testing and experimentation. Euclid (c.300 BC) and Archimedes (287–212 BC) developed the idea of axioms, or hypotheses, in mathematics and geometry. Given certain axioms, then certain consequences follow – hypothesis and deduction. But this approach was used in the abstract realm of mathematics. In the seventeeth century, Descartes

(1596–1650) elaborated this hypothetico-deductive method and laid the groundwork for its application in science. But it was not until the twentieth century that this hypothetico-deductive approach became central in the understanding of science, together with a full appreciation of the role of experimentation in actively testing hypotheses.

## THE TRADITIONAL 'INDUCTIVIST' VIEW OF SCIENCE

Aristotle's view came under more critical scrutiny as the philosophy of science developed in modern Europe. By and large, the inductivist view of science held sway and was further augmented. Among many contributions, we can take John Stuart Mill (1806-1873) as a prominent example from the nineteenth century. Mill argued that there were four primary inductive methods which could be used (for example, to distinguish accidental and causal correlations). These were agreement, difference, concomitant variations and residues.

As a fictional illustration of this in the social sciences, suppose we have induced a correlation between having the death penalty for murder and a reduced number of homicides. According to Mill, we could infer causation – that hanging deters homicides: if there are few homicides at times/places where the death penalty is enforced (*agreement*); there are many homicides at times/places where the death penalty is not enforced (*difference*); there are fewer homicides when the death penalty is enforced strictly and more when it is interpreted more leniently (*concomitant variations*); and presence/absence or variation in other possible causes (e.g. unemployment, marital instability) do not affect the number of homicides (*residues*).

Mill argued that the processes of inference and induction, could lead us to deduce causal relations. If these were verified – if they explained observations and other causal relations did not – then we could regard the hypothesis as verified. Mill cited Newton's inverse square law of force (that the gravitational attraction between two bodies reduces as the square of the distance between them – a crucial part of explaining planetary motion) as an example of a completely verified law. This law could then be considered 'true' in some absolute sense.

Mill's work epitomizes the 'traditional' or 'inductivist' view of the scientific method. In brief, this holds that science proceeds by collecting factual data through observation and by experimentation which serves to increase the observational data base. By inductive methods, generalizations and causal laws could be arrived at. In principle, induced laws could be completely verified if all the deductions from them were correct. This view held sway in many quarters well into the twentieth century. For example, Karl Pearson (who developed the well-known product–moment correlation coefficient) wrote: 'the classification of facts and the formation of absolute judgments upon the basis of this classification . . . *essentially sum up the aim and method of modern science*' (1892: 6; author emphasis).

A crucial part of the traditional view is that *hypothesis follows observation* (this refers to procedures, question 2 of our four questions at the start of the chapter). It also argues that *we can achieve completely verifiable, 'true' theories* (this refers to questions 3 and 4). Yet few modern philosophers of science accept either of these conclusions. In fact, most would argue that *hypothesis precedes observation* and that *we cannot achieve completely verifiable, 'true' theories*. Thus, the 'traditional' view has come to be radically overthrown.

## THE HYPOTHETICO-DEDUCTIVE VIEW OF POPPER

Karl Popper (1902–1994) has been one of the most well-known philosophers of science to attack the traditional view and to establish an alternative, hypothetico-deductive view (Popper, 1959, 1963, 1976, 1979, 1986; see Magee, 1982). Another well-known figure who has propounded similar views to Popper, is Peter Medawar (1915–1988). This hypothetico-deductive view also has a long intellectual history and as an example we can consider statements by Charles Darwin in the 1860s (quoted in Medawar, 1969: 11): 'I have an old belief that a good observer really means a good theorist' and 'how odd it is that anyone should not see that all observations must be for or against some view if it is to be of any service'.

From Darwin's notebooks we know that he was formulating ideas about evolution well before the publication of *The Origin of Species* in 1859. Even during the voyage of HMS *Beagle* (1831–6) he may have been directing his observations towards testing ideas that were fermenting in his mind. As Medawar (1969) put it, 'we cannot browse over the field of nature like cows at pasture'. If Darwin had gathered data randomly, this would not have provided nearly such good evidence for natural selection as the systematic data he did collect – on where fossils were found, on how the beaks of finches varied in different habitats, and so forth – which allowed him to confirm or disconfirm his hypotheses.

Popper holds that science and knowledge progress by advancing hypotheses, making deductions from them and using observations and experiments continually to test these deductions until they are falsified; then revising or changing the hypothesis to cope with this. (Note the increased role of experiments here explicitly to test hypotheses.) Hence, the hypothetico-deductive method: Hypotheses come first and observations follow; 'observations are interpretations . . . in the light of theories'. It is easy to underestimate the importance of this view, which is fundamentally different from the traditional view and itself leads to other differences. Essentially, it is saying that we do not collect facts, as Pearson had implied; we do not gather unbiased observations. Rather, we interpret our observations in the light of biases, preconceptions, hypotheses and theories. We choose which aspects of incoming stimuli to attend to and what interpretation to put on them. This view relates to some modern ideas on the psychology of perception and the psychology of development.

FIGURE 1.1   Ambiguous figures: old lady or young lady?

## Psychology of perception

The study of ambiguous figures, as in Escher drawings and visual illusions, or the interpretation of minimal sketches or cartoons shows that the human brain actively interprets visual (and other sensory) stimuli. Depending on our expectations and previous experiences, different people may experience a certain stimulus in different ways – as an old lady or a young lady in Figure 1.1, for example. Thus, preconceptions are biasing our observation.

## Psychology of development

There is a developmental history to our preconceptions. Ultimately, there is an evolutionary history in that our sensory systems themselves are 'biased' to respond to certain kinds of external signals (e.g. wavelengths in the visible light range; sounds in our audible range) because the 'hypotheses' that such signals were important were successful in the natural selection of our ancestors. Looking at individual development, a human baby has biases about which kinds of stimuli to attend to and readily develops hypotheses about human faces, about depth and about causal relationships. Jean Piaget's theory of cognitive development views the developing child as trying out hypotheses in the world. This is very explicit in his 'formal operational thinking' stage of adolescence, which is itself very similar to a Popperian view of scientific method in its testing of hypotheses. The individual scientist can be viewed as someone who carries out formal operational thinking systematically and consistently in his or her scientific domain.

Thus, Popper is saying that observation is 'theory laden'; that is, there are always hypotheses implicit or explicit in observation (even, ultimately, back to innate perceptual hypotheses in the newborn infant). However, this implies a different status to 'facts' than Pearson and the traditional thinkers had in mind. Facts or observations are open to reinterpretation in the light of a different theory. Also, a theory may fit the observations now, but future observations may disprove it – the deductions from a theory, even if satisfied now, may not always be satisfied. This leads to two related points:

1   A theory can never be verified in the sense of proved correct, but it can be falsified.
2   All knowledge is provisional, there is no absolute truth, but we can prefer one theory over another.

In forming these views, it is very likely that Popper was influenced by developments in physics at the beginning of the twentith century. For a long time, Newtonian physics held sway and seemed to provide a perfect explanation of force and motion and, via the inverse square law of gravitational attraction, of the motion of the planets and comets in the solar system. The predictions of this theory seemed very well confirmed. Yet there were a few anomalies, for example, the detailed orbit of Mercury, the innermost planet, was not exactly as predicted. Other difficulties were discussed. Physics entered a period of ferment at the turn of the twentieth century, which was resolved when Einstein's theories of special and general relativity (as well as the theories of quantum mechanics developed by Schrodinger, Heisenberg, and others) provided a totally new and different basis for understanding physical reality. In particular, Einstein's theories replaced Newton's as a basis for predicting planetary motion and did so better, for example, correctly predicting the orbit of Mercury.

If a theory as apparently well established as Newton's could be overthrown, what theory was safe? This was a dramatic example of how many prior confirmations do not safeguard a theory against future refutation. Effectively, Einstein had falsified Newton's theory. This did not mean that Einstein had achieved absolute truth – perhaps his theories will be overthrown in the future – but he had provided a better explanation than Newton.

This illustrates the final crucial point about Popper's view – that theories cannot be proved, but can be falsified, and that falsifiability is the criterion separating science from non-science. Using this criterion, Popper addressed directly the first of our questions at the start of the chapter, providing a 'demarcation criterion' which he claims can be used to separate (or demarcate) the sciences from the non-sciences. One can falsify Newton's theory, but one cannot falsify a painting. Paintings can be beautiful and valuable, but they are not science.

Popper placed much (scientific) value on falsifiability. He argued that highly falsifiable theories should be preferred to less falsifiable ones –

provided, of course, that they had not actually been falsified. Also, scientists should try to falsify their theories, rather than confirm them: 'the wrong view of science betrays itself in the craving to be right'. Planned experiments have a crucial role in attempts at falsification, potentially deciding whether one theory or perhaps another can be disproved. Using his falsifiability criterion, he also attacked two prominent theories in the social sciences – psychoanalysis and Marxism.

### Popper and psychoanalysis

Popper regarded psychoanalysis as non-science by the falsifiability criterion. (In fact, he regarded psychology generally as 'riddled with fashions, and with uncontrolled dogmas'.) He argued that psychoanalytic ideas could be used to explain any example of human behaviour; thus, they could not be falsified; therefore, psychoanalysis was not science. Grünbaum (1979) argued that, in fact, Freud's theories could make predictions which were in principle falsifiable; for example, that early severe toilet training would lead to an anal personality; and that some of these predictions were confirmed (not falsified) by cross-cultural studies.

However, Popper (1986) reiterated that 'every conceivable case [of human behaviour] could be interpreted in the light of Freud's theory'. He gave as example an argument attributed to Grünbaum, that a Freudian prediction is that 'if people do not repress traumatic experiences, then they will not become victims of neurosis'. Popper argues that this is untestable since who decides what is traumatic, and what is repressed: 'Who has never been hurt, never suffered a trauma? And who has not tried to get over it by forgetting about it – which means 'trying to repress it'? But if so . . . all [such] so-called predictions are untestable.'

### Popper and Marxism

Popper attacked Marxism, or Marx's theories, not for being unfalsifiable but because Marxists ignored the falsifications which had happened. In *The Open Society and its Enemies* (1945), Popper argued that Marxism predicted that only fully developed capitalist economies would become Communist (falsified: the principal Communist countries such as Russia and China were pre-industrial); Communist revolutions would be based on the industrial proletariat (falsified: Mao Zedong's revolution in China relied on the peasantry); capitalism should, through its own contradictions, lead to increased inequality, crisis and revolution (falsified: many capitalist countries have achieved less inequality through social democratic governments). Marxists ignore these falsifications and find 'excuses' to preserve the theory. Thus, according to Popper, Marxists abandon pretensions to be scientific. Popper more fundamentally criticized 'historicism' in the sense of any preordained prediction of history, given what he saw as our ability and responsibility to control our own destiny.

Popper's views have become very influential, not only in the physical sciences but in some areas of the social sciences. His views are a radical alternative to the traditional view and the emphasis on requiring prior hypotheses and then attempting to falsify them may seem a refreshing antidote to a lot of psuedo-science. However, it is worth noting that some traditions in science and in social science are not too compatible with this. In science, consider the work of Konrad Lorenz and Niko Tinbergen, Nobel prize winners in ethology (the study of animal behaviour). Ethologists emphasized the importance of getting rid of preconceptions when studying a species of animal. In order to enter the animals own experienced environment, or *umwelt*, one should try to discard (so far as possible) one's anthropomorphic expectations. Ethologists would acknowledge that prior hypotheses bias our perceptions, as Popper does, but unlike Popper they would see this as a hindrance rather than an advantage. They would argue that theories should emerge later, from immersion in the data.

This view shows correspondences to that of grounded theory in the social sciences. This is one way of treating qualitative data obtained from people through observation and/or interview. Again, a considered aim of this approach is that concepts, and subsequently theories, should emerge from an (as far as possible) unbiased immersion in what the environment or setting throws up in the way of data. Hypothesis testing is not rejected, but the intention is to go some way to the induction-deduction-testing cycle rather than the straightforward deduction-testing cycle which Popper espouses.

## ALTERNATIVE VIEWS OF KUHN

Popper's views have also been criticized more directly within the philosophy of science literature. A major protagonist to Popper has been Thomas Kuhn (1922–98), especially in his key work *The Structure of Scientific Revolutions* (1970). Kuhn agreed with Popper (and most other recent philosophers of science) in seeing observation as 'theory laden', and science as a problem-solving activity which cannot arrive at an absolutely verifiable truth. However, he disagreed about the role of falsifiability and about the criteria demarcating science and non-science. The main thrust of his view of science is summarized in Figure 1.2.

In his work, Kuhn paid much more attention than Popper to the history of science and the way in which scientists have actually worked. For example, he drew particularly on the development of modern chemistry from the earlier work of alchemists, as well as the development of physics. Kuhn characterized a mature branch of science as having an accepted 'paradigm' (a basic set of assumptions, or ways of problem solving). In a very early

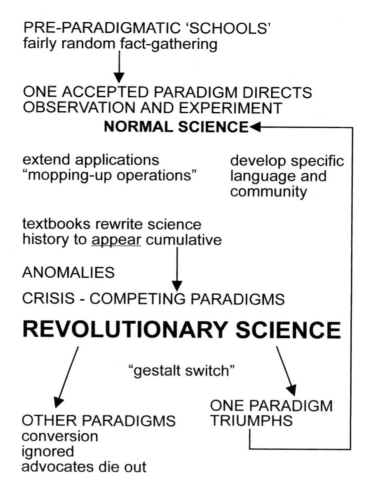

**FIGURE 1.2   A diagrammatic view of Kuhn's view of science**

stage, a discipline might be pre-paradigmatic, characterized by many schools which quarrel about fundamental issues, and by rather random fact gathering. With maturity, one paradigm is accepted and directs observation and experiment.

As an example of this shift, Kuhn pointed to the alchemists as being pre-paradigmatic. With the vague aim of seeking life-enhancing elixirs, or turning base metals to gold, they mixed anything to see what happened. Chemistry only became a science when Dalton proposed his atomic theory, and the concepts of particular elements made up of atoms of different atomic numbers and weights (which could not be transmuted). This provided a basic set of assumptions which could guide future work – the identification of missing elements, the examination of how particular elements combined, etc.

Kuhn here has advanced a demarcation criterion between science and non-science (question 2, at the start of the chapter), but one different from Popper's: a field is a science if it has a paradigm. Science is distinguished from non-science by being a problem-solving activity with an accepted paradigm.

This period of chemistry (or any other area where a paradigm becomes accepted, for example, Newtonian theories in physics, plate tectonics in geology) would be an example of what Kuhn calls 'normal science' (see Figure 1.2). This is a period of 'mopping-up operations' in which paradigm applications are extended. 'Mopping-up operations are what engage most scientists throughout their careers' (Kuhn, 1970: 22). Methodologies are developed and characteristic jargon appears which is accessible to those in the paradigm but not to others (in chemistry such terminology would be 'element', 'atom', atomic weight', 'atomic number', etc.).

Interestingly, Kuhn also looked at how normal science is transmitted to the wider community and taught to the next generation. He argued that textbooks characteristically reinterpret past history as leading to the current paradigm. For example, chemistry textbooks may portray the work of alchemists as leading to modern chemistry. Physics textbooks may portray Newtonian physics as leading on to Einstein's theories. In fact, Kuhn argued, these transition points are much more chaotic and unfocused than such simplified accounts would suggest.

Normal science continues, despite the existence of anomalies or falsifying instances. Kuhn argued that scientists are quite content to ignore difficulties while developing a new paradigm (for example, early chemists had to ignore the problem that certain elements had varying atomic weights which were not whole numbers – an anomaly only solved by recognizing the existence of isotopes, elements of the same atomic number but different atomic weight, itself only fully explicable by nuclear theory, much later). The paradigm is doing well generally, so why reject it because it temporarily fails in some areas?

The paradigm is not rejected unless, apart from anomalies accumulating, a potentially superior paradigm appears. 'To be accepted as a paradigm, a theory must seem better than its competitors, but it need not, and in fact never does, explain all the facts with which it can be confronted' (Kuhn, 1970: 17–18). This view is different from Popper's; rather than trying to falsify their theory, Kuhn suggested not only that scientists avoid falsifying their theories, but that this is a necessary part of normal science.

As can be seen, the role of falsifiability is limited in Kuhn's approach. All paradigms always have anomalies. But Kuhn obviously had to recognize that theories are sometimes falsified, or disproved; like Popper, he was very aware of Einstein's overthrowing of Newton's ideas. However, Kuhn described such events as a period of 'revolutionary science' (see Figure 1.2). Such a period comes about when an accepted paradigm, despite a period of development, has not dealt with anomalies, and indeed anomalies have begun to accumulate to an embarassing extent. At this point, competing paradigms may appear. There will be a period of some confusion or chaos, as the previous paradigm loses adherents, but no one new paradigm predominates. Eventually, one paradigm triumphs, in part through resolving some anomalies, but also perhaps through making some new successful predictions or appearing more precise or elegant. This new, triumphant paradigm then becomes 'normal science' in its turn (Figure 1.2). Adherents of the older, or alternative, paradigms are converted, ignored, or eventually die out.

Kuhn argued that each paradigm embodies such different assumptions that a 'gestalt switch' in perception is needed to move from one to the other. Just as in Figure 1.1 the switch from 'old woman' to 'young woman' requires a sudden, complete reinterpretation of the same stimulus information, so (Kuhn argued) a paradigm shift (for example, from Newtonian to Einsteinian theory) requires a complete reconceptualization, in new language, of information previously interpreted in the old paradigm. Kuhn also stated that competing paradigms are 'not only incompatible but often actually incommensurable' (1970: 103), that is, only partially comparable in logical terms. Proponents of different paradigms characteristically 'argue past each other', employing such different language and different basic assumptions that meaningful dialogue is difficult if not impossible.

Kuhn's work has inspired many thinkers in the social sciences who have taken up the idea of 'paradigm' enthusiastically, claiming that their area represents a new paradigm for their discipline (see Lambie, 1991; Peterson, 1981). However, Kuhn saw 'controversies over fundamentals' as 'endemic among, say, psychologists and sociologists' (1970: viii). He seems to have viewed the social sciences as at an early, pre-paradigmatic stage in science, though this was not discussed in depth in his writings.

In fact, the nature of a 'paradigm' has been one of the two major criticisms made of Kuhn's work (e.g. Lakatos, 1970). Kuhn defined paradigms as 'universally recognised scientific achievements that for a time provide model problems and solutions to a community of practitioners' (1970: viii). Besides the circularity of including 'scientific' in this definition of science, it has been pointed out that Kuhn provides many other explanations of 'paradigm' in his 1962 book, which vary appreciably (some 111 different definitions, according to Masterman, in Lakatos and Musgrave, 1970). Is it a grand theory, a localized hypothesis, a new tool or technique? Kuhn recognized the force of this criticism and in the Postscript to the second edition of his book (1970) distinguished between a more global meaning as 'disciplinary matrix', or network of shared conceptual assumptions; and a more localized meaning as 'exemplar' or useful problem-solving methodology.

The other main criticism of Kuhn's work related to the nature of paradigm change. Was Kuhn saying that such change was rational, or was it more due to fashion and social pressure? For Popper (as for more traditional philosophers of science), scientific change was seen as progress. New theories were more powerful than old ones, encompassing more known observations and successfully predicting new findings. For Kuhn, it was not so clear cut. Certainly, a paradigm gets into trouble when anomalies accumulate. But Kuhn stated that all paradigms have anomalies and falsification is in reality not used as a primary criterion for paradigm rejection. He states (1970: 8) that 'competition between segments of the scientific community is the only historical process that ever actually results in the rejection of one previously accepted theory or in the adoption of another'. This, together with the incommensurable nature of different paradigms, leaves open the door to suggestions that a paradigm shift occurs because one group of scientists is just more powerful or has more social influence than another.

Clearly science is influenced by social pressures. The history of Lysenkoism in the former Soviet Union (in which Lysenko, through his influence, promulgated what are widely held to be false ideas of effects of plant breeding) is one example. This and other examples could be dismissed as aberrations in science. Kuhn's work, however, has opened up a debate as to whether even normal science and the competition between paradigms is strongly influenced by such social forces. This debate has obvious relevance to the social sciences. So far as the philosophy of science is concerned, this debate has led to a defence of rationality in science (e.g. Lakatos, Bunge) and to further attacks (e.g. Feyerabend, Collins, and recent sociologists of science).

## VIEWS OF LAKATOS AND OTHERS

A compromise between the positions of Popper and Kuhn was advanced by Imre Lakatos (1922–74). Lakatos agreed with Kuhn that Popper was wrong in emphasizing falsification as the demarcation criterion between science and non-science; but he wished to reject the relativism that Kuhn was near to espousing. Lakatos sought for ways to keep Popper's ideas of scientific progress, while retaining Kuhn's insights into how science actually changes (Lakatos, 1970).

Lakatos distinguished three kinds of falsificationism in science:

1   *Dogmatic falsificationism*: this would be the repeated overthrow of theories by 'facts'; a single disconfirmation would lead to a theory being discarded. (This would clearly be pointless as a disconfirmation might later be shown to be due to some mistake, such as measurement error or faulty procedure. Popper in fact recognized this and was not as guilty of it as some of his critics imply.)
2   *Naive methodological falsificationism*: to safeguard premature rejection of theories, Popper says that 'criteria of refutation have to be laid down beforehand'. But Lakatos (like Kuhn) does not believe that science actually progresses this way.

# SCIENTIFIC RESEARCH PROGRAMME

PROTECTIVE BELT OF AUXILIARY HYPOTHESES

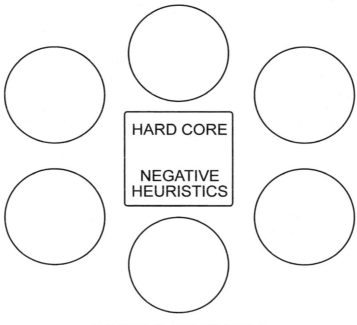

HARD CORE

NEGATIVE
HEURISTICS

POSITIVE HEURISTICS

**FIGURE 1.3   A schematic view of Lakatos's concept of a scientific research programme**

3   *Sophisticated methodological falsificationism*: according to Lakatos 'there is no falsification before the emergence of a better theory'. A theory T is falsified only if a new theory T' explains all the unrefuted content of T and makes further predictions, some of which are corroborated.

Lakatos's key concept was that of a a 'scientific research programme' (see Figure 1.3). A research programme encompasses a set of theories and methods which can change over time. However, there is a 'hard core' of very basic theoretical assumptions which do not change (for example, in chemistry, this could be atomic theory). This hard core would not be questioned by adherents of the research programme; indeed, they would defend them vigorously ('negative heuristics'). However, the hard core would have generated a range of 'auxiliary hypotheses'. These are much more open to question. They are the frontiers of the research programme, ideas which are being tried out and tested for their range and explanatory power. If they prove successful, well and good. If they do not, they will be jettisoned, or changed to accommodate anomalies or falsifications, without threatening the 'hard core'. These 'positive heuristics' of active testing and questioning complement the 'negative heuristics' used to protect the hard core assumptions.

Lakatos then saw mature science as a history of competing research programmes. His is a sophisticated conception of science which seems to advance beyond what Lakatos saw as the naive methodological falsificationism of Popper, retaining the insights of Kuhn into historical processes of competing programmes (similar to Kuhn's 'global' paradigms). Kuhn had emphasized the revolutionary nature of scientific change – to the extent that his approach was caricatured as seeing science as 'a series of widely spaced upheavals separated by lengthy dogmatic intervals' (Watkins, in Lakatos and Musgrave, 1970). Lakatos showed the extent to which each research programme also embodied positive heuristics of testing and debate.

Unlike Kuhn, Lakatos rescued the idea of rational progress, at least in part, by describing research programmes as 'progressive', or 'degenerating'. Rational criteria are available to decide whether a particular research programme is 'progressive' or 'degenerating'. A 'progressive' programme anticipates novel facts and produces novel theories, which have 'heuristic power'; changes in the auxiliary hypotheses are productive. A 'degenerating' programme, by contrast, patches up anomalies in ad hoc ways which do not generalize to other situations; changes in the auxiliary hypotheses are unproductive. Nevertheless, Lakatos concedes that there is necessarily some subjectivity in these judgments and also that, over time, what had seemed a degenerating programme may become progressive again (or vice versa).

These ideas have been applied to the social sciences (Friman *et al.*, 1993; Rowell, 1983). For example, Gholsen and Barker (1985) described traditional learning theory in psychology as a degenerating research programme. One could mount a similar argument for psychoanalysis or Marxism.

Similar ideas have been proposed by Larry Laudan (b. 1941), who argues that even the 'hard core' of a research programme can be modified over time. He also postulates a close and reciprocal influence between the philosophy of science and the history of science (Laudan, 1977).

By contrast, Paul Feyerabend (b. 1924) emphasizes the non-rational aspect of Kuhn's ideas of paradigm conflict. In this relativist position there are no logical grounds for preferring one theory over another one (Feyerabend, 1975). Kuhn's relativist views are developed further in recent trends in the sociology and history of scientific knowledge (e.g. Collins, 1985). This holds that 'the results of scientific experiments are more ambigous than they are usually taken to be, while theory is more flexible than most people imagine. This means that science can progress only within communities that can reach consensus about what counts as plausible. Plausibility is a matter of social context so science is "a social construct"' and that 'in a sociological or historical investigation, act as though the world does not constrain what scientists believe about it' (Collins, 1994).

The view that science is (just) a social construct is of course vigorously debated; for a critique of these views, see Bunge (1991, 1992). As Richard Dawkins put it:

> When you take a 747 to an international convention of sociologists or literary critics, the reason you will arrive in one piece is that a lot of western-trained scientists and engineers got their sums right. If it gives you satisfaction to say that the theory of aerodynamics is a social construct that is your privilege, but why do you then entrust travel plans to a Boeing rather than a magic carpet? As I have put it before, show me a cultural relativist at 30,000 feet and I will show you a hypocrite. (Dawkins, 1994: 17–18)

# QUESTIONS OF HERMENEUTICS: BEYOND EMPIRICISM AND POST-MODERNISM

*Nick Stevenson*

To write an introduction to something called 'hermeneutics' might at first glance appear to have little contemporary relevance. In an age that has come to be increasingly dominated by theoretical deconstruction, post-structuralism and post-modernism a concern for hermeneutics might seem old-fashioned. Yet the tradition of hermeneutics already occupies many of the assumptions of these better known trends and, in certain instances, offers powerful corrections to a number of theoretical evasions. On the other hand, much research in the social sciences continues to steer clear of dense theoretical disputes, aiming to give us a clear window on a changing world. Here my argument is that if post-modernism leads us astray then a naive empiricism fares no better. In summary, I claim that a hermeneutic disposition equips us well for a variety of different research agendas.

I want to start with the connection between so-called theory and so-called facts. I think that an encounter with a rich tradition like hermeneutics allows us a qualified scepticism about two positions that have gained a foothold in certain sections of the social sciences. The first is the mistaken view that we can present facts in such a way that is free of theoretical baggage. The desire to adopt such a position may come from a variety of motivations (including the avoidance of more political disputes). Such a view, as we shall see, inevitably blinds us to the notion that facts are also social constructs and that certain theoretical positions will inevitably prefer certain facts. The other position that hermeneutics asks us to distance ourselves from is a form of radical post-modernism. By this I mean the view that theoretical paradigms totally construct our view of the world. This would make much empirical work unnecessary as we would only find such material that reinforced our theoretical prejudices. The tradition of hermeneutics, however, construes social enquiry as a more dialogical form of analysis than such a position allows. This is not to argue that hermeneutics can give us the answer to everything or that there is not considerable dispute within its borders; more that a genuinely 'hermeneutic' approach continues to have much to offer present generations of social researchers.

Before moving on let me make two points. First, while the term hermeneutics sounds very grand and intimidating, it is actually meant to describe a rather mundane and practical activity. We all do hermeneutics. That is the practice of hermeneutics is concerned with the practice of interpretation. The aim of hermeneutics is to make clear an object of study or area of enquiry that is currently unclear and requires further clarification. Charles Taylor (1985) in this respect has argued that notions of interpretation are intimately connected with the need of human beings to make sense of their experience. Human beings, according to Taylor, have a need to position their experiences in narratives, to reflect on the kind of persons that they want to be and to form understandings of their relationships with nature and history.

Taylor argues that all forms of interpretation are an attempt to bring to the fore an underlying sense that is currently lacking. This activity presupposes at least three phenomena:

1   a field of texts, persons, documents or objects about which we can reasonably talk of their 'coherence' or 'non-coherence';
2   that we can make a distinction between the expressions of a particular group and the meanings that might be made clearer through further elaboration;
3   that these expressions are meaningful for a human subject.

In short, for Taylor what we call a successful interpretation is one that is able to make clear a meaning which was originally present in a confused or an unclear way. For instance, I remember when I first read the work of Raymond Williams I was unsure why certain terms like 'complexity', 'structures of feeling' and 'experience' had such resonance for him. I later discovered through much effort and further reading that Williams's attachment to these concepts had a multitude of interrelated sources connected with his own historical context, political position and individual particularity. It was only when I began to bring together Williams's personal and intellectual history that these notions began to resound with meaning. Take the idea of 'feeling': this was important as it spoke of the post-war New Left's desire to break with economistic Marxism, introduce an understanding of cultural relations, reconnect politics to humanist conceptions of the subject in defiance of the perceived brutalities of Stalinism and articulate an aesthetic dimension. So what am I seeking to demonstrate here? That after a period of reflection and confusion what initially appears strange and extraordinary can eventually make sense. In other words, simply having more information about Raymond Williams would be of little help unless I am able to link his expressions to interpreted meanings.

Now all this might, with further qualification, be accepted, but does it make for a correct or final interpretation? Hermeneutics resists such absolute formulations. What I am offering with respect to Williams is a particular reading of his life, intellectual context, worth, etc. This reading will be challenged, passed over and made sense of by other interpreters in the future. Hermeneutics then offers a vision of the academic project as always incomplete and uncertain, responding to new questions and problems in the quest for sense. Indeed, if my particular understanding of Williams was, as it well might be, disputed by others, the answer could only be more interpretation: that is, all things being equal, I would attempt to enter into debate with others to identity areas of consensus and dis- agreement, before either we decided we were never going to agree, one of us got bored, or indeed we actually changed our minds and gave up on old ways of thinking. This process of continual and never ending critique and counter-critique points to the extent to which intellectual life and our identities are dialogically constructed out of the ebb and flow of conver- sation. More specifically it makes us aware that in coming to interpret a text, social group or person we can only appeal to interpretations that refer to other interpretations; this is usually referred to as the 'hermeneutic circle'.

More often this is experienced by the practitioner as being related to the uncertain nature of our interpretations which have a degree of openness attached to them due to their inevitably provisional nature. Of course these interpretations can be said to 'harden up' during the course of finishing a particular piece of research, but they never lose their open quality. This is summed up by E.P. Thompson in writing about the practice of the historian when he describes his craft as 'less an experiment in historiography, than a way of muddling through' (Thompson, 1977: 71). There are then no clear rules that we can point to which will guarantee a correct interpretation. All hermeneutics is able to offer in this respect is a reminder that we may ourselves come to change our minds or that readers at some point in the future may find our conclusions absurd.

## BREAKING OUT OF THE CIRCLE

Against notions of muddling through, there have been various attempts to break out of the hermeneutic circle and offer more definite forms of knowledge. These can be characterized in two main ways:

1   rationalist attempts to offer up logical incontroversial truths (I think, therefore I am);
2   empiricist arguments that the case is not built upon interpretation but on so called 'brute data'.

I am particularly interested in the second of these arguments, which is usually associated with positivist or scientistic attempts to offer something by the way of evidence that cannot be questioned by another interpreta- tion. When I think of this argument I often picture a man in a white coat pointing to a row of figures, looking to the audience and insisting that the 'facts' speak for themselves. As should be obvious by now, hermeneutics argues that the debate over meaning cannot be brought to a halt in this way. This is because, at least at some level, social reality cannot be identified in abstraction from the languages that we use. This refers back to some of my initial remarks about theory and facts. Indeed this point has caused a great deal of confusion and upset in the social sciences.

Take the example of global warming. There are two positions to be avoided in this debate that can be connected to what I shall call subjectivism and objectivism. The first, along with hermeneutics, would argue that the way we seek to understand ecological processes is caught up with the language or cultural criteria within which we ourselves are enmeshed. So we might get a very different understanding of these processes from a radical ecological group and a government minister. Where certain critics have gone wrong, however, is to argue that such reflections can only be about the prejudices or individual perspectives of particular groups. Through a shared language both the government minister and the ecological group are trying to open out perspectives on the world in which we currently live. That is, while language does not mirror reality, it does of course refer to it. The other mistake in dealing with these arguments that is more strongly connected with empiricist claims is the objectivist illusion that we can know about global warming without taking the turn through language. The picture that is offered here is of reality standing apart from language. Of course the languages that we use help us picture the world that we inhabit. Post-structuralist and post-modernist writers of a variety of persuasions have helpfully pointed towards the textuality of nature; that is we need to attend to the historically shifting linguistic and cultural signs of nature. It is true that we can make no clear separation between the 'reality' of nature and the way that it is represented. The limits of our language are also the limits of our world. But, as Kate Soper (1995) has eloquently argued, 'this does not justify the conclusion that there is no ontological distinction between the ideas we have of nature and what the ideas are about'. Another way of expressing this view is that we can re-describe nature any way we might choose, but this will not ultimately affect 'real' processes of global warming and rising levels of pollution.

How then might we apply a hermeneutic sensibility to questions of this type without succumbing to a hard empiricism that suggests we could put complex cultural questions aside, or succumbing to the view that the 'natural' has disappeared into a post-modern simulation? Before we can answer this question we need to look more closely at the nature of language.

## LANGUAGE

As we saw, for most contemporary theories, and in this hermeneutics is no exception, understanding and interpretation emerge through a linguistic dimension. But if language cannot be described as subjective (held inside people's heads) or objective (standing apart from the social world) it might best be described as intersubjective. That is we refer to linguistic practices as intersubjective as they are bound up with everyday social practices, are changed by practical action and are constitutive of taken for granted social meanings.

John Searle (1969) provides a good example of intersubjectivity when he writes about the distinction between regulative and constitutive rules. If we take the example of a game of tennis then there are certain rules of conduct that are there to regulate the activity of the competitors and prevent foul play. On the other hand, tennis has a number of rules without which we could not imagine the game. These could be the practices of point scoring, serving, volleying and returning, all of which constitute the game of tennis. Just as language is neither objectivist nor subjectivist, so it is with the constitutive rules of tennis. Linguistic practices as constitutive practices make up a stock of shared background meanings that arise in the public spaces between people. For instance, we have to share certain background meanings that allow us to have a conversation or go to a lecture in the first place. The sociologist Garfinkel (Heritage, 1984) through his famous 'breaching experiments' attempted to reveal the extent to which human beings share a similar intersubjective web of pre-understandings when entering into conversations with others. For instance, in the next conversation that you enter, try asking 'why' each time your partner tells you something. The reason that he or she will eventually get annoyed is because you are breaking the taken for granted consensually held rules of what it usually means to enter into a conversation with another. In other words, social life is only made possible by the extent to which humanity shares certain background meanings that allow party elections, playing music and gossiping in the laundrette.

To take this argument a little further, understanding, then, always depends as we have seen upon background understandings. What happens when someone comes along who lacks the necessary background understandings? We have all come across irritating people who do not seem to understand that a good conversation has its own rhythm of turn taking and subtle intersubjective clues. Linguistic practices presuppose certain shared rules that enable us to 'go on' in a multitude of settings. Wittgenstein points to this when he says 'obeying a rule is a practice': that is an intersubjective practice can be illustrated if we think for a moment how we might persuade the boorish person who prefers the sound of his own voice to have a more mutual conversation. This might prove impossible as there is no fixed definition as to when it is acceptable within a conversation to talk for an extended period. This is something we just know how to do. There are, if you like, no abstract rules that govern what a good conversation is like that stand apart from the variety of contexts within which we talk to others. For Wittgenstein we will know how to have a conversation when we know how to follow the various shared conventions and rules that go into making a conversation. Again this points to a dialogical rather than a monological or disembedded view of the subject.

Wittgenstein was referring to questions of this order when he argued that there is no such thing as a private language. By this he meant that language and meaning are by their very nature public phenomena. To understand how our language works, we have to understand it as a shared intersubjective practice. Wittgenstein famously wrote:

> Our language can be seen as an ancient city: a maze of little streets and squares, of old and new houses, and of houses with additions from various periods; and this surrounded by a multitude of new boroughs with straight regular streets and uniform houses. (Wittgenstein, 1958: 8)

I think that this is a helpful metaphor. To think of language as being like a city in which we live means that we cannot take up a position 'outside' language. Second, we might think of the way new streets are added to our city as referring to the way a language might change historically without losing its essential character. Language, he seems to be suggesting, does not develop through changes in 'external' reality (he rejects a correspondence theory of language) but needs to be understood as a practice in its own right.

Returning to our ecological question then, how might these reflections help us? First, a hermeneutic approach would seek to point to the different discourses or language games that were evident in respect of different ways of representing nature. Then we could search for the areas of agreement or consensus that must exist for us to be able to come into a dispute over the natural order in the first place. This process of clarification might then enable the participants to discover they had more (or indeed less) in common than they originally thought. Again such a strategy differs from certain post-modern viewpoints that seek to emphasize the radical difference and incommensurability of different perspectives on nature. Such a view also differs markedly, as I have indicated, from more positivistic approaches that would ignore our shared intersubjective and cultural backgrounds altogether.

## SYMBOLIC CULTURE

The anthropologist Clifford Geertz (1973) adds an extra dimension to our discussion so far when he stresses the symbolic nature of culture that retains an openness to further interpretations by the lay actors themselves or the investigative social scientist. Here there is a need to distinguish between first and second order interpretations: that is, a separation needs to be made between the intersubjective meanings produced by the agents themselves (those whom we are investigating), and the sense social scientists make of these interpretations. Cultural expressions are meaningful for social agents as well as the researchers that study them. Often, as Anthony Giddens's (1984) notion of the 'double hermeneutic' implies, this situation is further complicated as the interpretative worlds and frameworks of the social sciences are not as separate from those of lay actors as many have traditionally assumed. For instance, anyone getting married these days is aware of the increasingly high divorce statistics that are transforming traditional family patterns within western democracies. In the large part, these are made available for us through the practices of the social sciences. According to Giddens's later work (1990) this produces a situation of radicalized reflexivity within the modern era: that is, 'expert' cultures are not only the property of academic communities, but are continually finding their way into popular discourses through mechanisms such as the mass media. This radicalizes Geertz's original model in that what is being offered is not only an interpretation of an interpretation, but a reflexive reinterpretation of numerous layers of reworked unstable cultural meanings. We might be tempted to read such features, as many sociologists and cultural theorists are doing, as opening out a culture of radical reflexivity. Such a view would suggest (put very crudely) given the expansion of communication systems and the decline of tradition more generally within modernity that we are living in a more hermeneutically complex age than ever before. On one level we could argue that such a view does away (in certain branches of the social sciences at least) with an ivory tower view of academic practice. If the actual research findings, ideas and concepts of the academy are constantly interrupting the shared understandings of lay actors, then such a view is difficult to maintain. Perhaps more seriously, however, this view disrupts clear boundaries and divisions between what Geertz called second and first order interpretations.

Again this returns us to the problem as to what a good interpretation might be. As might be expected, different writers give different pointers on this issue. According to Geertz, a good interpretation of a particular linguistic community is not governed by the author's cleverness but by his or her ability to take the reader to the 'heart' of the symbolically produced common meanings. Ricoeur (1981) similarly talks of a valid interpretation as being one that is 'verifiable'. By this he means that the interpretations which are offered must not only be probable, but be more probable than the others on offer. On this question, he continues, it is important to search for agreement, but that this may not be possible, and indeed the desire to have the last word is probably connected to a violent and indeed totalitarian impulse. For hermeneutics a good interpretation is less of a method and more a rule of thumb. Ricoeur goes on to argue that valid arguments 'proceed in a cumulative fashion through mutual reinforcement of criteria – which if taken in isolation would not be decisive – that is a good interpretation is one that is convincing' (Ricoeur, 1981).

These are obviously not hard and fast rules which will guarantee a good interpretation, but Riceour tells us that if our arguments move along in this fashion then we could well be on the right lines. Rather than pointing to how discursive paradigms secure a field of research or looking to theory-free factual evidence, such a view returns us to questions of debate and the clarification of an underlying sense, all of which can be associated with the hermeneutic circle.

## THE GADAMER-HABERMAS DEBATE

To close I want to turn very briefly to what I take to be the central contemporary debate within hermeneutics. While I can hardly do justice to it here, I hope at least to indicate why it has been so influential. This discussion takes as given many of the points I have been trying to make so far in respect of the nature of language, but more centrally addresses questions of relativism on the one hand and power and ideology on the other.

Habermas (1990) has argued that understanding requires what he calls 'communicative action'. For Habermas the very fact that we are language users means that we are communicatively able to reach an understanding with one another. He argues that in every act of speech we are capable of immanently raising three validity claims in connection with what is said. These three validity claims, he adds, constitute a background consensus of normal everyday language use in western society. The three claims – that are used by agents to test the validity of speech – could be characterized as: truth claims, normative claims related to appropriateness, as well as claims connected to sincerity. These intersubjectively-held validity claims mean that we should accept that 'in principle' our own perceptions and utterances have the same status as those who we are seeking to understand. We should, according to Habermas, open ourselves up to reciprocal forms of conversation without having previously decided who is going to learn from whom. This would entail giving up the perspective of the 'observer' for an equal partner in conversation. Second, the interpreter also has to grapple with the 'context' within which interpretations are offered, as we should not assume in advance that we necessarily understand the group's background assumptions. Finally, as language cannot be said to mirror the social world, it is better to say a good interpretation 'fits' or 'suits' the meanings of the social group in question.

Habermas is clear, along with most other versions of hermeneutics, that the process of interpretation is inevitably tied to the horizons or value judgements of the interpreter. This, however, raises questions regarding issues related to the objectivity or validity of our findings. There are two responses, according to Habermas, within the philosophical tradition we call hermeneutics, to this problem. They are empathy theory and relativism.

Empathy theory suggests that we place ourselves in the position of the social group or historical period we are investigating. This was indeed what an earlier branch of hermeneutics advocated. Schleiermacher's version of romantic hermeneutics suggests it was the task of the interpreter to understand the author better than they understood themselves (similarly

Dilthey wished to recreate the author 'behind' the text). Such a view then suggests there are no interpretative barriers to putting on the shoes of the person or persons we are currently writing about. For example, if we were in the process of writing the life story of my now dead grandfather William Stevenson we could attempt to tell his story as he might have wanted to tell it. The only limitation that might be imposed upon us by this view might be an unwillingness of existing family members to tell his story or a missing diary that might reveal crucial information. The point is that there are no necessary barriers to reconstructing the view of the author behind the text or person behind the life.

Gadamer (1974), however, famously sought to critique the positions that can be associated with empathy theory. His views are related to the cognitive dimension he calls Bildung. Put briefly, individuals and cultures can be said to be in the possession of Bildung, the extent to which they retain an openness to other forms of life. Bildung, or learning from others, while opening oneself up for experience, is opposed to dogmatism. Gadamer, in this respect, argues that our 'prejudices' are necessary to our forming an understanding. Prejudice does not mean, as it usually does in ordinary language, the refusal to accept the rational arguments of another in favour of that which has no justification. Prejudice is instead, in Gadamer's terms, those cultural horizons through which understanding is made possible. One sees through the horizons of one's cultural tradition in such a way as to reveal, draw comparisons with and reflect critically upon past historical periods and other cultures. By merging horizons with other 'experiences', both sets of cultural presuppositions are brought into question. To write in a spirit informed by Bildung is to be aware that the historical horizon in which one finds oneself embedded is not a fixed, final point. This involves the recognition that different generations and different authors will necessarily ask different questions of history and culture. Thus romantic hermeneutics and empathy theory turn out to be mistaken in that we can never gain access to the 'other' by imagining ourselves outside our own location within culture and society.

To return to the example of my grandfather's biography, it would make a great deal of difference who decided to write an account of his life. If it were written by me, his grandson, it might contain romantic tales of a street-fighting man who was a trade unionist, spoke fluent Urdu, fought in the Balkans and later in life took to growing beautiful flowers. Gadamer's point is that it is a mistake to argue that a more 'objective' account could be written by someone else. It is, if you like, our own projections and interests that make the subject alive to us in the first place. However, the biography I write and construct is written in the knowledge that others would form different understandings of my grandfather's life and should be written in the spirit of open inquiry and critical reflection. It is then not the point to write an 'objective' study, but to be aware as to how the process of writing and researching could well reshape the questions I want to ask and my most intimate projections.

Habermas argues, however, that Gadamer's position outlined above ultimately reproduces a form of relativism. This is because it asserts that different value orientations will produce different research questions. As we saw in the example, Gadamer's position is quite open to the charge that the biography becomes an invention of the biographer. Further, we may give up talking to others, under this rubric, as we would never agree given that we have radically different perspectives. It is true to argue that Gadamer suggests that we should search for a consensus with others (what he calls the 'anticipation of completeness') accepting that agreement may not be possible. Habermas, on the other hand, argues that the main reason why agreement is not possible is due to the operation of power and force. As we saw, there was nothing about the structure of language itself that prevents those involved in rational conversation from coming to an agreement with one another. If this is the case, reasons Habermas, then failure to reach an agreement with and understanding of another must be due to the operation of material factors outside language. Further, Gadamer overlooks the extent to which 'consensus' could equally be the product of force and ideology.

For Habermas, we should go beyond language to investigate the 'extra-linguistic' factors which shape cultural perspectives. A rational consensus on this view can only be achieved if language is not deformed by the operation of power and ideology. This notion is connected to what Habermas invokes through his critical court of appeal or 'ideal speech situation'. The ideal speech situation is best represented as communication with the absence of barriers. This can only be satisfied where there is an equality of opportunity to participate in communication and where a statement is only true if it could potentially command the free consent of everyone. Thus rational consensus can only be arrived at once everyone has a right of participation and where those involved in the conversation are concerned for the well-being (or exhibit empathetic sensitivity towards) his or her neighbour. In this way, Habermas aims to overcome relativism through the forging of a rational consensus.

How might Gadamer respond to charges of conservatism and relativism? First, on the question of force and ideology, Gadamer would make the obvious point that we can only become aware of so-called 'extra-linguistic forces' through language and conversation. While I think Habermas is more attuned than Gadamer to some of the social forces that might 'distort' communicative flows, the answer to the problem raised is more talk and interpretation. Second, I think Habermas has a tendency to view dis-agreement as being purely the result of power and domination. Gadamer, it seems to me, is much more attuned to the notion that we could have free and open discussion and still fail to reach an agreement . In short we might point to areas of ambiguity or interpretative conflict where we are simply unable to reach an agreement with others from different cultural, historical or social contexts. We might indeed be able to point to certain inter-subjective areas of consensus without ever being able to reconcile the numerous interpretations that exist concerning a certain issue. Here I take Gadamer's respect of pluralism rather than relativism as instructive. Bildung, despite Habermas's claims to the contrary, does not necessarily entail a relativistic conclusion that all cultures and forms of life are of equal value. The writer, alternatively, should engage with others in argument and debate developing insight into the variety of shifting perspectives that are available on a given issue. The enlarged mentalities that emerge from such a conversation are likely to clarify areas of disagreement, respect the difference of those involved in the conversation and, possibly, help us recognize exactly what the barriers to understanding and consensus are. Again to place the emphasis on what we might learn and the enlargement of horizons is, I think, to avoid charges of relativism.

If we take relativism to mean that one viewpoint is just as good as another, then Gadamer escapes this charge. To return once more to my grandfather's biography, a relativist position would suggest there are simply different biographies. Indeed this is what certain versions of post-modernism would try and argue. My grandfather's life would be viewed as a text that could be simulated from a number of radically different viewpoints. In that respect, there would be no way of privileging my account over that of other people. All we could do is point to the different discursive registers that are mobilized in trying to tell the story. One might be the story of a masculinist patriarch, another of working-class heroism and still a further of a dutiful grandfather. However, a Gadamerian approach would argue that the process of good biography writing would be the product of a dialogue with the past. The post-modern viewpoint could not ultimately prefer a dogmatic account of my grandfather's life suggesting he betrayed his comrades during the war which ignored evidence to the contrary. Such an account, within a post-modern perspective, could only point, as we have seen, to the different fictions about my grandfather's life. A more Gadamerian project would at least need to be open to the complexity of reconciling these different positions with one another, learning what I could through experience and reasoning and opening myself up to the critical interjections of others.

All of these issues remain important within theoretical perspectives in the social sciences. To end I just want to point to ways in which hermeneutics is likely to become more rather than less important in the modern world. First, the increasingly globalized and culturally hybrid world in which we live means that issues of cultural conflict, translation and interpretation are likely to become more and not less important in the future. While post-modernism through a discourse of fragmentation and difference retains a certain descriptive relevance, it is unlikely to be of much help in trying to foster common rules of intersubjective engagement. Whether locally, nationally or globally, there will be an increasing need to form common frameworks for cultural exchange, dispute and discussion. In this process hermeneutic understandings are likely to prove important in revealing the cultural specificity of the self and others: that is, the things we share and of course what holds us apart. One only has to remember the Gulf War to consider that misunderstanding and violence often go together. Said (1993) wrote of the forms of intersubjective misrecognition that characterized this conflict:

> Thus Muslims or Africans or Indians or Japanese, in their idioms and from within their own threatened localities, attack the West, or Americanisation, or imperialism, with little more attention to detail, critical differentiation, discrimination, and distinction than has been lavished on them by the West. The same is true for Americans, to whom patriotism is next to godliness. This is ultimately a senseless dynamic. Whatever the 'border wars' have as aims, they are impoverishing. One must join the primordial or constituted group; or, as a subaltern Other, one must accept inferior status; or one must fight to the death. (Said, 1993: 376)

Said's concern for ethnicity, global conflict and misunderstanding best characterizes the direction in which hermeneutic concerns and questions are likely to be of service in the future. What is not clear, to me at least, is that we can say the same of certain aspects of post-modernism which seemingly blandly celebrate human forms of plurality, or of more empirical orientations that remain on the level of description. In this respect, the continuing desire of hermeneutics to represent the plural nature of modern societies, along with a concern for social and historical contexts, continues to ensure its contemporary relevance.

3 FEMINIST METHODOLOGIES FOR SOCIAL
RESEARCHING

Sue Webb

> *Once upon a time, the introduction of writings of women and people of color were called*
> *politicizing the curriculum. Only we had politics (and its nasty mate ideology), whereas*
> *they had standards. (Robinson, 1989: 319)*

Such women's writing and research has the potential to disrupt traditional
ideas of how we create social science texts and knowledge (Becker, 1986;
Denzin, 1997; Haraway, 1988; Harding, 1986). It has called into question the
surgical gloves of objectivity that appeared to prevent contamination of
the research data by the researcher, and enabled the researcher to demarcate
his [sic] personal and public life. A spill-over between these personal and
public spheres has been recognized by many feminists who have struggled
to overcome the systematic ways that the researcher's power to construct
research stories has effectively silenced accounts that might change women's
lives (Fine, 1994; Ribbens and Edwards, 1998). The consequence has been a
focus on philosophical issues. This chapter will examine these issues, and
begin with a discussion of why feminist contributions to social research
should be considered. Some key features of feminist research will be identified by examining briefly how those who position themselves as feminists
have practised as researchers. This analysis will show that central to many
feminist accounts of doing research has been a distinction between method,
methodology and epistemology. The reader will be guided through
discussion of these terms and the chapter will describe how they have
been used by feminists to distinguish their research activities from those of
others.

**WHY LOOK AT FEMINIST ISSUES?**

As the tourist guide book says:

The institutions and organisations of Academia are masculinist in two closely
related senses. The first is that historically the knowledge makers, guardians and
teachers of this tribe have been male . . . The second is that knowledge is by

definition rational, scientific and universal. Those seminal characteristics are counterposed against those of emotionality, the natural and particular, and these and related characteristics – termed 'binaries' – are associated with the known characteristics of the sexes. Moreover, gender among the Academic tribe has both the power to magnificently increase the size and attractiveness (in the male) and can produce near invisibility (in the female). (Stanley, 1997: 2–3)

In focusing on gender among the Academic tribe, Stanley may be thought to be describing the antics and beliefs of some exotic society of the past and the account may be open to question. Alternatively, it may invoke feelings of identification with the writer, a feeling that one has visited this place before. Stanley's account may increase the understanding of one's experience of entering academia. This may be because fundamental to this type of feminist analysis of academic research and its communities is the view that women have been excluded from the knowledge-making process by men, and that the rules and regulations for constructing knowledge have been developed by and serve the interests of these men rather than women. Kramarae and Spender go further and claim that an achievement of this feminist scholarship that exposes the gendered construction of knowledge is that it 'explodes the traditional knowledge making practices, and their products' (1993: 1). They argue that an effect of feminism is that research has been unmasked, and that any understanding of research requires a focus on its philosophical assumptions, rather than on methods and techniques. In other words, it requires a focus on issues of epistemology (the criteria for determining what is acceptable knowledge) and ontology (one's claims about one's being or existence, and the effect this has on how the criteria for deciding what can be known about the world).

In essence the idea that research is a social activity and is affected by social organization and relationships of power, such as those between women and men, is a simple but challenging idea. It also resonates with other debates about positivism and empiricism and the discourse of the natural sciences, which include, for example, those within the philosophy of science that suggest science is a social practice (Kuhn, 1970), and those from the hermeneutics and interpretive traditions that argue that knowledge is partial and bounded by different perspectives (Habermas, 1972). Similarities can also be found with post-modern approaches that suggest that through its practice, which includes the production of research texts, research creates meaning and governs what can be known, and so a post-modernist account should seek to disclose this contingency and partiality of knowledge by critical reflexivity (Lyotard, 1984). As a consequence of these approaches, feminism along with these other philosophical approaches has had an impact on the way that topics have been conceptualized and investigated within many of the disciplines that inform social research, although the impact has varied (Kramarae and Spender, 1993).

## CHARACTERISTICS OF FEMINIST RESEARCH: METHODS, METHODOLOGY OR EPISTEMOLOGY?

In adopting these philosophical concerns, feminist approaches to research are more than a debate about methods. Instead they are about a way of *being* and *doing* research in which there has been a shared assumption about the need to place the diverse experiences of women at the centre rather than the margins of social investigation, and to deconstruct research that has neglected women's experiences or assumed that male experiences are universal (Hall and Hall, 1996). Such commonality of approach is evident in spite of the diversity of feminist thought and positions. Feminist researchers have shared a focus in making problematic informal and formal institutional structures, phenomena and texts, and the social relationships that have framed women's and men's situations and experiences, in order to develop theories that advance social justice for women (Olesen, 1994).

Abbott and Wallace argue, 'it is the way in which research is carried out and the framework in which the results are interpreted that determine if research is feminist or not' (1990: 205), but the question still arises about exactly how feminists have carried out research that provides a non-subjugated or, even as some claim, an emancipatory knowledge? Taking an empirical approach to this question one might use a range of methods to do the following: ask questions of feminists and non-feminist researchers; observe and listen to what feminist and non-feminist researchers do and say; examine feminist and non-feminist research documents looking for examples of similarities or differences in methods used, and for signs of similarities or differences in meaning and experiences. In addition, the researcher's interpretations could be examined reflexively and could be cross-checked with those who have been studied or by comparison with information from other sources. Reinharz (1992) undertook a similar investigation such as the one discussed above and she found that feminists had employed a 'multiplicity of methods [that] allows us to study the greatest possible range of subject matters and reach a broad set of goals . . . There is little "methodological elitism" or definition of "methodological correctness" in feminist research . . . Feminist research is amoeba like; it goes everywhere, in every direction . . . The amoeba is fed by the women's movement. The women's movement, in turn, is fed by women's outrage and hope' (Reinharz, 1992: 243–244). Arising from her investigation, Reinharz (1992: 240) has identified ten themes associated with feminist social research:

1 Feminism is a perspective, not a research method.
2 Feminists use a multiplicity of research methods.
3 Feminist research involves an ongoing criticism of non-feminist scholarship.
4 Feminist research is guided by feminist theory.

5  Feminist research may be transdisciplinary.
6  Feminist research aims to create social change.
7  Feminist research strives to represent human diversity.
8  Feminist research frequently includes the researcher as a person.
9  Feminist research frequently attempts to develop special relations with the people studied (in interactive research).
10 Feminist research frequently defines a special relation with the reader.

This empirical investigation suggested that 'method' may not be the distinguishing feature of feminist research and bears out the arguments of those who advocate that the nature of knowledge needs to be recast through a feminist praxis based on feminist ways of knowing (see, for example, Bowles and Klein, 1983; Stanley, 1993). In contrast, others have questioned the apparent essentialism of this argument (Barrett, 1987; Currie and Kazi, 1987) and have argued that by adopting appropriate research strategies and techniques 'reality' can be known (see also Hammersley, 1992). In these ways, a concern with techniques and methods has continued to underpin debates about feminist research, even though in many cases feminist research practice reveals a preference for qualitative rather than quantitative methods (Maynard, 1994; Olesen, 1994; Reinharz, 1983; Ribbens and Edwards, 1998). In order to understand this apparent contradiction between the practice of researchers who claim to be feminist and their writing about feminist research, something more than just an empirical investigation of their perceptions and methods is needed. Further consideration of the methodological and epistemological issues raised by feminists is required because decisions about the research tools used are frequently bound up with theories about how the research should be developed. For example:

> One reason it is difficult to find a satisfactory answer to questions about a distinctive feminist method is that discussions of method (techniques for gathering evidence) and methodology (a theory and analysis of how research should proceed) have been intertwined with each other and with epistemological issues (issues about an adequate theory of knowledge or justificatory strategy) in both traditional and feminist discourses. (Harding, 1987: 2)

## FEMINIST EPISTEMOLOGIES: FEMINIST WAYS OF KNOWING

The existence of different feminist discourses suggests there are distinct feminist epistemologies which provide frameworks for specifying the construction or generation of knowledge about the social world (see Harding, 1987; Lennon and Whitford, 1994; Stanley and Wise, 1990). Epistemological concerns are about the 'what' and 'how' questions concerning knowledge. These include questions about definitions of knowledge and the processes involved in its production, for example:

- What do we understand to be the nature of 'reality'?
- How do we specify what knowledge is?
- How do we recognize knowledge?
- How do we identify who are the knowers?
- By what means does someone become a knowledge producer?
- What are the means whereby competing knowledge claims are adjudicated and some rejected in favour of others or another?

The Enlightenment ideas discussed earlier in this book marked a radical shift in conceptualizations of the self and external phenomena (the subject and object binary). Traditional beliefs, feelings and emotional understanding were rejected for being partial and subjective responses, and knowledge became grounded in empirical investigation using scientific methods underpinned by inductive and deductive reasoning. The emphasis was on systematic and rigorous study to produce generalizable explanations that had been verified and tested. These ideas have had considerable influence in the social sciences in spite of the challenge from the hermeneutic and interpretative approaches which have stressed that knowledge of the social world is always a matter of understanding, and so is partial and iterative rather than comprehensive and cumulative.

Not surprisingly then, since epistemology is about 'how we know what we think we know' and because a characteristic of feminism has been diversity that has associated with women's cultural, social and historical locations, there has been a contestation of view within feminist epistemology just as there has been between feminists and non-feminists. For example, Harding (1987) identified three epistemological positions: feminist empiricism, feminist standpoint, and feminist post-modernism. Harding's approach distinguishes conceptually different feminist positions and ways of seeing the world and makes a contribution to our historical understanding by relating them to the context of the development of ideas within the women's movement.

## EARLY MANIFESTATIONS: THE FEMINIST EMPIRICIST APPROACH

In the 1960s and 1970s when 'second wave' feminism was claiming a political agenda based around women's absence from public life and confinement to the private by naming the personal as the political, identifying the gaps in existing research seemed fairly straightforward, although tendentious. The focus was on suggesting that there was a problem with existing knowledge about the world, particularly in the social sciences (see Millmann and Kanter, 1987), because the descriptions of social reality produced had been male centred and partial. Feminist empiricists questioned the validity of such knowledge for the following reasons: first, the topics investigated were masculine and reflected male experiences in the world; second, the theoretical frames reflected the structure of masculine

gender identity in the contemporary culture; third, the narrative constructed served the interests of men as a group, promoting their position
and subordinating women; finally, the whole symbolic order by means of
which knowledge claims were articulated, privileged male experiences
and conceptualized the female as lacking the characteristics associated
with masculinity.

An example that illustrates the problem of partiality can be found in some
of my own research on women shop assistants (Webb, 1990). In this study I
found that women shopworkers exhibited strong occupational identities
that included the notion of a 'career'. This finding was in contradistinction
to the claims of much of the previous literature about women workers. This
literature had suggested conceptualizing women's attitudes and experiences of paid work in terms of characteristics associated with their gender
rather than in relation to any features of the job itself (see Feldberg and
Glenn, 1979 for an example of this partial approach).

Feminist accounts which adopted the empiricist approach have been
concerned with redressing the partiality and distortions of previous
knowledge by 'adding women' into research. They also tended to assume
that although social reality is independent of the researcher, it could be
described more adequately by adopting an approach which included the
following foci. First, the gender balance could be redressed by searching
out lost women; identifying and studying invisible women; and identifying women's issues including their systematic subordination. An
example of this approach would be Lorber's (1975) study of women and
medical sociology which examined their invisibility as professionals and
their ubiquity as patients. Second, an avoidance of gender bias in research
could be made by focusing on the partiality of the 'context of discovery';
that is, the way questions are posed, as well as on the 'context of justification'; that is, the way research is conducted and explanations developed.
An example is the study by Finch and Groves (1982) of women as carers in
which the concept of work was reconfigured to provide understanding of
the unpaid and publicly unacknowledged work of women carers.

Further examples of such feminist approaches to knowledge construction can be seen in the work of Millman and Kanter (1987) and Eichler
(1988). In these texts the writers argued for research that examined men
and women from women's eyes. Millman and Kanter (1987: 30) illustrated
this by borrowing the story of the emperor's new clothes in order to
explain how it is that the women's movement could produce empirically
more accurate pictures of social reality by stripping away the 'covers and
blinders that obscure knowledge and observation'. Eichler summarized it
in this way:

> Such a new approach can be called a 'dual perspective', as opposed to a single
> (male) perspective. In the absence of a female perspective that is developed as
> well as a male perspective, applying a dual perspective necessarily involves
> investigating issues about which we thought we already knew enough.

We need to create baseline data sets that are comparable for men and women. This will mean, for quite a while, putting special emphasis on studying women rather than men, in order to start redressing the current imbalance. It also implies looking at both men and women from a female rather than a male perspective. Both sexes must be understood as gendered people. In the process, we will learn new things not only about women but about men as well. (Eichler, 1988: 45)

Eichler identified four primary problems that lead to sexism in research: first, androcentricity, which in its basic form is a vision of the world in male terms; second, overgeneralization in the language used or the concepts employed, which takes place when a study deals with one sex only but presents this as if it were of general applicability; third, gender insensitivity, which involves ignoring gender as a variable; fourth, double standards, when identical behaviours or situations are evaluated, treated or measured by different criteria. In addition Eichler suggested that three further problems can be derived from the four primary ones. These are sex appropriateness, familism and sexual dichotomism. Her purpose in identifying these seven problems was to enable researchers to overcome sexism and so Eichler concluded this text with a set of guidelines for non-sexist research practice which she suggested will enable researchers to 'see problems in a different light; new questions, new research agendas, and eventually new answers and new policies thus emerge automatically' (Eichler, 1988: 167).

The growth in feminist research in the USA and UK throughout the 1970s and early 1980s, which linked the private worlds of many women to the public sphere by making visible women's contribution as carers or the injustices of social and public policies (Olesen, 1994; Stacey, 1981), was evidence of the widespread acceptance of Eichler's prescriptions. However, adherence to a non-sexist approach was not sufficient to produce new and different research from a women's perspective. In spite of important contributions made by these feminist social scientists who have sought to 'add women' into research, 'feminist perspectives have been contained in sociology by functionalist conceptualisations of gender, by the inclusion of gender as a variable rather than as a theoretical category, and by being ghettoised, especially in Marxist sociology' (Stacey and Thorne, 1985: 301). In other words, Stacey and Thorne (1985) have argued that a positivist approach underpins Eichler's prescriptions and this they have rejected.

I would also argue that Eichler's research model fails to examine the relationship between experience, consciousness and theory and treats these distinctions as if they are unimportant. In other words, the model of non-sexist research is just as likely as sexist research to generate data that will appear 'seamlessly constructed' and the partiality of its production will not be apparent because Eichler does not encourage discussion of the role that the researcher plays in the structuring. Indeed, in my own research in the department store, my research story and how this intertwined with storytelling in the organization was a critical element in the formation of the account produced (Webb, 1991). In contrast, Eichler presents a technical or methods solution to an epistemological problem because she focuses on the operation of the research rather than considering that the partiality of knowledge is a problem about the contestation of the power of who can be a knower.

The critique of feminist empiricism provided here is embedded in a different model of knowledge generation. The critique presumes that there are different ways of conceptualizing objectivity in the social world and that different subject positions will be associated with different knowledge constructions. Harding (1987) suggested that this form of feminist commentary is associated with a second type of epistemology, the feminist standpoint theory and it is to this that I now turn.

## THE FEMINIST STANDPOINT THEORY

Feminists associated with this approach (see, for example, Hartsock, 1987; Mies, 1983; Smith, 1987) have argued that their critique of male-centred knowledge centres around differences in the conceptions of objectivity. This approach claims that the goal of objectivity in traditional research is masculinist and the pursuit of this goal has obscured the partial position of those constructing such knowledge. These writers considered 'bad science' to be an inevitable result of research conducted by those whose standpoint is privileged and not simply a mistake that can be rectified by 'adding women' in. In contrast, they suggested 'good science' is that which recognizes how the subjective position of the researcher affects the research process and its outcome and so these feminists would include researcher's subjectivity as a resource and an object of research. This approach emphasized the experiences of women; it articulated women's perspectives and attended to the research problems generated by women. In other words, their focus has been on the 'context of discovery' or the ways in which research questions have been formulated, as well as the 'context of justification' which refers to the ways in which research questions have been answered.

The Enlightenment idea of universal knowers who can stand outside of themselves and objectively develop research questions and examine the world without any partial perspective has been rejected. Feminist standpoint theorists have argued that all knowers are situated in space and time, and historically, culturally and socially. These features of their location or positioning have been intertwined with their sense-making and their explanatory formulations. Stanley and Wise (1993) have called this the interrelationship of their being (ontology) and their knowing (epistemology). They argued for a rejection of Cartesian binary ways of understanding the relationship between the body, the mind and emotions

(Stanley and Wise, 1993: 194). They stated that the Cartesian notion derived from Descartes of 'I think, therefore I am' suggests that knowing is necessary to being and to know involves overcoming a dichotomy between male and female ways of being and thinking in which the male is associated with rationality and the female with irrationality and emotion. They contend that for feminists being is part of knowing and is intertwined with it. Consequently, they argued that knowledge produced from an acknowledged subjective standpoint is less distorted than knowledge that does not reveal its partiality.

These ideas were explored in detail by Dorothy Smith, a Canadian sociologist who has written a series of influential papers arguing that sociology has been constructed around the kinds of knowledge and conceptual schemes that happen to be used by men for 'ruling' others. Consequently, Smith has argued that in learning to be a sociologist one learns 'its methods, conceptual schemes and theories [that have] been based on and built up within, the male universe (even when women have participated in its doing) . . . There is a difficulty first then of a disjunction between how women find and experience the world beginning (though not necessarily ending up) from their place and the concepts and theoretical schemes available to think about it in' (Smith, 1987: 86).

Smith went on to argue that this state of knowledge has arisen because:

It is a condition of a man's being able to enter and become absorbed in the conceptual mode that he does not have to focus his activities and interests upon his bodily existence. The structure of work and the structure of career take for granted that these matters are provided for . . . (and) Providing for the liberation . . . is a woman who keeps house for him, bears and cares for his children, washes his clothes, looks after him when he is sick, and generally provides for the logistics of his bodily existence. (Smith, 1987: 89–90)

As a consequence Smith suggested that the sociology that resulted from this mode of production is a body of knowledge 'based on organisation of experience that excludes theirs (women's) and excludes them (women) in a subordinated relationship' (1987: 91). In contrast Smith proposed a sociology that begins with different experiences of the world:

Women's direct experience places her a step back where we can recognize the uneasiness that comes in sociology from its claim to be about the world we live in and its failure to account for or even describe its actual features as we (that is women) find them, living in them . . . (and) Though such a sociology would not be exclusively for or done by women it does begin from an analysis and critique originating in their situation. (Smith, 1987: 95)

Similarly, writers such as Mies (1983) have suggested that when the standpoint is that of the oppressed, researchers have a view both of their own position and of the oppressors and so their accounts are more complete and less partial than 'malestream' ones. In other words, feminist standpoint theorists have privileged the subjectivity of the oppressed and have argued that research conducted from such a standpoint generates 'good science' because it includes the following three features:

- new empirical and theoretical resources: that is, women's experiences;
- new purposes of social science: that is to be transformative for women;
- new subject matter of inquiry: locating the researcher in the same critical plane as the overt subject matter. (derived from Harding, 1987: 9)

Harding summarized her argument as follows:

> It is features such as these three – not a 'feminist method' – which are responsible for producing the best of the new feminist research and scholarship. They can be thought of as methodological features because they show us how to apply the general structure of scientific theory to research on women and gender. They can also be thought of as epistemological ones because they imply theories of knowledge different from the traditional ones. (Harding, 1987: 9)

These feminist standpoint theorists have interwoven the private world of the researcher through the public activity of research and in doing so they have unsettled the power relationship between the researcher and researched. For example, following her work on interviewing mothers, Oakley, also a mother, argued that social research conventions about the uninvolved interviewer should be subverted by feminist interviewers so that women's voices can be heard. She argued this is achieved when 'the relationship of interviewer and interviewee is non-hierarchical and when the interviewer is prepared to invest his or her own personal identity in the relationship' (Oakley, 1981: 41). Similarly, the private and public worlds have been linked by Finch (1984) who has identified the issue of power relations in the research process and the responsibility of the researcher to exercise care to ensure the research is in women's interests:

> Initially I was startled by the readiness with which women talked to me . . . the ease with which one can get women to talk depends not so much upon one's skills as an interviewer . . . but upon one's identity as a woman . . . [But] there is a real exploitative potential in the easily established trust between women, which makes women especially vulnerable as subjects of research. (Finch, 1984: 72)

Others have used their own experiences as a personal resource to identify questions for research. For example, Haggis's (1990) discussion of how her upbringing in Australia, her experiences as a woman and her educational career all contributed to her interest in the exclusions surrounding women's experiences in colonialism and social change. Further reflections on the lived experience of research have also shown there may be a merging of the public and the private – the analytical and the emotional – as when Layland (1990) suggested that as mother of both a gay son and a straight son she was angered by homophobia and sexism, and so undertook an ethnography of a gay and lesbian youth group in order to explore the meaning and practice of masculinity.

These themes indicate a shift in focus towards an interest in epistemology and methodology and away from a concern with filling in the gaps in knowledge. Throughout the 1980s feminist researchers began to question 'who can know' and attempted to provide theoretical explanations for the inadequacies they perceived in knowledge claims that had not taken into account women's experiences. At the same time, feminist research was accompanied by a growing diversity of methods, and for some quantitative methods were no longer seen as the evil tools of positivism:

> If we begin from this position (that is a feminist epistemology) then it is possible to bring a feminist standpoint to a range of methods; we do not have to accept the 'scientistic' model of surveys or reject surveys as necessarily 'non-feminist'. (Kelly et al., 1995: 246)

These standpoint arguments have been very influential and for many feminists have come to mean that feminist research is considered to be that which is 'by women, on women and for women'. Yet, interestingly, Smith's (1987) contribution, which encouraged researchers to focus on women's daily experiences to generate the 'problems' requiring sociological explanation and a sociology that is for women, has spawned research that has revealed the multiplicity of women's experiences. In uncovering the partiality of knowledge this writing encouraged a further questioning of the universality of any claims to knowledge, whether they be from the standpoint of the privileged or from the oppressed. Smith herself acknowledged this when she suggested that such critical sociology would not be exclusively done for or by women and though women's experiences can generate important problems they do not offer any answers. Instead, she suggested the determinants of women's daily experiences are not to be uncovered directly from within the experiences, rather the experiences are a means of generating the conceptual procedures to explicate and analyse these experiences.

Furthermore in Smith's writing of the early 1970s we can see that she has begun to anticipate many of the critiques of the feminist standpoint theory offered by feminists in the 1990s (see Collins, 1990) as the following shows:

> Riding a train not long ago in Ontario I saw a family of Indians, woman, man, and three children standing together on a spur of a river watching the train go by. There was (for me) that moment – the train, those five people seen on the other side of the glass. I saw first that I could tell this incident as it was, but that telling as a description built in my position and my interpretations. I have called them a family; I have said they were watching the train. My understanding has

already subsumed theirs. Everything may have been quite other for them. My description is privileged to stand as what actually happened, because theirs is not heard in the contexts in which I may speak. If we begin from the world as we actually experience it, it is at least possible to see that we are located and that what we know of the other is conditional upon that location as part of a relation comprehending the other's location also. There are and must be different experiences of the world and different bases of experience. We must not do away with them by taking advantage of our privileged speaking to construct a sociological version which we then impose upon them as their reality. (Smith, 1987: 93)

Dorothy Smith's ideas provide a foretaste of the post-modern critique of feminist standpoint theory since they begin to recognize the heterogeneity of experience. Harding (1987: 187–188) identifies such critiques as a third manifestation of feminist epistemology and it is to this that I now turn.

## MORE RECENT MANIFESTATIONS: FEMINIST POST-MODERNISM AND OTHER ISMS

A third phase in feminist writings can be seen developing throughout the 1980s and 1990s in part in response to growing diversity within feminism through the challenges by black feminists, lesbian feminists and others, and in response to post-structuralism. The very philosophical and political arguments that had enabled feminists to develop a critique of the authority of male-centred knowledge carried with them the tools that led the voices of others, black women, lesbian women, disabled women, women from developing countries, and so on to question who can know and whose experiences are informing the knowledge produced. In other words, the epistemic authority of the feminist researcher's account began to be questioned:

> The feminist challenge showed the political dimension of acts of representation and made it impossible to ignore the power relations at the heart of knowledge production. However, to the extent to which feminism has moved from its moment of critique to that of construction it has become implicated within the power network. (Lennon and Whitford, 1994: 14)

Harding (1987: 188) suggested that feminist post-modernism created 'troubles' for the other feminist epistemologies that she identified because it raised the sceptical question of whether there can be a universal know-ing subject. This scepticism can be applied not only to the knowledge claims produced by the privileged but even to those who claim to be generating 'good science' because they are producing knowledge grounded in their experiences of oppression. Harding summarized the claims of the oppressed in the following way:

The empiricists and the standpoint theorists are both attempting to ground accounts of the world which are less partial and distorted than prevailing ones. In this sense, they are attempting to produce a feminist science – one that better reflects the world around us than the incomplete and distorting accounts provided by traditional social science. This science would not substitute one gender-loyalty for the others, but, instead, advance the objectivity of science. (Harding, 1987: 187)

In contrast, feminist post-modernism has questioned the Enlightenment project that involved a search for the truth and it has been 'derived from semiotics, deconstructionalism and psychoanalysis and the rejection of any notion of a more authentic self' (Stanley and Wise, 1990: 27). Such deconstruction has been applied to the category of woman so that variations in age, class, country, colour, sexuality and positions in power relations have served to undermine any homogeneity in the term feminism. Consequently, the very foundations of feminist politics and practice that have characteristically been rooted in women's experiences and exemplified by the slogan 'the personal is political', have been challenged (see, for example, Grant, 1993). The most explicit rejection of the idea that all women share common experiences has come from black feminists (see, for example, Brah and Minhas, 1985; Carby, 1987; Collins, 1990). This type of questioning has resulted in a recognition that any epistemological project which attempts to articulate female subjectivity and derive universal claims from women's experiences will be regarded as conflictual and contradictory. Therefore, from this perspective the notion of a 'successor science' (Harding, 1987) seems doomed.

While Harding's typology of three feminist epistemologies has been a frequent reference point for feminist discussions (Lennon and Whitford, 1994), there have been some dissenting voices. For example, Stanley and Wise (1993: 191) have argued that there is a spectrum of feminist epistemologies that shade into each other in people's actual work. They have suggested a different model of feminist epistemology that allows for contradictory views about the definition and generation of knowledge. From their work on lesbians in which they have suggested many complexities that were absent from some 'standpoint' accounts, they have argued that individuals are able to combine different elements, from apparently conflicting frameworks, in their research. This is possible they have suggested either because as researchers we fail to notice the conflicts since we do not think through the bases of the ideas with which we are working or, alternatively, we decide to work with the contradictions because these reflect the way we experience social reality:

Our feminist critique of knowledges argues instead for a materialistic, but not a Marxist, theory of knowledge, one irrevocably rooted in women's concrete and diverse practical everyday experiences of oppressions; and it insists that these analytic knowledges are reflexive, indexical and local: they are epistemologically tied to the context of production and are ontologically grounded. This is what we have earlier referred to as our feminist fractured foundationalist epistemology. (Stanley and Wise, 1993: 191–192)

In contrast to Harding (1987), Stanley and Wise (1993) have questioned the claim made by feminist empiricist and feminist standpoint epistemologies that they are producing privileged knowledge. They have suggested that some feminists such as black or lesbian feminists may be silenced by a typology of epistemologies that involves privilege in knowledge construction. They have accepted that 'on the surface, assuming the epistemological privilege of the oppressed is both attractive and plausible' (1993: 227) because these ontologies/epistemologies do provide a different view of what passes for reality and that it is a preferable interpretation to that provided by oppressor groups. However, they have questioned how one can compare competing knowledge claims from within the oppressed. They have posed the following questions: should we measure comparative suffering; and should we seek to identify those with the greatest degree of suffering to be the superordinate among the epistemologies of the oppressed? Stanley and Wise's argument is rather different from that of other feminist epistemologies because they have rejected the concerns of these other approaches. They have contended that empiricist and standpoint epistemologies are rooted in Cartesian notions of science and share an assumption that these feminist positions have a privileged access to descriptions and explanations of the 'real' social reality, either because of the training and techniques used, or because the researchers are from an oppressed group. They have concluded:

> Our view is that there are no foundational grounds for judging the *a priori* superiority of the epistemologies of the oppressed, nor of any one group of the oppressed, in relation to the production of 'knowledge' and the settling of its problematics, other than by comparing and judging the ontological bases of these epistemologies; and such a judgement is . . . ethically objectionable. There are however, acceptable moral and political grounds for finding one of these preferable, a rather different claim than that which is concerned with staking claim to a 'truer, more real reality'. For us the grounds are ontological: that is, that it better fits with a proponent's experience of living or being or understanding. Knowledge, as we have argued, is situated, specific and local to the conditions of its production and thus to the social location of its producers. (Stanley and Wise, 1993: 227–278)

A solution to these dilemmas rests in revealing how the research story and the voice of the researcher and researched are made public in research reports (Ribbens and Edwards, 1998). Here, feminist concerns chime with the crisis of legitimation explored by Denzin (1997) and with Lyotard's (1984) scepticism of the grand narratives of the European Enlightenment. Within these approaches, validity is regarded as the researcher's mask of authority (see Lather, 1994), and so deconstruction of these strategies for legitimation is advocated through polyvocal and multi-authored research stories, autobiographies and performance texts among other modes which make explicit the political practice of research (Lather, 1991; Stanley, 1990; Trinh, 1991). For example, by writing full autobiographies or reports in the first person, as in Stanley's (1990, 1994) discussion of the way 'a referral was made', which is an account from the inside (the carer's view) of how a social services department created an elderly statistic, and by including the angst, passion and emotion of the research process, the author-ity of the researcher's voice becomes apparent. In other words, it seems that feminist claims to science are just another story. Different women tell different stories and they each have validity.

For those readers who are beginning a research project for the first time, some may have found these ideas discomforting because they undermine the notion that a comprehensive account can be produced or that oppressed groups will always produce a 'successor science'. Others though may have found the ideas convincing, because they acknowledge that all ideas, descriptions and explanations about the social world are in part a reflection of who the researcher is, in terms of their sex, 'race', class and sexuality, whether they be feminists or not. Nevertheless, whichever of these views attracts, the contribution that these other more recent feminist frameworks make which you are likely to have found useful is the prescription to be reflexive about your role in the research process. As Reinharz has suggested:

> Feminists found that their troubling or puzzling experiences became a 'need to know'. Being an insider of the experience enabled them to understand what (some) women have to 'say in a way no outsider could'. Researchers who adopt this view draw on a new 'epistemology of insiderness' that sees life and work as intertwined. (Reinharz, 1992: 260)

You may think that being an insider gives you more insight into an experience and that you can draw on your own common-sense knowledge to help you to understand what is going on. This can have strengths; for example, in my study of the department store my experiences as a woman led me to recognize the sexism involved in the imposition by managers of different dress codes across the various departments of the store and between women and men (Webb, 1991). However, 'insiderness' can lead one to become blind to the ways one is using one's common-sense knowledge. This knowledge or commonality of experiences needs to be subjected to scrutiny just as the issues that appear new and different are noted for study.

Furthermore, if one accepts the idea of differences among social groups, including women, then the notion that one can always expect a link between the personal experience of the researcher and the research in which they are engaged could lead to ethnocentrism, particularly in cross-cultural research. Indeed, you may decide that there are some things that you cannot research because you are not an insider and you occupy a position of outsider that might exclude you from certain knowledges and experiences. In the department store, I worked as a shop assistant and my access to department management perceptions was limited by the work role I had adopted and by my gender (Webb, 1990).

You may have identified some research plans in which 'starting from one's own experience' seems inappropriate to you; you may also feel that it violates an expectation that a researcher be detached, objective and value neutral. Consider though some of the ideas presented in this chapter which may be summed up by Oakley (1974) when she suggested that much written in sociology at that time (the 1970s) was often a cover for patriarchy rather than value neutral knowledge. Whether you are male or female and whether you identify with feminisms or not, the arguments discussed so far in this chapter would suggest that one should distrust research reports which include no statement about the researcher's experience. Reinharz has summarized this concern in the following way:

> Reading such reports, (that neglect to include anything about the researcher) I feel that the researcher is hiding from me or does not know how important personal experience is. Such reports seem woefully incomplete and even dishonest. (Reinharz, 1992: 263)

# 4 RACE AND RACISM

*Peter Jackson*

This chapter aims to introduce some of the main philosophical issues in the study of 'race' and racism including the debate between essentialist and social constructionist perspectives, the question of academic neutrality versus political commitment, and the issue of our own positionality as researchers.[1] Given that the field of 'race relations' is such a politicized one, where debate is often highly charged and where emotions frequently run high, it may be best to begin with some definitions.

## RACISM

Following the sociologist Robert Miles (1982: 78), racism can be defined as an ideology that ascribes negatively evaluated characteristics (e.g. stereotypes about laziness or greed) in a deterministic manner to a group of people who are additionally identified as being in some way biologically distinct. There are several aspects of this definition that are worth exploring in more detail. Miles insists that racism is an ideology, a set of ideas and beliefs that reflects the material interests of those who articulate such views and which inform particular kinds of practice. Miles also insists that racism operates in a deterministic manner. Racism is not simply the belief in a casual or contingent link between social characteristics and physical traits. It is a belief in their necessary and inevitable connection: all Irish people are assumed to be unintelligent, all Chinese people to be industrious, or whatever. Finally, Miles insists that racism involves a belief in the social significance of genetically inherited or biological differences between human beings.

The advantage of Miles's definition is that it sets up a series of strict criteria for academic debate. The problem is that it rules out certain kinds of thinking that we might still consider to be racist. Consider, for example, Margaret Thatcher's comments in the run-up to the 1979 election:

> If we went on as we are, then by the end of the century there would be 4 million people of New Commonwealth or Pakistan [origin] here. Now, that is an awful lot and I think it means that people are really rather afraid that this country might be swamped by people with a different culture. And, you know, the British character

has done so much for democracy, for law, and done so much throughout the world, that if there is a fear that it might be swamped, people are going to react and be rather hostile to those coming in. (quoted in Jackson, 1987: 9)

According to Miles's definition this would not qualify as a racist statement: there is nothing here about the biological basis of human difference and no direct reference to 'race'.[2] Rather, the issue is expressed in cultural terms, referring to 'the British character' and to the 'different culture' of 'those coming in'. Yet one need only think about the history of public debate about British immigration, concern about the number of immigrants coming in and the phrasing of such debates in terms of flooding and swamping to realize that Mrs Thatcher's remarks contain a poorly concealed subtext about 'race' that many would define as racist. Enoch Powell used similar arguments about the inevitability of 'racial' conflict in his so-called 'rivers of blood' speech in 1968 (also characterized by a concern for the number of immigrants). Similar images recur in the reporting of the 'visa crisis' in 1986. On 15 October 1986, the *Sun* carried the following headline: '3000 Asians Flood Britain', the *Daily Mail* published a photograph with the caption 'Swamped: immigration officer is besieged by relatives seeking news of passengers', and the *Daily Express* headline ran 'Asian Flood Swamps Airport'. The recurrence of images of 'flooding' and 'swamping' is surely no coincidence and reveals the consistency of racialized thinking and its continuity over time.[3]

These incidents provide some significant insights into the nature of contemporary discourse about 'race'. Increasingly, racism is expressed in a cultural vocabulary, shorn of any direct reference to biology (see Blaut, 1992). Yet, as a *Guardian* editorial, 'Racism: the words and the reality', remarked in 1987:

> Race politics in Britain are increasingly conducted in a superficially non-racist code . . . Much of what the Conservatives say about the inner cities, council housing, education and, above all, law and order, simply cannot be understood any longer without appreciating its unspoken subtext on race. (*Guardian*, 15 April 1987)

Rather than thinking about racism as an inevitable feature of human societies where it is 'only natural' to be suspicious of people who are perceived to be different from ourselves, our responsibility as social scientists is to trace the specific form that racism takes in different places and at different times. For, as Stuart Hall reminds us, it is not helpful to define racism as a 'natural' or permanent feature of all human societies, arising out of a universal 'human nature':

> It's not a permanent human or social deposit which is simply waiting there to be triggered off when the circumstances are right. It has no natural or universal law

of development. It does not always assume the same shape. There have been many significantly different *racisms* – each historically specific and articulated in a different way with the societies in which they appear. Racism is always historically specific in this way, whatever common features it may appear to share with similar social phenomena. (Hall, 1978: 26)

Very similar ideas are expressed by the Director of the London-based Institute of Race Relations: 'Racism does not stay still; it changes shape, size, contours, purpose, function – with changes in the economy, the social structure, the system and, above all, the challenges to that system' (Sivanandan, 1983: 2). Such a perspective also leads to a rather different way of conceptualizing 'race'.

## RACE

The idea of 'race' has a very long history, but it took on much of its contemporary meaning during the age of imperialism in the eighteenth and nineteenth centuries (McClintock, 1995). Travellers' accounts and missionary tales of distant places and foreign people were avidly read 'back home', supplemented by the emergence of new scientific disciplines like natural history, anthropology and geography. From the eighteenth century it had been common to divide humanity into a series of discrete 'races' (Negroid, Mongoloid or Caucasian), associating physical traits (like skin colour, hair type and nose shape) with social characteristics (like leadership and the capacity for hard work). The Darwinian revolution in the mid-nineteenth century had an enormous impact on thinking about 'race', highlighting the continuities with our ancestors among the primates and popularizing the idea of an evolutionary sequence (with white men inevitably placed at the top of the evolutionary tree).

Victorian ideas about 'race' were often quite contradictory (Lorimer, 1979). Ideas about the 'noble savage' (popularized in novels like Edgar Rice Burroughs's *Tarzan of the Apes*, 1917) were juxtaposed with stereotypes of the 'comic buffoon' (popularized in music hall and black-face minstrelsy). Quasi-scientific ideas about racial classification and the supposedly degenerative effects of intermarriage led to the development of pernicious ideas about eugenics, in order to reduce the 'stock' of the 'lower types' of humanity and to increase the numbers of those with good 'breeding'. Gradually, however, in the twentieth century (not least because of the impact of racialized thinking in Nazi Germany), scientific ideas about the natural or biological basis of 'racial' difference have given way to a more liberal, social-scientific perspective on 'race relations'. Within this 'race relations' perspective the principal debate has been between those who adopt an essentialist position and those who adopt a social constructionist approach.

## ESSENTIALISM VERSUS SOCIAL CONSTRUCTIONISM

Essentialist approaches to 'race', as with gender, argue that there are fundamental differences between the 'races', based in human biology or in long-established and ineluctable tradition. Even where the cultural basis of human variation is acknowledged, essentialists assert that these differences are inherent and hence invariable over time. These ideas have been progressively challenged to the point where they are no longer a dominant way of thinking within the social sciences. Current social science thinking supports the idea that 'race' (and gender) are social or cultural constructions that reflect the ideas of the time in which they were advanced and support the interests of those who advance the ideas. In the nineteenth century, for example, a common construction of 'race' suggested that black people were well adapted to manual labour in the tropics. This was clearly in the interests of the plantation-owning classes, supported perhaps by pseudo-scientific arguments about the relationship between climate and 'race'. The following is an example of ideas that were prevalent until surprisingly late into the twentieth century:

> In the case of the Negro, climatic influences – acting direct and through the typical food – lead to the early closing of the 'seams' between the bones of the skull; and thus the development of the brain is arrested; and the adult is essentially unintellectual. On the other hand, he is naturally 'acclimatized' against numerous diseases and other conditions of life and work which are very adverse to the white man. He is, therefore, of great use as a manual labourer in a 'steamy' climate, e.g. on a cane-sugar plantation. ('The Races of Mankind', *Bartholomew's School Atlas*, 1921; quoted in Jackson, 1992: 138)

It is easy to feel rather superior about the blatant racism of the past and to assume that we are now much more enlightened. But rather than thinking of the history of ideas about 'race' as some kind of unilinear progression towards the present, we might focus instead on the continuities and discontinuities of racialized thinking over time. For example, ideas about the supposed musicality and sexuality of black people have been remarkably constant since the nineteenth century, as have ideas about Jewish avarice or Irish aggression. Similarly, as previously noted, Margaret Thatcher's argument about 'the British character' being 'swamped' by 'those coming in' can only be understood in relation to earlier debates about 'race'. From this perspective, racism can be seen to work as a kind of reservoir of ideas and images whose meaning derives in part from the way these ideas and images have been used in the past. Racism supplies a stock of knowledge, a 'pre-formed vocabulary' on which it is possible to draw selectively as occasion demands. For example, the word 'immigrant' has a particular meaning in British society with a particular set of connotations that derive from the period of large-scale immigration from the New Commonwealth and Pakistan in the 1960s and

1970s. The largest 'immigrant' group in Britain, the Irish, are rarely thought of as 'immigrants' in this sense, just as earlier groups of immigrants such as the Huguenots or the Jews were not 'racialized' in the same way as more recent arrivals from the New Commonwealth and Pakistan.

While there are clear continuities with the past, other aspects of racialized thinking can be shown to have varied over space and time, and between different social groups. For example, we would not now expect a British prime minister to speak openly about alleged differences in intelligence between the 'races'. (These ideas were, however, given renewed currency in the USA following the publication of Hernstein and Murray's (1994) controversial study of 'race' and IQ.) Rather than thinking about 'race' as a natural feature of human society, whereby humanity can be divided into a series of clearly defined and non-overlapping groups, a social construction approach obliges us to examine the specific form that racialized thinking takes in particular places and at different times. In the words of Marci Green and Bob Carter (1988), 'races' are made, not given; they are the product of history and society, not biology.[4] Our focus as social scientists should be on tracing specific processes of racialization, including the multiple ways that racialized ways of thinking combine with constructions of gender, sexuality, (dis)ability or other 'axes' of social difference, including divisions of class and nation (Anthias and Yuval-Davis, 1993). Once this perspective is adopted, the old sociology of 'race relations' is no longer a tenable academic object of study as there are no discrete and unchanging 'races' whose social relations can be studied. Rather, our job is to study particular processes of racialization as they have taken shape in different times and places.

### 'RACE RELATIONS' OR ANTI-RACISM?

With the development of a social construction approach to 'race', the liberal consensus about 'race relations' has been thoroughly unsettled, forcing academics with an interest in 'race' to redefine their own roles and responsibilities. As Stuart Hall charged in the early 1980s:

> Instead of thinking that confronting the question of race is some sort of moral intellectual academic duty which white people with good feelings do for blacks, one has to remember that the issue of race provides one of the most important ways of understanding how this society actually works and how it has arrived where it is. (Hall, 1981: 69)

From this perspective, 'race' is not something that only applies to marginalized groups within British society; it is not simply the preserve of so-called 'ethnic minorities'. Rather, racialized thinking is central to the definition of the nation and the cultural politics of 'race' is something that applies to everyone (Gilroy, 1987). Challenging racism, rather than studying 'race relations', came to preoccupy more and more social scientists during the 1970s as local government also developed a more self-consciously anti-racist agenda during the period of municipal socialism.

During this period the controversy arose about the label 'Black' which some activists sought to apply to people of both South Asian and Afro-Caribbean origin and descent, while others rejected this gesture towards inclusivity as failing to address the specificity of different ethnicities. While Tariq Modood argued that the label 'Black' 'requires too high a price in terms of loss of principle from anti-racists and sells short the majority of the people it identifies as "Black"' (1988: 397), others argued that 'Black' was a matter of political consciousness rather than a question of skin colour. The experience of the civil rights struggle in the USA and of municipal anti-racism in Great Britain was held to have given a new and positive meaning to the label 'Black', but which others found unacceptable in its apparent homogenization of 'ethnic' difference.

This controversy points to one of the possible limitations of the social construction approach: that it can be seen to deny or undermine the very basis on which particular forms of anti-racist politics have been effectively organized. If 'race' is held to be only a 'construction', some feel that its significance as a basis of oppression is being downplayed. If people wish to organize themselves politically around essentialist constructions of 'race', should academics be seen to oppose such moves? It is certainly possible to point to particular contexts in which the move away from essentialist conceptions of 'race' has had very negative political consequences, reducing the likelihood of indigenous people's land claims being upheld, for example. Academics with an interest in 'race' have therefore been forced to reconsider their position and to question whether their politics and their theories might be pulling them in different directions.

Similar debates have arisen among feminist social scientists where the turn towards post-modernism is viewed with suspicion insofar as it implies a moral relativism in which one standpoint or perspective is no more valid than another. The African-American feminist bell hooks cites a typical response from black people to the critique of essentialism, especially when it denies the validity of their political identities: 'It's easy to give up identity', she says, 'when you got one' (1990: 28). She suggests that we should be suspicious of post-modern critiques of the 'subject' when they surface at the particular historical moment when many subjugated people feel themselves coming to voice for the first time. She later describes the whole thrust of post-modernist relativism as 'the latest hip racism' (1990: 133), a suspicion that Nancy Hartsock expresses in rather more guarded fashion:

> It seems highly suspicious that it is at this moment in history, when so many groups are engaged in 'nationalism' which involve re-definitions of the margin-alized Others, that doubt arises in the academy about the nature of the 'subject', about the possibilities for a general theory which can describe the world, about

historical 'progress'. Why is it, exactly at the moment when so many of us who
have been silenced begin to demand the right to name ourselves, to act as
subjects rather than objects of history, that just then the concept of subjecthood
becomes 'problematic'? (Hartsock, 1987: 196)

For these reasons, academics have recently begun to talk about various
forms of 'strategic essentialism', whereby particular groups of people may
choose to adopt an essentialist label, despite its faults, for the positive
political purchase it offers. Racial or ethnic labels may be chosen as what
Hall (1992: 254) calls a 'necessary fiction', something that is recognized to
be constructed but which is treated in a temporary and strategic fashion as
though it were more fixed. Some will regard the implied distinction
between political and academic commitments as completely untenable;
others will accept that such contradictions are an unavoidable feature of
the increasingly positional politics of 'race'.


## A POLITICS OF POSITION?

Conventionally, of course, the adherence to a committed political position
is inconsistent with the neutrality and objectivity that is required of
academic inquiry. For others, the suggestion that academics can ever be
'neutral' is itself untenable, once the relationship between knowledge and
power is accepted. While many would accept that there is no contradiction
between political commitment and scientific rigour, few would now be
prepared to defend the 'neutrality' of social science. As a result, the politics
of academic research on 'race' has come to be debated with increasing
urgency. Writing in the radical journal *Race and Class*, for example, Bourne
and Sivanandan (1980) challenged academic researchers to abandon their
self-appointed role as the 'translators' of black cultures. They argued that
the position of neutral outsider or 'ombudsman' was no longer tenable. But
they also warned academics against adopting the equally problematic role
of uncritical 'cheerleader' to black resistance. How then should researchers
seek to 'position' themselves in relation to questions of 'race' and racism,
and how are we 'positioned' by our circumstances?

One response has been to throw off the cloak of scientific objectivity and
to explore the consequences of our own subjectivity: to accept that knowledge is situated and to take responsibility for our own position in relation
to those about whom we write. Such a process corresponds to what the
Italian Marxist Antonio Gramsci once described as a shift from a war of
manoeuvre to a war of position where, in this case, the play of identity and
difference is generating new kinds of identity. Though Gramsci himself
might not have approved, the contemporary form of this 'positional' war
has led to the increasing abandonment of conventional class-based politics
and the articulation of new forms of 'identity politics' around such issues
as gender, sexuality, race and the environment. Part of that process has

involved the identification of what Stuart Hall calls 'new ethnicities' (see Back, 1996).

Hall's 'new ethnicities' are articulated as part of a new politics of representation in the visual arts which have rejected the notion of an 'innocent' black subject. Instead, Hall seeks to uncover 'the extraordinary diversity of subjective positions, social experiences and cultural identities which compose the category "black"' (Hall 1992: 254). Despite the troubled history of the term, Hall argues that the word for such identities is 'ethnicity':

> If the black subject and black experience are not stabilised in Nature or by some other essential guarantee, then it must be the case that they are constructed historically, culturally, politically – and the concept which refers to this is 'ethnicity'. The term ethnicity acknowledges the place of history, language and culture in the construction of subjectivity and identity, as well as the fact that all discourse is placed, positioned, situated, and all knowledge is contextual. (1992: 257)

The new forms of ethnicity that Hall goes on to outline are forward looking to new alliances and possibilities, not backward looking to originary cultures or ethnic absolutism.

One consequence of these debates for white academics with an interest in 'race' is that we might begin to theorize our own ethnicities rather than focusing exclusively on the identities of various racialized Others. For too long 'ethnicity' has been seen as something that applies only to ethnic minorities, leading to a marginalization of 'ethnic' politics and turning the focus of attention away from those who, historically, have been responsible for the development of racist thinking and the practices that such ideas inform. There has already been some attention within cultural studies to the play of 'whiteness' in the literary imagination. In Richard Dyer's pioneering essay in *Screen* (1988), for example, 'whiteness' stands for virtually anything besides the position of racial privilege that it historically denotes. When not seen as a position of privilege, according to Dyer, 'whiteness' appears unmarked, colourless, bland, invisible, cultureless, everything and nothing, asserting its normativity (if it is required to assert itself at all). Toni Morrison provides a very similar list of the character of 'whiteness' in her reflections on American literature, abhorring the 'wilful critical blindness' that sees whiteness as mute, meaningless, unfathomable, pointless, frozen, veiled, curtained, dreaded, senseless and implacable (1992: 59).

Catherine Hall's (1992) work takes the argument a stage further, exploring specific historical connections between 'whiteness' and particular forms of male, middle-class Englishness. For those who are its subject bearers, 'whiteness' only becomes an issue when it is faced with some form of cultural other: during the Morant Bay rebellion in nineteenth-century Jamaica or as a reaction to New Commonwealth immigration to

Britain in the 1960s. The kind of politics with which 'whiteness' has been associated in Britain are of the most reactionary and barbarous kind: the National Front and British National Party, Powellism or, more recently, as part of a more generalized neo-fascist response across Europe. For Diane Jeater, this was the abiding problem of her childhood, growing up in south London, where being white did not seem to bestow an identity that could be linked to any kind of oppositional politics. In her attempt to speak from the specificity of her own circumstances, she argues that 'blackness' is not inherited as part of a fixed and separate cultural tradition, but 'out of the interactions between cultures and histories which could be traced back to both Europe and Africa' (Jeater, 1992: 114). From this historical position, she goes on to assert a notion of cultural hybridity as characteristic of her own British identity, a creative blending of apparently separate elements: roast beef and reggae music in her own memorable terms. Her ability to 'celebrate' the complexities and interdependencies of her diverse cultural heritages (1992: 118–119) may, however, still be thought to betray a position of cultural privilege. Finally, then, Ruth Frankenberg addresses this problem head-on, emphasizing the structural context in which such 'hybrid' identities are formed. Though interested in the diversity of ways of experiencing 'whiteness', she argues that the range of possible ways of living such an identity is delimited by the relations of racism at that moment and in that place (Frankenberg, 1993: 236).

## CONCLUSION

This chapter has sought to guide you through some of the main philosophical issues that are confronted in the contemporary academic study of 'race' and racism. It has shown the gradual demise of essentialist thinking about 'race' and the growing strength of an alternative social construction approach. But it has also sounded a note of caution concerning the unintended effects of an uncritical approach to the social construction of 'race' which may be politically disabling. The question of strategic essentialism was seen to have arisen in this context, whereby racialized thinking is accepted, in some circumstances and by some people, as a 'necessary fiction'.

It has also been argued that the academic study of 'race' and racism cannot be divorced from the wider politics of 'race', raising questions about our supposed neutrality as social scientists and the need for a more committed approach that retains its intellectual integrity. One possible line for thinking through these issues was discussed, concerning the notion of positionality, whereby all knowledge is situated and our own subjectivities as researchers also need to be theorized. For white researchers with an interest in 'race', it was suggested that a more historically and sociologically inclusive study is required whereby 'whiteness' is not excluded from the analysis. As with many of the key questions in social science theory and methodology, however, there are few (if any) 'right' answers. These are issues that have to be worked through in the context of each particular research project. They arise in one version or another with all social science research, but they take on a particular sharpness in the current context because of the highly charged and politicized nature of the study of 'race' and racism.

## NOTES

1  Throughout this chapter, the word 'race' appears in quotation marks to highlight the problematic nature of the term. 'Race' is approached here as a social construction rather than as a biological fact. Analysis focuses on the idea of 'race' (as an ideology), on various kinds of racialized thinking and on the consequences of such thinking. For further arguments in support of this position, see P. Jackson and J. Penrose, *Constructions of Race, Place and Nation* (UCL Press, London, 1993).
2  For subsequent developments in R. Miles's thinking about 'race' and racism, see *Racism* (Routledge, London, 1989) and *Racism After 'Race Relations'* (Routledge, London, 1993).
3  For an excellent discussion of 'race' and racism in contemporary Britain, see J. Solomos, *Race and Racism in Contemporary Britain* (Macmillan, London, 1993).
4  Biologists now accept that there is as much variation within each so-called 'race' as there is between them. For a review of the biological evidence on 'race', see S.J. Gould, *The Mismeasure of Man* (Norton, New York, 1981).

# PART II

# ETHICAL AND LEGAL ISSUES IN SOCIAL SCIENCE RESEARCH

Social science research covers a very wide field of studies and those who engage in research in the social sciences will find themselves in all kinds of different situations. No one can tell you exactly what you should do in all the circumstances that may confront you with an ethical dilemma, because it is quite possible that no one else has had to confront exactly that set of conditions before. One of the classic dilemmas, for example, is whether there are circumstances in which you breach the obligations of confidentiality to a respondent. Ultimately, therefore, you have to exercise judgement. But does this not mean that you are on your own and decide what to do as you go along? There are many precedents and examples of what should or should not be done. There are often guidelines, and there are laws that have to be observed, but above all there are ethical principles.

This part of the book deals with three highly problematic concepts – research, ethics and the law – and it is perhaps timely at this point to identify how these terms will be used. The term research covers a wide range of activity: the focus in the subsequent chapters is concerned with social scientific inquiry which is generally characterized by its systematic and theory driven nature (contrasted with, say, the kind of research that a journalist might undertake). As far as 'ethics' are concerned, while the matters considered here have a much wider philosophical context, the emphasis is on ethical principles as applied to the research enterprise. No attempt is made to deal with the whole field of ethics, as broadly conceived. Finally, the law will be evaluated as a particular ethical approach in survey research, and to assess the extent to which the law regulates research.

The discussion in the following chapters is essentially about understanding what ethical principles are and about translating them into practice. The principles are set out in Chapter 5 by Gerry Kent, but they underpin all the other contributions. Gerry also presents a number of cases which are used by way of examples of the ethical principles that he presents. This is followed by a chapter in which the underlying theme is research and power. In this chapter Iain Crow unpacks the various dimensions of power within the research context by a discussion of confidentiality, fraudulent research and accountability. An issue raised by many research students who are writing a theoretical thesis is that discussions about ethics and social research are not relevant to them. Iain addresses this issue and concludes that ethics are important, regardless of the nature of the project. While ethical considerations are more immediate and direct for research students engaged in empirical research, ethical considerations are also evident in theoretical work which can have indirect and longer term consequences. The chapter concludes with a discussion of the ethical and power dimensions inherent in the ownership and control of research.

In Chapter 7 Gerry Kent considers the important topic of informed consent, specifically what it is and how it is achieved. In Chapters 8 and 10 David Townend explains that the law constitutes a particular ethical position and looks at how legal concepts apply to various stages of the research process. He considers such matters as intellectual property rights and the ownership of research, and the protection of the researcher and others. In doing so he explains the researcher's obligations under the Data Protection Act 1998.

It is all very well for lawyers and social researchers to say what they think is right, but what does it feel like to be on the receiving end of research – to work in an agency that is often the subject of research? Anne Celnick was in this position as a research officer for the South Yorkshire Probation Service, so she knows what it is like to be approached by research students keen to pursue their inquiries into offenders, or the way the service works. She has also undertaken research herself, so is able to appreciate both perspectives. In Chapter 9 she considers how the demands of policymakers and practitioners may sometimes conflict with ethical principles, and provides some valuable advice about the kinds of issues that research students should think about when seeking access to organizations.

## SUPPLEMENTARY READING

Bulmer, M. (1982) *Social Research Ethics*. London: Macmillan.
Burgess, R.G. (1994) *The Ethics of Educational Research*. Basingstoke: Falmer Press.
Homan, R. (1992) *The Ethics of Social Research*. London: Longman.
Kimmel, A.J. (1988) *Ethics and Values in Applied Social Research*. London: Sage.
Punch, M. (1986) *The Politics and Ethics of Fieldwork*. London: Sage.
Sieber, J.E. (1992) *Planning Ethically Responsible Research*. London: Sage.

# ETHICAL PRINCIPLES

*Gerry Kent*

This chapter is designed to aid understanding of the underlying principles and issues involved in conducting research in an ethical manner. These principles apply to everyone in a wide variety of settings. Not only do they help to make decisions about research issues, but they also serve as a general guide for living in an ethical and responsible way. The aims of this chapter are (a) to provide a brief introduction to moral theory and (b) to illustrate how these principles apply to research. A fuller discussion of the issues involved can be found in Beauchamp and Childress (1994).

## WHY IS IT IMPORTANT TO KNOW ABOUT MORAL THEORY?

It is possible to design a scientifically sound piece of research which could contribute substantially to human welfare and to science itself. This research could, for example, lead to a better understanding of a socially important issue, such as the transmission of the HIV virus, or could lead to the development of a new intervention to reduce human distress. However, it could also be a research project which ought not to be conducted, because it could involve the violation of human rights or might result in some kind of harm. In such a case, a good piece of scientific research could not be performed because it is considered unethical. It can be useful to consider a (hypothetical) example to illustrate this issue. Consider the following possibility:

> You are a researcher who has received a grant from a charity to conduct research into HIV/AIDS. As part of your research you have been taking blood samples from people who are HIV+. On one analysis you find that a person who was previously HIV+ now has no signs of infection in his blood. You know that this has been recorded previously but is very rare. You think that by analysing his blood further you may be able to develop a vaccine or even an anti-body. However, the person refuses you permission to use his blood in this way.

This scenario presents a problem for the researcher. On the one hand, further analyses might yield significant results, but on the other hand this would involve going against the person's wishes. Each of these actions would have its own merits and difficulties. This is an example of an ethical dilemma, where there is no straightforward answer.

Is there a way of understanding this dilemma in formal terms? As shown below, knowledge about ethics and moral theory would not tell the researcher what to do and how to behave. Although ethics helps the researcher to understand better this ethically problematic situation, it only provides a framework for making decisions. Ultimately the researcher has to draw upon his or her values and experiences and the cultural context when considering what action to take in response to an ethical dilemma.

## THEORIES OF ETHICS

There are two overarching theories in ethical philosophy: deontological theory and consequentialist theory.

### Deontological theory

This term derives from the Greek 'deon', meaning duty. The most famous advocate of this approach was Immanuel Kant (1724–1804), who argued that morals ought to be based on obligations to others. According to this theory, we ought to follow natural laws and rights. Researchers ought to respect every human being, even if this could have some unfortunate consequences. According to Kant, the researcher should not conduct further analyses on the blood because this would go against the individual's wishes and rights.

### Consequentialist theory

This type of theory holds that we ought to produce the greatest possible balance of value over disvalue. The utilitarian philosopher John Stuart Mill (1806–73) is perhaps the best-known advocate of this approach. He argued that people should seek to act in accordance with the consequences of their behaviour and minimize suffering and maximize well-being. He might conclude that the researcher ought to conduct further analyses because the harm done to the individual person involved is minimal, yet the positive consequences for thousands of others might be great.

What kind of researcher are you? Would you tend to be a deontologist – giving individuals' rights the higher priority? Or are you a consequentialist – valuing the greater good over the individual? If asked, could you develop an argument to justify your choice of action?

## ETHICAL PRINCIPLES

In the early part of the twentieth century ethicists began to consider ethical dilemmas in a different way. Rather than argue between deontological and consequentialist approaches, they developed a set of four principles and four rules which can be used to guide ethical analysis. These principles are: anatomy, beneficence, non-maleficence and justice.

### Autonomy

We ought to respect the right to self-determination. At this point in western cultural development, this is the principle which is most often given priority when there is an ethical dilemma. The term autonomy comes from the Greek 'autos' (meaning self) and 'nomos' (rule, or governance). The idea here is that researchers have an obligation to recognize that a person has the right to agree or not agree to take part in a research project. Respect for this right forms the basis for attempting to ensure that informed consent is achieved.

### Beneficence

We ought to do good. This principle involves the obligation to take positive steps to help others. It provides an important justification and goal for researchers. Society funds academic research partly on the basis of furthering basic scientific knowledge, but also in the hope that the knowledge and understanding gained will ultimately be of a wider benefit.

On occasions, a conflict occurs between the principles of autonomy and beneficence. An example from medical care is when a patient decides to refuse treatment (the patient's right to autonomy), which a doctor believes is in their best interests (the doctor's obligation to do good for his or her patients – beneficence). The term paternalism (or, more often now, parentalism) is used when the principle of beneficence overrides the principle of autonomy. Similarly, a researcher may believe that a potential research project has such high value for society in general that a person's reluctance to participate ought to be overridden. As outlined further in the chapter on informed consent, paternalism is generally unacceptable from an ethical point of view since autonomy is often given the greater weight.

### Non-maleficence

We ought not to cause harm. This is the principle concerned with the obligation not to inflict harm or expose people to unnecessary risks. In terms of research, it implies that we should not involve people in experiments where detrimental effects on physical or emotional well-being are likely. Some of the notorious experiments shortly after World War II, where soldiers and civilians were exposed to radiation, are examples where this principle was ignored.

### Justice

We ought to ensure fair entitlement to resources. This is the principle which addresses entitlements: people should be treated fairly. It would be unethical, for example, for one postgraduate student in a department to be given many resources to do research while another is starved of accommodation, computing facilities or financial support. Another relevant issue for research students is that society provides funding for postgraduate study, even though this can imply a shift of resources away from individuals in low-paid jobs who have few prospects towards those who are most intellectually capable and whose future earnings might be considerably enhanced by training.

### RULES

Another level of ethical analysis involves what are termed rules. These are more specific guides to action than principles. These rules are seen as necessary for the development of trust between researchers and study participants. Like principles, however, they are not absolute. It may be ethical to override a rule if there is adequate justification for doing so. The four rules are: veracity, privacy, confidentiality and fidelity.

### Veracity

Veracity concerns telling the truth. Researchers have an obligation to provide accurate information about the nature of a study when enlisting potential participants. The rule of veracity regulates against the use of deception. For example, a potential participant should not be misled about the purpose of a study. Also, as discussed below, researchers have an obligation to report the results of their research truthfully, without tampering with the data or being selective in what they report.

### Privacy

Privacy concerns respect for limited access to another person. This means that people have the right to limit access to themselves, physically, emotionally or cognitively. Research participants grant access to their thoughts, feelings and behaviour when they agree to take part in a study, but not unlimited access. In an interview study, for example, an interviewee has the right to decline to talk about certain issues. A participant's willingness to disclose information might be affected by what will happen to information afterwards, a question of confidentiality.

## Confidentiality

Confidentiality concerns the right to control information about oneself. A person may grant access to information about him or herself, but this does not mean they relinquish control over the information obtained. A researcher should not divulge what has been learned to others without the individual's permission. This applies to both verbal communications and written records. All means of identification should be removed if the results are to be published in any form (including a thesis lodged in the library). Confidentiality can be violated in a number of ways. Some are obvious, as when there is deliberate disclosure or when there is negligence (e.g. leaving notes in a public place). A breach of confidentiality can also be less obvious, as when a researcher contacts potential research subjects from a confidential list, such as one held by social services.

This is not to say that the rule of confidentiality is absolute. Infringements of confidentiality can be justified in certain circumstances. This may occur when there is an obligation to fulfil another and more stringent obligation, such as when someone is likely to be harmed in a serious way. In such an instance, the researchers may have an obligation to disclose information to others without permission if he or she expected a person to be at risk of harm. A key point here is to have discussed any potential for a breach of confidentiality with the participant before data collection.

## Fidelity

Fidelity concerns promise keeping. Researchers make a number of implicit promises when they conduct a study, especially to be careful with information obtained and not to engage in fraud. Fidelity can be problematic in the case of clinical research. Although the clinical role is primarily concerned with a patient's welfare, a research project may be for society's benefit, not the patient's.

## ANALYSING ETHICAL DILEMMAS

These theories, principles and rules are helpful in understanding the difficulties faced by the researcher doing work on HIV discussed above. It

**TABLE 5.1   Alternative ethical analyses for the HIV dilemma**

---

**A   A justification for conducing a further analysis of the blood sample**

*Theory*: Consequentialist. We ought to maximize the common good.
*Principle*: Beneficence. We ought to do good for others.
*Rule*: Fidelity. The researcher has promised, implicitly at least, to conduct research for the benefit of society.
*Action*: Perform the additional tests on the blood in a search for a cure for AIDS.

**B   A rationale for not conducing a further analysis of the blood sample**

*Theory*: Deontological. We ought to respect individual rights.
*Principle*: Autonomy. Everyone has the right to decide what happens to their bodily tissue.
*Rule*: Privacy. Everyone has the right to control access to information about themselves.
*Action*: Do not perform the additional tests on his blood, perhaps missing an opportunity in the search for a cure for AIDS.

---

is possible to see how his or her dilemma is due to the conflicts between theories and various principles and rules, as shown in Table 5.1. By evoking a consequentialist theory, the principle of beneficence and the rule of fidelity, the researcher could justify further analyses of the person's blood, despite their objections. Conversely, by evoking a deontological approach, the principle of autonomy and the rule of veracity, the researcher might decide not to use the blood further, despite the possibility that the research might have widespread beneficial consequences for society as a whole.

The important point here is that the choice of action can be justified by the researcher. Whatever he or she decides, it is important that there be a strong rationale, consistent with moral reasoning, for the final choice. It is useful to repeat here that, at this point in western culture, autonomy is usually given the most weight in ethical analysis. A particularly strong argument would need to be made to override individual rights.

## FRAUD

Simply because the researcher in the above example could justify both courses of action does not mean that any behaviour is justifiable. Unprovoked harm to others is something which could not be justified. Fraud is another type of behaviour which is unacceptable. The social sciences are based on trust, particularly that researchers will collect information and report their findings honestly and openly. However, it is clear that this obligation to truth is sometimes disregarded, often to the detriment of society (Beecher, 1966).

Most researchers have been tempted to engage in fraud at some point in their careers. Studies have shown that at least half of undergraduates admit to cheating, including plagiarism, at some point during their time at university. It seems likely that the most important reason for fraud in research is that certain types of results are more valuable than others. All researchers are involved in furthering their careers as well as advancing science, and results which are publishable are more valued by colleagues, supervisors and journal editors than are results which have little apparent coherence or which do not correspond to hypotheses. It is relatively straightforward to ignore some results or slightly to tamper with data to 'massage' the findings.

Such actions are clearly unethical and can do great damage to others. They go against the principle of non-maleficence as well as the rule of veracity. Because research develops on the basis of previous work, fraud can have a knock-on effect, seriously affecting the well-being of later researchers, perhaps leading to the waste of resources.

# 6 THE POWER OF RESEARCH

## *Iain Crow*

## RESEARCH AND POWER

Let me start by posing some problems:

> Many less well-off people have debts. You are attempting to carry out a study which will examine ways of helping people with their debt problems. However, the only realistic way that you can get information about debt problems is through the files of a debt advice agency. Although the agency is willing to give you access to the files, it is impractical to contact all the individuals concerned and obtain their consent to abstracting data from their personal files. *Should you proceed with the study?*

> You are undertaking an ethnographic study of attempts to rehabilitate offenders who are in a hostel for ex-prisoners. The success of your study depends on gaining the trust of the hostel residents and them being able to confide in you. During the course of your studies you learn that one of the residents has hidden a sawn-off shotgun under the floorboards in his room. *What do you do?*

> You are undertaking a study of people addicted to heroin, which involves in-depth interviews with addicts. During the course of one interview a female respondent discloses that her partner sometimes hits her young child. She begs you not to tell anyone because, being a known addict, she already has problems with the social services department and she is afraid that her child will be taken away from her. *What is your response?*

The situations presented above are not hypothetical. They are based on real situations. The purpose of this chapter is to encourage the asking of questions about the ethical aspects of what researchers do. It considers the potential that research has to take information about people and use it in ways which they have no control over and which may be detrimental to their interests. The chapter looks at the various ways in which this can happen in different types of research. It does not offer simple solutions, but it does end by suggesting some of the steps that can be taken to deal with these situations.

## ETHICAL DILEMMAS

Among the first questions that any researcher should ask are: Why am I doing this? Why am I researching this particular topic? These are the kind of questions that are considered when discussing whether research can ever be value free. But they are also questions which affect the position that a person is likely to take when faced with an ethical dilemma. One's interest in a research topic may, quite legitimately, be influenced by a commitment to a particular cause, such as animal rights, equal opportunities or better health-care provision. But such a commitment may influence the extent to which you think that the goals of your research justify adopting certain methods, or withholding certain information. For instance, if you are carrying out a study of court cases to see whether the courts discriminate against black people, do you tell the magistrates that this is what you are doing, knowing that this may affect the way they react while your study is in progress? Not to do so may be considered unethical. You may adopt a pragmatic response that in this instance the greater good of overcoming racism justifies withholding information. Or you may decide that because you are committed to safeguarding people's rights, this has to extend to magistrates as well, and your principles will be compromised if you do not fully inform them about the subject of investigation. How you deal with such a situation will depend on whether you adopt a deontological or a consequentialist position, as outlined in the previous chapter.

After considering one's own motivation, another question to address is: Why should I be concerned about ethical and legal issues? Here I do have an answer to put forward: research has a lot to do with power. This manifests itself in various ways. At the most basic level research may be considered to be a form of alienation. Social scientists may be familiar with the Hegelian concept of *entfremdung*, whereby part of oneself is taken away and then stands over against you (Schacht, 1971: 1–7). The researcher is asking the person (or organization) they study to give away part of themselves. Alienation is linked with powerlessness (Coser and Rosenberg, 1967). In a questionnaire or research interview, information is taken from someone and may then be used by others. The donor of the information loses control over how the information is used. It is then only a short step to the abuse of this information. Market research firms carry out surveys according to a strict code of behaviour, but it is nonetheless the case that the information gleaned by market researchers is used in ways which manipulate the wants, needs and desires of the market. The term 'empowerment' is often used in relation to various kinds of social action. Research has the potential to empower people if it gives them the benefit of knowledge that will enable them to control their own destinies. But it is necessary to recognize that research also has the capacity for disempowerment.

## CONFIDENTIALITY

This alienating aspect of research is one reason why confidentiality is so important. Its importance is given legislative backing by the Data Protection Act 1984, which is considered further in Chapter 10. But the remit of the Act is limited, and in any event confidentiality has a social context which goes beyond the purely legal obligations. As an example of this, I have often been in the position of seeking access to confidential records in order to abstract data for research purposes. I have quite properly been asked to give an undertaking that the data will remain confidential. After one particular session discussing the preservation of the anonymity of their clients with a group of practitioners from different agencies I was invited to join them for a drink at the local pub. After a short while the practitioners' conversation got round to discussing particular clients that they knew, by name, in a public place with me and others in earshot. This illustrates how easy it is to slip into a lax attitude towards what those practitioners would undoubtedly regard in the abstract as an important moral principle, so that a gap appears between the principle and the practice of confidentiality. It also raises the question of how confidential is confidential? Does one share information with the members of one's work team? In the example I have given information was being shared with people in other agencies who were in the same profession. There is a danger that a professional culture, whether it be practitioners or researchers, means that it is permissible to share information with others of the same background. It is important to be clear about who will have access to confidential information, how it will be kept secure, how it will be disposed of when the research is finished, and to tell respondents what your intentions are.

## FRAUDULENT RESEARCH

Perhaps the most extreme form of abuse of power that can be perpetrated by researchers is data fraud. The extent of such fraud is unknown and probably unknowable, but there are clear instances of it happening. There are many types of fraud. Perhaps the most obvious is the deliberate manufacturing of results, where a study is reported which was never conducted. However, it is also fraudulent to 'massage' the results, by removing or ignoring data which do not fit the hypothesis the researcher is attempting to confirm. By ignoring the data from some participants, for example, or grouping certain data sets together, it may be possible to obtain a statistically significant result. Plagiarism is another type of fraud, where another's words or ideas are appropriated as the researcher's own work. Anyone who has done a statistics course will know something of the ways in which numbers can be mishandled and manipulated.

Lock (1993) provides several examples of deliberate fraud. Some of these had practical implications for the treatment of patients. For example, in

1987 a psychologist at the University of Pittsburgh faked data purporting to show that in mentally handicapped children stimulant drugs were more effective and had fewer side effects than the standard treatment with tranquillizers in altering their disruptive behaviour. The psychologist's report led to changes in therapeutic policy in Connecticut. The researcher was later charged with making false statements and sentenced.

The more subtle ways to misrepresent data can be illustrated by a personal example. Some years ago I was involved in work which looked at the effectiveness of training schemes for people who were unemployed. An important dependent variable in the study was what happened to participants when they left the training scheme: what percentages got a job, went on to further education or training, or remained unemployed. Inevitably there were a number of people for whom there was no follow-up information. One research group, which shall remain nameless, reported a higher proportion of leavers getting a job than another research group. However, their data did not include the 'no information' group, which had simply been omitted, thereby increasing the percentage in all other categories.

It is easy to condemn these kinds of misleading and fraudulent practices. But there are many pressures on researchers to report attractive data, and many conflicting obligations. On the one hand, researchers have obligations to their science. A postgraduate student has an obligation to be conscientious in collecting, interpreting and reporting results. However, he or she may also experience pressures to arrive at interesting results. There may be a belief that a study will be looked on more favourably by a supervisor and external examiner if the results are interesting. It is easier to publish positive results (which show an interesting effect) than negative ones. There can often be a temptation to massage data for career reasons, and the recognition of this temptation is an important first step towards safeguarding against it.

## ACCOUNTABILITY

It is, of course, possible to exaggerate the power of research. Some researchers may overestimate the importance of research, and others may complain that not enough notice is taken of their work. Researchers sometimes feel that governmental and other bodies do not take enough notice of their work and that this means that the exercise of power by authority is less informed. Nonetheless, further questions to consider are: How much power does research have? How much should it have?

The exercise of power that we all engage in by virtue of being involved in the research process cannot be avoided, however small it may appear to be. It is therefore important to consider its implications and consequently the obligations of the researcher. Students who have spent many hours in lectures, seminars and libraries may not appreciate when they first become involved in social research that they are engaged in something that can involve real consequences for real people. Research may, for example, affect:

- the giving or denying of treatment;
- the availability and distribution of resources;
- people's job prospects;
- whether or not people experience distress.

To illustrate the last point I would cite the example of a student who proposed giving patients a questionnaire about their doctor's treatment of them. To the student this was an undergraduate project; an important step towards getting a good degree. But to the patients concerned discussing their illnesses and other reasons for visiting the doctor might be a sensitive and disturbing experience; something which the student had not at first realized.

If research has consequences for the freedom and well-being of others, by what right do we engage in it? Research is often justified in terms of the pursuit of knowledge for its own sake, or by reference to the benefits it may confer. To whom, and who decides whether it is beneficial? Such questions direct our attention to the moral basis of research ethics. On the one hand there is the utilitarian, or consequentialist, position referred to in the previous chapter which underlies the 'greater good' argument. On the basis of this position one may feel justified in undertaking double blind drug experiments on some people without their knowledge because in the long term it will benefit others. A problem attendant on adopting such a position is that it may not always be clear who benefits most: the patients or the drug company. There is the further question of who decides what is in the general good, which brings us back to the accountability problem. An alternative position is the deontological basis for resolving ethical dilemmas. Adopting this position leads one to conclude that there are certain basic rights that should never be violated. These include the right of the researched to make their own choices about their freedom and well-being in as full knowledge as possible of the potential consequences. This may mean that certain research will not be carried out, and as a consequence the world may be denied important knowledge or benefits.

Thus a further question raised by the exercise of the power of research is, to whom are we accountable? Whereas the medical and legal professions have bodies that can revoke a practitioners right to practise, there is no similar regulatory body for social science research. Various discipline related bodies, such as the British Psychological Society and the British Sociological Association, have issued ethical guidelines, but these are not easily enforced. The development of ethical regulation has been strongest in those areas most closely related to medicine. The World Medical Association's Helsinki Declaration offers 'Recommendations guiding physicians in biomedical research involving human subjects', and medical schools invariably have ethical committees to vet research proposals, but the same cannot be said of social sciences.

## RESEARCH ETHICS AND VARIOUS KINDS OF RESEARCH

At this point I would like to pose a further question: Is there any research that does not have ethical implications? It may be thought that what has been said so far applies to those engaged in empirical investigations but that, since your research is predominantly theoretical or library based, such considerations do not apply to you. Is the 'pure' scholar exempt? Are ethical considerations more important for applied research than for theoretical research? For those engaged in empirical research the ethical implications may be more immediate and direct, but theoretical research may have indirect and longer term consequences. Theoretical work is often instrumental in setting research agendas and influencing policies, as happened in criminology in the late 1960s and early 1970s when the 'New Criminology' developed. The researcher engaged in writing a thesis on the contribution that a person now dead has made to twentieth-century thought still has obligations. As stated earlier, we all have an obligation not to distort, mismanage or, in the extreme instance, to concoct our research material, whether it comes from an experiment or a library book. Having said this, the different kinds of research that social scientists engage in do give rise to somewhat different ethical considerations, depending on the research design or method used. I would like to consider briefly some of the issues raised by particular methods.

## EXPERIMENTATION

Experiments in the social sciences are problematic because their effectiveness may depend on those taking part not knowing all the details (Box 6.1).

### Box 6.1  Experimental Research Designs and Ethics

One of the classic examples of this is the Milgram electric shock experiment. In this series of experiments the researchers recruited subjects, through public advertising, who were told that they were taking part in an experiment in learning. They were taken to a laboratory with an electric shock generator. The person who was to be the learner was strapped into an 'electric chair'. When the learner gave wrong answers to a question the subjects were instructed to press a button that would give the learner an electric shock. When this happened the learner exhibited the symptoms of someone in pain. The voltage was progressively increased each time the subject was instructed to press the button, until it was apparent that the learner was in an extreme state of distress. Subjects protested but were instructed to continue and did so, sometimes to the point where the setting on the electric shock generator indicated 'Danger: Severe Shock'. The level of shock at which each subject refused to take any further part in the experiment was recorded, and the experiment was repeated for different conditions, varying such things as the proximity of the victim, the closeness of the authority figure, and so on. The subjects were not told, however, that the button they were pressing was not connected to an electricity supply, and that the 'learner' was in fact one of the research team, acting as though in pain. The experiment was designed to investigate the extent to which ordinary people will inflict pain on others when instructed to by an authority: what the researcher referred to as a universal triad of authority, executant and victim (Milgram, 1965).[1] *Was such an experiment justified?*

Another kind of difficulty is raised by the controlled experiment where random allocation is used to assign participants to either a 'treatment' group or a 'control' group. This is often done in medical situations, but is more problematic where the 'treatment' is some kind of social intervention. There have been many attempts to 'treat' offenders in the hope of finding something that will be effective in reducing crime. But there is a question as to whether the way that offenders are dealt with can ethically depend on the requirements of research (Box 6.2).

### Box 6.2  Ethical Issues in Researching Offenders

Some years ago a juvenile court in the north of England adopted a system whereby delinquents who had been truanting from school were not dealt with by the court immediately but had their cases adjourned for a number of months, during which time their school attendance was monitored. What happened to them subsequently depended on their behaviour during the period of adjournment. This was nicknamed the Damocles experiment. In order to test its efficacy, juveniles were randomly allocated either to be given the Damocles treatment or to be dealt with in the normal way (Hullin, 1985). The procedure was controversial and eventually discontinued.

## COVERT METHODS

Ethnographic studies and studies using techniques such as participant observation often involve the researcher adopting a role within a group of people who are not aware that he or she is a researcher. There are many examples of this in sociology, one of which is a study of criminal subculture in the East End of London by someone who came from the East End. The researcher describes his method in Box 6.3.

---

**Box 6.3   Ethical Issues and the Use of Covert Methods**

While engaged in this part of my study my strategy was to exploit contacts who were acquainted with my pre-academic self . . . This necessitated total flexibility on my behalf, and a willingness to abide by the ethics of the researched culture and not the normative ethical constraints of sociological research. When someone telephones at six in the morning with the cryptic message that: 'I got a parcel going to Felixstowe; need a hand. I'll be round in ten minutes – alright?' the response, if richness and depth of data are at all important, can only be 'yes'. A refusal, or worse still an enquiry concerning the legal status of the 'parcel', would provoke an abrupt conclusion to the relationship. Consequently, I was willing to skirt the boundaries of criminality on several occasions, and I considered it crucial to be willingly involved in 'normal' business transactions, legal or otherwise. I was pursuing an interactive, inductive study of an entrepreneurial culture, and in order to do so I had to display entrepreneurial skills myself. Because of my background I found nothing immoral or even unusual in the dealing and trading that I encountered. However, I do not consider the study to be unethical, for the ethics that I adhered to were the ethics of the citizens of the East End. (Hobbs, 1989: 7)

---

This passage raises several interesting issues, for example, about the extent to which the researcher becomes involved in the world that he or she is studying. But what is of particular interest is the introduction of the notion of ethical values being relative: the 'normative ethics' of sociological study are contrasted with the ethics of the researched culture. Are ethical values relative, or are there some absolute ethical values that apply regardless of context? The answer to this question is likely to be even more crucial when those being researched are not a group within one's own society but people from a different society.

The Milgram experiment and the study by Hobbs are interesting because of what they have in common and what is different about them. In both studies the principle involved is that of informed consent: in neither case were the participants to the studies able to make an informed choice about whether or not to participate. But in other respects they are different. Both the Milgram experiment and the Damocles experiment derive their research methodology from a positivist approach to social research, in which the researcher is essentially attempting to replicate the conditions of natural science by controlling variables. Participant observation on the other hand owes no such allegiance to a positivist epistemology. Indeed, the researcher may be making a conscious attempt to adopt an interpretive research strategy. This helps to illustrate an important point: ethical considerations are not peculiar to a particular school of research.

## APPLIED RESEARCH

Some of the most acute and immediate ethical dilemmas are posed by applied research: that is, research where the primary aim is to produce practical or policy conclusions, and contribution to social scientific knowledge is secondary. A common type of applied research is the evaluation of some particular form of social intervention. The Damocles experiment is an example of applied research, and evaluation research often raises issues related to the adoption of an experimental or quasi-experimental design. However, evaluation research also raises other issues. There is frequently a considerable investment in a social programme. This investment is not just a financial one: there is often much personal investment in social projects. Consequently people's aspirations – and jobs – can be dependent on the results of one's research. The evaluator may therefore come under a great deal of pressure (some of it self-imposed) to produce favourable results. Other kinds of applied research assess the extent of social needs. Where people are being interviewed about such things as their need for care or assistance there is a danger of raising unwarranted expectations. The results of research may also be used to try to predict the likelihood of certain events occurring. An instance of this is the use of prediction techniques to assess the likelihood of reoffending by criminals which, since it is based on probability, runs the risk of being inaccurate in a proportion of cases, perhaps resulting in the release of a dangerous criminal, or the continued incarceration of a non-dangerous one. This is a specific instance of a more general problem for the applied researcher: to what extent is the researcher responsible for the ways in which others apply the results of their studies? Of course, one way out of such problems is to shun applied research. But in doing so there is the possibility that one may thereby be depriving people of considerable benefits, so the dilemma remains unresolved.

## ELITES AND OTHERS

Social research has had a tendency to focus most often on those in society who have least power: on consumers, students and pupils, delinquents, and so on. Over the years, however, attention has increasingly turned towards studies of the powerful: managers and their companies, teachers, judges and police chiefs. In such 'elite studies' the researcher may be interested in how elites use, and perhaps abuse, their powers. The question then arises as to whether the researcher has the same obligations to a powerful person or organization as to less powerful members of society. Should the researcher 'blow the whistle' despite having given assurances of confidentiality? Further problems may be raised where the researcher is dealing with organizations, or indeed communities, rather than individuals. Clarifying to whom any obligation is owed may then become a primary concern. In contrast to elite studies, some research involves the most vulnerable in society. In recent years, for instance, there has been a growing body of work in the field of child abuse. Although it may be inappropriate to regard some areas of research as ethically more important than others, it is becoming clear that particular considerations apply to such research, which may require special skills and training.[2]

Clearly this consideration of some kinds of research is not exhaustive. It is impossible to consider all possible methods and research strategies here. But I hope it serves to demonstrate that ethical dilemmas are not peculiar to some kinds of research rather than others.

## PROBLEMS RAISED BY THE OWNERSHIP AND CONTROL OF RESEARCH

The main theme underlying this chapter is research and power. In this context the ownership and control of research is crucial. In a later chapter the legal position is considered. But the control of research often has a social and political dimension as well as a legal one. In essence who is the research for, and how will it be used? Here I would refer back to the concept of *entfremdung*, the process of taking control of something that belonged to someone else, which raises concerns about three types of relationship:

- the relationship of the researcher with the subjects of research;
- the relationship of the researcher with the funder;
- the relationship of the researcher with the academic community.

### *Relationship of the researcher with the subjects of research*

Does the researcher have obligations to the subject apart from informed consent, privacy, veracity and fidelity? What about, for instance, telling those who have provided data about the results? Quite apart from the ethical consideration of giving back to participants some of that which was taken from them, providing feedback can also be regarded as a matter of 'research etiquette' and good professional practice. I have tried as far as possible to feed back the results of research that I have been involved in to those who took part in it. But this is not always easy. Practical considerations limit how much feedback can be given and in what form. It is seldom possible to give a full copy of the report to all the respondents to a very large survey. But it may be possible to tell respondents when they complete the questionnaire what is going to happen to the results of the study they are taking part in, and how they can find out about them if they wish. It is also possible to produce a brief summary of the results of research that can be sent to agencies, groups and individuals involved. However, it is not always clear to whom the feedback should be given. Researchers often gain access to information about individuals through an inter-mediary organization. Should feedback be given to this organization, when informants within it have commented negatively on its performance, and would this prejudice their relationship with that agency (or their job) if this became known?

## Relationship of the researcher with the funder

There has been a significant shift in recent years in the approach of some funding bodies towards research. Public bodies (government departments in particular) are much more likely than they once were to take a close interest in the research they have funded while it is in progress, and to determine what happens to it once it is finished. Hence it is important to have a clear understanding at the outset about the expectations of the parties involved. In the case of research commissioned by a public body or commercial organization this will often take the form of a contract, which therefore has a legally binding status. This does not always provide a clarity of understanding that is to the researcher's liking, since it may specify, for example, limitations on publication. The publication of work undertaken for government departments is governed by Crown Copyright. Even where there is no formal contract, there is likely to be a research proposal which can be regarded as having a similar status. It is therefore in the researcher's interests to spell out in the proposal such things as your right to publish and feed back the results of research.

Of course this means that there is considerable power in the hands of a funding body to control the results of research, especially if it comes up with results which the funders do not like. The consequence of this, in the long term, is to have a powerful effect on the whole research agenda of a field of inquiry. There has been a trend towards shorter term funding periods and to an emphasis on applied research which means that it is more difficult to get funding for fundamental work that may take a number of years to produce results. A criticism that has been made of British criminology in recent years is that, because funding has tended to be so heavily affected by Home Office priorities, the discipline has become dominated by what is called 'administrative criminology'. In addition many organizations have their own in-house research capacity – local authorities, social services departments, probation services, police forces, national charities, and so on. To some extent this is welcome – not least because it provides more job opportunities for social science research students. But undertaking research within an organization which has to be concerned first and foremost with its own management objectives, image and interests may place the in-house researcher in compromising positions where the demands of the employing organization are in conflict with ethical principles and the integrity of research.

## *Relationship of the researcher with the academic community*

Where does this leave a third relationship: that of the researcher with the academic community? Do we also have obligations to more abstract entities, such as science and the pursuit of knowledge, and to the research community as well as to the subjects and owners of research? Is there any longer such a thing as academic freedom? Does the in-house researcher have obligations to his or her profession as a researcher independently of his/her employer?

## DEALING WITH ETHICAL ISSUES

This chapter has been liberally scattered with questions, and I said at the outset that different situations need to be handled in different ways. To undertake a career as a social researcher it is necessary to become practiced at handling ethical issues. However, I also said that there are ways of handling such issues by applying certain principles. So it may be helpful to finish with some suggestions about what can be done to address ethical concerns and deal with ethical dilemmas.

The first suggestion is to ensure that you are familiar with the ethical guidelines produced by the body appropriate for your discipline. If you find that the body most concerned with your area of work has not produced any ethical guidance, then perhaps you should be asking why.

Next, I would stress the importance of planning and preparation in undertaking any research; try to anticipate what ethical considerations may arise. As researchers we may sometimes find ourselves placed in difficult positions. For example, a respondent may tell us something in confidence which we feel we cannot ignore because it concerns the well-being of others. But many more ethical issues are to do with research design or the use of particular methods and can be foreseen. The third of the three examples given at the beginning of this chapter – involving the drug addict with a young child – is a situation which it may have been possible to anticipate in advance. It is better to be prepared beforehand in anticipation of such situations than to deal with them as they arise. For instance, in this example the researcher needs to be aware of the limitations of his or her competence and may need expert backup for such an eventuality. A section of any research proposal should discuss the ethical aspects of the proposed study and explain how they will be addressed.

Third, it is important to consult and involve others. A research student, for example, would start by discussing ethical problems with his or her supervisor. In other situations there may be ethical committees and, if not ethical committees, professional and disciplinary bodies who may be able to advise. However, I hasten to add that involving others should not simply be an attempt to drop the problem on someone else. Ultimately the ethical obligation lies with the researcher.

For this reason I would also suggest that it is important that every social researcher is clear about their own personal moral position. Ethical dilemmas often arise, not because the researcher is wantonly disregarding ethical considerations, but because there is a conflict between moral principles. In several of the examples I have given earlier the need for confidentiality conflicts with the obligation to avoid harm: the researcher in a hostel for ex-prisoners who learns that one of them has a gun; the respondent who tells you in confidence that her partner abuses her child. In such situations one response might be to explain to the respondent that they have placed you in a situation where you have an obligation to do something to avoid harm to others, even if this puts the research at risk. More problematic is the situation where the potential good for the many that may ensue from research conflicts with the rights of the individual. One possible reaction is that one knows that the infringement of the rights of individuals is immediate and certain, whereas the potential benefits of the research are less certain and one is less able to judge their merits. I personally believe that it is important to be open and honest in talking about one's research: after all researchers rely on other people being open and honest with them in order to obtain valid data. Perhaps the most fundamental principle involves asking how we would want others to treat us and to treat others as we would wish to be treated. This is not, I admit, an answer to all ethical issues, but I find it a helpful starting point.

## NOTES

1  It is worth noting that the paper in which Stanley Milgram presented his results was awarded the Socio-Psychological Prize of the American Association for the Advancement of Science in 1964, showing that this was not some minor, insignificant study.
2  The Social Research Association has run a seminar, 'Asking the Unaskable' on undertaking research on 'sensitive' topics. A report can be found in the *SRA News*, May 1993.

# 7 INFORMED CONSENT

## Gerry Kent

The general aim of this chapter is to provide some background concerning the issues surrounding consent to participate in a research study. Sometimes this is called 'informed consent', sometimes 'real consent' and sometimes 'valid consent'. Whatever the term used, the intention is the same: to achieve a position whereby people who agree to take part in a research programme know what they are agreeing to and authorize you to collect information from them without any form of coercion or manipulation.

In order to say that a person has given informed consent, several essential conditions need to be met. While it might seem at first that these conditions are easy to meet, there are actually a number of complex and difficult issues involved. How, for example, can a person fully understand what is involved until he or she actually takes part? A person may initially agree to take part in an interview study, for example, but later encounter questions which he or she finds too personal to answer. Also, it is possible to put pressure on people to take part. It can be tempting to 'push' a person a little harder into agreeing to take part when recruitment is not going well. And how about children? Is it ethical to recruit a 5-year-old child into a study, even with a parent's agreement? These are important questions, since they bear on the right, that we all possess, to make decisions about what we do with our lives.

Some have argued that informed consent is a convenient myth – an ideal which cannot be achieved (Silverman, 1989). This may be so, but it should not stop a researcher from taking all possible steps to achieve the best possible outcome. Thus, the specific aim of this chapter is to outline the steps which a researcher needs to take in order to achieve informed consent from his or her research participants.

## WHAT CONSTITUTES INFORMED CONSENT?

Consent is needed to protect the important ethical principle of autonomy – the right to exercise self-determination. Having discussed some of the theoretical background to this principle in Chapter 5, it is possible to have a closer look at the specifics of consent. Five elements need to be met in order to protect this right: information; understanding; voluntariness; competence of potential participants; actual consent to participate.

## Information

The information given to potential research participants ought to include anything which could bear on their decision to participate. This is information which is important from the researcher's and the participant's points of view and would include facts about the purpose of the study, the procedures involved and risks and benefits which might result. This information might be given verbally if the procedures are straightforward and not threatening, or may require more detailed written information if the time commitment is large or if the study involves a degree of invasiveness.

One issue concerns the amount of information to give. Telling a participant every detail about the project is likely to be both tedious and unhelpful. Also, there will be times when an extensive explanation about the nature of a study will invalidate the results. For example, if a participant were informed about the researcher's hypothesis, the participant might provide information which he or she thinks the researcher would like to hear, rather than the truth. While deception is rarely justifiable, non-disclosure of a researcher's intent may well be needed.

## Understanding

Even if information is transmitted, it may not be understood. Some research notions, such as risk and randomization, are quite complicated. An example of how different people understand risk is provided by Sutherland *et al.* (1991). They first reviewed fifteen consent forms (discussed in more detail below) which had been used at the medical centre where they worked. The research studies involved trials for different forms of treatment for cancer patients, many of which carried a degree of possible harm. Several words to describe levels of risk were used, such as 'may occur', 'rarely' and 'possible'. Patients were then asked to indicate their understandings of the terms. There was a surprisingly wide variation in understanding. For example, some patients believed that 'rare' meant an adverse reaction could occur about one time in a hundred, but others believed that this could mean twenty-five times in a hundred.

Similarly, Snowdon *et al.* (1997) examined participants' perceptions of the meaning of randomization. In many empirical studies people are assigned to different groups on a random basis, so that initial differences between individuals are washed out by chance. Snowdon *et al.* interviewed participants after the study was completed and found that only a minority had an accurate understanding of what randomization meant. Most believed that whether they were assigned to one group or another was decided by the researcher in some way. Although every effort was made to ensure that the participants were informed about the nature of the study, this information was often misunderstood. Thus the key here is the participant's perspective and understanding of what will be involved.

## Voluntariness

Even if information is shared and understood, informed consent is achieved only if there is no coercion or manipulation involved. Researchers have many motives in conducting their studies. Although there is the desire to increase knowledge and commitment to the scientific enterprise, it is, of course, not as simple as this. Every researcher has a number of other personal interests and social obligations. He or she will want to finish their research work in time for submission and will need at least an adequate sample size. Such factors put pressure on researchers to recruit as widely as possible and may encourage them to place pressure on people to participate.

Even if there is no overt pressure, it is possible to use a degree of covert manipulation. There are many ways to encourage people to act in particular ways. An example of this is the foot-in-the-door technique. This involves making a small request first, and then later a larger one. Once people have agreed to the minor request they are more likely to agree to a major one (Freedman and Fraser, 1966).

Third, it may not be appropriate to approach all potential participants. This could be because they are currently distressed or if they believe that they could have something to lose by refusing. For example, a student might find it difficult to refuse to take part in a teacher's research project, lest there be some negative consequences on assessment. In some countries prison inmates cannot be employed in any research projects because of their inferior position within the institution.

## Competence of potential participants

A further condition for consent is that a person is legally competent. People who are demented or have learning disabilities and children under the age of about 11 may not be able to give fully informed consent. This has led some to take the radical position that research should not be conducted on such groups, since the achievement of informed consent is not possible. In practice, consent is usually requested from other parties, such as parents, which is termed consent by proxy. A researcher who wishes to observe children in a playground, for instance, ought first to approach parents for their permission.

Proxy consent brings its own difficulties. It is based on the assumption that the proxy consent giver is in a position to give an accurate view of what the research participant would wish to do if they were competent. However, there are several studies which have indicated that this assumption is often incorrect. For example, it is reasonable to assume that parents would be in the best position to give consent for their children, but this is not always the case, perhaps due to the parents' own beliefs and feelings (Manne et al., 1992).

**TABLE 7.1   A written consent form**

## Research Consent Form

**Title of Project**:

| | |
|---|---|
| Have you read the information sheet? | Yes/No |
| Have you had the opportunity to ask questions and discuss the study? | Yes/No |
| Have you received satisfactory answers to all your questions? | Yes/No |
| Have you received enough information about the study? | Yes/No |

Who have you spoken to? _____

Do you understand that you are free to withdraw from the study:

| | |
|---|---|
| • at any time | Yes/No |
| • without having to give a reason for withdrawing? | Yes/No |
| Do you agree to take part in this study? | Yes/No |

Signed _____ Date _____

(Name in block letters) _____

---

### *Actual consent to participate*

The final condition concerns the actual written or verbal consent. In many research projects, verbal consent is adequate, but when the project is invasive participants are usually asked for written consent. Written consent could be needed in the social sciences when, for example, there will be an interview on intimate topics.

A widely used consent form is shown in Table 7.1. Although this may seem long and complicated, it provides a clear format which attempts to ensure that all the important aspects of consent have been considered. By asking potential participants to indicate whether each of the conditions have been fulfilled, the researcher may be assured that every attempt has been made to achieve an accurate understanding of the procedures involved.

### HOW CAN INFORMED CONSENT BE ACHIEVED?

The above description of informed consent illustrates that it can be a complex procedure and difficult to achieve. In many respects no one can fully understand what will be involved in a study before they actually take part. Nevertheless researchers have an obligation to do their best to ensure that the size and nature of the commitment is as clear as possible to the people who give up their time and effort to help. This section of the chapter provides some guidelines about how to present information about a study to a potential participant.

**TABLE 7.2  A suggested format for an information sheet. These are the areas which are most likely to be of concern to research participants**

| |
|---|
| 1   What is the purpose of this study? |
| 2   Who is conducting this study? |
| 3   What will be involved if I take part in this study? |
| 4   Where and when will the study take place? |
| 5   What information will be collected? |
| 6   Do I have to take part? |
| 7   Can I withdraw at any time? |
| 8   Will all information be kept confidential? |

## Giving information

The essence of giving information in a way in which it can be understood – so that there is a shared understanding of what will be involved – is not an easy task. Because researchers have a vested interest in recruiting people into their studies, it is tempting to minimize the nature and size of the commitment involved. One way of attempting to ensure that people do have this shared understanding is to provide a written information sheet. This has two advantages. First, it helps participants not to be overwhelmed by information when they are first approached. If information is given verbally, it is possible that the participant will not be able to remember all the details involved. There are also advantages for the researcher. If the information is given in written form, it may be that the people concerned will make a firmer commitment to the project. Particularly for projects where sensitive issues are involved, it is important that people understand as much as possible and do not decide to drop out halfway through data collection. A suggested format for an information sheet is given in Table 7.2. An important point is that it is in a question/answer format. This format not only serves to break up the text but also people are more able to take in information if they read to answer a question rather than simply being given the information.

One point which is often overlooked concerns the format of the information sheet. It is helpful if the sheet has no jargon and contains few long words and sentences. About one-sixth of the general population is functionally illiterate and the average reading age is about 12 years, so it is important to keep the sheet clear and to the point. As recommended by Kanouse and Hayes-Roth (1980), there are several ways to increase the ease with which text can be read:

1   Use active rather than passive verbs.
2   Use concrete rather than abstract words.
3   State ideas explicitly rather than implicitly.
4   Use the same words consistently when referring to the same idea.
5   Use numbering when presenting facts.

6    Put old information at the beginning of a sentence, new information at the end.

There are also guidelines about typeface. The font size is also important, not only for those whose sight might be impaired but also for elderly people generally (Taub *et al.*, 1987). Poulton *et al.* (1970) suggest that the following are important:

1    Type should be at least 10 point.
2    Indenting the first line of a paragraph increases speed of reading.
3    Printing everything in capital letters reduces speed of reading.
4    Printing in italics reduces speed of reading.

The questions in Table 7.2 cover most of the likely relevant issues, although there could easily be others depending on the project. Two important questions concern the need to take part. Not only do people have the right to decline to take part (question 6), but they also have the right to withdraw at any time (question 7) without needing to provide a reason or justification. Even if a written information sheet does not seem necessary in a particular study, the verbal request should cover all of these issues.

## ETHICS COMMITTEES

Many departments in the social sciences have their own research ethics committees. Usually they consist of several members of staff who are charged with the responsibility of ensuring that there is a positive balance between the risks and the benefits involved in a research project. Many research projects carry little risk to participants, but there is always some effort involved and it would be unethical for a project to be conducted which is of no benefit whatsoever. Of course there does not have to be a major practical or theoretical benefit: one of the aims of postgraduate research is practice in designing and carrying out studies, which is itself of positive value.

Over recent years, there has been an increasing realization that ethical committee approval is needed for most studies in the social sciences. It is important to remember that these committees exist to support and facilitate research, and not to block or hinder projects. It is also useful to have someone who is not closely involved with a project to examine a proposal, because it is easy for researchers to miss issues when they are closely involved in the details.

Ethics committees are particularly interested in protecting the right of potential participants who may not be able to give informed consent for some reason, such as children or adults with psychological or psychiatric difficulties. In such instances they need to be convinced that the research has value. Here methodological issues can become important. Many would argue that a research project which is methodologically flawed in some significant way should not be carried out. They contend that a study which gives results that cannot be interpreted sensibly is a waste of the participants' time and effort.

8

# CAN THE LAW PRESCRIBE AN ETHICAL FRAMEWORK FOR SOCIAL SCIENCE RESEARCH?

*D.M.R. Townend*

There are two distinct types of question to consider when examining the relationship between the law and social science research. There are questions to be asked about the substantive law that exists and regulates social scientists in their work, which are addressed in Chapter 10 on legal issues. The other questions, which are equally interesting – especially in a book such as this – ask what the substantive law should look like which regulates social science research. These questions about the philosophy of law – Jurisprudence – are addressed in this chapter. They are questions which have tended to be the preserve of lawyers. However, it is proper that all those whom the law regulates should question the nature of those laws and inform the process of rule making. It is also the case that the law seems to suggest, by its language and institutions, an alternative form of ethical framework. It is equally appropriate to ask if this is the case. Here then there are two questions:

1   Is the law necessarily moral?
2   Does the concept of 'property' help when forming an ethical research stance?

## DOES LEGAL NECESSARILY MEAN ETHICAL?

The law makes a series of assumptions about its relationship with morality. Its language is riddled with references to the validity of law: for example, property is partly governed by the rules of 'equity', magistrates are known also as 'Justices', and disputes are paraded through the halls of the 'Supreme Courts of Justice'. This language goes further, since the underpinning principles of law equally use morally weighted labels: for example 'due process' and 'natural justice'. Thus, society conditions its members to equate 'the law' with a morally correct and therefore justifiable set of rules. Jurisprudence indicates that this is not necessarily the case (Adams and Brownsword, 1992).

### Is any given law necessarily morally correct?

A first response could be to follow a line suggested in a social contract theory or in a Marxist, historical perspective. In both, law is a function of a wider agenda: in the former, it is a vehicle of the mutual rights and responsibilities of the citizen to the state or collective; in the latter, it is a vehicle whereby power has been exercised, and is subject to change for external motives. These approaches do not go to the heart of the matter, which is the appropriate constraints to be placed upon behaviour, and the facilitation of greater participation and understanding of society.

### What is morality and what is the law's relationship with morality?

One answer might be to challenge the necessity for such a question and to suggest that, since this is a plural society with laws created by a demo-cratically elected parliament, then all laws are given moral force through those democratic processes according to the rules of pluralism. This is most attractive, especially for an acceptable multicultural explanation of morality. However, it relies upon the assumption that there is no external criteria of right or wrong: law is justified only internally through the will of the majority. Thus, a statute requiring, for example, all social science researchers to be imprisoned, if it is the product of the will of the majority through its proper processes, is a valid rule. Further, it assumes that all law is the product of the democratic system. Clearly, in the English precedent-based system this is not the case. Judges, through individual case decisions, create law, either through the interpretation of rules and their language or through judicially established principles. The judiciary is independent and unelected and therefore stands outside a purely democratic mechanism for moral justification for its rules.

Democratic pluralism then is arguably unsatisfactory in answering the question of the link between morality and law. There are two further and competing schools of thought in jurisprudence which address this ques-tion: *Legal Positivism* and *Natural Law Theory*. Both, it can be said, lead to a similar observation about the present rules on the statute book and in the case law. Legal Positivists, most notably H.L.A. Hart (Hart, 1961), would argue that there is no necessary link between law and morality. They would point to the array of laws that exist and the potential for creating new laws, and would conclude that there can be no claim that such laws are necessarily moral. These Legal Positivists could be described, perhaps, as pragmatists. If we assess the group of elements described as law, the elements exhibit no necessarily moral characteristics. From this, they conclude that there is no compulsion for laws to be moral. It may be the case, for the Legal Positivists, that laws could be created with a moral backbone, or that laws should at a later stage be judged against a moral code. However, there is no necessity that a 'law' be moral: Legal Positivists would have no problem with applying the label 'law' to any rule which its society would recognize as having authority. Natural Law Theorists, however, would have precisely that difficulty.

A Natural Lawyer would have no great difficulty in accepting that there is a body of rules which is colloquially termed 'laws'. However, he or she would require that for the term 'Law' to be applied in a technical and correct sense, a rule must be morally valid if it is make the jump from being merely a rule to becoming a 'Law'. In this part, it is easier to distinguish *law* in an amoral sense and *Law* in a law and morals connected sense. If, then, a rule is not moral, and therefore not a Law, arguably it should not be obeyed even if that would bring the sanction for breaking the rule. Natural Law Theory has many different proponents from many ages, taking widely different bases for the theory. The linking element is always, however, that Law-making is a moral enterprise. Thus, Law is perceived to be necessarily moral for scholars from Aristotle, through Augustine and Aquinas, to modern writers such as Beyleveld and Brownsword (1986) or Gewirth (1978). The theories all show that from an external rationale Law must conform to a code of morality: Law is prescriptive and, as such, is a form of ethics. Therefore, to a Natural Lawyer, a rule may be created by parliament, for example, concerning the incarceration of social scientists, and that rule may display all the elements of social and cultural authority, but it will not be a 'Law' unless it is also morally justifiable.

### How can one adjudicate between these positions?

It can be seen that there are a number of different answers to the question: Should law necessarily be moral? The central difficulty is one of adjudication between these competing theoretical positions, if, indeed, this is possible. Returning to the approaches which we have thought about, there are some indications of a framework for adjudication. The Anarchist or Pluralist would say that there is no prevailing morality; they are simply fashions, products of culture and history. To them, the question of adjudication would be a matter of prevailing social trends and opinions, and nothing more. The Marxist, Social Contractor or Legal Positivist would appeal to a form of obviousness. The Marxist would claim a self-evident historical analysis of the place of law. The Social Contract Theorist would equally claim self-evidence from the state of man. The Legal Positivist would claim authority in the weight given to law by the institutions which create it in any given society. The Natural Lawyer presents, and faces, a greater difficulty.

Natural Law Theory claims a necessity that Law be moral. It does not prescribe a particular morality, however, and thus creates a secondary problem of adjudication between moralities. Morality could be on the basis of faith, as is the case for St Thomas Aquinas (Kenny, 1980), or purely upon reason, as is the position of Beyleveld and Brownsword (1986). How can one judge between claims to moral superiority as between, for example, a utilitarian and a rights theorist? How can one claim a validity as between John Stuart Mill (Robson, 1965), Ronald Dworkin (1977) and John Rawls (1973)?

This is discussed at great length throughout Jurisprudence, and is perhaps for future consideration rather than detailed analysis at this point. Here it is sufficient to conclude that law is not necessarily moral and there is a constant debate raging as to whether rules should be moral. When laws are applied to social situations there can be no assumption that they are Laws (moral rules), which begs the question of why they should be obeyed and how and for what purpose they have been framed. This clearly goes to the heart of the question about whether the rules which apply to research guarantee or even assist in developing principled researchers.

## LAW AND ETHICS: USING THE LAW TO THINK ABOUT AN ETHICAL POSITION

Having established the distinction between Law (morally weighted) and law (rules without moral weight) in the previous section, from this point on *law* or *Law* will not indicate a moral weighting. The initial questions here have concerned the status of rules, and therefore the amount of weight which should be placed upon them by a researcher or other member of society. On the one hand, since they are rules, breach of the duties they create may result in the sanction of law. However, there is the issue which constantly hangs over law, namely, are the rights and duties created justifiable? As researchers, the concern should not only be to work within the law, but also to influence the creation of appropriate regulations for the research environment.

Unfortunately, the arguments presented so far seem to be inconclusive as to the relationship between the law and ethics. Perhaps another approach to the issue, by considering one of the central concepts of law, could provide an alternative set of questions about the nature of ethical behaviour. It also opens an interesting question of whether the law goes far enough in the rights and duties it creates for research regulation. The next question must be: Whom should the law protect in this area?

### *What are the elements which make up your life as a researcher?*

Some of the elements may be: gathering information and preparing thoughts for publications; discussion of ideas with others; forming research relationships with individuals and institutions to gain access to data and materials; or using computers and software to analyse data.

First, although not necessarily primarily, the individual researcher needs some sort of protection, some sort of security that when discussing an idea, it cannot be taken and used by another. He or she will require protection of his or her writing when it is published: some sort of control over the way it is treated and how it can be used. He or she will need some sort of clarity of expectations when dealing with the subjects of research: it is essential that the rules of engagement are drawn before starting work. The law provides some, but not all, of the answers to these problems.

Perhaps more importantly, the elements listed above, and many other areas of research, bring outsiders into the process. There are, for example, the individuals and institutions who will provide the data for the studies, the community of academics within which study is undertaken, employers and funding bodies, the broader academic community to whom the findings and analysis are ultimately presented, and the broader society which is influenced by the whole endeavour. Again, there is a clear need to regulate on behalf of these individuals. One of the constant themes of this collection is that research carries with it enormous power: it is certainly part of the law's role to regulate a proper exercising of that power and to guard against its abuse.

Three issues emerge from the above discussion: the ownership of data; the proper expectations of the researcher; and the wider expectations and rights of the society in relation to information and analysis developed – the consumer interests.

### Who owns the data which forms the basis of research?

Colloquially, 'property' means 'things'. When thinking of 'property', perhaps we think primarily of land, houses and fields, and of tangible goods, books, tables and chairs. If pushed, we would also consider shares in companies, bank accounts, and other intangible things, as 'property'. We would probably also talk in terms of 'my' or 'your' property, and in this we begin to approach the legal position. Law has a technical meaning for 'property', far removed from the colloquial, estate agent's use. 'Property' in law can be defined as the relationship between individuals about things. It is not the thing itself; the thing is the subject of the property. The relationships may be visible between two individuals, but a property right is properly described as the right of one individual as against the whole world. The law takes a broad view of the things which can be the subject of property, for example, a lease for a house, a copyright or patent. However, there are limits on the extent of property, albeit limits which are constantly under challenge from both technology and theory. Macpherson (1978) presents a useful set of essays on these issues.

Property is defined through a curious mixture of justifications. A strong line of justification stems from the thinking of John Locke (Laslett, 1964), namely that property – owning things and therefore a right to exclude others from enjoyment of those things – comes from the right to ownership of one's own body, and there is, therefore, a necessary right to the fruits of one's own labour. This individualist approach is challenged by the right of the wider society. A challenge within the labour theory, clearly advanced by Nozick, challenges the place of the individual within the wider scheme of labour (Hettinger, 1989). This refining influence is seen most clearly when discussing the right to property in inventions. Nozick points to the dependence of the individual upon the accumulated knowledge and labour of all members of the society, and suggests the purer form of deserts justification based upon added value. This point is best illustrated by thinking of the symphonies of Mahler. Could those great works have been written without the great composers writing before him – Beethoven, Mozart, Haydn, even Bach? Each genius wrote with knowledge of the culture and development of his predecessors and contemporaries, and this begs the question of the nature of originality and ownership.

The second challenge to Locke is more direct and from the Utilitarian school. Property to the Utilitarian could be justified on the basis of social benefit to the whole. Individuals will be encouraged to participate in and advance the whole of society if they are encouraged by the carrot that is a right to private ownership. The Marxist view would challenge this perception of the good of allowing the basis of removing and distorting the natural rights of ownership stemming from work.

The law, based upon consensus and pragmatism, has taken elements of all theories to justify the ownership of property. On the one hand, and enshrined in the United Nations Declaration of Human Rights, is a right to the fruits of one's labour. On the other, however, there are clear constraints upon unlimited ownership on the basis of the good of the public. Countless examples can be seen where the individual's ownership and rights over property are constrained by notions of the 'public interest' or the 'consumers' interest'. Property law relating to social science research is a good example of the law's constraining influence. The law, albeit indirectly through a notion of property, also begins to offer us an ethical position for research relationships.

### What is the 'property' in research?

Research concerns information. Information is gathered, interpreted, and presented. The information can be held in a variety of states by a number of individuals. In one of my own research projects, I spent some time studying the practitioners' understanding of a child's best interests in separation and divorce cases. If I consider the various forms of information which I used, I can see a great variety of 'ownership'. Some of them are included in the following: the courts hold and publish a variety of statistics about the area, notably the number of cases including children per annum; the law reports give verbatim accounts of each of the reported decisions from those statistics. I interviewed the individual professionals, solicitors, court welfare officers and conciliators to gain an insight into their role and perception of the process. One could also interview the individual parties and their children and record their histories, their stories about their divorce and separation. All this information forms different data sets, the issue becomes whether it can be said that information is the 'thing' which forms the basis of research 'property', and then how the law views the ownership of that information.

The law takes a pragmatic stance here. Once the information is crystallized into a permanent and discrete expression, then the law recognizes ownership of that expression. The expression is the thing which attracts property in the form of copyright. Thus, in the examples above, the Crown owns copyright in the published statistics about the courts, the law reporters and their employers own the copyright in the tangible report of the Judge's decision. This points towards the labour principle. The individuals or institutions and companies involved invest their expertise, time and capital into producing the expression of the data, and the reward is a property right – a right to control that expression. One must ask about the ownership position of the mother and father who offer their account of their divorce: who owns the history of the divorce? Here the law takes a rather different approach.

### Why shouldn't ideas be capable of being property?

As a researcher, one might take the view that since one expended effort in collecting the data, then it should be one's own property, and protected from third parties regardless of what one has proceeded to do with the information. There is clearly some mileage in this. The law, however, has taken a rather different view. In *Oxford v. Moss* ((1978) 68 Cr App Rep 183.) a student broke into the place where an examination paper was being kept secure and, it was alleged, stole the information on the paper – the questions as opposed to the physical document. The court considered the desirability of finding this to be the case. However, they felt that information should not be capable of being owned, and a charge of theft of the information was not upheld, the university being deprived permanently of no property.

This may seem a strange ruling on its face. Indeed, the Law Commission in their assessment of the principle (Law Commission, 1997) has suggested that the law is more concerned about the theft of the company furniture than the theft of the trade secrets of the company. However, if we consider the wider public interest *Oxford v. Moss* must be the correct decision. The law takes the view that society is only advanced through the sharing of information, and therefore only minimal constraints on ownership, sufficient to recognize and encourage the labourer to produce ideas and information, should be made. Imagine the constraints upon research if information was owned by individuals. The possibilities for broader concealment would become boundless; independent academic scrutiny would be impossible. Further, implications for invention and innovation would be devastating. Even the Law Commission, following their concerns indicated above, could not contemplate a full reversal of the *Oxford* decision. The Commission proposes that there should be a criminal sanction for the breach of a duty of confidentiality in the area of trade secrets. It has not gone down the track of a general creation of enforceable property in ideas.

There is also a pragmatic consideration behind the legal position here. It would be almost impossible to police a rule which allowed ideas to be owned. The courts would be full of disputing thinkers, contesting the claim to the basis of a new novel, or other idea. Defending one's own data would be impossible.

In copyright, pragmatically, it is impossible to say who first had the idea for the story, and so the law bases ownership on the expression of the idea. For example, first consider a public lecture. If the lecture is taped or verbatim notes are taken, then there is a copyright vesting in the lecturer. If the lecture is heard and the ideas are produced in the listeners' own words, then there is no breach. The same principles apply to the researcher hearing the histories of the interviewees. If the story is recounted and no notes are made and the researcher only draws general conclusions from what is said without using the words of the interviewee, then there is no form for the idea to find expression in, and there is no ownership. If, however, the interview is taped, then there is a copyrights created in the words and the recording. Further, personal information is regulated through Data Protection and the flow of ideas can be regulated by confidentiality.

The law points researchers towards a fundamental ethical principle about the place of research and the availability of ideas to the community. This prescribes our conduct from the public interest perspective but also recognizes a need for a flow of ideas. However, this leaves another question unanswered: How should researchers treat their subjects and view their relationships to information disclosed to them?

### How then should we treat the subject?

This could be answered by drawing together a number of the threads which have already been considered above. First, the legal position is not necessarily morally justified or correct. There are considerable gaps between the two positions, and therefore the legal reasoning may be inadequate for our particular ethical needs. Second, the law is not saying that there are no claims to rights for the subjects in relation to their stories. It is clear that there is a possible position that could entertain a property right to ideas; this would be found in the labour theory approach. The idea is an extension of the individuality of the subject and therefore should be his or her property. The law examines this and overrules it for pragmatic reasons and because of the greater rights of the society generally.

The legal position does not stop the research community reappraising the same equation presented to the law and questioning the ethical value of the law's position. I would suggest that there is a pure moral sense in which the subject of the research 'owns' the ideas which he or she discloses. This is not an ownership always recognized at law. However, it is one which fits well with the ethical concepts of proper academic conduct. The outcome of this use of the concept of ownership requires us to consider two questions, which clearly influence the way we treat the data once it is in our hands: What is a proper respect for the information which we have been given? Do the subjects hand over their moral claims to the ownership of the information on disclosing it to the researcher?

Perhaps the best principle is derived from a consideration of how we would wish information about ourselves to be used by another. This would be a similar consideration to Rawls's veil of ignorance principle (Rawls, 1973). The law has not provided an ethical framework. However, through considering ownership, we have been able to construct some ethical questions by examining the law's particular position.

## CONCLUSION

It is clear then that the law does not necessarily produce an ethical framework for social science research, since law-making does not necessarily produce moral rules. There are, however, in certain legal concepts, notably 'property', concepts which could underpin social science research since they produce a particular way of thinking about the relationships created within social science research between the members of the research community and the subjects of the research. It is now necessary to move on from these Jurisprudential questions to examine how the law regulates social science research in practice, and to ask if any of the rules produce the same ethical framework which is imposed upon the researcher by the research community.

# 9  ETHICS IN THE FIELD

*Anne Celnick*

This chapter begins by considering how differences in ethical perspectives may affect research practice. Particular emphasis is given to the role ethics can play in influencing the sanctioning of research by organizational gatekeepers. The chapter concludes with a discussion of some of the ethical issues which may arise for researchers engaged in policy-oriented research. The conclusions I reach and many of the examples I provide are drawn from my experience in the probation service both as a researcher and advising research students on requests for access.

## ETHICAL PERSPECTIVES

Social research which involves research from within a large organization can for a researcher based in an academic institution seem like being in a country whose culture is strange and alien. This is because although the same ethical principles may be held by the organization, its members may have a quite different perspective on how those principles apply compared with the perspective of an academic researcher. Despite the fact that it has been suggested that there is 'simply no consensus on key ethical questions' (Punch, 1986: 81), the ethical principles of autonomy, non-maleficence, beneficence and justice are as relevant to practitioners and managers in a wide range of professional settings as to researchers. Their interpretation and the relative priority accorded to competing principles will differ, however, because the professional values underpinning their practice and the context in which they operate are different. For example, Wenger (1987: 211) compares the academic ethos 'which places a high value on independence, intellectual autonomy and creativity' with 'the administrative ethos [which] is one of agency loyalty, formal procedures and respect for authority'. The effect of different priorities among ethical principles is that different professional groups are likely to experience different ethical dilemmas. The effect of different interpretations of ethical principles is that there are different definitions of what constitutes ethical practice.

### Differences in interpretation

The interpretation of the ethical principle of autonomy in relation to getting informed consent to an interview can be contrasted between a researcher and a probation officer. Defendants for whom courts require a pre-sentence report have little choice in the matter. If they do not co-operate, they may be remanded in custody. Probation officers, however, do not regard themselves as acting unethically by conducting interviews with them in these circumstances because it is part of the professional context in which they work. In contrast, for a researcher to impose an interview on someone without their willing consent would generally be regarded as unethical behaviour.

Different professional values also affect the interpretation of ethical principles. For example, researchers undertaking policy research may find that the organization resists publication of the findings. On the one hand, if the organization fears the findings will damage unfairly its reputation in the wider world, it may consider publication to be a breach of the principle of non-maleficence. On the other hand, the researcher is likely to see efforts to prevent publication as in breach of the principle of intellectual autonomy. Thus in Barnes's (1967: 206) view:

> Administrators are capable of defending their own interests much more effectively than are private citizens and hence the effects of anthropological publications rarely constitute a serious threat to them . . . it would be regrettable if ethnographers were able to publish only manuscripts approved by the administration.

Although in this instance Barnes is referring to governments, the principle could also apply to large organizations.

### Differences in priorities

The second effect of different ethical perspectives, the existence of different priorities among ethical principles, can also be the source of conflict between professional groups. For example, a probation officer may become aware that an offender is doing casual work while claiming welfare benefits. Because probation officers see that it is more difficult for someone with a criminal record to find reasonably paid work and know that surviving on benefits over an extended period is extremely difficult, they experience an ethical dilemma whether or not to report the person to the authorities.

It could be argued that this is unlikely to be experienced as a dilemma for the police because their professional values emphasize the beneficence of the public rather than of the offender. This difference can lead to an uneasy relationship between police and probation officers, the former regarding the latter as unprincipled for 'siding' with offenders.

A further complication is that, although individual professions may have codes of ethics, the application of the code is ultimately a matter of individual judgement in relation to the particular circumstances of the case. Consequently, different members of the same profession may reach different conclusions.

## Value of understanding differences between ethical perspectives

Differences in ethical perspectives are of more than academic interest to those researchers whose research brings them into contact with people. Understanding how the people involved with the research (whether as gatekeepers or subjects) approach ethical questions and the values they bring to ethical decisions can both facilitate the research and contribute to its quality in a number of respects.

First, in the process of obtaining permission for access or in requesting information, this understanding may help the researcher to foresee and avoid potential areas of concern for the organization. For example, an approach to the probation service to seek access to sex offenders for a piece of research would be likely to be turned down if there was no evidence in the application that the researcher would be sensitive to and knowledgeable enough about issues of sex offending to make risk of harm to themselves, the offender or victim unlikely.

Understanding the perspective of others can provide a guide to what methods may and may not be acceptable. This can influence the choice of methods for the research. For example, in a sensitive area such as research involving work done by probation officers on domestic violence, requests for access to case records would be more likely to be successful than a request to be put in touch with victims, again because of the perceived potential for further harm to them.

Finally, an understanding of the professional context and values of an organization can help the researcher understand what might otherwise be inexplicable behaviour. This may give a better insight into the material gathered and how it should be interpreted.

For example, when studying how probation officers operate in the court setting, a probation officer was observed to suggest to the magistrates that they remand a defendant for several weeks for the preparation of a report rather than pass sentence immediately. This was despite the fact that the defendant himself had indicated to the court that he did not want a further delay. The explanation for this apparently uncharacteristically unsympathetic attitude to the defendant was that the magistrates were proposing to impose a sentence which in the officer's view was overly harsh in the circumstances. He was aware that the case for a more lenient sentence could only be fully made in a written report. In his view, then, both justice and beneficence to the defendant would be promoted by an adjournment. Without an understanding of how professional values were operating, it would have been easy to conclude falsely that the officer was not concerned about the defendant's well-being.

This section has described how different ethical perspectives can arise and the importance for researchers of understanding the ethical perspectives of the people involved in their research. The next section will consider the part played by ethical questions in decisions on research access.

## GATEKEEPING ACCESS

As Lee (1993: 120) observes, getting access is usually the one part of a study which is only ever written from one side. What is lost thereby are the understandings of those who are being researched or being studied. In this section, I shall explore from the perspective of those being researched, the place of ethics in gatekeeping access to research subjects or in the provision of information.

Those responsible for giving permission for access have ethical duties towards both the employees of the organization and their client group. Neither the benignity of the research nor the researcher's ability to avoid causing harm to employees or client group can be taken for granted. For example, in relation to staff, incompetent research can, at best, mean wasted resources through time spent co-operating with it. A poorly designed questionnaire is unlikely to produce the information it was intended to collect, so that the time spent by the organization to ensure completion, and thereby reducing resources for its business, would be wasted. More tangible damage could result if the processing and analysis of the data were done incompetently. Inaccurate findings might then be used to inform policy decisions.

Researchers are likely to be sensitive to ethical considerations in relation to the clients of the organization but they may be less aware of ethical questions in relation to its employees. It is important to recognize that damage to the organization may result in damage to its individual members, since their livelihood is bound up with it.

In relation to the granting of access to the clients of the organization, the organization must satisfy itself that ethical principles are not likely to be breached through granting access. For example, when the probation service received a request that officers should encourage compulsive gamblers to refer themselves via their GP for an experimental programme, it had a duty to check that the programme would not be likely to harm them. If the researcher had also wanted to interview those individuals, the service would have had an ethical duty to protect confidentiality by ensuring that the interviewer was not simply given a list of names but could only contact individuals by indirect means via the probation officer concerned.

Wilkins points out that 'prisoners' rights are rarely a matter of concern to the authorities until someone wants to do research on prisons' (1986:

38). Unfortunately, organizations are not always as conscious of ethical considerations in relation to their own behaviour towards clients as they ought to be. Even if, as a result, the ethical criteria applied in relation to access for research purposes appear to be more stringent than those required of staff, it must still be right that they are in place.

Personal contacts may provide an easy route into an organization but should not be used to avoid following the proper procedures for getting access. Both the ethical duties of the organization and the ethical duties of the researcher to the organization mean that the researcher should ensure that the organization, and not just the individual member at the point where access is required, gives informed consent to research involving its work or its staff. At the same time, the organization can be said to have an ethical duty in relation to promoting the pursuit of knowledge and ought not unreasonably to refuse access or information.

## Access procedures

While procedures differ between organizations, there are likely always to be some formal arrangements by which access should be sought. In a bureaucratic organization with a hierarchy of authority the level at which access is granted may vary with the nature of the research; small-scale student projects may be authorized at a local level while research involving more people in the organization will require permission from the centre. Although formal procedures may seem unnecessarily bureaucratic and time consuming to the researcher, from the organization's viewpoint, they are intended to protect its interests:

1   *Managing staff time*: although an individual research request may require relatively little time from staff, it may be one of many such requests, all adding up to a substantial additional workload. Central consideration enables this to be controlled consistently and according to organizational priority. For example, requests from students at local academic institutions may be given priority over those from outside the area or priority may be given to research which appears likely to have some benefits for the organization.

2   *Preventing duplication*: it helps neither the researcher nor the organization if staff are asked to give the same or similar assistance to two different researchers since the co-operation afforded is likely to be reduced. Sometimes, in-house work may be planned to cover a similar topic and unless this can be co-ordinated with the external research, the results may be compromised.

An example of this was when lack of co-ordination led to a situation in which the same group of staff was required to complete three quite separate but similar questionnaires from different sources. Not surprisingly, the third (which might have resulted in suggestions for improved service to women offenders) got a particularly poor response rate.

3   *Application of consistent and informed judgements about research requests*: requests for access may be examined centrally against pre-determined criteria. Criteria used by gatekeepers may differ from organization to organization but the three important ones are likely to be the evidence that the research will be done competently, ethical considerations and resource implications for staff. In relation to the last, it is worth noting that researchers often underestimate greatly the time the organization will have to spend on co-operating with the research. For example, there may be no quick way to identify which clients fit the researcher's specification or information may not be held in an easily accessible form.

### Ethical considerations for the organization

As we have seen, the judgement that the gatekeeper has to make when considering a request for access is whether the benefit of co-operating with the research (both to the organization and the wider community) out-weighs the cost to the organization. S/he must also consider questions of data protection: how the research process and its findings might impact on the agency. Last, but very importantly, ethical issues have to be examined. For example, what arrangements can and will be made by the researcher to ensure confidentiality and for getting informed consent from subjects, whether these are the staff of the organization or its clients?

In reaching conclusions about these issues, an important factor is the gatekeeper's view of the researcher's probity, that is, how far can the researcher's word be trusted. Will s/he keep to the undertakings made to satisfy the organization's concerns or will these be abandoned once access has been obtained to research subjects or material? If the researcher is unknown to the gatekeeper, the judgement may be made on the basis of the reputation of the researcher's supervisor, academic institution or organ-ization, or on impressions gained from contact with the researcher.

Two contrasting examples illustrate this point. The first demonstrates the importance of personal knowledge of the researcher where the research is potentially contentious. As part of the aims, the research was designed to examine the extent to which probation services were rationally managed. Clearly if the researcher were to find this not to be the case, that could be damaging to those services if it became common knowledge. On the other hand, not only was there the potential for local probation services to learn from the research, but it could be argued that there was a public interest in it being carried out. The crucial factor in the decision to agree to co-operate was that the researcher was personally known and there was confidence both in his ability to do the research well and in his probity. Agreement was reached with him that representatives of the service would be able to comment on his draft report and it was believed that although the findings might turn out to be critical, they would be fair.

In the second example, the probation service received a proposal which did not appear, on the face of it, to be well designed to achieve its stated ends. The request for access came from an unknown researcher at an institution whose reputation was also unknown to the gatekeeper. In the letter requesting access, the researcher listed among his forthcoming publications an article in an academic journal which by chance the gate-keeper had been asked to assess and on which no decision on whether or not to publish had been made. Strictly speaking then, the researcher had been untruthful in his representations. Consequently, not only was there a question mark over the standard of the research but also over the researcher's probity. The result was that access was not given.

Since judgements are likely also to be made on the basis of past experience, trustworthiness in the sense of telling the truth and keeping promises is an ethical duty on researchers in relation to other researchers. For example, access was given to a postgraduate student to do some research in the organization which involved extra work for staff. At the time, the view was taken that the findings of the research would be useful enough to the organization to make the effort worthwhile. Unfortunately, the student did not complete his research. That experience resulted in the organization being less generous in the level of assistance offered to researchers subsequently.

Another problem created for researchers by other researchers is failure to provide the organization with an account of their findings or a copy of their report, even when this was promised at the outset. This means that agreement to co-operate is usually decided on the basis that minimal use of resources is required because the expectation is that there is likely to be little direct benefit for the organization.

Understanding how decisions are made may enable the researcher to negotiate access even after a refusal. For example, if the refusal is based on an assessment that the costs outweigh the benefits for the organization, it may be possible to amend the research proposal so that less is required from the organization's staff and other resources.

Researchers also need to take care about the way they conduct their research. If they appear not to be respecting the values of the organization, future researchers are likely to have more difficulty getting access. Respecting the values of an organization is not always as straightforward as it might seem. What do you do, for instance, if respecting an organiza-tion's values will be demonstrated by not publishing the findings? As Berry *et al.* (1986: 85) point out: 'Research findings are not value neutral and often challenge the conceptions of the very members who gave consent for the research to be conducted.'

If the consequence of carrying out a particular piece of research appears likely to result in difficulties for future researchers, it could be argued that there is a duty to consider whether or not that consequence is justified by the potential value of the research. It perhaps calls for a high degree of altruism from a researcher in this situation to reach the conclusion that his or her findings will be of less worth than those of future researchers, but student researchers in particular may need to pay particular attention to that question. After all, they themselves may want to return to the organization to do more advanced work. Sometimes the problem can be avoided by anticipating it and negotiating with the organization a compromise position, for example, additional safeguards to ensure anonymity.

In the following example, the consequences of publishing findings were to prevent further research for a considerable period. The research involved a study of sentencing in a magistrates court by eminent researchers but the findings were held by the chief magistrates clerk to be damaging to its reputation for justice. Subsequent requests for research access on however a limited scale and on whatever topic were refused for many years. In this case, the findings were important and the decision to go ahead with publication can be argued to have been ethically correct.

Finally, in this section, the following examples illustrate how the decisions about granting access may be made. The first example is a hypothetical case of two different students applying for access. One is a student training as a probation officer at a local university and the other is a student teacher from another area. Both are interested in circulating a questionnaire to be completed by offenders about their attitudes to adult education. The findings will be used as the basis of the required dissertation for their course.

The judgement is likely to be that the limitations of both surveys mean that the findings will not add to existing knowledge. Moreover, whatever the view of the student on the simplicity of the questionnaire, taken as a whole, the organization will have to put the equivalent of several days work into identifying suitable people, copying the questionnaire, chasing up returns, etc. However, assuming that the questionnaire did not pose any ethical problems, some efforts would be made to grant a request (with certain qualifications such as size of survey) from a student probation officer on the grounds that the organization has an interest in relation to their training, particularly at a local institution. If, on the other hand, the request is from a student teacher, it would probably be refused.

The following two examples are of letters written to probation services asking for co-operation. The first shows how a researcher can maximize their chances of getting access by foreseeing and dealing with the organization's probable concerns.

> *Survey of sexual victimization among men*
> We intend to ask men who are currently being supervised by Probation Officers to complete a . . . questionnaire . . . We hope the questions have been phrased sensitively and would emphasize that subjects will be free to withdraw consent to participate at any stage of the study . . . The survey has been approved by [named] Ethics Committee and has been designed in a way to cause minimum

embarrassment or distress . . . We shall endeavour to cause minimum disruption to your probation officers should you agree to co-operate in the study. Our research assistant would be available to offer immediate support and guidance on further counselling or services which might be required should anyone become distressed during the course of the computerized interview.

The mention of approval by an ethics committee can be particularly useful.

The second letter concerns a request in which access was refused. Compared to the first, there is little evidence of an understanding of the difficulties which may arise. It appeared that one purpose of the research was to identify people for whom the service offered by the applicant might be appropriate, and attached to the letter was information about the cost of membership, leaflets and tapes, so there appeared to be at least some indication of a financial interest.

> Anxiety disorders among those on probation
> [Named organization] is a registered charity helping those who suffer from anxiety disorders . . . The reason we would like to carry out this survey relates back to a call I received from a probation officer . . . he was interested in the work we do as some of the people he saw did have anxiety disorders . . . and wanted help for them . . . Through this questionnaire we hope to find out how much anxiety there is among probationers . . . We would then like to train probationers so that they can set up a helpline under the auspices of [named organization] to offer telephone counselling.

In this section, the process by which gatekeepers may reach decisions on requests for access from external researchers has been described. In-house researchers may not experience difficulties in getting access to their subjects but they too must resolve ethical dilemmas. This is the subject of the final section in this chapter.

## ISSUES FOR RESEARCHERS INVOLVED IN POLICY-ORIENTED WORK

The difficulties and some of the ethical dilemmas involved for external researchers who undertake policy research have been well documented (for example, Bulmer, 1982; Wenger, 1987). In-house researchers share some of those problems and have to find ways of resolving them. Although there are similarities, one difference stems from the ease of access to research data for in-house researchers which may obscure the ethical issues involved in getting informed consent. For example, an in-house researcher was required to evaluate a programme for men who had been violent toward their partners and one of the methods chosen was to observe sessions. Participants were informed why the researcher was there but were not asked to give consent. It appears that, at the time, it did not occur to anyone that this might be necessary. Some might argue that it was not and that the responsibility of the organization to ensure its practice is evaluated outweighs the ethical requirement to get informed consent. Others would disagree.

Such experiences tend to confirm the suggestion by Gallagher *et al.* (1995) that ethical issues have been generally ignored in social research, at least where in-house research is concerned, for one of the reasons they propose, namely that benign consequences are assumed to follow.

The same authors also point out that resolution of ethical dilemmas is not just a philosophical problem for researchers: 'ethical principles have methodological and practical implications which may be critical in deciding how an ethical dilemma is dealt with' (Gallagher *et al.*, 1995: 303). They describe three different approaches to resolving ethical dilemmas:

> The *expedient* (avoiding the problem): abandon the research or choose a different methodology to avoid the problem, or let the ethics committee decide on the appropriate course of action. In some instances none of these options will be practicable.
> *The value-driven*: the researcher uses her/his own value system to decide which of conflicting ethical principles should win. This carries the problem that values are linked to professional background and gender and also that individual values may be no more than a reflection of self-interest. This makes it essential to check decisions with someone detached from the problem.
> *The pragmatic*: the relative importance of each conflicting principle is assessed. This has similar limitations to the value-driven approach because the assessment will depend on the value system of the person making the assessment. Nevertheless, the authors favour this approach because they believe it encourages ethical principles to be viewed from the perspective of their significance in a research setting as well as from a philosophical angle. (Gallagher *et al.*, 1995: 303)

The following are examples from the probation service of the use of each of these three approaches. All relate to ethical dilemmas in getting informed consent.

### Expedient approach

The dilemma in this instance was whether to go ahead with the evaluation of a 'dispersed' hostel without the full consent of staff involved; on the grounds that it would contribute to good practice in this area of work (that is, the ethical principle of beneficence in relation to offenders took precedence over getting informed consent from staff).

Offenders can be sent to probation hostels either as a condition of a probation order, as a condition of their bail from court or as a transition from custody back into the community. The traditional hostel is one large building with communal dining and recreational areas, with food prepared for residents and staff on site to supervise and assist them. For some time an experiment had been going on locally to place offenders in bedsitters in houses rented and managed by the probation service which were visited on a daily basis by hostel staff. No evaluation of the effect of this dispersed model had been undertaken at the stage when decisions were pending about its future. The understanding of the staff of the dispersed hostel was that it was to close and they were upset and worried about their future. At this point, the researcher was asked to evaluate the effectiveness of the dispersed hostel. It was suspected that managers might use any negative findings to justify the closure of the hostel and ignore the positive ones. If that happened it would feed into the view common among staff that research was simply a threat to preferred ways of working rather than a means of learning how to improve practice. The result could be that it would be more difficult in future for in-house researchers to get consent and co-operation from staff in research initiatives.

The dilemma was resolved by choosing to undertake only a limited study of the dispersed hostel, recording its history and what staff saw as its strengths but not attempting to produce an objective evaluation of its effectiveness. Some would argue that taking this kind of expedient approach is a sensible compromise, but others might regard it as intellectually dishonest.

### The pragmatic approach

The question of getting informed consent from staff in research not just authorized but required by managers of an organization can appear to be somewhat theoretical. As Punch says:

> The 'subjects' of research may not even have been consulted by superiors about the presence of a researcher . . . and may not be in a position to refuse to co-operate. To negotiate access and consent with everyone would be almost futile and would become absurdly complex if some said 'yes' and some said 'no'. (Punch, 1986: 37)

In this example of a pragmatic approach, the in-house researcher was asked to assist managers reaching decisions about the use of resources by examining the way in which different geographical divisions organized work with courts to see which worked best. It was known that the number and grades of staff differed, but nothing was known about the effects of different arrangements. For the researcher, the complicating factor was that at the time this research was to be done it was known that cuts in funding would mean that a number of posts throughout the organization would be lost. Consequently, an examination of the differences in working arrangements in court could be seen as a potential threat to an individual's job.

The method chosen to carry out the study was observation of practice in courts, informal discussion with staff and semi-structured interviews with managers. Where people are suspicious about the researcher's motives, there is a danger that the results obtained will be incomplete or qualitatively poor. Steps had to be taken to make the research acceptable to informants who had been informed by managers that they must take part. This was easiest to do where the researcher was already known to staff as someone who could be trusted to be fair. Where the researcher was not personally known to staff, special efforts were made to inform staff what was planned and to reassure them that they would have an opportunity to comment on the draft report. At the same time it was important to make it clear that the researcher was not in control of how the results would be used.

Punch admits that: 'Unconsciously or semi-consciously you do "lie through your teeth" and dissemble in order to gain acceptance and get at the data . . . [this is] inevitable and irreducible but not the same as consciously and covertly dissembling' (1986: 33). The use of personal relationships in the way described above might be seen as a form of deception or a pragmatic approach to getting the research done.

### The value-driven approach

As part of an evaluation of an experimental probation project, the researcher wanted to interview probationers about their experience. The dilemma was how to get informed consent, but at the same time ensure that at least some probationers were interviewed in the time available. The solution chosen was to write to the individuals concerned explaining the purpose of the interview and suggesting a suitable date and time when they would be called on. They were told that unless the enclosed reply-paid response was returned indicating they did not want the researcher to visit or that the suggested time was not convenient, they would be visited. There was a further opportunity to withhold consent since, knowing when the researcher was coming, the person could arrange to be out or not answer the door. If there was no response when the researcher called, no further contact was attempted.

Arguably, this does not constitute truly informed consent. However, the judgement was reached that getting information from the consumers of the service was a very important aspect of the evaluation without which decisions about the future of the project would be flawed. The value placed on that outweighed the value placed on fully informed consent.

In this chapter, after considering different perspectives on ethical principles, I have described two roles in relation to research ethics: first, the role of the organization's gatekeeper to research access; second, the role of the researcher undertaking research within that organization. What I hope has become evident is that, although it may be easier to make ethical judgements about someone else's research than about one's own, the ethical considerations remain the same.

# 10 HOW DOES SUBSTANTIVE LAW CURRENTLY REGULATE SOCIAL SCIENCE RESEARCH?

## D.M.R. Townend

In Chapter 8 on legal issues, the theoretical contribution of the law to defining an ethical framework for social science research was discussed. It was suggested that there was perhaps little coherent ethical thinking behind the law: that the law came from a variety of sources in this area, all created for different purposes, and because of that lack of coherent attention to the regulation of social science research, the law did not give a developed ethical framework. The law, however, does give a number of legal rules which regulate the social science researcher at all levels within his or her career, and this chapter deals with the substantive laws which affect our work.

The chapter is organized into two parts. The first introduces each area of the law and explains something of how it works in practice. One of the most important areas, and one which has recently undergone massive reform, is the area of data protection, which is addressed first. An equally important area of law relating to research is intellectual property law, which is the second area for consideration. The remaining issues of importance to the social science researcher are defamation and contract law, which are considered third. Clearly there are wider issues which could be considered, for example, the legal relationship between a student and his or her university or issues of employment as a researcher after postgraduate study. These go beyond the immediate scope of this book and will not be addressed in this chapter. Having identified and explained all the substantive law which may regulate the social science researcher, the second part of this chapter places each of the substantive laws in the context of a research programme to give a clearer understanding of when the law applies to the researcher.

As has been said above, the law regulates the professor and the PhD student equally, and the description of the law in this chapter will be of use to those who are old hands, but especially to those who are starting out in the field. It is important to note that this chapter serves as a general introduction. It is designed to give an understanding of the type of law which protects the researcher and his or her subject, his or her writing, thesis and publications, and the materials of others. It is possible that legal issues will arise during your degree or project. The postgraduate is in the same position as all academics in that the community of scholars in which he or she works has a wealth of experience upon which to call for advice. Further, it is possible that there are lawyers in one's institution who would be prepared to give advice. One's union is also a useful source of information and often legal advice.

## FREEDOM OF INFORMATION AND THE PROTECTION OF DATA

In England, according to Halsbury's Laws, 'liberty of the subject is an implication drawn from the principle that the subject may say or do what he pleases provided he does not transgress the substantive law or infringe the legal rights of others' (Halsbury's Laws, 4th edn: 729). It has already been noted that there is no single statement of the law relating to social science research, making the researcher's life perhaps awkward, but little more. In the realm of civil liberties, and therefore in the realm of access to information, it should equally be apparent that there is no single statement of the law concerning the rights of citizens; English law exists without written constitution or modern bill of rights (Dworkin, 1990). This has a much more serious and, some would suggest, sinister implication, especially to those whose concern is understanding the development of society and calling its development to account.

While certain aspects of the life of the citizen in relation to the community and the state are regulated, for example by the Magna Carta of 1215, the Bill of Rights of 1688, the Act of Settlement of 1700 and through the international treaties on Human Rights to which the UK is a party, there is much that could be described as unregulated and secret. Access to information is traditionally in this latter category. There are two distinct freedom of information areas within the protection of data and both could be directly relevant to the social scientist: access to state information and access to personal information.

### Access to state information

State information is very carefully controlled. The government makes decisions and takes risks using information which influences the daily lives of the citizen. Access to such information is important for democratic scrutiny. The strict control of information was seen in cases such as *Spycatcher* or Clive Ponting, or in more recent arenas such as the Gulf War or the Balkan conflict. Considerable attempts were made in the 1990s to develop a more 'open government' ethos (Birkinshaw, 1993; White Paper, 1993). However, arguably, many difficulties remain in gaining access to government and other state information. Certain statutory duties were placed upon local government to hold registers of information, or to disclose certain information to the public. Duties arise through public law principles of natural justice, requiring a duty to give reasons for decisions made against individuals having a particular grievance (not a general duty to give reasons for decisions), and public clamour and political pressure can be brought to bear to gain public inquiries into decision-making. Public authorities have always been regulated by parliamentary scrutiny and the public records systems, but are such vehicles adequate protection?

Information is placed into the public domain by the state, be it politicians or civil servants. The process of legislation requires debate into the appropriateness of proposed measures, and this process gives rise to a number of opportunities for the publication of information. First, the proposals are presented in justifying papers, first Green Papers, moving to firmer proposals in White Papers, or at parliamentary committee stages. These are published at the command of parliament (hence, Command Papers), and show useful explanations of policy. They concern policy and do not disclose vast amounts of information. Likewise, ministers are under parliamentary scrutiny. Written and oral questions can be made to the government requiring replies. Again, published, these could be seen as exercises for diplomatic writing classes rather than for the free flow of information in the public interest. The principle seems to be grossly paternalistic and fuelled by an intense fear of the 'enemy'.

Control of choice of information for disclosure is therefore the key. But, you may say, parliamentary papers are held in the Public Record Office. The case is, however, that under the Public Records Act 1967, public access to papers is only granted thirty years from the placing of documents in the Office. Further, the Act itself allows selectivity in the documents filed in the Office. Now, this could be seen as manipulation, but perhaps it is only realism and leads us to a more difficult conclusion about the potential benefits of a Freedom of Information Act.

In November 1999 a Freedom of Information Bill was introduced to Parliament. It proposes a right to access information held by 'public authorities'. Further, such authorities must act to make information available through 'Publication Schemes'. The proposals retain the thirty year rule and the secrecy of information concerning national security or information likely to prejudice the economy. On their face, the proposals appear a great advance in open government, however, there is room, perhaps for cynicism. Control still vests with those gathering and developing the information and hence the effect of a right to such information has little effect upon the secret state.

The likelihood of full disclosure of all information is inconceivable: first, on the grounds of national security – retained in the 1999 scheme for freedom of information; second, on the ground of the cost of publication of all decisions and the bureaucracy which would thus be created; finally, since it is not in the nature or interests of a competitive political system and system of government (with departments of government competing against each other for limited funds) to concede the power of information to their opponents. The Freedom of Information (FoI) proposals seem to rely on a knowledge of the availability of information. Fishing trips are not encouraged in the proposals.

Further, beyond the traditional concepts of the state, and rooted in commerce, the quasi-state is emerging through the operation of commercial interests. This is well documented in writing on 'globalization'. It is argued by public lawyers that this quasi-state is different to the position of the public state since it is not part of the democratic state based around the provision of a framework for private interests: commerce is, to a very large extent a matter of private interest and therefore outside the issues of public law. This is all absolutely correct. However, there is an alternative analysis that large companies and other institutions of commerce have enormous control over the lives of citizens, be they employees or simply members of society generally. It is equally the case that there are enormous issues of secrecy and the proper use of power over the 'citizens' of the commercial state which stand beyond the simple regulation through private law. There is a need to develop a proper administrative law of these new states within states and, it is argued here, issues of secrecy are an excellent starting point for that discussion. In commerce, rights to secrecy are justified on the basis of the sanctity of competition. At the heart of this secrecy is the fact that disclosure of information into the public domain is a matter of choice and that all those involved with the information are sworn to secrecy through the Official Secrets Act 1911 as amended by the 1989 Act, and through Theft Acts (Birkinshaw, 1990: 25–65). It is almost impossible to think that rights of access to information would be extended into the private arena. In a capitalist economy, commerce can always control the disclosure of its information on the grounds of competition. In an increasingly privatized state, this control becomes more invasive to individuals' lives.

### Access to personal information

The realm of personal information is rather different. The holders of information on individual citizens are legion, regulation of them is, however, piecemeal. If we return to the confusion in English law about the distinction between owning pure information and owning rights to exploit the benefits of one's ideas, we can see the origin of this difficulty: there is confusion as to whether individuals can own information about themselves. This problem is addressed in the European Convention on Human Rights, article 8, which gives the citizen a right to respect of their private and family life. This would point us towards two elements: first, it would suggest a right to privacy; second, it would seem to require a right of access to information held about the individual.

Professor Birkinshaw, when considering the obligations placed upon the law from international treaties relating to privacy suggests: 'There is no doubt that our law falls short of the protection of privacy envisaged in article 8 of the European Convention on Human Rights. There is no statutory or common law right to privacy as such' (Birkinshaw, 1990: 209). As such then, social science research is unencumbered by laws of privacy of the individual citizen (*Lord Bernstein of Leigh v. Skyviews and General Ltd* [1977] 2 All ER 902). Even after the Human Rights Act 1998, the position is likely to remain the same. If, however, the self-regulation of the press by the Press Complaints Commission does not continue to prevent the excesses of the media, this could change radically.

Recent developments seem to suggest a reshaping of the law in relation to civil liberties through the Human Rights Act 1998. Arguably this will be limited. The 1998 Act places the European Convention on Human Rights in English law. Wadham and Mountfield (1999) indicate that the vast majority of legislation must be applied in the courts through the requirements of the Convention and with an acceptance of case law from the European Court on Human Rights. However, for our purposes, the Convention is not applied directly against a private individual. It will 'have an indirect effect on the outcome [of litigation], because the court will be obliged to interpret statutes so as to conform to the Convention wherever possible; must exercise any judicial discretion compatibly with the Convention; and must ensure that its application of common law or equitable rules is compatible with the Convention' (Wadham and Mountfield, 1999: 3). On its face, article 8 of the Convention appears to give a right to privacy. Wadham and Mountfield argue that this would not be a correct reading of the right and that, rather, to apply the article 8 rights the violation must be outside the law – for example, relating to confidentiality or data protection – and not be an action required in a democratic state (Wadham and Mountfield, 1999: 96). This leaves open a number of important questions about the future of privacy: should the individual citizen have a right to privacy, or is the resulting loss to the freedom of information too high a price to pay, especially in the field of social science research?

## DATA PROTECTION

Personal data is an increasingly important commodity in a consumer society. This has a number of implications for the protection of the individual, and therefore for regulation. Personal information often forms the basis of data which is used in social science research, and therefore the regulations concerning personal data are of great importance. The issues which have concerned the law are around a respect for the individual subject of the data and, because of that individual, a respect for the data which is held. The individual is respected in that both the material kept about the individual must be accurate and open to scrutiny and challenge and the individual has certain rights to access the data. This reflects that the freedom of the individual is greatly influenced by the decisions which are taken by others with the use of the material and also that the individual makes decisions about him or herself having access to the same data. Further issues relate to the purposes for which data is collected and used, and the security of the environment where the data is stored. In English law, certain types of personal information such as medical or credit information have been regulated specifically from the mid-1970s and early 1980s. Data Protection was first added to the statute book in 1984 and was recently completely revised under the Data Protection Act 1998. The new Act is in force from 1 March 2000.

### Definitions under the Data Protection Act 1998

There is a similarity of language between the Data Protection Acts of 1984 and 1998, but the concepts and effects are so radically different under the new law that it is best to forget the 1984 Act and start afresh in the area (Carey, 1998: 21). The Data Protection Act 1998 prescribes the manner in which data is kept and the use to which it is put. 'Data', under the 1998 Act, has a much wider coverage than that of the 1984 Act. Under section 1 of the 1998 Act, data includes information which is processed by automatic equipment for data processing (DPA 1998: s. 1(1)(a)), is recorded with the intention that it should be processed by means of such equipment (DPA 1998: s. 1(1)(b)), is recorded as part of a relevant filing system or with the intention that it should form part of a relevant filing system (DPA 1998: s. 1(1)(c)), or forms part of an 'accessible record', for example, health, education or other accessible public records (DPA 1998: s. 1(1)(d)). The most important part of this definition is the third element, the 'relevant filing system'. This system is clearly defined in the first section of the Act to include any set of personal information which is not kept or manipulated by electronic means, but is easily accessible by reference to the individual such that specific information about an individual can be accessed. This inclusion of manually kept and processed data sets addressed one of the major criticisms which was levelled at the 1984 Act. The automated processing distinction drawn under the initial legislation perhaps could be seen to have its roots in the concerns about the computer age which the Younger Committee felt bound to address. However, it was certainly an artificial distinction to draw (Younger Committee, 1972). There is clearly no real distinction between holding personal information in an automated system or a manual system for the subject of the information. The same issues and expectations of access, accuracy and security will prevail. The 1998 Act is, then, a most useful step forward.

Again, by section 1 of the 1998 Act, anyone who 'determines the purposes for which and the manner in which any personal data are, or are to be, processed' is termed a 'Data Controller'; anyone who processes personal data on behalf of a data controller is named a 'Data Processor'; and anyone who is the subject of personal data is a 'Data Subject'. There is a development of the principles of the 1984 Act in the definition of 'personal data' in the 1998 Act. 'Personal Data', which is the relevant data for the Act, is defined as information about a living individual who is identifiable from the data or from data in the hands of the data controller which, in conjunction with other information either already in the hands of the data controller or which *is likely to come into the possession of the data controller*, makes the individual identifiable from the mixture of the data (DPA 1998: s. 1). An example of the mixing of data to create a data set which allows the identification of an individual could be where a data controller holds a data set about ten individuals numbered one to ten which has had all names, addresses and other personal markers removed, and then she holds another file with the names of the individuals listed each at the same numbers one to ten. The 'is likely' clause covers a situation where the second file subsequently falls into the data controller's hands. 'Data' includes the data controller's opinions about the individual or intentions of the data controller or other person in respect of the individual.

This 'personal data' definition is clearly very far-reaching. The most important issue will be the interpretation of the 'is likely' clause above. This has interesting implications. How will the clause apply to material which could become individually identifiable should certain other facts fall into the hands of the researcher data controller? This will perhaps be interpreted with some form of 'reasonably foreseeable' test. The more interesting questions will no doubt be debated when material does fall into the hands of the data controller which, when added to material already kept, makes individuals identifiable in the data set. Clearly, in such a case the actual event makes the possibility more than likely in one sense since the extra information is in the hands of the data controller, but there must be room to argue successfully that although the additional material did come to light, the event was not foreseeable, and so the data controller could not be liable for any breach of data protection duties prior to the emergence of the data. This may seem a ridiculously legalistic point, but there are clearly issues of how the data protection duties relating to identifiable personal data apply for any unidentifiable data if 'is likely' is interpreted without some sort of reasonably foreseeable element for the actual emergence of subsequent clarifying data.

The 1998 Act develops the scope of the data protection principles in relation to manual as well as automated, identifiable personal data. It expands the meaning of identifiable personal data to situations where it may be 'likely' that clarifying data may fall into the hands of the data controller making information about an unidentifiable individual become information about an identifiable individual. These show a depth in the new Act; a maturing of the data protection legislation towards a true privacy in personal information for the individual. There is a further development which is to be welcomed in the wide definition of 'processing' of data under the 1998 Act. 'Processing' includes almost any dealings with data. By section 1, it includes obtaining, recording, holding, 'or carrying out any operation or set of operations on the information or data, including –

(a) organisation, adaptation or alteration of the information or data, (b) retrieval, consultation or use of the information or data, (c) disclosure of the information or data by transmission, dissemination or otherwise making available, or (d) alignment, combination, blocking, erasure or destruction of the information or data'. As can be seen, the interpretation of processing covers the vast majority of uses of data or information.

The Data Protection Registrar, created under the 1984 Act, by the 1998 Act becomes the Data Protection Commissioner (to become 'Information Commissioner' by the FoI Bill 1999). Behind the Commissioner there remains the bureaucracy which maintains the data protection register and investigates breaches of the Act. Further, there is a Tribunal which deals with appeals in the area.

## Data protection principles and legal processing of information

Having established the definitions of data and the individuals involved with the processing of information covered by the Act, the 1998 legislation again follows the pattern of the 1984 Act, in that the rights and duties under the 1998 Act largely flow from the *Data Protection Principles* (DPA 1998: s. 4 and Schedule 1). Carey notes that the principles look similar to the 1984 Principles, but that they are radically different when interpreted through the new definition of 'processing' (Carey, 1998: 21). The principles are much more far-reaching than the previous legislation.

The first principle states that personal data must be processed fairly and lawfully. Further, it states that personal data 'shall not be processed unless at least one of the further conditions of Schedule 2 is met' and, where the data is 'sensitive personal data' – which includes data about an individual's race, gender, sexuality, or political and religious beliefs – it cannot be processed 'unless at least one of the Schedule 3 conditions is also met'. Thus, all processing must be fair and lawful: processing includes 'obtaining' data and is therefore as broad in its scope as the previous legislation. Schedule 2 requires compliance with at least one of the following conditions:

1  The data subject has consented to the processing.
2  The processing is necessary in performing a contract to which the data subject is party or in taking steps to create such a contract.
3  Beyond contractual obligations, the data controller is compelled to process the data because of another legal obligation.
4  Processing the data protects the 'vital interests of the data subject'.
5  The administration of justice, government or public body, or duties conferred by statute, require the data to be processed.
6  The data controller or third party to whom the data is disclosed require the processing of the data for their legitimate purposes which are not prejudicial to the 'rights and freedoms' of the data subject.

Schedule 3 requires that where sensitive data is processed, alongside compliance with the general duties under Principle 1 and Schedule 2, at least one of the following conditions must be present:

1   The explicit consent of the data subject to the processing has been given.
2   The data controller has a legal right to process the data through employment.
3   The processing of the data is in the data subject's vital interests and consent cannot be gained, or processing is in a third party's vital interests and the data subject unreasonably withholds his consent.
4   The processing is carried out by a non-profit-making organization, or a body that 'exists for political, philosophical, religious or trade-union purposes'.
5   The data subject has taken deliberate steps which have resulted in the data becoming public information.
6   The processing is necessary for work relating to legal proceedings, legal advice, or defending legal rights.
7   The administration of justice or government, or duties conferred by statute, require the data to be processed.
8   The processing is necessary for medical purposes and is conducted by a health professional or other person who owes the same duty of confidentiality.
9   The processing enables a furthering of racial equality and respects the freedoms and rights of the data subjects.

The requirement that data be processed 'fairly' is addressed in Part II of Schedule 1. It is not an exhaustive definition, but it does highlight that the method by which the data is acquired must be fair and lawful. In particular, the person from whom the information is gained must not be 'misled or deceived' (DPA 1998: Schedule 1 Part II para. 1(1)). The definition of fairness also indicates that a data controller has not acted fairly if the data subject is not given the identity of the data controller and any of his or her representatives, the purpose for which the data processing is intended, and any further information which is required to allow the data to be processed fairly (DPA 1998: Schedule1 Part II para. 2(3)). This must be done within a 'relevant time', if it is not disproportionately difficult to observe. When considering the meaning of fair and lawfully processing, one should remember that the guidance in Part II of Schedule 1 is a starting point to understand the principles only, and that the meaning of processing is so very broad under the 1998 Act that it covers all practical dealing with personal data from initial collection to its final destruction.

The first data protection principle, above, must be observed by researchers. Researchers have certain exemptions under the 1998 Act and the second data protection principle does not apply when the processing is for research purposes (DPA 1998: ss. 27–39). The exemption is not a complete exemption for researchers and, for example, where the data has been gathered for a health or educational purpose, the researcher must ensure that the information has been gathered appropriately and that the transfer of the data to the researcher is within the law. Further, it remains to be seen exactly where the line is to be drawn between research and commercial or other activity for the Act. The second data protection principle is that personal data may only be processed for specified and lawful purposes. A process is 'specified' by giving notice of the process to the data subject or to the Commissioner.

The third principle applies to researchers who process personal data and it seeks to safeguard the integrity of the data subject. The data held must be 'adequate' and 'relevant' to protect the subject from incomplete analysis, for example, this will be important in ensuring material is adequate for a decision about the data subject. However, the amount of data held cannot be excessive for the purposes of the processing which the data controller is to carry out. It is in this second area that the case law under the 1984 Act focused, establishing the principle clearly that the data controller cannot amass vast data banks over their needs.

The fourth principle again protects the integrity of the data subject, placing a duty on the data controller that 'personal data shall be accurate and, where necessary, kept up to date'. As Carey indicates, the requirement is that the data controller should take 'reasonable steps to ensure accuracy of the data', and reasonableness will depend upon the facts of each case (1998: 34). The fifth principle continues the themes of the third and fourth principles: personal data should not be kept for longer than is necessary for the data controller's purpose. This fifth principle does not apply to research (DPA 1998: s. 33).

The sixth principle draws into the data protection principles the other rights of the data subject which are created in the 1998 Act. For the purposes of this principle (DPA 1998: Schedule 1 Part 2 para. 8), the rights of the data subject are: the right of access to personal data for the data subject (DPA 1998: s. 7); the right of the data subject to give notice to the data controller to stop processing personal data about him or herself where such processing would cause unwarranted and substantial damage or distress to the data subject or another (DPA 1998: s. 10); the right to prevent information about the data subject being used by a data controller for direct marketing (DPA 1998: s. 11); and, the right to object to certain decisions being made about the data subject solely on the basis of automated decision-making (DPA 1998: s. 12).

In section 33 of the Act, which creates the exemptions from the data principles for research, it is clear that when the personal data held by a data controller about a data subject are held for research purposes, when there are no decisions to be made about the individual through the processing of the data, when the individual data subject is not identifiable in the findings made available from the research or statistics, and when no 'substantial damage or distress is, or is likely to be, caused', then the data is exempt from the requirements to allow the data subject access to the data held about him or herself. It is equally clear that the remaining rights of the data subject must be observed by the researcher. Should a researcher be served with a notice to stop processing data concerning a data subject, then within 21 days a written reply must be given which indicates an acceptance and compliance with the data subject's request or the reasons why the data controller does not agree to comply with any part or the whole of the data subject notice (DPA 1998: s. 10 (3)).

The seventh and eighth principles, both binding upon researchers, relate to the security of personal data. The seventh principle is that 'appropriate technical and organizational measures shall be taken against unauthorized or unlawful processing of personal data and against accidental loss or destruction of, or damage to, personal data'. The notes on interpretation of the principle in Schedule 1 Part II paragraph 9–12 of the 1998 Act show a number of safeguards for both the data controller and the data subject. For the former, there is an element of reasonableness: the data controller 'must ensure a level of security which is appropriate' to the damage which would be caused by a breach of the security principle and the 'nature of the data to be protected'. This clearly invites the courts in interpreting the security requirement to look to the importance of the information and the relative costs of protection. Security for the data subject's information is the high priority of the Act and therefore the new security principle reflects the change from purely automated to automated or manual data systems in the language of the principle. Simply keeping the files closed on a desk in a locked room will not be adequate security for personal information. Likewise, where the data controller uses data processors to process the data the relationship must be formal, using written contracts which outline the authority of the data controller in determining the extent of the processing and requiring the same level of security for the data is required of the data processor as is required of the data controller him or herself. Further, the choice of data processors must be made with a view to the security of the data. The eighth principle reflects the fact that origin of the 1998 Act is a European Directive. Data may only be taken out of the European Economic Area when the territory to which it is taken has an adequate level of data protection for the data subject.

The data protection principles impose a series of duties upon the data controller to respect the personal information about the data subject. As we have seen, and following the exemptions in the 1984 Act, the researcher has relaxed duties compared to the commercial data controller in relation to the data subject's rights of access to the information processed, the length of time that the data can be stored, and the notification of the purposes of processing. These elements are limited to some extent where the research makes decisions which directly damage or otherwise directly affect the data subject. It must equally be noted that while there are exemptions at law, the professional ethics of researchers must draw them to a code of treatment of personal data which looks very similar to the data protection principles.

### Further duties on the data controller and sanctions

In the analysis of the Data Protection Principles, the major rights of the data subject have been indicated. The data controller is under a further considerable duty. He or she must register by 'notification' to the Commissioner who maintains a register of data controllers. The requirements for notification are outlined in section 16 of the Act, and include the name and address of the data controller, the type of data that is to be held and the purpose for the processing of the data, and the intended recipients of the data. A failure to notify the Commissioner before any processing of data occurs is a criminal offence. This appears very onerous for the researcher in, for example, a university. Discussions with the data protection authorities reveal that even if the university or research institution is registered, then individual researchers who are data controllers, would be required to register separately and individually for work undertaken as part of the university work. They would, clearly, have to observe the duties under the Act. Equally, if the research being undertaken fell outside the general work for the university or research institution, for example, the work was under contract for an outside body, then the data controller (the researcher) would have to register. The Registry is extremely approachable and the easiest way to clarify an individual position or to register is to contact them directly by telephone.

The Commissioner is required under the Act to enforce the data protection principles. Where a data controller is in breach of the principles, the Commissioner may serve him or her with an 'enforcement notice'. This requires the data controller to comply with the principles. It outlines the nature of the breach and gives time limits within which the processing must stop or come within the scope of the principles. The Commissioner may also order that data be corrected or destroyed. Further, when an individual feels that they will be adversely affected by the processing of data, the Commissioner is empowered to make inquiries and may require the data controller to give information about their processing of the data through the 'information notice'. A failure to comply with a notice is an offence under section 47 of the Act. An appeal against a notice may be made to the Tribunal.

It can be seen that the Act not only sets out a series of rights and duties concerning the protection of data, but also creates an agency of enforcement which has real teeth. This has been a brief introduction to the new law in the area. Since the Act is very recent at the time of preparing this chapter, there are still areas of interpretation which are not clear or available. It can be seen how important it is that researchers should observe the law on data protection. It must be stressed that assistance from the Data

Protection Registry or from a lawyer should be sought to clarify the application of the Act to specific social science research projects and work.

## INTELLECTUAL PROPERTY RIGHTS

Intellectual property (IP) protects as the intangible product of the human brain (Phillips and Firth, 1995: 3). The law relating to IP is one of the fastest growing areas, not least because it is concerned with innovation and the commercial exploitation of ideas. The area covers copyright, moral rights, confidentiality, all of which are of concern to researchers, and also patents, trademarks, and passing off, which do not directly concern the social science researcher (Cornish, 1996; Holyoak and Torremans, 1998).

### Copyright

The most pertinent of the substantive IP rights to the social science research field is undoubtedly copyright with its derivative, the moral rights. Copyright has grown up in two traditions. The UK tradition emerged from the advent of mass printing, increased public literacy, and a resulting explosion of the publishing industry. It was seen as a necessary protection to allow those who printed and published literary works to avoid unfair competition and, like so much of IP law, it emerged from a practice of censorship. The continental system took a radically different perspective. Their copyright protection grew up from a focus on the right to the protection of an individual's creativity. Thus, the continental law concentrated more intently upon the creative processes of authors or painters (etc.), and their right to exploit the products of their creativity. Both systems granted rights which extended beyond the particular owner's life, introducing a sense of legacy in the creative property.

The current English law is a compromise between the hard commercial sense of the early UK law and a recognition of the rights of the artist from the continental perspective. This occurred, at least, since this area attracted international agreements to respect the rights created in other jurisdictions: see especially in this area the Paris Convention 1883 and the Berne Convention 1886 with its subsequent amendments (notably Paris, 1971).

Copyright, today, vests in any literary, musical and artistic works. This has been extended reflecting new technology, and therefore includes recordings, analogue and digital, film, computer software, alongside the traditional elements of books, writing, paintings, sculpture, and music (CDPA 1988: s. 1). This then is the protection of the purely creative, whereas patents and trade marks concern the realm of the industrially inventive. Writing, publishing and seminar papers are all in the realm of copyright.

Further, it should be noted that this protection of the creative could be described as primary copyright and alongside this are available secondary copyrights for publishers, those who take the created work and place it widely into the public domain. Thus, here record producers and publishing houses, broadcasting organizations and other third parties can own copyrights in created works. A third dimension to the scope of ownership is that a number of copyrights can exist in the same created work. Thus, a film can have rights vesting in the scriptwriter, the author of the book from which the idea was developed, the director and the actors, the production house and their staff, in the composer of the musical score and in the recording of that score. The list of copyrights and their owners is endless as each part of the process is undertaken. The interesting consideration relates to the transfer of rights and the relative bargaining power of individuals within the process.

A copyright exists in any item which falls within the statutory definition of copyrightable without further action by its creator (CDPA 1988: s. 3–8). It is not a registrable right, it simply vests in the statutory owner (CDPA 1988: s. 9). This makes life very simple for the creator, and rather difficult for the user of copyright material, since there is no central statement of who holds interests in the particular copyright. Imagine, for a moment, the position of financing the film. The client is prepared to purchase an interest in the film, and a major job is to investigate the ownership of interests and the mortgages already taken out on the copyrights. One cannot look to a register, and the task will soon take on nightmare proportions.

A copyright vests in copyrightable material. The types of enterprise which fall into this category have already been considered: there is another fundamental element to the issue of what is copyrightable. A copyright cannot vest in an idea (CDPA 1988: s. 3(2)). The policy reasons for this choice were discussed in Chapter 8 on the law in this book; here is the practical outworking. Copyright bites only upon the expression of the idea. Thus, a lecture contains ideas, but only when it takes a permanent form of expression is there a work capable of vesting a copyright in the lecturer or other person. Thus, if the lecture is written in the form of verbatim notes, or is otherwise recorded, perhaps in a student's shorthand notes or on his or her tape-recorder, then that expression becomes the property of the lecturer. In the case of the tape, there is also a right vested in the actual tape in the owner of that tape as well. A lecture given without notes, however, if not recorded in anyway, is not copyrightable; its property dies with the echo of its words.

A copyright is a finite property right, inasmuch as its duration is prescribed by statute. Once granted, it lasts for primary copyrights (those vesting in the author or director and producer) the author or director's and producer's life and seventy years thereafter; in secondary rights (those created from acts deriving from the primary act of creation) the duration is generally fifty years from the year of the publication (CDPA 1988: s. 12). Prior to the extension of the copyright period, the duration of copyright was the life of the author and fifty years thereafter. The extension of the copyright period has, consequently, had the effect of reviving some copyrights which were previously out of copyright. The Duration of Copyright and Rights in Performances Regulations 1995 (S.I. 1995 no. 3297), which amended the duration of copyrights under the Copyright Designs and Patents Act 1988, indicate the position for those who are using revived copyright materials in collections and publications (Cornish, 1996: 350–357). For those dealing with revived works – where the author died between fifty and seventy years ago – in their research, the effect is best thought of as simply bringing the works back into protection: revival of a copyright gives the work full protection again.

A further concern must be around infringement of copyright. A copyright vests the power to copy a work in the copyright owner (CDPA 1988: s. 16), and therefore any unauthorized act of copying or producing work can give rise to an action for infringement of copyright (CDPA 1988: s. 96). It is not an infringement of copyright to copy for private study purposes (CDPA 1988: s. 29). Likewise, copying in a critical work does not constitute an infringement (CDPA 1988: s. 30). These two enterprises thus allow much scope for the researcher. There is, however, clearly a fine line where information is copied for commercial purposes. A 'reader' in a particular area, using others' published extracts, is clearly over the line. Quoting others in the context of an analysis in a book for publication could be said to be just within the line, although extent would be a crucial consideration.

Enforcement of copyright can take many forms. Clearly, the underlying requirement upon which a judgment is made depends upon showing that an unauthorized copy (i.e. without licence from the owner or statutory exemption) has been made by the individual. Prior to judgment an injunction can be granted to stop the publication or distribution of the infringing material, and if an infringement is found, then damages and account of profits can be ordered against the offender. Criminal sanctions may also apply where the infringement is for commercial ends.

Within the academic sphere, copyright could be seen to be the rather thick end of a wedge which concerns the proper treatment of others' work. Plagiarism is the thin end of that wedge. The ethical requirements of plagiarism, the unattributed use of another's work as one's own, are well rehearsed in academe. This, in academe, can attach not only to expression but to ideas. A best practice could be to view the use of another's thoughts and toil as their property, certainly, and therefore sacrosanct, but also as the basis upon which analysis and criticism can be based. Therefore, regurgitation becomes unnecessary since attribution must be given to all other ideas in order properly to facilitate a discussion, and to allow the formation of new ideas and concepts. A distinction should be made again, however, about the use of pure information and of ideas. Here, information (e.g. about the terms of an act of parliament) is in the public domain, whereas the particular expression and the ideas and analysis of the information is protected by plagiarism rules. Plagiarism rules are much stronger than legal regulations surrounding copying, since they go much further than simply protecting the expression of the work. Each discipline within academe has its own understanding of plagiarism and reference should be made to those rules. Here the interesting point to see is that the legal protection of the social scientist is not as extensive as the professional ethics which surround him or her.

## Moral rights

When one owns the whole of a copyright, then one controls the use of the creator's image and reputation. When, therefore, one is misrepresented, a copyright owner can sue for breach and protect one's reputation through the permissions granted to use the work. However, if the copyright has been assigned away from the author, then the control of reputation is lost to its true owner. Continental law, with its focus upon the creator, recognized this danger, and vested in the creator who gave up his or her copyright (given that often that was not a real choice for them) moral rights to protect the abuse of his or her reputation independently of the copyright. In English law, these rights were not introduced fully until 1988 (CDPA 1988: ss. 77–89).

By the 1988 Act, once the creator of a copyright work assigns his or her right to that copyright, and as we have seen this is not uncommon, he or she is left with some residual protection. The moral rights are non-assignable even if a contractual term claims a transfer (CDPA 1988: s. 94), but can pass to a third party on the death of the original owner (CDPA 1988: s. 95). There are four moral rights. The right to privacy in certain commissioned photographs does not concern us directly. However, the remaining three are of great importance. First, an author or director of a copyright work has the right to be identified as such in any use of the work (CDPA 1988: s. 77). Second, the author or director of a copyright work can object to derogatory treatment of the work (CDPA 1988: s. 80). Treatment here includes most dealing with the work, although its exact terms have been the focus of intense discussion in the courts. Third, a person has the right to object to the false attribution of a work to his or her name (CDPA 1988: s. 84). These rights then protect the integrity of the author. Since they apply to copyright work, author is taken to have a broad definition, covering literary, dramatic, musical and artistic work, as well as film and other media within the arts (CDPA 1988: s. 1).

It could not be the case, however, that the law would allow unbridled rights to the author in English law. Moral rights can be waived and the right to be identified as the author or director, the strongest of the rights, must be asserted before it can be enforced (CDPA 1988: s. 78). Clearly, this allows those negotiating with the author to obtain a deal where the copyright will be assigned but where the moral right will not be asserted. However, it appears that in the book publishing world, at least, this clause is not yet required generally, and authors assert their rights in a standard declaration at the front of the book, referring to their rights under the 1988 Act.

## Confidentiality

This is a central area in both commerce and research. As has been seen, copyright protection exists for the published form of an idea. The same is true for the ideas contained in inventions and trade marks, given that they are regulated by a first to file patent system and the trade mark registration system. However, in both research and commerce, novelty in presenting and exploiting ideas is fundamental and in both ideas are taken and used by competitors. The law allows individuals to protect their ideas prior to publication through the law of confidentiality.

This poses us with an ethical difficulty. Within the university, indeed within any researching community, the temptation, indeed the duty, is to share concepts for the advancement of the community. Academics are raised to give papers, to discuss ideas and to learn from each other. Indeed, the very system of apprenticeship with a supervisor encourages that mentality, and it must be the correct method for the development of ideas. There is, however, a great danger in adopting this practice, since not all are scrupulous. Perhaps it goes beyond that. If the enterprise is to attempt to develop original thoughts and present them in papers, it necessarily means that, like sponges, researchers soak up ways of thinking. Fledgling ideas are shared and ownership is as much collective as individual; individual approaches are formed in the theatre that is one's subject. There is, therefore, a question of where the individual ends and the collective begins. This, however, can be seen as a matter of degree for the application of the following rules. There is a distinction to be drawn in the application of confidentiality in academe and in a company, where within the company an acceptance of shared information would be presumed, but externally the walls of secrecy would be very thick.

Confidentiality law is not a substantive IP right, rather it is a specific application of contract law and Equity (Law Commission, 1997). It is found not in statute, but in case law. It should be noted, from the case following the disclosure of private facts concerning the marriage of the Duke and Duchess of Argyle by one of the parties after their separation (*Argyle v. Argyle* [1967] Ch 302), that this area of law is not simply for commerce, but any relationship which develops an expectation that the information is not to be disclosed. The ownership or control of information is being achieved here through the recognition of a relationship between the parties which creates a duty to maintain the secrecy of the information. Either expressly, or by implication from the circumstances of the disclosure, the party disclosing the information can impose a duty of confidentiality over those to whom the disclosure is made. For example, if company X invites a potential customer to view a new prototype fountain pen which X has developed, X can stop the customer taking the ideas contained in the design and producing the fountain pen themselves or disclosing the invention to competitors by expressly creating a contractual or equitable agreement with the customer – making them sign an agreement offering disclosure if secrecy is maintained. Alternatively, the circumstances of the disclosure – the manner and behaviour of company X – could be said to imply a duty of confidence on the customer: for example, taking the customer into a room with an appropriate notice on the door and employing an appropriate dialogue which could be said to place the customer under an inescapable duty of secrecy once the customer had accepted the opportunity to hear or see the confidential information.

There are dangers here. First, can there be adequate compensation for a breach? Clearly, the customer runs a severe risk to their own reputation within their community for dishonour. However, the great new idea with its potential for exploitation has been ruined and the compensation may not be able to reflect what could have been the company's market position without the disclosure. The hope would be that prior to the unauthorized disclosure, an injunction could be gained on the basis of the parties' relationship to stop the disclosure. Gaining knowledge of an impending disclosure would be a matter of extreme luck. Further, if one relies upon implied contracts there is an inherent risk. The implication is made by a court, and therefore will be made at a time when another seeks to use or disclose the information, or has already done so, and without express agreement, there is the danger that the courts will view the circumstances and feel that there has not been a sufficiently clear duty placed upon the other party. Thus, at all times, disclosure should be made with an express undertaking of confidentiality between the parties.

There are exceptions to the general application of the rule of confidentiality. The courts will not entertain claims of confidentiality where it is in the public interest that a disclosure has been made. This, however, places great discretion and political power in the hands of the court. For example, should the question of the disclosure of side effects of drugs be a matter of whether the courts feel that they are serious enough to warrant disclosure when a researcher is given information by a company?

By way of conclusion, clearly confidentiality depends upon the type of product or ideas. In some areas, for example, in engineering, once a product is placed on the market or displayed at a trade fair or the like, all secrecy is lost since the product itself discloses its secrets and reverse engineering is possible. In other areas, for example, most notably in the case of a strong employer such as Coca-Cola, secrecy can be maintained through contractual agreements and severe non-disclosure policies, and the product is secure within the fragile frame of the trade secret. Research work could fall in the middle ground. By strong use of contracts and implied terms during the secret, pre-publication stage, the ideas can be protected for the individual. After publication, the monopoly is granted for the expression, with the trade-off for society that the information is available for external use and scrutiny.

## DEFAMATION

Viewers of the many satirical comedy programmes on TV will be familiar with the concept of defamation – 'allegedly'. Essentially, defamation is a civil wrong concerning the protection of a living individual's reputation against false accusation by a third party. Defamation takes two forms, written or otherwise permanent defamation (libel) and spoken or otherwise transient defamation (slander). Thus, a TV or newspaper allegation could be libellous, while a comment made in a meeting could be slanderous. Our concern is that unsubstantiated claims or allegations in the research publications or discussions are equally under the rigours of this law. Further, it is an area of little clarity and often high awards of damages.

The golden rule in defamation is that the truth cannot be avoided, but it is in perceiving the truth that the trouble lies. The defamation occurs where a statement is published 'which reflects on a person's reputation and tends to lower [him or her] in the estimation of right-thinking members of society generally or tends to make them shun or avoid him' (Winfield and Jolowicz, 1994: 312). Thus, it is this which has to be proved usually before a jury. The interpretation concerns both the manner of the delivery and the receipt of the delivery. Further, it can only concern the individual subject of the allegation. The allegation causing the reduction of esteem in the eyes of the reasonable can be direct or by innuendo.

There are a number of defences to defamation claims. First, one could claim that the allegation was true, judged on the balance of probabilities. Second, one could claim that the remark was 'fair comment', since the elements of honest criticism, an expression of opinion and fairness rather than a basis in fiction, is perhaps a good thing for mature individuals and a mature society. Further, certain jobs give rise to a privileged position with regard to the claim. Comments made in parliament cannot be defamatory, nor those made in court, and perhaps in a relationship of privilege, for example, as between a solicitor and a client. Once defamation is proved, a duty to compensate attaches to the conduct. This could be mitigated by offering a settlement including a public apology, but the duty would still remain.

## CONTRACT

Contract is the area that will be most familiar already, and yet the least considered. Already, today, it is likely that one will have made a series of contracts – contracts for the supply of perhaps a morning paper or a bottle of milk, a contract to travel on a bus or to buy a cup of coffee. These relationships are myriad, but they all share essential elements, as do the contracts surrounding the research enterprise of access, funding and responsibility to the subjects. Further, the relationship between an employer and employee is subject to specialist contractual regulations.

All contracts could be said to concern the transfer of property or services between individuals. There are essential principles to be observed whether the contract is implied or express (Adams and Brownsword, 1995). There is an assumption of an equality of bargaining power. From this develops the maxim 'let the buyer beware'. A centrally important feature of this property transfer is that it generally only conveys a right upon the parties to the agreement, the principle of 'privity of contract'. Equally, consideration – something of value – must flow from each side of the agreement. That is not to say that the bargain must be objectively reasonable since there is an assumption of a freedom of parties to enter whatever terms of a bargain they should chose. Breach of contracts can give rise to damages, or a requirement of specific performance of a duty, through breach of one or more of the terms of the agreement. Depending upon the severity of the breach, the obligations of the 'innocent' party could be destroyed by a breach of a term.

The starting point for all contracts is the offer and acceptance. A may offer terms to B; B's acceptance of the offer will constitute the contract. It may be that prior to this, as part of the negotiation, one of the parties indicates that there may be a possibility of a contract, without offering terms – the invitation to treat. The next stage is an offer, rather than an acceptance, since the control of the subject matter of the contract has not been placed at risk of acceptance by the invitation.

It should be noted that, while there is a presumption of the freedom of the individual to enter into a contract and that in a free market all players are considered equal, there is an element of paternalism which can be brought to bear upon a contract. First, there are rules regarding fairness. Once an obligation is accepted and an individual acts in reliance of the agreement, then the contract becomes irrevocable. If the obligations become impossible, for example, the goods for sale are destroyed, then the parties cannot be forced to continue with their obligations. Further, statute provides a realistic approach to the power differences between consumers and providers of goods and services in the Unfair Contract Terms Act 1977 and also in the Unfair Terms in Consumer Contracts Regulations 1994. In cases of extreme unreasonableness of bargaining power, certain obligations within contracts can be overruled. Thus, a contract made with an unrepresented composer to work exclusively for one record company and to sign over all his or her intellectual property rights in return for a very small wage may be considered unfair if it is a consumer contract. George Michael's case rather indicates that there are, however, different perceptions of fairness.

Therefore in the research environment there is an assumption of a freedom to enter and negotiate the terms of contracts. Exceptionally, unfair terms may be struck out. The major areas of impact will lie in funding and employment especially in short-term, employment contracts, but also most importantly in the area of IP and access agreement.

When considering copyright, the possibility of assigning or transferring rights was indicated. This is often the way with publishing contracts and the like. This could be seen as the great power of the publishing house securing a best deal for itself. Alternatively it could reflect the great risk a publishing house takes in investing in a book, especially for an esoteric area and from a relatively unknown writer. Perhaps one would not be surprised that some publishing deals require the assignment of all IP rights in return for a fixed fee. Perhaps, even, the research funding body will require a similar transfer, largely so that it can control the dissemination of the information gathered and analysed. The best advice is to reflect on the importance of controlling the information, but also on the fragility of the balance of getting published and retaining full copyright control of the work. Once again, seek advice whenever possible from those with experience – senior academics and lawyers.

As to access, as a researcher one will negotiate mostly informal contracts concerning access to institutions or data. The nature of confidentiality has been considered. Once again, this is a question of balance. Negotiate from the position of one's integrity. Do not agree to what one cannot undertake to provide. Respect the terms of any agreement. Research is about power and is very visibly so in contractual relationships. When gaining access to large institutions, they have the power to require particular commitments, they have the commitment to themselves and their confidentiality requirements and have the finance to enforce their requirements. In the position of gaining access to an individual, perhaps to a resident in an old people's home whose recollections of the war in Sheffield one wishes to hear, one will have enormous power. This becomes a matter of professional integrity that the duties and obligations are undertaken with the same respect.

## FITTING THE KEY ELEMENTS INTO THE RESEARCH PROCESS

The key legal concepts which concern social science research have already been introduced. They must now be placed into a framework of research as they might apply to social science research, for example, when undertaking postgraduate study by research. In order to do this, I have adopted a crude model of the periods of the research enterprise, as follows:

- gathering information;
- processing information;
- publishing information.

Alongside this, the subject of the legal protection must be considered. There are two possibilities here: the rules can apply to how one should deal with another's property – perhaps another researcher's published or unpublished work, or the property of the subject of an empirical study. Alternatively, the rules could protect one's own research against the actions of a third party – for example, when discussing a research idea with colleagues or at a conference, gaining a correct attribution for one's work, or negotiating a research contract.

## Gathering information

*The protection of others*   Perhaps the first element of other individuals' work that one could use is the published work in the field. Clearly, this will be subject to copyright and, perhaps, to moral rights. Where this is the case, the fair dealing rules apply for making copies of copyright work, research work perhaps coming under the exemption of private study and the CLA licence. The work of copyright owners and the authors must be attributed. Seeking permission for work analysed in a thesis will usually be unnecessary, since such treatment falls within the scope of fair dealing. However, as in the case of biography or 'readers', larger pieces of work used outside the context of comment may cause difficulties.

Unpublished work, for example, theses or papers from other people, although not commercially published, will still attract copyright protection since they are in a tangible form. The area of research work which may be outside the scope of copyright protection is the interview, and the use of material from a discussion. The position of the taped research interview and of ownership in the subject of one's research has been discussed . The effect would be one copyright in the words and another in the recording. However, since the researcher will have entered into a research contract, be it express or implied, there will be an implication of permission to use the material for the research purposes outlined. Thus, a best practice approach is to explain clearly what one expects to do at the beginning of your relationship with the subject and, if necessary, create a document outlining the extent of the permission and the extent of what one would wish to do and get a signed licence.

*Confidential information*   Clearly, this rule of thumb will change where the research involves access to confidential information. In such cases, perhaps where one gains access to company records or even to the product development departments of a company, then the requirement will undoubtedly be for a formal undertaking on the use and disclosure of information. The best practice here is to try to use any discussion to retain one's academic freedom, but this is always balanced by your desire to gain access to the data. At once there is the conflict: the data is only available under strict conditions and the conditions make using the data for research impossible. Make a firm agreement, leaving as little room for uncertainty as is possible, and then stick to the terms agreed, since the penalties for breach can be great in either express or implied contractual situations. The onus would be upon the company to make the confidential nature of the material clear. However, the easiest position to adopt is one of caution and openness about what one wants to know and plans to do with the knowledge.

*Protection of oneself*  Gathering information produces copyright works in the physical expression of the data which one collects. Thus, one's research questionnaire, and the completed forms have copyright value, as do drafts of ideas and perhaps even one's notes, if they can be described as literary works.

The biggest problem at the earliest stages of research, from the point of view of protecting oneself, is the protection of one's ideas. An interesting research project and interesting initial findings could be rich pickings for the unscrupulous. However, the natural need in academe is to discuss and analyse with colleagues. One's discussions, especially those informal discussions outside one's department, should be couched in terms which make plain the confidential nature of the material. Disclosing and discussing ideas is clearly important in academe and the possibility and desirability of owning ideas in themselves has been rejected earlier in the chapter. However, data is rather different and should be protected.

## Processing and storing

*Protection of others*  There are certain legal relationships which are entered without great concern. For example, the software we use for storing data and for processing it is made available under licence from the copyright owners. These have specific terms and conditions which are accepted through use. These issues will not be considered here in any great detail. The legal dangers start when an individual modifies or copies a program: the former is very specialist, the latter is outlawed other than to back up an original disk. Databases may be subject to copyright if their compilation requires sufficient skill, and may be subject to a Database right if they are substantial works.

Data protection, however, as has been seen, is of great concern to research. This is a key protection for certain research subjects. If one's research entails the storage or processing of personal data, then one must follow the data protection principles outlined above.

*Protection of oneself*  At this stage of research, most of the protection needed is from copyright. A number of literary works are always generated in the process of analysing and developing research. Each draft of the thesis or papers, each seminar paper, the tables for analysed data, if they are one's own original work, are usually copyright works. The problem in proving ownership of that copyright work is one of proof. This can be overcome cheaply through the use of the postal service. Important works created, prior to their publication in a finished thesis or report, should be sealed and sent to oneself by registered post. On receiving the parcel, keep it unopened. This should provide sufficient evidence of the chronological supremacy of one's claim over the material, if the postmark is clear (if it is not try the process again).

## Publication

This is the most difficult area, since it covers a wide number of the heads already discussed above.

*Protection of others*  When preparing work for publication or writing a thesis, one must examine it to ask: 'Am I making claims about individuals which are defamatory?' 'Am I drawing conclusions from the materials which could be construed as a slur upon the individual's character (for example, the director of a particular institution within which you have gathered information)?' Humour is often the worst culprit for unguarded defamation, so are the asides within the law? Clearly, a thesis should be about presenting a supportable reading of the information. Therefore the defence of fair comment should always be able to prevail in the writing – would it?

A second consideration must be copyright. Is the material gained from other people correctly attributed? If one has used other people's research frameworks or perhaps extensive examples, or even a cartoon for the cover, it is necessary to obtain permission for the use of the material. Further, have one's confidentiality obligations been observed?

*Protecting oneself*  Before the work is published, one usually owns copyright in it, although this may depend upon particular contractual undertakings around, for example, funding or employment. With that ownership, it may be possible to enter into a book agreement to exploit the ideas and hard work and study. Clearly, this is a situation which is open to the rigours of a free market contract. The balance is always the amount of one's rights one is prepared to sacrifice for the chance to publish one's work. Clearly, the copyright may be the first right to fall. The publisher is taking a risk, especially with a new author, and needs to have some security over the return. Thus, it is not uncommon to be required to relinquish the copyright in book contract, or in producing a chapter for a book. Journal articles are rather different, depending upon the journal.

There is an alternative thought on such assignment of copyright: if one retains the copyright, would one have the financial ability to maintain it should it be breached? Clearly, if the copyright is retained the moral rights available for one's protection to a certain extent guard against adverse publication by your publisher. One's publisher could maintain one's assigned rights against the world, something which one could not contemplate alone. This is a difficult balance since one's reputation is paramount, and one should guard it as fiercely as possible. This is most problematic when one submits work to the hands and judgement of an editor.

As to asserting one's rights, declarations to assert moral rights can be seen in most texts after 1988. If a copyright is assigned (or indeed generally), and the contract allows one to assert one's moral right of paternity, this can be done by a simple declaration of assertion of rights under the Copyright, Designs and Patents Act 1988 (CDPA 1988: s. 78). In UK law, one does not need to use the copyright sign ©. However, its inclusion with a date of the copyright and the owner's name could assist worldwide protection.

## CONCLUSION

It can be seen that there is a considerable weight of law which has direct influence upon the social science researcher. There is equally a distinction to be drawn between the rules which are created by the profession and academe to regulate the practice of social science and the laws which impact upon the same area. One clear cause for this imbalance is that the laws have been created generally, without specific reference to social science. This could be remedied by opening the debate about regulation to include regulators and members of the research community. There are two further questions, however, which might indicate why the law should be different to the professional ethical standards of social science research. Should the law regulate to the same high ethical standards as are exacted by the profession? Would it be proper to use the full weight of legal sanction, and the financial resources of the state, to protect, for example, the plagiarized academic? Such questions should find their answers in a full debate across the social science disciplines and not from the lawyers alone.

## ACKNOWLEDGEMENTS

I am grateful to my colleagues Professor John Adams, Roger Brownsword and Dr Jeffery Goh, Norma Hird and Dr Margaret Llewelyn for their comments on Chapters 8 and 10 in this volume. The errors remain my own.

# PART III

# GETTING STARTED

It is absolutely crucial that research students develop a high level of information management and search skills early on in the life of a thesis. Literature searches are the building blocks of a PhD, the foundation upon which all the other material rests. Effective literature searches should highlight 'gaps' in the existing literature which will enable research students to construct an original project. Comprehensive and up-to-date searches will also add to the overall quality of a thesis. Not undertaking literature searches effectively can result in a student duplicating the work of others and therefore not producing an original project. Failure to keep track of the most recent literature can also result in a thesis appearing dated. The inability to produce a relevant set of references will also hinder attempts at writing, since the ability to write a first chapter will be dependent on having a substantial number of literature sources on which to base the account.

Despite the importance of information and search skills in getting a thesis off to a good start, research students often perceive this element of training as having a very low status. There is an assumption that literature searching and the management of the results is a straightforward, unproblematic activity. In reality the task to review the relevant literature required for a good quality thesis has never been more difficult. The sheer size of the task which confronts today's research students as a result of developments in information technology and ever-increasing number of databases is enormous. More than ever before there is an onus on students to get themselves organized. Systematic ways in which literature searches can be organized to enable students to make the most effective use of their time are discussed in Chapter 11. A core skill which students need to acquire is the ability to build search strategies in ways which are appropriate for on-line searching. Some of the detailed and technical terminology which researchers have to master before searching databases are explained and demonstrated. By the end of the chapter students should be aware of the systematic steps required to build a literature search.

Alongside the skills required to search for relevant literature are appropriate methods of documenting searches. Not having a good system for recording the results could have the effect of students wasting time duplicating searches. Since huge numbers of references are often generated, there is pressure on research students to develop the ability to assess each of the items. Some of the time-saving ways in which the usefulness of material generated can be effectively evaluated are discussed in this chapter. Similarly, the ability to make notes and record references in ways which are easily retrievable is also crucial. Some of the strategies which students can adopt to do this are critically evaluated. The final section of the chapter is devoted to referencing systems. It is important that any references cited in the thesis conform to a consistent style. In this chapter the Harvard system of referencing is extensively illustrated.

## SUPPLEMENTARY READING

Cooper, H.M. (1998) *Synthesizing Research*. London: Sage.
Gash, S. (1989) *Effective Literature Searching for Students*. Aldershot: Gower.
Hart, C. (1998) *Doing a Literature Review*. Milton Keynes: Open University Press.
Orna, E. and Stevens, J. (1995) *Managing Information for Research*. Milton Keynes: Open University Press.

# 11 USING LITERATURE TO SUPPORT RESEARCH

*Dawn Burton*

Information search and information management skills are the fundamental building blocks of all research projects. Johanson (1997) suggests that in many ways creative researchers function like information managers in the way they collect, assimilate and communicate knowledge. The importance of research students having an in-depth knowledge of literature search techniques and associated skills is acknowledged by the Economic and Social Research Council (ESRC). In its Guidelines on research training for postgraduate students it states:

> At a suitably early stage in the student's research career, departments will be expected to include training for all students in certain basic skills. These are likely to include the identification of library resources and how to use them; training in other bibliographic sources and methods; methods for keeping track of the literature; the use of annuals, thesis, journals, conference proceedings and semi-publications; the maintenance of a personal research bibliography. (ESRC Guidelines, 1989: 13)

Barry (1997) believes that research students have the greatest need for information skills of all university students. She argues that their need to acquire such skills is even more acute than for established academics because of the requirement to develop a comprehensive and up-to-date review of the literature in a doctoral thesis; and because research students often lack the information reserves of established academics, such as personal contacts with well-informed colleagues which may act as a short cut to developing information skills. Johanson (1997: 107) even goes so far as suggesting that networks are more important than 'documentary sources or reports of previous research'.

The need to undertake quality of literature searches early on in the life of a thesis is important for three main reasons. First, a thesis should be based on original research. If students have not surveyed the relevant literature adequately, they are unable to ascertain whether anyone else has researched the same issue in the same way. As a result they cannot be sure whether their proposed research is in fact original. It is a nightmare scenario for a research student to be eighteen months into a project only to find that someone else has already researched the same issues and in the same way. In that situation the onus will be on the student to amend their work to make it different and original. Second, students need to have a thorough knowledge of the general area in which their project is located. This in-depth knowledge should point to 'gaps' in the literature which will then help to establish the scope, context and parameters of a thesis. As a result of not searching the appropriate literature effectively, some students have difficulty in identifying original research issues and can start to panic and lose confidence. This is not a situation in which most research students would want to find themselves. Finally, the information unearthed by literature searches must be up to date and comprehensive and be continued throughout the whole period of the research project. It could be the case that a paper published twelve months into the thesis could change the project's direction. However, at some stage students need to commit themselves to a specific project and stick to it.

Despite the important contribution of literature search techniques to a good quality thesis, very often students need to be persuaded that the relevant skills need acquiring (as I know all too well). There is a sense in which research students take comfort from the fact that their information skills are good and have proved successful in the past, otherwise they would not have gained the appropriate qualifications to be able to study for a PhD. Often the problem is one of students underestimating the different magnitude of researching for a PhD as opposed to a dissertation or a piece of coursework (similar parallels can also be drawn with writing a thesis, see Chapter 28). The issue of skills acquisition can be further compounded by the limited advice which is given to some students about how to go about the task. This issue has been raised by Gash:

> Students may arrive at the stage of embarking on a Ph.D. or MSc thesis without ever having had to do such a search or having received any advice or instructions as to how it can best be done. They are then very often at a loss to know how to go about the task, and sad to say, many supervisors also have very little idea how to perform a systematic search. As a result, it frequently happens that this essential task is neglected or virtually ignored by many students. (Gash, 1989: 2)

Barry (1997: 231) further questions how research students are going to acquire appropriate information skills. She notes that the electronic information skills of supervisors has not been the subject of a great deal of scrutiny. What little evidence exists, suggests that many are 'novice searchers, conducting very simple single word and author searches on databases'. The ability of supervisors to help students develop appropriate information skills is also dependent on the way they are supervised. David and Zeitlyn's (1996: 6.15) research on the context in which bibliographic skills were acquired by science, social science and humanities research students found that social science students (in this case confined to economists) were 'less integrated' with and 'regulated' by their supervisors, and as a result were less likely to develop alternative literature search strategies by using a variety of different information sources.

Traditionally, it has been librarians who have been extensively involved in teaching research students the relevant literature search techniques (Newton *et al.*, 1998). Librarians are well suited to this task because of their professional training; investigating and evaluating sources is an ongoing part of their job, and they have a unique insight into academics' information skills through dealing with their enquiries (Johanson, 1997). However, the increase in the range of skills required by researchers in an electronic information age, combined with increasing student numbers, suggests that many librarians will not be able to continue to provide a comprehensive training infrastructure without significant changes in the way they are resourced. This situation may lead to students being given tuition on a narrow range of searching techniques, while neglecting other problems which can be more problematic such as obtaining references, recording what has been read, and citing literature in a professional manner (Gash, 1989). Barry (1997) also suggests that there needs to be a negotiated division of labour between librarians and supervisors. In her view, librarians are best suited to provide training to enable students to make judgements about information, whether that be evaluating quality, filtering out excess and focusing on specific needs, whereas supervisors are best placed to advise on academic content. Other research suggests that confusion about the division of labour between academics and librarians in this area of work can fall foul of poor communication, which can lead to research students missing out on training opportunities provided by library staff (David and Zeitlyn, 1996). This appears to be a case of the right hand not knowing what the left hand is doing.

What the brief review above has demonstrated is that research students can find themselves in a variety of organizational contexts, with completely different systems for providing tuition in information skills. However, in most organizational contexts librarians, supervisors and computing staff will be involved. The most important piece of advice that can be given to research students is to find out as soon as possible after registering where the different areas of responsibility lie, so that you can source appropriate help when you need it.

Since information search and information management skills as they apply to PhD work are so huge and diverse, the objectives of this chapter are necessarily modest. The focus will be on providing an overview of the most important issues associated with using literature to support research by outlining the steps which need to be undertaken in building literature searches; providing examples of how literature searches can be constructed; strategies for recording searches; and finally, referencing literature in appropriate ways.

## LITERATURE SEARCH AND INFORMATION SKILLS IN AN ELECTRONIC AGE

The information skills required of academics in an electronic age are of a different magnitude to those required in a traditional information age.

Hodge (1995: 10) argues that post-modern postgraduates need 'prosthetic ears and eyes' to enable them to connect electronically into a global community and abandon scholarship which was reliant on being self-contained, highly literate individuals. Barry also highlights this contrast:

> Identifying and locating individual resources in the traditional library was a finite task, bounded by the limitations of the collection and called mainly for the ability to navigate library catalogues and shelf classification system. Identifying and locating sources in an electronic world on the other hand, may be an almost infinite task. As we continue to make the transition from a traditional to an electronic age, the need for information skills intensifies. (Barry, 1997: 239)

The main stages which researchers work through remain the same in IT and manual based searching. Orna and Stevens (1995: 36) describe these stages as: defining information needs; locating sources of information to meet needs; transforming useful information to internal knowledge; storing the relevant information; managing the store of relevant information so that it can be retrieved when the researcher needs it. However, what has changed dramatically for today's researchers is the complexity of the tasks associated with each of the different stages, given the large increase in information available.

It is crucial that research students make the most effective use of their time. An initial registration period of three years (for full-time research students) may appear to be a long time at the start of a thesis, but most students find it a demanding task to complete in three years. The quantity of literature available to search is almost too big to be within conception. There are a quarter of a million books available in each language, another quarter of a million books in England, another quarter of a million books in the USA, another quarter of a million books in the other English-speaking countries of the world. An important consideration for researchers is how to use a variety of data sources to find the required information. In addition to books and journals there are lots of other sources of information such as newspapers, theses, research reports, computer databases, and so on. All this information is actually clamouring for your attention and only by organizing your searching and reading are you going to be able to find a way of controlling it.

Another consideration is that using just one library could result in your literature search being of an inadequate standard since most universities are limited by the number of books and journals they can purchase. Inter-library loans are a useful service because they provide much wider access to the relevant literature. That said, the status of research students and their allocation of inter-library loans requests are extremely variable across departments, disciplines and universities. The frequency with which research students can request items also varies, so some students are allowed to request one item per day, others might have a total for the year, while others do not have access to inter-library loan vouchers at all.

Students need to enquire in their department about their allocation. Another useful way of accessing material is through on-line searches that provide full text rather than abstracts which are obviously particularly good sources of articles.

Many universities also organize trips to some of the large national libraries, such as the British Library at Boston Spa. Research students should enquire in their department or the library about such trips, and if they do not exist perhaps think about organizing a visit themselves. Using other university libraries is another option, but students should check in advance that the library they wish to visit is 'open' to students from other universities. Some libraries are 'closed' to other university students and card technology is used to reinforce this policy. In such cases students will need to write to the library concerned and ask permission. Other libraries do allow outside researchers to use their facilities but a charge is made. One final point to remember is that libraries exist to serve the reader. Gash (1989: vii) notes that libraries are exhibiting a tendency to become obsessed with the development and contemplation of more and more complicated systems, many of which are distinctly user unfriendly. She provides the following advice: 'Try not to become intimidated – either by the system or the librarians. Remember, if it was not for you, both would be out of a job!'

## STEPS IN BUILDING LITERATURE SEARCHES

Being organized and systematic in your approach to literature searching is an important consideration. As long as your searches are thorough, it will not really matter in what order they are undertaken. However, an example of how they might be approached is set out in Table 11.1. Literature search techniques can be broadly defined as on-line or off-line. On-line searches enable researchers to search databases using a computer. As a result of developments in technology large databases can now be used in an inter-active way and accessed by large numbers of users simultaneously. Development in national international networks has enabled users all over the world to have access to a huge number of databases. The use of the Internet and electronic journals and libraries has contributed to the huge resources available to research students. By contrast, off-line searches require users to perform manual searches by using abstracts or microfiche.

Gash (1989) has set out what she considers to be some of the advantages and disadvantages of on-line searching (see Table 11.2). Advantages tend to be the speed with which significant numbers of databases can be searched. Interactive searching enables the researcher to modify searches based on previous findings which makes database searching a flexible option. Some of the disadvantages are that systems vary in accuracy, which can result in inappropriate or insufficient output. Problems can arise from the author's poor description of the research design; lack of appropriate indexing terms

**TABLE 11.1   Literature search strategies**

| Stage | Source to search | Document types retrieved |
|---|---|---|
| Stage 1 | Library catalogue | Books, pamphlets, reports, conference papers |
| Stage 2 | Book bibliographies | Books, reports, conference proceedings and other monographic publications |
| Stage 3 | Abstracting and indexing journals | Journal articles, reports, conference papers, occasional books |
| Stage 4 | Current awareness services | Journal articles |
| Stage 5 | Special indexes, e.g. TSO, international labour organizations, World Bank | Reports, conferences, thesis, official publications |
| Stage 6 | Institutions and people, e.g. Current Research in Britain (CRIB) | Almost anything |

*Source:* Gash, 1989.

**TABLE 11.2   Advantages and disadvantages of on-line searching**

| Advantages | Disadvantages |
|---|---|
| Speed of retrieval<br>Range of databases that can be searched | Poor and inconsistent indexing can cause problems in obtaining comprehensive searches |
| Multiple sources of access to references, i.e. greater number of keywords than manual records | Retrospective searches are often limited in year span. Manual searches go back much further |
| Printouts are often available, thus does not require note taking | Bias occurs because there can be tendency for searches to have US focus; and in some disciplines on-line databases can be poorly developed |
| Interactive searching means that the search can be altered as a response to results and therefore flexible | You have to be taught how to use the system and it can be some time before you become proficient in using it |
| Current awareness facilities: facilities include retrospective searches and future items | On-line searches can often produce large amounts of irrelevant references which are time consuming to read through and difficult to manage |
| Downloading: useful for printing out abstracts or full text papers | |
| Document delivery: printed journal articles can be ordered in time and mailed to the user | |

*Source:* Adapted from Gash, 1989, Chapter 3.

in the thesaurus; and inaccuracies in assigning indexing terms (Boynton *et al.*, 1998). Some journals are indexed in computer databases and a few of them are indexed in two, three or four. However, the overlap between computer databases is surprisingly small. On-line retrospective searches are often more limited in time span than manual searches. Bias can also occur as a result of some databases having a very specific US focus. Another issue can be that database originators tend to change their operating systems on a fairly regular basis which necessitates the user negotiating a new format and commands. Some researchers also believe that an extensive reliance on computerized searches makes the chances of accidental discovery less likely than if browsing in libraries. Cooper (1998) recommends that students browse in libraries before undertaking computerized searches. This might serve to expand the student's conception of what is important, which can then be built into a search strategy.

Using the Internet for very specific purposes, such as searching a well-established organization's home pages, can prove incredibly valuable and time efficient. 'Surfing' the Internet in the hope of finding some literature of relevance is a riskier strategy and can be very time consuming. Huge amounts of sources tend to be generated by Internet searches, most of which will prove to be completely useless. For these reasons many universities are actively discouraging students from using the Internet in this way. Cooper (1998) also draws attention to the fact that many freely available electronic journals on the Internet do not use peer-review procedures. Research students should be well aware of this fact and critically evaluate the quality of such papers. However, the advantage which electronic journals do have over paper journals is the much shorter time they take to be published once they have been accepted. This characteristic may mean that the data they contain is more up to date than that contained in paper journals, some of which have a two or more year publication lag (see Chapters 29 and 30).

What the discussion above demonstrates, is the need for research students to acquire skills which will enable them to develop a multiple mode approach to literature searching. It would be a mistake to think that some of the older more traditional forms of searching have been made obsolete by on-line searching. As Barry (1997: 229) indicates, 'students will still need to be encouraged to pursue traditional methods of information access, such as face-to-face contacts, conference attendance and browsing in libraries in tandem with IT methods'. Because of the variety of literature available and the diversity of places it might be located, it makes sense to get to know about the resources available at your own university library and identify staff who can help.

## UNDERTAKING THE SEARCH

The first steps in successful literature searching are to formulate your search terms and then to develop a strategy. A first step is to identify key words or phrases where more specific details such as authors or journal titles are unknown. For example, if references are sought on the following topic: 'How far did industrialization change the character of cities in nineteenth-century Europe?', the following would be suitable keywords for an initial search:

> industrialization
> cities
> nineteenth century
> Europe

However, you might need to specialize further by naming countries or widening the search by substituting urban for cities. Other things to consider are spelling differences, for example, industrialiZation, industrialiSation, labor, laboUr, and correct handling of hyphens and apostrophes. Different databases handle hyphenated words in different way. So for example, if the keyword 'nineteenth century' does not retrieve any records, the term will need to be broken down into its two components. An important skill to develop is being able to think of alternative ways in which search queries can be described. This is particularly important if an initial keyword search does not retrieve a sufficient number of relevant records. Alternative keywords could be synonyms (words with the same meaning) and related terms (terms with similar meanings). For instance, alternative keywords for a more focused approach or widening the search for the topic above could be:

> industrial revolution
> industrial economy
> capitalism
> European cities
> towns
> urban regions

A strategy that is well thought through will make the search more accurate and will maximize the number of relevant references retrieved. The aim is to avoid retrieving irrelevant references and too many or too few references. Whether the results of a search are perceived as too small or too large will depend on the expectations of the researcher.

Once key words have been identified, a useful next step is to determine the relationship between them. Boolean operators, sometimes called logical operators, are used to combine keywords in your search query and help you to achieve a more accurate search. The Boolean operators are AND, OR and NOT:

> AND finds records that contain all of the search terms.
> OR finds records that contain at least one of the search terms.
> NOT eliminates all those records containing a search term.

Some databases use different symbols for Boolean operators, for example:

+ = AND
, = OR
– = NOT

Therefore you need to check the documentation of Help Screens which pertain to each specific database. So, for example, if you have too few references, search-broadening tactics may be: to use alternative keywords (synonyms or related terms); make more use of Boolean OR to combine keywords; and make less use of Boolean AND to combine keywords.

To ensure that all references containing a search term or its derivations are retrieved, it can be helpful to use truncation to substitute for one or more letters in a word. Truncation ensures that all possible endings of a word will be identified. It is particularly useful for plurals. The symbol or wildcard to denote truncation varies from database to database but it is usually either an asterisk (*) or a question mark (?). For example, if you enter industr* as your search term, you will retrieve records containing:

industry
industrial
industrialize
industrialism
industrial revolution
industrialisation
industrialization

If you enter only indu* you will also retrieve:

induce
inducement
indulge
induction

Obviously this final set of records is irrelevant and demonstrates that truncation needs to be used with care. Wildcard symbols operate in a similar way to truncation. Usually defined as a question mark (?) or asterisk (*) they can be used anywhere in a search term as a substitute for one or more letters. If lab*r is entered as a search term, records containing the US spelling, labor, and the British spelling labour will be retrieved.

## DOCUMENTING LITERATURE SEARCHES

It frequently does not occur to students to keep a record of what has been done in the course of a literature search as distinct from what references have been found. (Gash, 1989: 69)

Gash makes a very good point here and most researchers, at some time or another, will have fallen into this trap. Many academics do not adequately document their searches, yet this is extremely important, especially when searching on-line databases which are updated several times a year. Not keeping a record of the searches conducted could mean that valuable time is wasted replicating previous activities. Having an exercise book set aside for this specific purpose could prove extremely useful. Such a document should include:

- the title and location of the source to be searched;
- the year (and month where applicable) from which the search is to start and finish in that source;
- the search terms used with that source;
- the volumes/issues that have been searched;
- the volumes/issues that remain to be searched.

How references are recorded is a matter of personal preference. Two options are possible: a manual paper-based system, or a computer software package. Record cards are easy and convenient to use and are flexible in the sense that they can be taken anywhere. So, for example, having read a journal article in the library you can immediately write up a record card while the key points are still fresh in your mind. There has to be a decision made at some stage whether it is worth the effort to set up a computer program for this purpose, especially if the user is not particularly experienced at using computer software. That said, there are several advantages of using computers to document references. Some of the advantages and disadvantages are set out in Table 11.3. Whichever

**TABLE 11.3  Advantages and disadvantages of using computers to document references**

| Advantages | Disadvantages |
|---|---|
| Computers are good at handling large databases. If for some reason you think you will have many references it could be a good strategy. | Computer records require access to a computer, and are therefore not as flexible as manual systems. |
| Computer records can be manipulated in a more sophisticated way than manual records, e.g. by undertaking key word searches. | Computer records could generate more work. First, noting the reference manually then transferring it to a computer database. |
| Once the references have been put on disk then they can be moved across to another file and used in your bibliography. | The searcher is dependent on printouts to search for duplicate references. The need to review printouts is a chore. |
| If most of the literature searches are on-line searches, then information can be downloaded and stored in an appropriate file. | It is difficult to browse looking at a computer with only one record being shown at a time. |
|  | For some reason the system might lose data hence the need for back-ups. |

method you choose to use, you need to ensure that you have recorded the relevant information. The relevant details include:

- the complete bibliographic reference;
- the source where the reference was found;
- location and availability;
- whether the item has been read;
- annotation or abstract.

## EVALUATING THE USEFULNESS OF MATERIAL GENERATED BY LITERATURE SEARCHES

The more sophisticated and extensive methods of searching the literature have become, the more emphasis there is on researchers to make quick and effective judgements about the usefulness of particular items that are unearthed. As a result, researchers need to acquire highly developed scanning abilities. The scanning process for each item should take no longer than four or five minutes (much less if possible), during which time the importance of the document should be ascertained. As far as initial appraisal is concerned, a good starting point is noting the author's credentials, whether in relation to their previous publications, work experience or place of employment. If your supervisor has mentioned the author's name and if he or she has been frequently cited in other academics' work these are all good indicators of quality. The date of publication is also a useful piece of information. There needs to be a judgement made as to whether the theoretical framework and/or the data are in fact out of date. However, it should be remembered that many older papers can be classified as 'classics' and are extremely important to cite. As far as books are concerned, the edition could be an important factor. Generally speaking, the later the edition the better. The name of the publisher is also worth noting. Certain publishers have the reputation for publishing different types of work and of varying degrees of quality.

Once a feel of the quality of the source has been ascertained, a decision needs to be made whether or not to read the document. Gash (1989) outlines what she considers are five main elements of the scanning process, focusing on the most significant features of the item:

1  *Abstract or author's summary*: this will hopefully sum up what the article is about and the main conclusions. Some abstracts are so good that often you learn little more from reading the whole article.
2  *Introductory paragraphs*: these should set out the scope of the article and what debates are being addressed.
3  *Concluding paragraphs*: hopefully these will summarize the most important points and highlight areas for future research.

4   *Illustrative material*: illustrative material could include graphs, tables, diagrams and photographs, etc., which summarize key findings.
5   *Section or paragraph headings*: these usually indicate the main topics and the thread of the argument, which enable key information to be selected out.

Following this process will enable you to decide fairly quickly whether the item is important and therefore central to the thesis topic, useful as background reading, or of no use whatsoever. If you decide you want to read the article or report further, a very quick content analysis should be undertaken. In this situation you need to evaluate whether the work updates other sources that you have read, or provides any new information. At this point decisions need to be taken as to whether notes should be made of the article content. Many research students often ask how they know when they have read enough literature to enable them to complete their literature review and move on to the next stage of designing their project. The answer is when you get to the point of undertaking literature searches and very little, if any, new, useful material is being generated.

When sources yield useful items you need to make notes. It is often difficult to extract some ideas from books and papers, particularly during the early stages of the project when you are reading around the literature fairly widely, as a precursor to narrowing down and focusing in on a specific area. During the early stages it is useful to photocopy key articles as much as you can. When you are reading text you are reading it in the hope of finding something useful which fits in with your research project at that point in time. However, it is often the case that during the first few months you might want to change the emphasis in your research project, so you might be reading papers looking for something a little different. That said, Orna and Stevens (1995) provide some useful tips on note taking. Their advice is always to ensure that you make an accurate note of bibliographical details. This is a very simple task, but it is surprising how easy it is to forget some part of the reference. Your lack of accuracy over referencing will catch up with you when you compile your thesis bibliography. Going back over literature to complete reference details is very tedious, time-consuming work which can easily be avoided. Highlighting in colour or large letters at the top of the page the theme/topic which is relevant is also a good idea since it will help to retrieve information quickly.

As far as note taking is concerned, avoid copying large chunks of text. The purpose of note taking is to extract material which is directly relevant to your specific research area. Summarizing complex ideas can be quite a demanding task, especially for overseas students whose first language is not English, but it is an important skill to acquire. You might also be accused of plagiarism if you use another person's work and only change a few of their words in a particular passage. If you wish to use direct quotations, make sure you note accurately the page number where the quote is located. Finally, it is extremely important that you use appropriate 'vehicles' for documenting notes, such as notebooks, loose leaf binders and cards. Bell (1996: 29) suggests that there is considerable merit in using cards. They are easy to sort and to reclassify; they are all the same size so easy to handle; and they are likely to stand up well to wear and tear. However, you may wish to use one of the computer-based systems that was discussed above.

## CITING YOUR REFERENCES

There are two main methods of citing the literature which are generally used:

- References are indicated in the text by the author's surname and the year of publication. The sources are collected together at the end of the thesis presented in alphabetical order of authors (usually known as the Harvard citation system).
- References are numbered consecutively in the text and the sources are collected together at the end of the thesis in the order cited (Vancouver system).

You should check in your department whether or not there is a 'house' style which you are required to use. If you are free to choose the most commonly used method of citing references is the Harvard system. The following section gives examples of how the Harvard system should be used in a variety of writing situations.

## HARVARD SYSTEM

The following notes are based on British Standards BS1629:1976 and BS5605:1990.

When writing up a piece of work you will need to cite (quote) the bibliographical references of all documents you have used or to which you have referred. It is very important to be consistent and accurate when citing references because the references may need to be traced at a later date by someone else who reads your work. The same set of rules should therefore be followed every time you cite a reference.

References need to be cited in two different places: first, at the point at which a document is referred to in the text of the work; second, in a list at the end of the work.

## CITATION IN THE TEXT

All statements, opinions, conclusions, etc. taken from another writer's work should be acknowledged, whether the work is directly quoted, paraphrased or summarized. In the Harvard system cited publications are referred to in the text by giving the author's surname and the year of publication in one of the forms shown below.

- If the author's name occurs naturally in the sentence the year is given in parentheses: In a recent study Harvey (1993) argued that . . .
- If the name does not occur naturally in the sentence, both name and year are given in parentheses: A recent study (Harvey, 1993) shows that . . .
- When an author has published more than one cited document in the same year, these are distinguished by adding lower case letters (a,b,c, etc.) after the year and within the parentheses: Johnson (1989a) discussed the subject . . .
- If there are two authors, the surnames of both should be given: Matthews and Jones (1992) have proposed that . . .
- If there are more than two authors, the surname of the first author only should be given, followed by *et al* in italics or underlined: Wilson *et al* (1993) conclude that . . .

## ELEMENTS TO INCLUDE IN THE LIST OF REFERENCES AT THE END OF A WORK

Bibliographical references describing the documents cited are given in a list at the end of the text. In the Harvard system, the references are listed in alphabetical order of authors' names. If you have cited more than one item by a specific author they should be listed chronologically (earliest first), and letter (1993a, 1993b) if more than one item has been published during a specific year. Whenever possible, elements of a bibliographical reference should be taken from the title page of the publication rather than from the front cover. Each reference should use the elements and punctuation given in the following examples.

### *Reference to a book*

Elements to cite:

- Author's surname, initials
- Year of publication
- Title in italics or underlined
- Edition (if not the first)

- Place of publication
- Publisher
- White, R., 1988. *Advertising: what it is and how to do it*. 2nd ed. London: McGraw Hill.

### Reference to a contribution in a book

Elements to cite:

- Surname of contributing author, initials
- Year of publication
- Title of contribution followed by the word *In*: which should be in italics or underlined
- Author or editor of publication, (initials, surname) followed by ed. or eds. if relevant
- Title of book in italics or underlined
- Edition (if not the first) or volume number if part of a series
- Place of publication
- Publisher
- Year of publication of book
- Page number(s) of contribution
- Wright, P., 1986. Reactions to an Ads contents versus judgments of Ads impact. *In: J. Olsen and K. Sentis, eds. Advertising and consumer psychology*. Vol. 3. New York: Praeger, 1986, 108–117.

### Reference to an article in a journal

Elements to cite:

- Author's surname, initials
- Year of publication
- Title of article
- Title of journal (in italics or underlined)
- Volume number and part number (with the latter in parentheses)
- Page numbers of contribution
- Greco, A.J. and Swayne, L.D., 1992. Sales response of elderly customers to point-of-purchase advertising. *Journal of Advertising Research*, 32 (5), 43–63.

### Reference to a conference paper

Elements to cite:

- Surname of contributing author, initials
- Year of publication

- Title of contribution followed by the word *In:* which should be in italics or underlined
- Editor of conference proceedings (initials, surname) (if applicable) followed by ed. or eds
- Title of conference proceedings (in italics or underlined) including date and place of conference
- Place of publication
- Publisher
- Page numbers of contribution
- Silver, K., 1989. Electronic mail: the new way to communicate. *In:* D.I. Raitt, ed. *9th international online information meeting, London 3–5 December 1988,* Oxford: Learned Information, 323–330.

### Reference to a publication from a corporate body (e.g. a government department or other organization)

Elements to cite:

- Name of issuing body
- Year of publication
- Title of publication (in italics or underlined)
- Place of publication
- Publisher
- Report number (where relevant)
- Independent Television Commission, 1991. *The ITC code of advertising standards and practice.* London: ITC.

### ACKNOWLEDGEMENT

Information on the Harvard system was provided by Academic Services Group, LIS, University of Bournemouth.

# PART IV

# QUALITATIVE METHODS: DESIGN, DATA COLLECTION AND ANALYSIS

This section is wide ranging in its approach to qualitative research and includes theoretical foundations of qualitative research; qualitative research in practice; using computers to analyse qualitative data; and writing up qualitative data. Chapter 12 addresses the link between philosophical approaches to qualitative research and qualitative research methods. Simon Holdaway explores the theoretical foundations of qualitative research and uses symbolic interactionism as an example. Since this chapter makes links between a distinctive philosophy of social research and research methods it should be read in conjunction with the material presented in Part I which addresses philosophical approaches to social science research.

The majority of chapters in Part IV focus on the practical application of a variety of qualitative research techniques. Chapter 13 provides an insight into the use of participatory research. Although not a widely used method in the social sciences, participatory research is growing in popularity because of its ability to provide in-depth collaboration with subjects and facilitators. Wanda Thomas Bernard's account of using participatory research is particularly valuable because her project is a fairly rare example of a researcher undertaking cross-national, qualitative research which in her case involves the use of participatory research groups in the UK and Canada. The focus of her research is survival and success as defined by black men and will be particularly valuable to research students undertaking work in the area of ethnicity and race. This chapter could be usefully read in conjunction with Chapter 4 by Peter Jackson who explores the contribution of 'race' as a distinctive philosophical approach to social science research and Chapter 24 by Dawn Burton who assesses the importance of ethnicity and race in the context of secondary data analysis.

The use of focus groups in social science research is a relatively new phenomenon, although the technique has been well established as a market research method for some time. Because the technique is relatively new in academic research, researchers are still exploring different ways in which focus groups can be used to the best effect. Caroline Oates used focus groups in her research about women's magazines in Britain. In Chapter 24 she outlines some of the practical issues which need resolving prior to using the technique and some of the problems which can be encountered in the process of using focus groups. Caroline concludes by setting out what she considers are the main strengths and limitations of using focus groups in academic research.

Unlike participatory and focus group research, in-depth interviewing is a well-established and frequently used data collection technique in social science research. In Chapter 15 Matt Stroh explores the issues which need to be considered before choosing interviewing as a strategy; the different approaches to interviewing which are available to researchers; and some of the practical issues which can arise during and after the interviewing has taken place. The material contained in the chapter is based on his PhD thesis which researched individual's attitudes to environmental issues.

Case study research is another well-established method of researching in the social sciences. However, although the method is widely used, there is no definitive definition of what the term case study actually means across the social science disciplines. Unpacking the different definitions of the term case study and case is the starting point of Chapter 16. The problems of conceptualizing case studies as purely qualitative research and the various types of case study designs that are available to researchers are discussed. Some of the practicalities of conducting case study research are considered by Dawn Burton in relation to her research on human resource management practices in the financial services sector. In the final section of the chapter some of the main objections which are levelled against the method and strategies for dealing with them are evaluated.

While design and data collection techniques in qualitative research have attracted a considerable amount of attention, the process of qualitative data analysis has frequently been marginalized. The mass of data which often arises from using qualitative methods has led to discussions about ways in which data can be more effectively managed and analysed. Whether or not it is advisable to use computers for the purposes of data analysis has become a very topical issue, particularly in the context of an ever-increasing array of software being developed for this purpose. In Chapter 17 Matt Stroh considers some of the philosophical and practical issues which research students should consider prior to using computer software to analyse their own data.

In Chapter 18 Peter Jackson discusses another data management issue which many research students using qualitative methods have difficulty with and that is writing up their findings. It is a cause of concern for many research students that they have lots of data, but they do not have a clear idea how to present them. Peter Jackson addresses the writing up question in three ways: by making some general points and observations about writing; considering theoretical issues about textual strategy and in particular the politics of representation; and finally making some practical suggestions about writing up based on his own research experience.

## SUPPLEMENTARY READING

Bryman, A. and Burgess, R.G. (1993) *Analyzing Qualitative Data*. London: Routledge.

Marshall, C. and Rossman, G.B. (1989) *Designing Qualitative Research*. London: Sage.

Mason, J. (1996) *Qualitative Researching*. London: Sage.

Morgan, D.L. (1988) *Focus Groups as Qualitative Research*. London: Sage.

Shaffir, W.B. and Stebbins, R.A. (1991) *Experiencing Fieldwork: An Inside View of Qualitative Research*. London: Sage.

Silverman, D. (1993) *Interpreting Qualitative Data*. London: Sage.

Strass, A. and Corbin, J. (1990) *Basics of Qualitative Research*. London: Sage.

Wolcott, H.F. (1990) *Writing Up Qualitative Research*. London: Sage.

Yin, R.K. (1994) *Case Study Research: Design and Methods*. London: Sage.

# 12 THEORY AND METHOD IN QUALITATIVE RESEARCH

*Simon Holdaway*

There is a clear view within the social sciences that methods of research are discrete, to be separated from social theory and the activity of theorizing. Within the context of teaching about methods of research, curricular often seem to suggest that a set of useful research tools is contained in a toolbox, the contents of which are to be purposely removed, one by one, for instruction about their application. This tool, a questionnaire perhaps, is suitable for this project. Another tool, participant observation, say, is removed for another project, and so on. Each research method is seen to be a vital tool for use with the job at hand.

Some social sciences, psychology for example, have a rather smaller set of research tools than others, sociology would be a good comparison. The former subject prefers to restrict its collection of research tools to what is regarded as the precision of experiments and questionnaires, along with an array of accurate measuring devices. Practitioners of sociology, which also has a long tradition of research based on qualitative data, needs systematic, observational and related research tools as well as questionnaires.

The adequacy of this view of methods of research as a discrete subject is questioned in this unit. My argument is not that we need to extend the range of research tools available, applying them in number to extract the maximum amount of data from the social world. The practice of what is called 'triangulation' is not part of my argument (Bulmer, 1984). My fundamental point is this. All methods of research are underpinned by a social theory of one type or another. Methods of research are not a discrete subject but unavoidably and necessarily related to social theory.

## LINKING THEORY AND RESEARCH METHODS

There are two main ways in which methods of research and theory are related. First, all methods of research imply a particular view of the human being. They imply a particular philosophical anthropology (Hollis, 1977). This means that a method of research places a stress on the active or passive nature of human beings; on the extent to which action is influenced by social factors or by reflective thought; on the nature of mind, therefore, and on the relationship between mind and action. Crucially, one's primary method of research implies a theory about the extent to which social relationships and other phenomena are meaningful, which draws our attention to a distinction made in social theory between behaviour and action (Weber, 1949). Action is meaningful. Behaviour is more repetitive, a response to external or internal forces. Finally, methods of research imply ideas about the extent to which the thoughts and behaviour of human beings, as individuals and/or as members of groups, institutions and societies, are determined by external social forces (or internal states). Are then human beings in any sense able to determine for themselves their thoughts and actions?

These are not exclusive emphases to be identified clearly with any one method of research. They are viewed more appropriately as points on a continuum running from behaviour to action, for example. It is nevertheless very important for researchers to reflect upon the extent to which their methods imply a philosophical anthropology, which may be so taken for granted within their discipline that it is rarely questioned. Experimentation in psychology, for example, is in some university departments regarded as the only 'scientific' method available and the philosophical anthropology it assumes is accepted as 'common sense'. The use of questionnaires is similarly regarded in some areas of sociology. It is taken for granted. Feminist methods are premised on a number of anthropological assumptions, many untested and assumed to be 'given' (Gelsthorpe, 1992; Hammersley, 1992). The upshot for a research student beginning to develop a research project is the benefits of reflecting on the ways in which chosen methods of inquiry define the nature of the subject of your research. You should learn to question what your discipline takes for granted about methods of research and the implicit, theoretical assumptions that underpin them.

The second way in which methods of research and theory are intertwined is in the notion of social order that particular methods of research imply. Notions of social order are also related to philosophical anthropology which, as we have seen, is concerned with the extent to which social structures determine the behaviour (or action) of an individual. We should ask, therefore, whether our method of research implies a view of social order in which social structures transcend and in some senses constitute the individual. Or are social structures interpreted, forming the basis of but not straightforwardly determining human action as they resonate within the mind of an individual, constructing and reconstructing a society?

Are we able to read off the meaning of action from a prior analysis of social structures, a class-based, gender-based analysis, for example, or should we place human diversity and its documentation in a more prominent position? Do we assume that a test of statistical significance based on data from a questionnaire survey is adequate to tell us about the diversity of views that have been constrained by the number of answers it was possible to give to a particular question; to the ways in which answers have been constrained by coding; and the ways in which findings have been constrained by the supposed validity of statistical tests of significance and deviation (Cicourel, 1964)? These types of approach to research, and the methods on which they are based, may well distort the social world. We need to reflect carefully on the ways in which our methods of research can redefine the phenomena we seek to research and to which we hope to be faithful.

## THEORETICAL FOUNDATIONS OF QUALITATIVE RESEARCH

To illustrate these points I will use some pretty stark examples from sociology, my own subject. They are stark illustrations because I am mindful that students taking this course come from many different disciplinary backgrounds and may not be used to dealing with the central questions I am asking. The illustrations are nevertheless salient for all the social sciences. The example I have chosen is Durkheim's research on suicide.

In *The Rules of Sociological Method* and his related, empirical study *Suicide*, Emile Durkheim illustrated clearly one, dominant view of theory and its relationship to a research method (Durkheim, 1952, 1982). At root, Durkheim argued that 'social facts should be treated as things'. The suicide rate, for example, should be regarded as thing-like, an object with changing proportions but an object that can be measured nevertheless. When the shape of the object changes, the proportions of the change can be measured and expressed numerically. Quite simply, if the recorded rate of suicide is found to have risen in a particular period of time, it has risen indeed. If the rate has decreased, it has decreased: 'social facts should be treated as things'.

Having defined the object of his study, the rates of suicide in France, the society in which he was interested, Durkheim then went on to identify factors of direct relevance to changing rates of suicide. He found, for example, that rates of suicide in rural areas were lower than those in urban areas. Suicide rates were higher among Protestants than Catholics. They were higher among people living alone than among members of families living together. The inference from the data was that some variables, that some (for the purposes of research) 'thing-like' phenomena, were having what might be a direct effect upon levels of suicide. Durkheim was identifying objective forces playing upon individuals, leading them to a greater or lesser propensity to commit suicide.

In Durkheim's analysis, changes in the social structure orchestrated changes in suicide rates. Changes in social structure orchestrated behaviour, the act of suicide. The more a society is structured to foster a normative balance between integration and individualism, the more stable the suicide rate. The more a society emphasizes integration to the exclusion of individualism, the higher the suicide rate. The more individualism is emphasized to the exclusion of integration, the higher the suicide rate. The more a society is in a state of anomie, a concept Durkheim developed to describe a state of constant flux and uncertainty within a society, the higher the suicide rate. Stable suicide rates are found in societies with a 'natural' balance between integration and individualism. The key point is that individual action, in this case suicide, is caused by changes in the social structure, which is wholly external and prior to mind, meaning, personal reflection and action.

Durkheim's method of research was a classical one. Define the phenomenon to be studied. Measure it, as if an object, using the appropriate tool from one's research methods toolbox. Refine the measurement in relation to other object-like variables and, through statistical analysis, express, numerically and then in prose, relationships between the variables that appear to be significant. The final objective of research is to make law-like statements about the causes of changes in the suicide rate.

Individual states of mind were of no interest to Durkheim. The meaning of events or processes of mind that lead a person to commit suicide were also of no interest. The task of the sociologist (and, by implication, the social sciences) is to describe and analyse the effects of external, causal factors that act upon the individual and determine action – even the most individualistic action one can identify – suicide. It is possible for the social scientist to, as it were, read off the meaning of events that lead to a suicide by measuring the social forces that transcend individual consciousness.

Let us now look more closely at the theoretical assumptions implicit in this type of research. In this study, human being are more played upon than reflecting upon the constraints they perceive to be acting upon them and then acting in the light of their understanding of those constraints. One or a number of causal factors that act upon the individual and determine their actions (even the most individualistic action one can find, suicide) have been identified. The security of our methods of research reassures us about the validity of our findings. It is possible to read off and understand the meaning of events that lead to a suicide by measuring the social forces that transcend individual consciousness.

The view from Durkheim is one of a very deterministic understanding of human beings. It is of a passive human being whose behaviour reflects social structural change. The philosophical anthropology implicit within this view is of social structures constituting human kind. Passivity rather than activity is the keynote. Notice too that we have a model of social order, of social structure, now apparent in this theoretical view. The social order is an objective phenomenon, it transcends individuals. It is constantly in the ascendancy and it is causal. Individuals living within a particular social structure are more determined than determining their actions. Durkheim went on to argue that levels of societal integration have a direct relationship to rates of suicide in a society. Unless that level of integration is normative, suicides will occur in excessive numbers.

Now, the research method that flows from this anthropology – put all too starkly and simply – is of a social world that can be reduced to variables. A social phenomenon is defined to facilitate its measurement. Data are gathered and measured, probably by statistical means. By various manipulations, tests of significance and so on, initial hypotheses are generalized until, ideally, law-like statements are made.

You should recognize this positivist approach to research methods, often assumed without reflection to be the method of social science. At worse Durkheim's approach, which you should know as current within many different social sciences, is captured in the edict 'if you can't measure it, neglect it'. The view is found in questionnaire studies where the researcher selects the appropriate variables, defines them within questions to be asked to a number of respondents, selected according to some pre-defined criteria. People, objects one might say, who come within the parameters of the criteria are then suspended in time and space while questions are asked. The answers to predetermined questions, called 'data', are then analysed to determine their statistical significance and as general a set of numerical and, later, written statements as it is possible to make are written.

All of these aspects of social science follow from the method which Durkheim and many others working in a very wide sweep of social science have raised to the status of security. Along with related methods, they form the core of the research toolbox. To depart from their use often requires special pleading. Other methods of research might be acceptable in some circumstances, but their utility will be assessed against the benchmark of the standard research tool kit. The research tool kit, however, is not a neutral set of instruments. Each one implies a theory, a philosophical anthropology, a notion of social order. Theory and method cannot be separated.

## AN ALTERNATIVE VIEW: QUALITATIVE RESEARCH METHODS

Durkheim chose to study suicide because it presented the most difficult challenge to his methods of research and to his fundamental theory that changes of individual behaviour are directly related to changes in the social structure of a society. Clearly, it was not possible for him to arrange semi-structured interviews with his research subjects or to engage in participant observation of some type. His neglect of the meaning of suicide and the ways in which rates of suicide may not in any fundamental sense reflect the incidence of or changes in the number of suicides has been the focus of criticism of his work.

This critique, with its different methods and different theories, has not been concerned with the extent to which an objective social order determines the behaviour of individuals. Rather, the critical research has been concerned with the ways in which human beings, relating one to the other, interpret acts that might be associated with death, attribute particular meanings to deaths, believe a particular version of 'common sense' about death and suicide. In other words, there has been an interest in the ways in which an aspect of the social world, suicide, has been constructed. There has been an interest in the social construction of the suicide rate.

Jack Douglas in the USA and Max Atkinson in England have asked, for example, how has the suicide rate been constructed by the personnel of the various agencies involved in attributing the meaning of 'suicide', a legal category, to a death that could have been interpreted as natural (Atkinson, 1971, 1979; Douglas, 1967, 1971)? They have extended their research further back than the published formal rates of suicide to analyse social processes that precede their publication, taking into consideration coroner court judgments, pathologists' decisions, the common-sense views of suicide held by mortuary assistants, by police coroners' officers, by relatives and by others concerned with deceased persons and, finally, with the deceased person's own ideas about their death as expressed in written notes and other forms of communication.

The formal rate of suicide is the end product, it is argued, of a long chain of human decision-making within which various officials and other people concerned with an apparent act of suicide employ different types of knowledge of events – medical, legal, emotional, prejudicial, stereotypical, and so on, and on – which lead to the classification of an act as suicide. However, the formal rate of suicide, the statistic of each suicide and, aggregated, the rate of suicide is the end product, an object-like phenomenon, that shields the social processes, the negotiations based upon the selection and reflection on the available evidence. Research should focus on the social processes and related meanings of phenomena that are contained in mundane and professional knowledge that lead an act to be defined as suicide and then appear in the official statistics.

From this perspective it is necessary for the social scientist to inquire into the ways in which what appears to be an objective world is constructed: common-sense views brought to the consideration of whether or not a person intended to take their own life, which might amount to whether or not a note was left, or a judgement, albeit on the basis of hearsay, that a person appeared to be upset in the days before their death. So deaths that could have been defined as 'natural' are constructed in such a way that they are attributed with the meaning of 'suicide' and then become part of what Durkheim would regard as an objective reality, a formal rate of suicide articulated by an objective social structure.

Within this view we have a very different understanding of human beings and the nature of social order, of social structure. We have a view of human beings attributing meaning to the social world as they reflect upon the social context, the written, verbal, physical and other clues available to them. The apparent truth of what has happened to a person who has died is negotiated in relationship with others. Relatives and police officers, coroners and doctors and others discuss in different contexts the available evidence, vying with and yielding to various accounts of events, weighing them in the balance of professional and more mundane knowledge. The human being is active, conscious, more acting than acted upon by external social structures or internal mental states. There is a view here that processes of mind are central to social scientific inquiry, that it is necessary to suspend belief in the apparent objectivity of measures that regard social phenomena as 'object-like' and to analyse the social processes that construct the apparent appearance of objectivity.

Further, the notion of social order implicit within this alternative approach to social science is one in which the social world, the social structure, is constructed by human action. Constant negotiation between people constitutes the apparent, commonsensical status of social structure that Durkheim placed in a central position. That which appears to be rock solid betrays a reality that, on closer inspection, is seen to be constructed and reconstructed by human action. Common sense and other forms of knowledge certainly constrain the ways in which events are interpreted, but there is no sense in which an objective social structure acts as a straitjacket. Social reality is rather tenuous, dependent upon human action to sustain it.

The methods of social science that follow from this view are rather different from those of the quantitative social scientist. Semi-structured interviews in which mundane views about motive, about ambiguous events, and so on are probed sensitively. Unstructured interviews might be preferred because it is thought that they allow a less restricted articulation of opinion. Periods of observation might be undertaken, in the case of studies of suicide in mortuaries, coroners' courts, the offices of coroners' officers, police stations. Any written evidence will be combed to discover and analyse the meanings presented. The central task is to describe and analyse the dominant meanings expressed in letters and notes, for example, by those who have died.

These methods are designed to document the ways in which the apparently objective phenomenon of suicide is constructed. They define social phenomena in a particular way that begs a theoretical view of social order and the nature of human beings. We again find a clear link between theory and method.

## SYMBOLIC INTERACTIONISM

I now want to discuss further the social theory that has informed much of what I have said about the links between research methods and social theory. Symbolic interactionism is not the only theory (many prefer to call it a perspective rather than a theory) that could be discussed, but it has been one of the major bases of qualitative social research (Plummer, 1979; Rock, 1979).

The primary reference for the perspective of symbolic interaction is George Herbert Mead's *Mind, Self and Society* (Mead, 1934). Here we find Mead influenced by one of his Chicago colleagues, the psychologist John Watson. Watson was a behaviourist, who argued that human behaviour could be analysed in terms of stimulus and response. Watson was solely interested in behaviour. His method of research was experimental. Mead, working in the department of philosophy at Chicago, pitted himself against Watson's ideas, arguing that he was merely concerned with behaviour, with behavioural outcomes, leaving mental processes in which meanings were attributed to phenomena completely unresearched. This was wholly inadequate from Mead's point of view.

Mead drew a distinction between *significant* and *non-significant* symbols. A non-significant symbol is behaviour that is immediate, seemingly a response to one or more stimuli. It is habitual, almost automatic. The behaviour of animals is like this. Significant symbols, however, are the basis of human relationships and their use sets human beings apart from animals. Human beings have created and continue to recreate a world of symbols, crucially linguistic symbols that reach beyond an immediate situation, relationship, or other context. Symbols expand meaning from the present to link discrete events and objects, to relate different points in time, to creatively anticipate the future, to harmonize and enrich ideas.

From this perspective, the social world is not intrinsically meaningful. *Meaning* is created as human beings relate to each other, taking into account past and anticipated future experience. Meanings are created in interaction with others and therefore negotiated. The concern is with social processes. Any relationship which can be conceptualized in terms of social processes can have diverse meanings for those involved in it and to those who observe it. The meaning of a relationship can change as people relate to each other in different contexts. Meaning, the use of symbols, inter- actions, negotiation and contextualization are all basic ideas of symbolic interaction.

Further, Mead argued that in childhood we learn to '*take the role of the other*'. This is to view the world from the perspective of those who are physically present with us and those who are remote from us. Again, Mead's ideas suggest that we routinely take into account a wide range of symbolic and instrumental factors as we relate to each other, as we seek to understand the social world.

How is this possible? Is there some biological constitution of the human being that facilitates this ability to 'take the role of the other', to create meaning, to use symbolic language, and so on? Mead recognized that the physiological structure of the vocal chords and related organs is the basis of language. Biology and the social world are in this sense interdependent. However, there is no sense in which human behaviour is tied to biology in a fixed relationship.

At the heart of Mead's thought is the notion of '*the self*', by which Mead conceptualizes a social process with two aspects, the '*I*' and the '*Me*'. It is essential to keep in mind that Mead was describing a social process of mind when he talked about the self. Human beings have the capacity, which they continually employ, to interact with other people and with themselves. We can address ourselves and ask about the possible meanings of an event, a relationship, whatever. Importantly, we can ask what might be the most human of human questions, 'Who am I?' 'Who am I in relation to these people?' 'Who do these people think I am?' I might be a university lecturer, which might denote one meaning in the context of the lecture hall, another at a party, and another in conversation with friends? The answers to this and other questions about meaning are not discovered once and for all but in a process of dialogue between the 'I' and the 'Me'. They refer to the particular contexts within which they are asked.

The 'I' is my response and my response alone to events, relationships and so on. Mead said that we surprise ourselves, by which he meant that to some extent we cannot anticipate, predict, plan our action. The 'Me', however, is my response to the meanings which others have placed upon similar relationships, objects and events to the one I am presently concerned with. This is the historical framework of constraint, of sedimented meanings, perhaps regarded as common sense, that provides me with a lexicon of rules, meanings, predictions, and so on, to which the 'I' continually responds. Symbolic interaction is therefore an internal and external dialogue during which the world of relationships, objects and events is sustained as meaningful.

Mead did not clarify precisely the meaning of the self and you will find different interpretations of it, ranging from a view that the 'I' is similar to Freud's notion of the 'id' to a claim that he engaged in metaphysics (Meltzer *et al.*, 1975). The key point for me, however, is that Mead assists us to move away from a highly deterministic social science, from a social science in which human beings are but the embodiment of a transcendent social structure, the role scripted clearly by a society, the dominant meanings predetermined by a group playing a sum-zero power game. Mead cautions us about any type of reductionism. There is in his work a tension between the individual and the societal spheres of action. Human beings are active rather than passive, they are capable of creativity, never finally determined by power structures, roles, or any other conceptual straitjacket found within the social sciences. The task of the social scientist is to describe and, through systematic methods of research, analyse the meanings of the social world, as it is understood by the members of a group, an organization, or some other collectivity. This implies the description and analysis of social processes that lead to the construction and sustaining of the meanings to which members of collectivities hold as adequate and true.

These ideas give us a clue about Mead's philosophical anthropology – activity, consciousness, meaningfulness, negotiation, interaction, self-reflection are all stressed. There is also a view of social order implicit in his writings – interaction, constructions, reconstruction and negotiation, the unfinished, a dimension of the immanence of social structures as well as their transcendence come into view. The subject matter of social science is thereby defined and which requires the deployment of particular methods of research.

## METHODS AND THEORY: A UNITY

Mead emphasized the place of social processes within human relationships, which suggests that our methods of research should document the ways in which the meanings of relationships (and other phenomena) are constructed and sustained. We are not interested in the snapshot album that suspends the social world in time and space, presenting a picture of this statistical relationship, that test of significance, and so on. We have to observe, perhaps participate in the world of those whom we are researching, to relate the construction and sustaining of meanings through time and across the spatial contexts within which they are discovered.

Further, our interest is in the mundane world, which is another reason for a researcher's observation of and participation within it. The emphasis is on other people's worlds, which might mean that we need to sit rather lightly on a number of taken for granteds of our chosen social science. We must concentrate on what other people find meaningful, not what sociologists, psychologists, economists and so on have found useful to their disciplines.

Our questions must therefore sensitize us to discover the range of meanings attributed to a subject of interest, to the contexts within which the same meanings might change, to their relevance to action, and so on. Our methods of research should therefore preserve the natural world which is regarded as taken for granted by the people we research, not distort it by placing people in a distinct context, like that of an interviewer with a questionnaire, or in an experimental laboratory, or, as it were, by the use of a preconceived theory that interprets every nuance of meaning in, say, class-based or engendered terms. The cardinal rule is to be sensitive to and faithfully describe the commonsensical world of others, which for the social scientist means as minimal an intervention into their life as seems practical and possible.

It takes time to observe and gain insight into other people's lives. Qualitative research cannot dash in and raid peoples' minds in the belief that the rich symbolism of the social world has been captured adequately. We should avoid 'smash and grab' raids in the name of social science. Anthropologists typically spend considerable periods of time living among groups of people, precisely to familiarize themselves with the language used, with the diverse meaning of phenomena and with the complex relationship between word and action in the contexts of the society they seek to study (Carrithers *et al.*, 1985). The fear is that without close observation and interaction one simply glosses over the complexity and diversity of the world one seeks to study.

William Foote Whyte, another Chicago scholar whose *Street Corner Society* is probably the best example of the type of research methods I am advocating, decided to undertake research on youths, especially gangs, in an Italian quarter of Boston, Massachusetts (Whyte, 1943). Whyte went to live in a community house, explaining that he was interested in writing a book about the Italian quarter in which it was situated. He made friends with people living there, especially with Doc, a man considerably older than himself who wanted to introduce Whyte to the neighbourhood and its people. Doc provided some pretty good advice to this doctoral (sic) student. He told Doc to stop asking all those 'what', 'why', 'when', 'where' questions. Just listen. So Whyte learned a basic rule of qualitative methods of research – observe, be patient, listen and you will see and hear about other people's worlds. The time to ask questions is when you have become sufficiently familiar with the context observed and skilled in interpreting its apparent meanings.

An example of this idea is found in Whyte's discussion of the structure of relationships within gangs of Italian youths. Instead of using some kind of quantitative measure, or asking questions about the subject, Whyte noticed that the youths always bowled in the same order when at the bowling alley. Then it dawned on him that the order of bowling reflected the power structure of the gangs, the status of members and the roles they played. Not a single question was asked by Whyte to document and analyse this part of his research project – he kept his mouth shut and his eyes and ears open. His ideas then developed.

None of these ideas suggest that the methods of qualitative research are unsystematic. It is essential to demonstrate how one has arrived at research conclusions. The ways in which possible bias has been countered, observations recorded, the analysis has been conducted when sifting and sorting the mass of data that typifies qualitatively based research, and many, many other aspects of research need to be described and to some extent rendered capable of replication. Qualitative research is to this extent systematic if not what is classically regarded as 'scientific' by many social scientists (Meltzer *et al.*, 1975).

## THE BASIS OF QUALITATIVE RESEARCH

The basic point we return to is this – methods of research used by social scientists must be designed to document adequately the richness and diversity of meanings people attribute to phenomena. They must allow us to document the ways in which meanings are constructed, negotiated within particular social contexts and become regarded as taken for granted. Our methods of research must therefore allow us to suspend belief in the givenness of phenomena, to perceive the frailty of the social world and to appreciate the ways in which that frailty is created into what is taken for granted and has integrity for the people we are studying. Our methods of research follow from an understanding of the subject matter of the social sciences. Theories of social science imply methods and methods of research imply theories.

# 13 PARTICIPATORY RESEARCH AS EMANCIPATORY METHOD: CHALLENGES AND OPPORTUNITIES

*Wanda Thomas Bernard*

This chapter explores the use of participatory methods in academic research. It begins with a discussion of the key elements of participatory research, and a dialogue about its implementation through a case study of the process used for my doctoral study: 'Survival and Success: As Defined by Black Men in Sheffield, England and Halifax, Canada'. The chapter concludes with a critical evaluation of participatory research. I begin with a brief discussion of participatory research.

## PARTICIPATORY RESEARCH

Research is the production of knowledge about a given subject matter, and people who produce and control such knowledge increase their power to deal with the particular issues involved. Participatory research is a process in which a group documents and analyses their collective experience of a social problem, placing it in a wider context of social, economic and political cause and effect, and integrating knowledge from outside the limits of their immediate experience (Bernard, 1996). Participatory research is a process of critical and reflective inquiry, which holds hope for the marginalized; it gives voice to those who are usually silenced and empowers people to analyse their experience as a means of effecting change. Maguire states:

> The alternative paradigm concept of uniqueness brings the focus of research back to individuals and groups in the particular social context being investigated. The purpose of research is shifted from constructing grand generalizations for control and predictability by detached outsiders to working closely with ordinary people, the insiders in a particular context . . . to understand their realities. (Maguire, 1987: 26)

Participatory research has been used in many different forums, including community development and evaluation research. While definitions and degree of participation varies, most proponents of participatory

research define it as a process of systematic inquiry with trained researchers and those normally considered 'subjects' actively engaged in a collaborative project. They collaborate on the research topic, the collection and
analysis of data and the dissemination of results (Bernard, 1996; Hall, 1993;
Maguire, 1987; Reason, 1988a; Whitemore, 1994). The major focus in participatory research is the active involvement of participants, raising their
consciousness, and empowering them to reconceptualize the identified
problems and to identify action strategies. Maguire describes participatory
research as:

> a method of social investigation of problems, involving the participation of
> oppressed and ordinary people in problem posing and problem solving. It is an
> educational process for the researcher and participants, who analyze the struc-
> tural causes of named problems through collective discussion and interaction.
> (Maguire, 1987: 29)

Participatory research has been described as an effective tool that
enables marginalized people to become aware of their collective power, to
create knowledge about their experience, and to take action. Participatory
research was originally developed in the work of Paulo Freire, who used
techniques of consciousness raising and conscietization with rural peasants
of Brazil to help them challenge the oppressive conditions under which
they were living (Freire, 1972). Ralph (1988) concurs with this perspective
and argues that participatory research empowers oppressed people, giving
them the essential information they need to advocate for change in their
conditions. Those normally studied become full participants as active
agents in the research.

Hall describes participatory research 'as a process which combines three
activities; research, education and action' (Park *et al.*, 1993: xiv). Working
from the bottom up, participatory research enables participants and
researchers to work collaboratively to create knowledge and understanding about the problem under study, and to take action for change. As such
it challenges traditional research hierarchies, and those normally studied
are empowered to challenge the oppressive conditions they are living
with. Co-operative inquiry can also break down the traditional distinction
between the role of the researcher and the role of the subject. Subjects are
co-researchers and they devise, manage and draw conclusions from the
research.

Dialogue is central to participatory research and to be effective researchers must break down the traditional hierarchies to enhance dialogue with
participants. It often requires a re-conceptualization of power and the fair
use of power. Ristock and Pennell (1996: 10) posit that researchers should
'minimize power inequities in all relationships, including the research one,
through critical reflection and openness to criticism from others'. In my
participatory research with men of African descent, I began with an
unpacking of my role as an insider–outsider and critically reflecting on the

power inequities that existed between us. According to the men I did manage to break down some of those perceived and real barriers. The following quotation is illustrative of the men's assessment of my work with them.

> Wanda you were able to motivate us to work on this project and to stay with it. You were motivating in a way that was encouraging and not demanding. Even though you brought the original idea to us . . . this was our research, we owned it . . . we appreciated your ability to clearly articulate and represent our views in the written report. (Halifax Research Working Group and Sheffield Research Working Group)

The type of involvement in participatory research may vary, but to be considered participatory a project must involve some degree of active involvement of participants as agents in the research. This may be limited to consultation during various stages of the research or total involvement and ownership, as was the case in my research. Reason (1994) informs us that while participatory research is relatively easy to espouse, it is challenging genuinely to practise. Maguire (1993) contributes to this debate with her reflections on doing participatory research as a doctoral student. She argues that the demands of academia are contradictory to the expectations required for genuine participation in research. During my research project I was constantly troubled by the contradictory demands. I quote from my personal diary:

> I am worried that the thesis examining board will challenge the participatory methods that I used. I have written the thesis, to satisfy the academic requirements, yet the research belongs to the men. I have used a lot of 'first voice' throughout the text. How will this be perceived by the examining board? I am worried that they will not see it as 'academic enough'. More important, how will I deal with their criticisms of the work? (Personal research diary, 1995)

Maguire (1987) has named the androcentric bias evident in the participatory research literature. To address this, Maguire established a framework for feminist participatory research. It critiques both positivist and androcentric underpinnings of dominant research; gender, 'race', culture and class are at the centre of issues, and in the entire research process. Maguire argues that explicit attention should be paid to gender in the evaluation and reporting of research (Maguire, 1987: 105–108). To this I would add that 'race', class and culture also need to inform the research, particularly data analysis. The inclusive practice of feminist participatory research allows for the inclusion of more voices in the research. Maguire (1987) also advocates for the involvement of research students as partners in the entire research process, to increase the potential for more equitable distribution of the benefits of the research. Ralph (1988: 37) concurring with this perspective, argues that if we are truly committed to empowering those we study, then this [participatory research] is an essential tool to master.

The central focus in feminist participatory research is the involvement of subjects as co-researchers into the study and resolution of their perceived problems. Social change and transformation are the ultimate goals, which result when people develop an increased awareness about their own resources and power, which facilitates their taking action. Some consider it a more scientific method of research because participation of the community in the research process facilitates a more authentic analysis of their social reality. The researcher is a committed participant and learner in the research, not a distant observer. In the next part of this chapter I set out the key tenets of participatory research and describe the method and process used in my doctoral study to illustrate the implementation of each tenet.

## THE KEY TENETS AND ELEMENTS OF PARTICIPATORY RESEARCH

Table 13.1 sets out the major differences between traditional and participatory research approaches. In this chapter, each of the participatory

TABLE 13.1   Participatory action research versus traditional research

| Element | Participatory action research | Traditional research approaches |
| --- | --- | --- |
| Problem identification | Done by community or group experiencing the problem | Often done by outside person/external researcher |
| Decisions about how the research will take place | Done by community | Usually done by the researcher |
| Methods of gathering information | Wide variety of methods are used (group meetings, workshops, surveys, use of drama and song, kitchen table meetings, storytelling | Usually interviews and questionnaires |
| | Focus on collective/group response | Focus on individual responses |
| | Adaptable to each community or situation | Usually very inflexible |
| Analysis and interpretation of data | Emphasis on group problem-solving and interpretation | Analysis done by external researcher often without consultation from the community/group |
| How results are used | Direct application where possible by community, planned action to push for change in the system | Not usually part of the process; a report is written to document findings with little ownership by people in the community |
| Feelings of community group involved | Fun, lots of involvement and sharing, learning, enlightened process, informal | Perpetuates status quo; often makes no difference in the lives of people in the community; they feel exploited; process is stiff |

Source: BLAC, 1994: 8.

research elements that are identified here are discussed in detail, using my doctoral research as a single case study to illustrate the application of the research methods and to analyse its effectiveness.

## PROBLEM IDENTIFICATION

My doctoral research 'Survival and Success: As Defined by Black Men in Sheffield, England and Halifax, Canada', was an exploratory cross-national participatory action project with black men from the two countries. The research set out to explore their experiences and conceptualizations of survival and success. Although the initial problem was identified by me as part of my doctoral programme, the participatory methodology was selected as the most effective way to engage black men in an exploration of the issues that impacted on their lives. My emphasis in this Africentric feminist participatory research project was the full participation of black men as co-researchers. This was rooted in my assumption that when people in a given situation do their own research to discover ways to improve their situation, they increase their power to act on the knowledge they generate and prevent others, normally considered experts, from expropriating or exploiting their knowledge, thereby gaining more power over them.

Although it is asserted in the literature that in good participatory research the problems are identified by the community under study, it is also recognized that people in the community often lack the confidence, skills and resources to do the research. Researchers committed to social action and critical perspectives in research should be encouraged to engage with communities and community groups to do participatory research. However, such projects must be fairly negotiated and begin with a critique of the power inequities and a willingness to share that power. Ristock and Pennell (1996) remind us that power influences all relationships, and the research relationship is no different. As noted earlier, I began this research with a critical examination of the power inbalances inherent in our research relationship: doctoral student/community co-researchers; insider–outsider woman doing work with men; academic professor–community members; perceived and/or real class differences.

The research was initiated by me, as a doctoral student, and costs associated with the work were paid by me, as part of my overall educational costs. In addition, we raised funds to assist the Research Working Groups (RWGs) with travel to the respective conferences. In each site, community groups donated the use of space for our meetings and the conferences. The theme of the research was identified in my original research proposal, which was developed for my university admission and funding. The RWG members identified the specific areas to be addressed and designed the questionnaires that were used. Control of the research design, the questions, the analysis, the sample and dissemination of the results remained with RWGs.

I agreed to participate in this research project because when I read Wanda's proposal, I saw there the opportunity to truly participate in something worthwhile. Every year I am approached by University students who want to interview me to learn something about the 'Black experience'. A few years ago I vowed to never again participate in such projects because nothing comes back to us. This research gives me an opportunity to have a say in what is done, how it is done and what will happen to the results. (SRWG member)

The problem identified for study in this research was an examination of the survival strategies used by black men, to bring consciousness awareness of those positive strategies to the men themselves, to the black communities, and others in society at large. We also sought to develop a critical understanding of what success meant to black men. The study was conducted by black men, with other black men. In addition, the views of black women and other allies were heard through the conferences. This inclusive process enabled the voices of a larger group of participants to be heard.

## RESEARCH DESIGN AND PROCESS

The entire research process was conducted from December 1992 to September 1995. Decisions were arrived at through group discussion and consensus at the (RWG) meetings. An interactive process was established and all voices and opinions were heard, respected and acknowledged throughout the research. As one RWG member stated: 'We had here an environment where we could agree and disagree, and take on board useful debates about some tough issues. This was a valuable exercise.'

The project began in Halifax with a preliminary review of the literature, the development of the research proposal and recruitment of black men to participate in the HRWG. The involvement of black men in the RWG allows for active participation of the 'subjects' of this study in the entire research process, building in face and catalytic validity.

HRWG members were recruited, using a snowball sampling method. The following criteria were established: aged over 19; meets the preliminary definition of success; has grown up in Nova Scotia; is willing to donate time, energy and personal expertise to this study; is interested in jointly exploring the issues as set out in the proposal in a broad context; be from a range of socio-economic groups; and be from a range of age groups. Most of these men remained active participants throughout the entire research process, reinforcing my stated principle of ownership of and involvement in the research by the men themselves.

A total of six men participated in the HRWG and were from diverse backgrounds, different age groups, and worked in a range of careers. The one thread that linked them was their active involvement in their community or in the larger struggle for black equality, and/or their concern about the future of black men. One of the men in the group was my partner, an African Canadian man to whom I have been married for over twenty years. His involvement in the research brings my subjectivity into plain view. His involvement was essential, as my initial interest in the work grew out of struggles and triumphs in our relationship. I was later informed by the Sheffield RWG that his involvement and commitment to the research served as a motivating factor for them, as it reinforced the positive benefits of addressing the issue of the marginalization of black men: 'I knew that this was an important piece of work . . . it had to be for Sonny to give up everything to participate in it with Wanda and move to Sheffield' (SRWG).

I met with each RWG member following his agreement to participate in the research. I gave him a copy of the preliminary research proposal and we discussed the broad parameters of the research, the aims and objectives; the time frame and expectation of RWG members. During our bi-monthly meetings from February to August 1993, the HRWG collectively reviewed key themes arising from the literature review; developed the Halifax questionnaire; refined the research proposal; and generated a list of men to be interviewed and to participate in the focus groups. We decided to use multiple data gathering techniques to achieve triangulation of the data. We also built in a series of member checks to reduce the potential for false consciousness. I would interview the RWG members and they would each interview four men from a list they had collectively generated.

My fieldwork in Sheffield began approximately one year after I began the work in Halifax. This involved the establishment of a Sheffield RWG from cold contacts. The same selection criteria was used, with the exception of residency. Members were expected to have been born in England, or to have spent a considerable part of their lives here; to be currently living in Sheffield; and to be black, of African origin.

I had no prior knowledge of black people or black communities in Sheffield. Consequently, I had to rely on referrals from my supervisor, an African colleague at the University, and friends whom I had met on a prior visit to the University of Sheffield in 1992. A snowball sampling method was also used in Sheffield. The merits of the research were positively received by all of the groups we contacted. For some, there was a feeling of 'this is long overdue'. Primarily, people responded to the positive tone of the research, the participant involvement and the action orientation. The result was that we were able to recruit five men to participate in the Sheffield RWG, including my partner Sonny Bernard, who formed an important link between the Halifax and Sheffield RWGs. The research process proved generalizable and transferable. A copy of the research proposal was given to each volunteer, followed by a meeting with him, to explain the research process in greater detail.

The Sheffield RWG met twice a month from January 1994 to June 1994 and completed the following tasks: reviewed preliminary analysis of

Halifax data; revised the Halifax questionnaire; developed the Sheffield questionnaire; conducted their interviews; planned the conference; participated in the comparative analysis of the data and the conference; and commented on the draft conference report. Changes were made to the Halifax questionnaire, taking into account reflections based on the Halifax data analysis and the nuances of the Sheffield population.

I conducted interviews with each of the Sheffield RWG members and trained them to conduct their interviews. Each was asked to conduct three interviews from a list of potential interviewees that they had generated. The interviews were conducted in May–June 1994 in preparation for the joint meeting of the Halifax and Sheffield RWGs which was held in June 1994.

Conducting this research as a doctoral student placed me in a somewhat precarious position. As a black woman doing research with black men, I was an outsider–insider. The potential conflicts, power inbalances and competing role demands were particularly highlighted in defining my role in the RWG. After much dialogue, we agreed that my role would be that of a facilitator. I would arrange the meeting times and location, facilitate discussion and take notes at each meeting. While I attended all meetings, I was not a member of the RWG. In participatory research, the principal researcher is seen as an educator, a motivator, a facilitator (Park *et al.*, 1993). I fulfilled each of these roles in this research project: 'Wanda was able to encourage and motivate us in a way that was positive and not demanding' (HRWG member). 'Wanda you have shown great skill in your ability to work with these men in such a positive, affirming manner and to work within the confines of academia' (African Centred Research Group Member).

## DATA GATHERING

The information was gathered through in-depth individual interviews, using a detailed questionnaire, through focus groups, and at the Sheffield Conference by the RWG members and me. Each of these methods are discussed in some detail below.

### Interviews

I interviewed each of the RWG members and they each interviewed other black men, from a list that they had generated. The RWG members conducted three to five interviews and transcribed them. Each interview was described as an in-depth conversation. A structured questionnaire was used as a means of ensuring some consistency in the data gathered during this phase of the research. Most of the questions asked were open ended, which allowed for more dialogue between the interviewer and interviewee. Most of the interviews were tape-recorded, which facilitated less interruption in the interview for extensive note taking.

## Focus groups

A focus group is a carefully planned discussion designed to obtain perception on a defined area of interest in a permissive, non-threatening environment (Krueger, 1988: 18). Focus groups are used to engage participants in focused discussion of an issue and to produce qualitative data that provide insights into the attitudes, perceptions and opinions of participants (Krueger, 1988: 30). Focus groups are used at several levels in data gathering in this research. The major advantage of using focus groups in data collection is that it allows the researcher to obtain data from a large number of participants in a short time span. Additionally, it enables the researcher to observe interaction between group members. Focus groups enable us to discover the link between individual condition and social position. However, focus groups are not based in natural settings. There is also the potential of participants influencing each other in the focus group, and the issue of possible domination by one or more of the group members. Another factor is the limited control which the researcher has over the discussion and subsequent data which is produced.

The real value in using focus groups in this project was that they served a useful function in data triangulation. This process allowed me to test the focus of the research, the data collected and the analysis for its representatives and generalizability. Lofland and Lofland suggest that group interviewing may be most productive on topics that are reasonably public and have the advantage of allowing people more time to reflect and to recall experiences (Lofland and Lofland, 1984: 14).

Focus groups were used on several levels in my research with black men. The Research Working Groups (RWGs) were focus groups. The Halifax RWG was interviewed as a focus group, using the questionnaire that we had designed, as a field test of the research instrument. Focus groups were held in both sites to discuss the key issues to focus on in the research, to test the questionnaire, to get additional interpretations of the research data, and as a means of member checks regarding the data analysis.

In addition, two focus group sessions were held with a young black men's group in Sheffield called the Black Youth Organization (BYO). This group is comprised of young African-Caribbean men who formed a collective to offer mutual support and to provide a forum for discussion of shared issues, interests, problems and ideas. The first focus group session with them was used as an opportunity to discuss the research, the Halifax findings and the planned conference. This group provided a useful cross-generational analysis of the identified issues and perceived solutions affecting black men. The BYO participated in the Sheffield conference by presenting a play which highlighted some of their identified issues and survival strategies. A follow-up focus group session was held with this group to provide further analysis of the Sheffield data from the conference and interviews. A member of the Sheffield RWG attended each of these focus group sessions.

### The conferences

It is argued that the key in participatory research is involvement of the community in data gathering and analysis. In this research, conferences were organized as a way of involving a wider range of people in the problem definition, analysis and follow-up actions.

The first conference on black men was organized in June 1994, in conjunction with the visit of the Halifax co-researcher audience, building thereby another level of member checks into the research method. The main work was done in ten workshops, which functioned as focus groups and were facilitated primarily by members of the two RWGs and other community resource people. The objective of these workshops was to have a wider community of black men discuss and analyse the issues which impact on their lives; the survival strategies which they have used; their definitions of success; and to engage in discussions about the development of future options which could help create new pathways of opportunities for young black men.

One hundred and twenty people attended the Sheffield conference; the majority of those in attendance were black men. Lather (1991) suggests that the true goals of action/participatory research are self-understanding and self-determination through research participation. This conference, indeed this research, is an indication of how these are actualized. As a result of the conference, a follow-up action group was organized in Sheffield to facilitate the implementation of the conference recommendations.

A second conference was held in Halifax in May 1995, attended by approximately 250 people, 65 per cent of whom were black men, with a programme similar to the Sheffield conference. This three-day event was organized to coincide with a visit to Halifax by the Sheffield RWG members for a second joint RWG meeting and review of the thesis draft. This conference provided an opportunity to discuss some of the issues facing black men with a wider audience and at the closing plenary I presented the principal findings of the research. These findings proved generalizable as they were consistent with the themes that emerged in the workshops.

The conferences allowed for a greater number of black men, black women and allies to engage in the research and potential actions. A limitation, however, is the reality that the use of the 'conference' as a medium inadvertently excluded some men, including some that were interviewed.

Other options should have been explored to ensure that all potential voices were heard. An RWG member put it succinctly:

> I would try and get the people that were interviewed by the RWGs more directly involved . . . these people should be well aware of the contribution that they have made to [this] research project and anonymity could still be maintained. They should be made to feel that they can be part of the solution. By doing this perhaps they would encourage others to become part of the solution as well. (HRWG)

Despite these limitations, the multiple techniques used for data gathering and analysis did enable us to 'get closer to the truth' (Whitemore, 1994).

## DATA ANALYSIS AND INTERPRETATION

I did the initial analysis of the data, picking out the broad themes. These were further analysed by the SRWG, and jointly by the two RWGs. I wrote up the first draft of the research, which was reviewed by the RWGs and discussed at our second joint RWG meeting.

Most proponents of qualitative research advocate for the simultaneous conduct of data collection and data analysis. This type of process is said to produce a better quality analysis. The final stage of data analysis and writing should be a synthesis of all one's ideas.

> Data analysis is the process of bringing order, structure and meaning to the mass of collected data. It is a messy, ambiguous, time-consuming, creative, and fascinating process . . . Qualitative data analysis is a search for general statements about relationships among categories of data; or builds grounded theory. (Marshall and Rossman, 1989: 112)

In this research, I used an inductive approach to the analysis, identifying the salient categories that emerged from the data and developing concepts and categories. Further analysis was done to identify additional patterns and meanings. The focus groups, the conferences and RWGs all served as multiple opportunities to conduct member checks to test the accuracy of the data analysis. Strass and Corbin (1990) postulate that using the grounded theory method, phenomena is discovered, developed and provisionally verified through this process of systematic data collection and data analysis. Triangulation of data collection and data analysis helps to establish trustworthiness, face validity and catalytic validity.

## DISSEMINATION AND USE OF RESEARCH FINDINGS

The results of the research were disseminated at the Halifax conference, in workshops in Sheffield, other major cities in Britain, at conferences throughout Canada, and at local community-based sessions. A summary report on the findings was made available to the black communities in an accessible format. The two conferences were videotaped and the conference proceedings edited. These are available to the communities at cost and can be used in education programmes in both countries. The results have also been of benefit to educators, social workers, policymakers, government, youth workers, in community development and in the development of the black community

## RESEARCH METHODOLOGY AND PROCESS

All research needs to be evaluated and I thought it most appropriate to conduct a participatory evaluation of this research. During the writing up phase of this research I conducted follow-up interviews with each of the RWG members as another means of achieving face validity. I was also interested in having the co-researchers conduct a participatory evaluation (Park, 1993) of the participatory research process. RWG members evaluated the project through individual interviews and HRWG, SRWG and joint RWG meetings.

Learning took place on a number of levels in this research. On a micro level, the RWG members gained skills in conducting research from start to finish. They learned how to construct a questionnaire, draw up a study sample, conduct interviews, data analysis, conference planning, group facilitation and editing. They also experienced individual and collective consciousness raising, about themselves, each other and other black men and women. Through this research they experienced personal and professional development.

On a macro level, two groups of men, from two continents, met, networked, shared experiences of struggle with racism and oppression, survival and success. Change occurred in the two universities, Sheffield and Dalhousie, as a result of this research. Both participated in the respective conferences and new initiatives have resulted at each site. The RWGs formed into an organization at each site and developed follow-up plans in their home locale. Future work will be done in consultation with existing groups, who will determine how best to use the research findings.

A critical question that encouraged me throughout this research was 'who benefits?', as I wanted to engage in work that would benefit the black community in some way. Participatory research has two objects: to produce knowledge and action directly useful to a community; and consciousness raising or conscientization, to empower people through the process of constructing and using their own knowledge, for their own benefit (Reason, 1994). It is empowering to see that the process has worked; the black community has already benefited from this work, as have black men and women, white allies, academics and educators. Many others benefited as the results were disseminated more widely.

All RWG members named the opportunity to come together as a group, and later as two groups, to talk about common issues and share experiences as the most significant part of the research process. They stated that they felt included in the entire process; they owned the research and they gained a sense of individual and collective empowerment as a result of having participated:

> That we got together as a group to talk about issues . . . that we did not feel like an object, a passive object of the research, but like people. This was valid interaction where we found out things about ourselves that we had in common, and things that needed further study . . . This got people talking about their innermost feelings. It was very useful. [The research] was conducted in an atmosphere of comradeship . . . these are friends, not research abstracts . . . serious, but also able to enjoy because of the lighter side, like coming together that night at Darcy's . . . that was really good. (SRWG)

> I enjoyed working as a group in an ongoing way. Research participation usually involves a one or two hour interview, with no feedback . . . the fact that we have linked as two distinct groups, plus come together on two occasions is good . . . I have a feel for people involved on the other side, have got to know them on a personal level, and have an understanding of the issues. One of the highlights for me is the high level of commitment in the group; everyone attending meetings and doing the work! This encourages you to participate. I also liked the opportunity to speak to other people on the [PhD] course, being given the opportunity to participate in the academic circle. (SRWG)

These views are consistent with my evaluation that the process has facilitated both personal and professional development. When asked what they would change if participating in similar work in the future, most stated that they would change nothing. Two members said they would be more active in the entire research process, others stated they would work harder at fund raising. One RWG member stated he would try to get those who were interviewed more involved in other aspects of the research. Finally, one participant stated that he would deal with some of those more sensitive issues, such as homosexuality, and interracial relationships, and ensure that really experienced facilitators led workshops on topics such as these:

> I would try and make sure that those sensitive issues were handled by people who were really experienced . . . this research got us talking about some tough issues, now we need to take it further. (SRWG)

This assessment of things to be changed in future work is evidence of the type of learning that has occurred for individual RWG members during the research process. Education is one of the goals of participatory research and through this participatory evaluation I asked the RWG members to name their most significant learning. Most named the experience gained from learning about each other's experiences, and those of black men and black people more generally in two countries. The collective consciousness about the survival strategies and the redefinition of success was significant for all participants. A common theme in the biographies of the RWG members is their involvement in community. However, through this research most became more determined to engage in action strategies to deal specifically with the issues affecting black men. Finally, for some members of the group, involvement in this work has helped to inspire them to return to further and higher education; four members are currently enrolled in programmes.

> I learned that black men and all black people continue to face deep struggles to become successful. [This] has opened my eyes even more to the injustices we face and the fact that there is a great need for us [black people] to work together. (HRWG)

> Through this research I have gained a better understanding and empathy for those black men who do not survive . . . and I am more determined to do something to help them. (HRWG)

The RWG members have all stressed that one of the most positive, and unanticipated outcomes of the research was the opportunity to talk to other men about their own feelings, issues and experiences of struggle, survival and success, as self-defined.

## AFTERTHOUGHTS

Maguire (1993) says that researchers should get involved in a problem that they feel passionately about. I have argued that it is not only important to feel passionate about a problem, but one must be willing to use one's skills and resources actually to do something about that which you feel so passionately (Bernard, 1996). My lived experiences as an African Canadian woman influenced my choice of research topic and my commitment to social action and change underpins my choice of methodology. My goal was not simply to do research on black men's experiences, but to work with black men and engage others in a process that would facilitate change. The participatory research methodology clearly enabled me to do this. Those who participated in the research have been personally empowered to do and to act; they gained knowledge, information and experience that has led to action. The Sheffield and Halifax conferences and the focus groups brought larger groups together at each site, many of whom have expressed a desire and willingness to be part of the solution to their identified problems.

The participatory evaluation of the research supports the theory that research, knowledge and education can lead to action. This research model could be called emancipatory research, or research for empowerment. Change took place during the research process and other changes will happen as black men come together with black women and other allies to plan strategies that will enable black men and black communities to survive and succeed. A non-participatory research methodology would not have mobilized so many people in such a short time span. Participants' evaluations of the two conferences are a good indication of the value and significance of this research methodology, particularly its ability to empower those normally studied.

> As the mother of four sons, I've been encouraged to do and to act. Thank you for an enlightening conference, and the opportunity to spend time talking about black men in a positive light. (Halifax conference evaluation)

Attending to process is one of the most important aspects of participatory research (Whitemore, 1994). We created an open, direct system of communication in this research which helped to facilitate the process. Challenged both by my status as an insider–outsider and doing this work as a doctoral student, I had to pay careful attention to the ethical dilemmas and the potential for power imbalance and conflicting demands. Some of the methods and time lines that were necessary to fit the academic requirements may have limited the scope of the work which we were able to do. The lack of funds to do follow-up work and the absence of an organizational structure or support was an obstacle that did not receive enough attention. My location in Halifax enables me to get closer to the ongoing work of the participants, but there is no support for maintaining the contact cross-nationally.

The RWG members each conducted interviews, transcribed them and gave them to me for initial analysis. Some information was undoubtedly lost through the transcription process. A useful follow-up exercise might be a series of in-depth case studies based on this research material. More connection should have been made between those interviewed and conference participation. According to one HRWG member, many who were interviewed did not attend the Halifax conference, citing the thirty-dollar registration fee as a contributing factor. These men could have been invited to participate at no fee, as was the case at the Sheffield conference. The time span may have been a contributing factor, as the Halifax interviews were conducted in 1993, with the conference in 1995; whereas most of the Sheffield work was completed in 1994.

Despite the limitations, this model allows the researcher to tap into the real-life experiences of those who are the subjects of the research. Through sharing and collectivizing those experiences, participants were enriched, encouraged and empowered to take charge of their own lives and to do something about the issue being studied. The model provides opportunity for the acknowledgement of 'first voice' experiences and facilitates the visibility of those normally outside the mainstream. The active involvement of participants in problem posing and problem solving ensures the continuation of work initiated through the research. In this model power rests with the researched, not the researcher. Social work skills such as group facilitation, communication, understanding group dynamics, an analysis of oppression and a commitment to the empowerment of others (Whitemore, 1994) were particularly useful in the conduct of this research.


## THE CHALLENGE IN DOING PARTICIPATORY RESEARCH FOR ACADEMIC CREDIT

When considering the use of participatory methodology, the central issues to be addressed are time and costs. Participatory research is very time consuming and a very lengthy process (Maguire, 1987; Park *et al.*, 1993, Reason, 1988b, c). Frequently used with marginalized groups, the issue of availability of resources is a constant worry and threat to the research. What funds are made available for this type of emancipatory research and from where? Whitemore (1994: 97) argues that participatory research requires more time, as one is required to go beyond the immediate task, particularly when working with groups that are marginalized from the mainstream.

Also an issue is the question of validity, which has been the subject of much debate. Rooted in the positivist paradigm, the notion of validity is difficult to discuss in the context of participatory research, because as a holistic and evolving process it becomes difficult to deal with in all phases of the research. The actual process of establishing the validity of participatory research must also be participatory, taking the form of participatory evaluation (Park, 1993: 17), which I attempted to employ in this research. The conclusions of co-operative inquiry are valid if they have the quality of being well founded on the experiences of the co-researchers as co-subjects. The coherence of the conclusions is also a criterion of validity. A central skill required to achieve validity in co-operative inquiry is the bracketing procedure. This bracketing allows for the suspension of the concepts and categories and interaction of ideas in the research, experience and presentation.

Building on the work on validity done by Reason and Rowan (1981) on the 'objectively subjective' inquiry and Guba and Lincoln (1981) on the three techniques for assessing validity: triangulation, reflexivity and member checks, Lather (1991) presents four validity requirements for action-oriented, emancipatory research:

1   *Triangulation*: critical in establishing data trustworthiness, moving beyond multiple measures, to include counter patterns and divergence.
2   *Construct validity*: operate within a conscious context of theory building. Systemized reflectivity must reveal how *a priori* theory has been changed by the logic of the data.

3  *Face validity*: recycling description, emerging analysis and conclusions back through at least a sub-sample of respondents; acknowledge potential of the notion of false consciousness to limit the usefulness of member checks.

4  *Catalytic validity*: represents the degree in which the research process reorients, focuses and energizes participants toward knowing reality in order to transform it, a process Freire (1972) called conscientization. (Lather, 1991: 65–69)

I utilized Lather's (1991) validity techniques in this research to help increase the legitimacy of the knowledge that was produced. Triangulation and face validity were achieved through the use of focus groups at each site, the Sheffield conference and the consultations with the RWGs regarding data gathering and analysis. Face validity was also achieved through presentation of the findings at the Halifax conference. A reflexive account of the findings was reflected in the analysis to achieve construct validity. The planned actions emerging from the research and those that occurred during the process are evidence of catalytic validity.

Whitemore (1994) questions the notion of 'truth' or validity and argues that the quest for truth is challenged by barriers such as 'race', gender, class and culture, and should not be ignored. Simple matching on any one of these, in my instance 'race', cannot overcome these barriers; they can never be eradicated entirely. However, a participatory process can help to permeate and reduce the effect they have on achieving 'truth'.

The research was managed and directed by the RWG members; they decided which issues to cover, based on their own experiences. The RWG members were selected based on criteria that I had set out in the research proposal. They used the same criteria to select other black men to interview. The fact that the men interviewed men whom they knew could be interpreted as an ability to get closer to the truth, to further our understandings of the issue under study. However, this may also be interpreted as interviewer influence regarding how questions were asked and the emphasis on certain issues, based on their own experience of survival. We tried to deal with this in the research through the training, piloting and the structured questionnaire. There were times during the data analysis when I questioned the meaning of certain statements, and if conducting the interview myself would probably have probed to get clarification. However, in participatory research the researcher has to be prepared to have the process directed by the participants themselves.

Participatory research stimulates self-reliance, raises consciousness and affirms the knowledge that people have about their own experience. This work contributes to the existing body of knowledge about participatory research, as it challenges both the androcentric bias (Maguire, 1987) and the Eurocentric bias. It is evidence of an inclusive research methodology that does empower those normally excluded from decision making in research.

As an Africentric feminist, I am concerned about the oppression of all people and I was concerned that my doctoral research project should be research for empowerment. I had to be aware of my own baggage and how this would influence my work with these men. My insider–outsider status enabled me to understand 'race' oppression, from a location of experience, but I had to be open to understanding the different location of the black male experience. Through this research, the participants and I have become empowered to assume responsibility to transform not only ourselves, but to help create positive change in the structures of society. Collins (1990) believes that knowledge is essential to the empowerment of oppressed people, and that knowledge is about individual and collective consciousness, which can lead to social change.

This research has implications for academia. It challenges traditional Eurocentric perspectives and argues that an Africanist approach is more holistic and inclusive. It brings participatory research into mainstream academia, whereas this methodology has traditionally been marginalized (Hall, 1993), developed mainly to third world countries and in community-based research. Maguire addresses the problem of doing participatory research with historically marginalized people within the confines of academia, particularly for PhD students (Maguire, 1993). Issues of ownership, power and decision making are crucial and must be addressed by the co-researchers.

There are also standards and procedures for doctoral research set by the university that are totally outside the student's control. For example, PhD research is expected to be an individual piece of work. However, participatory research calls for the active involvement of participants (Maguire, 1987, 1993; Park et al., 1993; Reason, 1988a). It presents a challenge to PhD students to reconcile these conflicting expectations. In this research I have taken full responsibility for the writing, but the RWG members controlled what was written. They reviewed the thesis draft. Their comments were shared in joint and separate meetings, individual sessions and in writing. These were reflected in the final thesis.

These are some of the barriers that I have had to overcome in developing a truly authentic collaborative, participatory research methodology. The proponents of this approach will need courage of conviction, personal strength, persistence, assertiveness and a determination to work towards the goal of liberation. We will also need support. Effectively to challenge structural oppression, we need to work collaboratively (hooks, 1984) and reconceptualize the definition of power.

I began this research with a desire to bridge the gap between academia and community and to engage in work that was going to be of direct benefit to African communities. This research is evidence of our ability to establish powerful links between academia and the community. It is a good example of empowerment, where the tools of academia have been effectively shared with a marginalized community; where the traditional power of the researcher has been completely transformed. Using participatory research in this way forges links between academia and community, linking community need with academic resources. Such an approach encourages academia to be more responsive to communities who want and need research that will be of direct benefit to enhancing their knowledge and hence their power base. It should facilitate a meaningful exchange between academia and the community.

The research has empowered many who have participated to engage in future action that will help to liberate black men, black women and black communities. As an Africentric feminist I do believe that there is power to act individually and collectively (Collins, 1990). However, I feel that what is often lacking is awareness and a critical analysis of the issues and necessary action. This research is a model that can be used by others to help communities engage in a process that will enable them to create self-awareness, collective consciousness and develop strategies for change. As a tool for emancipation, participatory research is one way to engage people in a process that aims to challenge oppressive structures that define and control their lives.

# 14 THE USE OF FOCUS GROUPS IN SOCIAL SCIENCE RESEARCH

## Caroline Oates

In the social sciences, the focus group is becoming an increasingly frequent technique for interviewing research participants, but despite this recent popularity, there is some uncertainty about what the term 'focus group' actually means. There are several books devoted to the definition, use and analysis of focus groups (Morgan, 1988, 1993; Stewart and Shamdasani, 1990), yet the term remains vague and is often used interchangeably with others such as 'group discussions' or 'group depth interviews'. This chapter will identify the key characteristics of focus groups, consider their appropriate uses and illustrate their application with an example from research on readers of women's magazines in the UK. The chapter will then conclude with a discussion of the advantages and disadvantages of using focus groups.

## WHAT IS A FOCUS GROUP?

Focus groups have been used by market researchers since the 1920s (Basch, 1987) and by social scientists since the 1940s. Merton was the first to use this technique in his research on the public's reaction to morale films during World War II and he coined the phrase 'the focussed interview' (Merton and Kendall, 1955). Since their original use by Merton, focus groups have become widely used. Thus, there is some confusion as to the nature of a focus group and how it is distinguished from other methods of group interviewing. Kitzinger (1994: 103) has defined focus groups as 'group discussions organised to explore a specific set of issues such as people's views and experiences of contraception, drink driving, nutrition or mental illness'. The group is focused in the sense that it involves some kind of collective activity such as viewing a film (as in Merton's original research), examining a health education message or reading magazines. But what distinguishes the focus group technique from the wider range of group interviews is 'the explicit use of the group interaction as research data' (Kitzinger, 1994: 103). Thus, although focus groups can provide insight into the experiences of individual participants, their value lies in the opportunity to analyse the interaction between participants (Catterall and Maclaran, 1997). This is the key to focus group research and what makes it such an insightful technique. As Morgan suggests, 'focus groups are useful when it comes to investigating *what* participants think, but they excel at uncovering *why* participants think as they do' (Morgan, 1988: 25). Focus groups can achieve this because the participants not only articulate their views and experiences about a particular topic, but also explain to the other members of the group why they hold those views. Such interaction occurs as participants question each other, or challenge views which might differ from their own. Participants are obliged to expose the reasoning behind their own opinions, allowing the researcher to explore and record such interaction. As participants think and reason out loud, their changing attitudes within the context of the group can be documented (Catterall and Maclaran, 1997). Not only do focus groups provide space for interaction between participants, but they also allow the researcher to access sites of 'collective remembering' (Kitzinger, 1994: 105). By using preformed groups (a practice discouraged by market research manuals but common in academic research), Kitzinger explored how people talked about AIDS within the various overlapping groups in which they normally operate. The advantage of using participants who knew each other meant that friends or colleagues were able to relate comments made in the focus group to events in their everyday, shared lives. Thus, Kitzinger was able to tap into fragments of interactions which resembled naturally occurring data. Further, using pre-existing groups is appropriate because groups form a social context in which ideas are nurtured and decisions made. However, it must be remembered that focus groups are artificial situations and therefore the data is not completely natural – the groups are deliberately constructed for the purpose of gathering data. A focus group is more than a group interview or discussion because of the *community of interest* shared by the group and the use of *participants' interaction* as research data.

## WHEN SHOULD FOCUS GROUPS BE USED?

Although focus groups can be used to produce quantitative data (for example, they can be systematically coded via content analysis; see Stewart and Shamdasani, 1990; Lunt and Livingstone, 1996), they are almost always used to collect qualitative data. This is one of the strengths of focus groups – their production of rich data in the participants' own words. But this can also be seen as a failing of focus groups in their inability to yield hard data. There are also concerns over representativeness. However, all techniques of data collection have their limitations and the key to using focus groups successfully is to ensure they are consistent with the objectives and purpose of the research. According to Kitzinger (1994), focus groups are invaluable for grounded theory development, that is focusing on the generation rather than the testing of theory and exploring the categories which participants use to order their experiences. Focus groups put the emphasis on the participants' ways of understanding, their language and what they feel is important. Focus groups can also be used with sensitive topics, although not all writers would agree. Kitzinger (1994) suggests focus groups are appropriate for discussing issues like AIDS because they provide safety in numbers and the company of others who share similar experiences. Schlesinger *et al.* (1992) used focus groups with women to explore issues around films and violence. Focus groups can also be used with populations that may be seen as particularly sensitive: for example, Buckingham (1987) held focus groups with children to explore the meanings in the television soap opera *EastEnders*. Therefore, they can be used for a variety of purposes and with different populations.

Focus groups can be used alone or combined with other methods. Lunt and Livingstone (1996) suggest that the use of focus groups as a self-contained method is becoming more frequent in the social sciences. However, focus groups can be combined with other sources of data in the triangulation method, where different forms of data on the same topic are collected. For example, Radway (1987) used focus groups and individual interviews together in a wider research study to inform her of how women read and use romantic fiction. Jackson and Holbrook (1995) utilized a number of different methods in their research design, including focus groups, and discuss how these methods worked in their study of shopping and identity. Thus, focus groups can be used without additional methods or can be part of a wider research study. Stewart and Shamdasani (1990) sum up the more common uses of focus groups:

1   Learning how respondents talk about the topic of interest.
2   Generating research hypotheses that can be submitted to further research and testing.
3   Stimulating new ideas.
4   Diagnosing the potential for problems with a new service or programme.
5   Obtaining general background information about a topic of interest.
6   Interpreting previously obtained quantitative results.


## FOCUS GROUPS IN PRACTICE

In this section, I shall discuss my own research using focus groups. This will raise several questions about the practical issues involved in the focus group method and how they might be resolved in relation to other research. This section should also enable readers to judge whether the focus group approach is appropriate for their own research projects.

## Background

The focus groups used in my study were part of a research project investigating women's use of certain weekly magazines. During the 1980s the previously staid domestic women's magazine market had been transformed by the launch of three new titles, *Prima*, *Best* and *Bella*, all owned by German publishers. A fourth title was added to the list in 1990 when *Take a Break* was launched. These four magazines were an immediate success and spurred British publishers like International Publishing Corporation (IPC) to respond by creating new magazines to compete. In addition, existing titles were given an overhaul to bring them up to date and the tactics used by the German publishers were imitated by the British. As a result, the weekly women's magazine market became more homogeneous as other titles copied the style and content of *Best*, *Bella* and *Take a Break*.

At the same time as the revolution in the magazine market, the academic approach to popular culture was undergoing change. Notions of the audience were beginning to be problematized. Rather than investigating the content of media forms and then inferring an ideal reader, writers like Morley (1980) had begun to explore the audience itself, looking at how readers/viewers responded to media messages. From the idea of a passive audience, which had been the accepted paradigm, came the idea of an active, critical, knowing audience, opening the way for studies on how people watched *Nationwide* (Morley, 1980) or read teenage magazines like *Jackie* (Frazer, 1992). This change in audience perception, combined with the new magazines and the changing role of women in society, prompted a sociological analysis of how women were reading and using *Best*, *Bella* and *Take a Break*, and whether the magazines could be identified in any way with the backlash against feminism concept (Faludi, 1991).

Given my research topic, it was appropriate to consider focus groups as a means of gathering data. Women read magazines in various social locations, as well as at home and because they discuss magazines with friends or colleagues, interviewing in a group situation seemed particularly suitable. Previous research on women's magazines had focused on the content. My intention was to explore the reading of magazines and how women made sense of them. The interaction between participants would be valuable and the research would take a different approach from previous studies.

## Access

One of the main problems in choosing the focus group method is the question of access – and this brings further associated problems:

- Where do you find your target population?
- How many groups do you need?

- How many people should be in each group?
- Should you use new or preformed groups?
- Does the composition of the groups matter?
- What location would be best for the group?
- Should you tape-record the group?
- Should you use questionnaires in conjunction with the focus group?

Having gradually realized that all these issues needed to be dealt with, it became clear why nobody had used focus groups in an academic research project with magazine readers before (although the magazines do have their own, very thorough research agendas which are conducted by market researchers using focus groups). The chief obstacle was access. Although millions of women read *Best*, *Bella* and *Take a Break*, there were no obvious means of contacting any of them. My uncertainty about how to access and then use focus groups was by no means unusual. Because previous researchers have rarely described their methodology, it was difficult to find others' experiences of using focus groups. Recently, there has been recognition of this omission and writers such as Holbrook and Jackson (1996) have detailed their own difficulties and uncertainties about using focus groups.

After having worked my way through several possible options, I decided to approach women I knew from my previous jobs in schools and a bank. This would mean using pre-existing groups, but I felt this would be an advantage when discussing magazines, because the intention was to access the everyday and taken-for-granted uses of magazines between readers. Using existing friendship networks seemed to be an ideal way to tap into the normal routines and uses of women's magazine reading. In her recent book on magazine readers, Hermes (1995) used not only friends but family for her interviews. Therefore, previous studies have used people known to the researcher, but this should not be allowed to restrict the sample if diversity is required. A recognized option is to start with friends or colleagues and then snowball to unknown others. (Snowball sampling is discussed more fully by Burton in Chapter 21.) Once all my existing networks had been utilized I snowballed to related groups, for example, playgroups and mother and toddler groups, via my original contacts.

### Size and number of focus groups

When the access issue had been resolved, the number of focus groups required and how many people should be in each had to be arranged. In a sense, the latter question was already decided. Although it is suggested that the ideal number for a group is between eight and twelve (Stewart and Shamdasani, 1990), there may be little choice for the researcher. Given that I was returning to old workplaces, I really had to accept however many women happened to be in the staffroom at the time. Fortunately, there always seemed to be an appropriate number, and if there were too many it was possible to split them into two groups. For example, a local playgroup held their meetings in a small room which was adjacent to the church hall, so it was feasible to carry out two focus groups in succession. Carrying out the focus groups led to the conclusion that the recommended size of between eight and twelve members for each group is too high – a more manageable number is between six and ten.

The number of focus groups needed depends on the required amount of diversity among participants and the use of different locations. Knowing that women's magazines are read in a variety of situations, I felt it would be informative to conduct focus groups both at work and at leisure, and also with readers of different ages and backgrounds. It was a case of covering a wide range of readers with different characteristics. Knodel (1993) has formalized this process of difference by suggesting that groups be organized according to *break* and *control* characteristics. Control characteristics are common to all groups, and break characteristics differentiate groups from each other. Thus, for my research, all group members had the common characteristic of being women and also readers of women's magazines, but break characteristics included age and family position. Incorporating break characteristics into the research design is necessary for contrasting views between subgroups and also for establishing common views.

A useful means of deciding how many focus groups to run is suggested by Lunt and Livingstone (1996) who advise that the researcher should continue to run new groups until the last group has nothing to add, but simply repeats previous contributions. For my own study, I found that fourteen focus groups were appropriate.

### Researcher as interviewer

Before returning to the schools and bank, I had written to or contacted colleagues to explain my research and ask permission to carry out a focus group. Having received permission, I prepared a schedule of questions or topic areas to ask in the group. This schedule needs careful preparation and the role of the researcher in leading the discussion has to be acknowledged. The researcher provides the agenda for discussion by virtue of her role in the group. Participants look to the researcher (or moderator) for direction, particularly at the beginning of the focus group. When the researcher suggests a new topic or area by asking a certain question, the group tends to comply. It is up to the researcher to decide how much she wants to direct the group and she needs to be flexible with the interview schedule. Some groups need little direction after the discussion has started, while others need frequent questions. It depends on whether the researcher has specific information needs or whether the aim is to learn about what the group thinks is important. These issues will be determined by the broader research agenda and the information required. At the very least a list of topic areas is recommended, which serves two purposes: it helps to reduce the researcher's nervousness, particularly in the first few groups; and it gives a broad outline to the discussion, preventing it from straying into unrelated areas.

### Location of the focus group

Choosing the location for focus groups can be quite a problem. In many of the books about focus groups, it is assumed that there will be money to pay for the hire of a room which is specially designed for hosting focus groups. This is unrealistic for many researchers and there may be little choice in location. The focus groups I carried out in the workplace usually took place in the staffroom of the bank or schools, and those in leisure situations had to be in any available room. Sometimes shortage of quiet space posed problems, particularly in the mother and toddler groups. The lack of a quiet, separate room meant that the women were constantly interrupted by their children and the noise level was high. The focus groups carried out in these groups tended to be much shorter than any of the other focus groups. The average time is usually between one hour and an hour and a half, but the shorter ones lasted for thirty minutes only. Therefore, it is important to check before finalizing a potential focus group that there will be a suitable space which is quiet. Otherwise the level of recording may be too poor to allow for the tape to be transcribed.

### Use of materials

As suggested earlier, one of the defining characteristics of a focus group is its use of materials to facilitate discussion and interaction between participants. I used *Bella*, *Best* and *Take a Break* for this purpose, with a number of similar weeklies included for comparison and articulation of difference between titles.The same magazine issues were used for every focus group, thus allowing potential analysis of both similarities and differences between groups in relation to the same stories or articles. Having the magazines there served further purposes in addition to facilitating interactive discussion. At the beginning of the group, members sometimes felt self-conscious about voicing their opinions and so the magazines 'broke the ice' as the women looked through them together or recalled certain issues they had already seen. If some women were familiar with only one or two of the titles, it was an opportunity for other members of the group to explain why they liked the magazines. At any awkward moments when conversation tailed off or began to drift into other unrelated topics, the magazines could be used to draw attention back to the relevant topic. Kitzinger (1994) noted that use of card games or vignettes served to 'warm up' participants, encouraging them to engage with one another, but this has the disadvantage that some people do not like such games and might be made to feel uncomfortable. The advantage of using magazines was the familiarity of them to participants and the instant shared reference points of being a *Take a Breakie* or a *Best* or *Bella* fan.

### Group dynamics

Each focus group has its own dynamics and it is difficult to predict how the members will interact. Carrying out two focus groups, one after the other, at a mother and toddler group, illustrated how similar groups may differ. The first group was vocal, interested and lively, with many new points about magazines I had not considered. Yet the second group was quiet, unenthusiastic and not very interested in the magazines they read. Both kinds of groups can present problems to the researcher: the first kind because there is often a dominant member who tries to take over the conversation, or because the conversation is so fast and loud that it is difficult to keep track of people's comments and explore interesting points which may arise; the second because the researcher has to work that much harder, and impose more of her own agenda onto the discussion.

Reading theoretical books about focus groups gives the novice researcher the impression that all groups run smoothly, with well-modulated conversations and polite members taking it in turns to speak. The reality is very different. There will be times when the tape is untranscribable because of the number of people talking at the same time, or because two people at the other end of the table are having their own private conversation. Running a focus group takes practice. There is a fine line between letting people have their say, allowing the discussion to degenerate into an incomprehensible noise, or being so in control that there is no interaction whatsoever between the participants. It is advisable to have one or two practice sessions first with friends, just to get the feel of knowing when to speak or how to prevent one person from dominating the discussion.

### Recording the focus group

The use of tape recorders in recording the focus group discussions has already been mentioned and I suggest that these are essential (but see Chapter 22 for an alternative view of recording). All my focus groups were taped as it is impossible to take notes as well as moderate a group, and this is also distracting for the participants. A small recorder, placed discreetly in the middle of the table, is soon forgotten after the first few nervous comments and it leaves the researcher free to concentrate on the interaction. It also means the researcher can quote verbatim from participants when writing up the research.

This latter point introduces the issue of confidentiality. Permission has to be obtained from the group before taping and it has to be explained that the outcome of the research might be published. The use of pseudonyms for group members is essential, but to ensure the participants can be identified on the tape when transcribing, it is useful to get each person to state their name at the beginning of the discussion. This also helps the moderator in addressing participants and gets the conversation going. It is helpful to transcribe the tapes as quickly as possible after doing each focus group and also to write brief notes after the groups about the discussion or any particular comments which were unusual. Morgan (1988: 63) calls these 'field notes' and suggests they are an essential element of focus groups because they are both part of the data collection and a preliminary form of analysis.

### Use of questionnaires

In my research project, I designed a questionnaire to elicit both personal details and details about the participants' reading habits and use of other media in addition to women's magazines. The purpose of this information was to allow comparisons between participants according to their different characteristics (for example, to see if women without children read magazines differently to those with a family). Where possible, these were given out before the focus groups were held so that participants would have time to think a little about the magazines they read. The use of these questionnaires became rather haphazard. Sometimes they were administered before the focus group, sometimes afterwards and in one group some of the women had reading and writing difficulties and the questionnaires had to be abandoned altogether. Thus, use of questionnaires to acquire background details, while useful for identifying participants' age, occupation and marital status, needs to be organized within the research design, where the relevance of participants' characteristics should be decided. Being consistent and always distributing the questionnaires before the focus group begins is the most advantageous strategy, as this helps the participants to start thinking about the topic (although the questionnaires should not be too long as participants may lose interest). For a discussion of the most appropriate way to use questionnaires in focus group research, see Morgan (1988).

### SUMMARY OF ADVANTAGES AND DISADVANTAGES OF FOCUS GROUPS

### Advantages

1   Participants can react to and build on the responses of other group members.
2   Focus groups allow the researcher to interact directly with respondents.

3   They allow the researcher to obtain rich data in the participants' own words.
4   They provide data from a group of people more quickly than interviewing individuals.
5   Focus groups are flexible in their suitability for investigating a wide range of topics.
6   They are suitable for use with children.
7   The results of a focus group are accessible and understandable.

## Disadvantages

1   The small number of respondents limit generalization to the wider population.
2   The results may be biased by a particularly dominant group member.
3   The open-ended nature of responses may make interpreting results difficult.
4   The researcher as interviewer may influence the responses of the group members.

(Adapted from Stewart and Shamdasani, 1990)

## CONCLUSION

Focus groups are a rich source of qualitative data for the social science researcher and as such are an attractive and popular method of data collection. But they are not particularly easy to use. The researcher needs to have means of access to willing participants and also to have the skills to interview and moderate those participants. This chapter has raised some of the issues involved in using focus groups as a research method and has discussed some of the main advantages and disadvantages. As with any issues in social sciences, there are no right or wrong ways of doing focus groups. It is up to the individual researcher to design their own study and to use focus groups appropriately. Clearly, they are better suited to certain kinds of research questions than others. This chapter should have helped to explain when focus groups are most useful and whether they should be incorporated into the researcher's own design.

# 15 QUALITATIVE INTERVIEWING

*Matt Stroh*

The purpose of this chapter is to raise the pertinent issues that should be addressed when considering qualitative interviewing in a research methodology. It is important that the research is well planned for it to be effective. For example, it is important to know what sort of data interviews produce and, from that, the ways in which qualitative interview material can or cannot be used to generalize findings. With the relatively small number of interviewees that will be able to be interviewed within the constraints of a single research project, the choice of participants needs care. Other elements of planning require the researcher to devise and test an effective interview schedule and also require the researcher to be fully aware of their own impact on the direction of the research conducted.

Each of these topics is potentially huge, so there will only be space here to introduce the key issues of each. There are an increasing number of texts offering advice to the interviewer, though few cover all of the topics addressed here. Noteable exceptions are Cook and Crang (1995) and Valentine (1997) who provide a useful overview of the practicalities of interviewing, but say little about analysing interview data, although this is covered by Crang in the same publication. Initially, though, I will outline the key differences between a qualitative interviewing approach and a questionnaire survey methodology.

## QUESTIONNAIRE VS. INTERVIEW

Interviewing is a research strategy that aims to move away from fixed answer questions. The difference between an interview approach and a questionnaire approach can be seen by drawing on examples from my PhD research. The thesis 'Social Constructions of Green: Accessing Popular Attitudes Towards the Environment', aimed to explore public perceptions of the environment and green issues and stressed the importance of exploring and including public interpretations in environmental policy. These ideas are resonant with Macnaghten and Jacobs (1997) who argued that there has to be a resonance between political discourse and the lay perception of 'sustainable development'. Their research suggested that what they term 'political salience' is needed for people to want to act pro-environmentally:

In the debates surrounding the meaning and policy implications of sustainable development, the question of its political salience has been remarkably neglected. Do voters actually support it? Of course the lack of a clear policy programme makes the strict notion of 'support' premature. The issue is more meaningfully expressed therefore in terms of whether the public *identify* with the concept of sustainable development and the analysis underlying it. (Macnaghten and Jacobs, 1997: 5; original emphasis)

There was a need for a methodological approach that could go some way toward remedying the neglect of an exploration of salience. A qualitative methodology can explore the 'actor's definition' and 'how people act [which gives] meaning to their own lives' (Eyles, 1989: 207). This allowed for a project that could access understandings and interpretations of 'actors', members of the public, within the specific context of constructions of green. Indeed, an objective of qualitative methods is to access the 'world' in the terms of those people being researched. This was a necessity in my research and I would advocate more qualitative research in policy evaluation (see Löfstedt, 1995). An important step toward achieving the required salience is a good understanding of lay (i.e. general public) perceptions and attitudes.

In order to explore these perceptions to question whether the public identified with sustainable development and environmental issues more generally, a questionnaire survey could have been conducted. However, 'questionnaires are . . . usually standardised; they are not tailored to individuals' circumstances' (Valentine, 1997: 110). They lack the sensitivity to be able to explore difference, inconsistency and, often, meaning and argument. A questionnaire has other strengths though. A questionnaire would have been able to explore a large number of people's views, but the depth of research would have been limited as a result of its inherently standardized approach. For example, to begin to understand whether the public identify with environmental issues, it is vital to explore what they understand by the environment and what they see themselves as doing to be pro-environmental. A questionnaire could have had a series of open-ended question such as:

- What do you understand by the word 'environment'?
- What do you do to be pro-environmental?
- And how often?
  Daily/weekly/monthly/less often/never?

While providing some of what I needed, the approach would not have allowed me to follow up immediately people's responses and to explore the contradictions and inconsistencies that are part of everyday life. For example, a number of respondents talked of their concern for recycling, which would probably have emerged from the questions posed above. Some participants were avid recyclers, but nearly all drove a car, even when public transport was a realistic alternative option, and did not practise ethical or green consumerism. In some aspects, then, these people could be categorized as pro-environmental, but this has to be balanced against less positive behaviours and attitudes in other spheres which only became apparent during the interviews. Very early in the project it became clear that these inconsistencies were going to be very common. They make it nearly impossible to classify any one of the respondents, and all of the respondents showed some degree of inconsistency. A questionnaire would have been less likely to identify these inconsistencies and certainly would give little scope for discussing them with each of the respondents in the depth provided by an interview-based technique. Valentine considers the problem of questionnaires:

> The tendency of questionnaires surveys to ask a rigid set of simple questions which 'force' or push the respondents' answers into particular categories, which they may not have thought of unprompted or many not want to use, is just one of the reasons why researchers often choose to use interviews either as a supplement or as an alternative to a questionnaire survey. (Valentine, 1997: 110)

To use my example above, it may be that people only recycled certain products: glass bottles, aluminium cans or newspapers. They would be hard pressed to fit inconsistent behaviour within a simplified categorization of behaviour:

> Well, I recycle newspapers nearly everyday inasmuch as I keep them, and take them to the recycle bins every month. But with aluminium cans, we've got a thing at work where I can drop them off as I finish them. I didn't realise you could recycle tin cans, perhaps I should look into that. And I suppose I don't recycle plastic bottles, but that's because we try to avoid them wherever we can.

This respondent recycles variously, daily and never, which would make a typology of his behaviour difficult, and he would face difficulty ticking a single box to represent his recycling behaviour. It is good that he recycles as much as he does, but less good, on the face of it, that he never recycles tin cans or plastic bottles – except that from this interview material it is easy to see why. This 'why', his justification, is vital to the understanding of this interviewee. If the answers had been given in a questionnaire, only a narrowly focused snapshot of his behaviour would have been available and a very different conclusion about his level of pro-environmental behaviour would have been drawn.

This is the key advantage of interviews over a questionnaire approach. Interviews will provide answers to the 'why' questions rather than just the 'how many' or the 'how often' of this example. Interviews aim to be a conversation which explores an issue with a participant, rather than to test knowledge or simply categorize. Thus, the two approaches can answer different research questions. In a study of the development of a new recycling centre, it would be important to know how many people recycle in order to assess the appropriate size of centre and the facility required. Therefore a quantitative survey would probably be the most useful. If the project is more interested in exploring why people do or do not recycle or, as in my project, what people understand by pro-environmental behaviour in general, a qualitative interview approach will be far more apt. The uses of interviews in various research projects are now widespread and widely accepted: 'Interviews are used so extensively by sociologists that Benny and Hughes have referred to modern sociology as "the science of the interview"' (Burgess, 1991: 101).

There are a number different research tools that fall under the interviewing banner which are all useful in different situations:

1   *Focus group interviews* in which a number of people are interviewed simultaneously. Group interviews are very interesting because they provide an opportunity to work with a group of people's ideas and can lead to interesting discussion between participants. However, one-to-one interviews are easier to arrange, requiring only the researcher and one participant to find a mutually convenient time, as opposed to the difficulties associated with trying to organize a group meeting.
2   *One-to-one interviews* which give the researcher the opportunity to explore an individual's opinion in depth. The focus of this chapter will be one-to-one interviews, which are probably the most often employed interviewing approach.
3   *Oral history interviews* in which elderly people are interviewed to get the view of someone who lived through a historic event.
4   *Interviewing elites* in which gatekeepers or special people are interviewed, such as members of parliament, or a key council officer.

Because they are relatively simple to organize, it should be possible for the researcher to arrange one-to-one interviews to try out interviewing techniques relatively simply.

## KNOWING WHAT TO ASK

Interviews should try to be made into conversations. To achieve a conversation, it is important not to sit in the interview setting and ask a series of closed ended questions. *Closed ended questions* are in the same style as written questionnaires. At their most limiting, they demand a box to be checked to indicate the participant's response, or a yes/no answer to a question. What is needed is an approach that allows you to ask *open-ended questions*. These are questions that demand a long answer to a question. Rather than allowing the participant to respond with a 'yes' or 'no,' they require the interviewee to answer the question more extensively. In semistructured interviews this type of question is helpful because it tends to generate a verbose, argued response to a question. Consider the difference between these questions:

1   Do you use recycling facilities very often?
2   How often do you use recycling facilities?

Question 1, an example of a closed ended question, can be responded to by a simple yes or no. Question 2 is a more open-ended example, but still only requires a short answer – 'weekly' or similar. There is a need for questions which will generate longer answers:

3   What do you think of the recycling facilities round here?
4   What would make you use them more?

These questions ask the interviewee for more information about their opinions and attitudes, but would probably still elucidate the answers to questions 1 and 2 in the process. The questions need to be open ended, but they also need to sound natural. Everyone would have a slightly different way of asking these questions, which is why an interview schedule lists prompts and themes for the interview rather than simply a series of questions. It is also important to realize the role of the researcher in the interview and to take note of where a leading question has been posed:

5   There are a lot of recycling places round here, don't you think?

As well as being closed ended, this is a leading question which is likely to sway the interviewee's response. I will show later that interviewees pick up even on individual words used by the interviewer. The leading nature of this question is therefore bound to affect their response. It is important to bear in mind the difference between open- and closed ended questions and to be aware of the potential effect of leading questions when devising what will be covered in each interview (for further examples of structuring questions in an interview, see Burgess, 1991: 111–117). Remember that it will only be possible to conduct a limited number of interviews, so it is important to practise to achieve an open-ended questioning style to ensure the interviews are as productive as possible.

## KNOWING WHO TO ASK

Time is the main constraint to the number of interviewees. All interviews are time consuming to conduct due to their very nature (with interviews for my PhD, for example, ranging from 40 minutes up to over three hours). Therefore it is only possible to interview a small number of people. Thus, the careful choice of that group is vital. Actually conducting the interviews can be time consuming, but the analysis and transcription also needs to be taken into account. While planning my PhD research approach, my supervisor recommended an allocation of one week per interview to allow for the time it would take to transcribe and analyse. At the time I thought that would be far too much time, but my supervisor was proved right. At one week per interview, 30 one-hour interviews, analysed in depth, can take 30 weeks (i.e. six months). There is also time to be added for actually recruiting participants, which means 30 to 40 interviews becomes a realistic maximum. This calculation assumes you plan to analyse the material in quite some depth, but can be used as a helpful guide to what can be accomplished in a qualitative project. For the research I was conducting, participants' perceptions, understandings of meaning and interpretations were the most important, which required a detailed analysis even down to the level of use of metaphor and structure of argument in some cases.

The analysis can be a lengthy process, but so can getting people to the interview. The time it takes to recruit interviewees can be far longer than anticipated. I have found that people have had difficulties understanding the worth of their contribution, especially, it seemed, when being asked for an interview rather than simply completing a questionnaire. At first the interview can appear threatening. From their point of view, someone coming round to their house to 'chat' about, in my case, environmental issues, particularly when they did not see themselves as at all expert, is often a problem.

Only a small number of people can be interviewed, so they need to be selected with care. For my thesis I listed the factors which I deemed pertinent to the project and from that made sure that at least one of the participants fitted into each category. I chose various professions, various ages, varying degrees of environmental activism, and a mix of men and women. The 'categories' which I devised at the outset of the research and from which at least one representative in the group of participants was chosen were:

*Parents and non-parents*
*Age:* limited to above 18; but includes pensioners
*Employment:* wide range of occupations, within scope of middle class
*Gender:* both
*Urban/rural dwellers:* particularly clear in Sheffield where people can choose to live in the Peak District or the city itself
*Political activity:* a range of positions, right to left and environmental

The 'sample' of participants that I researched was selected to represent diversity and variety within certain parameters. These parameters were generated from the literature and from the aims of the research. The research participants are not a representative, typical sample, but they did allow me to explore a number of subject positions with a larger group. I explored possible interpretations and meanings of 'green' rather than providing a definitive meaning (see Cook and Crang, 1995: 11–12) among a group of 30 interviewees. With such time constraints and the small number of interviewees, a common concern is the extent to which it is possible to generalize or draw conclusions from this type of material.

## DRAWING CONCLUSIONS FROM INTERVIEW DATA

Qualitative interview material is non-numerical and therefore conclusions cannot be drawn which will be based on statistical inference. The research question must be posed in a way which does not demand any statistical hypothesis testing. What qualitative research can offer is an understanding of people's 'life-worlds', trying to understand situations from the perspective of those being researched. To achieve this, it is important to acknowledge the difference in the role of the researcher in an interview-based project compared to a positivistic, numerical project. To understand other people's social worlds:

> One would have to take the role of the actor and see his [sic] world from his standpoint. This [qualitative, interview-based] methodological approach stands in contrast to the so-called objective approach so dominant today, namely that of viewing the actor from the perspective of an outside, detached observer . . . the actor acts toward his world on the basis of how he sees it and not on the basis of how that world appears to the outside observer. (Blumer, 1966, cited in Burgess, 1991).

In other words:

> Using this perspective it therefore becomes essential to gather statements made by participants with a view to examining the various dimensions of the situation that they construct. It is also important to focus upon ongoing patterns of interaction. (Burgess, 1991: 4)

An exploration of these interactions is the basis of qualitative research, and a project based on interviews must be researching a topic which is at least partially interested in these kind of issues. Qualitative methods are a sensitive way of exploring meaning and understandings:

> Qualitative Methods [are] ways of examining the social world, whereby central importance is given to the actor's definition and behaviour . . . While different methods vary in their precise detail, and while there are important differences in the conceptual derivations and backgrounds of the methods, all share the view that it is the task of research to uncover the nature of the social world through an interpretive and empathetic understanding of how people act and give meaning to their own lives. (Eyles, 1989: 207)

The depth and richness of the findings of qualitative methods compared to the breadth of data produced by quantitative approaches do not lend themselves, nor do they require, a statistically representative sample (see

Brannen, 1992; Bryman, 1992; Hammersley, 1992, 1993). Clearly, the relatively small number of interviewees in a qualitative project could not provide an adequate basis for inferential statistics. The inferences that can be drawn from qualitative data are termed 'common sense' or logical, rather than statistical (Cook and Crang, 1995: 10–13; Mitchell, 1983; Wallman, 1983). Qualitative approaches do not aim to produce 'laws' or generalizations in the same way as quantitative methods. It has even been argued that generalizability is a concept which is at odds with qualitative approaches per se:

> The emerging view shared by many qualitative researchers appears to involve several areas of consensus. First of all, there is broad agreement that generalizability in the sense of producing laws that apply universally is not a useful standard or goal for qualitative research . . . Second, most researchers writing on generalizability in the qualitative tradition agree that their rejection of generalizability as a search for broadly applicable laws is not a rejection of the idea that studies in one situation can be used to speak or to help form a judgement about other situations. Third . . . current thinking on generalizability argues that thick descriptions (Ryles, cited in Geertz, 1973) are vital. (Schofield, 1993: 207)

Note that generalizability is not the same as validity or reliability. To be valid, in the research design it is important to consider what the group of participants can offer to inform the issue being considered. The participants researched must be selected for their diversity and variety within certain parameters. In my PhD research, for example, I was exploring possible interpretations and meanings of green rather than attempting to provide a definitive meaning (see Cook and Crang, 1995: 11–12). Methodological approaches such as large-scale surveys which produce numerical data provide generalizations and inference through statistics. Qualitative approaches are then fundamentally different, but this does not make them less valid, provided that the researcher is confident of the rigour of their approach (for a discussion of levels of rigour in qualitative research, see Baxter and Eyles, 1997). It is important to be clear about what an interview-based project can offer and to be sure that this approach is appropriate for the research issues under exploration.

## ON GETTING IT WRONG

Qualitative interviews should be seen as interviews trying to achieve a dialogue. They do not aim to ask a series of questions of the respondent, but rather to engage them in a 'conversation with a purpose' (Burgess, 1991). In semi-structured interviews the locus of power in the interview is difficult to establish (see Pile, 1991; Smith, 1988). These semi-structured interviews attempt to be a conversation. There is dialogue between the researcher and the researched and there is, to varying extents, acknowledgement that bias and subjectivity will play a part in the conversation, as would be the case in a 'normal' or 'natural' conversation. The extent to which interviews can provide a natural dialogue, however, is oft debated in the literature (see, for example, the exchange between McDowell, 1991; Schoenberger, 1991; Pile, 1993).

While power relations in a questionnaire approach are regarded as relatively fixed, they are more fluid and complex in an interview context. This again needs to be borne in mind when conducting and analysing the material. While the researchers are in a position of power inasmuch as they have organized and initiated the interviews, they are, at least to an extent, at the mercy of the respondents to answer their questions in a frank and open way. While this does not in itself redress the balance of power in the interview situation, it does pave the way for a discussion that can problematize (rather than take for granted) issues of power. Subjectivity and bias will be present. The interviewers are directing conversation and their interjections will have an effect on the interviews. In my research, for example, there were a number of occasions where I very obviously, but also very unintentionally, shifted the tenor of the conversation: examples of where I obviously got it wrong and my subjectivity was very obviously having an impact on the interview.

Interviews that go badly are often the result of poor interviewing style. This is evident in the following examples taken from my PhD research. Dorothy, a middle-aged university administrator, was one of the earlier interviews conducted. The interview provides an example of where my interviewing technique was clearly at fault and reflection and hindsight gave me a chance to refine my technique in later interviews. I stopped Dorothy's train of thought on at least two occasions by being unintentionally sarcastic. The first was related to her interest in the Girl Guide movement, which she suggested was an important grounding in 'life skills', an organization that provides a set of ideals which girls, she suggested, would take into later life. This was important for the research, addressing her understanding of how people gain ideologies and ideals from childhood, in this case using uniformed organizations for education and a means to instil 'solid values'. Because of my interjected comments, however, this strand of discussion was terminated:

*Dorothy*: But the solid values from Baden-Powell days still remain, and I think . . . um, and certainly what girls learn through Guiding does tend to stick with them throughout life, even though they go away from Guiding and . . . they'll remember things from Guiding days . . .
*Matt*: How to make those things to stick your wellies on . . .

On another occasion, 'humour' again interrupted her train of thought. She was beginning to articulate her version of civic responsibility and the need for collective responsibility when I completely inopportunely digressed to talk about Margaret Thatcher's involvement with the 'Keep Britain Tidy' campaign. This digression once again stopped the flow of important material:

> *Dorothy*: Er, er, I also feel quite strongly about, it's not terribly green, but just about rubbish. And where you throw it and how much better for the world if people put their rubbish in the right places . . . and there'd be a lot less thrown by the wayside.
> *Matt*: [*laughing*] Our Maggie Thatcher was there . . .
> *Dorothy*: Well, she was, yes . . . you notice that if you go to other countries how much. The whole, place seems, er, more cared for and loved, kept clean and tidy . . .
> *Matt*: . . . throwing her litter in the bin.

On both occasions, valuable data were lost. Rather than the interview being an open and frank discussion, discussion remained stilted and awkward. This was due, I am sure, to nerves on my part which I coped with on this occasion with what I took to be humour. The interview had started badly because Dorothy was being defensive and I had found her difficult to talk to from the outset. She may have been wary because my introduction to her was through a senior colleague of mine and a friend of hers and she may have feared that they might read what she said (which would not have happened without data being first anonymized).

There were other examples where my supposedly humorous interjections stemmed the flow of data. With Jenny, a trainee accountant in her mid-thirties, I stopped the interview topic under discussion as she was beginning to explore issues which could have been used to inform my critique of expertise and knowledge, but again I prevented the discussion. She had been talking about unleaded petrol, which I suggested was being linked, through benzene additives present, to a higher risk of cancer.[1] I should have waited to see whether she had knowledge of the possible risk, and certainly not responded as I did:

> *Matt*: Have you had it changed to unleaded and all that?
> *Jenny*: What the car . . .? It is unleaded . . .
> *Matt*: But now apparently you get cancer . . .
> *Jenny*: Well, you never know where you are you see, do you?
> *Matt*: That's the latest one!
> *Jenny*: Mm, mm.

I had effectively closed down that avenue of discussion and had to move the interview to a different topic.

Brian, a surveyor in his late fifties, was discussing the effects individuals can have in improving the environment and was beginning to talk about the importance of peer attitudes. These were important insights to the analysis of dis-/em-powerment, central issues to my thesis:

> *Brian*: Seeing other people having that sort of attitude . . . Therefore, it's got to be a general process . . . even if people who use cars leave it at home once in ten days . . . I reckon that a 10 per cent reduction in traffic would make a tremendous difference . . .
> *Matt*: Yes . . .
> *Brian*: . . . particularly to a City like Sheffield. And it's not much.
> *Matt*: And I'd get run over less often . . .
> *Brian*: Very often I try to leave the car at the office one day a week . . .

It is clear to see how my interjection and use of the word 'often' influenced what Brian went on to discuss, with his use of 'often' in his reply. This level of influence was a concern to me and I tried to avoid providing such interruptions in later interviews. Experiences like these were accommodated and responded to as the data collection phase of the project progressed, and should be used as lessons if about to embark on interview research. I had to make a conscious effort not to alienate people's view and to establish and maintain the all-important rapport by not resorting to humour (and particularly sarcasm and asides) when under pressure in interviews. I also had to make it clear to the interviewees that they were not in any way being tested, which a number seemed to expect. It is important to ensure that the interviewee is clear about the structure of the interview. On more than one occasion I fell foul of a participant expecting to be subjected to a questionnaire rather than a conversation about the environment. The other interviews were largely more successful and allowed me to explore the realm of interpretation and understanding in participants' own terms.

The importance of building rapport in the interview cannot be over-stressed. A 'bad interview' can be disheartening and will also produce data of both lesser quality and quantity. A bad interview can be the result of the interviewee as much as the interviewer and highlights the issue of power relations and the importance of realizing the complex interaction in the interview situation. Interviews are difficult to get right: there are a lot of demands placed upon the researcher and one way to alleviate some of the pressure is to plan well. A vital part of that planning must be the interview schedule.

## PLANNING THE INTERVIEW

### The interview schedule

The conduct of interviews seems to be, like much of the fieldwork process, a 'messy' and idiosyncratic business (Brannen, 1992: 3). To give order to this 'messiness' and unpredictability and to provide structure and guidance to the interviewer, the interview should be based on an interview schedule which acts as a prompt. This prompt is a series of topics to be covered rather than a formal list of questions. A list of questions to be asked in a questionnaire can be helpful if you plan to use the interview to obtain factual data: for example, for details of an event rather than attitudes toward it. My PhD research needed to access issues about personal identity and interpretation and so needed a schedule that would allow me to explore them. People do not think in terms of personal identity and it is therefore inappropriate to ask questions directly on the topic. As such, the interview schedule covers issues such as the ascription of responsibility for environmental change. This gives access to the participants' understanding of relational identity between themselves and the government, for example. Accessing theoretical and academic issues in a way that is meaningful to the participants is the challenge of preparing the interview schedule.

To devise a schedule, list all the topics in which you are interested and then try talking them through with colleagues to see whether and in what ways it is possible to introduce them into a 'normal' conversation. Keep a log of these conversations and use it as a basis for preparing a list of themes which you will take into each interview. This list should include prompts about each theme in case a free-flowing conversation proves difficult to establish. I chose to write some of these prompts apparently as questions. However, these questions were ones I needed to be able to answer from the data rather than a series of fixed questions I asked interviewees.

Two questions that I did always pose as written were the opening and closing questions. These, I found, were the two most important parts of the interview. To begin with the interviewee (and probably the interviewer) will be nervous and unsure what to expect. I was invariably nervous about how the interview would progress (see, among others, Pile, 1991, 1993 for the importance of building rapport with the interviewee). Starting with a very general question was very helpful. Although it may seem odd to start with 'What do you understand by green?' because of the vast array of possible responses, it always generated some discussion and also gave me information I could use later in the interview to phrase more questions. For example, if the interviewees talked about recycling as part of their interpretation of green in their reply to my opening question, I could then ask how often and what they recycled and go on to ask what would make them recycle more often.

The closing question was equally important, to ensure that the interviewee has a sense of 'closure' rather than drifting to an end. Again, it was a comfort to me to know that I did not have to devise a closing question to end the interview on the spot. The issue of confidence in your interview schedule is key to the interview being a success: being clear in your mind what you must cover in the interview, which entails learning the schedule.

I still had the schedule to hand just in case. It can be useful having the schedule on paper so that the interviewee can see the structure of the interview and know what is to be asked of them. Unless they asked explicitly, though, I chose not to show them the schedule. There is no hard and fast rule about this, but it should be considered as part of the issue of 'informed consent', whereby the interviewees know what is expected of them (see Chapter 5 on ethical principles).

The schedule used for my PhD research is shown in Box 15.1. Although it could be improved, it was a suitable tool to obtain interview data. Four broad topics with a number of sub-themes gave material for interviews that lasted on average over an hour, although they varied in length from around 30 minutes to over three hours.

---

**Box 15.1   Interview schedule**

I   **Definitions – introduction, general questions and access to questions of conception of environmental crisis**
A   *'Green'*
  1   'Let's start with a very general question. What do you understand by the term green?'
  2   What can you do to be 'green'/What do you do to be 'green'/What could you do to be more 'green'/Why don't you go further?
B   *Environment*
  1   What is this environment we are 'safeguarding' (or whatever phrase is employed) – if they don't use the word, leave until later and then ask for definition?

II   **To access question of responsibility and also role of policy and government**
A   *Origination of impetus*
  1   Where does the impetus for change come from/Where should it/ Where/Who would be most effective?
B   *Politics*
  1   Do environmental matters affect your vote/What role do you think political parties have to play?
C   *Responsibility*
  1   Whose role is it to make changes?
  2   What is the role of industry/Business/Media (separate questions if not mentioned)?

III   **Consumerism and decision making**
A   *Consumerism* (if not covered under what one can do to be green, above)
  1   Who takes the decisions about what to buy in your house?
  2   Is the environment a consideration/What other issues do you take into account when shopping?

**IV Concluding questions**
*A Influences*
    1  What has been greatest influence in making you turn more 'green' or
       less (thinking of media or children, etc.)?
*B General closing questions*
    1  Moving on to other areas – do you think in the same way about your
       family, or about religion, as you do green?

With only a list of topics to act as a prompt, the pressure is placed upon
the interviewer to listen and respond to the interviewee. I have already
shown that interviews can go wrong in a number of ways, and in many
respects this is to be expected. The interviewer effectively has to ad lib
through the interview without the luxury of a list of fixed questions to
which to refer. While ad libbing, they have to be listening and responding
to the interviewee as well as covering the topics necessary to collect the
required data. This takes considerable skill and practice on the part of the
interviewer:

> [This] approach requires particular skills on the part of the interviewer. First, it is
> essential to listen carefully in order to participate in the conversation, to pose
> particular questions on topics that have not been covered or need developing.
> Secondly, it is important not to interrupt the person or persons who are being
> interviewed . . . Thirdly, interviewers need to monitor their own comments,
> gestures and actions as these may convey particular meanings to those who are
> interviewed which may advance or impede the interview. (Burgess, 1991: 111)

With so many pressures in the interview, it is almost impossible for the
interviewer to record the content of the interview directly onto paper.
To remedy this problem, interviews should be tape recorded wherever
possible. Small, unobtrusive cassette recorders are not expensive and
should be regarded as an essential tool of the qualitative researcher. As
well as convenient and labour saving, Pile suggests that a verbatim transcript is the only way to achieve a full qualitative analysis:

> An analysis of language can only be carried out with confidence if there is an
> entire record of a conversation. Hastily scribbled notes . . . are not accurate
> enough to be used in this way. Tape-recorded sessions provide the only viable
> data for this kind of analysis. (Pile, 1990: 217)

Tape-recorded interviews, it is suggested, provide a far more reliable
record of the interview than note taking. It is also suggested that interviewers are less likely to try to lead an interviewee in some circumstances:

> It is worth pushing hard to tape. Notes are not only very slow but open to
> doubts about validity. When in Britain police interviews went from contem-
> poraneous note-taking to tape-recording, detectives found that the average

interview times fell dramatically. An interview that took four hours with note-taking now took half an hour. The quality of responses also became more factual, and accusations of 'verballing' – putting words into the respondent's mouth – fell to virtually nil. (Fielding, 1993: 146)

While tape recording is undeniably helpful, it cannot record mannerisms or other non-verbal events during the interview. Therefore, it is important to note such events and to spend some time after each interview completing a research diary in which comments on the interviewee's mannerisms or other non-verbal communications can be stored to be used later in the analysis.

## INTERVIEW DATA ANALYSIS

It is important to consider the analysis procedure from the outset of the research project. First, it must be realized that qualitative methodologies produce a mass of data, far more than can be used in one project. Therefore, data need to be sorted and managed into what is useful for the project being undertaken and what has to be discarded. This process needs to be well planned to ensure rigour and reliability (see Baxter and Eyles, 1997).

There are various approaches to analysing the text, which depend not least on what you hope to get from the interview data. If you are exploring theories or concepts developed in other sources of data, then your analytical approach will be predetermined: you know what information you need from each of the data. If, like my project, you are interested in exploring interpretations and attitudes and are not in any way 'testing' preconceived theories, then a more grounded approach is required. In its purest form, this is a system whereby the research themes all emerge from the data and is described in detail in Strauss (1987) (also see Glaser and Strauss, 1967; Burgess, 1991: 180–181). The sheer amount of unstructured data means that an organizing system is needed into which material can be broken down into manageable chunks. These sections of data, or chunks, can then be sorted. This is usually done through a coding procedure in which chunks of text are labelled, or coded, and then stored by these codes. There will not be the space here fully to discuss interview analysis, but it is important to be aware of at least the stages involved.

Strauss (1987) advocates a 'grounded' approach to qualitative data analysis in which codes are allowed to emerge from the data, rather than being established before the research is conducted. This is a crucial difference between interviews and questionnaire approaches. With a survey, the 'codes' are pre-set into the questionnaire before it is distributed rather than emerging from the data later in the process. For qualitative data analysis a process is required that can draw these codes from the material at various levels: from the level of what people say, in terms of argumentative structure, the words they use and in the interview as a whole. There is also a need to compare and contrast between interviews. These various scales are difficult to incorporate into the analysis: there is the level of metaphor, at the individual word level and also within each sentence. There is also the scale of the interview as a whole and, simultaneously, the level of the structure of arguments, again both at a small scale and larger scale within each interview text. Also, there are themes which emerge in importance over a number of texts. To keep all of these levels of analysis in a system-atic and rigorous order can be obtained by the use of a dedicated com-puter package, although this approach should not be adopted without careful consideration of the implications (see Chapter 17 and Crang, 1997). In order to manage all the levels of analysis during the coding, I adopted the following procedure:

- Read/listen to each interview through in full in order to get an overall feel for its whole content and what the concerns for the participant were.
- I circled words and phrases that seemed to recur in the text. Using this approach, if a participant, say, kept coming back to questions, issues or particular experiences, these would be clearly highlighted ready for the next stage.
- Using the circled words and phrases I began to link these together. I began the actual process of coding as I categorized the words and phrases, and also the more abstract argumentative structures at work in the interview.
- I began the theory-building stage of the research as I began to link the codes together, in order to ascertain what general themes were emerging from the text.

This system allows the researcher to get from the specific concerns of the participant through to the more general concerns present in all the texts, and to explore inconsistency and difference at various levels (for more detail on the process, see my thesis, lodged at University of Sheffield).

The next stage of the analysis was to extract the most pertinent codes on which to focus for the thesis. It is important to choose the thematic focus of the analysis with care. As well as codes which emerge from the data, using a system similar to the above, Tesch (1990) suggests that there are other sources from which the final themes can emerge:

> In interpretational analysis, there are at least four sources from which the beginnings of an organising system can be derived:
>
> a The research question and sub-questions
> b The research instrument(s)
> c Concepts or categories used by other authors in previous related studies
> d The data themselves. (Tesch, 1990: 141)

I would also add a fifth 'cultural/social context'. A combination of these sources gave rise to the codes that went on to structure my thesis. The interviews were explored in the initial phase to ensure that the participants' constructions of the terms and definitions were being listened to. These were then combined with themes that emerged from the literature. Some were discarded after careful evaluation, because there will always be too many interesting avenues to explore. The next phase of the analysis involved entering the thematically coded data into the software package, but before then I had to determine which codes spanned all of the interviews, or were to prove the most interesting for inclusion in this write-up of the project. As is always the case in qualitative research, with its depth, there are many themes that cannot be fully covered in a thesis because of the limit of space. Once themes have emerged from the data, it is important to code all the interviews in these themes. It becomes immediately apparent whether the code/theme only applies to a small proportion of the interviews, or to all the project. The themes which are only found in a small number of interviews may still be important, but it is often the case that qualitative researchers can unintentionally overplay themes which seem particularly interesting and discover too late that there is little material to substantiate findings. It is therefore vital to keep referring back to the original data to clarify and refine the themes.

This has only been the briefest of introductions to the analysis process. The key issues to bear in mind are:

1   Qualitative, interview-based approaches always produce more data than it is possible to include in a research project.
2   A rigorous and systematic procedure is needed to manage and effectively analyse qualitative material.
3   There is now some useful guidance in the literature on analysis (Burgess, 1991; Crang, 1997; Dey, 1993; Strauss, 1987; Tesch, 1990 and that presented above), but each scheme will need refining and applying to an individual project's needs.
4   It is vital to allow codes to emerge from the data as well as from a priori established ideas from the literature. It is then important to check the substance of these emergent codes by constantly referring back to the original interview texts.

## LIMITATIONS

Interviewing provides a wealth of rich data. The data can allow access to people's opinions and attitudes. They are particularly useful in the exploration of difference and inconsistency and in an examination of the 'why' as well as the 'how many' and 'how often' questions more suited to a questionnaire project. But the approach is not without its problems.

First, there is the difficulty of recruiting people. It is difficult to know who to recruit, knowing which people will suit the research aims most appropriately and how to convince people that their contribution is worthwhile and important. This is due not least to the length of time that an interview will take. The analysis is also very time consuming. As I suggested earlier, and found through experience, on average a week per interview is a good estimate.

Devising an interview schedule can prove problematic. It is difficult to devise topics which can form questions without them becoming leading questions. It can be easy to focus on the topic which is the main object of the research too soon in the interview. In my project, as I have described above, I found it best not to talk explicitly about the subject matter being researched. Rather, other questions and topics gave rise to interesting data on the issue of identity. Burgess (1991: 111–117) provides examples of types of questions to use in interviews.

It is difficult for researchers to find it easy to accommodate the interactive nature of interviewing. The researcher will affect the interview in many ways: the effect of a man interviewing a woman, for example, needs to be considered. Some topics may be difficult or inappropriate to discuss. Men should probably not talk to women about experience of rape, needing to be sensitive to the participants' harrowing experience, for example. At all stages in the interviewing process it is very important to acknowledge explicitly not only the interviewer's influence on the proceedings, but also to realize that the participants have a role in shaping the research as well. To overcome this at least in part in my research, although I set an initial interview schedule, I was influenced by the participants in the project as it progressed and adapted the interview schedule accordingly.

Once the data have been collected, there is then the problem of analysing them, both in terms of what the analysis can provide (i.e. how inferential and/or generalizable are the data) and in terms of how to approach the data initially. The former is overcome by an understanding of the type of data which interviewing and qualitative methods in general provide; data whose quality comes from their depth rather than breadth. The latter is overcome by devising an analysis system before the research is under way. There is an emerging literature suggesting methods for analysis (for examples, see Burgess, 1991; Cook and Crang, 1995; Crang, 1997; Dey, 1993; Tesch, 1990), and these should be consulted. I do not think it can be emphasized enough that it is crucial to consider the analysis of the data before they are collected.

## CONCLUSIONS

Despite its limitations, interviewing provides rich and worthwhile data. Many topics would benefit from more use of the exploration which interviewing allows. It offers the opportunity to sit and listen to people's concerns and opinions at a level inaccessible to a questionnaire. That is not to say that surveys do not have their uses, but to reiterate their short-comings, the data produced are different and should be used to answer different research questions.

It is important to follow the decision-making stages presented in this chapter. You have to be sure that the material you need is appropriate to this methodological strategy. There is a need to be clear about whom you will interview and why. It is important to plan the interview topics with care. There is a need to allow time to test and pilot the interviews, both to check the topics in the interview schedule and also to allow a refinement of your interviewing style. Finally, it is vital that the analysis process is well planned, rigorous and systematic. A chapter of this length can only provide an introduction to these topics and I would recommend drawing on the experiences of others presented elsewhere in this volume, and also making wide use of the references.

## ACKNOWLEDGEMENTS

My PhD research was funded by the Economic and Social Research Council, award no. R0042932433, and the University of Sheffield, to whom I am most grateful. My thanks to Dawn Burton for comments on an earlier draft of this chapter and to my supervisor, Peter Jackson.

## NOTE

1 Later this link was made between additives to the higher octane 'super unleaded' intended as a replacement petrol for vehicles not designed to run directly on unleaded fuel.

# 16 THE USE OF CASE STUDIES IN SOCIAL SCIENCE RESEARCH

*Dawn Burton*

Case studies are one of the most popular methods of conducting social science research. Despite their popularity there is not a unanimous view across the social sciences about what constitutes a case study. A clarification of the different definitions of the terms case and case study is the starting point in this chapter. There is also a problem of conceptualizing case studies as purely qualitative research and some of the reasons for this view will be assessed prior to exploring the different case study designs available to researchers. The main focus of the chapter is concerned with documenting some of the practical issues associated with conducting case study research, by using examples from a case study of human resource management practices in the financial services sector. Finally, in the concluding section some of the objections which are often levelled against case study research are discussed.

## WHAT IS CASE STUDY RESEARCH?

Within the social sciences, the case study is one of the most frequently applied research designs. Despite the widespread use of case studies there is little consensus about what the term actually means. What is clear is that the definition of what constitutes a case study has changed over time and varies between social science disciplines and individual researchers. For some researchers case study research includes a single case, otherwise the research is regarded as comparative and not case study research. Other researchers consider that the number of cases is not an important issue (see Table 16.1). A central concept used in social science research is the idea of having cases as the building blocks for data collection and analysis. However, there is also some controversy as to what should be regarded as 'a case'. A case has been used to describe as diverse entities as an individual, an organization, a country and a continent. A case can also comprise an event such as some aspect of organizational change, or implementing a new programme. Indeed, the question of what is actually a case has generated a whole book debating the issue (Ragin, 1992).

An additional debate is whether cases should be conceptualized as empirical units or theoretical categories (Ragin, 1992). *Realists* would take the view that cases are either given or empirically discoverable. In other

TABLE 16.1   Some defintions of case study research

| Author | Discipline | Definition |
|---|---|---|
| Becker (1968) | Sociology | Participant observation of groups and group behaviour |
| Lijphart (1971) | Politics | Comprises only one case, no generalizations can be made |
| Runyan (1982) | Psychology | The presentation and interpretation of detailed information about a single subject, an event, culture or individual |
| Mitchell (1983) | Anthropology | A detailed examination of an event or events which the researcher believes exhibit the operation of some identified theoretical principle |
| Platt (1988) | Sociology | One or more cases, but the number of cases in each category is not significant; the unit case may be a person, small group, community or event |
| Yin (1994) | Organizational studies | An empirical enquiry that investigates a contemporary phenomenon in context; when the boundaries between the phenomenon and the context are not clearly evident, multiple sources of evidence are used |

Source: Platt, 1988.

words cases do exist out in the world and they just need to be found. This is in contrast to the *nominalist* view which argues that cases are theoretically and therefore socially constructed by researchers for the purposes of carrying out their investigation. A second concern relates to the generality of case categories. If case categories are developed during the course of the research through interviews and other methods, under these circumstances cases are highly specific to the particular research project. In this situation case categories are 'grounded' in the data and the content of cases may not be known until the empirical part of the project is complete. A rather different approach would view case categories as existing prior to the research, and not unravelled by the research process. These general categories are those viewed as legitimate by the social science community such as gender and social class. In this second instance, cases are theoretically constructed prior to the research being undertaken.

What unit of analysis you use in your project is your decision, but since there are competing definitions of the terms case and case study, it is essential that you are clear about the approach you have chosen and give appropriate reasons for your choice. Once you have agreed on a working definition you need to clarify a number of other issues. One factor relates to the issue of boundaries, specifically who or what is included and excluded and why. Another issue relates to time scales: when is the case study going to begin and end and is the time scale significant in some respect. You will also need to determine the limits of the data collection and analyses. Particularly crucial is the ability to compare your research with previous data, which by implication requires that you operationalize your research issues in similar ways, or if not you should make deviations from previous studies clear and they should be legitimated.

## QUANTITATIVE AND QUALITATIVE DICHOTOMY

The concept of case study is frequently associated with qualitative research, indeed the term qualitative research and case study research have often been used interchangeably (Burgess, 1991). In some instances there has also been confusion with case studies being linked with ethnographies or participant observation (Yin, 1994). Some researchers would not accept that case study research is purely qualitative research and would argue that case studies can legitimately be undertaken utilizing both quantitative and qualitative research techniques. Furthermore, Ragin (1992) suggests that the quantitative and qualitative dichotomy is not as wide as is often believed. He illustrates the point by using the example of two researchers both undertaking case study research in one organization, one taking a qualitative approach and the other a quantitative approach. Both the researchers use semi-structured interviews as their preferred method of data collection and ask similar questions. Both use the interviews to make sense of practices within the organization. The qualitative researcher analyses the interviews by coding text whether that be sentences or phrases, and uses quotations to prove or disprove various theoretical propositions. The researcher taking a quantitative approach also codes the interview data, but with a view to constructing a dataset which can be analysed using an appropriate statistical programme. At the end of the project both researchers produce data about the organization and both make sense of their findings by integrating them to previous research, thereby moving forward academic debate. Both researchers have undertaken case study research, but the process might be described differently by them. The qualitative researcher has only one case, whereas the quantitative researcher has many cases.

Case study research is flexible and not necessarily about conducting qualitative research. Case studies can and should include numerical measurement, where appropriate. Research designs can and do include single and multiple cases studies. Data may include documentary sources, archival letters, direct observation and participant observation. Case studies can also be used in longitudinal research with case studies being conducted on a continuous basis, or with periodical follow-ups. The concept that case studies can include quantitative and qualitative techniques has led to different types of case studies being defined. Some of these different classifications are discussed in the following section.

## DIFFERENT TYPES OF CASE STUDY RESEARCH

Yin (1994) argues that there has been a popular misconception that case studies are only appropriate for the exploratory phase of an investigation, with surveys more suited to the descriptive phase and experiments the only way of conducting explanatory causal enquiries. By contrast he suggests that there are three different types of case studies – exploratory, descriptive and explanatory – which are capable of adapting to a range of research problems. Which type of case study should be used depends on a range of issues such as the type of research question posed, the extent of investigator control and the degree of focus on contemporary as opposed to historical events. That said, Yin (1994: 1) suggests that some research situations may warrant a preferred approach: 'In general, case studies are the preferred strategy when "how" or "why" questions are being posed, when the investigator has little control over events and when this focus is on a contemporary phenomenon within some real life context.'

Hakim (1992) provides another classification of case studies: descriptive, selective and experimental. *Descriptive* case studies can be used to illustrate cases thought typical or representative. Descriptive case studies can also be exploratory if there is little existing research on the topic. In policy-oriented research descriptive case studies can be used to illustrate good or bad practice. If a considerable amount of literature already exists on a topic, *selective* case studies can be used to focus in on particular aspects and provide a very rich and detailed account and thereby refine our knowledge. Finally, *experimental* case studies can be used as an alternative to conventional experimental designs, by assessing behaviour in a real-life setting. The experimental isolation method within a case study methodology involves specifying factors to be included and excluded and thereafter identifying one or more settings in which they are or are not present.

Having identified definitions and characteristics of case study research, a worked example of one case study will be used to illustrate some of the practicalities of undertaking case study research.

## CASE STUDY EXAMPLE

### Background

The case study to be outlined formed part of a research project which was designed to assess human resource management policies in the banking industry in Britain. During the 1980s the banking industry had become increasingly competitive as a result of significant regulatory change. The project aimed to uncover the effect of regulatory change on working practices, specifically the extent to which the industry had become more consumer oriented. A review of the previous research in this area revealed that most of the studies had utilized a quantitative approach by conducting surveys, either mail surveys or structured interviews. In addition, the basis of the survey data was often a response from human resource managers or other senior managers and did not represent the views of employees in branch offices. The case study methodology was employed for three reasons. First, it was a different methodological approach from that which had been used before and was therefore a useful contrast with previous studies. Second, the case study approach was more suited to the issues which I wanted to address. I wanted a more in-depth approach to investigate what effect policies designed by head office staff were having on the practical day-to-day activities of the employees in the branches. Finally, I thought having face-to-face contact with respondents and undertaking research in an organizational setting would be more interesting than mailing out questionnaires to anonymous people whom I did not know and ana-lysing the results thereafter.

### Negotiating access

Securing access to people, organizations and data is necessary for the successful completion of any research project, but it is particularly crucial in case study research where the researcher may wish to spend a considerable amount of time with relatively few individuals or within a limited number of settings. Burgess (1988) suggests that several factors are significant in the process of negotiating access in case study research. The first important issue is sponsorship. If researchers are sponsored, they should critically evaluate their sponsorship and recognize that it may open doors in some contexts and have the exact opposite effect in others. It follows that if the sponsor is an 'independent' body, researchers should make the most of this fact and stress that there is no hidden 'political' agenda. If the nature of the sponsor is likely to cause difficulties, then a response to address some of these issues should be thought through in advance. A consideration of the behaviour of 'gatekeepers' (individuals who have the power to grant or withhold access) is also a major access issue. In Burgess's (1991) study of two schools, head teachers determined when researchers could visit the school, where within the school they were allowed to visit, with whom researchers spoke and for how long. The third significant issue is that of membership roles. He notes that many of the characteristics of the researcher, such as age, sex, social class, social status and ethnicity, can and do have an important impact on whether access is granted or withheld. During the research process it is inevitable that the researcher will come to know some individuals better than others. Burgess suggests that friendships made during the research project can significantly affect which avenues of access are opened and closed during the research process.

Undoubtedly a convincing self-presentation is crucial. Difficulties can arise when one cannot determine in advance what image should be pre-sented (Shaffir, 1991). As sociologists, Crompton and Jones had the dilemma of how to present themselves when approaching organizations for access:

> We had to endure long and often unsuccessful vetting by mostly suspicious management before we could even commence fieldwork. The problem is worse for those who carry the label 'sociologist'. Increasingly, the ill-grounded tirade from some sections of government and the media against sociology and its practitioners has made negotiating access to work organisations even harder. Some have retreated into more 'acceptable' niches – management scientist, organisational analyst. We stuck (perhaps obstinately) to 'sociologist'. (Crompton and Jones, 1988: 68)

This dilemma is perhaps more acute for research students. What titles are appropriate vary between researcher, research student, doctoral student, member of a department or graduate school.

The access issue was particularly difficult in the context of financial institutions where competition and confidentiality are important considerations. These features, together with the fact that there are relatively few British high street banks from which to choose, made the access issue particularly difficult. The difficulties of gaining access to British banks had already been documented. In their research into human resource policies in banks, Crompton and Jones (1988) stress the importance of identifying power holders as soon as possible to avoid protracted negotiations with 'gatekeepers' who are not in a position to make access decisions.

Having identified that access was going to be an important consideration in my project, a summary of the research aims and objectives, along with brief details of the research design, were prepared and sent to the research and development departments of all the major high street banks. All the documents were prepared using the university's headed notepaper. Overall, the response to the mailing was very poor. Most organizations did not respond and those that did suggested that in order to conduct the research I would need access to information that might reveal bank strategies which were designed to provide a competitive advantage and as a result were confidential. Another barrier was that most banks have their own research departments which undertake quantitative and qualitative research. As a result they did not feel that they needed to be involved with any other projects. Ironically, one organization indicated that it was collaborating on a similar project to mine with another university.

At this point the research was in danger of folding. Without gaining access to an organization the project could not continue. The approach at the head office level was clearly unsuccessful, so a different strategy was adopted. I knew that most banks had local area offices which in many respects mirrored the activities undertaken at head office level. I sent the same details to the personnel manager of just one bank (the one where I had my own account) asking whether or not I could undertake a small-scale study to help with my PhD. Two weeks later the telephone rang and I was given an immediate go-ahead. This one action resurrected the project and arrangements were made to visit the bank and start the research. From start to finish, negotiating access to a bank had taken six tense, not to mention nerve-wracking, months. This experience highlights the point that negotiating access should be done as soon as possible for it can be a lengthy process. It is clearly important to develop an access strategy as early as possible. The only preconditions placed upon me were that the bank should remain anonymous and that it should receive copies of the findings.

### Research design

My research design was negotiated with the bank's operations manager. I asked that three branches should be included in the study. Three branches were chosen because I estimated that I could manage the data which would be generated. The three specific banks were chosen because they were examples of small, large and medium-sized branches. Three different geographical locations were also chosen: a large city, a market town and a medium-sized town. I considered that this combination would provide as comprehensive an overview as possible. A six-part research design was proposed including:

- a small number of face-to-face, semi-structured interviews with key informants who were senior managers and could provide a general overview of the organization and its strategy;
- a mail questionnaire sent to all the employees in the three branches;
- semi-structured, face-to-face interviews with 25 per cent of employees in the branches;
- interviews with a small number of corporate and small business managers in the area;
- content analysis of documentary sources – specifically the bank's training handbooks and leaflets which gave an indication of the image it was promoting to both consumers and staff;
- contextual analysis of the phyical environment of the bank's branches: use of atmospherics such as the way space is used, the furnishings and other decor and colours gives an important indication of the changing nature of the consumer–bank relationship.

This research strategy was accepted by the bank. The use of all these methods together gave a rounded and multidimensional account of the changes in working practices at the bank.

The order in which the different methods were used was an important consideration. I already had quite firm ideas about what sorts of questions I wanted to ask in the interviews with employees and on the questionnaire which had been generated from reading the relevant literature, and some which replicated from other projects. However, I needed to ensure they made sense within the context of the organization in which the research was to be conducted. In the first interviews with senior personnel I checked out the terminology used at the bank and the systems that were in place so my questions made sense to employees. The next activity was to distribute the questionnaire to all employees in the three branches. The reason for the survey questionnaire was to give me an overall view of human resource policies as viewed from the employees' point of view. The results were then to be analysed and interesting and unexpected trends in the data were followed up in the semi-structured interview with the 25 per cent of employees in the branches which focused on four or five main themes. Finally, interviews with small business managers were conducted at the end of the project so I could compare human resource policies in the business banking with personal banking. The analysis of documentary sources and the interiors of the bank offices were undertaken on a continuous basis.

Once I had ensured that the questionnaire was compatible with the procedures and practices at the bank, it was piloted. The piloting process was undertaken on my behalf by senior managers (at their insistence) who distributed the questionnaire to six employees and then fed back the results. The questionnaire was highly structured with most of the responses having been precoded. As part of the piloting process the time taken by employees to complete the questionnaire was noted. It took ten to fifteen minutes to complete which was regarded as acceptable. The operations manager fed back results of the pilot to me and stressed that questionnaires must be completed on a voluntary basis. Although the briefing about the pilot was adequate, I would have preferred to have been in control of the piloting process and to have had results fed directly to me.

The questionnaire stage of the research presented a number of challenges. It was my preference to distribute the questionnaires to the branches in person so I could introduce myself and the project and hopefully improve the response rate. However, it was the bank's policy to distribute them centrally. While this practice saved me time, it did have its disadvantages. The main problem was that the questionnaires were not always delivered to the appropriate destination, specifically some of the sub-branches associated with the large branches were omitted. Employees were provided with a plain brown envelope in which the responses could be returned to me at the university. No names were placed on the questionnaires, but the responses from different branches could be identified by a code. A response rate of 65 per cent was obtained, which was neither exceptionally good for a workplace survey, nor particularly low. Overall, the questionnaire worked well but there was one question which did not work as effectively as I wanted. This related to whether or not individual employees had received performance-related pay the previous year. Unfortunately, only managerial level employees received performance-related pay; clerical employees being given prizes in the form of goods instead. As a result the question could not be analysed in respect of clerical employees. Had I been in control of the piloting process, the ambiguity might have been picked up. The responses were analysed using SPSS.

The interviewing stage of the project was the point at which I was most visible as a researcher. Until that point employees had only known of my existence through the questionnaire and accompanying letter which had been distributed centrally on my behalf. How I presented myself to managers and employees was therefore important. Gurney (1988) has provided some extremely good advice for female researchers. She suggests that a researcher's appearance can affect their interactions with subjects and it is therefore best practice to conform to the dress code of professional women working in that setting. She also points out that researchers should know as much as possible about the roles occupied by men and women before starting the research to avoid later difficulties. All employees at the bank wore a uniform which was a smart business suit. I decided to dress in a similar style so I would blend in more easily. As far as gender relations in banks are concerned, it is well established that roughly equal numbers of men to women work in the British banking industry. I therefore knew that I would not be a lone female in the branches. What is also evident is that men overwhelmingly hold occupations at the higher levels of the occupational hierarchy. This factor made some of the women in the study slightly suspicious of my motives. One female even said, 'You're not one of these ambitious women are you?' The bank had adopted a policy whereby it had begun to employ graduates, some of them women. It later emerged that the female graduate who had worked in the bank was not particularly popular. On the other hand, men at the bank were used to dealing with women as subordinates and therefore treated me in a rather paternalistic way.

Managers were asked for their help in identifying respondents with the characteristics that I required in my sample. I felt that equal numbers of men to women would be appropriate, given that there was a more or less equal distribution of men and women in the organization. I also wanted to comment about the relationship between human resource policies and gender. Age was another important variable and broad age bands were constructed and quotas of individuals in the appropriate age bands were chosen. Finally, employees at different levels in the occupational hierarchy were identified to give as comprehensive a view as possible. Once suitable employees were identified, there was the problem of availability. In busy commercial organizations lunch breaks, holidays, sickness and the intensity of work may mean that several visits are required to conduct a relatively small number of interviews. The interviewing element of the project took much longer than anticipated because of these interruptions, even though the interviews had been designed to last approximately twenty minutes. The managers at the bank were most concerned that in fact the interviews did only last twenty minutes and, unknown to me, they were timing them. This issue came to light when one particularly interesting interview went on for thirty-five minutes, at which point I was told, 'It would be better if the interviews were shorter rather than longer.'

There was also a problem of having suitable accommodation in which to conduct the interviews. The ideal situation is to have a confidential setting in which the researcher can build up the trust of the respondent. While researchers can request an office or other place in which interviews can be conducted without being overheard by others, a suitable setting is not always available. During this project most employees were interviewed in an office out of earshot of other employees, but others had to be interviewed at their desks, in the counting room, or in the safe.

The lack of a suitable room in which some of the interviews could be conducted raises wider issues about anonymity and confidentiality. It is not clear how anonymity can be guaranteed in a small organization, when others can see who has been interviewed and who has not. Similarly, in many instances it is difficult to guarantee confidentiality in settings where there are limited numbers of subjects. Good researchers use a strategy of feeding information from earlier interviews into questions for subjects who are subsequently interviewed. In the setting of the bank branches, the existence of a very hierarchical occupational structure meant that only certain employees had access to specific information. Feeding back information gained from one employee and posing it as a question to another to check it out and obtain a different insight often reveals the identity of respondents. In some instances this took the form of a confrontation. As one employee said of another, 'I know who told you that, it was Bill wasn't it?' This situation presents a difficult dilemma for researchers and needs to be handled diplomatically. As a researcher it was ethically appealing for my respondents to be anonymous and for the information they gave to be confidential. It was clearly the case that in practice this was difficult to implement.

It is always a dilemma whether or not to tape-record interviews and it is an issue which researchers have to consider within the context of the research setting and how the data is to be analysed. None of the interviews with bank employees were recorded. The bank was of the view that taping was not in the best interests of the employees. I also felt that some of the issues about which I was asking were slightly controversial within the context of the bank and I wondered how forthcoming employees would have been if they had been taped. Writing comprehensive notes at the time of the interview is difficult and is certainly a skill which one needs to cultivate. With hindsight, if the interviews had been taped they would have provided more quotes which would have been very enlightening. But on the other hand, the tapes would have had to be transcribed, which is a time-consuming and laborious process.

## OBJECTIONS AGAINST CASE STUDIES

The most frequently cited objection to the use of case studies in social science research is the issue of representativeness, which raises the question of the extent to which the research findings can be generalized to a wider population beyond the case study. There are two approaches to deal with these types of criticism. The first approach is to accept the criticism and modify the case study research design accordingly. The second way forward is to defend the research design as being a legitimate research strategy on philosophical grounds. If we want to accept the criticisms and modify the research design, there are a number of strategies which can be used. One approach is to study more than one case. Evidence from multiple case studies is often more compelling and more robust than single case studies and enable the results of the studies to be compared and contrasted and some tentative generalizations made. It should be acknowledged that in some disciplines (for example, political science and anthropology) multiple case studies would be regarded as comparative research and not case study research. Another way of combating the criticism of generalizability is carefully to choose a case or cases which are typical and contain certain cluster characteristics which are representative of other cases. The problem with this practice is that the researcher may want to study a particular case because it is unusual in some way. A further defence of case study research is that it usually involves the use of multiple evidence from a wide range of sources. Case studies therefore provide rich and detailed accounts. The defence on philosophical grounds would focus on the fact that the principal use of case studies is to test theoretical propositions – the relationship of the case study findings to theory is of primary importance – not comment about the generalizability to populations and universe. Case studies are about making analytical generalizations and not about making statistical inference. To attempt to make statistical generalizations from case studies is inappropriate and uses a research design in a way for which it was not intended. An additional objection levelled at case studies is the lack of rigour. Yin (1994: 21) suggests that: 'Too many times, the case study investigator has been sloppy, and has allowed equivocal evidence or biased views to influence the direction of the findings and conclusions.' A further complaint levelled at case studies which Yin has identified is that 'they take too long and result in massive, unreadable documents'. It should be stressed that these criticisms could be made of any badly designed and executed research project and are not confined to case study research.

## CONCLUSION

Case studies are an extremely flexible method of conducting social science research and this flexibility contributes to the attractiveness of the method. This said, it would be wrong to assume that because case studies are popular they are an easy research design with which to work. Yin (1994: 55) suggests that 'the demands of a case study on a person's intellect, ego, and emotions are far greater than those of any other research strategy'. Difficulties arise for a number of reasons. First, data collection procedures in case studies are frequently not routinized, unlike a highly structured survey where consistency in the delivery of the questionnaire is crucial. In case studies a premium is placed upon question and listening skills, being adaptive and flexible and having a good grasp of the issues in order that an appropriate focus is maintained. Second, case studies often require the interviewing of 'key informants' such as professionals, public officials and other power holders. Elite interviewing requires a great deal of preparation on the part of researchers, not to mention confidence in interviewing individuals with a higher status than oneself. In this sense, case studies are extremely demanding psychologically. Third, a high degree of research expertise is required by researchers where a wide range of methods has been used. The continuous interaction between the theoretical issues being studied and the data collected also requires constant monitoring. Finally, a practical problem relates to the presentation of the case study data, in particular which data is to be given prominence and how it all interacts together needs to be carefully considered.

# 17 COMPUTERS AND QUALITATIVE DATA ANALYSIS: TO USE OR NOT TO USE . . .?

## Matt Stroh

## QUALITATIVE DATA ANALYSIS: MESSY AND IDIOSYNCRATIC

There are various approaches to collecting qualitative data, but there is still a relative paucity of literature on how to analyse the data generated. The analysis process is complex, laborious and time consuming. Computers can offer a solution to the problems of drudgery and resultant potential for error in a manual system. However, the adoption of a computer in the analysis process, especially a dedicated package, should be a considered and careful decision. The use of dedicated packages is not without critics, and their criticisms need to be addressed before embarking on a computer-assisted qualitative data analysis process.

There are few guidelines to qualitative data analysis, so qualitative researchers are largely forced to devise their own analysis scheme. One of the rare constants in qualitative data analysis is usually recourse to Strauss's 'grounded theory' (1987), a scheme which attempts to ground all concepts and analysis in the data themselves. Through an elaborate – and largely prescribed – coding strategy, inference emerges from the data. However, rather than prescribed or dictated in this way, qualitative research is usually regarded as creative: 'the creativity of the qualitative research process – which implies contingent methods to capture the richness of context-dependant sites and situations' (Baxter and Eyles, 1997: 505).

The few texts which are written on qualitative data analysis suggest that it is the very intuitive, idiosyncratic and creative nature of the approach that has led to the neglect of advice on the analysis process. Qualitative researchers expected literally to immerse themselves in their data, to get close to them and to feel part of them – which literally they are if they have guided interview discussions or conducted an ethnography, of course. The analysis process needs to reflect this closeness to the data, but there is an expectation that qualitative research will necessarily produce order out of chaos:

> Piles of paper spilling from the desk across the floor and strewn over every available surface: such is the archetypal image of the qualitative analyst at work.

Of course, this shrewd paragon of academic virtue knows exactly where every-thing is and can always find a particular piece of paper within moments: the supposed chaos is more apparent that real. This image is comforting but hardly credible. In the real world the chaotic mass of papers spread across the room is a recipe for confusion, error and frustration. In practice, the analyst depends on storing and filing data in an organised and systematic way. (Dey, 1993: 55)

The tenet of qualitative analysis has been, then, Anselm Strauss's grounded theory (see Burgess, 1984; Glaser and Strauss, 1967; Strauss, 1987; Strauss and Corbin, 1990). However, the practice of qualitative research is very different. The aim of Strauss's grounded theory is an elaborate theory resulting in abstracted categories, with these categories having evolved from the data rather than a priori. A number of commentators have argued that the practice needs to become more like the theory, with qualitative researchers becoming more concerned with questions of order and rigour rather than creativity and piles of paper. The fascination with the creative elements of the qualitative process, some argue, is still a result of wishing to be seen as anti-positivist:

Until recently, qualitative researchers have tended to focus more on what criteria should *not* be used to evaluate their work – the standards used to judge positivistic-quantitative work – and less on what they should be looking for to determine the rigour of qualitative research. (Baxter and Eyles, 1997: 521)

Subjectivity, close involvement in the research itself, effects of posi-tionality of the researcher and such like are the antithesis of a quantitative approach and Baxter and Eyles argue that this is why qualitative research-ers like to hold on to these concepts. Tesch, however, argued that the neglect of detail on the analysis process is because analysis is still judged in positivist terms:

For the most part, concrete ways of handling data have been passed on from one researcher generation to the next by word of mouth. It is not very glamorous to talk in a scholarly book about piles of paper, stacks of index cards, newsprint sheets on one's living room walls, and coloured pens. Many novice researchers simply, and sometimes to the point of exhaustion, experiment until they have invented their own scheme. (Tesch, 1990: 128–129)

It is not 'scholarly' to talk about the piles of paper so vital to a qualitative approach. However, this paucity of guidance has led the likes of Eyles and Baxter to question the rigour of the qualitative approach. Similarly, Dey argues that qualitative researchers should be concerned with organization and system. Some have taken this search for order onto computers. Lynn and Tom Richards, developers of the software package NUD•IST,[1] note that their interest in using computers originated from the need to store, manage and sort the mass of data that Lynn had been generating in a research project:

[The project] had already amassed a vast quantity of very rich, very unstructured material: informal interviews, field notes and taped discussions. This material obviously exceed the capacity and flexibility of manual systems for handling qualitative data. (Richards and Richards, 1994: 146)

Mere bulk was the immediate problem. The data records of a year of unstructured interviewing and field notes from participants were formidably bulky, and in various paper forms (typescript, field-note diaries, hand-written accounts). To control this increasing volume of records had become a high priority. Filing systems and methods of identifying different types of data seemed at times the major preoccupation of the project staff. (Richards and Richards, 1994: 147)

With the increasing amount of data, the supposedly rich and creative analysis process was becoming just the task of sorting the data into categories. This resulted in the researchers on the project expecting no more of the analysis:

The . . . project quickly showed that the code-and-retrieve method is not only a technique of data control but also one of data retention. Researchers' language showed this: the data had become 'stuff', physical stuff that must be put somewhere, not ideas to be explored. (Richards and Richards, 1994: 150)

Like Baxter, Eyles and Dey, Richards and Richards argue that the very language of qualitative research is concerned with order:

The language of qualitative research methods is imbued with the metaphors and methods of creating and ordering ideas by classificatory categories. The task of the researcher is presented as finding and exploring categories and patterns of categories in unstructured, even chaotic, records. To do so is to make sense of, understand, expound and illuminate, the records. (Richards and Richards, 1995: 80)

I do not agree that qualitative research is always about 'order'. The analysis phase must be rigorous, however, and acknowledge the need to manage data effectively. There are qualitative projects when the search for order and pattern is inappropriate: there could be more benefit in a search for inconsistency, for example. Qualitative data are by their very nature chaotic, but it should not necessarily be the task of the qualitative analyst to impose order on this chaos; rather to find a system of data management which can work with rather than against this characteristic. Computers provide an obvious means to manage and work with a mass of data.

## COMPUTERS' POTENTIAL FOR STORAGE AND MANAGEMENT OF QUALITATIVE DATA

The important issue in the literature is the management of the massive amount of material that qualitative methods produce. These data may be field notes, documents, verbatim transcripts, diaries or oral histories.

Qualitative researchers, have previously resorted to various manual systems, with varying degrees of success. The advent of affordable and powerful computer storage solutions has led to the computer being viewed by some as a 'natural' progression from the manual filing systems (see Richards and Richards, 1995).

## Practical problems

Computers are now part of everyday life, used to word process or compute statistics in seconds. People are now accustomed to their power for storage of large amounts of textual and numerical data. Although useful attributes for the management of qualitative material, the application of a computer in management has a number of implications for the analysis of data. For example, computers dictated the ways in which data can be stored: until recently they had to be on-line, usually as straightforward typed text. This requirement excluded the easy analysis of video recordings, documentary sources and audio cassettes directly. On-line data can be stored directly on a computer. Off-line data, on the other hand, cannot be stored on the computer in an accessible form: for example, newspaper or magazine articles and pictures. Sometimes, however, it is possible to scan in graphic representations of these documents, but they cannot be edited, searched or manipulated in the same way as a word processed text file. This distinction is important: we are quite used to working with textual material on computers in word processors or e-mail, but less so working with video. The computing power required to run lengthy video and audio clips is also prohibitive for widespread use.

As well as practical problems, the sorting and managing of data on computers is called in question. There are concerns about what the computer can offer to the next stage of analysis: the so-called 'coding' or sorting of text and the later retrieval and comparisons between these codes, categories or labels (so called 'theory building'). Some software packages simply allow for data management and retrieval (at base, this can be achieved on a word processor, of course). Others allow complex searches of the data, providing a detailed 'content analysis', while some allow researchers to 'build theory' from the data.

## Typology of computer packages

Different packages offer different functions and opportunities for assistance in the research process. There is no one 'accepted' computer package that is best or the most helpful to everyone, but rather there are a number of different types of software package available for analysing qualitative data. Whatever type of package is being considered for use, it must be realized that computers themselves do not analyse qualitative data. They can help in a number of ways, but still require the 'thinking' and analytic structure supplied by the researcher. They do not necessarily make the job any easier, as I will detail below. They can help us to be more effective, arguably rigorous and systematic, but, above all, make the analysis different to a manual approach. Researchers can be freed from the administrative tasks of data management, allowing them time to focus on the data analysis:

> A common misapprehension is that in some way the programs do the analysis for you, or produce some sort of concrete results on their own. The programs do not magically produce correct results, or for that matter 'results' at all. The results are the connections, patterns and explanations *you* draw out of your materials – not something produced by the computer. (Crang, 1997: 187)

Some programs simply replicate the manual approach of cutting chunks of data, assigning them a code and storing them – and then offering the researcher an easy way to retrieve the assigned text at will. Some provide complex search functions while others, to which Crang refers, allow 'theory-building' functions, which can be mistaken for programs that will deduce inference and results for you. The programs available for qualitative data analysis can be split into six categories:

- word processors;
- text retrievers;
- text/database managers;
- code and retrieve programs;
- theory builders;
- conceptual network builders/graphical mapping packages.

The software packages mentioned will, over time, be updated and altered, but the genres themselves are still helpful guides. Precise details of each package can be found in a number of texts, starting with Miles and Weitzman (1994) and more recently Kelle (1995). As Pfanffenberger rightly notes:

> Specific programs come and go . . . but software genres – such as, for instance, key-word-in-context concordance programs and text-oriented database managers – remain remarkably stable – with, to be sure, occasional (but only occasional) accretions of some genuinely new phenomenon . . . To put the point another way, from the perspective of sufficient distance (and detachment) one sees that the noisy hyperbole of the marketplace . . . disguises the fact that the generic types of software have been around for some time. (Pfanffenberger, 1988: 11)

Each of the genres of analysis package and the programs themselves excel in different arenas. Above all, remember that each program (bar the word processors, obviously) was written with a specific analysis in mind, often resulting from a specific research project or research question. It is usually possible to find work by the package's author that details this (see Dey, 1993; Richards and Richards, 1995; Seidel, 1991; Tesch, 1990).

## Word processors

This is the package with which most computer users are familiar. The functions available range from the simplest text processor to desktop publishing presentation features. Most allow the user to type text into the computer, perform basic 'cut and paste' of blocks of text, correct mistakes and alter document structure. More complex packages include the latest Word-for-Windows type with grammar checker, sophisticated spell checker, find and replace text features, advanced formatting capabilities, the ability to insert and manipulate pictures and images, and built in e-mail and fax software. Word processors offer the power and versatility for textual data input and basic management of material. They are the entry point for most dedicated qualitative data analysis packages because they allow us to type in our transcripts and 'export' them in a format which other computer packages can understand. For transcribing tape-recorded interviews, writing up field notes or diaries they prove invaluable. They are now also taken for granted and users assume they have no effect on the data inputted, other than, perhaps, through spell-checking and formatting. However, commentators have raised concerns.

Modern word processors even cause problems just at the level of data entry and the subsequent use of the data in a dedicated package. The problem with all the functions of software such as Word for Windows is that the formatting of the saved document is particular to that package. The basic format of text interchange is still based on the original ASCII format (American Standard Code for Information Interchange), but in addition to the words and punctuation are myriad other pieces of information about text style, font size and now even colour of the text. It is still possible to save as 'raw text', or just as ASCII. In Word, this is achieved by selecting the 'Save As' command from the 'File' menu and saving as 'Text Only'. WordPerfect, for example, is similar, but even this relatively simple process highlights the need for the user to be relatively competent in application of the word processor software to be able merely to export the data in a useable format.

Word processors can be used to assist manual analysis, which is the approach opted for by many qualitative researchers. Word processors, however, lack the ability to attribute a code word to a section of text easily, although they can search text for embedded words. One way round the problem is to use the multitasking that windows-based systems allow. A number of files can be opened simultaneously, with each representing a code or theme of analysis, and segments of interview data copied into each file. The name of each file can represent the category or 'code' assigned, and it is then possible to sort and explore these files. However, there is still the issue of how to reference back to the original document in order to be able to explore its context, which was the main problem of the manual approach.

Reid (1992) suggests ways in which the 'find' and 'macro' capabilities of advanced word processors (basically recording a set of key strokes which, say, find a particular word, copy the sentence and then paste it to a new location) can be used in the code and sort process. In this way, word processors can be used for searching text for all occurrences of a word or words, and this can be enhanced by typing code words in the text, possibly preceded by an '@' symbol and searching for that. It is not a particularly efficient approach, can be very time consuming and often leads to mistakes. It is also difficult to keep a record of exactly where each extract comes from, and even harder to change the coding scheme once it is in place.

Word processors can also only work with on-line information. They are designed for text to be in a typeable form, although the more sophisticated packages (such as Word for Windows) do allow some audio clips to be imported and some have drawing capabilities so that sketches and maps made in the field can be included. Furthermore, the find features of word processors are designed to help typists search relatively brief documents rather than search the often very long texts with which qualitative researchers have to work (with a one-hour interview, verbatim transcribed, often reaching 30,000 words – multiply that by the number of interviews and you have a very large file to find words in). Speed, then, diminishes rapidly with larger files.

Word processors have their uses. They can manipulate interview transcripts, for example. They allow data to be typed in and then exported to a dedicated package, although most of their advanced functions hinder rather than facilitate this data exchange. Word processors can be used to perform data management functions without recourse to a dedicated package, but this can be as time consuming and as prone to error as a manual approach. Crucially, word processors do not provide one of the most useful functions offered by dedicated packages: the ability to refer quickly and easily back to the document from whence data were taken.

### Text retrievers

These are programs which can solve the problem of the slow speed of text searches in word processors. They are specifically designed to search a lot of text as quickly as possible, either in one or a number of files. The text is stored in its original file, but will need to be saved in an appropriate format. The speed increase achieved over word processors is due to the use-specific nature of the packages. Worth looking for in text retrievers are the ability to retain the context of words found (say, five or more words either side) and an ability to produce rudimentary statistics of word counts, percentage of text which is found and the like. Examples include Metamorph and Sonar Professional.

### Text/database managers

These result in a massive increase in speed compared to the above two genres. They may be able to access video and audio tape if it is suitably referenced. Examples are ask-Sam, Orbis and Zyindex.

### Code and retrieve programs

These programs provide the functions needed to work in the grounded theory tradition. They are suitable for researchers more interested in meaning and depth ascribed to data by the analyst, rather than automated categorization found through content analysis. Packages of this genre are able to attribute code (for that also read index, category or label) words to sections of text (although what constitutes a section varies and is sometimes user definable: the word, sentence, line, paragraph or other definable 'unit'). The software is then able to 'retrieve' the code words and place them in a separate location for further study later. Crucially, the link between the locations of the extracted coded data and the original text are maintained. Thus, this takes the place of an advanced manual system of data coding, storage and subsequent retrieval. These packages will require you to 'import' your data to them in a particular format (see difficulties with word processors above). It can sometimes be difficult to change data after they have been imported to the package.

These packages are often able to carry out the features of the text retrievers, but the key to this genre of software is the retrieval of codewords attributed by the researcher and not just words and phrases present in the text, which in text retrievers are found through searches of the data. These code and retrieve packages are able to 'export' the examples of each code ready for writing and analysing in a word processor. Examples of this genre of software are The Ethnograph, Kwalitan and QUALPRO.

### Theory builders

These are the most advanced and feature laden of the packages available, which does not necessarily make them the best or most appropriate to every project. Incorporating the features of the software above, these packages enable the researcher to compare codes and, in their own terms, begin to build theory. This theory building is not simply in terms of positivistic hypotheses, although it does allow, for example, to see whether men of certain ages are more likely to agree or disagree with a proposition than women of the same age. They differ from positivistic analysis because they also allow for theories such as 'do people who talk in a particular way about neighbours talk about family in the same terms?' The key to being able to conduct these qualitative theory-building exercises is the codes (indexes, categories) into which data are categorized (for examples, see Dey, 1993; Richards and Richards, 1995; for a very helpful guide to NUD•IST see Gahan and Hannibal, 1998).

Although the theory-building functions can seem helpful and enticing at the outset, they may be a far cry from the grounded, data-driven approach that characterizes much qualitative research. However, with care and foresight, it is possible to use the theory-building functions as part of a grounded theory approach, which is certainly the intention of the developers (Richards and Richards, 1995). It is often the case, however, that the code-and-retrieve functions of these packages are most useful to qualitative researchers, while the theory-building functions never get used. However, some of these theory-building packages are far more 'user friendly' – ATLAS/ti and NUD•IST, for example – than the code-and-retrieve packages. Many prefer to use them for this reason alone. Another example of this genre is HYPER-research.

Both NUD•IST and ATLAS/ti also have capabilities for graphically displaying the code structure, called the index tree in NUD•IST and network in ATLAS/ti. NUD•IST is based around an index structure which is hierarchical. At the 'top' of the tree are two or three categories, say, 'Base data' and 'Interpretation'. Below base data you would find categories such as 'Age', 'Sex, 'Race', 'Occupation', and/or other pertinent characteristics. Below interpretation would be, depending on the project's focus, 'Family' and 'Neighbourhood', and below 'Family' titles such as 'Positive toward', 'Feels pressured by', and 'Negative'. NUD•IST is very hierarchical in this way, assuming that each 'node', as they are called, is related as in a family tree: thus you get children, parents and siblings. In the above example, 'Family' is the parent of 'Feels pressured by', a child of 'Interpretation' and a sibling of 'Neighbourhood'. The more subtle links between codes, for example, 'Is related to' or 'Is nothing to do with', are explored through the theory-building functions whereby the analyst is able to interrogate the coding scheme. These functions allow the analyst to 'search the index tree' and perform a range of functions, including searching for overlap between any number of codes, to not present in one or in none. ATLAS/ti, through its network facilities, allows the researcher to place different connections between the 'nodes' visually, in order to build up a graphical representation of relationships between concepts, ideas and interpretations of the researcher. Examples of these connections include 'Belongs to', 'Leads to' or 'Is a part of'. The NUD•IST tree is a good way to order the codes, whereas ATLAS/ti is an interesting and some find powerful and useful way to graphically display the connections between the codes.

## Conceptual network builders/graphical mapping packages

These are programs which enable the researcher to build the conceptual frameworks and maps of which NUD•IST and, to a greater extent, ATLAS/ti, are capable. They do not store the data as such, but represent the ideas or codes and relationships between them. Examples of this software, as well as ATLAS/ti, are SemNet and Inspiration.

Computer packages can be useful in a number of ways. However, they can be of no more use than the user puts them to; create a bad coding structure and analysis will be limited by it. Remember, computers do not produce results as such, they merely take some of the laborious data management tasks away from the researcher. The computer system will probably highlight problems in a management system earlier, however, and because of the ease of coding there is more chance of the analyst making the effort to remedy the problems sooner. For example, at the beginning of a project, data may have been sorted by interview type (focus group or one-to-one interview), or by gender, and it may prove later in the project that some other factor is more important, possibly ethnicity or sexuality of respondents. With a computer-based system which allows for rapid recoding, the researcher is more likely to have the time to recode rather than list the interest in the 'further research directions' section of their conclusions.

Beyond data management, the theory builders and conceptual mapping packages prove invaluable to some. But however complex the computer package, it is vital to retain a sense of the tenets of the qualitative approach being used: its fundamentally messy and idiosyncratic nature. The power of computers and the potential they offer is undeniable. Dey (1993), Reid (1992), Richards and Richards (1994) and Tesch (1990) all make convincing arguments for the power of the computer in successfully managing qualitative data, but this unashamed wholehearted embrace of the potential of computers in qualitative research is not without its sceptics. It should be noted, however, that much, but not all, of the literature on using computers to analyse qualitative data is basically pro-computers in some way. Often, the literature is written by the developers themselves (for example, Dey (Hypersoft), Richards and Richards (NUD•IST), Seidel (The Ethnograph) and Tesch (Hyper Research)), although there are notable exceptions (Fielding and Lee, 1991; Kelle, 1995; Miles and Huberman, 1994). For many critics, concerns and criticism begin with society's infatuation with computers and computing itself which, they suggest, blinds researchers to the culture of computing they become complicit with. It is easy to forget that using a computer immediately sets a particular relationship between researchers and their data. A number of commentators have gone on to suggest that the epistemological history of computing through its association with a positivistic, numerically-based tradition must be recognized and overcome before embracing the use of computers in qualitative research.

## COMPUTING CULTURE

Computers are now in every sphere of work and domestic life – Internet addresses adorn advertisements and for many e-mail is now part of everyday life. However, for a long time computers were rightly associated with a particular social group. The complex, large, mainframe computers now largely consigned to the history books made access to computers very privileged, and the mechanics of computer machinery has been a predominately masculine culture. Labels such as 'nerd' and 'hacker' and the schoolboys who write computer software and make their millions perpetuate such associations (see Gilbert, 1995; Tesch, 1990: 168–169). This raises concerns for the use of computers in an analytical approach which purports to be sensitive to difference, aware of the positionality of the researcher and hopefully not sexist. The history of computing, imbued with gendering as some would argue, may be seen by some to be at odds with the concerns at the core of qualitative research. Some have argued that knowledge and the use of computers was a male 'rite of passage'. Men become 'trapped by the machine'. These concerns over gendering resonate with concerns about qualitative researchers becoming infatuated with the power of the software facilities available to them. In interviewing dozens of personal computer users, Turkle encountered some men who seem to have become trapped by the machine: 'The world they had conquered – a world of amateur programming and adventure games – bore little relation to the world of social relations and did nothing to improve their confidence there' (Pfaffenberger, 1988: 22–23).

This is a part of a wider argument in which Pfaffenberger rightly posits the computer and technologies as:

> not a thing, an object to external behaviour. On the contrary, technology *is* social behaviour. If technology is social behaviour, then in assessing its impact we are not talking about the impact of a 'thing' on 'society.' We are talking about the *relationship between one form of social behaviour and others* (Mackenzie and Wajcman, 1985: 3). This relationship is complex, shot through with meaning, indeterminate, and – one might add – a perfect subject in itself for interpretive, qualitative analysis. (Pfaffenberger, 1988: 17; author emphasis)

The use of computers, and the gendered relationships they represent, reflect culture and social relations more widely. The historical and epistemological baggage that computers carry with them must be considered in exactly the same way as a researcher thinking carefully about whether to adopt a positivistic or qualitative approach and the philosophical baggage of each:

> Many human geographers point to computing's close association with certain kinds of research epistemologies . . . A predominantly male computer culture was bolstered by an epistemological perspective taken from developmental

psychology (notably that of Jean Piaget) which held that formal, abstract, logical and symbolic reasoning was the most advanced and powerful form of human cognition. (Gilbert, 1995: 2–3)

The link between a masculine computing culture and a positivist (and therefore anti-qualitative approach) is evident in the very label 'computer':

> Maybe it's the name that causes . . . concerns. If we had called them 'all purpose machines' or the 'symbol handling machines' instead of christening them with the math-sounding 'computers' we might not misrepresent them so often in our minds. There is no doubt that our perceptions can make us misread our own experiences. (Tesch, 1990: 168)

As a qualitative approach must acknowledge, language is imbued with meaning. In this case, the computer label refers to the rhetoric of positivist, quantified, numerical data processing, and it is difficult for this to be challenged. 'Technology is social behaviour,' Pfaffenberger reflects. In this case the social behaviour associated with technology and access to knowledge about computers have been gendered. To use the technology, then, may be seen to be perpetuating these gendered social relations. Such deep concerns often manifest themselves in a sense of alienation and distrust of computers. Users overlook the fact that computers are inanimate and do not make decisions (nor, remember, can they produce results for the user automatically). Rather, the interaction is actually with the computer program and thus with the developers of the software package.

Computers are just machines, programmed by someone who is trying to second-guess our needs as users rather than someone trying to trick us into making mistakes and losing work (though it is very difficult to remember this at times). The history of computing and its present-day usage is one of perceived issues of power, control and access to knowledge, based around a series of 'computing myths' (after Tesch, 1990: 168–169). When trying to overcome these fears, it is important to:

> recognise that the 'minds' of our computers are really the minds of their programmers. People often act as if they were trying to comply with the expectations of their computers; if something goes wrong, they feel somehow at fault, as if they have failed the computer. It is always the other way around: the minds whose programs we are using have let us down. They have sought to imagine what we would want and need in our applications, and have missed.   (Tesch, 1990: 173)

> The programmer, through the program, is our point of contact with computers: Whenever you do anything at all with your computer . . . you must use a program. Each program is nothing more, and nothing less, than the reflection of the mind of the person (or persons) who created it. The moment you call up a program you are beginning an interaction with another mind (or group of minds). (Tesch, 1990: 172)

Qualitative analysis packages are always developed by qualitative researchers who have found the functions of computers useful during their own work. To an extent, then, the functions available should be those that the qualitative researcher needs. However, to reiterate, it is easy to become enticed and infatuated with functions rather than to use them critically. The user becomes aware of the functions available and assumes them to be of use, rather than approaching each with 'critical awareness' and caution. It is important at all stages of the decision to use computers in the analysis process to be aware of what they can offer and the implications this will have. The history of computing may be important if you agree that computers will affect your relationship with your data – or you may dismiss the concerns. Whatever decision, it is important to realize what computers can be useful for and what to be cautious about. To some, the concern is that computers not only alter the relationship between researcher and data, but add an insurmountable distance, which is fundamentally at odds with the 'closeness to data' so treasured in qualitative research (see, for example, Crang, 1997; Tesch, 1990).

## 'DISTANCING' THE RESEARCHER FROM THE TEXT?

The main use for computers in the analysis process has already been outlined: in assisting with, rather than replacing, manual methods of analysis by allowing a convenient, efficient and labour-saving means of storing analytical categories or 'codes' and the manageable storage of the data. More controversially, they can also automate some types of analyses. The automation in-built to text retrievers and theory-building packages includes complex searches for words or phrases which can, in a quasi-statistical manner, provide information about frequency of words or phrases as a percentage of the whole text document (say, an interview) or as a percentage of the project as whole. This information would be virtually impossible to obtain with a manual approach and for this type of analysis the power of computers is self-evident. The word search approach has its uses, but fits best with traditional 'content analysis' which was concerned with such quasi-statistical data (word counts, etc.).

To achieve a more 'grounded' analytical approach, more 'meaning' and interpretation oriented in the approach, the ways in which the computer can assist and complement 'manual' approaches are key. To remain in some way true to the tenets of grounded theory, they should still allow for the creativity and intuitive nature of the qualitative approach, rather than replace it by purported computer-driven rigour and order. However, even the assistance they provide to a well-considered and reasoned manual approach is the subject of much debate because of the ways in which the computer transforms manual methods (see Dey, 1993: 55–57; Richards and Richards, 1991):

A new technology supports a new way of writing. The computer cannot think, but it can help me to think, and even to think differently from how I used to think. Some things I have always done, I can now do quicker and more efficiently; such as correcting mistakes. Some of the things I now do, such as continually restructuring the text, I wouldn't dream of doing without the computer. (Dey, 1993: 55)

The computer gives the researcher a different relationship with their data than through manual approaches. This is true even from the level of writing field notes or interview transcriptions on computer. For instance, it is difficult very easily to include sketches and annotations made in the field (see, for example, Cook and Crang, 1995), although there are now graphic capabilities in word processors and more specialized programs that are helpful. As a result of the very nature of word processors, there is reliance on the text rather than illustration and annotation. When text is written it is viewed differently – on a screen in 30-line segments rather than on A4 or bigger sheets of paper, which can literally immerse the researcher as Dey suggests. On a computer it is difficult to view many pages at once because of screen limitations and impossible to scatter notes on the floor or desk, to make notes in the margin, or to cross out mistakes in a way that allows us to see what has been changed; although as software becomes more complex records of revisions are now possible on computer. The main difference is that the user is able to correct mistakes, not worry about spelling until later and move text sections around at will. As this is being written, I do not have to think about presentation or spelling and can rework sections as I wish – cutting and pasting, changing font type and size, while at all times the document looks all but finished. The completed article is always but a keystroke and printer (or e-mail these days) away from completion, rather than a hastily drafted manual version which needs typesetting and reworking. In qualitative analysis, this gives the result of completed analysis too soon – the text is transformed into a document even through a word processor. Some deliberately try to make their work look unfinished by not justifying the text until a final draft, or purposely using an unattractive font when working on initial drafts of analysis to avoid being sucked into the presentation and formatting power of computers. All of these concerns are valid at all stages of data analysis – from initial transcripts, through computer-based analysis to report writing later in the process.

Computers can offer the potential for the researcher to lose sight of the 'ends' and purpose of qualitative data analysis, instead becoming fixated on the means offered by the software available. It is important to remain critically aware and, crucially, fully conversant with the mechanics of the qualitative analysis process so that a check on the computer's involvement can be maintained. It is definitely worth evaluating a manual approach before embarking on the dedicated package route (for guidance see Burgess, 1984; Cook and Crang, 1995; Crang, 1997; Strauss and Corbin,

1990). It is the distance that computers place between the researcher and data which is of most concern. The traditional image of the qualitative researcher is one of being literally immersed in their data, surrounded by piles of paper, allowing, supposedly, creativity to flourish. The reality is, as Dey suggests (1993), somewhat different. The piles of paper become insurmountable obstacles to analysis, preventing the researcher from being able to make sense of the data, being lost in its mass, rather than inspired by its richness. Although computers do offer the means to manage data, vitally important to Richards and Richards (1995), for example, the picture conjured of the paperless office is somehow alien and threatening. Computers make researchers look at their data differently. With the interface with the data through the computer, researchers often feel distanced from their data, a criticism John Seidel, the developer of the Ethnograph, has had levelled at his software:

> One concern of the author [of a paper he had recently read] was that the use of the computer had separated him from his data. I was quite shocked. The design of the Ethnograph is intended to keep returning the researcher to the data . . . I had envisioned that the Ethnograph would be a vehicle for enhancing the researcher's relationship with the data. (Seidel, 1991: 114)

To Seidel, computers should facilitate closeness to data, not add any distance. They should simply manage some of the more mundane tasks of data analysis, freeing the researcher to focus on the creative elements. He goes on to suggest that rather than diminish the paper involved in the process, the reality should be different:

> Another researcher called me up and said that he missed having his piles of Xeroxed copies and note cards lying around. He felt that he was missing something. I told him not to worry. The program did not eliminate or reduce the number of piles of paper. Rather it simply organised and multiplied them. In no time at all he would be swimming in paper. (Seidel, 1991: 114)

Here, the developer of the software has an attitude very close to grounded theory, which was evident in earlier versions of his Ethnograph software in which it was only possible to code off-line. NUD•IST has allowed on-line coding for some time, which to Seidel adds distance between researcher and data. It is important to keep notes of findings, thoughts and ideas and hopefully, with a computer-based approach, the piles of paper should be analytical rather than administrative. It is important to keep these considerations in mind when developing the analysis process. Although apparently trivial, they are key decisions in the adoption of an appropriate, rigorous and defensible research strategy. Computers can be very helpful to the research process, particularly in data management, but they have their drawbacks:

- They can lure the analyst toward use of functions which were apt for the software developer, but may be at odds with the researcher's theoretical approach. For some this is particularly true of 'theory-building' functions.
- Researchers can be distanced from their data, relying on perceived automation of analysis, rather than retaining the closeness of the data so vital to qualitative data analysis.

However, computers are useful and their adoption should be considered, but used with care. There are a number of questions that are helpful to ask as part of this decision. These are in addition to what might be regarded as 'normal' ethical considerations such as confidentiality, informed consent and the anonymity of respondents, as well as the implications of computer-stored material and the UK's Data Protection Act.

## DECIDING TO USE A DEDICATED SOFTWARE PACKAGE

Using a software package can be very rewarding. The laborious tasks of data handling can be managed by the software, leaving the researcher free to analyse rather than administrate. However, it is vital that a number of issues are considered first: type of computer user; type of data; time considerations; analytic process.

### Type of computer user

It is important to establish whether you are already computer literate, and therefore likely to be able to use new software relatively quickly, or someone less confident with computers who will have to devote more time to learning a new package. Weigh up this evaluation carefully. It is all too easy to dismiss computers as unwieldy, unfriendly and alien and, therefore, to conclude that they can be of no use to your project. Take some time to read experiences of people similar to yourself (start with Tesch, 1990: 167–175). If you are less confident using computers it will help to know someone who can offer advice. If this is not possible spend some time working with the demonstration versions of many packages which are readily available over the Internet. You also need to consider whether you are accustomed to Apple Macintosh or IBM-PC based systems and choose a package available on the platform of your choice accordingly. NUD•IST, as an example, will run on both, whereas other packages are platform specific.

### What data will the project produce?

For computers to be useful, the data have to be in a form appropriate to the software, meaning that the data will usually have to be on-line. This is fine for typed interview transcripts and 'memos' or annotation about non-verbal communication in the interview can be added in most of the advanced packages. Videos or the tape recordings themselves will be more problematic. Thus, the first issue to consider is whether there were plans to type up transcripts or to store them in other ways. This also has several implications. It will be important to differentiate between methodological strategies in a multi-method project, so the ability to tag data will be required. It is possible to apply 'headers' to documents in NUD•IST, for example, and The Ethnograph allows for 'Case Histories' of each document. Try the software before purchase (which can be costly) to make sure that among the array of available functions are the ones you need – again highlighting the importance of planning the analysis strategy before even turning on a computer!

### Time considerations

Qualitative interviews are usually tape recorded and transcribed in varying levels of detail. To transcribe a whole interview will run to many pages of text and take a long time. It may well be tempting to only transcribe the 'relevant' sections, but in a grounded approach it is rarely possible to ascertain what will be relevant until well into the analysis process. If there are plans to work in a grounded theory tradition, there is a need for a management or coding scheme that can evolve with the project. With a manual approach, sections of text could be transcribed and the rest of the tape noted or referenced. Computers may save time in the management of the data and in retrieval and storage, but may add to the time taken to collect and prepare the data for analysis because they usually require on-line complete transcriptions to work to best effect (although verbatim transcripts are not the sole domain of computer-assisted analysis).

### Analytic process

The analytical resolution is an important consideration. It may be appropriate to analyse at the level of a word, a line of text, a paragraph, by the response to set questions or by theme. This level of analysis will dictate the size of 'text unit', which is the smallest level of text it is possible to code. Some software dictates the minimum size of a text unit while others are more flexible. Once the data have been coded they have effectively been taken out of context and placed at a coding point (similar to cutting up the text literally and placing in a coding file, as per a manual system). When the coded material is retrieved, the context of the extract can be vital. Some programs are better at 'spreading' the data once they have been coded or 'de-contextualized'. NUD•IST, among others, allows the user to specify the number of text units either side of the extract to be 'spread' when retrieving coded data, which is a very useful feature.

To reiterate, it is vitally important to have planned the analysis procedure from the outset. If there are to be elements of content analysis, look for software that can perform the text searches easily and quickly. It is worth considering whether you are working with an evolving or an a priori coding scheme. For some research projects it is very clear from the outset what the categories for the data will be and the researcher will then classify data to the already set codes. In other words, you work with a priori codes. A project which 'evolves' needs a package that allows codes to be added and changed as it progresses. NUD•IST's background is in a project where the developer had found manual filing systems too fixed, so it allows the structure of the coding system to be easily manipulated, as does ATLAS/ti (see Richards and Richards, 1995). However, be wary of using the features of a package just because they are there. Be clear about your approach from the outset and only change this after careful consideration.

When all these issues have been addressed you should be able to consider using a computer to assist in the analysis of your qualitative data. The choice of package itself is difficult. Address the various problems and try to work out what features are needed. Miles and Weitzman (1994) document the packages available, and the WWW and other sources can be very helpful in finding demonstration versions, as can specific newsgroup discussions. Individual packages may come and go but the broader questions and issues that should be considered will remain the same. To reiterate:

- The computer is a powerful means to store and manage data.
- The computer does not do the analysis for you, but helps with aspects of it.
- It is very important to understand the mechanics of qualitative data analysis before using a computer package that automates some of the process.
- Computers do not necessarily save time: they do, however, allow you to focus on the analysis of the data rather than the management of them.

**NOTE**

1  NUD•IST stands for Non-numerical Unstructured Data: Indexing, Searching and Theorising. The developers claim that the origin of the acronym was accidental.

# 18 WRITING UP QUALITATIVE DATA

*Peter Jackson*

This chapter has three main aims:

1 To make some general points about *the process of writing* (asking why so many people find it difficult to write and what we can do to make the process less painful).
2 To consider some *theoretical issues about textual strategy* (how writing raises important questions about the politics of representation and what strategies we might use to address these issues).
3 To make some *practical suggestions about 'writing up'* qualitative research.

Put slightly differently, this chapter will ask: *Why* do we write? *For whom* do we write? *How* do we write? Although it will concentrate on the written word (on textual strategies), several of the issues apply equally to questions of visual representation (using photographs, maps and other illustrative material). This chapter includes a case study drawn from a recent ESRC-funded research project on consumption and identity concerning the social use of two north London shopping centres.[1] It concludes with a discussion of some practical strategies for writing up qualitative research (see also Wolcott, 1990).

## WHY DO WE WRITE?

Perhaps it is significant that this chapter comes towards the end of a module on qualitative data collection and analysis. The implication is that writing up is the final stage in a sequence that begins with data collection, proceeds through analysis and culminates in a phase of writing up and disseminating the research findings. Maybe it is simply that we all tend to put off writing as long as possible. Writing is often a painful process that many people hate, or which they only enjoy retrospectively, when it is finished.

My own perspective is very different. I argue strongly against the conventional, linear model of PhD research which begins with research design and literature review, proceeds through a phase of data collection or fieldwork, and ends with a period of analysis and writing up. In my experience this model simply does not work. Writing is nearly always postponed and the completion of the PhD is as far away as ever, the cardinal sin to be avoided at all costs. The preferred alternative is *to write early and write often*; to get into the habit of writing; to write for different audiences; to force yourself to write; to give yourself deadlines and meet them; to get other people to read your work (not just your supervisor); to be prepared to rewrite over and over again (much easier these days with the almost universal availability of word processing).

In an effort to inculcate this habit, a former colleague of mine got his students to write something personal about themselves and then to tear it up and throw it away. This often caused them considerable distress: they felt that what they had written was a part of them, something precious and permanent. But the method was designed to show that nothing we write is sacred; that it is always provisional. Once this lesson is learnt, it becomes much easier to write, safe in the knowledge that our work can always be revised or even dispensed with altogether as our ideas change and progress.

Another reason for writing early and often is that we often do not really know what we think until we have tried to write it down and communicate our ideas to someone else. It is good practice to write something for your supervisor(s) to read before every meeting, even if only a couple of pages the night before. It helps clarify your thoughts, gives your supervisor(s) something to respond to, records the progress of your work and helps set the agenda for your meeting. Two rules of thumb might be that *it's never too early to start writing* and that, with PhD research, *it's always later than you think* (writing up always takes longer than you anticipate).

When you write, you should always write with a purpose and with a sense of your audience in mind. George Orwell's autobiographical essay 'Why I Write' (1946) lists four reasons for writing, besides making money:

- sheer egoism (the desire to seem clever);
- aesthetic enthusiasm (the desire to shape an experience);
- historical impulse (writing for posterity);
- political purpose (to push the world in a certain direction).

'And looking back through my work,' Orwell concludes, 'I see that it is invariably where I lacked a political purpose that I wrote lifeless books, and was betrayed into purple passages, sentences without meaning, decorative adjectives and humbug generally.' While you may not agree with Orwell, it is certainly worth asking yourself periodically why are you writing a PhD? Who is it for? And who (apart from your examiners) do you want to read it?

## FOR WHOM DO WE WRITE?

The question of audience (who will read our work) raises some complex problems about the politics of writing (and also applies to questions of visual representation). For more than a decade, the social science literature has been full of heated debates about the 'crisis of representation' (Marcus and Fischer, 1986). The debate concerns whose ideas are selected for discussion, whose voices are heard and whose are marginalized or silenced. The issue is a response to various political and intellectual movements, within feminism, post-colonialism and various kinds of 'history from below'. It is related to the linguistic and cultural turns in the social sciences (as described by Chaney, 1994). The debate raises questions for us as social scientists about our rights and responsibilities with regard to those whose lives we try to represent, to change or improve.

The 'crisis' came first in anthropology where there is, perhaps, the biggest gulf between those who represent and those whose lives and cultures are represented. Clifford Geertz (1973) has described the whole disciplinary endeavour of anthropology as involving 'the interpretation of cultures', an act of translation in the broadest sense. Culture, according to Geertz, is about inscription, about writing things down. 'The culture of a people,' he insists, 'is an ensemble of texts, themselves ensembles, which the anthropologist strains to read over the shoulders of those to whom they properly belong' (1973: ix). This is, of course, a profoundly political process, reflecting the discipline's colonial past. Any ethnographic work inevitably raises questions about the power of representation: Who is represented and by whom? Who controls access and to whom is it denied? Even the concept of 'ethnography' that anthropologists employ is deeply ambiguous, applying not only to the process of fieldwork and data collection ('doing ethnography') but also to the product of that research (an ethnography), whether in the form of a book, a film or an academic paper.

The 'crisis of representation' has led social scientists to engage in various experimental methods of writing, employing different textual strategies that are designed to overcome (or at any rate reduce) some of the problems associated with conventional narrative structure (Sayer, 1989). For example, there is a rich debate about (auto)biography within sociology, history, geography and anthropology (Okely and Callaway, 1992; Stanley, 1992), as well as experiments with multiple narratives (e.g. Pile and Rose, 1992), 'angry writing' (Keith, 1992) and 'polyvocality', the attempt to record many different voices rather than a single story (e.g. Crang, 1992). These are all part of current attempts to demystify the process of qualitative research. But it is important to remember that experiments with textual strategy will never be adequate to deal with some of the wider questions raised by the politics of representation which involve the entire process of research (from seeking funding, choosing a topic, deciding on a research strategy, collecting data, writing up and disseminating the findings). These questions come more sharply into focus when we consider the actual practice of writing.

## HOW DO WE WRITE?

In this section, I shall refer to a case study from my own recent research. I shall use it to raise a series of questions for you to think through in relation to your own research. The case study concerns the social use of two north London shopping centres (Brent Cross and Wood Green) and aims to explore the relationship between consumption and identity. The project has a number of phases: a questionnaire survey at the shopping centres, a series of focus groups at youth, senior citizen and community centres in and around Wood Green and Brent Cross, and an intensive year-long ethnography at the household level also in the Brent Cross–Wood Green area. Here, I shall be drawing on the initial round of focus groups in the Wood Green–Tottenham area.

The method is described in detail elsewhere (Holbrook and Jackson, 1996). Briefly, it consists of holding informal discussions for around one and a half hours with groups of people who are already acquainted with one another from their membership of various kinds of community groups. The discussions are prompted by a loose agenda of topics (people's likes and dislikes for different kinds of shopping, their preferences for high street shopping, markets and malls, etc.). The conversations are tape recorded and transcribed in full. What issues arise in analysing and writing up such qualitative material? Let us begin with a couple of examples. The first comes from a Wood Green youth club:

*Bev*: Do the young men here go shopping in Next or places like that?

*James*: My mother gets me Next underwear . . . [*laughter, giggles*]. My Next underwear [*emphasized, more laughter and giggles*]. Designer boxer shorts. What's wrong with that? . . .

*Bev*: Do you think the young men here take more care with their appearance than older men?

*James*: Yeah. In day-to-day life, like, some people like to look good all the time. But with me, I only like to look good when I'm going out, or if I'm going to meet someone, or if somebody's coming to visit me. I jump into the bath and have a good wash and stuff like that . . .

*Efua*: Yeah, and put your new underwear on.

The second extract is from a Tottenham mothers and toddlers' club:

*Peter*: Can you think about a recent shopping trip that you went on that you really enjoyed? . . .

*Jane*: With two kids in tow, it's no enjoyment . . . It's alright when you're going to get something they want [the children]. It's when you want to look at something that they get fed up.

*Deirdre*: Yeah, but don't you find, this is my problem always: I go out shopping for myself, and I say, right, this is it. I'm going out today to get something for myself. And I will come back, guaranteed, with something for everyone else at home except what I want. Always. I always intend going out, it's like I get money for Christmas or birthday or whatever, and I decide, right, that's it. I'm going out and spending this on me. And I go out and I see something and I think, oh yeah, that would be nice for Kylie [her daughter]. And then I think, I can't get something for Kylie without getting something for Jason [her son]. And then I think, I've got something for them now I've got to bring something home for Paul [her husband] . . . I come back and I'm lucky if I get, say, an eyebrow pencil or an eyeliner out of it. But I intended to go out and spend maybe £30 or £40 on myself and I go out and spend on everyone else and I'm lucky if I get two quid out of it.

Qualitative material of this kind can be interpreted in a variety of ways. For example, my research associate (Bev Holbrook) and I disagree about how to interpret the first extract. I argue that James's interest in clothing and appearance is indicative of changing gender roles and identities. Traditional models of heterosexual masculinity have not allowed men to take pleasure in their own appearance or to enjoy looking at other men. Far from signalling an ambivalence towards traditional masculinities, however, Bev Holbrook read the extract as confirmation of a long-established pattern of male narcissism and display (see Simpson, 1994). James is performing for an audience of female admirers, even if in this case the subject of the performance is clothing (bought for him by his mother).

Similarly, in the second extract, a number of interpretations could be advanced. In this case, a group of young mothers is discussing the pleasures and pains of different kinds of shopping, recalling their enjoyment of shopping for themselves before they had children, when they had more disposable income and fewer family responsibilities. But there is also an argument here about the loss of personal autonomy as women's individual identities are surrendered to those of their children and husbands, as they invest both financially and emotionally in their children's future. At one level, the loss of autonomy is resented; at another, they derive considerable pleasure from this sense of inter-generational investment.

These are just some of the possible interpretations that might be made of these extracts. If this was your project and you were considering how to analyse and write up this kind of material, what questions would you need to ask yourself? Here, I suggest a number of possible questions and indicate some of the issues that you might like to consider in relation to your own research.

### What does the reader need to know about the research context in order to make sense of the data?

How much background information would a reader need to know about the social backgrounds of those who contributed to these discussions? What difference does it make that the first group was mixed gender, conducted by the female researcher (Bev) on her own, and that the second session was women only, except that both Bev and myself (Peter) were present as 'facilitators'? How much more do you need to know about how the groups were recruited, whether the participants knew each other beforehand, how much the conversation was 'steered' towards certain topics, whether the researchers had a clear 'agenda', what the participants were told about the purpose of the group, and so on. Following on from that, there is the question of attribution.

### How should individual quotations be attributed?

In the extracts, participants are identified only by their first name (including the first names of the researchers). Would it make a difference if the researchers were referred to only by their initials, or as 'interviewer', or not at all? Should a list of all the participants be included, with notes on their social backgrounds, or should individual quotations be attributed with some relevant details in brackets (e.g. 'Deirdre, a 30-year-old Irish single mother'). What characteristics are relevant to include here (age, race, gender, occupation)? What are the implications of different strategies?

### To what extent should the data be 'cleaned up'?

Opinions vary as to whether transcripts should be presented in full (as an appendix, for example) or whether brief extracts such as those quoted here are sufficient. Should the extracts include every hesitation, every 'um' and 'er' of the participants? Silences and hesitations can be revealing about the topics that people feel comfortable talking about and those they have more difficulty discussing in public. But if you include every hesitation, every stumble over words, there is a danger of breaking up the flow of a conversation, or of making participants seem less articulate than they really are (or less articulate than the researcher).

### How would the sense of these extracts change if the researcher's questions/prompts were omitted?

Some researchers omit their own contributions from the discussion or give only brief summaries of them. To what extent would this distort the meaning of such discussions by disguising the researcher's role in 'framing' a particular conversation, or the extent to which they asked leading questions or even put words into people's mouths? Can the researcher's words be analysed in the same way as other participants, or do their contributions have a different status?

## *(How) would the sense be affected by using longer (or shorter) extracts?*

Some researchers use very brief extracts, sometimes quoting two or three participants in support of a single point, often without individual attribution. How does this differ from quoting longer extracts, perhaps of a page or two, with a much fuller description of the speakers? Do different kinds of analysis, or different research questions, require different kinds of writing strategy? Would it be appropriate to offer two or more interpretations of the same extract(s)?

## *Is it acceptable to re-arrange the extracts?*

Would it be acceptable, for example, to leave out a few lines (or words) and to indicate that this had been done by the use of ellipses (. . .)? How much could be left out in this way without distorting the meaning? Would it be acceptable to run together two or more extracts from the same speaker, omitting interruptions from other members of the group? Would it be acceptable to rearrange the sequence of a set of extracts in order to improve the clarity of an argument or to support a particular point? How far are you trying to reproduce a conversation as it 'actually happened' or are you merely trying to reflect the 'spirit' of a particular conversation? (After all, some researchers refrain from using a tape recorder and rely on their memory to reconstruct conversations after the event.) Are you a purist or a pragmatist in this respect?

## *Should you return your analysis to your respondents?*

Should participants be sent a copy of the transcript to check its reliability? Or should they be sent a summary of the topics covered? Should they have the right to edit the transcript if they feel their contributions have been misrepresented? Should we share with them the analysis we propose to make since it is based on their conversations? Should they have the right to challenge our interpretations or to prevent us from publishing things that they may feel do not adequately reflect their own views? Should they have a right of veto? If they do not agree with our analysis, does that invalidate our interpretation? Say, for example, that we wish to argue that some of the women respondents are exploited by their husbands or that they lack economic independence. Would we feel unable to argue this if the respondents themselves do not feel exploited? How independent is our analysis of the 'common-sense' interpretations of those who participated in the research? Or, as Liz Stanley and Sue Wise put it (1993: 200), are the participants in our research on the same critical plane as the researcher?

These are some of the questions that inevitably arise in writing up qualitative research. There are no 'right answers' to many of these questions, but it is our job as social scientists to ask ourselves difficult questions and to come up with working solutions that we can defend both ethically and in terms of our disciplinary and professional standards. Many of the questions indicate that writing up is not separate from analysis. Rather, the writing process involves a series of strategic decisions, each of which has both pros and cons. We can only resolve questions of writing strategy when we are clear what the research questions are and when we know why we are writing and who we are writing for. Let me conclude with some more practical thoughts about writing up qualitative research.

## SOME PRACTICAL STRATEGIES

Let us assume that the practical details of coding and analysing transcripts have been covered elsewhere. (If they have not, then Strauss's *Qualitative Analysis for Social Scientists*, 1987 provides a useful, if sometimes over-elaborate, guide.) Here, I want to focus on various strategies for identifying themes and structuring an argument in terms of possible chapter or section headings. There are at least three possible strategies.

First, it is possible to write up a project as a kind of 'natural history' of how the research was conducted. If the research involved a questionnaire survey followed by a series of in-depth interviews, then the structure of the thesis can follow the same pattern: the research findings can be reported in the same order and using the same categories in which the data were collected. This is probably the easiest strategy but it is also rather unimaginative.

A second more challenging strategy is to select a number of 'themes' around which to report the results. In relation to the previous extracts, for example, one could structure a chapter around questions of gender, around changing 'family values', or the practical problems of shopping with small children. These themes might 'emerge' from the (analysis of the) data or, more likely in my view, might reflect the original aims of the project and the theoretical issues that underpin the research.

A third and more ambitious strategy is an extension of the second. Having conducted a series of interviews or focus groups around a number of themes (differences between high streets and shopping malls, the pleasure and pain of supermarket shopping, variations between men and women consumers, etc.), the writing up can be structured around a different set of themes at a higher level of abstraction.

In some research I supervised about urban redevelopment in London, for example, the thesis was ultimately structured around two meta-themes concerning 'imagining communities' and 'making monuments'. It is here that drawing on the theoretical and conceptual apparatus of your discipline can make a real difference, bringing the writing alive and lifting the analysis above the more mundane level of simply reporting your results.

## CONCLUSION

This chapter has raised a number of issues concerning the writing up of qualitative research. It has shown that the process raises complex ethical considerations about the politics of representation, as well as more practical issues of textual strategy and style. It suggests the benefits of beginning to write early in the life of a project rather than leaving the writing up to a much later stage. It has considered a number of different strategies for writing, each of which raises questions about the relationship between 'theory' and 'empirical' research, and between researchers and those whom we research. As with most issues in social science, there are few if any 'right answers'. Methodological questions can only be resolved once the research problem is adequately specified. Only when you know what you are trying to say will it be possible to write persuasively and with conviction. Conversely, writing may help to clarify your ideas, to identify what you know and what you may still need to find out. In my experience, writing is an iterative process where you begin with a rather poorly defined question and gradually, through several stages of writing and rewriting, come to clarify your objectives and narrow your focus. The sooner you can define the problem and identify the 'story' you want to tell, the easier will be the writing process and the more satisfying the result. Practice may not lead to perfection but it is probably the best means of achieving steady improvement, increasing the pleasures of a process that many people still find intrinsically painful. Even for those who hate the process of writing, there is nothing quite like the satisfaction of having written.

## NOTE

1  The research was funded by ESRC (award no. R000234443). For further details of the project, see Miller *et al.* (1998).

# PART V

# USING COMPUTERS FOR QUALITATIVE DATA ANALYSIS

The purpose of Part V is to introduce you to the use of ASR/Scolari's qualitative data analysis package. NUD•IST, version 4. This acronym stands for 'Non-numerical, unstructured data – indexing, searching and theorizing. The package is a 'theory builder' in the typology presented earlier in the book. The software allows a researcher who is working with qualitative data the facility to import them, manage and store them, and analyse the data using a relatively simple user-interface.

Chapter 19 will take you through the necessary steps to type in some data on a word processor, format and introduce it for use in the NUD•IST package, and become familiar with the workings of the package. It differs from the tutorial that is included in the NUD•IST package because the lessons will take you through the data entry phase. The NUD•IST tutorial is helpful for exploring the more advanced theory-building functions once you have become familiar with the basics presented here.

This hands-on course is designed for a computer novice, so more advanced users may well be able to make quick headway through the early sections. The demonstrations and instructions offered here will be based on the version of NUD•IST operating on an IBM-PC in a MS Windows 98 environment.[1] The look of NUD•IST and some commands may be different on the Apple Macintosh version, but will still be transferable in the main.[2] The only assumed knowledge here will be at the level of familiarity with the MS-Windows 98 platform, including basic file management through the Windows Explorer and basic application of the Word-for-Windows word processor which will be used to enter data initially. As with all computer instruction, it is difficult to cater for every level of user. It is advisable to read through the entire chapter before even using the computer. Make sure you differentiate between instructions for use in the lesson itself and additional information which is provided for you to make further use of when you come to use NUD•IST for your own project in the future.

Because of the varied nature of computers available within the IBM-PC genre, it will be assumed that the package has been installed. This is simple on a stand-alone PC, merely a case of entering disk 1 of the NUD•IST installation set, clicking on the 'Start' button, selecting 'Run' and then typing:

```
A:setup
```

and then following the on-screen instructions. It is important to note the folder that the package installs to, as will become apparent later. This lesson will assume that it is on the C: drive, in a folder, 'NUD•IST'.

## AIMS OF THE LESSON

Although NUD•IST is a 'theory builder' that incorporates functions which allow complex search and evaluation procedures within the coding framework, it can be used very effectively as an easy code-and-retrieve package. The introductory lesson presented here will focus on the functions useful for code-and-retrieve, that most researchers should find apply in any qualitative project. Other authors can be consulted about the more complex theory-building functions (for example, Gahan and Hannibal, 1998; Miles and Huberman, 1994; Richards and Richards, 1991, 1994, 1995). There are problems with using computers in the analysis of qualitative data. Among other wise words, Gahan and Hannibal note:

> Some researchers harbour the desire that a computer will somehow do away with the need to engage with data – that the computer will distinguish the important bits and make the links between these bits. For another group of researchers, it is the underlying fear and anxiety that the computer will indeed take over the data and do things to it! (Gahan and Hannibal, 1998: 1)

In the following lessons that make up Chapter 19 the aim is to dispel both myths. NUD•IST allows you, the researcher, to distinguish the important 'bits', or segments of data – it does nothing to the data unless you ask it to. NUD•IST allows you to make sense of these by categorizing or coding the material and provides an easy to use 'tree' structure to manage the data. It does not take over and it does not do the analysis for you. However, it is a powerful research tool which you should consider using if you are embarking on a qualitative project. Once you have considered a package such as NUD•IST, you may decide to reject it because it is not helpful to you or appropriate to your project, but this needs to be an informed, considered decision.

Chapter 19 will take you through the basics of what is needed to conduct the code-and-retrieve elements of the analysis of an interview-based research project using the package and introduce you to the theory-building component through:

- formatting data ready to import them into NUD•IST;
- building a coding scheme, termed indexing in NUD•IST;
- applying this scheme to the data;
- search and manually coding data;
- an introduction to the theory-building functions;
- instruction on exporting the coded/indexed data reports to a word processor.

The examples and data presented, for simplicity's sake, will all be assumed to be taken from interview transcripts. Bear in mind that NUD•IST can work in a similar manner with any on-line material, including field diaries and data retrieved from an archive. It can also work well with off-line data, for which a suitable referencing system would need to be devised (see NUD•IST reference manual for more details on this approach). NUD•IST is brimming with complex functions, but is designed for use by a wide audience. The Windows interface makes it relatively user friendly.

This chapter is designed for the computer novice and also the qualitative data analysis novice. You will be directed to particular functions which should prove useful to know if you were to go on to use the package for your own work. Gahan and Hannibal's (1998) guide is a useful next step for those who wish to explore the functions and capabilities of the package more fully than there is space to here. Chapter 19 aims to give you the confidence to be able to use the package in a way which is appropriate and helpful for your research. It will enable you to go on to experiment with your own data and to make critical use of the manual, Gahan and Hannibal's guide, and the on-line NUD•IST tutorial included with the package. It is not designed to be a replacement for, but a complement to, all of these resources.

## NOTES

1  This will be familiar to many users of Windows 95 and Windows NT, but is considerably different in appearance to Windows 3.x.
2  Gahan and Hannibal's (1998) NUD•IST guide is based on the Macintosh version of NUD•IST v.4.

## SUPPLEMENTARY READING

Dey, I. (1993) *Qualitative Data Analysis: A User Friendly Guide for Social Scientists.* London: Routledge.

Fielding, N.G. and Lee, R.M. (1998) *Computer Analysis and Qualitative Research*. London: Sage.

Gahan, C. and Hannibal, M. (1998) *Doing Qualitative Research Using QSR NUD•IST*. London: Sage.

Miles, M.B. and Huberman, A.M. (1994) *Qualitative Data Analysis: An Expanded Sourcebook*. London: Sage.

Popping, R. (1999) *Computer-assisted Text Analysis*. London: Sage.

Richards, L. and Richards, T. (1991) 'The transformation of qualitative method: computational paradigms and research processes', in N. Fielding and R. Lee, *Using Computers in Qualitative Research*. London: Sage, pp. 80–95.

Richards, L. and Richards, T. (1994) 'From filing cabinet to computer', in A. Bryman and R. Burgess (eds), *Analyzing Qualitative Data*. London: Routledge, pp. 146–172.

Richards, L. and Richards, T. (1995) 'Using hierarchical categories in qualitative methods', in U. Kelle (ed.), *Computer-aided Qualitative Data Analysis: Theory, Methods and Practice*. London: Sage.

Tesch, R. (1990) *Qualitative Research: Analysis Types and Software Tools*. Basingstoke: Burgess Science Press.

Weitzman, E.A. and Miles, M.B. (1995) *Computer Programs for Qualitative Data Analysis*. London: Sage.

# 19 USING NUD•IST VERSION 4: A HANDS-ON LESSON

## Matt Stroh

### LESSON 1   PREPARING DATA FOR NUD•IST

NUD•IST requires data to be formatted in a particular way for it to be imported. Here, we will type in data, format and save them appropriately, and import into the NUD•IST package. The extracts that we will work with are adapted from my PhD research, which explored people's attitudes to the environment. These are only short extracts to avoid extensive typing. They may be appended by extracts of your own.

NUD•IST requires text to be saved as ASCII, which is text stripped of all formatting characters, thus cannot be emboldened or italicized text because this will be lost when imported into NUD•IST. The procedure for saving as ASCII text will be detailed later. First, we need to type in the text that we will work with.

- Open Word for Windows.
- Ensure that the font is set to 12 point.
- Then type in the following text:

```
MATT: . . . what do you think of when people talk about the
   environment?
CLARE: Just outside really. [. . .] And living space.
MATT: And what do you make of politics?
CLARE: Well, I haven't a lot of time for politicians. I don't
   like politics in local councils you see. I don't think that
   should be in at all.
MATT: Right.
CLARE: I don't think there should be any party politics in
   local - I think you should vote for somebody who you know
   has got a good head on him, or, brain. [. . .] And would -
   would see things - Well, I'd vote for somebody who I
   thought saw things the way I saw them.
```

This is the basic text of the interview with Clare you will be working on. As well as interview text itself, NUD•IST allows the user to include

'Headers'. These headers contain information about the interview which will be displayed whenever the interview is displayed. For this document, pertinent information will be some background information on the interviewee, the type of interview, the location and the date of the interview. The way NUD•IST differentiates headers from interview text is through the use of the asterisk. NUD•IST will look for the first line of text without an asterisk, and takes all that precedes it to be a header. To add a header to Clare's interview, add the following lines *before* the text you have already typed.[1]

```
* Clare, late 50s, retired school teacher
* One-to-one interview
* 1st April, 1997
* Her house, living room
```

Once this has been typed, it is time to save the interview. To create the required ASCII text in Word for Windows use the 'File' menu, and rather than saving normally, click on 'Save As' (Figure 19.1).

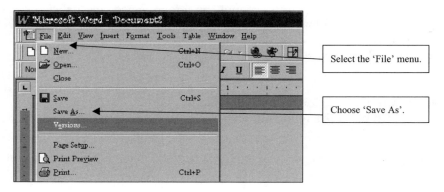

**FIGURE 19.1  Using 'Save As' in Word**

Text units are the basic unit of analysis in NUD•IST. These text units are the smallest scale of analysis. This basic text unit might be individual words, sentences, lines of text or paragraphs. The size of text units is set by placing a 'hard carriage return'. This is achieved by pressing 'Return' or 'Enter' and thus starting a new line, as you do at the end of a paragraph.

'Soft carriage returns', which do not constitute text unit breaks in NUD•IST are those which the word processor adds to text automatically as you reach the end of a line within a paragraph.

When you come to use NUD•IST for your own work, if the text unit was to be the paragraph, you would click on save as 'Text Only'. If, however, you want the text unit to be a line of text, click on 'Text Only with Line Breaks'.

For this project, we will work with lines as the text unit, so select 'Text Only with Line Breaks', but you should experiment and consult your analysis strategy and research aims for an appropriate level of analysis (Figure 19.2).

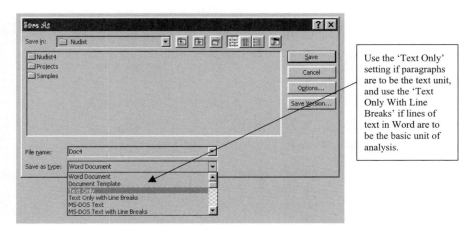

**FIGURE 19.2   Saving as 'Text Only'**

Call the document 'Clare' by typing her name in the filename box. Select a location to save the document that you will be able to remember, and click on 'OK'. Word will warn you that formatting will be lost, which is precisely what we need to transfer the data to NUD•IST, so click on 'Yes' to continue.

Once this has been completed, you need to type in the other interview data we will work with. You need to follow the same procedure for the following documents for Andrew, Anthony and Dorothy. Remember to work in 12-point font, to include the header as I have complete with the asterisk, save as 'Text Only with Line Breaks' and to save the documents in the same location as the 'Clare' document that you have just saved.

```
* Andrew, mid 20s, school teacher
* One-to-one interview
* 21st April, 1997
* His house, living room


MATT: So you enjoy the countryside then? In what ways?
ANDREW: . . .The thing is I live in this contradiction. What
    I like is to go out into, onto this hillside and enjoy the
```

fact that no-one else is there. [. . .] And that's what
everyone else wants to do, but I'm there ruining that. . .
MATT: Yeah.
ANDREW: You know, and it's this contradiction in my mind the
whole time; things like the Duke of Edinburgh. The whole
point of the Gold Trip is that you're away in a wilderness
area. You're a self-sufficient unit going out into this
area where there aren't roads, car parks, help, telephones,
all the rest of it. But the very fact that you're going out
doing that, is wrecking it for somebody else. And you know
there's a limit to the number of people that can do that.
Coz if everyone wanted to do it, there wouldn't be a
wilderness area any more . . .


* Anthony, environmental voluntary worker, mid 30s
* One-to-one interview
* 1st March, 1997
* His place of voluntary work, office


MATT: How about what it is we're looking after. What is the
environment? What is included?
ANTHONY: . . . well, the environment is everything isn't it?
It includes everything.
MATT: . . . good answer! . . . [laughter] . . .
ANTHONY: Yeah . . . I can only come back to the political side
of it again because sometimes it's uncertain as to what the
environmentalists are after.
MATT: Mm huh
ANTHONY: all right? . . . what type of society they're after.
MATT: Mm huh
ANTHONY: How they want production to be organized. . .


* Dorothy, late 40s, homemaker, active member of env'l group
* One-to-one interview
* 12th April, 1997
* My office


MATT: And what about the preservation and management of those
kind of areas, then?
DOROTHY: Yes. It's unfortunate that, in some ways, now we have to
have special footpaths put on them. But on the other hand if it
stops the mountain eroding then, if you want to go . . . I don't
think, the right answer is to prevent people from going and
enjoying. . . [. . .] then so be it. ..

At the end of the process, you should end up with four documents, Clare, Andrew, Anthony and Dorothy, all saved as Text Only with line breaks in the same location. These are now ready to incorporate into the NUD•IST system. Once you have completed these tasks, close Word and we are now ready to begin using NUD•IST itself.

## LESSON 2   STARTING NUD·IST

To run NUD•IST, click on the start button, select 'Programs', then 'QSR NUDIST' and then click on the NUDIST icon. If you have not already entered the required registration details you will prompted to do so before the package will start. Once you have entered these details, you may need to restart the package. Once that process is complete, you will be presented with the opening screen (Figure 19.3).

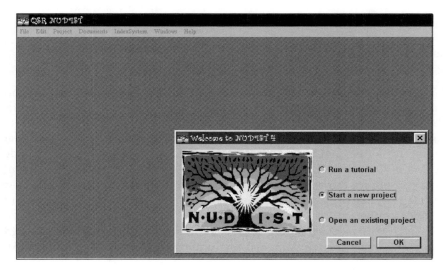

**FIGURE 19.3   NUD·IST opening screen**

We will open a new project called Environment, so click on 'Start a New Project', and then 'OK'. NUD•IST will move you to its 'projects' directory. Type 'Environment' in the filename box and click on 'Save'. Enter your name as requested. (NUD•IST allows multiple users to work on a project. It is useful to know who has coded and analysed what, so NUD•IST keeps a track of users' names.)

NUD•IST will then open the 'Node Explorer' and 'Document Explorer' window. The basic system of organization within NUD•IST, as will become increasingly apparent is the 'Index Tree'. Figure 19.4 shows a 'working' NUD•IST screen shot which will explain this.

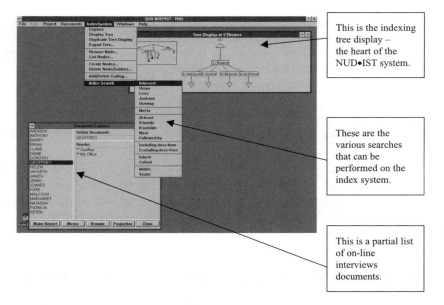

This is the indexing tree display – the heart of the NUD•IST system.

These are the various searches that can be performed on the index system.

This is a partial list of on-line interviews documents.

**FIGURE 19.4   NUD•IST at work**

The indexing tree is the core of NUD•IST's code-and-retrieve and theory-building functions. Each point on the tree diagram is called a node. The nodes can either just be labels, or they can contain coded data. Data can be pasted to any node, as we'll do later. The tree has a root, oddly at the top for a tree, and branches. These nodes can be looked at in the 'Node Explorer', but first data need to put into the system. The 'Document Explorer' allows the user to see the documents included in the 'Project'. At this stage of our project (called 'Environment') there are no documents and no nodes either.

As NUD•IST will be telling you in the Node Explorer window, to add documents open the 'Documents' menu and select 'Import' (Figure 19.5).

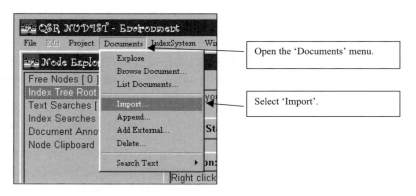

Open the 'Documents' menu.

Select 'Import'.

**FIGURE 19.5   Introducing documents to NUD•IST**

Once a project has been created it creates a series of directories, one of which is 'Rawfiles'. This is the NUD•IST term for ASCII text saved from a word processor ready to import. However, we created the documents before we created the project, so will need to navigate to wherever you saved the files in Word. Once you have found them, select 'Clare.txt' and click on 'OK'. NUD•IST will then prompt you for a name for the file, and here you should type the interviewee's name, Clare. Click on 'OK' to proceed. Once you have done this, Clare will appear in the Document Explorer. Click once on 'Clare' and you will see the header information appear. This can be very useful for identifying and jogging your memory about the interview details (Figure 19.6).

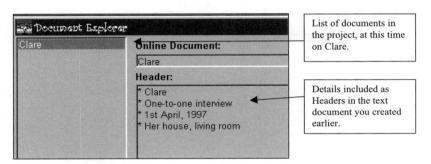

**FIGURE 19.6   Document Explorer**

There are various buttons on the Document Explorer you should look at:

- *First click on 'Browse'*, which will open the document in the 'Document Browser'. Note that it is relatively difficult to change text once it is entered into NUD•IST, so check through the document at this stage for any errors and, if necessary, remove the document from the Project, using the 'Delete' option back on the 'Documents' menu. It is possible to amend individual text units, but any edits that are complex are worth doing back in the word processor before any coding and analysis has begun. Clicking on browse also opens the 'Indexing Palette'. This is used when coding and editing the document. We will work with this more later, but for now note that the 'Edit' and 'Insert' text unit functions are located here. Close both the Document Browser and Indexing Palette by clicking on the 'X' on the top right of each.
- *'Properties'* opens up an information dialog, which tells you when the document was introduced and last worked on ('modified'), and again reminds you of the header information. It also tells you how many text units the document is – Clare's interview is 13 text units long in my version, and this will vary slightly depending on how the margins, etc. were configured on your machine. The number of text units can be useful at this stage for confirming that the document saved from the

word processor correctly. If you have a document with far fewer text units than the number of lines of text, chances are you saved it just as 'Text Only' in the word processor, thus making each text unit equate to a paragraph rather than a line of text. If this is the case, delete the document from the project (Documents menu, then delete), reopen it in Word, and resave it following the instructions above. You can use the Properties dialog to change the name of the document. It may be the case that it gets entered incorrectly, or that you later interview another Clare and need to differentiate the two. Simply overtype the 'Clare' in the name box, and then click on 'OK'. NUD•IST will ask you to confirm the change. Clare is the right name, so do not change it, but just exit the dialog by clicking on 'OK'.

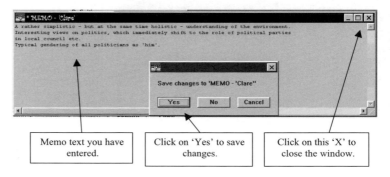

| Memo text you have entered. | Click on 'Yes' to save changes. | Click on this 'X' to close the window. |

**FIGURE 19.7   Memoing Clare**

- *'Memo'* is one of the most useful features of NUD•IST (Figure 19.7). This allows you to attach any sort of textual information to both documents and also individual nodes. For a document memo, you would use the feature to store ideas or comments about the conduct of the interview that may have bearing on the analysis. As the project progresses, you would begin to use this to store ideas about possible themes in the interview, or perhaps as a reminder to check on something later. Recording the progress of qualitative analysis is vital, and memoing is an important part of the process. You should add a memo to the Clare document to practice. To do this, click on 'Memo' and then 'Yes' to create a new memo for Clare. A new window will open on which you can type a memo. Add the following comment to this memo window:

```
A rather simplistic - but at the same time holistic -
   understanding of the environment.
Interesting views on politics, which immediately shift to
   the role of political parties in local council etc.
Typical gendering of all politicians as 'him'.
```

After typing the text, click on the top right 'X' on the memo window to close it, and then 'Yes' to save changes:

- *'Making Reports'* is a function central to the way NUD•IST operates. Creating Reports is the way the user retrieves information from NUD•IST. To see coding held at a node, you 'make a report' in much the same way as in a manual system you would go to a file and open it up and see what is stored there. Documents can be 'reported on' to review work which has been carried out on them. You have been using Word earlier in this lesson, so should configure NUD•IST to save reports in a Word format. Open the Project menu now. Select 'Preferences' and 'Reports Files' and then click on Microsoft Word.

- *Next you will create a report.* At this stage you have added a memo to the document, Clare. As we progress you will add coding, or indexing as it is termed in NUD•IST. Although the focus of your analysis will be the coding, stored at Nodes on the index tree, it is important also to explore and be reminded of how text units of the interview documents have been coded. This is useful if only to highlight any omissions in the coding procedure. Click on 'Make Report'. A dialog will open asking you what you would like NUD•IST to report to you. For now, ensure the 'No Coding' box is checked (after all, we haven't added any as yet!), and make sure the Document Header, Memo and Text boxes are checked (Figure 19.8).

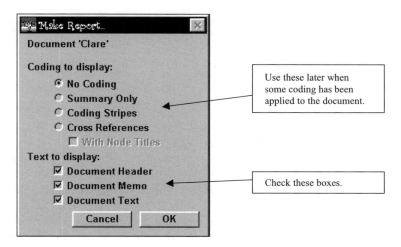

**FIGURE 19.8   Making document reports**

- *Click on 'OK' to continue.* NUD•IST will ask what text range you would like to report on, which for this document can be all the text units (this will probably vary from the 13 text units I had when using the data provided as a result of margin and other settings in Word). In larger documents NUD•IST may limit the amount you can review in

NUD•IST itself and offer you the option of saving the report for review in a word processor. Click on 'OK' and the document report will appear showing user information, which should be your name, the project name and the time the report was created. This is important for logging development of analysis as the project progresses. The report browser then displays the header, memo and numbered text units, in my case from 1 to 13. If you had selected less than the full document, it would calculate what percentage of the document you were viewing (Figure 19.9).

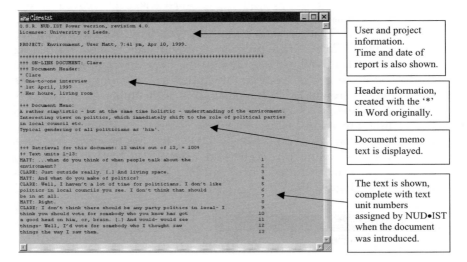

**FIGURE 19.9    Document reporting on Clare**

- *Clicking on the top right 'X' will close the report*, prompting NUD•IST to ask whether you wish to save the report. Click on 'Yes' in this instance. NUD•IST will open the file manager dialog. You should use the file manager to navigate to the 'Projects' and within it the 'Environment' directory. This was automatically created when we entered the title of the new project. Thus, if you start a project entitled 'PhD' or 'Research', a directory will be created with that title by NUD•IST, which is where the working for your project will be stored. If you haven't done so already, double-click on the Environment folder to select it. This will display the folders NUD•IST created for the project (note the RAWFILES directory we could now use to save new text documents from Word).
- *Double click on 'Reports'* and then enter the document name as 'Clare Report', then click on 'Save'. This saves the report as a text file which you should now look at in Word. Close down NUD•IST (select the File menu, then Quit), open Word and then open the file you just created in NUD•IST. In Word, select the File menu, then Open, then

navigate to the NUDIST directory, through PROJECTS, ENVIRON-
MENT and into REPORTS. To see the text file you just saved in
NUD•IST you may have to ask Word to look for 'All Files' in the 'File
Type' box. Then double-click on the 'Clare Report' file to open it. You
may be asked to click on 'OK' to convert the file from text only. The
file will now open in Word. This is the same procedure that you will
need to use later in the lesson to explore coding and other analysis of
the data. Note that because NUD•IST is compatible with many types
of word processors, the reports are saved as text only, stripped of
formatting, so to include reports in papers etc. will need time allocated
to reformat them.

- *Close the report and reopen NUD•IST*. Now that the project has been
  established, select 'Open an Existing Project' and choose 'Environment'. The 'Daycare' project which may be listed is part of the
  NUD•IST tutorial. You should find yourself back with the Node and
  Document Explorer windows open.

So far we have only introduced one of the four interview documents.
We now need to introduce the other interview documents you created in
Word. Do this now as you did for Clare: remember: documents menu,
import, find the file, give it a name and check it quickly in the Document
Explorer where you should see the header information . . . Once this has
been done for all three other documents, they should all appear in the
Document Explorer and should each be checked for errors using the
'Browse' facility. By this stage you are able to use NUD•IST's basic
functions. You can:

- create new projects in NUD•IST;
- format documents and import them into NUD•IST;
- explore documents using the Explorer in NUD•IST;
- create memos;
- make and save reports, and then view them in Word.

The next stage is to add coding to the imported text and store that in the
index tree.

## LESSON 3   CODING WITH NUD•IST

Qualitative approaches produce thousands and thousands of words,
which have no obvious analytical structure. The codes chosen need to be
both meaningful and helpful. Using codes and breaking down the data
and placing them at the codes is a means to make a mass of unstructured
data manageable. The codes need to make sense of the data and give the
researcher a means to organize and categorize the large amount of data.

> Calling a tree a tree, whether it's a young apricot or an old oak, or a Christmas tree, is a matter of forming categories or classes of things in our mind and sorting real objects into them. (Tesch, 1990: 135)

In exactly the same way as trees are all classified under one heading, data need to be sorted into meaningful and useful categories called codes.

Qualitative research usually involves some degree of the researcher exploring the text for themes that inform the choice of codes which emerge from the data. Other approaches, such as content analysis, require the researcher to search the text for words and phrases. NUD•IST allows both, which you will get the chance to see here. Before this, however, it is important to understand and be able to use NUD•IST's indexing tree. The tree is a hierarchical organizing system for data, based on an upturned tree. There is a 'root' at the top, with branches sprouting below it – similar to a flow diagram. In qualitative analysis the root will sprout, usually, two branches: 'Base Data' and 'Interpretation'. Under 'Base Data' you would place codes such as 'Gender' and 'Age'. Under 'Interpretation', you would code thematic interpretation of the data.

Although the tree-like scheme is simple to follow and use and makes a simple data management tool, it is not necessarily the most analytically useful. Some find it too constraining and would rather have the ability to display more links between categories than just 'Belongs to' or 'Owns', which are the only links you can show in a hierarchical tree. Other links might be 'is related to', 'causally affects', 'has nothing to do with', or 'contradicts'. Rather than displaying this variety of links between nodes on the basic tree, NUD•IST allows complex searches of the tree and uses them to make the links between coded data. It is important to be aware that the organizing system used for data is the main constraint on the way they can be analysed. A poorly planned management system will most likely result in poorly analysed data. (See Chapters 15 and 17 for some advice, and also Cook and Crang, 1995; Dey, 1993; Tesch, 1990; and Baxter and Eyles, 1997 for the importance of planning and rigour in qualitative research.) So, for your own project you would need to plan an organizing system that could be incorporated on the tree system at the heart of NUD•IST. Before data can be coded, then, it is important to become familiar with the manipulation and operation of the indexing tree.

### Taking control of the tree

If NUD•IST is not already running, start the package and open the 'Environment' project we have been working on. The Node Explorer shows the tree in one form. To see the tree more graphically, open the 'IndexSystem' menu and click on 'Display Tree'. At this stage, you will only see the root. We need to create two 'children' for the root. On the hierarchical system NUD•IST uses, it is easy to apply a familial metaphor.

Nodes can be seen to spawn child nodes beneath it; thus, a node will have siblings (brothers and sisters), a parent node, and possibly children too. To exemplify this, we will create children from the root. On the tree display, click on the 'Root' node. A pop-up menu will appear. Select 'Create Node'. A dialog will appear asking you to name the node and to define it if you wish. Note that you can also 'Make Report' on the node and memo in exactly the same way as we did with the Clare document earlier. There is also the 'Code' option to which we shall return. For now, in the dialog call the node 'Base Data' and in the 'Definition' note that the node will store basic information about the interviewees (Figure 19.10).

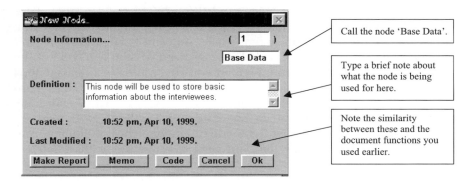

**FIGURE 19.10   Creating nodes**

Click on 'OK'. NUD•IST now creates the node, but it can take a short while for it to be shown on the tree display. If it does not appear, double-click on upper left-hand-side of the tree display itself – at the moment this will appear to be an empty box, but will eventually show an outline of the whole index tree. You should now see the root with one branch, leading to the base data node you just created. Click on the 'Root' again, and create a node for 'Themes'. This will store thematically coded analysis. Create this in the same way as previously. Select 'Create Node', enter the name of the node and basic information in the next dialog, then check it appears on the tree display. You will now see that the tree shows both nodes you have created, and the purpose of the inset tree display should be becoming clearer.

We now need to create further nodes. Under 'Base Data' we need to add nodes for gender, and thus male and female, and also for age. Click on 'Base Data' and then 'Create Node' and work though the process above to create two children: gender and then age. Under gender create nodes in the same way for male and female. Under age create nodes for 20–39, 40–49 and 50+.

To move around the tree is relatively simple. Clicking on the big arrow that appears under 'Base Data' after you create the gender and age nodes allows you to move down a level. Later, an arrow up will appear, and this will take you back to the root or to the next level up the tree depending on which you choose from the mini-menu that will appear. You will get more practice as the course progresses. If you lose sight of the index tree, use the 'Windows' menu to bring it back into view.

Remember that gender and age are siblings, thus should both be created from the 'Base Data' node, whereas the gender and age categories are their respective offspring, so you should create them *from* the gender and age nodes. Again, if you find the tree is not being displayed properly, double-click on the upper left side of the tree display window.

If you have made a mistake it should be simple to remedy. It is easy, for example, to end up with 'Gender' branching directly from the root rather than from 'Base Data', or for 'Men' and 'Women' to end up from 'Base Data' rather than 'Gender'. To solve these problems, think of the indexing tree as you would a Word document when you want to cut-and-paste, and therefore move, a segment of text. Thus, we need to 'cut' a section of the tree and 'paste' it to the relevant node. If you haven't made a mistake thus far, well done! You need a mistake to work on, so create a node from 'Base Data' called mistake. Next, click on the 'Mistake' node, or whichever node is actually in the wrong place, choose 'Cut' and it will go. Note that you could actually delete either just that node or any branches of the tree from it, but for now I will assume that you need to move rather than delete a node. So, 'Cut' the node.

When you cut anything, nodes or text, it is stored on the 'Clipboard'. In NUD•IST, this is called the 'Node Clipboard' and can be viewed at any time by using the Node Explorer. So, click on 'Node Clipboard' on the Node Explorer and you should see details of your 'Mistake' node (Figure 19.11).

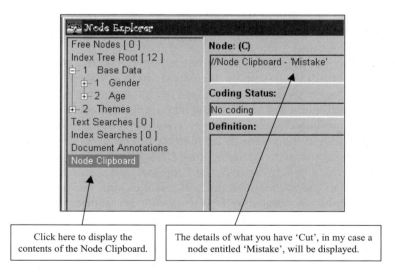

FIGURE 19.11   Node Clipboard

You can use this to check you have cut the right node. Once you have confirmed you have cut the right node move back to the tree display. If you are correcting an error, you need to find where the node needs to be. If you are working with a 'Mistake' node navigate to the 'Gender' node, click on the node and the pop-up menu will appear. Select 'Attach', which is the equivalent of the 'Paste' command in Word. If you have just added a mistake node, admire your work and then click on the mistake node and 'Delete' and then 'Node' from the menu. If you find you have more mistakes to correct, repeat the above procedure.

Use the 'Window' menu to bring the tree back into view. When you have created the nodes, the tree should look as shown in Figure 19.12.

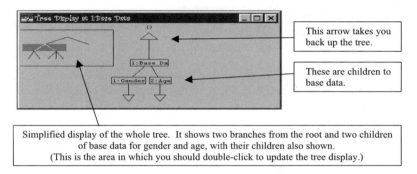

FIGURE 19.12   Tree Display window

The display in Figure 19.12 shows the two children of the root node and the split into base data and themes. Under base data, there are nodes to store basic information about the interviews of gender and age of the interviewee. There may be other pertinent information that could be added here – in a multi-method project, different types of interview might be an important distinction; or political affiliation or income of the interviewees in some cases. Basically, these are nodes at which the complete interviews will be coded: the whole of Dorothy's interview should be under 'Female', and also in the '50+' category. To add a whole document to a node is simple in NUD•IST. Move round the index tree until you find the '50+' node. Click on it and the pop-up menu will appear. Click on the first line of the menu, which should read '3: 50+' (Figure 19.13).

Once you have done this, a node dialog will appear. For this exercise we will use the 'Code' button. Click on this and the coding dialog will appear. Here you can select a document (by name), a node address and the numbers of the text units to be coded. The node address is simple to work out. From the root there are two branches. The one that was created first is numbered '1'. Thus, base data should be '1' and themes '2'. Under base data two children were created: gender and age. Assuming age was created first, this will be number 1, and age 2. The node address for age is

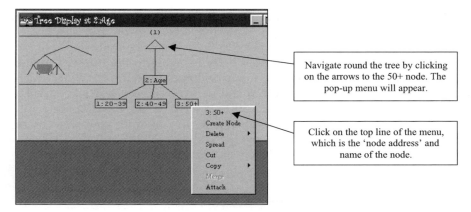

**FIGURE 19.13   Adding coding**

thus: (1 2). It is the second node under base data, which is number 1 from the root. Gender would be (1 1). '50+' is the third node created under age, and is thus the node address of (1 2 3) which NUD•IST displays in the coding dialog.

It is important to familiarize yourself with this node identification system for use later. For now, though, we need to add the whole of the Clare document to 50+. So, either type in 'Clare' in 'Document Name', or choose 'Select' to choose Clare from the document list, and also check the 'Entire Document' box in the coding dialog. Click on 'Add' to complete the procedure. NUD•IST will then code the entire Clare document to the (1 2 3) node. One confusion here is that NUD•IST assumes you will use the coding dialog to perform a number of coding operations at once. Thus, once you have coded Clare to the 50+ node, the same coding dialog reappears. There are no other interviews to be stored at 50+, but Clare needs to be coded to 'Female', and it is possible to do this by simply entering the node address in the coding dialog – this should be 1 1 2 (note the space between each number). If you are unsure, click on 'Select', next to 'Node Address' and the Node Explorer window will appear. Like Windows Explorer's ability to explore layers of files and folders on your hard disk, you can expand the branches of the tree by clicking in the little '+' sign next to 'Base Data' then the '+' next to 'Gender' (Figure 19.14).

Once you have selected the node in the Explorer, the node address will be placed in the dialog – (1 1 2) in this case. Again, click on 'Add' and the entire document will be coded at that node. This should be repeated for all the documents at the relevant nodes, using both the node and document select options.

Once you have coded Andrew to '20–39' and 'Male', Anthony to the same, and Dorothy to the appropriate node we need to check the coding has been applied correctly. To exit the coding dialog, click on 'Stop'. The coding could be checked by making a report for each document as we

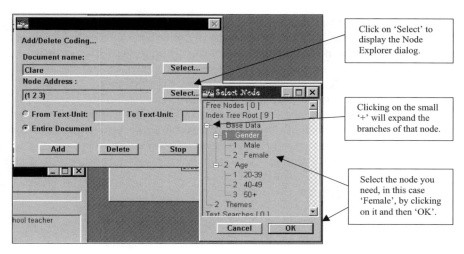

**FIGURE 19.14   Selecting nodes in the Explorer**

have done previously, to check which text units are coded where (in this case it should be all text units at the nodes), or a report can be generated at the nodes themselves, which we shall try now. The Node Explorer, at the top left of the NUD•IST screen, will also allow us to make a quick check on what is coded where. This works in the same way as the base data branches which were expanded when you were adding coding. The Node Explorer also shows some basic information about each node. For example, clicking on the 'Base Data/Male' code will tell you that 2 documents are coded there, comprising 25 text units (Figure 19.15).

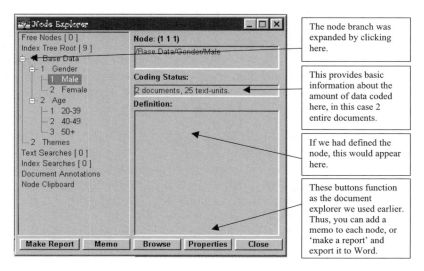

**FIGURE 19.15   Node Explorer**

The Node Explorer allows you to work with the nodes in the same way that the Document Explorer worked with documents: so you can check on the properties of the node; make a report to export to Word for editing; or browse the contents of the node. At this stage, each of the nodes will merely contain the entirety of the documents coded there, because we selected 'Entire Document' during the coding process. This has simply categorized entire documents by gender and age. Class, income or other factors may also be worth categorizing in some projects. However, most qualitative data analysis requires the researcher to explore the data and to code shorter extracts by theme. Now you have a basic understanding of the tree structure and can use the Node and Document Explorer, you are ready to begin to code the documents thematically.

### Coding segments of data in NUD•IST

There are a number of methods of adding coding in NUD•IST. You have already seen how you can add coding from the Document Explorer by opening a document, clicking on 'Properties' and then 'Code'. You then select the node address and the number of text units and coding is adding (at this stage you have only added entire documents, of course). The same dialog can be accessed from the Node Explorer, from which you select a node, click on 'Properties' and then, as before, 'Code'. Another route to this dialog is from the 'IndexingSystem' menu, and selecting 'Add/Delete Coding'. NUD•IST contains this variety of methods to meet individual researcher's needs. For some, it is important to be able to index one document to a number of places relatively quickly, as we have done with the base data nodes. Thus, you would want to select the document and be able to index from there. You could do the same from each node if you knew which documents were male interviewees and so forth. The 'IndexSystem' menu option can be useful if you have manually indexed the interviews off-line. In other words, you have made a report of an entire document, printed it out and then used a highlighter pen or other manual approach to coding and want to add particular segments of text to particular nodes. You would have the text numbers already on the print-out, and should be able to learn their indexing node addresses relatively quickly (or you can choose the 'Select' option in any case).

There is another way of adding indexing which can speed the process, although some feel that it can detract from the qualitative analysis process (see in particular Seidel, 1991). This is on-line coding, which we shall now work with. Before we can do that, we need to develop the other half of the indexing tree and give ourselves some themes. Therefore, you will need to create nodes under themes. Display the index tree ('IndexSystem' menu and 'Display Tree') and then find 'Themes'.

To navigate around the tree, click on the large arrowheads – if you click on an up arrow you will be given the choice on a small pop-up menu to go straight to the root or just one level up the tree. Clicking on a down arrow will take you to the next level down.

When there, click on 'Themes' and then 'Create Node'. In this tree structure, the nodes here should be the analytical themes of the project. For the few extracts we have here, we can consider the importance of the role of the individual as opposed to government – what I would term 'Active Agent', which can either be individuals or politicians at this stage. So create a node 'Active Agent' – done by changing the name. Add a definition that says, 'Who's role to be active in encouraging change?' Click on 'OK' and an arrow down should appear from 'Themes'. Click on this to move down the tree. Then we need to create two children from 'Active Agent', the first 'Individuals', the second 'Politicians'. Click on 'Active Agent', then 'Create Node' for each (Figure 19.16).

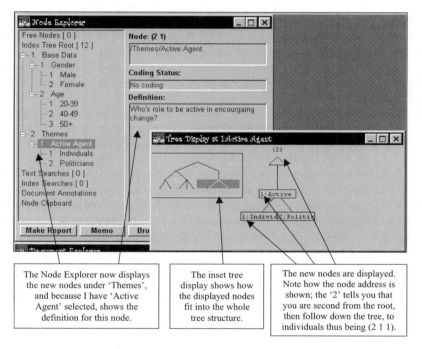

| | | |
|---|---|---|
| The Node Explorer now displays the new nodes under 'Themes', and because I have 'Active Agent' selected, shows the definition for this node. | The inset tree display shows how the displayed nodes fit into the whole tree structure. | The new nodes are displayed. Note how the node address is shown; the '2' tells you that you are second from the root, then follow down the tree, to individuals thus being (2 1 1). |

**FIGURE 19.16   Nodes created under 'Themes'**

### On-line coding

To code extracts of data on-line, that is on-screen, without having to print it out first is very simple in NUD·IST. We have created some nodes, so we know what we are looking for in the data. In a whole research project, you would obviously have more nodes and more themes to explore. With NUD·IST's tree display, it is easy to see whether you have too much complexity and too many branches. Eventually you need to whittle down the number of useful codes to three or four for a PhD thesis, with three or four analysis chapters. Obviously each code would have sub-themes but avoid a colleague's example, who became infatuated with the simplicity of clicking on text and adding coding and ended up with over 1,500 code-words. Before devising analytical codes, which you have seen to be very easy to do, think hard about why you need another theme and write yourself a memo justifying the choice. Suggestions for some of the analytical process can be found elsewhere in the collection, but for now we will focus on the mechanics of using the software.

So, we have an interest in who the 'Active Agent' is perceived to be and divided this into 'Individuals' or 'Politicians'. Those with an interest in gender studies can draw parallels between these and private/public gender divides. It will be interesting to compare the opinions on this issue between the men and women in the project. Please note that this is just a snapshot of example data you are working with that will show the principles of using the computer and not offer substantive conclusions on the issue. There is a need to trawl through the data and code according to whether the interviewees are ascribing responsibility to themselves (individuals) or politicians.

We can explore the text using the Document Browser. The indexing palette opened at the same time as the document, you may remember, and this is what we will use to code the interviews. So, using the 'Document Explorer', click on the first document, Andrew, and then choose 'Browse'. The text of the interview, complete with header information will be displayed, and the indexing palette will also open. The interviewee to me appears to be concerned about their impact on the environment, and seems to be taking personal responsibility for that. They are not expecting politicians or any policy to change their views, and this is particularly emphatic in Andrew's comment that:

```
10   it. But the very fact that you're going out doing that,
     is wrecking it for
11   somebody else. And you know there's a limit to the
     number of people that can
12   do that. Coz if everyone wanted to do it, there wouldn't
     be a wilderness area
13   any more . . .
```

He realizes that he is personally having an effect, and his actions need to be changed. The exact numbering of the lines will vary from computer to computer, and this depends on margins set in your word processor. Before embarking on your own project, it is worth experimenting to get the line of text to fit on one of NUD•IST's lines (around 75 characters per line). Concentrate here on finding the text itself rather than on the exact line number which is what we need to code to the 'Active Agent/Individual' node.

So, highlight the text in the Document Browser and then click on 'Add Coding' on the indexing palette. You then need to enter the node address, or use 'Select' to navigate through the tree as you have done before to find the node.

If you were to click on 'Free Node', you could attach text to a new node which NUD•IST would create for you. This facility is designed for you to be able to have an idea while looking through the text and not needing to add to the tree right away. These free nodes are displayed in the Node Explorer and can then be renamed and cut and attached to a location of your choice: these are nodes for 'work in progress', if you like.

For now, though, we know the node – address 2 1 1 (note, this may be slightly different if you have previously made an error and cut and attached nodes earlier). Click on 'OK' and the text will be coded to that node. It is no more complex than that to use NUD•IST as a basic coding package. Of course, you then need to be able to retrieve your coding. This is the real power of the computer package over a manual system in which you may have to search through files containing literal extracts from interviews.

### Retrieving coding

It is possible to retrieve the coding in a number of ways. Here I will show you how to use the tree and the Node Explorer. To use the tree, click on the tree display and navigate through the tree, using the large arrows, remember, from the root down to the 'Themes/Active Agent/Individual' node. If you can't see the tree display, use the 'Windows' menu and select 'Tree Display'. If the tree display is not listed, go to the 'IndexSystem Menu' and select 'Display Tree'.

Click on the 'Individual' node and the pop-up menu will appear. Click on the name of the node, the top line of the menu, and the node dialog will appear. Click on 'Make Report' which, remember, is the way in which NUD•IST allows us to view work, and to export it to a word processor for further analysis. The Report dialog gives a number of options. You can use this to show general information about the node (the 'Show General Data for this Node' options), but we are interested in the coding which is stored at the node. This is accessed through the 'Show References for this Node' options. Check the 'With Headers' and 'With Text' options for now. Click on 'OK' and NUD•IST will retrieve all the data stored at the node, and then produce a report which will show the project information, user name and date. Because you asked it to, it will show the document header for any coded data stored at the node, at this stage only data from Andrew, of course, and then the coded extract – in my case from lines 10–13. NUD•IST also provides other information:

```
Total number of text units retrieved = 4
Retrievals in 1 out of 4 documents, = 25%.
The documents with retrievals have a total of 13 text units,
    so text units retrieved in these documents = 31%.
All documents have a total of 45 text units,
    so text units found in these documents = 8.9%.
```

We have indexed only part of 1 of the 4 documents to this node, amounting to 25 per cent of the project. The coding is 31 per cent of the total of all the documents indexed here (only from one document which is 4 units of 13 indexed), and only 8.9 per cent of the data as a whole. For content analysis, these statistics are vital. For more grounded approaches they are also very important. They allow the researcher to check the extent to which ideas they have about the data are borne out by the whole project, or only apply to small elements of it. It is easy to get carried away with a topic which seems to be of great academic interest, but these statistics may show that there is little data to substantiate the ideas. Thus, the figures can be very revealing, even if they are not directly useful to the final analysis of the material. Close the report (click on the top right 'X'). You might choose to save the report for future reference, or just click 'No' to delete it.

The next stage is to code the other documents appropriately. You have already carried this out once: remember, use the Document Explorer, choose the document, select 'Browse' and the document and indexing palette will open. Then you can highlight the text and use the palette to 'Add Coding' and then select the appropriate node. Remember to close each interview browser after use or else it is easy to end up with many windows open simultaneously, which can get confusing very quickly (click on the 'X' to close each unnecessary window). The text that you should code is listed below.

Anthony has very clear views about the importance of formal politics, so the following should be coded at 'Themes/Active Agent/Politicians':

```
6  ANTHONY: Yeah. . . I can only come back to the political
   side of it again because sometimes it's uncertain as to
   what the environmentalists are
7  after.
```

Clare is also very clear on her views of politics, but in this case is far less convinced by them, so should be coded to 'Themes/Active Agent/Individual'.

```
4  MATT: And what do you make of politics?
5  CLARE: Well, I haven't a lot of time for politicians. I
   don't like
```

6 politics in local councils you see. I don't think that
  should
7 be in at all.


Although it might be inferred that she expects politicians and policy-makers to be important for appropriate environmental management, in the extract from Dorothy there is nothing really conclusive about her views on politics, so there will no coding for this document.

By the end of the procedure you will have a number of text units coded to the two nodes: 'Individual' or 'Politician', reflecting the concerns of the interviewees. To check these, use the Node Explorer to expand the branches under 'Themes' until summary details for the two nodes can be viewed. For individuals this amounts to 2 documents and 8 text units, and for politicians only 1 document and 2 text units. Dorothy has not been coded to either, explaining why only 3 documents appear in total.

To retrieve the coded material, highlight the particular node in the Node Explorer, click on 'Browse' and the data will be displayed. Note how for 'Individuals' both document headers are shown as well as the coded text, which makes remembering who said what that bit easier. What this approach gives you is access to the data you have coded. Working with such small sections of data, it is easy to remember the context from which the coded extracts were taken. When you get to work with longer inter-view documents, it will be harder to remember. NUD•IST allows you to 'spread' the retrieved text units to aid your memory. Whenever you open a document or node browser, the coding palette is opened too. One option on here is 'Spread'. With the node browser open, highlight any line of interview text and click on 'Spread'. When prompted, spread the text to 5 units either side of your selection. The browser will then display more text either side of the extract. To remove the spread, click on 'Unspread'. Although apparently unnecessary at this level of demonstration, it is one of the most treasured facilities in qualitative data analysis software. Rather than manually having to find the interview transcript, follow a reference back to the exact point from where an extract was taken and see what was either side of it, possibly just to jog your memory, it can be performed in NUD•IST virtually instantaneously. When you have tried spreading and unspreading another text unit, close the browser by clicking the 'X'.

To generate a report to export the coded material use the 'Make Report' function. In the Node Explorer, click on the 'Themes/Active Agents/Individuals' node. Then click the 'Make Report' button. This brings up a familiar dialog. As you become more familiar with NUD•IST you will begin to find other features useful. One is worth highlighting here – coding stripes. Ordinarily, you would spend more time than we have coding the text. Codes will regularly overlap and some data would be coded to more than one place. For example, Clare's comments that have just been coded to 'Individuals' might also be worth coding in a section on local versus national politics. Andrew's comments on wilderness, currently coded to 'Individuals', would probably merit coding to a node on 'Understandings of Nature' or similar. 'Coding stripes' allow you to view these overlaps very simply. When selected, NUD•IST ascribes up to 26 different labels to codes you specify – checking the coding stripes box brings up a dialog automatically, in which you can choose which overlaps you are interested in. Down the margin, NUD•IST then displays a letter per code, and it becomes very simple to see that, for example, a unit of text is coded in three different places. I have added some extra coding to Anthony to demonstrate how this works in practice (Figure 19.17).

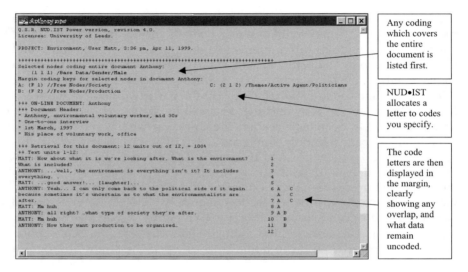

**FIGURE 19.17   Coding stripes**

Back to the task in hand, generating a report on the node 'Individuals': as before, check the 'With Headers' and 'With Text' boxes and click on 'OK'. You should see the coded data from Andrew's and Clare's interviews, line numbered and with the document headers. Once you have examined the report, click on the 'X' to close it, and there's no need to save it when prompted.

Having completed these tasks, you are now in a position to be able to perform most of the basic functions for coding and retrieving data:

• develop and manipulate the index tree;
• use the Node Explorer to browse nodes and generate reports;
• know how to spread retrieved data;
• work with the Document Explorer in a similar way;
• examine and code documents, in their entirety and in small sections;
• are aware of some of the other functions, such as code striping.

Although these procedures will become routine when you have become more familiar with the software, they can be confusing at first. If you do not yet feel confident about using these functions, it is worth taking time at this point to explore the functions you have used and, if necessary, work back through the procedures presented here.

When you are happy with the process, you are ready to continue. You know the basics of NUD•IST. The last part of the chapter will work through the text search functions of the software and introduce its theory-building 'index system search' capabilities.

## LESSON 4   ADVANCED FUNCTIONS

### Text and index searches

There are two approaches to coding text available to the qualitative researcher: manually sorting through and coding data, as you have done in the previous section, and some sort of automated coding. You have already performed this as well – automatically coding entire documents to, for example, gender nodes. NUD•IST can also perform other auto-mated searches for words and phrases contained in the documents them-selves. For many the power of the computer to perform text searches is key to their research. The method is not always appropriate for all projects and bear in mind that just because the computer can perform text searches very quickly and easily, it is not always suitable. The facility's use depends on the theoretical background to the project. However, the computer can scan many lines of data very quickly to find words or phrases which may be key to your research question.

To perform a text search in NUD•IST is relatively simple. Click on the 'Documents' menu and select 'Search Text'. This will display three options: 'String Search', 'Pattern Search' or 'Special Characters' (Figure 19.18).

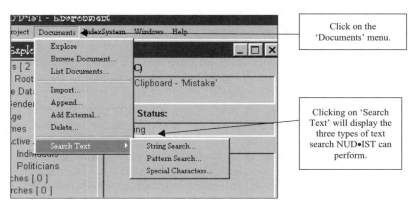

**FIGURE 19.18   Text search functions**

To introduce you to the mechanics of text searching we will only use 'String Search' for now. This type of search allows you to find words and phrases in the data. A 'Pattern Search' allows you to find groups of words, such as beautiful, attractive and pretty. It can also be used to find words with a common root such as friends, friendlier, friendliest, friendly. There is a series of complex operators for these functions which can be found in the manual and in the 'Help' function. For now, though, we examine string searches. Select 'String Search' from the list. It will open the search text dialog. There are a number of available options (Figure 19.19).

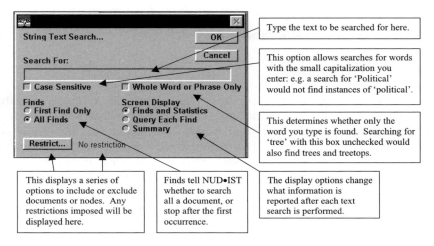

**FIGURE 19.19   'String Search' dialog**

We will try a string search for 'Environment'. Type 'Environment' in the 'Search For' box. Leave the whole words UNchecked – this means that we will also find derivatives, such as environmental, environmentalist and environmentalism in the interview text. There is no need to 'restrict' this search, but this function could be useful in some projects: a search for the use of a certain word in men's interviews and then women's interviews, for example. To facilitate that restriction, you would need all the interviews coded to appropriate 'Base Data' nodes, which provides a fine example of the importance of a well-planned organization system. Now click on 'OK' to perform the search.

NUD•IST will search all the text of the four interview documents and display a report and the Text Search Node Explorer window (Figure 19.20).

In Figure 19.20, only two of the four documents contained the text. If you were to spread the results you would find that it was me (the interviewer) who used it in the interview with Clare. Obviously with more data there will be more chance of a find, but this demonstration does serve to highlight some of the limitations of the approach. I for one would

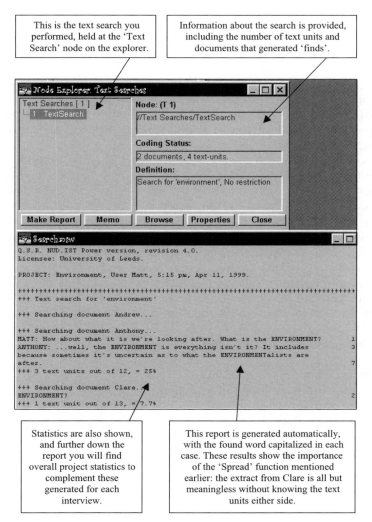

This is the text search you performed, held at the 'Text Search' node on the explorer.

Information about the search is provided, including the number of text units and documents that generated 'finds'.

Statistics are also shown, and further down the report you will find overall project statistics to complement these generated for each interview.

This report is generated automatically, with the found word capitalized in each case. These results show the importance of the 'Spread' function mentioned earlier: the extract from Clare is all but meaningless without knowing the text units either side.

**FIGURE 19.20   Results of 'Text Search'**

advocate a manual, grounded approach to coding data. Having said that, in my research I found the text searching facility useful for pointing me toward new areas of analysis. After coding a number of interviews in depth I found a number of words that seemed to be important, but I needed an idea of how often they appeared in other interviews. Rather than trawling through each interview, I was able to instigate a text search and found some useful material to explore. Close the report (click on the 'X'), saving it if you wish. You can use the text search explorer in the same way as the document browser, adding memos and checking on the properties of the search. Now 'Close' this text search window.

You will note that the text search you have performed is stored in the main Node Explorer window, under 'Text Searches'. You can browse and use the palette to spread them again from here should you wish. Note that the searches are also pasted onto the node clipboard, meaning that you can simply attach the text searches to anywhere on your indexing tree. The node clipboard provides an easy way to spread the data before you attach it anywhere. Simply *right* click once on the 'Node Clipboard' label and a pop-up menu will allow you to select 'Spread'. Select 5 text units either side and 'OK'.

For now, we will attach the text search under 'Themes', so go to the tree display (opening it on the 'IndexSystem' menu if it is closed), navigate to 'Themes', click on it and then select 'Attach' – in exactly the same way as you attached the 'mistake' at the beginning of the session, remember. Clicking on 'Attach' will prompt NUD•IST to ask whether you want to copy the contents of the node clipboard to the 'Themes' node, so click on 'Yes'. This will now attach the node clipboard data to this node. Under themes will now be the 'Active Agent' node and a 'Text Search' node, which you can rename by clicking on it once, and on the top line of the pop-up menu. You can also browse the text at this stage should you wish, or generate a report to export to Word. Close down the node dialog by clicking on 'OK'.

You have now learned how to:

- perform complex text searches;
- use the various options for searching;
- browse and spread the results;
- attach the results of the search from the clipboard onto the coding tree.

The final section of the lesson will introduce the theory-building functions of the NUD•IST package.

### Theory building: searching the index system

As well as providing a convenient means to store coded data, the index tree performs another function. Through a series of complex search functions of the index system itself, not the data, note, NUD•IST can 'build theories' from the data. For example, it is possible to explore whether women have spoken about the active environmental agent being the individual, as would be expected from conventional wisdom and gender stereotypes. This is done by comparing the overlap of data held at the 'Base Data/Gender/ Female' and 'Themes/Active Agent/Individual' node. A similar search can then be performed in '/Politicians' against '/Male' for comparison.

These functions facilitate exploring the relationships and inconsistencies in the indexed data. They allow you to explore whether data that are indexed in one place are indexed in another; or whether data that are indexed in 'a' is near to data in the original document indexed in 'b' and/or 'c'. Using complex combinations of 'Boolean' operators (basically AND, OR and NOT) as well as a number of operators unique to a package of NUD•IST's complexity, it is possible to search for overlaps of indexed data, for data that is common to two nodes, data that are in only one of two nodes and many more.

To view the available options, open the 'IndexSystem' menu and select the 'Index Search' option. This will open a long list of search functions. The use of each function is detailed in the NUD•IST 'Help' and the users' manual. Within the confines of this lesson, there is only time to familiarize you with one function. The function you will use is often the most useful because it looks for overlaps between data coded in two places, enabling a theory about whether men think differently to women, for example, to be explored easily.

Open the 'Index Search' menu and select 'Overlap' (Figure 19.21). 'Overlap' finds instances of coded data held at all the nodes selected. You can also restrict the search. A restriction would mean that you could explore the overlap between two *thematically* coded nodes, and restrict finds to men or women. Here though, we will be using the overlap of the 'Female' node to the 'Individuals' node. Do this by 'selecting' these nodes as you have done before and ensuring that they appear in the 'Overlap' box. Click on 'OK' and NUD•IST will perform the search and then open a Node Explorer dialog. Click on 'Browse' to view the results. Click on the 'X', top right of the window, to close the browser now. Then choose 'Close' from the 'Node Explorer: Index Searches' dialog.

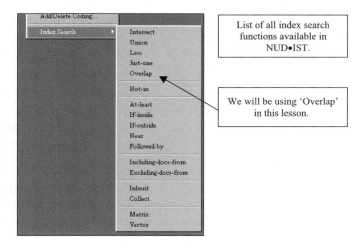

**FIGURE 19.21  NUD•IST 'Index Search' functions**

For a single search, it is relatively simple to browse the text after the search, as you have just done. When you are conducting a number of searches, it is more useful to use the Node Explorer to browse the searches, spread the results if necessary and then incorporate them into your indexing tree.

To do this, look at the Node Explorer. Like other searches, you can browse the find, using this to 'spread' the results if necessary, and generate a report to export the results. On the Node Explorer window, one Index Search will be noted, which contains the results of the search you have just performed. Double-click on 'Index Search'. This will then expand the branch beneath it to show any index searches – at this stage it should only show the one you have just performed. Right-click on this and a pop-up menu will appear. You can now spread the data and then 'cut' it to 'attach' to a point on your index tree. At this stage there is no need to spread the data, and we will cut it in just a second.

It is worth noting that the same functions can also be performed on the node clipboard. The difference is that only one search will be stored on the clipboard, overwritten by subsequent searches. If you are conducting a number of searches, you can perform each and then come back to browse and save them as necessary.

Now, select your index search and then cut the search from the Node Explorer. Using the tree, navigate to 'Themes' and attach it under 'Themes' on your index tree. Now carry out a similar search for 'Males' and 'Individuals'. Use the 'IndexSystem' menu, 'Index Search' and select 'Overlap'. Then select the appropriate nodes and perform the search. Cut the search from the Node Explorer and attach it to the 'Themes' node. You should then browse both and compare the results. It will show, in this case, that the theory is difficult to prove, with Andrew appearing to support an individual active agent as well as Clare. What it can show, though, is that conventional wisdom was not right on this occasion – gender does not appear to predict which agent the interviewee will favour. This would be interesting to follow up as more data became available in a full project.

You have now completed all of the exercises to enable you to begin to use NUD•IST in your own work. Close the package by selecting 'Quit' from the 'File' menu, saving the changes to the project when requested.

Now that you have completed all of the exercises you are well equipped to move on to the in-built NUD•IST tutorial, or try to evaluate the package with your own data. There has not been the space to take you through the whole package, but you should now be in a position to transcribe your own qualitative material, format it appropriately, use NUD•IST as a code-and-retrieve package and be able to explore the theory-building functions in more depth. You should have learnt how to:

- prepare and import data into NUD•IST;
- ascribe memos to text;
- develop and manipulate the coding system;
- manually code data and store it at nodes;

- search data using NUD•IST's search functions;
- navigate the theory-building functions of the package.


## WHERE NEXT?

The features of the package are varied and very useful in a range of qualitative projects. However, it is worth heeding John Seidel, the developer of another data analysis package, *The Ethnograph*:

> In my contacts with qualitative researchers I have discovered that many seem to have become infatuated with the ideas of collecting and managing large volumes of data. For better or worse, the application of computer technology to the analysis of qualitative data has become a means of aiding and abetting this infatuation. (Seidel, 1991: 109)

It is easy to become used to the speed and apparent convenience of the packages available. NUD•IST, for example, can handle far more documents than would have been possible in a manual system. They can be searched for text at the click of a mouse, and the data neatly stored on the index tree. The thought of manually coding hundreds of documents is not, however, appealing or even feasible. It would be impossible to maintain the required rigour or enthusiasm and the user would soon resort to automated searches to ease the task. For many projects, automated text searches are perfectly adequate. In fact, NUD•IST also contains basic programming functions which could be used automatically to introduce documents, attach them to nodes and even perform a number of text searches in one go (see the 'Help' facility in NUD•IST for details and examples). However, for a grounded theory approach, which requires codes to emerge from the data, the limitation is set not by the capability of the software, but the researcher, and it is vital to bear this in mind. With that caveat, use the lessons presented here to familiarize yourself with the software and apply it with care to your own projects.


## NOTE

1  In some versions of Word, it will automatically replace asterisks with bullet points. To turn this off, select the 'Tools' menu, then 'Autocorrect' and then click the 'AutoFormat as you type' tab you will see. Then uncheck the 'Automatic Bulleted Lists' box.

# PART VI

# SURVEY RESEARCH IN THE SOCIAL SCIENCES: DESIGN AND DATA COLLECTION

Quantitative research techniques are a distinctive approach in social science research of which social science researchers should have a thorough knowledge. Many researchers who prefer to use qualitative methods often question why it is necessary to learn about techniques which they mistakenly believe they will never use. The reason why it is important to have an appreciation of a range of methods is because there may be occasions when research students need to evaluate and interpret the quality of publications in their research area in which a quantitative approach is used. Unless research students have knowledge of quantitative methods they will be unable to thoroughly review all the relevant literature in their research area and will certainly not be able to evaluate it. Part VI will concentrate on providing information about designing and conducting surveys since they are the most widely used quantitative technique in academic research. The material presented in the subsequent chapters should therefore be read in conjunction with Part I which gives an insight into the philosophical basis of quantitative methods and Part VII which provides detailed tuition about how to prepare quantitative data for analysis, and procedures for analysing data using a variety of statistical techniques.

Chapter 20 concentrates on design issues in survey research. The survey method process is often depicted as a linear and relatively straightforward activity in the methods literature. This interpretation is highly misleading since a host of complex factors need to be taken into account. Mistakes made at the design stage of a research project can be very costly, so it is important that research students spend time designing a project which is simultaneously practical and fulfils their research needs. A wide range of factors impinge on the survey design process and those discussed include operationalizing concepts and constructing indicators; evaluating alternative survey designs; combining quantitative and qualitative research;

ethical issues and survey research; researcher safety; and some of the main criticisms of survey research and how they might be dealt with.

The purpose of Chapter 20 is to provide a broad overview of a range of design issues associated with survey research. The subsequent chapters concentrate on the different stages of the survey research process. Sampling strategies are the basic building blocks for survey research. Flawed sampling could seriously undermine survey results. The discussion in Chapter 21 focuses on distinguishing between various types of probability and non-probability sampling and evaluating their advantages and disadvantages. Another issue addressed is sources of error in survey research, especially those related to sampling errors and sampling variability. Finally, the chapter concludes with a discussion of an issue raised by many research students: how large a sample should be. Unfortunately, there is no definitive answer to this question, but some guidelines relating to sample size are provided.

A variety of data collection techniques are available to survey researchers. Choosing a method of data collection can therefore be quite a dilemma for research students who may have limited research experience. In Chapter 22 particular attention is given to factors that need to be taken into account when choosing a specific method, some of which may include the types of questions that need to be asked, the abilities of respondents and acceptable levels of response. The advantages and disadvantages of a range of techniques are considered, whether they be some of the more traditional methods (such as face-to-face interviewing and mail surveys) or by using some of the newer information technology applications (for example, computer assisted personal interviewing, CAPI, and e-mail).

Designing questionnaires is a highly skilled area of research. Since many of the technical criticisms of survey research are directed at badly designed questionnaires, it is important that research students put a great deal of effort into this activity. Chapter 23 aims to provide research students with an overview of the major issues associated with questionnaire design. Some of the practical elements of questionnaires such as questionnaire layout; designing questions; wording questions; scaling techniques, and survey reliability are discussed. Other aspects associated with the design and use of questionnaires which are given much less attention are conducting pilot studies and different ways in which survey results are presented. This chapter concludes by examining both of these issues.

The final chapter in Part VI is devoted to secondary data analysis. Important advances in computer hardware and software, combined with more organized and user-friendly systems of obtaining datasets from national archives, have facilitated a much more buoyant interest in secondary data analysis as a research technique in its own right. The starting point in Chapter 24 is to evaluate competing definitions of what secondary data analysis is, prior to considering some of the advantages and disadvantages of its use. Since there are huge numbers of datasets currently available from which to choose, research students need to assess very carefully which one(s) out of a selection are appropriate for their project. By way of aiding students to make the right choice, a check list is provided with factors which need to be included in the decision-making process. The chapter concludes by working through a practical example of analysing the General Household Survey to assess differences in pension scheme membership among ethnic groups.

## SUPPLEMENTARY READING

Converse, J.M. and Presser, S. (1986) *Survey Questions*. London: Sage.
De Vaus, D.A. (1993) *Surveys in Social Research*. London: UCL Press.
Fowler, F.J. (1993) *Survey Research Methods*. London: Sage.
Hague, P. (1993) *Questionnaire Design*. London: Kogan Page.
Hakim, C. (1992) *Research Design*. London: Routledge.

# 20 DESIGN ISSUES IN SURVEY RESEARCH

*Dawn Burton*

The purpose of this chapter is to provide an overview of the main design issues involved in survey research. The first issue to be addressed is the survey method process. Undertaking survey research is often depicted as a linear and straightforward process in many methods texts. This approach is highly misleading and is illustrated at the beginning of the chapter by a discussion of the ways in which concepts and indicators can be operationalized. A range of different survey designs are available to researchers and some of the advantages and disadvantages of several different options are evaluated. An alternative research strategy is to combine the use of surveys with other methods. The process of using different combinations of methods is called triangulation. An exploration of the merits of combining quantitative and qualitative data is considered. Ethical and safety issues are also important aspects of survey research, yet they are rarely addressed in the research methods literature. It will be argued that both have important research design implications. The final section of the chapter focuses on some of the criticisms of survey research. Students need to be aware of potential criticisms when designing a project, not when it has been completed. It is unlikely that a researcher's philosophical standpoint will be a point of negotiation or compromise, since the survey method has very firm roots in positivist or more broadly defined foundationalist philosophy. However, it may be possible to modify some part of the design or data collection process as a response to criticisms or concerns about the use of surveys.

## SURVEY METHOD PROCESS

Whichever type of survey research design is used, the process is the same and is set out in Figure 20.1. The starting point for any academic research should always be social science theory, specifically, a theoretical debate which the researcher wishes to address. Once a theoretical debate has been identified, research students need to construct a hypothesis, an idea or set of ideas that can be tested. Concepts then need to be operationalized so they can be measured by the use of indicators. A sample of cases, whether individuals, households, documents, video recordings or some other unit of analysis, is selected using a relevant sampling technique. At this stage

**FIGURE 20.1   The survey process**

designing a reliable data collection instrument becomes important and once constructed it is used to collect relevant data. Analysing the data and reporting the results are the final stages. The results of the analysis are then used to accept or reject the original hypothesis which can in turn be used to modify social theory.

This might appear to be a straightforward process, but in reality it is fraught with tensions. A first problem relates to the definition and operationalization of concepts. De Vaus (1996: 48) describes concepts as 'abstract summaries of a whole set of behaviours, attitudes and characteristics which we see as having something in common'. However, it is often the case that concepts are contested, in the sense that they have no fixed meaning. One important challenge for researchers is to define concepts in appropriate ways. One way of clarifying concepts is to obtain a range of definitions, such as those used by other researchers, or lay definitions and classify the results into categories before choosing one which appears appropriate. An alternative way forward would be to collect together previous definitions and search for common elements which would form the basis of a definition. A much easier approach would be simply to use a definition which already exists. Once a concept has been established, then indicators have to be developed which reflect the concept in question, but in some cases this is easier said than done. Carley (1981: 90) notes that 'many indicators are poor proxies for the phenomena they purport to reflect'. The suitability of particular indicators which reflect a specific concept is another area of debate. The extent to which concepts and indicators are contested is clearly evident in the example below relating to social class.

### Theory, concepts and indicators in practice: an example using social class

The practice of officially classifying the British population has a long history going back to 1851. A recent ESRC initiative (see Rose, 1995) has focused on drawing together the existing classifications of social class in order to assess which are the most appropriate. The Registrar-General Classification Scheme (RGCS) has its roots in the 1920s. The underlying assumption of the RGCS is that society is divided into a hierarchy of occupations. The British population were allocated to one of five different social classes (professional; managerial and technical; skilled occupations: non-manual and manual; partly skilled; and unskilled) on the basis of their occupation. The location of occupations in the hierarchy depended on their standing in the community. As from 1980 this classification was changed by the Office of Population Census and Surveys so that social class was directly equated with occupational skill, or specifically the competencies required to perform a particular job. Very few changes are made with regard to which occupations are included in which social class categories. Individuals are assigned to social classes according to a threefold process:

> First, they are allocated an occupation group, defined according to the kind of work done and the nature of the operation performed. Each occupational category is then assigned as a whole to one or other social class and no account is taken of differences between individuals in the same occupation group, e.g. differences of education level or level of remuneration. Finally, persons of particular employment status within occupational groups are removed to social classes different from that allocated the occupation as a whole. Most notably, individuals of foreman status whose basic social class is IV or V are reallocated to social class III. (Rose, 1995: 2)

The RGSC has been widely used for over sixty years. However, perhaps the most interesting issue for academics as far as the discussion about indicators is concerned is that occupations are allocated to social classes by the RG staff and other experts, and not in respect to any specific social theory. As a result of some of the inadequacies of the RGCS, some researchers favour a different classification. One of these alternative definitions is based on socio-economic groups (SEG). However, the problem with the RGSC and SEG is that both classifications are based on paid employment and as a result ignore 40 per cent of the population comprising: housewives, the unemployed, the retired and other economically inactive groups.

Other researchers reject the concept of class analysis altogether because it is perceived as a static approach to what are actually dynamic social processes. The Cambridge Scale (see Prandy, 1990) favours a much broader approach integrating social and economic factors which together provide a measure of social stratification and social inequality. The scale measures a combination of respondents' occupational friendship and marriage scores to produce scale measures of the outcome of different jobs and the lifestyle associated with them. Other academics argue that it is consumption and not employment related factors which is the most powerful organizing principle in contemporary society (see Baudrillard, 1988).

What the brief discussion about defining and operationalizing social class has demonstrated is that concepts and indicators are highly contested. As far as social class is concerned, indicators will be informed by the theoretical framework which is favoured and conceptual frameworks are likely to differ in the importance they place on particular indicators. As Payne *et al.* (1996: 3.3) suggest, the issue of the relationship between the concept social class and relevant indicators is a complex one. There is 'no more a single "social indicator movement" than there is a single school of class analysis'. Research students need to be aware of concept and indicator ambiguity and provide a clear rationale for their choices. Similar dilemmas and debates are evident at each stage of the survey process and these are discussed in the following section.

## DIFFERENT TYPES OF SURVEY DESIGNS

How researchers go about the process of selecting a survey design is very much related to the aims and objectives of the project in hand. At a very general level, Fink (1995:14) describes surveys as ways of producing 'information to describe, compare, and predict attitudes, opinions, values, and behaviour based on what people say or see and what is contained in records about them and their activities'. Whereas McCrossan (1991) suggests that information collected in surveys can be divided into four categories: people's physical condition, such as health and use of medical services; behaviour, such as smoking and drinking habits; social and economic circumstances; and their attitudes and opinions. Often a survey will include questions of all four kinds of issues. Ackroyd and Hughes (1983) characterize surveys into four distinct categories: factual; attitudinal; social psychological and explanatory. Factual surveys were among the first to be undertaken and focused upon the material well-being of respondents rather than their attitudes or opinions. Attitudinal surveys were designed with a particular interest in finding out what subjects thought of various issues including their material well-being. Social psychological studies took attitudinal surveys a step further by trying to predict how people would behave. Finally, explanatory surveys attempt not just to predict behaviour but to explain it.

A rather different typology would make the distinction between descriptive and explanatory research designs. Descriptive research is fairly straightforward and merely describes the process whereby researchers collect data which identifies trends. There is no attempt to explore or explain why a phenomenon occurs, but just to state that it does. Descriptive research could therefore be described as low-level, relatively unsophisticated research. However, it could be the case that where very little is known about a particular subject, descriptive research could make an original contribution to existing knowledge which is one of the defining features of a PhD (see Chapter 28). It is therefore important not to dismiss descriptive research as of being of little academic or practical value. Explanatory research designs are more sophisticated than descriptive ones. Researchers undertaking explanatory research are concerned with causal processes, explaining why social behaviour occurs in some instances and not others. The aim in explanatory research is to develop good explanations for observable patterns in the data.

There is a range of explanatory research designs which researchers can use: classic experimental design; quasi-experimental design; cross-sectional design; longitudinal designs.

## Classic experimental design

The classic experimental design is one in which the researcher selects two or more groups with matched characteristics. One group is assigned as an experimental group and the other as the control group. The experimental group is subject to an intervention and the control group is not. The results of the two groups are then compared and contrasted before and after the intervention. If both groups were the same to start with and at the end the experimental group exhibits different behaviour to the control group, then we can draw the conclusion that changes in behaviour were due to the intervention. De Vaus (1996) suggests that there are a number of problems which confront social science researchers wanting to use an experimental research design. First, in some situations it may not be possible to obtain repeat measures for the same group. This issue is relevant for all research designs which have repeat sessions built in. Second, it can be difficult to obtain a control group. Third, in some situations practical and ethical considerations make it inappropriate to use experimental intervention (see Chapter 6).

## Quasi-experimental design

Quasi-experimental research designs are sometimes referred to as non-equivalent control group designs. In some situations it is not possible accurately to match groups prior to undertaking the research, hence the term non-equivalent. In this situation the researcher tries as much as possible to match groups and then tests the strength of the intervention.

## Cross-sectional design

The cross-sectional design uses data collected from at least two groups at one point in time and compares the extent to which they differ. So for example, respondents are usually chosen for their personal characteristics whether that be age, gender ethnicity or other defining feature. Sampling respondents with different characteristics allows researchers to compare the attitudes and behaviours of different sub-samples. Cross-sectional research designs are widely used in social science research.

### Longitudinal designs

The final set of research designs are longitudinal designs. Menard (1991: 4) describes longitudinal designs as research in which:

- data are collected for each item or variable for two or more distinct time periods;
- the subjects or cases analysed are the same or at least comparable from one period to the next;
- the analysis involves some comparison of data between or among periods.

The main types of longitudinal techniques are:

1 *Prospective panel designs* where the same group of people is surveyed at more than one period in time.
2 *Quasi-panel designs* are similar to the prospective panel design except that different groups of subjects are used at specified intervals, trying to match characteristics of the initial sample.
3 *Retrospective panel designs* involve asking to recall events at different points in their life at only one meeting.

What research design is most suitable for a particular project depends on a whole range of factors, such as time constraints, the abilities of subjects and the nature of the research problem to be addressed. Obviously surveys which are longitudinal in design require more long-term, sustained commitment from researchers than do cross-sectional designs. Longitudinal studies also require a great deal of financial support to make subsequent studies feasible. It is for both of these reasons that few longitudinal surveys are undertaken by academic researchers and many of those that are tend to be based on the secondary analysis of large, national sample surveys. While longitudinal studies would appear to be more detailed than cross-sectional studies, there are problems interpreting the findings. As Menard (1991: 6) explains: 'The distinction between time and age as conceptually distinct continua along which change may be measured can pose serious problems of interpretation in the study of change.' There is also a problem of panel attrition in prospective panel designs. For example, some individuals might die between one measurement and the next, others may wish to drop out, and others might not be traceable. In retrospective designs, problems can arise from the failure of individuals to recall past events, information, or behaviour. Panel conditioning is also an issue. The effects of repeat panel testing may affect the internal validity in quasi-experimental designs so that the researcher ends up measuring this effect.


## COMBINING QUANTITATIVE AND QUALITATIVE RESEARCH

Another option open to research students is to combine quantitative and qualitative data. It has traditionally been the case in social science research that it is unacceptable to construct research projects which mix quantitative and qualitative methods. Fielding and Fielding (1986: 23) suggest that: 'Advocates of particular methodologies have been concerned more with asserting or defending their accustomed lines of inquiry than with indicating the possible points of convergence with other approaches.' The degree of generality of macro approaches often leads to the view that it is suggestive and requires more rigorous, detailed investigation. It might be the case that smaller scale, qualitative work can bridge the gap. Carley (1981: 174) notes:

> Objective social indicators are based on counting the occurrences of a given social phenomenon, and subjective social indicators are based on reports from individuals about their feelings, perceptions and responses. Neither type, used alone, has managed to give us an accurate 'window' on reality, and they are best developed and used in conjunction. (Carley, 1981: 174)

Indeed this whole debate has given rise to ethnostatistics, 'the study of the construction, interpretation, and display of statistics in quantitative social research' (Gephart, 1988: 9). It has become more acceptable in recent years to combine quantitative and qualitative research (see, for example, Bryman, 1993) and the process is known as *triangulation*. As Cohen and Manion (1989: 269) indicate: 'Triangulation may be defined as the use of two or more methods of data collection in the study of some aspect of human behaviour.'

So what might some of the benefits be for research students in combining quantitative and qualitative research? Qualitative approaches can assist quantitative work in a number of ways: by providing hunches or hypotheses to be tested by quantitative research; as a mechanism for validating survey data; interpreting statistical relationships and deciphering puzzling responses; to help construct scales and indices for survey items; and offering case study illustrations. While survey data can identify individuals for qualitative study and representative and unrepresentative cases (Bryman, 1993; Fielding and Fielding, 1986). Cohen and Manion (1989) suggest further advantages of triangulation can occur in circumstances: when a complex phenomenon requires analysis; when some controversial aspects need investigating; when an established approach provides a limited and perhaps distorted picture; and where the researcher is engaged in case study research.

Using more than one method to examine the same research question enables researchers to strengthen the validity of their findings if both are shown to provide mutual confirmation (Bryman, 1993). However, while being supportive of the mixed methods approach, Fielding and Fielding (1986) stress that the use of multiple methods is not an absolute guarantee of the validity of the findings and in fact using multiple sources can increase the chance of error. This issue is particularly relevant when the use of various research methods produce different results. Cohen and Manion (1989) suggest that there is often a dilemma about which of the research findings are to be given more weight when drawing conclusions.

## ETHICAL ISSUES IN SURVEY RESEARCH

> Every survey engages ethical concerns in terms of protecting respondents' confidentiality. Similarly, all surveys engage ethical concerns in terms of informed consent, to which the main threat is deception. (Presser, 1994: 446)

Ethical concerns are present in all research designs and go beyond data collection to include analysis and publication. Despite the centrality of ethics to survey research, it is rarely considered as an issue in its own right. Presser (1994: 457) argues that concerns about ethics in market survey research are cyclical and are 'concentrated around the occasional times when the profession is under attack or its code is undergoing revision'. As far as academic survey research is concerned, researchers usually require the help of volunteers and you should inform respondents fully of the extent to which you require their co-operation before beginning your data collection phase. Only when respondents are in possession of all the facts can they make a fully informed decision to help (see Chapter 5). You should also provide details about who you are and where you come from. Respondents are often sympathetic to students, especially if you tell them you are studying for a qualification. Tell respondents who is sponsoring your research, if you are funded by a research council, the university, or are self-funded. You should make the most of this and present yourself as 'neutral', 'unbiased' and without an axe to grind. Carley states:

> The academic researcher is often concerned with research quality and the pursuit of knowledge for its own sake. The policy analyst, on the other hand, is usually directly or indirectly for government or private institutions interested in enlightening or influencing decision-making, and he/she must be very careful and explicit about what values and whose values are injected in the analytical process. (Carley, 1981: 103)

If you are funded by a company, industry or other organization, you should declare this at the start. If you think this may present problems, make sure you have worked out an appropriate response (see Easterby-Smith *et al.*,

1995 for some useful advice on doing research with private companies). It is good practice to provide a brief description of your proposed research to respondents, either by letter or verbally. Co-operation must be voluntary and respondents should be told that if they do not want to answer all the questions, that is fine, even if it causes problems for your research project. The Social Survey Division of the Office of Population Censuses and Surveys, which undertakes a range of large-scale, national surveys in Britain, always provides the following information to respondents:

1   The name of their organization.
2   The name of the department on whose behalf the survey is being undertaken.
3   An explanation of how the person/household came to be selected.
4   The purpose of the survey and the uses to which the information will be put.
5   The confidential nature of the enquiry: the identity of respondents will remain anonymous and findings will be presented in a way so that no individual can be identified.
6   The voluntary nature of their co-operation (McCrossan, 1991).

Having identified that ethical considerations are important, it needs to be acknowledged that some categories of respondents require careful consideration, such as children, the mentally ill, prisoners and other vulnerable groups. Working with vulnerable groups raises a range of ethical issues which are discussed at length by Sieber (1992) and she gives this advice on undertaking research with children (Box 20.1).

---

**Box 20.1   Doing research with children: some considerations**

As a research population, children and adolescents are special in several respects:

(a)   They have a limited psychological, as well as legal, capacity to give informed consent;
(b)   they may be cognitively, socially, and emotionally immature;
(c)   there are external constraints on their self-determination and independent decision-making;
(d)   they have unequal power in relation to authorities, such as parents, teachers, and researchers;
(e)   parents and institutions, as well as the youngsters themselves, have an interest in their research participation; and
(f)   national priorities for research on children and adolescents include research on drug users, runaways, pregnant teenagers, and other sensitive topics, compounding the ethical and legal problems surrounding research on minors. (Sieber, 1992: 11)

Confidentiality is a central issue in the research process. Singer *et al.* (1995) suggest that researchers make a number of assumptions about confidentiality in survey research: that concern about confidentiality reduces response rates or quality; if concern can be reduced or eliminated, it is possible to improve response rates; assurances of confidentiality reduce concern; and therefore assurances of confidentiality increase or improve the response rate. Singer *et al.* (1995: 71) tested these assumptions when researching sensitive behaviours such as those which are defined as illegal or socially disapproved of. They found that 'when sensitive questions are asked, stronger assurances of confidentiality produce better results 74 per cent of the time . . . when questions are not sensitive, confidentiality assurances produce better results only 35 per cent of the time'.

Their broad conclusions are that assurances of confidentiality do affect response rates, whether measured as item non-response, response rate, response quality and whether assurance is verbal or technical. However, these effects are much greater where sensitive questions are being asked. It goes without saying that if you have assured respondents that information given to you will be confidential and they will remain anonymous, you must keep your word. The issues of confidentiality and anonymity apply to the data collection, analysis and presentation phases of the research. If you have assured confidentiality, you must protect respondents. This can be done in a number of ways. Think carefully about the setting in which the survey will be conducted. Will your respondent be heard by others? You can minimize the links between answers and identifiers such as names, addresses and detailed characteristics of the individual, group, or organization. Completed questionnaires/survey results should only be seen by individuals directly involved in the project. If you wish others to view the data, you must make sure all identifiers are removed. Any individuals who could identify respondents should not be allowed to see the data. For example, if you have asked employees to complete a self-administered questionnaire, this must not be viewed by their superiors. The use of plain brown envelopes or pre-paid envelopes can be a useful strategy to employ. You need to take care when presenting survey data. Analysing small categories could give away the identity of respondents. Once the data has been collected, it is the researcher's responsibility to keep it safe by making sure it is securely stored or destroyed. The latter should not be undertaken unless your supervisor agrees.

Most respondents co-operate with researchers because they believe that they are doing something worthwhile by helping you out, and that it is for a good cause. However, you may be confronted by the attitude 'what's in it for me?' As a research student, you are not in the position to provide money, prizes or gifts to respondents, and even when such things are offered they do not necessarily work (for a discussion see Singer *et al.*, 1998). An experiment using the gift of a ballpoint pen to improve response rates in a US door-to-door survey did lead to a higher rate of granting an interview at the time of the first visit, but mostly in the lower socio-economic groups. An added advantage was fuller responses to open-ended questions early on in the interview. However, these effects were short lived and did not have as powerful effect in subsequent visits (Willimack *et al.*, 1995). The usual incentive offered by academics is to provide, on a free-of-charge basis, an executive summary of the research findings. Above all, you should not overstate the benefits of the research to respondents to gain their co-operation. Such a strategy is promising something that you cannot deliver and could get you into trouble.

## PERSONAL SAFETY AS AN ISSUE IN SURVEY RESEARCH

Researchers have to be realistic when designing surveys. There is no point in designing a project which looks great on paper but which could be dangerous to undertake. The hazards of undertaking fieldwork have not been extensively discussed in the research methods literature. When issues of safety are considered in the research methods texts, they tend to refer to respondent's safety, such as whether they feel vulnerable to opening the door to strangers in the evening (see, for example, De Vaus, 1996). Researcher safety is an important but neglected issue in the research methods literature. This omission has been noted by Lee (1995: 10): 'Concerns about the health of the researcher rarely surface in the sociological literature. There are some scattered references to the onset of physiological symptoms – diarrhoea, nosebleeds, and vomiting – produced by the psychological stresses associated with fieldwork.'

However, the growing awareness of the physical well-being of other professionals such as teachers and social workers is facilitating discussions about the difficulties of undertaking 'dangerous' fieldwork. Lee distinguishes between two kinds of danger which could possibly arise during the research process: ambient and situational. He suggests:

> Ambient danger arises when the researcher is exposed to otherwise avoidable dangers simply from having to be in a dangerous setting for the research to be carried out . . . Situational danger arises when the researcher's presence or actions evoke aggression, hostility, or violence from those within the setting. (Lee, 1995: 10)

Obviously a researcher's exposure to violence during the research process will vary according to the nature of the project. Those at most risk include researchers who are undertaking a project in a violent setting, or where interpersonal violence and risk are an everyday occurrence. Under some circumstances it can be the actual existence of the violence which attracts attention from social science researchers. Moore (1996: 6.9) found that violence in inner city Liverpool had a number of implications for the conduct of survey research. First, the fear of crime made householders less willing to open their doors or go out in the evening, which made it difficult to gain access to respondents. Particularly problematic were 'dangers posed by young people on the streets and drug-related crime'. Second, hostility against researchers had built up over a number of years. This was in part a reaction against research undertaken by government departments in that location, such as the Department of Health and Social Security, the results of which were perceived to have a detrimental effect on the people living in the area. Anyone who remotely looked as though they were an official was treated with suspicion and researchers were no exception; some had also suffered threats of violence.

The potential for researchers to find themselves in uncomfortable positions where they may feel their safety is being compromised is not unique to survey research. However, there are reasons why some types of survey research could pose more of a threat to personal safety than other methods. First, probability sampling requires researchers to interview any case which is chosen at random. Where personal interviewing is concerned, researchers have no choice as to whom they interview since that is determined by the logic of the method. This could mean that individuals might be selected as part of the sample that interviewers might otherwise have tried to avoid because of the respondents' undesirable personal characteristics. It is also the case that researchers using probability sampling techniques might make many more attempts to reach individuals chosen during the selection process. De Vaus (1996: 114) provides the following advice: 'If a respondent is not at home, call back up to four times. Call twice on different weekdays, once during the evening and once at the weekend.' Problems can arise with night visits and researchers need to consider whether they feel safe about undertaking research which may involve entering someone's home in the evening. A second issue, is that the samples involved in survey research tend to be fairly large. The more individuals that are approached, the greater the likelihood that you might find one which is difficult to deal with.

In order to undertake effective research, researchers need to feel comfortable. This may mean avoiding night calls and the use of weekends instead for respondents who are not available during the day on weekdays. It is a good idea to use public places to conduct your survey rather than someone's home. If you enter someone's home always make sure you memorize the exit route Telling other people where you are going and who you are meeting is also useful. Avoid giving out personal details such as your home address and/or telephone number. Always use your office address, unless there is a very exceptional reason not to. If you do not feel safe collecting your data on a face-to-face basis, use a different method such as postal questionnaires or a telephone survey. It is an important rule of undertaking research that you do not take unnecessary risks.

## CRITICISMS OF SURVEY RESEARCH

It is very important that research students are able to evaluate their chosen research method(s). The methods section of a thesis should contain a critical evaluation of why a particular approach was adopted over another, and not simply state the methods that were used and how they were implemented. Questions about the chosen methodology and method are also popular in vivas. It is therefore extremely important for research students to have a good understanding of what the advantages and limitations of particular approaches are before designing research projects so that perhaps some of those potential criticisms can be dealt with at an early stage. It is unlikely that a researcher's philosophical standpoint will be a point of negotiation or compromise since the survey method has very firm roots in positivist or more broadly defined foundationalist philosophy (see Chapter 1). However, it may be possible to modify some part of the design or data collection process as a response to criticisms or concerns about the appropriate use of particular methods.

Criticisms of survey research can be classified into three main categories: philosophical, technical, and political (see De Vaus, 1996 for an extended discussion of all three). The philosophically based criticisms tend to focus on these points:

- Surveys cannot establish causal links between variables.
- Surveys are incapable of getting at the meaningful aspects of social action.
- Surveys merely assess a particular aspect of some social phenomenon without placing it in a context in which actions occur.
- Surveys often assume that human action is determined by external forces and neglect the role of human action.
- Survey research is based on a rigid science model of hypothesis and significant testing which involves little imagination or creative thinking.
- Survey research is empirically based which contributes little of theoretical value.
- Some things are not measurable by surveys.

These criticisms directly relate to the philosophical debate about whether or not human behaviour can be studied using the same methods as those used in the sciences. These issues are discussed at length in Chapters 1, 2 and 12. If in doubt it might be useful to read these chapters again.

In addition to rejecting survey methods on philosophical grounds, criticisms also focus on technical issues. Babbie notes that the standardized approach which is integral to survey research is little more than attempting to put 'round pegs in square holes':

> Standardised questionnaire items often represent the least common denominator in assessing people's attitudes, orientations, circumstances, and experiences. By designing questions that will be at least minimally appropriate to all respondents, you may miss what is appropriate to many respondents. (Babbie, 1989: 110)

This point has also been noted by Hughes (1976: 191): 'The very coding procedures and question formats used in surveys serve to reduce the variety in individual responses to fairly clear-cut, firmly bounded categories necessary for variable analysis.' The result is that often surveys can appear superficial in their coverage of complex issues. Another of Babbie's (1989) criticisms relates to the inflexibility of surveys. It is standard practice that once the final survey instrument has been constructed, it should remain the same throughout the project. This scenario is unlike qualitative research where the researcher would be encouraged to explore new ideas and issues that arise during the research process. Finally, Babbie believes that surveys are artificial: what they measure is not social action, i.e. what people do, but what they say they do, have done, or will do. The technical critique also focuses on the view that surveys are too statistical, reduce interesting questions to incomprehensible numbers, and that methods used to analyse data can leave a lot to be desired. This view is articulated by Hammersley and Gomm:

> There is still a common tendency to treat the validity of numerical data as given despite their constructed character and sources of potential bias built into them. Furthermore, statistical techniques are sometimes used as if they constituted a machine for transforming data into valid conclusions. This is certainly not to suggest that all quantitative researchers are naive in these respects; but there is a strong tendency for simplistic methodological ideas to survive in practice long beyond the time that they have been consciously abandoned. (Hammersley and Gomm, 1997: 2.7)

In defending the use of questionnaires in survey research, De Vaus (1996) suggests that many of these criticisms are true in instances where questionnaires have been used but were inappropriate for the task in hand; where questionnaires have been poorly designed; and when they have been inadequately piloted. He also highlights the fact that questionnaires are not the only method for conducting surveys, or indeed the only method of undertaking quantitative research. However, De Vaus (1996: 355–356) does suggest that researchers would be well advised to focus on the logic and meaning of statistical results rather than displaying their ability to make use of the most recent statistical 'toy'. He adds: 'Survey researchers ought to try to demystify statistics and not hide behind them. A determined attempt by survey researchers to communicate results and make them accessible is sorely needed.' This issue may be more about the presentation of statistics in user-friendly ways than the statistics themselves. Perhaps if some of these issues were attended to, criticisms of the use of statistics would be reduced.

The political criticisms of survey research focus on two main issues. First, survey research is intrinsically manipulative, by giving power and control to those who undertake such work which they can abuse. A second criticism is that survey research does not produce knowledge about reality, but is an ideological reflection whose acceptance furthers particular interests (De Vaus, 1996). It could be argued that these political criticisms are more relevant to the large-scale government surveys and the production of 'official' statistics, and therefore might be more applicable to the analysis of secondary data than to surveys which are being undertaken by research students (see Chapter 24). Conceptualizing statistics as organizational products (Thomas, 1996) and subjecting 'official' statistics to close scrutiny (May, 1993) are important ways in which researchers might diffuse some of these criticisms.

What might be of more relevance as far as research students are concerned is the impact that official surveys may have on the willingness of respondents to co-operate in future research. Just such a situation confronted Moore (1996) when he found that residents in the poorer parts of Liverpool were reluctant to participate in research because they had felt the negative consequences of previous government surveys in which they had participated by being labelled as scroungers. Obviously the use and abuse of statistics can be practised in any research project which raises considerable ethical issues (see Chapters 5, 6, 7, 9). The temptation to present results in particular ways is perhaps more of a danger when the research is being funded by a sponsor who is also an end user, rather than a research council (see Chapter 28). However, even research councils have been criticized for pandering to the needs of end users when making decisions about funding research. Indeed outside agencies are actively recruited to referee research proposals (Rappert, 1997). This said, it does need to be acknowledged that being influenced by the requirements of end users is not unique to survey research.

There are a considerable number of criticisms which can be levelled against the use of surveys and research students need to be aware of these when designing their own surveys so that some of them may be overcome, or at the very least be acknowledged. It does need to be recognized that many of the criticisms of survey research are true of poorly designed surveys.

# 21 SAMPLING STRATEGIES IN SURVEY RESEARCH

*Dawn Burton*

The purpose of this chapter is to introduce some of the issues confronting research students when they have to decide how to go about the process of selecting a sample. The first issue to be addressed is whether in fact students do need to select a sample, or whether it is possible for a census to be undertaken. However, since most researchers engaged in survey work tend to select a sample, most of this chapter is devoted to understanding the various types of sampling strategies available. A number of issues are addressed including the distinction between probability and non-probability sampling; various different types of probability and non-probability sampling; and a consideration of when some sampling strategies might be more appropriate than others. Finally, the chapter will conclude by discussing some of the issues associated with sampling error in surveys and how they might be minimized.

## CENSUS OR SAMPLE?

Sometimes it is possible for researchers to survey all the cases in a specific population when the number of relevant cases are small. Surveying all cases in a population is called undertaking a census. A census is what researchers should aim towards, if at all possible. For example, to survey all twenty organizations which manufacture a particular product is manageable. For practical reasons researchers are not always able to undertake a census and therefore need to take a sample drawn from a relevant population. In some respects sampling can be a better strategy than undertaking a census. Several advantages of sampling are:

- data is often cheaper to collect because of the smaller numbers involved;
- fewer people are needed to collect and analyse the data;
- sample surveys are frequently quicker to administer, analyse and process;
- having fewer cases make it possible to collect more data about each.

Sampling approaches fall into two broad categories: probability and non-probability sampling. Choosing between these approaches is a matter

TABLE 21.1   Issues in sample design

| Issue | Criterion | Implication |
|---|---|---|
| Population definition | Consistency of target population and study population | Study population yields biased results by including members not in target population or leaving out members who are in target population |
| Sampling method | Sample selection equally likely to select any member of study population | Sample methods yield biased results if some study population members are more likely to be selected than others |
| Precision of estimate | Estimate precise enough to inform policy decision | All samples yield estimates, not exact figures. Lack of precision can impact on the decisions to be made |

Source: Henry, 1990: 11.

of evaluating the issues of validity and credibility, against a realistic assessment of alternatives both in time and effort. The choice of sampling technique is extremely important since statistical theory and tests are used in survey research to assess whether or not the null hypothesis can be rejected or upheld. Statistical tests are sensitive to sample size, sample error and sample selection. Flawed sampling can therefore seriously undermine research findings. Three of the most important sampling issues and their implications are summarized in Table 21.1. First and foremost is population definition. Researchers need to consider carefully what population is to be sampled and then ensure the sampling strategy is consistent enough to produce accurate results. Second, probability sampling techniques require that all subjects have an equal probability of being selected. If inappropriate methods are used the sample could be biased, which will undermine the research findings. Finally, the precision needed to prove or disprove a hypothesis, or theoretical assumptions needs to be given consideration.

## PROBABILITY SAMPLING

The distinction between probability and non-probability sampling has been succinctly summarized by De Vaus (1996: 60): 'A probability sample is one in which each person in the population has an equal, or at least a known, chance (probability) of being selected while in a non-probability sample some people have a greater, but unknown, chance than others of selection.'

Probability samples are often regarded as preferable by survey researchers because they are more likely to produce representative samples and facilitate estimates of sample accuracy which allow inferences to be

TABLE 21.2 A survey of probability sample designs

| Type of sampling | Selection strategy |
| --- | --- |
| Simple random | Each member of the study population has an equal probability of being selected |
| Systematic | Each member of the study population is either assembled or listed, a random start is designated, then members of the population are selected at equal intervals |
| Stratified | Each member of the study population is assigned to a group or stratum, then a simple random sample is selected from each stratum |
| Cluster | Each member of the study population is assigned to a group or cluster, then clusters are selected at random and all members of selected clusters are included in the sample |
| Multistage | Clusters are selected as in the cluster sample, then sample members are selected from the cluster members by simple random sampling. Clustering may be done at more than one stage |

Source: Henry, 1990: 27.

made to a wider population. There are several different types of probability sampling techniques which are set out in Table 21.2. The rest of this section will be concerned with drawing out some of the main features of this group of sampling techniques.

## Simple random sampling

Statistical theory states that the most reliable way of obtaining a representative sample is to use random sampling whereby each case, whether that be an individual, household, or organization, has an equal probability of being selected. The objective is that 'the measurement of a particular variable can be generalized, with a calculable degree of confidence, to the population from which the sample was drawn' (Elliot and Ellingworth, 1997: 2.1). In order to construct a probability sample, it is necessary to use a sampling frame. A sampling frame might consist of a list of all the employees in a factory, or households on the electoral register in a particular location, and so on. Once an accurate frame has been located or constructed, each case in the sampling frame should be given a number. Cases should then be chosen at random until the required number of cases which comprise the sample have been selected. Simple random sampling is usually deemed to be sampling without replacement. This means that once a case has been selected, then it should not be returned to the pool and hence not be eligible for selection again. This is in contrast to selection with replacement, whereby the case is returned to the pool and is eligible for reselection.

Problems with random sampling occur for a number of reasons. The first relates to the precision of the sampling frame, specifically, whether in fact all possible populations which should be included are accurately represented. If there is some doubt about the adequacy of the sampling frame, the sample cannot be accurately described as a probability sample. In implementing a random sampling strategy, the researcher has no choice whom they interview. Researchers need to consider whether this strategy is practical or desirable. Selection with replacement strategies have the undesirable property whereby selecting a particular case several times can occur. Finally, in practice many large-scale surveys do not use random sampling because of the excessive costs associated with sample selection and instead opt for a compromise which often utilizes stratified, multi-stage, random sampling (Elliot and Ellingworth, 1997).

### Systematic sampling

Systematic sampling refers to the process whereby the researcher knows the number of cases in the sampling frame and has chosen an appropriate sample size. The researcher then divides the number of cases in the frame by the sample size and selects every $x$ case (known as the sampling interval). For example, if the total number of individuals in the sampling frame is 120 and the researcher wished to interview a sample of 40 individuals, the sampling interval would be 1/3 indicating that every third person in the frame would be interviewed. The starting point for the selection of cases is chosen at random.

Problems can arise in systematic sampling if the sampling frame is ordered in a way that might reflect a trend, which would then affect the characteristics in the sample: for example, a list of employees ordered by age, or income. The sampling interval might correspond to a particular characteristic of the population: for example, if every twentieth house was sampled and they were all at the end of a street, this could be problematic if you wanted to interview people about their neighbours.

### Stratified sampling

Stratified sampling is a modification of simple random sampling and systematic sampling techniques but includes an extra process. Stratified sampling involves identifying individuals with certain 'target' characteristics (for example, age, gender, ethnicity, etc.) and then drawing a sample, using simple random sampling or systematic sampling techniques, from each of the groups. This strategy is useful if the aim is to compare groups. The sampling technique requires that subjects in the sample are reflected in the same proportions as those in the population. Stratified sampling is widely used in social science research.

**TABLE 21.3   An example of multi-stage cluster sampling**

| | |
|---|---|
| Stage 1 | Divide the city into a number of districts which could either be electorates or census districts |
| Stage 2 | Divide each of the districts into blocks using an up-to-date street map |
| Stage 3 | Draw up the list of all households in each of the blocks |
| Stage 4 | Select households to include |
| Stage 5 | Select people within each household to interview |

## Multi-stage cluster sampling

The sampling strategies already discussed in this chapter have limited use when a sampling frame does not exist. They are also not appropriate for sampling a geographically dispersed population. Multi-stage cluster sampling requires the researcher initially to draw a sample from a large population and then select out progressively smaller populations until the required number of cases are included in the sample. So for example, multi-stage sampling might be used to select a sample of households in a particular geographical area by using the stages set out in Table 21.3.

### LIMITATIONS OF PROBABILITY SAMPLING

Probability sampling becomes highly problematic if the information required to construct a sampling frame does not exist. This limitation could mean that researchers might miss out on important areas of research being undertaken, for example, deviant types of behaviour (Coomber, 1997). The inability to construct a suitable sampling frame of users on the Internet is one reason why it is not a suitable vehicle for constructing probability samples of the general population (Schillewaert *et al.*, 1998). If an adequate sampling frame needs to be constructed from scratch it can be a labour-intensive enterprise and a judgement needs to be made about whether it is worth the time and effort. Problems can also arise if a sampling frame exists but is deficient in some way. For example, it has been argued that the Electoral Register is not necessarily a good sampling frame for the British population because young people, the transient and ethnic minority groups are less likely to be included (Elliot and Ellingworth, 1997). It may also be the case that the population is so widely geographically dispersed as to make cluster sampling inefficient. Finally, if not undertaken extremely accurately, probability sampling can generate a significant number of different types of error. Bryman and Cramer (1993) suggest that response rates on sample surveys are sometimes so low that the issue of representativeness between probability and non-probability samples is often not as great as one might expect. Even where random samples have been selected, factors such as non-response may adversely affect a sample's representativeness.

**TABLE 21.4  Some non-probability sample designs**

| Type of sampling | Selection strategy |
|---|---|
| Convenience | Select cases based on their availability for the study |
| Most similar/ dissimilar cases | Select cases that are judged to represent similar conditions or, alternatively, very different conditions |
| Typical cases | Select cases that are known beforehand to be useful and not extreme |
| Critical cases | Select cases that are key or essential for overall acceptance or assessment |
| Snowball | Group members identify additional members to be included in the sample |
| Quota | Interviewer select sample that yields the same proportions as the population proportions on easily identified variables |

Source: Henry, 1990, p. 18.

## NON-PROBABILITY SAMPLING

A range of non-probability sampling techniques are available to researchers. Kalton (1983) has used threefold classification to summarize different non-probability techniques: haphazard, convenience, or accidental sampling; judgement or purposive sampling or expert choice; and quota sampling. Within each of these categories there are a number of designs. Henry (1990) provides a more extensive typology which is summarized in Table 21.4. In the following section of the chapter, some of the characteristics of non-probability sampling techniques will be discussed in more depth.

### Quota sampling

Quota sampling is a widely used market research technique. We have probably all had the experience of avoiding market researchers with clipboards standing on street corners. Quota sampling attempts to approximate or represent the population characteristics by dividing the sample according to a number of specific characteristics such as gender, age and social class. The distributions of each of the groups in the population can be ascertained by using census data. Interviewers are then required to collect data which meets the *quota target*. The quota targets might be to sample 10 men and 10 women, 10 of whom are in the age range 20–30 and 10 in the range 40–50, as Table 21.5 illustrates. This example is very simple and straightforward. However, quota sampling can become very complicated when additional variables are introduced. Quota sampling techniques are examples of non-random or non-probability sampling because the interviewer chooses any case which fits the criteria. Therefore human judgement enters the selection process.

**TABLE 21.5  An example of quota sampling**

| Age | Men | Women | Total |
|-----|-----|-------|-------|
| 20–30 | 5 | 5 | 10 |
| 40–50 | 5 | 5 | 10 |
| Total | 10 | 10 | 20 |

Kent (1993: 52) suggests there are a number of advantages of using quota samples:

- They are quicker, cheaper and more straightforward to administer than random samples.
- They do not require a sampling frame.
- The sample size and quota composition are usually achieved.

Quota sampling is usually quicker to implement than other strategies for two main reasons. First, for in-home quotas (calling on people in their own homes) no call backs are necessary because the researcher continues on until the requisite number of respondents have been included. For street quotas, there is no travelling time between interviews. Second, the procedures for drawing up samples are very easy because no sampling frame is required. In terms of cost per interview, quota samples are much cheaper than many other sampling techniques.

While there are certainly advantages to quota sampling, Kent also identifies a number of disadvantages:

- There is a considerable potential for bias.
- There is more variability between samples than using other techniques.
- The application of probability theory to such samples is questionable.
- The sample may not be representative of the population as a whole or the locality in which the sampling was undertaken.

Bias can be introduced in two ways: that generated by interviewer behaviour and a high level of non-response. Usually it is the researcher's responsibility to choose respondents at the sampling point. This practice can lead to bias as interviewers may select individuals whom they believe will be the easiest to interview. These characteristics can change according to the preference of particular researchers which makes the problem of bias even more complex. The issue of non-response is largely hidden in quota research. As long as the quotas are filled, there is no need to declare the level of non-response (for example, individuals who refuse to participate) as substitutions are allowed. Levels of non-response and reasons for non-response can have important implications for research conclusions. Kent estimates that, at best, quota samples have an effective response rate of 25–30 per cent. A final problem is that accurate population proportions may not be available, which makes quota sampling extremely difficult. For example, if census data is to be used as a basis for constructing quota categories it could be out of date as the census is only undertaken every ten years. At a more micro level, localities may be subject to major social, economic and political change. The data upon which quota estimates are based may therefore not be representative of anything concrete.

### Multi-purpose sampling

An existing survey can sometimes be used as a vehicle for reaching the target population. Multi-purpose sampling can take two forms:

- *Piggybacking* – using the sample of an existing survey.
- *Amalgam* – join forces with other researchers to identify a larger number of subjects.

   Piggyback sampling would appear to be a useful way of enlisting the help of other researchers in identifying a suitable sample. It has the advantage of saving time in identifying an appropriate sample, especially when respondents might be hard to reach for one reason or another. Despite these advantages there are two main problems with piggyback sampling. First, there is the issue of confidentiality, such as giving respondents' names and perhaps addresses to other researchers. This in turn raises ethical issues about informed consent (see Chapter 5). Second, the original survey sample may not necessarily be the ideal vehicle for a subsidiary study.

   Amalgam sampling raises another set of issues about ownership of the data and publishing responsibilities and rights. There is the other possibility of researchers having different priorities and agendas for the research project which might only emerge once the project has begun. Punch (1986) describes a situation where academics nearly came to blows about disagreements concerning the priorities of a research project. Since research students are in a position where their thesis is going to be judged on originality and is a product of their own work, both of these sampling strategies need to be evaluated within that wider context. Supervisors should be able to advise on appropriate ways forward.

### Networking or snowball sampling

In network sampling the researcher establishes contact with a suitable respondent, then asks that respondent for other contacts with the required characteristics. Network sampling is particularly useful when respondents are highly stigmatized or vulnerable, which can make them more difficult to reach. In network sampling there is a great deal of emphasis on the researcher to prove that they are a bona fide researcher and some security features might have to be built into the research design. Network sampling often requires the researcher to work through intermediaries and there is the possibility that the link person may misinterpret the aims and objectives of the research. Accurately explaining the aims and objectives to all involved is therefore crucial. Another concern is that it is often difficult to keep track of refusals if working through intermediaries. It could easily be the case that refusals might be reported when in fact no contact is made (Lee, 1993). There is also a problem of bias. Networks tend to be homogeneous in their attributes, rather than providing links to others who have different social characteristics (if that is what is required). It is therefore good practice for researchers to pace and monitor very carefully the referral chains which they generate.

### Outcropping

Outcropping is a method of sampling the target population in a geographic location or area in which they routinely congregate with a view to surveying them. The areas in which they might meet could be a coffee bar, a red light district, or some other place. Some disadvantages are that if the chosen location has a high turnover, data capture may be difficult. As with network sampling, there is no guarantee that a sample drawn from a particular setting is representative of the wider population beyond the sample.

### Advertising

If all else fails, advertising is a way of obtaining a sample. However, major problems arise because of the lack of control over who responds, both in terms of representativeness and suitability. If advertising is to be used via an established route (for example, newspapers, radio, television), a press release must be constructed. Some notes of guidance may be required regarding press releases:

- Press releases should be no longer than a side of A4.
- They are best handled by the university press office, which will usually have names and addresses of all relevant contacts at hand. In fact, it is best if guidance from the press office is sought as early as possible. Press releases should state very clearly the objectives of the research, who the target sample is, what the research findings will be used for, and how individuals should proceed if they wish to help out.

- There is no guarantee that press releases will be taken up at all.
- Press releases can be distorted, and represented in a way not intended by the researcher. Beware!

## THE UTILITY OF NON-PROBABILITY SAMPLES

Non-probability sampling is a useful method of sampling under some circumstances, indeed on occasions it may be the only method available. Where the researcher is specifically interested in respondents within the sample as opposed to making wider generalization or inference, the non-probability method is likely to be more appropriate. In exploratory research, a non-probability sample would also seem to be a suitable choice and could perhaps take the form of a small pilot study with the results being integrated into a larger probability sample at a later date. Limited resources, inability to identify members of the population and the need to establish the existence of a problem all justify the use of non-probability sampling. Lee (1993) notes that sampling becomes more difficult the more sensitive the investigation, as potential respondents have more to hide. Less visible individuals are more difficult to sample. Obtaining a sample of respondents who have characteristics which are rare is more difficult and costly to sample than individuals who display frequently occurring behaviour. Sampling subjects over a wide geographical area is likely to improve representativeness, but the financial costs of doing so may be excessive.

While there are clearly advantages of using non-probability samples, there are also disadvantages. Henry (1990) notes that as a result of the subjective nature of the selection process involved in non-probability sampling, there is concern about the generalizability of the findings to the wider population. There is a risk that the findings will not be valid because of bias in the selection process. Kalton argues a similar point:

> The major strength of probability sampling is that the probability selection mechanism permits the development of statistical theory to examine the properties of sample estimators. Thus estimators with little or no bias can be used, and estimates of the precision of the sample estimates can be made. The weakness of all non-probability methods is that no such theoretical development is possible. As a consequence, non-probability samples can be assessed only by subjective evaluation. Moreover, even though experience may have shown that a non-probability method has worked well in the past, this provides no guarantee that it will continue to do so in the future. (Kalton, 1983: 90)

## SOURCES OF ERROR IN SURVEY RESEARCH

As with all research processes, there is potential for errors to occur in survey research. Sources of error fall into two main categories: non-sampling errors; sampling errors.

## Non-sampling errors

Non-sampling errors arise as a result of decisions during data collection and are not directly related to the selection of the sample. Non-sampling errors can take a variety of forms.

*Response errors* These occur when respondents give 'wrong' answers. Response errors may occur due to dishonesty, poor memory, or misunderstanding, among others.

*Interviewer errors* These refer to the inaccurate recording of the response given by subjects, making mistakes, or asking questions in a non-standard fashion.

*Non-response errors* These are generated by inadequacies in the research process. Non-response errors can result from subjects who refuse to provide data, those who are asked to provide data but who are unable to undertake the required task and, finally, those whom the data collection procedures did not reach; therefore not providing individuals with an opportunity to respond. High levels of non-response can have serious implications for inference; the extent to which findings from the sample can be generalized to a wider population. For example, if a survey yields response rates of 10–25 per cent of a sample, the final sample bears little relationship to the original sample as those responding are self-selected. Whereas if a response rate of 95 per cent is achieved in a probability sample, the final sample is still very similar to the population as a whole. Fowler (1993) suggests that there are different types of bias associated with different methods of data collection. For example, mail questionnaires are more likely to be returned by individuals who are particularly interested in the project. As a result low response rates can be significantly biased in ways that are directly related to the purpose of the research. In addition, better educated people tend to send back mail questionnaires than those who are less well educated. Bias resulting from telephone and personal surveys tends to focus on availability. For example, if a survey was undertaken on weekdays between 9am and 5pm the likely scenario is that individuals without jobs (unemployed, retired and housewives) would be over-represented in the sample.

There also tend to be lower response rates in cities than in suburbs and rural areas, which is largely a result of the disproportionate number of single people living in cities who can be difficult to contact; the nature of housing, specifically the greater number of individuals who live in flats, which makes access difficult; and the fact that some areas in the centre of cities are undesirable places to conduct fieldwork, especially at night. Researchers cannot assume that non-response is unbiased and it is not always obvious in what ways non-response is biased, which makes it difficult to counteract. The ideal solution is to reduce the non-response by amending data collection techniques such as varying methods and undertaking systematic follow-ups.

*Processing errors*   These are coding and data entry errors. Constructing a comprehensive coding book and having in place quality control procedures should reduce such errors.

### Sampling errors

Sampling errors directly relate to the sample selection process. Sampling errors can be divided into two main groups: *systematic error* (or *bias*), and *random error*. Hammersley and Gomm provide a useful statement of the difference between the two:

> Bias is generally seen as a negative feature, as something that can and should be avoided. Often, the term refers to any systematic deviation from validity, or to some deformation of research practice that produces such deviation. Thus, quantitative researchers routinely refer to measure or sampling bias, by which they mean systematic error in measurement or sampling procedures that produce erroneous results. The contrast here is with random (or haphazard) error: where bias tends to produce spurious results, random error may obscure true conclusions. (Hammersley and Gomm, 1997: 1.6)

Systematic error usually occurs as a result of one of the following: the selection process was not random, when it was intended to be; the selection of respondents was made from a list that did not cover the whole population; and non-respondents were not a cross-section of the population.

Random error relates to the error which can arise as a result of the sample size. The larger the sample, the less random error there is likely to be as the sample is more likely to be representative of the population from which it was drawn. A sample used to estimate a variable that varies widely in the population will show more random sampling error than for a variable that does not.

Quite controversially, Hammersley and Gomm (1997: 1.7) argue that systematic error does not always occur by accident and that it can also include 'a tendency on the part of researchers to collect data, and/or to interpret and present them, in such a way as to favour false results that are in line with their prejudgements and political or practical commitments'. This may include the positive tendency to report findings that promote false conclusions, or exclude from consideration other conclusions which include the truth. They argue that the abandonment of the positivist, or foundationalist's, view of error and the adoption of a more radical post-foundationalist approach leads to a much more complicated view of error with the causes of systematic error being defined in different ways. Whereas previously it was considered as relying on logic, it becomes 'deviance from communal judgements' about what is reasonable and unreasonable behaviour in the pursuit of knowledge, with these judgements being open to dispute and frequent revision. They acknowledge that there will always be the potential for systematic error and that some of it will be non-culpable by virtue of the fact that the researcher was unaware that the knowledge being relied upon was erroneous or dysfunctional which inadvertently led to wrong conclusions. However, it is also the case that some systematic error will be culpable, in the sense that researchers are judged to be in a position where they should have been aware that an assumption on which they were relying had an unacceptable chance of being erroneous and therefore held the possibility of leading them astray.

## HOW LARGE SHOULD A SAMPLE BE?

The issue which tends to concern research students undertaking survey research more than any other is how large a sample should be. This is a very sensible question, but unfortunately there are no definitive answers. However, there are some guidelines:

1   Of particular importance are time and resource constraints. There is no point in designing a project which looks brilliant on paper, but is just not practical. It is usually best to keep projects relatively small scale, something you feel happy with, and you feel you can do well rather than being over-ambitious. The temptation to work with a large sample can result in students spending longer than anticipated collecting and processing data, rather than analysing and linking it to contemporary debates. The lack of in-depth analysis is likely to be picked up on at some stage, especially in a viva. It is therefore very important to keep your sample to manageable size.
2   As a general comment the larger the sample, the greater the degree of accuracy. In effect the *sampling error* (the difference between the sample and the population which are due to sampling) can be reduced by increasing the sample size. After a certain level, gains via increase in accuracy are curtailed (see Fowler, 1993; De Vaus, 1996 on this issue).
3   You need to bear in mind the issue of non-response and adjust your sample accordingly. If non-response rates are high, you will need to increase the size of your sample to compensate. Alternatively, a critical evaluation of your data collection methods will be required. You should have an indication of non-response rates from your pilot study.
4   A final issue relates to the type of analysis you wish to conduct. Specifically, how many cases are required in each sub-group. Unless you have enough cases in each of the sub-samples in which you are interested, your analysis will be limited.

# 22 DATA COLLECTION ISSUES IN SURVEY RESEARCH

*Dawn Burton*

A range of data collection methods are available to research students who wish to conduct surveys. The purpose of this chapter is to highlight some important factors which need to be taken into account prior to choosing a particular data collection method, before critically evaluating some of the conceptual and practical issues associated with using different techniques. The data collection methods discussed in this chapter include some of the relatively new information technology based approaches such as Computer Assisted Personal Interviewing (CAPI), Computer Assisted Self-Interviewing (CASI) and the use of e-mail, in addition to some of the more traditional methods such as face-to-face interviewing and mail surveys.

## FACTORS TO CONSIDER WHEN CHOOSING DATA COLLECTION METHODS

Given the range of data collection methods available, it is often a dilemma for research students to choose which one, or which combination to use. Two main issues are relevant to the decision-making process. The first factor relates to the theoretical debates which the research project is seeking to address and how various methods of data collection can deliver the required information. A second important issue could be the methods used in previous research. You might want to choose the same methods as other researchers with the aim of replicating previous research designs. Alternatively, you might wish to choose a different approach in the hope that using different methods will shed more 'light' on a particular area. These two issues are your main starting point. However, in addition to having an overall data collection strategy, there does need to be an appreciation of some of the practicalities associated with various data collection methods. There is no point in designing a project which looks fabulous on paper, but which is difficult if not impossible to put into practice. Making mistakes at the data collection stage could prove very costly in terms of wasted time and effort. If you are in any doubt, you should be prepared to pilot more than one method and then compare the results. A number of factors should inform the final choice.

### How are you going to select your sample?

If your sampling list/frame has good mailing addresses, telephone numbers, names and other relevant details, then research students have a choice of which methods of data collection to use. Fairly obviously, you cannot conduct a mail survey without accurate addresses. If all the sample are not on the telephone, or if some have ex-directory telephone numbers, these two factors will make a telephone survey problematic. The way you select your sample has important implications for the feasibility of different methods of data collection and vice versa.

### How able are the respondents?

The abilities of the target population have important implications for the choice of data collection method. There is no point in using a self-administered questionnaire with individuals who have difficulty in reading and writing, for example, children, ethnic minorities whose first language is not English, or people with learning difficulties. Depending on the nature of the research project, less obtrusive methods might be more appropriate such as observation or content analysis. There has to be a good match between data collection methods and the abilities of respondents. A comprehensive pilot study should shed some light on these issues.

### How motivated are potential respondents to take part in the research project?

At some stage you will need to make a judgement about how motivated potential respondents will be to participate in the research project. Highly motivated subjects might be happy to complete a self-administered questionnaire and a good response rate might be obtained. Face-to-face interviews might be more appropriate in the case of respondents who have little interest in the project but whose views are nevertheless important to obtain; for example in the case of elite interviewing. Individuals who are fairly reluctant to take part may provide a short telephone interview but not a face-to-face interview.

### What sorts of questions do you want to ask?

If you wish to ask lots of open-ended questions, self-administered questionnaires are not necessarily appropriate. Face-to-face interviews are far better at eliciting data to open-ended questions. Self-administered questionnaires are better at generating information from highly structured questions where respondents are required to tick an appropriate box. Another important factor might be whether or not respondents wish to be anonymous. If you want to ask highly sensitive questions then a self-administered questionnaire could be preferable to a face-to-face interview. At best face-to-face interviews preserve confidentiality, whereas self-administered questionnaires facilitate confidentiality and anonymity.

### What level of response is acceptable?

As a general comment, the higher the response rate the better. You must make a judgement about which method is likely to give you the response rate you require. On average, higher response rates are usually obtained for face-to-face interviews than either telephone or mail questionnaires. However, it does need to be recognized that response rates which are cited for particular methods often relate to aggregate percentages. Every research project is unique and ultimately it is the pilot study which should give a clearer understanding of what methods are the most fruitful and whether any adjustments to sample size are required. In extreme cases it may be necessary to use different data collection methods to meet the needs of different individuals in the sample.

### Are you under any financial constraints?

All research students are under some degree of financial constraint. In a commercial research setting mail and telephone surveys tend to be more cost effective than personal interviews which are more labour intensive. However, unless research students have a budget allocated for mail and telephone expenses, personal interviewing may be a cheaper option. Overall response rates are frequently better with face-to-face interviews. What might appear to be a cheaper option per each response might not always be the cost-effective option when response rates are entered into the equation.

### How much time have you allocated to collect your data?

The secondary analysis of existing data does not require any time for data collection as the data has already been collected and processed for another purpose. Collecting data by using telephone and e-mail surveys takes less time than most other methods, but face-to-face surveys frequently provide higher quality data. You need to make a judgement between quality of data, time and costs.

## *How widely available is appropriate computer hardware and software?*

An increasing number of computer applications are being used to assist in the collection of data in surveys, whether via Computer Assisted Personal Interviewing (CAPI) or Computer Assisted Self-Interviewing (CASI). Obviously some of these new methods require appropriate hardware, software and appropriate information skills on the part of the researcher. Since many of these systems are new, there is not a significant methods literature about the practicalities of using these approaches. While their use could be perceived as being novel and innovative there are obviously certain risks attached to using them which should be very carefully evaluated.

Which data collection methods you choose will be a trade-off between time, cost, the nature of the project, your abilities and those of the subjects. In order to evaluate which method(s) is best for your project, you need to be fully aware of a range of possibilities, since a popular viva question often requires students to give reasons why they chose one particular form of data collection over another. The next section assesses the advantages and disadvantages of a range of survey data collection techniques in an attempt to provide some guidance on this issue.

### FACE-TO-FACE INTERVIEWS

Face-to-face interviews are perhaps the most sociable way to collect survey data, unlike telephone surveys and self-administered questionnaires – at least you see the respondents. There are a number of advantages to face-to-face interviewing compared with other means of collecting survey data. Face-to-face interviews are probably the most effective way of enlisting the co-operation of most populations. Other advantages relate to what is termed interviewer administration, including answering a respondent's questions; probing; prompting; and the facility to use complex question sequences. Face-to-face interviews are a multi-method of data collection. The interviewer can note down observations and in effect build up a contextual analysis and respond to visual cues of the respondent. It is far easier to build up a rapport and a relationship of trust with subjects on a face-to-face basis. Longer interviews are possible on a face-to-face basis than by telephone and they are preferable for asking open-ended questions. Material that needs to be shown to respondents can be properly presented during a face-to-face interview. These materials might include a list of options from which subjects have to choose, or a photograph to look at and then comment. If you have questions of a sensitive nature, using a card can be a useful device. The card in Box 22.1 was used in a OPCS survey to prevent embarrassment and allow the respondent to chose a number rather than say out loud the actual response. Finally, interviewers can usually persuade respondents to complete an interview and the quality of data generated is usually superior to that obtained by other methods.

**Box 22.1   Example of response card**

Since marriage have you and your husband used any of these methods to prevent you becoming pregnant?

SHOW CARD B                                    Yes     1 ASK a
                                               No      2 GO TO Q100

(a)   Which methods have you used?

1    Withdrawal (the man is careful and pulls out before climax)
2    Sheath, condom, Durex, French letter
3    The pill
4    Diaphragm, cap or Dutch cap
5    Coil, loop or intrauterine device
6    Chemicals, spermicides, 'c' film
7    Rhythm or Safe period
8    Female sterilization, tubes tied or male sterilization, vasectomy
9    Abstain (not having sex for several months to avoid getting pregnant)
10   Any other method

There are obviously considerable advantages to face-to-face interviewing, but it should be noted that interviewing is difficult to do well. The interviewer is on the one hand trying to be 'standard' in his or her approach but also needs to react to individual circumstances. Interviewing is a process of social interaction which is highly artificial in its outcome, including the answers, which might be influenced by the sex, age, accent and personality of both interviewer and respondent. McNeill suggests:

> Interviewers have to strike a careful balance between establishing the kind of relationship with respondents that will encourage them to be frank and truthful, and avoiding becoming too friendly so that respondents try hard to please. Friendly but restrained is a phrase used to describe this attitude. (McNeill, 1989: 39)

Holstein and Gubrium (1995) summarize other issues which have been drawn to the attention of researchers to enable them to conduct successful survey interviews:

> The interviewer must shake off self-consciousness, suppress personal opinion, and avoid stereotyping the respondent. Learning the interviewer role is also a matter of controlling the interview situation to facilitate the candid expression of opinions and sentiments. (Holstein and Gubrium, 1995: 11)

A similar scenario has been outlined by McCrossan:

Throughout the interview your aim is to avoid saying anything which could influence your informant's answer in any way but at the same time to show enough appreciation and interest to ensure that he makes a genuine effort to provide accurately the information which you want. (McCrossman, 1991: 64)

Researchers also have to make a judgement about whether they feel that they are able to undertake face-to-face interviewing, given the nature of the study. In some instances it is not easy to become psychologically/ emotionally distanced from the subject (see also Kleinman and Copp, 1993; Hunt, 1989 on this issue). Warren raises this point in relation to ethnographic work, but it equally applies to survey research:

I was asked recently to get involved in an ethnographic study of protective custody in women's prison. As in men's prison, protective custody is used mainly to keep women who have killed or battered their own children from being attacked by other inmates. As a new mother, I knew that I would not be able to approach such a setting without distress, so I declined the opportunity. (Warren, 1988: 60)

It also needs to be recognized that, because of the need to be physically present with the subject for the period of the interview, personal interviewing can be time consuming and is highly dependent on the availability of respondents. In constructing an interview programme you need to consider: the length of the interview, including allowances for interviews taking longer than expected through interruptions; for example: relatives visiting; pressure of work; travelling time; cancellations; and holiday periods, your own and the respondent's. If you are going to tape the interview and transcribe responses to open-ended questions, you need to allocate time to do that. Lack of careful planning about which respondents to interview at what time and where could mean that the data collection phase takes much longer than anticipated.

It is probably inevitable that at some point you will be refused an interview, or an interview will be prematurely terminated. This is not a particularly pleasant experience and is one which you could take very personally. The Office of Population Census and Surveys gives some very good advice to researchers in the event of a refusal.

When you have had a refusal or refusals try not to let it lower your morale in such a way that your dejection and lack of confidence show to other people as you call on them. This could easily lead to another refusal. After a refusal it is often helpful to think about the approach you employed. There are a number of questions which you can ask yourself:

- Were you dressed in any way unsuitably for the area?
- Were you calling at an unconventional time for the area, for example, too late in the evening?

- Were there any indicators, which you missed or ignored, that the time of your call was awkward for your informant?
- Was there anything inappropriate in the way in which you introduced yourself and explained the survey?
- Did you react sensibly and quickly to his/her attitude and the ideas which he/she expressed? (McCrossan, 1991: 65)

You can hopefully limit the premature termination of interviews by ensuring that the respondent is fully aware of the purpose of the research project and the types of issues to be addressed before the interview begins. This should be standard practice in all interviewing procedure and informed consent is discussed at greater length in Chapter 7.

## COMPUTER ASSISTED PERSONAL INTERVIEWING (CAPI)

New developments in specialized computer software and the widespread availability of laptop computers have facilitated what has become known as Computer Assisted Personal Interviewing (CAPI). All of the issues discussed above about interviewing are relevant to CAPI, but as a result of inputting data directly into a computer at the time of the interview, other issues are raised. The first large-scale use of CAPI in Britain occurred in 1987 when it was used for the Labour Force Survey, although the use of computers in the interviewing process has its roots in the USA in the 1970s when they were first introduced as an aid in telephone interviewing. Martin and Manners (1995) have highlighted the differences in the process required between using paper-based questionnaires and CAPI. The advantages of CAPI over more traditional methods focus on the fact that because the questionnaire is pre-programmed, there should be no routing errors which might lead to the interviewer missing out relevant sections of the questionnaire. Another advantage is that software programmes enable the data to be checked immediately for errors and thereby improve data quality. A third advantage is that systems offer the possibility to formulate more complex question sequences. Finally, there is no separate data entry phase since, once the interview is complete, the data is in a form which is ready to be analysed, thereby reducing the time between conducting fieldwork and analysing the results. As a result in CAPI developments, its effect on the interviewing process is beginning to receive a considerable amount of coverage in the research methods literature. Three main issues tend to dominate the discussion: the effects of the computer on the interview situation; the attitudes of interviewers towards using the systems; and the effects on the behaviour of respondents. All three issues have been extensively discussed by de Leeuw and Nicholls (1996). The rest of this discussion will therefore be confined to documenting their main findings.

There are a number of possible effects that the presence of a computer can have on the interview situation. One issue might be that respondents perceive that there is less privacy, particularly when there is a mistrust or unfamiliarity with computers. What they term as the 'big brother' effect could lead to more refusals and a higher incidence of socially desirable answers to sensitive questions. Alternatively, the opposite view might apply, whereby the use of a computer could lead to the expectancy of greater privacy because answers are directly typed into the computer and cannot be read by anyone other than those for whom the data is intended. Interviewers may feel more confident about using computers and therefore behave more professionally, which could result in the respondent having more confidence in the interviewing procedure. One possible negative effect is that the requirement upon the interviewer to type answers to questions may lead to less eye contact between interviewer and respondent and as a result interviewers could miss important non-verbal reactions of respondents. If the computer is placed between the interviewer and respondent, the physical distance might be greater than in conventional paper and pencil interviewing and may hinder the rapport between the two parties. However, the opposite might also be true. If the software takes over the responsibility for routing complex question sequences, the interviewer can pay more attention to the respondent and the social processes involved in interviewing.

As far as empirical research on the effects of CAPI on respondents is concerned, very few negative reactions have been reported. When directly asked for their views, respondents tend to react positively and prefer CAPI to traditional methods, finding it amusing, interesting and demonstrating a greater degree of professionalism on the part of the interviewer. There have been few reports of problems associated with lack of eye contact or social interaction. Respondents also tend to be more positive about data protection since responses are input directly into a computer and are perceived as being more confidential. It has also been reported that respondents commented that being asked about sensitive issues was less unpleasant. Interviewers' perceptions of using CAPI also tend to be positive. Researchers tend to appreciate the support that good systems provide and having a sense of professionalism which derives from working with a computer. Two main difficulties were mentioned: problems with grasping and keeping track of the overall structure of the questionnaire, given that computer systems operate on a screen, rather than page orientation; the difficulties which can arise in typing lengthy responses to open-ended questions. A further issue highlighted by Martin and Manners (1995) is that it is difficult to operate CAPI while standing.

CAPI systems provide an alternative method of data collection which has received considerable positive feedback from respondents and researchers. However, it needs to be acknowledged that it is not a panacea for good quality data. This point is made by de Leeuw and Nicholls (1996: 13–14) when they note that CAPI systems 'require one to do almost everything that is needed with a good paper and pen interview, and to add extra efforts in computer implementation, in testing the questionnaire, in designing an ergonomic screen layout, and in extra interviewer training'. As far as research students investing their time in designing a CAPI system are concerned, it should be treated with extreme caution unless they are endowed with excellent IT skills and have access to considerable support if things go wrong. Using a system which already exists is another issue and could provide a useful research training experience.

## SELF-ADMINISTERED QUESTIONNAIRES

If face-to-face interviews are time consuming and costly to undertake, self-administered questionnaires are the opposite as a result of subjects completing a questionnaire themselves. Given the same length and objectives, it is estimated that a self-administered questionnaire costs 50 per cent less that one administered by telephone, and 75 per cent less than one administered by personal interview (Bourque and Fielder, 1995). However, to be effective it is absolutely crucial that self-administered questionnaires are easy to use: respondents do not usually have the benefit of research training; they do not tend to be motivated to do the job well; and they are generally not selected on the basis that they are good at form filling. Several considerations should be taken into account when designing self-administered questionnaires:

- Self-administered questionnaires should be self-explanatory; there is no place for ambiguity.
- Closed questions work best; for example, ticking and circling responses. Open-ended questions often produce vague, incomplete answers.
- The questionnaire should be well set out, clear and uncluttered.
- Skip patterns should be kept to a minimum because they can confuse.
- Explicit instructions should be given about the procedure for returning questionnaires; a prepaid envelope should be provided if they are to be posted back.

The advantages of self-administered questionnaires are that they are cheap, quick and provide relatively easy access to geographically dispersed subjects. They also provide respondents with the opportunity to consider their response, for example, to look up records and ask other people. The anonymity of self-administered questionnaires may mean that individuals are more predisposed to answer questions on sensitive issues. Questionnaires preserve anonymity, at best interviews preserve confidentiality. Using the postal system avoids the hassle of non-contacts, i.e. people not being in when the interviewer calls. Other advantages are that respondents can complete the questionnaire at a time convenient to them and because there is no interviewer, there is no interviewer bias.

On the negative side of the equation, the use of self-administered questionnaires lacks the personal touch of a good interviewer, but a well-worded covering letter can help to compensate for this. The answers given by respondents must be accepted as final. There is no facility to probe or seek clarification from respondents on self-administered questionnaires, which can be a serious limitation in exploratory research. Nor are they appropriate where spontaneous answers are required. When respondents fill in the questionnaire they can see all of the questions, so different answers cannot be treated as independent. How does the researcher know who completed the questionnaire? This method requires a high trust relationship between researcher and respondent. Response rates can be pretty poor with rates as low as 20 per cent not uncommon. Self-administered questionnaires are only really practical in literate communities where respondents have the skills to complete them. Excellent mailing addresses and a good postal service are needed to send out and have questionnaires returned. Mail questionnaires are therefore appropriate for use in many advanced societies, but not for some developing countries where poor postal services exist.

## COMPUTER ASSISTED SELF-INTERVIEWING (CASI)

Computer Assisted Self-Interviewing (CASI) has been designed for many of the same reasons as CAPI, especially in respect of collecting data on sensitive issues. CASI can take the form of Disk by Mail (DBM); taking computers and programs to respondents or asking them to attend a specific location where computers are already set up; and by e-mail. The ability to use DBM is dependent on the target population having access to a personal computer. DBM response rates vary between 25 and 75 per cent, but rates of between 40–50 per cent have been reported without using a reminder. A similar mail survey using no reminders could be expected to yield response rates of approximately 35 per cent (de Leeuw and Nicholls, 1996). Early research also suggests that CASI is proving useful in eliciting responses to sensitive questions in some samples. The research by Wright *et al.* (1998) on smoking, drug and alcohol use in the USA found that pen and paper and CASI yielded similar response distributions as a whole for their sample of 12–34-year-olds. However, their respondents who were aged 12–18 years of age were significantly more likely to report undesirable behaviour using CASI than pen and paper. Reasons for this difference were attributed to a more positive attitude towards, and more familiarity with computers within this age group. Younger people tend to be more trusting of technology in general and have less concerns over its misuse.

The Internet and e-mail are promising methods of conducting survey research as the proportion of the population who own computers and have Internet access increases. It is obviously a research method in which academics have a particular interest given that most have free access. Current levels of the population with access to e-mail make it an inappropriate method for undertaking general population surveys. The personal characteristics of users and non-users also tend to be highly differentiated along the lines of social class, gender, age, income and ethnicity (Selwyn and Robson, 1998). However, e-mail is highly suitable for use with some samples such as company employees, where e-mail access can be as high as 100 per cent. Despite the obvious potential of e-mail as a survey methodology because of its costs, speed and early recognition of valid addresses, recent research suggests that response rates are not as high as mail surveys (42.6 per cent to 70.7 per cent respectively) (Schaefer and Dillman, 1998). There is also a possibility that e-mail response rates will decline as the amount of 'junk' e-mail increases. Other potential problems are that e-mail messages can be quickly deleted or saved in a file never to be read again (Thach, 1995)

The level of response rates in e-mail surveys is an important issue which researchers need to confront. There is some evidence to suggest that the more attempts are made to reach respondents, the higher the response rates. Multiple contacts are therefore essential for e-mail surveys to be successful. A review of e-mail surveys in the existing literature suggests that the average response rate for e-mail surveys with a single contact is 28.5 per cent compared with 41 per cent for two contacts and 57 per cent for three or more contacts. Apart from being an important survey method in its own right, its potential in mix mode communication also needs to be evaluated. The cost and speed advantages of e-mail make it highly suitable for a first approach. Thereafter, researchers may wish to use more expensive methods until the required level of response has been achieved. Where respondents have particular mode preferences, offering additional response formats could improve response rates (Schaefer and Dillman, 1998).

Obtaining acceptable response rates from e-mail surveys is one issue. Of equal importance is the quality of data that is generated. Unfortunately there is not a comprehensive body of literature to shed light on the issue of whether individuals respond differently to questions by e-mail rather than mail. Both methods involve self-administered questionnaires; therefore one would expect the quality to be similar. Early research suggests that levels of non-response are higher for e-mail items, but others indicate that the length of answers to open-ended questions is higher using e-mail. This perhaps indicates that entering answers via keyboard rather than writing by hand might be preferable for some respondents. Schaefer and Dillman's (1998) research indicated that 69.4 per cent of respondents to e-mail surveys completed at least 95 per cent of the questionnaire, compared to 56.6 per cent who completed a paper mail questionnaire. The responses to the last question which asked respondents to provide any further information had a 12 per cent higher completion rate for the e-mail survey and the responses were more extensive: an average of 40 words compared to 10 words via mail. Their research also documented differences in response times between mail and e-mail surveys. On average e-mail responses took a little over 9 days to be returned compared with 14 days by mail. Around 17 per cent of e-mails were returned the same day and over 50 per cent of the completed questionnaire e-mails were returned before one completed mail questionnaire was returned.

A final issue in the use of e-mails as vehicles for surveys concerns respondent anonymity. Responses via e-mail invariably include details of the respondent's name and address. Depending on the nature of the survey, anonymity might not be a problem. However, surveys which question respondents about sensitive issues might be more problematic and place more emphasis on researcher assurances of confidentiality. Just such a situation occurred in Coomber's (1997) research with drug dealers using Internet responses. His solution was to set up software which filtered and then recorded the responses to the e-mail questionnaire but not the respondents e-mail address. An associated issue in workplace surveys is the ability of employers to install software to enable them to read employees' e-mails. How this lack of confidentiality affects e-mail survey response is an important issue and one which needs to be addressed in the research methods literature.

## SURVEY RESEARCH BY TELEPHONE

Telephone surveys have not been very popular among academic researchers. Indeed until relatively recently they were positively discouraged in some research methods texts and ignored in others. It was not until market researchers demonstrated the benefits of telephone surveys in the 1970s that they took off (Frey, 1989). In business and other organizations telephone interviewing has become standard. Market research organizations are also extensive users of telephone interviewing, both to identify and interview quota samples of consumers (Thomas and Purdon, 1995). Telephone surveys are becoming more widespread and acceptable for a number of reasons:

- The extensive use of telephones in advanced societies.
- Telephone surveys as a research method have gained status.
- As a result of the difficulties encountered with traditional face-to-face interviews such as people being unavailable and high labour costs.
- The difficulty of conducting research in diverse geographical locations.
- Telephone surveys provide a quick method of data collection.
- By comparison with other methods telephone surveys are relatively inexpensive.

In addition to being a useful research method in its own right, a telephone survey can be used for other purposes, including prodding non-respondents to return mail questionnaires. Telephone surveys can also provide a low-cost screening facility to identify respondents with the required characteristics and exclude those that have not. Using the telephone to give advance notice that questionnaires are to be sent often leads to a better response rate than otherwise might have been achieved by sending a letter. Obtaining the co-operation of respondents before sending a postal questionnaire is a good idea, especially if you want to ask for responses over the telephone.

Some of the advantages of telephone interviewing reflect the norms of telephone usage. People are predisposed to answer the phone when it rings and it is not very socially acceptable to hang up. When interviewing respondents on the telephone you usually have their undivided attention, which can be a considerable advantage. People are used to being active participants in telephone conversations, so telephone interviewing is a natural extension of most people's everyday behaviour. Telephone surveys provide a cheap, quick method of data collection which is fairly easy to co-ordinate and administer. There is an argument which suggests that telephone surveys do not suffer from interviewer effects as much as face-to-face interviewing. Hence respondents are less likely to give a socially desirable response. Telephone interviews are also useful for interviewing powerholders in organizations who are often short of time and will perhaps give a short interview over the phone rather than setting aside time for a face-to-face session.

Some of the disadvantages of telephone surveys include the difficulty of selecting a probability sample because of inadequate lists of telephone numbers (see also Chapter 21). There can also be problems in sampling some populations. In Britain 10 per cent of the population does not have a telephone. This 10 per cent comprises individuals in deprived groups including: young adults, the unemployed, low income families and single parents. It is often the case that social science research would want to include individuals with those characteristics and accurately report their views. However, perhaps more significant are individuals and households who choose to have ex-directory numbers. Approximately 25 per cent of the British population have an ex-directory number and their profile is different from the general population. This group tend to be young, live in cities, and young women living alone are over-represented. Response rates also tend to be higher for face-to-face than telephone interviewing and more telephone interviews are terminated early (Thomas and Purdon, 1995). It is not unknown for researchers to find that four times out of ten the phone will ring but an interview will not be possible. There are also multiple reasons why an interview does not take place which need accurately reporting. A comprehensive listing of these has been documented by Lavrakas (1987) and some of the categories include:

| Code | Explanation |
| --- | --- |
| 1 | No answer after 7 rings |
| 2 | Busy after one immediate re-dial |
| 3 | Answering machine (residence) |

| 4  | Household language barrier |
|----|---|
| 5  | Answered by a non-resident |
| 6  | Household refusal |
| 7  | Disconnected or other non-working |
| 8  | Temporarily disconnected |
| 9  | Business, other non-residence |
| 10 | No-one meets eligibility criteria |
| 11 | Contact only |
| 12 | Selected respondent temporarily unavailable |
| 13 | Selected respondent unavailable during fieldwork period |
| 14 | Selected respondent unavailable due to physical/mental handicap |
| 15 | Language barrier with selected respondent |
| 16 | Refusal by selected respondent |
| 17 | Partial interview |
| 18 | Completed interview |

Other problems are that telephone interviewing is not particularly good at accessing elite groups and researchers can end up being diverted to gatekeepers. Nor is telephone interviewing always a good method for accessing people who are physically or sensorily impaired in some way. There can be problems in conducting long interviews – twenty to thirty minutes is about average before interviewer fatigue sets in (Lavrakas, 1987). It is impossible to use visual aids over the telephone and there can be a need to overcome the possible anxiety of the subject as there are no visual clues of the status or social background of the caller. Frey and Oishi (1995: 114) do argue that the voice of the interviewer is important in overall response rates. They note little is known about the impact of voice quality except that 'interviewers with slightly louder tones and the ability to pronounce distinctly have better response rates'. Finally, the telephone is not a good approach for asking complex questions and can result in shorter, truncated answers to open-ended questions (see also Thomas and Purdon, 1995).

## CONTENT ANALYSIS

Content analysis is a systematic and empirical method which has been developed for analysing documentary data. It is most often used for analysing written data, for example, newspapers and magazines. However, it can also be used to analyse visual and audio material. Abercrombie *et al.* provide the following definition:

> The analysis of the content of communication, which involves classifying contents in such a way as to bring out their basic structure. The term is normally

applied to the analysis of documentary or visual material rather than interview data, but the same technique may in fact apply to the analysis of answers to open-ended questions in survey research. (Abercrombie *et al.*, 1988: 50)

The use of the method involves six basic steps (see Ball and Smith, 1992):

- Select a topic and determine a research problem.
- Select a documentary source.
- Devise a set of analytical categories.
- Formulate an explicit set of instructions for using the categories to code the material.
- Establish a basis for sampling the documents.
- Count the frequency of a given category or theme in the documents sampled.

Content analysis enables researchers to use a standardized technique to analyse large amounts of data over a long time span. It is an unobtrusive research method, thus avoiding the problems of researcher effects associated with reactive methods such as interviewing. If documents are freely available, for example, newspapers, there are few access problems for the researcher.

Some of the disadvantages associated with content analysis are that there can be an over-emphasis on standardization, rather than attempting to recover the communicator's intent in publishing a particular type of picture, photograph or text. The process of categorization isolates those elements of the communicative message determined by the researcher's theoretical relevancy, which has led to the criticism that content analysis isolates and fragments the data – a process which decontextualizes the message. Content analysis highlights repetition as the mark of significance, when the significance might involve the meaning of a particular item.

# 23 QUESTIONNAIRE DESIGN

*Dawn Burton*

The most widely used survey instrument across the social sciences is the questionnaire. It is for this reason that this chapter focuses on questionnaire design. The chapter is very practical in its approach and a range of issues will be addressed including forming and wording questions; different types of questions; ordering; questionnaire design; survey reliability; undertaking pilot studies; and presenting findings.

## GETTING TO GRIPS WITH DESIGNING SURVEY QUESTIONS

Fowler (1993: 69) argues that 'Designing a question for a survey instrument is designing a measure not a conversational inquiry . . . Good questionnaires maximize the relationship between the answers recorded and what the researcher is trying to measure.' In one sense survey answers are merely responses that are elicited in an artificial situation which is orchestrated by the researcher. Indeed the contrived nature of the interaction between the researcher and respondent has been one of the main criticisms of survey research as Hughes (1976: 192) notes: 'the survey rarely deals with behaviour that is a response to a behaviour setting, but rather with behaviour elicited in a response to stimuli within settings'. Despite this criticism, surveys can provide important insights into human behaviour providing they are carefully designed. The extent to which questions are good measures relates to the degree of question reliability. When a number of respondents in the same situation answer a particular question they should all answer it in the same way. The extent to which there is inconsistency of response across respondents is reflected in the degree of random error and the measurement is therefore less precise. Another major issue in question design is the relationship between what the researcher is trying to measure and the answers provided by respondents. The correspondence between answers and true values has implications for validity. The key to designing a reliable research instrument is that researchers must be consistent in their approach to measurement by asking respondents exactly the same questions and that they record those answers in a systematic fashion. If respondents do not all perceive questions to mean the same thing, then that could be a reason for different responses. In extreme cases it may be necessary to use different questionnaires for different subgroups. The more general the sample, the more this can become an issue since there will be more variability in factors such as age, educational experience, socio-economic group and culture, among others.

Increasing the validity of factual reporting is crucial. Fowler (1993) suggests that respondents provide less than accurate responses under four circumstances. The first is when they do not understand the question. This can be particularly problematic because not everyone will own up to this, or indeed seek further clarification which provides the researcher with a hint that there could be a problem. The temptation on the part of the respondent is to guess what the question is asking and provide an answer which may not be correct. One alternative is to design open-ended questions for those topics which appear problematic and then construct categories which reflect the range of responses provided. However, it should be noted that this is a very labour intensive and time consuming task, especially if large numbers of respondents are involved.

Two other circumstances which can lead to respondents providing inaccurate answers are: if they do not know the answer, or they cannot recall the answer but do know it. If respondents are being asked a factual question about themselves and cannot answer, you are possibly dealing with a design problem and the question needs thinking through again. It may be appropriate to ask respondents why they cannot answer and then change the question to one which requires less detail and is easier to answer. An alternative perspective would be to help respondents estimate answers or allow them to ask other people such as family or work colleagues to help with details. Allowing time for individuals to respond would need to be built into the research design by using self-administered questionnaires or following up a face-to-face interview with a telephone call. A final reason why individuals do not accurately report in surveys is quite simply because they do not wish to answer particular questions in an interview context. This is most apparent in asking questions which are of a sensitive nature. In this instance it is important that the researcher makes it clear they will not personally judge responses that are given and that accuracy is the most important thing. Promises of confidentiality and anonymity can also be a useful strategy.

Fowler (1993: 71) argues that good questions mean the same thing to every respondent, appropriate responses to the questions are communicated consistently to all the sample, and that the question and answer process is entirely scripted. In a similar vein Hague (1993) suggests that researchers should ask themselves four important questions when drafting survey questions:

- Will this question be understood in the way I intend?
- How many different ways could this question be interpreted?
- Is this question likely to annoy, intimidate or offend?
- Is there a better way of asking the question?

One way of making sure that questions are understood and mean the same thing to all respondents is to use familiar words that they understand. After months of reading around the relevant literature you will have become used to expressing yourself in specific ways, perhaps using academic terminology or jargon. You need to make sure that this does not work its way into survey questions. Something which may be common to you after months of reading and being engrossed in your project might completely baffle the subjects. Refrain from using sophisticated or uncommon words. Keeping it simple is the key. As a matter of course you also need to avoid ambiguous words. Words such as 'often', 'usually' and 'frequently' lack precision. They could be interpreted in a whole range of different ways by respondents. You must express exactly what you mean.

It is always a good strategy to keep questions short and to the point to avoid respondents misunderstanding what you mean, or having to remember too much information at once which can confuse. To improve the accuracy of reporting make the questions specific, by pinning down events to times, places and periods. It is a good strategy to avoid questions which include a negative concept in them. Questions phrased in the negative are usually more difficult to understand than those phrased in the positive. The first of these questions is easier to answer than the second for just that reason: 'Are you likely to visit the cinema in the next week?' 'Are you unlikely to visit the cinema in the next week?'

Another trap that some researchers fall into is to ask hypothetical questions which are a waste of time and tell you little of any importance. For example: 'If the housing market improves in the future, do you think you might put your house up for sale?' Where answers are required of a sensitive nature, desensitize questions by using response bands. For example:

| Age | Income |
|-----|--------|
| 20–29 | £15,000–20,999 |
| 30–39 | £21,000–26,000 |
| 40–49 | |

but make sure fixed responses do not overlap:

| Age | Age |
|-----|-----|
| 15–20 | 15–20 |
| 20–25 | 21–25 |
| 25–30 | 26–30 |

## DIFFERENT TYPES OF SURVEY QUESTIONS

### Closed questions

One distinction between survey questions is whether they are open ended or closed. Within the closed question category there are questions which generate a dichotomous response, multi-choice questions and those which require respondents to choose a response from a scale. The types of questions you want to ask also have implications for the format of the response, which in turn has implications for the way in which the data can be analysed. The simplest type of question generates a *dichotomous response* which admits only the answers Yes or No with additional spaces for Don't Know. For example:

Does your car have front-wheel steering?
Yes                     . . . 1
No                      . . . 2
Don't Know              . . . 3

*Multiple choice* answers facilitate closed and pre-coded answers. Several alternative responses are listed and the respondent is asked to make a selection from those provided. It is important to have a complete list of choices. The respondent's recollection can be helped by showing him/her a card on which all the alternatives are stated rather than having to remember them all. For example:

What is the highest level of education that you achieved?
Secondary School        . . . 1
Sixth Form              . . . 2
University (u.g)        . . . 3
University (p.g)        . . . 4

Using *scaling techniques* in questionnaire design is a skill which definitely needs to be acquired. It is not the intention to explore scaling techniques in depth in this section, but to provide an overview of some issues to consider. A more detailed account of scaling techniques is provided in *Scale Development* (DeVellis, 1991). He is quite critical of the ways in which some researchers use scales. He notes: 'Researchers often throw together or dredge up items and assume they constitute a suitable scale. A researcher not only may fail to exploit theory in developing a scale, but also may reach erroneous conclusions about a theory by misinterpreting what a scale measures' (1991: 9). Several different types of scaling techniques are used by researchers.

*Likert scales* are commonly used in social science research. In this instance respondents are presented with a statement and then required to choose a response indicating varying degrees of agreement or disagreement:

Eating British beef is an essential component of a healthy lifestyle.

| 1 | 2 | 3 | 4 | 5 | 6 |
|---|---|---|---|---|---|
| Strongly disagree | Moderately disagree | Mildly disagree | Mildly agree | Moderately agree | Strongly agree |

*Semantic differential scales* are associated with attitudinal research. The use of semantic differential scales requires the respondent to be presented with some sort of stimulus and then asked to choose from paired adjectives at opposite ends of a continuum. There are usually seven or nine lines which represent a particular response as shown below. Respondents are asked to choose one of the lines on the continum which reflects their view on a particular issue.

British Beef  
Safe ____ ____ ____ ____ ____ ____ ____ ____ ____ Unsafe

*Visual analogue* scales are very similar to semantic differential scales. The difference is that respondents are presented with a continuous line upon which they place a mark according to their attitude. For example:

British Beef  
Safe _____ Unsafe

One issue which often faces researchers is how many response categories a scale should have. Obviously large numbers of response categories mean more work for the researcher. The time required to undertake the coding and data entry needs to be evaluated in the context of what 'extra' the precise nature of the scaling will add to the findings. Another related issue is whether the number of responses should be odd or even. DeVellis (1991: 66) suggests this 'depends on the type of question, the type of response option and the investigators purpose'. However, that said, an odd number permits a response which sits on the fence, i.e. neither agree or disagree, whereas an even number usually prompts a judgement one way or the other.

## Open-ended questions

Open-ended questions provide a response format that gives respondents the freedom to provide any answer which they care to make. The researcher then has to make sense of the responses given, construct appropriate categories and then code the categories so that the data can be statistically analysed. Even a very simple question such as 'What do you do in your spare time?' could generate a substantial number of responses which would need documenting very carefully. Dealing with open-ended questions can be very time consuming, but they can often be the most important questions on the survey by offering important and unpredictable insights into human behaviour.

## QUESTIONNAIRE LAYOUT AND DESIGN

Questionnaire layout is important for both the interviewer and interviewee. As far as the interviewer is concerned, a questionnaire is a working document, or as Fowler (1993: 71) suggests 'a protocol for one side of the interaction'. A questionnaire should not just be a list of relevant questions but also include instructions about how the interview should proceed to ensure that all interviews follow the same path. In the case of self-administered questionnaires, the format is even more crucial since respondents usually provide the relevant information without assistance from a researcher. There can be no ambiguity when designing self-administered questionnaires. If you are in doubt about how to construct a good questionnaire format, the best advice is to go and take a look at a completed version, preferably one which has been used successfully. However, sometimes this can be easier said than done since most academic journal articles do not provide a copy of the survey instrument. A more productive strategy might be to obtain a copy of questionnaires and associated documentation which supports one of the large government surveys or a very reputable academic survey, many of which are held in the Economic and Social Research Council's Data Archive at the University of Essex and can be provided to research students at minimal cost.

Here are some guidelines which will help in constructing your questionnaire so that the layout is simple but contains all the essential elements you need. Every questionnaire should have a title so it can be easily identified by all concerned: the researcher, respondent and data processor (where this function is undertaken by someone other than the researcher). Questionnaires also need to be given a unique identification number and a space should be provided to record appropriate details such as the name and address of the interviewee, place of interview, the date, and the time taken to administer the survey (see Figure 23.1). Space is at a premium when designing questionnaires, first because long questionnaires can put subjects off and second because they can be expensive to print. An alternative suggestion is that questionnaires should be printed on only one side of each page as people can miss questions that are printed on the back (De Vaus, 1996). As a general principle, try to avoid making questionnaires any longer than necessary. This said, you need to ensure that you have left sufficient room for vital information. A classic mistake is not leaving enough space for documenting the answers to open-ended questions. Remember that you or respondents will be writing the answers to open-ended questions by hand which usually takes up far more space than typed text. You also need to set up your page layout to include coding information to facilitate data processing. Usually a 3 cm margin containing the relevant number of coding boxes on the right-hand side of each page of the questionnaire is appropriate.

Typeface is an important consideration when constructing questionnaires. People read lower case sentences much more easily than UPPER

```
                                    Identification number: _____

   Title of project:_____

   Name of subject:_____

   Place of interview: _____

   Date of interview:_____

   Start time _____ Finish time _____

   Name of interviewer_____
```

**FIGURE 23.1  Questionnaire details**

CASE SENTENCES, so avoid capitals. It also makes the interview process easier if the questionnaire differentiates between words that the interviewer is to read to respondents and words that are instructions. Differentiating instructions and text can be undertaken using a variety of techniques by using **boldface**, <u>underlining</u> or *italics* or a different sized font. It is important to ensure that all the words the interviewer has to say are written down, for example, transitions, introductions to questions and explanations. Any optional wording should be located in brackets (his/her). Any probes that are used also need to be written down and questions where they are used need to be noted for future reference. It is also important to ensure that *branching questions* are obvious, for example:

Do you drink wine?   Yes   ☐
                     No    ☐      If no, go to section 10

Branching questions should be double-checked in case too many questions have been inappropriately excluded.

Another important set of considerations relates to the ordering of questions. Questions at the beginning of a questionnaire should verify that subjects with the requisite characteristics have been chosen. There is no point asking a respondent to answer a questionnaire and then finding out at the end that they did not have the characteristics you wanted. Questions should flow easily from one to another. Where appropriate they should be grouped into specific areas under headings and follow a logical sequence. It may be helpful to lead respondents into questions: For example, 'Now, if you don't mind can I ask you a few questions about . . .' The questionnaire should have an obvious path to assist the thought processes of respondents. This will help them to anticipate what questions they might be asked next, focus their minds and perhaps help them to sustain interest.

It is advisable to move from general issues to questions which are specific. Start with questions that are easy to answer and leave the more difficult or threatening ones (if there are any) until later. Taking this approach lets respondents get into their stride and prepares them for complex questions at the end. It is important to build up respondents' confidence and make them feel relaxed. While undertaking an interview may be nerve-racking for the interviewer, this is also true of respondents, many of whom will never have been involved in academic research before. Try to avoid posing difficult and sensitive questions at the beginning of the interview as there is a strong possibility that this may result in it being abandoned.

Finally, an issue which concerns many researcher students is where demographic questions (age, sex, income, marital status and so on) should be located within the structure of the questionnaire. There is no easy answer, but here are two different points of view. Some researchers are of the opinion that they should be placed at the end. They argue that many individuals find answering demographic questions boring and it will put them off and they might become disinterested. It is also the case that some respondents will find questions about age, income, etc. sensitive, which may cause reluctance to answer the questions. Researchers who favour such questions at the beginning argue that these types of questions are easy for the respondent to answer and so build up their confidence to carry on. Another reason for locating such questions at the beginning is that in the case of mail questionnaires, people who return incomplete questionnaires tend not to complete the final questions so that a lot of valuable demographic information is lost.

## SURVEY RELIABILITY

Although the advice above will hopefully help in developing good quality questionnaires, no survey or test is 100 per cent reliable, but some are clearly more reliable than others. Litwin (1995) suggests there are three ways in which researchers can determine survey reliability:

- test–retest/stability;
- alternate form/equivalence;
- internal consistency.

### Test–retest

Test–retest reliability is the most commonly used measure of survey reliability. This procedure involves having the same group of respondents answering the same survey at two different points in time and then comparing the responses. In effect the researcher is measuring how stable the responses are and to what extent they are reproducible. Correlation coefficients can be computed to compare the two or more sets of responses (see Chapter 26 for more information on this form of analysis). Test–retest reliability is normally undertaken for the whole of the survey, but can be used on specific questions or groups of questions. Care should be taken to avoid selecting items of scales that are likely to change over time as this will produce low test–retest reliability scores. The issue of practice effect is also of significance. Researchers should be aware that if subjects are asked to complete the survey instrument several times, they may become familiar with the items and merely reproduce their previous responses.

## Alternate form

Alternate form provides one way in which researchers can minimize the practice effect. One easy way is to shift the order of the responses. On multiple choice scales, some respondents tend to answer few questions conscientiously, then finding that they are choosing around the middle category on the scale, go on to give that response (or perhaps one category more positive or negative) all the way down the page. This can be overcome by reversing the polarity of items at irregular intervals, so the 'best' response is not always in the same place. Hence, a consistent expression of attitude will need a varying response on the form. This technique is best used when test–retest points are close together which requires respondents to read the questions carefully. Another technique is to change the wording of the response sets without changing the meaning. So, for example, number of days is substituted with number of hours: 1–2 times per day or every 12–24 hours. Yet another position is to change the actual wording of the questions.

## Internal consistency

Internal consistency provides an indication of how well different items measure the same issue. Although the use of one item on a questionnaire to assess the respondents' view about a particular variable is quicker to implement, asking more than one question and comparing the responses provides richer and more reliable data.

## UNDERTAKING PILOT STUDIES

In designing survey questions researchers rely on help from a variety of sources. As a general rule the more help you can attract from as many relevant sources as possible, the easier the process can be. Drafting a set of questions to facilitate feedback from fellow academics and supervisor(s) is an important starting point. It is essential that supervisors take a look at potential questions for they will have an in-depth knowledge of your particular research area and therefore be able to make a judgement about whether the questions you have constructed adequately address the important debates. However, it is sometimes the case that although supervisors have an extensive knowledge of a particular research area, they have limited experience in designing questionnaires. Constructing questionnaires is a skill that researchers develop by working on a variety of projects. If at all possible you should try and seek the help of academics who have experience in this area of work. They will often be able immediately to spot errors in layout or in the wording of questions and so on since they will probably have made some of the same mistakes in the past. Another useful source of help is fellow students. It is often a useful exercise, particularly in the case of self-administered questionnaires, if you ask them to complete one. Although they might not be able to answer some of the questions, they will be able to comment on whether they could navigate their way around the questionnaire easily.

In addition to asking for advice and help from your immediate academic community, help from outside universities is usually required. For example, focus group discussions with individuals having a similar profile to the final sample can be a useful way of refining questions, finding out what information individuals have access to and helping identify key words and terminology which are meaningful to respondents. Taping the focus group may prove useful since it will allow you to replay excerpts of dialogue which will enable study of the way in which respondents express themselves. How to conduct focus groups is a skill in itself and is discussed in more detail in Chapter 14. Interviewing selected key informants is also a useful strategy. Individuals in positions of authority can be a good source of information, not only about how to phrase questions to make them meaningful and provide advice about specific terminology, but also to give you an indication of the possibilities and limitations of the data collection method you have chosen. Key informants should be used wherever possible. They may even undertake to organize a pilot study on your behalf and provide some feedback.

It is quite possible that you may not wish to design all your own questions but rather replicate some that were used in other research. This approach is fine but you should take a critical view towards using another researcher's questions rather than accepting that they provide good measures. If you intend to apply questions which have been used previously but in a different setting, they may prove not to be as productive as you first thought. It is always a good idea to include some questions of your own in any event, since one of the quality indicators of a thesis is originality.

As a matter of course you should always carry out a pilot study – a small-scale replica of the main study. A question which research students often ask is how many respondents should be included in the pilot. Fowler (1993) indicates that survey organizers generally undertake 20–50 interviews during the pilot testing phase of questionnaire development.

However, ultimately researchers have to consider a range of factors when deciding how many interviews to undertake. One factor is the time that has been allocated to this particular activity. Many research students would find it very time consuming in their already tight PhD schedule to undertake so many interviews as a pilot. Another relevant factor is how successfully the piloting process is going during the first few interviews. If the questionnaire appears to be easy to administer, respondents understand the questions and can answer the questions sensibly and accurately, then a small number of interviews is all that is required. Extensive piloting needs to be undertaken if problems emerge. Fowler (1993) suggests that three factors indicate when something is wrong: whether or not the interviewers read all the questions as worded; whether subjects ask for clarification of the questions asked; and whether or not the respondent gives an inadequate answer which requires probing. He suggests that where one of these occurs in 15 per cent or more of pilot interviews the affected questions are likely to produce distorted data. Obviously the weaker the questionnaire, the more it will have to be revised and the further will need to be piloted. However, it needs to be said that it is far better to make mistakes at the piloting stage than in the main survey.

Pilot studies are useful for a number of reasons. By way of a check list, you need to determine the adequacy of your sampling frame; assess non-response rates; evaluate the suitability and effectiveness of the data collection method you have chosen; and establish the adequacy of the questions – do they work? Are questions understood by respondents? Should some questions be removed? You also need to check that you understand the answers which respondents provide. You need to evaluate whether the questionnaire 'flows', do questions 'fit' together and is the transition from one section to another smooth? Do question filters which direct respondents to skip questions actually work? Make sure they do not lead to subjects skipping more questions than necessary. It is important to evaluate the layout of the questionnaire, for example, is there enough room to write the responses to open-ended questions? You need to have a clear idea how long it takes to complete the questionnaire so you can advise potential respondents. This also enables you to estimate how long the data collection phase should take. The pilot study is also the place to judge respondents' interest and attention. If subjects become bored, perhaps you need to use shorter questions or a greater variety of questions. Finally, you need to determine whether the codes chosen for pre-coded questions are appropriate and construct codes for open-ended questions.

## PRESENTING THE RESULTS

It is usually the case in methods texts that a significant amount of attention is placed on collecting data and analysing the results, but how to present the results to readers in interesting and informative ways is given a very low profile. Bell (1993) provides some useful advice and illustrations about different ways in which quantitative data can be presented and anyone particularly interested in this area should consult her book *Doing Your Research Project*. The advice presented in this section is not exhaustive, but provides guidelines about some of the main presentational issues. First, you need to make absolutely sure that the data you write up is precise. It is pointless to be accurate at the data collection and analysis stage and then to make mistakes when writing up. Mistakes are very easy to make, especially when writing up detailed statistical data. Where you refer to your data in the text, make sure you signal to the reader where it comes from, for example: 'Table 1.2 indicates . . .'. Try to be creative when presenting statistical data. Think about using pie charts, bar charts, histograms and graphs rather than relying on statistical tables. Often the shape of distributions is as important as the statistics.

The format you use to present tables, figures and so on should be consistent and you need to number them consecutively, so, for example, in Chapter 1, tables could be numbered Table 1.1, 1.2, 1.3, etc.; in Chapter 2, Table 2.1, 2.2, 2.3, etc. Axes should be clearly marked and all tables and figures should be given a title and a source. Are you going to write the appropriate questions underneath the table? It is a lot easier if you leave figures and tables out of the thesis until the very end. If you write a journal article, figures and tables need to be placed on separate sheets of paper. Details about journal style are usually set out on the inside of the current journal cover and these issues are discussed at length in Chapter 30.

# 24 SECONDARY DATA ANALYSIS

## Dawn Burton

The preceding chapters have focused on the process of designing and administering surveys to meet the researchers' requirements, thereby creating a unique dataset specific to a particular project. Secondary data analysis is the process of exploring survey data which already exists. Although a research method in its own right, secondary analysis has not always had a high profile in the methods literature and its use within social science disciplines is highly variable in Britain (Bulmer, 1980; Dale *et al.*, 1988; Platt, 1996). In recent years the availability of an ever-increasing range of datasets lodged in archives and developments in information technology have contributed to a more buoyant interest in secondary data analysis. The purpose of this chapter is to provide some clarification about the different ways in which the term secondary analysis has been defined; give an indication of the availability and sources of secondary data in Britain; and evaluate some of the advantages and disadvantages of using secondary data. The final section of the chapter highlights some of the practical issues which can confront researchers when embarking on secondary analysis using a large multi-purpose dataset.

## WHAT DOES THE TERM SECONDARY ANALYSIS MEAN?

One of the earliest definitions of secondary analysis is provided by Hyman (1972: 1) as 'the extraction of knowledge on topics other than those which were the focus of the original survey'. A more comprehensive definition is provided by Hakim:

> Secondary analysis is any further analysis of an existing dataset which presents interpretations, conclusions, or knowledge additional to or different from, those presented in the first report on the inquiry as a whole and its main results. (Hakim, 1982: 1)

However, Thomas (1996: 42) questions the view that secondary analysis is about the re-analysis and further analysis of data in ways which differ from the first report, by indicating that many of the major surveys are increasingly designed with a range of other users in mind, not just those of the originators. As a result, he questions the idea that a particular dataset can generate one general report and that thereafter any other analysis constitutes secondary analysis. Dale *et al.* (1988: 4) provide an even broader definition as the 'analysis of data by anyone other than those responsible for its original commissioning or collection'. They also note that secondary analysis is not just confined to survey data, but that the term can be widened to include official records, tape-recorded interviews and video recordings. All of these methods of data are free standing and well documented which allows them to be open to secondary analysis. By contrast, the re-analysis of transcripts of unstructured interviews or ethnographic field notes do not easily lend themselves to secondary analysis as the researcher becomes, in part at least, the research instrument and the results are filtered through their own understanding of the social situation and the context in which the research dialogue occurs.

Researchers can use secondary data analysis in two main ways: as an alternative to undertaking primary empirical research, or as one element in a research strategy. The simplest approach to secondary data analysis is to use a single dataset, whether that be in order to replicate another researcher's results, or to use the data to address a completely different set of issues. A more complex undertaking is to analyse more than one dataset. As a result of the huge increase in datasets becoming available, researchers frequently have the option of analysing several datasets. For example, one of the large continuous datasets such as the General House-hold Survey has data going back to the 1970s, thus facilitating longitudinal analysis. As a result of pan-European and international collaboration, datasets also enable researchers to investigate cross-national issues. Another reason to analyse a variety of different datasets is that together they may provide a more detailed, comprehensive account. For example, there are four main datasets in the public domain which ask respondents about their savings and investment decisions (General Household Survey, British Household Panel Survey, Family Expenditure Survey, Family Resources Survey). Providing that each of the surveys provides a slightly different insight, analysing more than one survey could prove well worthwhile. Using secondary data analysis as one element in a research strategy can also be productive. For example, qualitative research might be used in a complementary way by shedding light on issues which were not addressed within a particular survey. This strategy was used in my own research and is discussed further at the end of the chapter.

## ADVANTAGES AND DISADVANTAGES OF SECONDARY DATA ANALYSIS

There are many advantages of using secondary data analysis as a research technique. Dale *et al.* (1988) argue that an important strength of secondary analysis is its ability to replicate studies and reanalyse data from a different perspective and within a different theoretical framework. Hakim (1982: 16) suggests that secondary data analysis enables researchers 'to think more closely about the theoretical aims and substantive issues of the study rather than the practical and methodological problems of collecting new data'. The sheer size of the samples used in many of the large datasets opens up a range of possibilities which would otherwise not be open to many established researchers, let alone research students. Platt (1996: 9) suggests that without using secondary analysis 'it is almost inconceivable that a graduate student's thesis could initiate a study using a national representative sample'.

The range of topics covered in existing datasets is also enormous. The large-scale, multi-purpose nature of some of the datasets makes them ideally suited to addressing debates about major social, political and economic change. An additional advantage is that some of the datasets have samples which are so large that they contain respondents which might otherwise be inaccessible or difficult to reach. Where continuous surveys are available, they enable researchers to conduct longitudinal research. Longitudinal research is very difficult for research students to undertake effectively within a three to five year registration period if they had to collect the data themselves from scratch, and the time scale would be extremely limited if they did. Even for experienced researchers, longitudinal studies are limited because of constraints on adequate levels of funding. Where funding is forthcoming follow-up studies can be very problematic because of the loss of contact with the original sample, or because individuals no longer wish to be involved in the project (for example see Moore, 1996). For these reasons the secondary analysis of datasets which go back many years is a very attractive option, as is the variety of data included which cover many areas of interest to social scientists (see, for example, Dex, 1991, on life and work history analysis).

Cross-national and comparative research defined as the examination of particular issues in more than one country also becomes a feasible option with the advent of large national databases. For example, Jarman *et al.* (1999) were able to analyse international variations in gender and occupational segregation in 38 different countries by analysing one International Labour Organization dataset (see also Hakim, 1991, on using the European Labour Force Survey). Despite the obvious attractions of using secondary data to undertake cross-national research, researchers should be aware of some of the limitations. Hantrais suggests that accessing comparable data and having working definitions of concepts and research parameters can be problematic:

Since much of the international work carried out at the European level is not strictly comparative at the design and data collection stages, the findings cannot then be compared systematically. Data collection is strongly influenced by national conventions. Their source, the purpose for which they were gathered, the criteria used and the method of collection may vary considerably from one country to another, and the criteria adopted for coding data may change over time. (Hantrais, 1996: 3)

Malhortra *et al.* (1996) also note that data from highly industrialized countries are likely to be more accurate than those from developing countries. The social and political context in which the data was produced also need to be taken into account. For example, many developing countries attempt to attract overseas aid by overstating economic factors which make their economy appear healthier than it is in reality (Czinkota and Ronkainen, 1994). The lack of sophisticated data collection systems in some countries may lead to estimates being reported which can result in unacceptably high margins of error. While Jarman *et al.*'s (1999: 17) cross-national examination of occupational segregation found: 'Since occupations that are predominantly male have received more attention from researchers and government statistical organizations, they have tended to be classified more finely. In contrast, women's occupations have tended to be classified in large umbrella categories'. (See also O'Reilly, 1996.)

On a practical level, secondary analysis is a useful method when results are needed quickly because the design, data collection and data input functions have already been undertaken. Invariably, secondary research is often a more cost-effective option which adds to its appeal. Finally, the quality of data obtained from large-scale surveys tends to be good because research originators specialize in undertaking the same survey year after year. Researchers working on the project also tend to be experienced and well trained. As a result of the data being already collected there are few access negotiations to be undertaken which can often be time consuming to resolve in primary research. Access in relation to secondary data is focused on obtaining the relevant dataset, and that can usually be organized fairly quickly by using a small number of key contact personnel. Ethical issues associated with analysing secondary data are not an area which has been extensively discussed, even in texts which are devoted to ethical issues and the research process (see for example, Sieber, 1992). Where ethical issues do exist in secondary research, they tend to relate to the analysis of small sub-sets of the data and focus on the anonymity of respondents (Dale *et al.*, 1988).

There are a considerable number of features of secondary data analysis which are very attractive. However, researchers must be very clear in their own mind that secondary data analysis is an appropriate method for addressing their own specific, research problem. This point is emphasized by Proctor (1993: 257): 'There is always a temptation for the subject of the research to be determined by what is convenient rather than by what is scientifically important, and the balance of effort between data collection and data analysis makes this particularly dangerous in planning secondary analysis.' Thomas (1996: 2) also argues that statistics should be conceptualized as organizational products and researchers need to be critical of the 'categorizations used and the data creation procedures followed'. He adds that even if statistics are systematically produced they are not necessarily scientific. While May (1993) argues that official statistics can reveal as much about particular organizations' priorities and the discretion afforded to individuals as the behaviour documented in the survey. However, Bulmer (1980) argues that as long as researchers are aware of these socio-political issues, official statistics are a valuable resource.

It does need to be recognized that not all surveys are of the same quality in terms of validity and reliability. Large nationally representative datasets and official surveys are often better than non-official studies and smaller scale surveys. In addition to these factors, sample size, sampling design and response rates all need to be given careful consideration. Another potential problem is that researchers undertaking the secondary analysis have no control over the questions that are asked, in effect it is an 'off-the-peg' approach rather than the 'haute couture' method of designing a survey which fits your unique project's aims and objectives. The definitions and categories that have been used also need to be carefully evaluated. If the survey definitions/categories are not compatible with those which the researcher wishes to use then this could be a problem, although it should be pointed out that some data categories can be reorganized. Other problems can arise if survey originators do not provide comprehensive technical reports which can lead researchers to make erroneous conclusions (for example, see the dialogue between Elliot and Ellingworth, 1997, 1998 and Lynn, 1998, on the issue of sampling error and response bias in the 1992 British Crime Survey).

Other problems relate to data handling difficulties. Some of the datasets are so huge that they can take quite a long time to set up before any analysis can be conducted. The datasets often require access to substantial computing space which can be in short supply at some universities. Finally, good statistical and computing skills are required to undertake some of the more sophisticated types of analyses. The ESRC provides tuition in quantitative techniques via summer schools at the University of Essex that research students can attend on a free of charge or highly subsidized basis, which might prove helpful.

## SOURCES OF SECONDARY DATA

The existence of large datasets is not a new phenomenon. A population census has been a regular decentenial exercise since 1801 in Britain and 1790 in the USA. Some of the traditional uses of large-scale surveys were measuring of public opinion for newspapers and magazine articles; as a way of understanding political perception and opinions to help political candidates in elections; and finally, by market research organizations that wanted to understand consumer preferences and interests (Fowler, 1993). More recently, large-scale surveys have entered a new stage exemplified by a move from central government statistics derived from records towards an emphasis on sample surveys. An important factor as far as secondary analysts are concerned is that many of the government-funded surveys are in the public domain and provide a wealth of information on a whole range of variables. Thomas (1996: 9) suggests that 'nearly every important area of activity and attitude in the British population has now been the focus of a major national survey'.

There are many sources of secondary data in Britain and the number of outlets producing statistical data are increasing all the time. Official statistics are one important source of data. The Business Statistics Office produce *Business Monitors*, an important source of trends in industry. The Office of Population Censuses and Surveys produces a range of continuous and multi-purpose datasets such as the *Family Expenditure Survey* and the *General Household Survey*, among others. The Central Statistical Office produces a number of multi-source publications such as *Social Trends* and *Economic Trends*. Other official sources are the European Community, the United Nations, the International Labour Organization and local government. Non-official sources could include trade unions, banks, market research organizations, professional institutions, chambers of commerce and so on. Kent (1993) distinguishes between four different types of secondary data:

- published articles in journals, books, newspapers or magazines;
- statistical data generated from government and other sources;
- data purchased from business publishing houses, market research companies or advertising agencies;
- data generated by a result of day-to-day operations.

The secondary analysis of survey data is a growing trend in Britain and the USA and is reflected in the increasing number of articles based on secondary data (Platt, 1996). This trend is being facilitated by the development of national statistical archives and the agreements made between these archives on exchanging datasets, and developments in computer technology which make the secondary analysis of datasets more manageable. The main source of datasets in Britain is the Economic and Social Research Council's Data Archive, based at the University of Essex. The Archive holds a wide range of large-scale datasets in addition to some machine readable qualitative data. In order to investigate whether the Archive holds any datasets of interest you need to access its home page on the World Wide Web.

The process of ordering a dataset from the Data Archive is fairly straightforward since most of the important details of the relevant datasets and the procedures for ordering are located on the Archive web pages. Data can be provided in a number of forms such as being downloaded directly into a user's work space, by disk or CD-ROM. The data can be formatted in a variety of ways to enable users to choose a format which is compatible with the program to be used for the analysis (see Ward and Dale, 1995 for information on software packages for statistical analysis and Chapters 25, 26 and 27 on using SPSS for Windows). Users can choose to receive a copy of a whole dataset or request a sub-set which focuses on a specific part of the data which is of interest. The latter option is usually best because variables are limited, the data is easier to handle and requires less computing space to analyse. The ordering process can be completed on-line or through the post. You need to remember that the Archive does not provide computing support once the data has been delivered. You may need the help of computer support staff at your own university to help you set up the dataset and make sure you have enough computing space to run sophisticated analyses.

## ISSUES TO CONSIDER WHEN CHOOSING A DATASET

Choosing a dataset has become much easier in recent years as a result of the establishment of archives and the implementation of user-friendly search systems. The ESRC Data Archive provides extensive details of all the datasets held, the years which the data covers and descriptors giving an indication of the types of questions asked. With such an array of information at your fingertips, careful thought needs to be given to dataset choice. The important factors involved in choosing datasets has been extensively discussed elsewhere (see Dale *et al.*, 1988; Stewart, 1984). An abbreviated version by way of a check list includes: sampling procedures; method of data collection; documentation availability; research originators; publications; year(s) to be used.

*Sampling procedures and the nature of the population sampled*  If researchers wish to make generalizations and inferences from the sample, then it is important to know whether in fact the sample is representative and of what population.

*Method of data collection*  It is important to know the methods used for the purpose of data collection since they will affect response rates and the kinds of questions that can be asked.

*Response rates*  Researchers need to know the level of response in order to make a judgement about whether it was acceptable. There are no hard and fast rules about acceptable levels of response, but OPCS tend to achieve response rates of approximately 83–85 per cent, against which other levels of response can be measured. Of equal importance is information about characteristics of non-respondents which can introduce an element of bias in the data.

*Availability of documentation*  Most datasets require some form of documentation to enable researchers to understand important elements of the survey process. At the very least researchers need to obtain a copy of the questionnaire and a description of the sampling techniques used. It is also helpful to have a knowledge of the instructions that were given to interviewers, especially in relation to probes. How coding frames were constructed and used, especially where open-ended questions are concerned, is important. The ways in which non-response has been coded is also crucial: for example, whether those to whom the question did not apply have been distinguished from those who did not answer, and what codes (if any) have been used for missing values.

*Research originators*  Researchers undertaking any form of secondary analysis have to rely on the accuracy and integrity of the data source. Research originators have responsibility for quality control procedures and the methodological work. Therefore their reputation does have considerable implications for the quality of the data. The interview schedule and the quality of available documentation are usually good indicators of the quality of the data.

*Publications generated from the dataset*  It is a requirement that publications which have been generated using datasets from the ESRC Data Archive are deposited in the Archive. Comprehensive lists of papers provide a good insight into the datasets and the way they have been used and may also reveal some areas which would benefit from further analysis.

*Year(s) to be used*  Many of the datasets held in the Archive are annual surveys and go back many years. The question of which year(s) to choose is an important consideration. A number of factors are worth considering. First, it is always best to work with data that is as up to date as possible. Second, the choice of data must relate to the suitability of the questions asked vis-à-vis the nature of the research project. Some surveys have special topics of interest on a one-off basis and they are worth looking out for since, if it is a topic in which you are interested, many more questions will be asked. If the intention is to undertake longitudinal analysis the problem can be more complicated as questions can change from one year to the next and for some years questions might be dropped altogether.

## THE ANALYSIS OF SECONDARY DATA IN PRACTICE

### The dataset

The dataset used for the purposes of this example is the General Household Survey (GHS). The 1992–3 dataset uses responses from around 27,000 individuals in households throughout Britain. Each year interviews are undertaken at approximately 13,000 addresses. At these addresses all persons aged 16 or over living in private households are interviewed. The sample is distributed over England, Scotland and Wales in such a way that different kinds of areas and households are represented. Similarly, fieldwork is undertaken throughout the year so that the survey can measure such things as seasonal changes in employment, use of health services, and so on. Data collection is by face-to-face interview. The dataset is available from the Economic and Social Research Council and the Archive can provide a tailored version of the dataset to meet researcher's individual needs rather than providing the entire dataset.

## The project

The GHS was used in my own particular project to assess pension scheme membership among ethnic minority groups in Britain. Within the context of this project, the secondary analysis of an existing dataset offered several advantages. The first advantage was cost effectiveness. The GHS provided a massive amount of information at minimal cost. The most expensive item was the copy of the questionnaire that was administered and the coding book. Second, undertaking research with ethnic groups is not an easy task. Not all members of ethnic minority groups speak English. There can be difficulties gaining access to certain populations and cultural differences can be problematic. To conduct a sample survey using interviewers from different ethnic groups would have been a difficult, expensive, not to mention a highly complex undertaking. A third problem in undertaking a sample survey from scratch relates to the geographic location in which various ethnic groups have settled. It is well established that there are distinctive ethnic minority settlement patterns in different regions and localities in Britain. While these patterns are documented in the census, undertaking research in several different localities to access different ethnic groups would have been logistically difficult to organize. The biggest advantage of the GHS for my purposes was that it documented the respondent's ethnicity and asked questions about occupational and personal pensions scheme membership. The analysis of the GHS was a good option.

## Sample size and categories used

The first task in beginning to analyse the data was to assess how many individuals were included in the survey in the age range 18–65, which I decided was the age group to be studied because it is the main age range of the working population in Britain. The results indicated that there were 19,373 respondents within that age category which is a considerable number of cases. An additional consideration was that only subjects who are employed will be paying into a pension scheme. The sample therefore has to be further refined to include just employees who totalled 9,837. The numbers of respondents in each of the ethnic groups who were employed is provided in Table 24.1.

**TABLE 24.1   Economic status by ethnic group**

|  | White | Black | Indian | Pakistani/ Bangladeshi | Other |
|---|---|---|---|---|---|
| Employed full-time | 6,393 | 80 | 98 | 24 | 73 |
| Employed part-time | 2,118 | 25 | 19 | 7 | 16 |
| Self-employed | 1,266 | 2 | 28 | 10 | 1 |
| Government scheme | 60 | 2 | 5 | n/a | 1 |
| Unemployed | 1,000 | 29 | 27 | 27 | 27 |
| Economically inactive | 3,243 | 45 | 69 | 64 | 49 |
| No response | 2,234 | 17 | 11 | 5 | 26 |
| Total | 18,567 | 200 | 257 | 139 | 210 |

Source: General Household Survey, 1992–3.

The next step was to find out how many individuals of different ethnic groups were included in the sample I wanted to analyse. The GHS listed 10 ethnic groups: White, Indian, Pakistani, Bangladeshi, Black Caribbean, Black African, Chinese, Arab, mixed origin and Other, but in some categories the numbers were so small that ethnic categories had to be combined. In the end the categories were recoded to just five ethnic groups: White, Black, Indian, Pakistani/Bangladeshi and Other. Having to recode ethnic categories in this way was not particularly satisfactory, when the whole point of the project was to investigate ethnic differences. However, this was a necessary procedure since even when the groups were combined there were still relatively few respondents in each of the ethnic categories.

### Types of questions asked

An additional concern when analysing secondary data is that the researcher does not have control over what questions are asked. Careful consideration therefore needs to be given to the adequacy of the questions for the purpose for which you intend to use the data. The questions which were asked on the subject of pensions on the GHS were as follows.

Does your present employer run a pension scheme or superannuation scheme for employees?
Yes
No
DK

Are you eligible to belong to your employer's pension scheme?
Yes
No
DK

Do you belong to your employer's pension scheme?
  Yes
  No
  DK


So do you think it's possible that you belong to a pension scheme run by your employer, or do you definitely not belong to one?


  Possibly belongs
  Definitely not


Intro: Some people arrange pensions for themselves, for which the contributions are income tax deductible. These schemes are called 'personal, private or portable pensions'.


Do you at present have any such arrangements?
  Yes
  No
  DK


Do you contribute to the scheme?
  Yes
  No


DNA (not in employment)


Does your employer contribute to the scheme?
  Yes
  No


Have you ever had any such arrangements?
  Yes
  No
  DK


Obviously the questions on the survey were very basic and more questions would have been useful, but as they stood they were adequate within the scope of the research. The research was exploratory in nature. To my knowledge no research had previously been undertaken on this issue in Britain. If the topic had previously attracted a considerable amount of attention, the data would have been of little value as it would have been too basic to add anything significant to existing debates.

## PRELIMINARY ANALYSIS

As far as men are concerned, occupational pensions are held in the highest percentage in the White category in which 43 per cent of respondents held an occupational pension, compared with 40 per cent in the Indian category and 41 per cent in the Black and 32 per cent in the Other category. By far the lowest levels of occupational pension scheme membership were in the Pakistani/Bangladeshi group where only 21 per cent had a pension. A similar distribution to that of occupational pensions is observable in relation to personal pensions. The highest levels were found in the White category at 27 per cent, the Black and Indian categories at 18 and 26 per cent respectively, with 25 per cent in the Other category. By far the lowest level of personal pension scheme membership was again in the Pakistani/ Bangladeshi group where only 9 per cent of respondents had a personal pension. Few respondents had both an occupational and personal pension. As far as women and pension scheme membership was concerned there were also considerable ethnic differences.

The highest levels of occupational pension membership were in the Black category at 40 per cent which was virtually the same proportion as the male figure. The percentages for the White, Indian and Other category varied between 29 and 33 per cent. Personal pensions were held in the highest proportion in the Indian and White groups at 19 and 15 per cent respectively. There were no female Pakistani/Bangladeshi women in the sample, which reflects the absence of these women from the labour market because of cultural and religious factors. As with the men in the sample, few women had both an occupational and personal pension but a higher proportion of women than men were without an occupational or personal pension (see Table 24.2).

A logistic regression procedure was undertaken to explore the relative effects of ethnicity compared to other personal factors (age, gender, colour, education, marital status, socio-economic group) and employment-related features (industrial sector, number of employees in workplace, whether respondent worked full or part time, income). The regression analysis indicated that six factors were significant in predicting personal pension scheme membership. In order of significance they were: economic status (whether part time, full time or self-employed); industrial classification; number of employees in the organization; socio-economic group; net weekly earnings; and ethnic origin. Nine factors were significant in predicting occupational pension scheme membership. In order of importance they were: number of employees in the establishment; economic status (whether employees worked full time or part time); industry; age; socio-economic group; net weekly earnings; sex; educational qualifications; and colour of respondent. Ethnicity was not significant in predicting occupational pension scheme membership, nor was country of birth. It was very interesting that being non-white as opposed to white was a significant factor, whereas for personal pensions ethnicity rather than colour was significant.

**TABLE 24.2**   Occupational and personal pension scheme membership by ethnicity and gender* +

|  | White | | Black | | Indian | | Pakistani/ Bangladeshi | | Other | |
|---|---|---|---|---|---|---|---|---|---|---|
| **Men** | | | | | | | | | | |
| Occupational | 2,274 | (43) | 20 | (41) | 34 | (40) | 7 | (21) | 23 | (32) |
| Personal | 1,443 | (27) | 9 | (18) | 22 | (26) | 3 | (9) | 18 | (25) |
| Both | 305 | (6) | 1 | (2) | 1 | (1) | 0 | | 2 | (3) |
| Neither | 1,261 | (24) | 19 | (39) | 28 | (33) | 23 | (70) | 28 | (40) |
| Total | 5,283 | (100) | 49 | (100) | 85 | (100) | 33 | (100) | 71 | (100) |
| | | | | | | | | | | |
| **Women** | | | | | | | | | | |
| Occupational | 1,634 | (33) | 28 | (40) | 21 | (29) | 0 | | 18 | (32) |
| Personal | 851 | (15) | 10 | (10) | 14 | (19) | 0 | | 7 | (11) |
| Both | 157 | (3) | 4 | (7) | 2 | (3) | 0 | | 1 | (2) |
| Neither | 2,211 | (49) | 26 | (43) | 32 | (49) | 0 | | 29 | (55) |
| Total | 4,539 | (100) | 60 | (100) | 65 | (100) | 0 | | 53 | (100) |

\*   Figures relate to working population between the ages of 18 and 65.
+   Percentages in brackets.

*Source:* GHS, 1992–3, author's analysis.

## Supplementary research

The GHS demonstrates different patterns in pension purchase within certain ethnic groups and that ethnicity in the case of personal pensions and colour in relation to occupational pensions are statistically significant in predicting pension purchase decisions. In this research project the secondary analysis of a large dataset was useful but the method alone was not a sufficient basis for a whole research project. The reasons for this were threefold. The first problem was that there were not enough questions to gain a comprehensive insight into pension purchase decisions. For example, the survey did not question respondents about their attitudes to and reasons for purchasing a pension, but merely asked whether they had one and what type it was (occupational or personal pension). A second difficulty was the small sample sizes in some of the ethnic groups. This feature meant that ethnic categories had to be combined, which is not particularly useful when ethnicity is the most important variable being measured. The third problem was that in some of the ethnic groups numbers were very small which caused difficulties in making generalizations or inference to wider populations beyond the sample studied. This said, it should also be added that without the dataset researchers would still know next to nothing about ethnicity and pension scheme membership. The secondary analysis of the data was a starting point upon which other research can build.

In order to obtain a more comprehensive view of the situation of ethnic minorities with regard to pension scheme membership, two additional telephone surveys were undertaken. The first was a telephone survey of trade unions in order to see if they were aware of any ethnic differences in pension scheme membership and to evaluate any policies they had in place to combat inequality in this area (see Burton, 1997). The second telephone survey focused on financial institutions with the specific aim of evaluating how they marketed pensions to different ethnic groups (see Burton, 1996). The findings from both the telephone surveys supported the General Household Survey data to the extent that the issue of ethnic minorities and pensions had been marginalized.

## CONCLUSION

It is undoubtedly the case that secondary data analysis is a research technique which is destined to become more influential in the future. The setting up of archives, the increasing number of statistical surveys being undertaken at national and international levels, software development facilitating more sophisticated analyses, and a growing awareness of analysis techniques have resulted in the techniques becoming a focus of discussion. Secondary analysis could be an appropriate way for research students to access relevant data which is cheap to obtain, free of access difficulties and does not require the collection or processing of data. Secondary data can be used alone or in conjunction with primary research. A further advantage of secondary data analysis is that it could prove a useful method for academics at the beginning of their research careers who are frequently without extensive funding to continue researching and publishing.

# PART VII

# QUANTITATIVE DATA ANALYSIS

Data analysis can be an all-absorbing pastime. I have been involved with quantitative methods in social science research for the last eight years and sometimes I feel that I have only scratched the surface, but I am not trying to put you off. In his cookbook Marco Pierre White, the famous London chef, says that if you want to cook well your money would be better spent on something other than a cookbook, but on the other hand if you wanted some inspiration then his book was a good buy. Like cooking, you cannot learn quantitative data analysis straight out of a book. It takes time to gain the necessary knowledge and experience.

Some people are introduced to quantitative data analysis early on in their undergraduate programmes. Other students are exposed to quantitative data analysis techniques as postgraduates. The coming chapters are not and cannot be a comprehensive account of quantitative data analysis techniques. This is because there is a vast array of methods and a raft of different computer software packages available to undertake analysis. The only way to learn quantitative data analysis and to become competent with a statistical software package is to attend a taught course and to back it up with background reading and practice. Like Marco's book, the following chapters will not teach the readers as much as they might probably like to learn, but I hope that they will give you a little bit of inspiration.

Over the past five years I have spent much of my time teaching research methods to undergraduates and postgraduates. In Chapters 25, 26 and 27 I have concentrated on the topics which appear, to me at least, to be the most prominent within social science research. I have tried to introduce them in a way which will be understandable and I have drawn heavily on my teaching experience and the feedback which students have offered.

The concepts and the issues are presented alongside instructions on how to use the computer software package SPSS. There are many other packages now on the market but within the social sciences this is one of the most popular and widely available statistical analysis packages. You can find out more about SPSS on their web site {http://www.spss.com}

Chapter 25 looks at **descriptive statistics** and Chapter 26 at **inferential statistics**. The final chapter assumes that the readers have got to grips with these concepts and will now want to begin their own analysis. Chapter 27 introduces the issues around data coding and data entry using SPSS.

# 25 DESCRIPTIVE STATISTICS

*Vernon Gayle*

## STATISTICS

After the initial panic and terror which many social scientists experience when they hear the word *statistics*, one of three definitions is conjured up. The original meaning of the word is 'State-istics', facts and figures which are collected by and for the state. In modern times statistics have become a branch of 'applied mathematics', and most British universities offer statistics degrees. The third definition is a 'statistical test'. In terms of data analysis, as social scientists, we are interested in applying statistical tests to social science data.

In social science data analysis there are two types of statistics in which we are interested. The first category are known as *descriptive statistics* and the second category are known as *inferential statistics*. As the name suggests, descriptive statistics describe something such as a characteristic of the sample. In a general sense we are used to descriptive statistics, such as a percentage of people who display a certain behaviour, or the average income of a particular social group, and so on. Inferential statistics, as the name suggests, allow us to infer or make some inference about an aspect of the social world. Most social research projects use a mixture of descriptive and inferential statistics.

Statistics that are concerned with only one variable at a time, for example, age or gender are known as *univariate statistics*. Statistics that are concerned with two variables, for example, the relationship between gender and levels of education are known as *bivariate statistics*. Statistics which are concerned with more than two variables, for example, the relationship between gender and ethnicity and levels of education are known as *multivariate statistics*.

A variable that explains an outcome is known as an *explanatory* or *independent variable*. It is typically denoted by the symbol X. A variable which measures an outcome is known as a *dependent variable* and is typically denoted by the symbol Y.

| Y variable | X variable |
|---|---|
| A Level result ⟵ | Social class |

## THE DATA

In the next two chapters the examples and the analysis is undertaken from data extracted from the Youth Cohort Study of England and Wales (YCS). This is a major programme of longitudinal research designed to monitor the behaviour and decisions of representative samples of young people aged 16 to 19 as they reach minimum school leaving age and either stay on in education or enter the labour market. The survey collects information on the young people's experiences of education, training and work as well as information on their aspirations, their family and their personal circumstances. Cohort members are contacted by post three times. The three sweeps of data collection are undertaken at yearly intervals, when the young people are 16–17 (sweep 1), 17–18 (sweep 2) and 18–19 (sweep 3).

## THE DATA FILES

The data files can be downloaded from the web http://www.stir.ac.uk/appsocsci/vernon/datafiles2.htm. (There are a full set of instructions on this web page.)

| ycs.sav variables | ycs2.sav variables |
|---|---|
| IDENT – Case Number | IDENT – Case Number |
| GRADES exam grades (end of 5th form) | GENDER gender |
| FAMCLASS highest RG social class (mother or father) | GRADES exam grades (end of 5th form) |
| GENDER gender | PAY1 FT job Weekly take home pay age 17–18 (measured in £) |
| PDEG Either parent has a degree | PAY2 FT job Weekly take home pay age 18–19 (measured in £) |
| OWNRENT parents own their own home | |
| PRIVSCHO Attended an Independent school | |
| SIBLINGS (Number of siblings) | |
| DEGREE studying for a degree in sweep | |
| ED16_17 Education 16–17 | |
| ED17_18 Education 17–18 | |
| ED18_19 Education 18–19 | |

**GETTING STARTED IN SPSS**

These instructions assume that you know a little about computers and operating in a Windows environment. To open a file in SPSS see Figure 25.1.

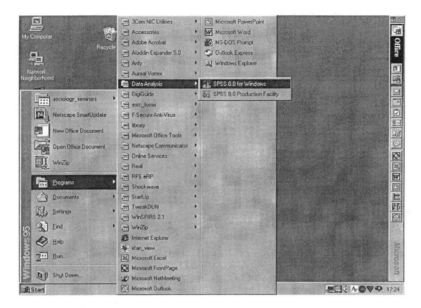

**FIGURE 25.1    Starting SPSS**

Most people have their own profiles set up in Windows 95 so their screens all look different. To open a data file go to the **Start** buttom at the bottom left of your screen. Choose SPSS from the relevant menu for your set-up (this is sometimes in **Data Analysis**).

Choose **Open an exiting file**.

Select the required file by moving the pointer onto a file (e.g. ycs.sav) and click on it. Then click on **Open**.

The frontmost window in which a grid is displayed is the 'Data Editor' window (Figure 25.4). This is where data are entered or changed, and it is the window you will be using most during the rest of this exercise. Each column of the grid represents a variable (typically a question) and each row, a case (often a respondent). The second window, entitled 'Output1', is used by SPSS for displaying the results of statistical analyses (see, for example, Figure 25.10). The large window in the background is called the 'Application' window (or sometimes the 'Main' window) and its main use is 'to hold everything together'. To toggle (switch) between windows go to **Window** and click on the window you require.

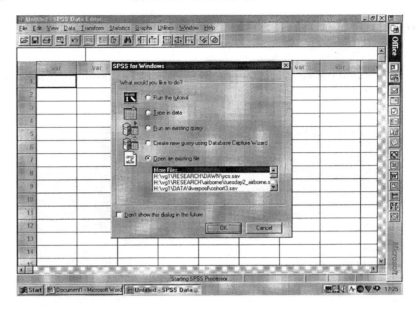

**FIGURE 25.2   Opening an existing file**

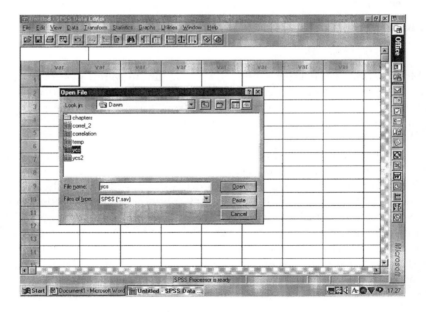

**FIGURE 25.3   Choosing a file**

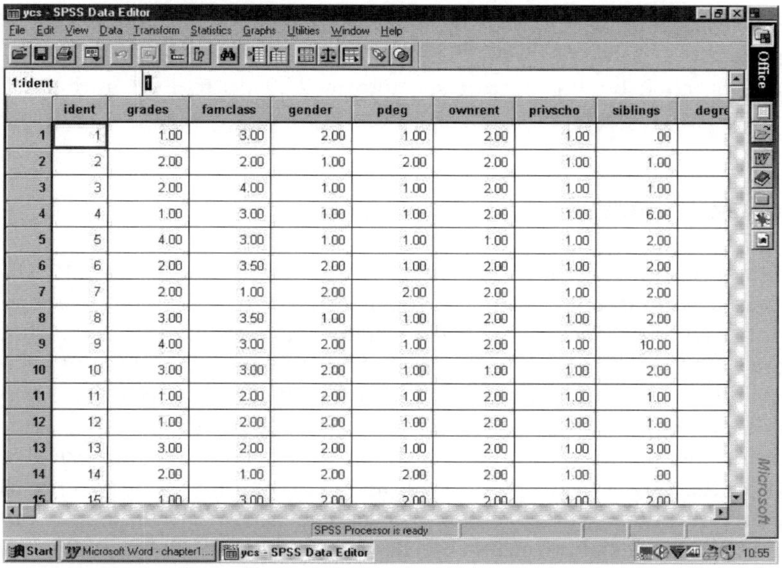

FIGURE 25.4   The youth cohort study data in the data editor window

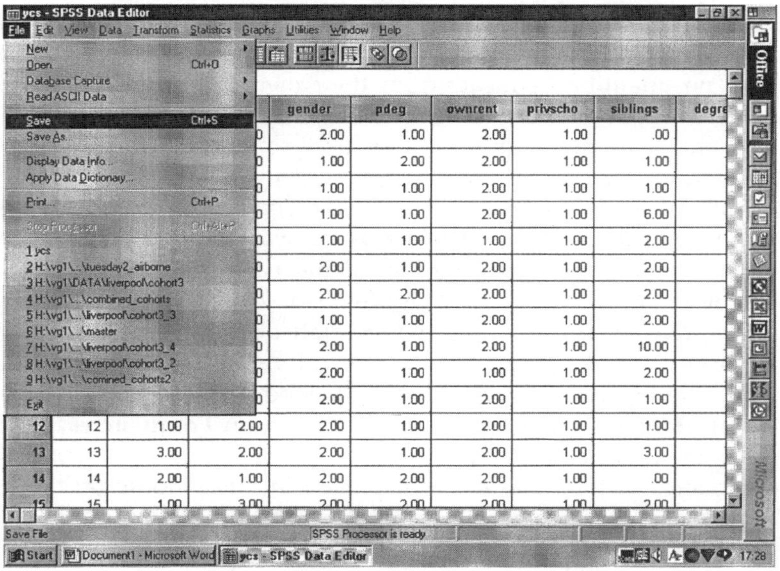

FIGURE 25.5   Saving a data file

To save a file go to **File** and then to **Save** and save in the normal Windows 95 fashion.

When undertaking analysis it is a good practice to have your word processor or a notepad open. To cut and paste output from SPSS into documents, click on the output see Figure 25.9 go to Edit and the Copy objects and then paste as usual in your word processor.

## DESCRIBING A SINGLE CATEGORICAL VARIABLE

The analysis and the comprehension of categorical data, especially data in tables, is a fundamental skill for social science researchers. Many of the questions which appear on social science surveys collect data that are *categorical* and can be measured on a *nominal scale*. In nominal scales numbers (called codes) are used to identify an attribute, or category. Numbers provide convenient labels in much the same way as postcodes label areas. But like postcodes the numbers used on nominal scales have no numerical significance in their own right. We would never dream of adding two postcodes together! Nominal or categorical scales, are easy to understand. For example, after having undertaken a survey, if you wanted to distinguish between responses from men and women, for the purposes of analysis, you might want to assign the males to a category labelled 1 and females to a category labelled 2. The use of numbers in this case does not mean that 1 is larger than 2. Nor does it imply that 2 is twice as large as 1. Numbers are merely a convenient way to organize the data. The main issue to grasp is that in nominal scales the numbers used are arbitrary. They are convenient labels and have no quantitative meaning in their own right. Numbers used in nominal scales are not 'measurement' in the strictest sense of the word. The only mathematical operation that can be performed on them is to count the number of times they occur (the frequency). The simplest way to describe a categorical variable is to report the frequencies, or raw scores, which fall into each category of the variable. A more useful way to describe a categorical variable is to report the percentages that fall into each category of the variable.

Open the data file ycs.sav (see Figure 25.4).

The **Frequencies** procedure provides statistics and graphical displays that are useful for describing many types of variables. For a first look at your data, the Frequencies procedure is a good place to start.

Click on **Statistics**, then on **Summarize**, then on **Frequencies**. You will now be in Frequencies dialogue box.

The variables in the dataset are displayed in the window on the left of the **Frequencies** dialogue box. It is possible to scroll up and down the list.

Click on *highest RG Social Class (mother or father)* and 🔹 to move this over to the **Variable(s)**: box.

Click **OK**. This will produce the frequencies for the *highest RG Social Class (mother or father)* variable in the Output1 window (see Figure 25.8).

The first column of the table records the categories of the variable (*highest RG Social Class (mother or father)*). These are the familiar categories of the Registrar General's Social Class Scale.

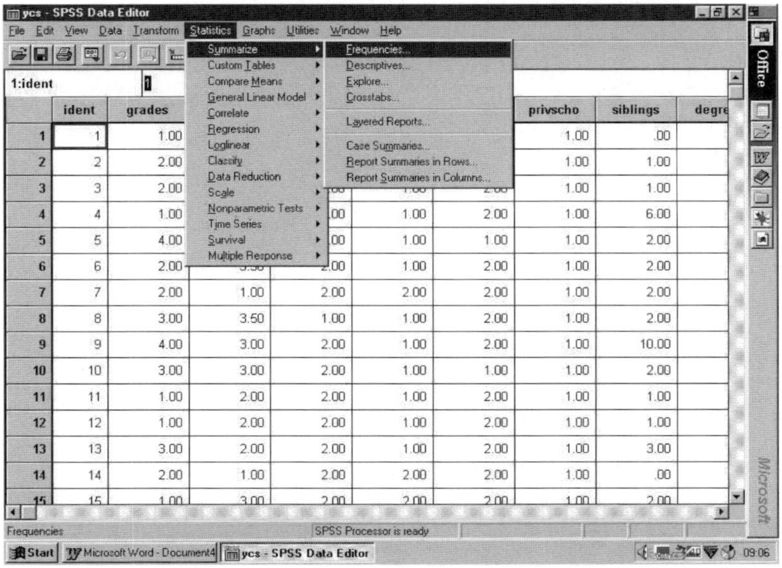

FIGURE 25.6 Selecting the frequencies command

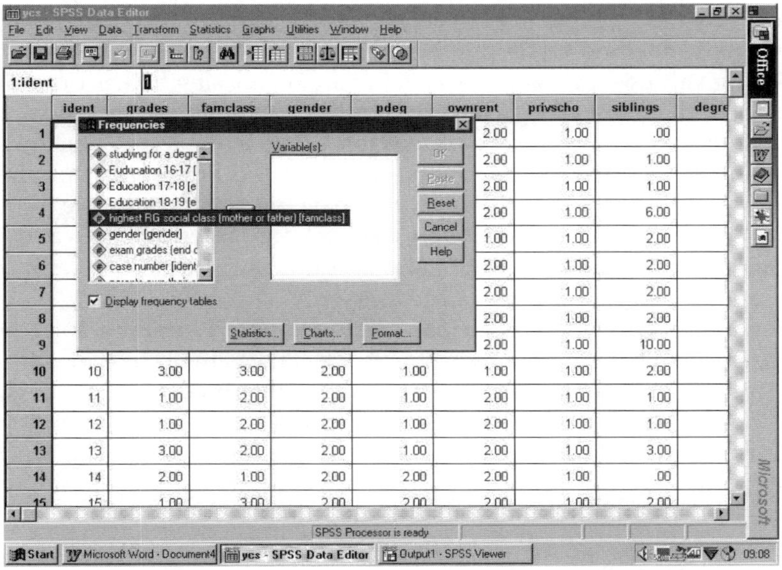

FIGURE 25.7 Selecting variables in the frequencies dialogue box

**Frequency** – This next column of the table reports the frequencies, or number of young people, in each social class category (e.g. 722 young people have a parent in the professional social class).

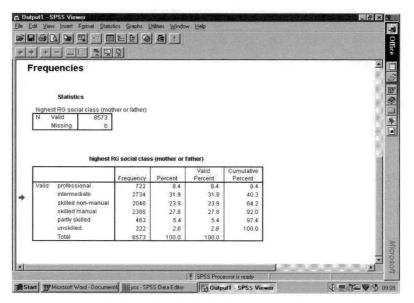

**FIGURE 25.8    Frequency output in the SPSS viewer**

**Percent** – The next column of the table reports the percentage, or proportion, of young people in each social class category. Using percentages is a very useful method of describing a categorical variable.

**Missing values** – In this example there are no missing values but in some sets of data there are cases which do not have a value for a given variable. SPSS will construct a row to represent this category which is labelled as

**Missing** in the first column of the table. In the **Frequency** column the proportion, or percentage, of cases which have a missing value are reported.

**Valid Percent** – For some analyses we are only interested in valid cases (i.e. those cases without missing values). The **Valid Percent** column of the table reports percentages for valid cases only.

**Cumulative Percent** – The final column keeps a running total of the percentages. This is sometimes useful as we can easily deduce that 40.3 per cent of the young people have parents in the intermediate or professional social classes (i.e. 8.4 per cent + 31.9 per cent).

From the Frequencies Dialogue Box it is also possible to construct bar charts, pie charts and histograms by clicking on the Charts Command.

## DESCRIBING CATEGORICAL VARIABLES

### Data in tables

The simplest way to represent the relationship between two categorical variables is to produce a table of frequencies. In the sections below we will be using SPSS to construct a series of tables using the data from the Youth Cohort Study. The example which we will be looking at is an exploration of the relationship between gender and participation in post-compulsory education (age 16–17).

The outcome in which we are interested is whether or not a young person has remained in education aged 16–17. This is the Y variable. We are attempting to see if a young person's gender explains this outcome. Gender is our explanatory or X variable.

To begin the construction of tables and the analysis of the data you must read in the data from ycs.sav

Click on **Statistics**, then on **Summarize**, then on **Crosstabs**. You will now be in the **Crosstabs** dialogue box. (Figure 25.9).

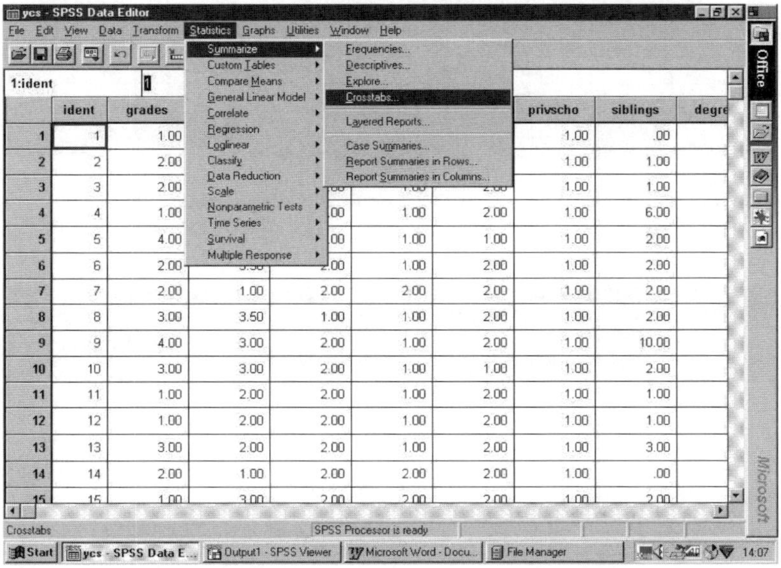

**FIGURE 25.9  Selecting the crosstabs command**

Click on *Gender* and [▸] to move this into the **Columns**: box. Click on **OK**. This will produce a crosstabulation of **Education 16–17** by **Gender** (Figure 25.10).

The simplest table is a two-by-two table (2 × 2). The raw scores, or frequencies, are hard to interpret especially when the cell frequencies are large. Calculating percentages is often more useful as they can be interpreted more easily.

We will now construct a table with column percentages. Click on **Window**, then click on **1 ycs – SPSS Data Editor**. This will bring you back to the **Data Editor window**. Click on **Statistics**, then on **Summarize**, then on **Crosstabs** (Figure 25.11).

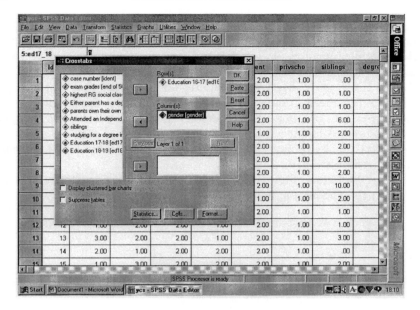

**FIGURE 25.10   Selecting variables in the crosstabs dialogue box**

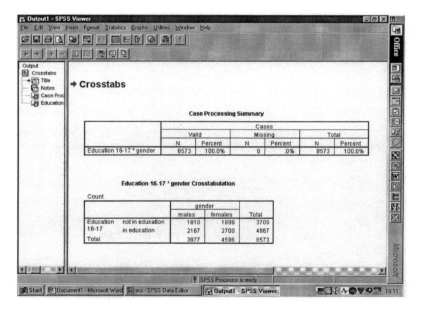

**FIGURE 25.11   Crosstabulation of education, 16–17 by gender**

It is sometimes difficult to interpret tables with large frequencies in each cell. In these circumstances it is better to use percentages.

To produce a table with percentages click on **Cells** at the bottom of the **Crosstabs** dialogue box. We are now in the **Crosstabs: Cell Display** dialogue box. Click on **Observed** to deselect. Here we select the percentage required from the **Percentages** dialogue box at bottom left-hand corner. Click on box beside **Column**. Click on **Continue** and then **OK** when you return to the **Crosstabs** dialogue box to run the procedure (Figure 25.10).

We have constructed the table to show column percentages. Conventionally, tables were constructed with the independent or explanatory variable (X) on the horizontal margin and the dependent variable or outcome (Y) on the vertical margin. Using this convention and calculating column percentages allows us to interpret the relationship between X and Y easily (Figure 25.12).

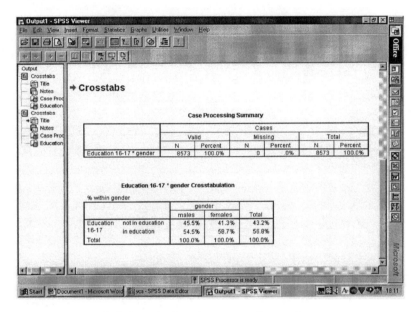

**FIGURE 25.12  Crosstabulation of education, 16–17 by gender row percentages**

The table can now be interpreted more easily than when raw frequencies are used

- 45.5 per cent of the young males in the survey were not in education when surveyed at age 16–17.
- 54.5 per cent of the young males in the survey were in education when surveyed at age 16–17.
- 41.3 per cent of the young women in the survey were not in education when surveyed at age 16–17.
- 58.7 per cent of the young women in the survey were in education when surveyed at age 16–17.

Using this table we can begin to examine the relationship between gender and education in another way (Figure 25.13).

- 48.8 per cent of the young people in the survey who were not in education when surveyed at age 16–17 were male.
- 51.2 per cent of the young people in the survey who were not in education when surveyed at age 16–17 were female.
- 44.5 per cent of the young people in the survey who were in education when surveyed at age 16–17 were male.
- 55.5 per cent of the young people in the survey who were in education when surveyed at age 16–17 were female.

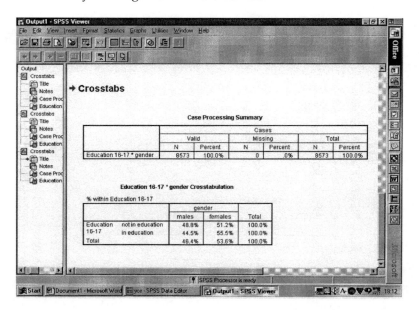

**FIGURE 25.13 Crosstabulation of education, 16–17 by gender row percentages**

To get the big picture we have calculated total percentages. This is the proportion of cases that fall into a particular cell. This is sometimes useful when we wish to report the characteristics of a sample (Figure 25.14).

- 21.1 per cent of the young people in the survey were male and not in education at age 16–17.
- 25.3 per cent of the young people in the survey were male and in education at age 16–17.
- 22.1 per cent of the young people in the survey were female and not in education at age 16–17.
- 31.5 per cent of the young people in the survey were female and in education at age 16–17.

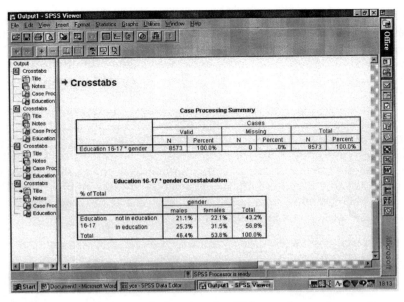

**FIGURE 25.14   Crosstabulation of education, 16–17 by gender total percentages**

In this section we have constructed basic tables in SPSS and presented the information in a variety of ways. The appropriate presentation of the data is very much dependent on what you wish to communicate to the reader. The data used in tables should be clearly labelled and word processed when presented in research reports and publications.

## DESCRIBING CONTINUOUS VARIABLES

There are two kinds of measurement scales with which social scientists have to work. We have already come across categorical data and are about to meet up with continuous data.

Continuous scales are generally ordered, so that it is possible to speak of 'more' or 'less' of what it is that is being measured according to the value on the scale.

If there is no true zero (for example, temperature where we have Celsius and Fahrenheit scales with arbitrary zero points), then we have an *interval* scale at best. Put simply, when a thermometer using either of these scales reads zero we can't say that there is no temperature in the room.

If there is a true zero point on a scale then that gives a *ratio* scale. It is possible to speak meaningfully of a data point of (say) 20 being twice as high as another data point with a value of 10.

Many continuous measurement scales in social science are interval scales rather than ratio scales. The difference is captured succinctly by asking the question: 'Are the data still meaningful if a fixed value (say *50*) were added to each score?' For much data on attitudes or preferences, scales are arbitrary and such an adjustment would not matter. By contrast data measured in pounds and pence are changed fundamentally by adding or subtracting a constant. Quantities measured in money terms are usually on ratio scales.

Open the file ycs2.sav using the usual procedure. This is another extract of the Youth Cohort Study of England and Wales. There are about 2,500 cases in this set of data . The first variable is an identification variable. The second is the young person's gender. The next measures the exam grades which the young person obtained in their final compulsory year of school. The next two variables are related to the young person's full-time employment. Pay1 measures their weekly take-home pay age 17–18. Pay2 measures their weekly take-home pay age 18–19 (Figure 25.15).

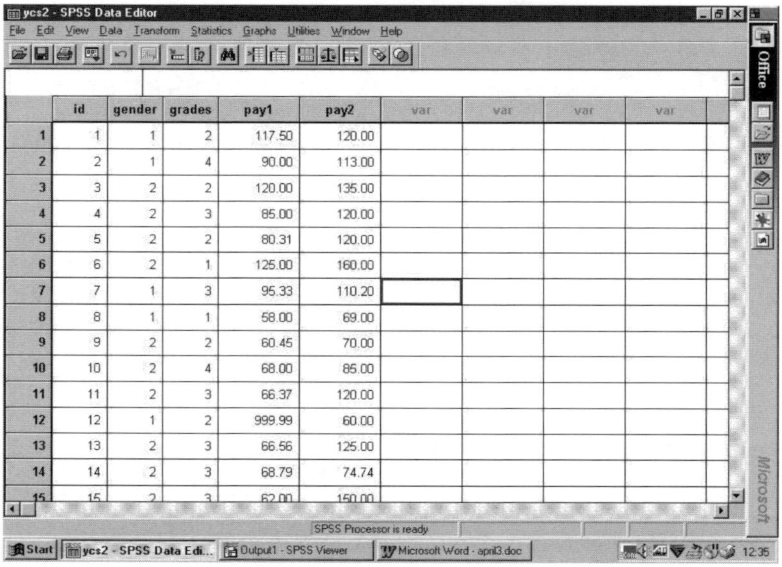


| | id | gender | grades | pay1 | pay2 | var | var | var | var |
|---|---|---|---|---|---|---|---|---|---|
| 1 | 1 | 1 | 2 | 117.50 | 120.00 | | | | |
| 2 | 2 | 1 | 4 | 90.00 | 113.00 | | | | |
| 3 | 3 | 2 | 2 | 120.00 | 135.00 | | | | |
| 4 | 4 | 2 | 3 | 85.00 | 120.00 | | | | |
| 5 | 5 | 2 | 2 | 80.31 | 120.00 | | | | |
| 6 | 6 | 2 | 1 | 125.00 | 160.00 | | | | |
| 7 | 7 | 1 | 3 | 95.33 | 110.20 | | | | |
| 8 | 8 | 1 | 1 | 58.00 | 69.00 | | | | |
| 9 | 9 | 2 | 2 | 60.45 | 70.00 | | | | |
| 10 | 10 | 2 | 4 | 68.00 | 85.00 | | | | |
| 11 | 11 | 2 | 3 | 66.37 | 120.00 | | | | |
| 12 | 12 | 1 | 2 | 999.99 | 60.00 | | | | |
| 13 | 13 | 2 | 3 | 66.56 | 125.00 | | | | |
| 14 | 14 | 2 | 3 | 68.79 | 74.74 | | | | |
| 15 | 15 | 2 | 3 | 62.00 | 150.00 | | | | |

**FIGURE 25.15 Youth cohort study data file 2**

Click on Statistics, then click on **Summarize**, then on **Frequencies** to display the dialogue box (Figure 25.16).

The variables are listed in the box on the left. Click on the **FT job: Weekly take home pay age 17–18 [pay1]** variable and then click on the ▶ to select. Make sure that you click on the **Display Frequency Tables** box on the left to deselect this option. If you don't you will get a listing of all the values of the **FT job: Weekly take home pay age 17–18 [pay1]** variable. In small studies this might be useful, but in large studies like the YCS, the frequency table is not useful. Click on **Statistics** at the bottom of the **Frequencies** dialogue box (Figure 25.17).

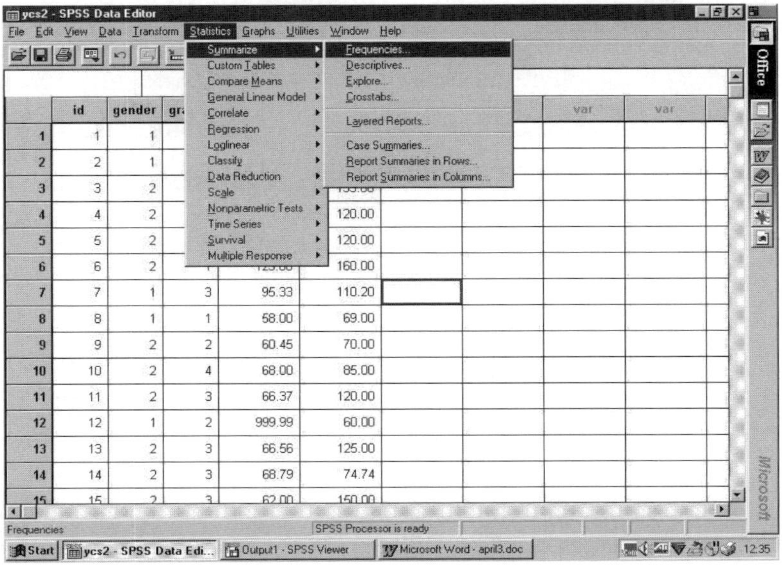

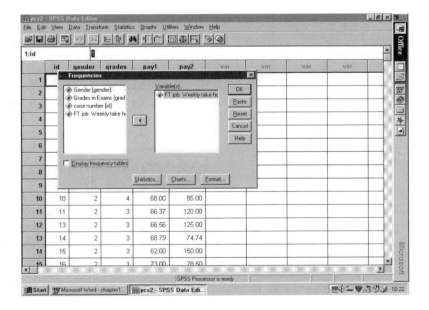

**FIGURE 25.16 Selecting the frequency command for continuous variable**

**FIGURE 25.17 Selecting a continuous variable in the frequencies dialogue box**

Click on the **Ra̲nge**, **M̲inimum** and **Ma̲ximum** check boxes within the **Dispersion** dialogue box. Click on **Continue** and then on **OK** to run the procedure (Figure 25.18).

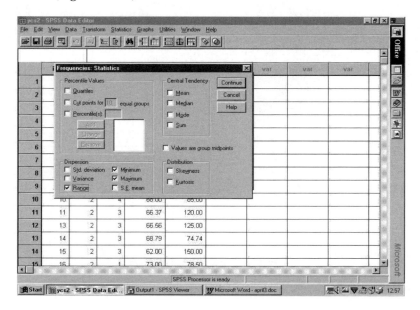

**FIGURE 25.18    Selecting measures for a continuous variable**

**Range** is the distance between the **Maximum** and the **Minimum** scores. From the simple measures of dispersion which we have calculated we can see that the lowest weekly income, when they were aged 17–18, for these young people was £30 per week. The highest weekly income was £300 per week. The distribution of incomes was from £30 per week to £300 per week, a range of £270 per week (Figure 25.19).

When we seek to summarize a large set of data, the obvious starting point is with an index which places or locates the data as a whole: in general high, middling or low on a scale. Most people will take such a summary measure as somehow 'typical' of the sample, although that may be misleading.

Click on **S̲tatistics**, then click on **S̲ummarize**, then on **F̲requencies** to display the dialogue box. Click on **S̲tatistics** at the bottom of the **Frequencies** dialogue box. Click on the **M̲ean**, **M̲edian** and **M̲ode** check boxes within the **Central Tendency** dialogue box. Click on **Continue** and then on **OK** to run the procedure (Figure 25.19).

**Mean** is the average value formed by adding all the scores and dividing by the number of scores. From our analysis we can see that the **Mean**, or average, weekly income for these young people when they were age 17–18 was £75.33.

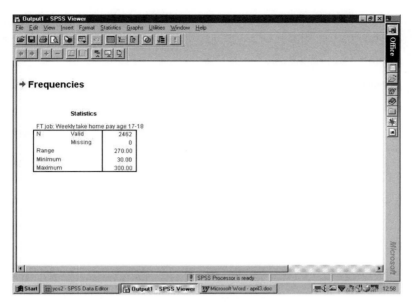

**FIGURE 25.19  Range of weekly take-home pay for respondents aged 17–18**

**Median** is the score that divides a set of scores in half. If scores are placed in rank order, 50 per cent of scores lay below or at the median. The median is sometimes referred to as the fiftieth percentile. The **Median** level of income was £70.00 per week. The median is the score that divides a set of scores in half. If the income of each of the 2,462 young people were ranked (i.e. placed in order), half of the incomes would lie below the median and the other half above. The median is a good summary measure as it is less sensitive to shape of the distribution (an issue which we will return to below).

**Mode** is the most common observation among a set of scores. The **Mode** or most common level of weekly income is £70.00 per week. The mode is the only suitable measure of central tendency for categorical data. When calculated for a categorical variable the mode denotes the most popular category (Figure 5.20).

Click on the **Statistics**, then click on **Summarize**, then on **Frequencies**. Click on **Statistics** at the bottom of the **Frequencies** dialogue box. Click on **St̲d. Deviation** and **V̲ariance** in the **Dispersion** dialogue box. Click on **Ske̲wness** and **K̲urtosis** in the **Distribution** box. Click on **Continue** then **OK**.

Most samples of data will contain some variability around a central value, some people scoring higher than others. How much spread there is around a measure of location is a valuable way of capturing something of a data set as a whole (Figure 25.21).

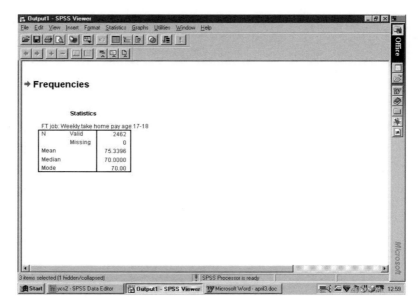

**FIGURE 25.20    Measures of central tendency weekly take-home pay for respondents aged 17–18**

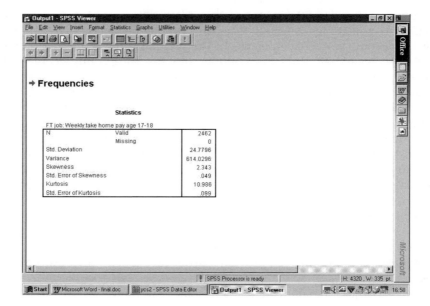

**FIGURE 25.21    Summary measures of the distribution of weekly take-home pay for respondents aged 17–18**

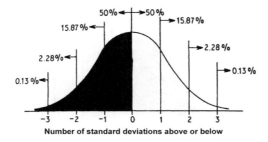

**FIGURE 25.22** **The normal distribution**

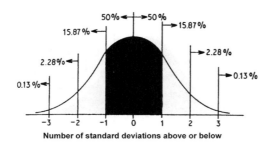

**FIGURE 25.23** **The normal distribution scores within 1 standard deviation**

## Standard deviation/variance

The standard deviation measures average spread around the mean. It is the most typical distance (or deviation) of scores from the mean. It is formed by working out the average squared deviation around the mean (this is called the *variance*) and then taking its square root. The *standard deviation* helps us to assess how reliable the *mean* is as a *measure of central tendency*. A large standard deviation indicates a lot of spread in our distribution and therefore the mean is a less reliable indicator of a typical value in our distribution. When a mean is reported it is good practice to also report the standard deviation.

Here is a little more statistical theory which will enhance our understanding of the standard deviation.

In the *standard normal distribution*, the bell curve, 50 per cent of the scores lay above the mean and the other 50 per cent below the mean (Figure 25.22). The shaded area in the bell curve represents half of the distribution.

Of the scores 15.87 per cent are more extreme than 1 standard deviation to the left of the mean and 15.87 per cent of scores are more extreme than 1 standard deviation to the right of the mean (Figure 25.23).

Of the scores 2.28 per cent are more extreme than 2 standard deviations to the left of the mean and 2.28 per cent of scores are more extreme than 2 standard deviations to the right of the mean (Figure 25.24).

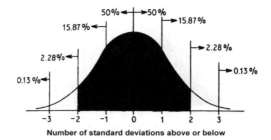

**FIGURE 25.24　The normal distribution scores within 2 standard deviations**

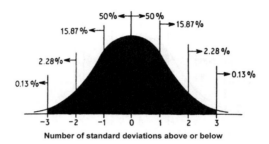

**FIGURE 25.25　The normal distribution scores within 3 standard deviations**

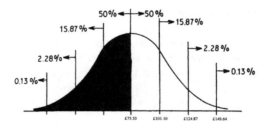

**FIGURE 25.26　The normal distribution and weekly take-home pay for respondents aged 17–18**

Of the scores 0.13 per cent are more extreme than 3 standard deviations to the left of the mean and 0.13 per cent of scores are more extreme than 3 standard deviations to the right of the mean (Figure 25.25).

Returning to the **FT job: Weekly take home pay age 17–18** variable, the *mean* was £75.33 and the standard deviation £24.77. Using a little statistical theory we can now make some assessment about the distribution of weekly take-home pay for the young people in this extract of the YCS (Figure 25.26).

Any young person that takes home more than £124.87 per week can be regarded as having a high level of take-home pay. This is because their take-home pay is more than 2 standard deviations above the mean.

Statistical theory tells us that 95.44 per cent of scores fall within 2 standard deviations either side of the mean.

Any young person that takes home more than £149.64 per week can be regarded as having a very high level of take-home pay. This is because their take-home pay is more than 3 standard deviations above the mean. Statistical theory tells us that 99.74 per cent of scores fall within 3 standard deviations either side of the mean.

## Symmetry/skewness

The next important characteristic of the shape of a set of data is the extent to which scores are distributed evenly around a central value, i.e. whether the data are symmetrical. This feature is important because extreme values at either end of a distribution may indicate gross errors, for which reasons should be sought and correct values inserted if this is appropriate.

Data which are strongly *asymmetrical* are less reliably described in terms of summary measures of location. It is possible to examine the symmetry of the distribution by plotting the data. If a dataset is large it becomes quite difficult to assess the symmetry by eye. To overcome this problem there is a single summary measure of *skewness*. A positive value for the measure of skewness means that the distribution is skewed to the right. That is, there are some large observations which will be pulling up the value of the mean. Conversely, a negative value for the measure of skewness means that the distribution is skewed to the left. There will be some small observations which will be pulling down the value of the mean.

Returning to the **FT job: Weekly take home pay age 17–18** variable, the mean was £75.33 and the standard deviation was £24.77. The maximum weekly take-home pay for this distribution of young people was £300.00 per week. We know that this value is extremely large being more than 3 standard deviations above the mean. The minimum weekly take-home pay is £30 per week. This is less than 2 standard deviations below the mean. This suggests that the distribution of weekly take-home pay is positively skewed (i.e. skewed to the right). This is confirmed by the *skewness* statistic which has a positive value (2.343).

The ratio of the skewness to its standard error (*Std. Error of Skewness*) can be used as a test to see if the distribution is *normal*. This is known as a *test of normality*. If the ratio is less than −2 or greater than +2, then the assumption of the normality of the distribution can be rejected. This test is rarely used or reported in social research.

## Kurtosis

This is a characteristic of data which is often reported by statistical packages, but is almost never used to describe the shape of a set of scores.

It refers to the extent a distribution is broad and flat or peaked. A distribution which is very peaked will tend to have many values close to the mean.

Peaked distributions are called *leptokurtic* and the summary statistic will have a positive value. Flat distributions are called *platykurtic* and the summary statistic will have a negative value. A bell-shaped distribution is called a *mesokurtic* distribution and has the value zero.

The ratio of the kurtosis to its standard error (*Std. Error of Kurtosis*) can be used as a test to see if the distribution is *normal*. This is also know as a *test of normality*. If the ratio is less than $-2$ or greater than $+2$ then the assumption of the normality of the distribution can be rejected. This test is rarely used and is almost never reported in social research.

## CONCLUSION

In this chapter we have been introduced to categorical data and data measured on continuous scales. We have used SPSS to describe a single categorical variable and then constructed a series of tables which have described the relationship between two categorical variables. The analysis and comprehension of categorical data is a fundamental skill for social science researchers.

Less data in the social sciences are collected on continuous scales, but in order to have an all-round understanding of the data analysis an appreciation of describing continuous data is also important. In the final section we used SPSS to describe a single continuous variable. In the next chapter we will extend our understanding of both categorical and continuous data analysis by moving from descriptive statistical analysis to some basic inferential statistical techniques.

# 26 INFERENTIAL STATISTICS

## Vernon Gayle

In social science data analysis there are two types of statistics in which we are interested. The first category are known as *descriptive statistics* and we met some of these in the previous chapter. The second category are known as *inferential statistics*. As the name suggests, descriptive statistics describe something such as a characteristic of a sample. In a general sense we are used to descriptive statistics, such as a percentage of people who display a certain behaviour, or the average income of a particular social group, and so on. Inferential statistics allow us to make some statistical generalizations about an aspect of the social world. Most social research projects use a mixture of descriptive and inferential statistics. However, for pedagogical reasons we often consider inferential statistics as a step up from descriptive statistics.

## PROBABILITY

The concept of probability is integral to inferential statistics. At a simple level, a probability can be considered as the likelihood of an event happening. *Probabilities take on values between zero and one.* A probability of zero means that an event will not happen. Conversely, a probability of one means that an event will definitely happen. A probability of 0.5 means that there is an even chance of the event taking place or it is equally likely to occur or not.

Probability
| 1 | 0.5 | 0 |
| Event will | | Event will not |
| occur | Evens | occur |

Therefore if there is a 0.75 chance of rain today it is more likely that it will rain than remain dry. In recent years TV weather people have begun to talk in percentages. Therefore we often hear that there is a 75 per cent chance of rain, i.e. the probability of rain is 0.75.

## HYPOTHESES

Hypotheses are a core concept within statistical methodology. An hypothesis is a *'proposition that is advanced for testing or appraising a generalization regarding the real social world'*. In a general form:

- The *null hypothesis (H₀)* states that there is no structured or systematic difference between two groups in our experiment.
- The *alternate hypothesis (H₁)* states that there is a structured or systematic difference between two groups in our experiment.

Consider a researcher who is interested in whether gender has an influence on young people remaining in education aged 16–17. The researcher would have available a set of data. Obviously this would include the subject's gender (male or female) and whether or not the young person was in education when they were age 16–17. In this example the *null hypothesis (H₀)* is that there is no structured or systematic difference between young men and young women in terms of their educational situation at age 16–17. In this example the *alternate hypothesis (H₁)* is that there is a structured or systematic difference between young men and young women in terms of their educational situation at age 16–17.

Within the hypothesis testing paradigm our goal is to assess the probability of the null hypothesis being correct. The diagram below is helpful in making the decision whether or not to reject the null hypothesis.

| Cannot reject $H_0$ | | Can reject $H_0$ |
|---|---|---|
| $P = 1$ | $P = .05$ | $P = 0$ |

Statistical tests help us to decide which hypothesis is true. Conventionally, when the likelihood of a null hypothesis being correct is less than 5 in 100 (i.e. $p < .05$ or 5 per cent) we can reject it.

If the probability of the null hypothesis being correct is greater than 5 in 100 (i.e. $p > .05$ or 5 per cent) then we cannot reject the null hypothesis.

Returning to our example above, education at age 16–17, if we calculated a statistical test from our data and it revealed that the probability of the null hypothesis being correct was $p=.03$ then we could reject the null hypothesis at the $p=.05$ level.

### Analysing categorical data

Let us return to the issue of examining the relationship between gender and whether or not a young person remains in education at age 16–17. In the last chapter we crosstabulated the *Gender* variable and the *Education 16–17 [ed 16_17]* variable using data from the ycs.sav data file (see Figure 25.11).

This crosstabulation produced the simplest table, a two by two table (2 × 2). The raw scores, or frequencies, are hard to interpret especially when the cell frequencies are large so calculating percentages is often more useful.

We have constructed the table to show column percentages (see Figure 25.12). Conventionally, tables were constructed with the independent or explanatory variable (X) on the horizontal margin and the dependent variable or outcome (Y) on the vertical margin. Using this convention and calculating column percentages allows us to interpret the relationship between X and Y easily (see Figure 25.11).

At the risk of being repetitive:

- 45.5 per cent of the young males in the survey were not in education when surveyed at age 16–17.
- 54.5 per cent of the young males in the survey were in education when surveyed at age 16–17.
- 41.3 per cent of the young women in the survey were not in education when surveyed at age 16–17.
- 58.7 per cent of the young women in the survey were in education when surveyed at age 16–17.

But what does this tell us about the relationship between gender and young people staying in education? We can see that a greater proportion of young females remain in education aged 16–17 than young males (see Figure 25.12).

- 54.5 per cent of the young males in the survey were in education when surveyed at age 16–17.
- 58.7 per cent of the young women in the survey were in education when surveyed at age 16–17.

This represents a difference of 4.2%. In statistics we refer to this as an *observed difference*.

However, in our sample there are different numbers of young men and women. There are also different numbers of young people in education and out of the educational system. This presents a problem. How do we know that the observed difference between young men and young women, with regard to staying in education aged 16–17 is real and not just a product of chance fluctuations due to the sample we have drawn. Well what is required is a statistical methodology to separate *structured* or *systematic* features in the data from *random* features in the data.

Consider for a moment that a researcher had collected data on the subject of gender and staying on in education. The following crosstabulation would be very easy to interpret. Clearly there is a gender difference, all the

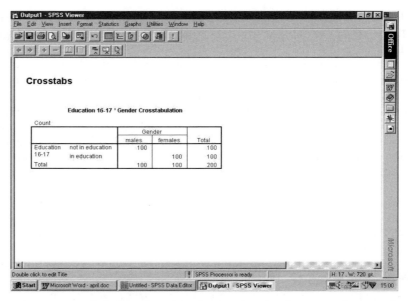

**FIGURE 26.1    Crosstabulation of participation in education for respondents aged 16–17 by gender**

males had left education and, by contrast, all the females stayed on in education at age 16–17 (Figure 26.1).

Consider for a moment, that a second researcher had collected data on the subject of gender and staying on in education. The following cross-tabulation would also be very easy to interpret. Clearly there is not a gender difference, equal numbers of males and females had left education and stayed on in education at age 16–17 (Figure 26.2).

Sadly, these two extreme situations are very unlikely in empirical social science research. In real research projects something between these two polar extremes usually occurs. Statistical methodology can, however, help us separate structured or systematic features in the data from random features. A little bit of statistical theory can help us understand the process. Let us put our research question more formally:

- *The null hypothesis*: $H_0$ = There is no structured or systematic difference between young men and young women in terms of staying on in education aged 16–17.
- *The alternate hypothesis*: $H_1$ = There is a structured or systematic difference between young men and young women in terms of staying on in education aged 16–17.

We can see that a greater proportion of young females remain in education aged 16–17 than young males.

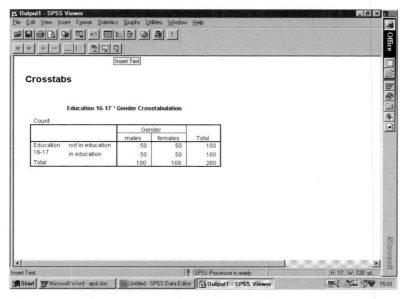

**FIGURE 26.2  Crosstabulation of participation in education for respondents aged 16–17 by gender, no association**

- 54.5 per cent of the young males in the survey were in education when surveyed at age 16–17.
- 58.7 per cent of the young women in the survey were in education when surveyed at age 16–17.

This represents an *observed difference* of 4.2 per cent.

However, in our sample there are different numbers of young men and women. There are also different numbers of young people in education and out of the educational system. The statistical solution to this problem is to consider what the table would look like if there were no structured or systematic differences between young men and young women in terms of being in education when surveyed at age 16–17. This is referred to as constructing expected frequencies. The formula for calculating expected frequencies is very simple:

$$E = \frac{\text{Row total} \times \text{Column total}}{\text{Grand total}}$$

In our crosstabulation of education age 16–17 and gender, 1,810 young men were not in education. What would this figure have been if there was no difference between young men and young women? Remember we have different numbers of young men and young women in our study and different numbers of young people stay in or leave education aged 16–17. Well, the formula can help us answer this question.

**Education 16-17\* gender Crosstabulation**

Count

|  |  | gender | | Total |
|---|---|---|---|---|
|  |  | males | females |  |
| Education 16-17 | not in education | 1810 |  | 3706 |
|  | in education |  |  |  |
| Total |  | 3977 |  | 8573 |

For the males not in education cell of our table: the row total = 3706; the column total = 3977; the grand total = 8573

$$E = \frac{3706 \times 3977}{8573} = 1719.2$$

In a similar fashion it is possible to construct expected frequencies for each of the four cells of the gender and education aged 16–17 table.

| Category | Observed | Row Total | Column Total | Grand Total | Expected Frequency |
|---|---|---|---|---|---|
| Males not in education | 1810 | 3706 | 3977 | 8573 | 1719.2 |
| Males in education | 2167 | 4867 | 3977 | 8573 | 2257.8 |
| Females not in education | 1896 | 3706 | 4596 | 8573 | 1986.8 |
| Females in education | 2700 | 4867 | 4596 | 8573 | 2609.2 |

It is possible to use SPSS to construct a table of expected frequencies (Figure 26.3).

Click on **Cells** at the bottom of the **Crosstabs** dialogue box (see Figure 25.10). We are now in the **Crosstabs: Cell Display** dialogue box. Look at the **Counts** dialogue box at top left-hand corner. To get a table of expected values click on box beside **Expected**. Click on **Continue** and then **OK** when you return to the **Crosstabs** dialogue box to run the procedure.

In a nut shell we have two tables. One contains *observed* or real values and the other contains *expected* values (Figure 26.3). What we need to do is to consider the issue of the difference between observed values and expected values in a formal statistical fashion.

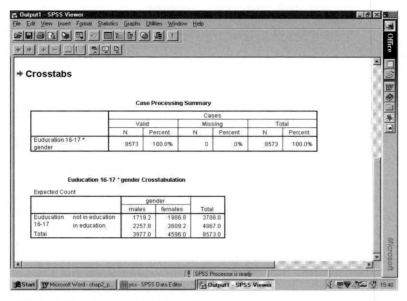

**FIGURE 26.3  Table of expected frequencies**

The *chi-square test* $\chi^2$ is a measure of the distance between the two tables. A big chi-square value denotes a big distance and a small chi-square a small distance. The formula for the chi-square test is:

$$\chi^2 = \sum \frac{(O - E)^2}{E}$$

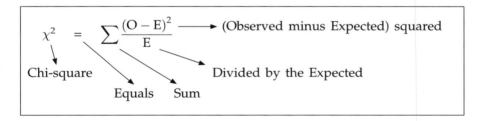

For each cell in the table we need to:

- calculate the difference between the *observed* and the *expected* frequency for each cell;
- then square this figure;
- then divide it by the expected frequency for the given cell.

| | Males not in education | Males in education | Females not in education | Females in education |
|---|---|---|---|---|
| O | 1810 | 2167 | 1896 | 2700 |
| E | 1719.2 | 2257.8 | 1986.8 | 2609.2 |
| (O−E) | 90.8 | −90.8 | −90.8 | 90.8 |
| (O−E)$^2$ | 8244.6 | 8244.6 | 8244.6 | 8244.6 |
| (O−E)$^2$/E | 4.79 | 3.65 | 4.15 | 3.16 |

The sum = 4.79 + 3.65 + 4.15 + 3.16 = <u>15.75</u>

This figure can be obtained using SPSS. Click on **Statistics** at the bottom of the **Crosstabs** dialogue box. We are now in the **Crosstabs: Statistics** dialogue box. To calculate chi-square click on the box beside **Chi-square**. Click on **Continue** and then **OK** when you return to the **Crosstabs** dialogue box to run the procedure (Figure 26.4).

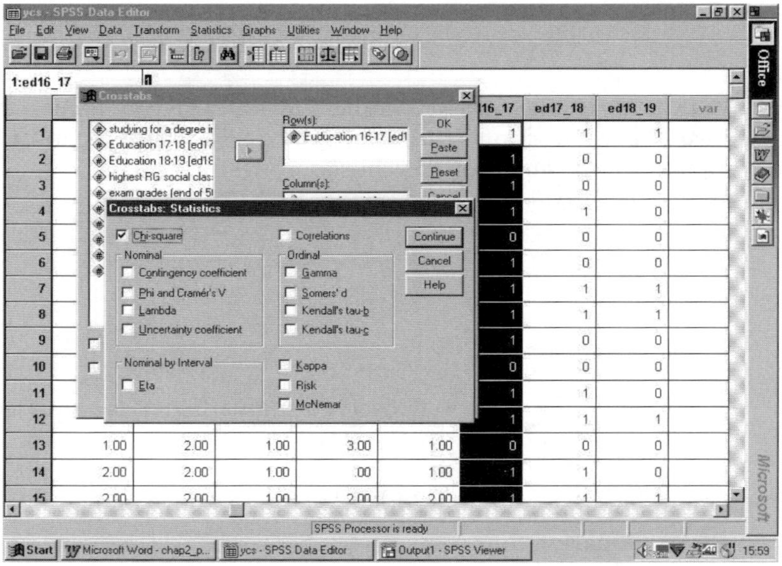

**FIGURE 26.4  Computing chi-square using SPSS**

The first table is the now familiar crosstabulation between gender and education at 16–17. SPSS calls the chi-square test **Pearson Chi-Square**, because Karl Pearson developed the chi-square test. SPSS has calculated the value of chi-square as 15.75 (Figure 26.5).

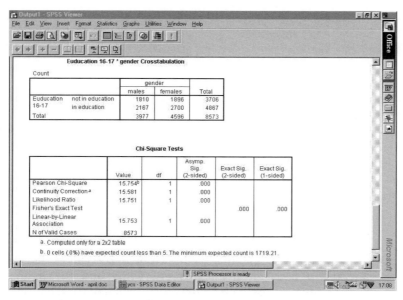

**FIGURE 26.5 Chi-square output for the crosstabulation of education by gender**

In addition to Pearson Chi-Square, SPSS also provides some other statistics. The **Continuity Correction** is a special calculation of chi-square for 2 × 2 tables. It is a slightly more conservative estimate of chi-square. In practice, in many situations when empirical data analysis is being undertaken the continuity correction is roughly equivalent to Pearson Chi-Square. However, there is a debate about it's functional value. The continuity correction is sometime known as *Yates' Correction* after its inventor.

The **Likelihood Ratio** is an alternative to Pearson Chi-Square. In large samples this statistic will be roughly equivalent to Pearson Chi-Square as in our example.

**Fisher's Exact Test** is a test for 2 × 2 tables with very small sample sizes. An assumption of the chi-square test is that no cells will have expected frequencies less than 5. Tables with expected frequencies less than 5 only occur when the sample size is small. Small samples should generally be avoided as they are less representative, but when they are used Fisher's Exact Test is an appropriate alternative to Pearson Chi-Square.

In footnote **b** SPSS reports the number of cells which have expected frequencies less than 5 and the smallest (minimum) expected frequency of any cell in the table. With large samples the minimum expected frequency assumption is generally not violated so presents no problem when social researchers use the chi-square test.

**Linear-by-Linear** is a chi-square test for two continuous variables which is seldom used in social research.

We can summarize the chi-square test:

*A big chi-square = Big difference between the observed data and the expected frequencies*
*A small chi-square = Small difference between the observed data and the expected frequencies*

So far so good, but how do we decide when a chi-square value is big or small? Given the calculation which we have seen above it would be unreasonable to expect the same chi-square values for tables with different dimensions. What we do is compare the chi-square value to the size of the table. The calculation for the size of the table is known as the *degrees of freedom (df)* of the table and it can be computed as follows.

$$df = (\text{Number of rows} - 1) \times (\text{Number of columns} - 1)$$

So our $2 \times 2$ table had $(2-1) \times (2-1) = 1$ degree of freedom.
The question still remains, how big is a big chi-square? This is determined by the relationship between the chi-square value and the degrees of freedom. Good statistical textbooks will have a chi-square table. In principle these all work along the same lines.

| df | $\chi^2 = .05$ | $\chi^2 = .01$ |
|----|----------------|----------------|
| 1  | 3.84           | 6.64           |
| 2  | 5.99           | 9.21           |
| 3  | 7.82           | 11.34          |
| 4  | 9.49           | 13.28          |
| 5  | 11.07          | 15.09          |
| 6  | 12.59          | 16.81          |
| 7  | 14.07          | 18.48          |

The table is an extract of a chi-square table. The reader looks down the column which denotes the required significance level. In social sciences we conventionally use the 5 per cent level, $p = 0.05$. This is the shaded column in the table. The reader then looks down the table to appropriate number of degrees of freedom for the table which is being analysed.

In our example the gender by education age 16–17 table has 1 degree of freedom. The *critical value* for 1 degree of freedom is 3.84. A $\chi^2$ value which is bigger than (or equal to) the *critical value* can be considered as a big chi-square value.

*A big chi-square = Big difference between the observed data and the expected frequencies*

The chi-square value for our table was 15.75, which is much larger than 3.84. Therefore we can consider this a large value of chi-square. What does this mean for our null hypothesis?

| $\chi^2$ < Critical value | $\chi^2$ => Critical value |
|---|---|
| Critical value | |
| \|----------------------------\|---------------------\| | |
| Cannot reject $H_0$ | Reject $H_0$ |

If the value of chi-square is less than the critical value then we *cannot reject the null hypothesis*. Therefore, we can substantively conclude that there is no structured or systematic relationship in the data. If the value of chi-square is (equal to or) greater than the critical value then we *can reject the null hypothesis*. In our example 15.75 is clearly greater than 3.84 so we can reject our null hypothesis:

> {$H_0$ = There is no structured or systematic difference between *young men* and *young women* in terms of staying on in education aged 16–17}

Substantively we can conclude that there is a structured or systematic difference between young men and young women in terms of staying on in education aged 16–17. Young women are more likely to stay in education aged 16–17.

An alternative and more practical way of assessing our hypotheses is to use probability theory. We have a difference between our observed frequencies and our expected frequencies (measured by our chi-square value). Is this a structured or systematic difference? One way of answering this question is to consider what is the probability of differences as extreme as those between our observed frequencies and the expected frequencies occurring by chance. It is possible for us to draw the chi-square distribution in much the same way as we were able to draw the normal distribution (bell curve). The shaded area in the graph shows values of chi-square which are above the critical value or *critical point*. These are extremely high values of chi-square (Figure 26.6).

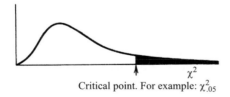

Critical point. For example: $\chi^2_{.05}$

**FIGURE 26.6**

The probability of a chi-square value being (equal to or) greater than the critical value is p < =.05. Conventionally, this is known as either *p = .05* or *the 5% level*. Alternatively, this can be considered as a 5 per cent chance. With some complicated mathematics it is possible to convert the chi-square value for a given number of degrees of freedom into a probability. SPSS and other statistical analysis software does this automatically.

**Chi-Square Tests**

|  | Value | df | Asymp. Sig. (2-sided) | Exact Sig. (2-sided) | Exact Sig. (1-sided) |
|---|---|---|---|---|---|
| Pearson Chi-Square | 15.754[b] | 1 | .000 |  |  |
| Continuity Correction[a] | 15.581 | 1 | .000 |  |  |
| Likelihood Ratio | 15.751 | 1 | .000 |  |  |
| Fisher's Exact Test |  |  |  | .000 | .000 |
| Linear-by-Linear Association | 15.753 | 1 | .000 |  |  |
| N of Valid Cases | 8573 |  |  |  |  |

[a] Computed only for a 2×2 table
[b] 0 cells (.0%) have expected count less than 5. The minimum expected count is 1719.21.

The fourth column of the **Chi-Square Tests** table is labelled **Asymp. Sig.**, which is short for the statistical term asymptotic significance. The *probability* or *p value* for the given statistic is reported in this column. The probability for the Pearson chi-square in our analysis is $p < .000$.

Cannot reject $H_0$                   Can reject $H_0$
(not significant)                     (significant)

|—————————————————————————|————————|

P = 1                               P = .05       P = 0

If p is greater than $(p >).05$ then *we cannot reject the null hypothesis*. If p is equal to or less than $(p = <).05$ then *we can reject the null hypothesis*.

Clearly, in our analysis of the relationship between gender and participation in education aged 16–17 *we can reject the null hypothesis at the p=.05 level*. Substantively, we can infer that there is a structured or systematic relationship between gender and participation in education aged 16–17 for this group of young people. Gender has a *significant* influence on staying in education aged 16–17. Young women were more likely than young men to stay on in education aged 16–17.

We have used statistical methodology to make an inference about our data. We have seen how the chi-square test is used and interpreted. We have also seen how probabilities can be derived from the test and interpreted. The appropriate presentation of the data is very much dependent on what you wish to communicate to the reader. The data used in tables should be clearly labelled and word processed when presented in research reports and publications! Good analysis of data in tables will report *chi-square values, degrees of freedom* and *probabilities*.

## MEASURES OF ASSOCIATION FOR DATA IN TABLES

The chi-square test is bound up with testing our hypotheses. Concluding our analysis at the interpretation of the chi-square test is sufficient in many instances, but we may wish to take the analysis further. Suppose we want to know the degree to which our explanatory variable and our independent variable are related or associated. What is required is a *measure of association*. For a two by two (2×2) table *Phi* $\phi$ is the appropriate measure of association.

Phi $\phi$ is the square root of chi-square divided by the sample size

$$\phi = \sqrt{\chi^2/n}$$

For tables larger than 2×2 *Cramer's V* is the correct measure of association:

$$V = \sqrt{\chi^2/nt}$$

where $n$ is the sample size and $t$ is either (row − 1) or (column − 1) whichever is smaller. For a two by two table Cramer's V is identical to Phi. Phi and Cramer's V vary between zero and one

A value for Phi or Cramer's V which is close to zero is considered as a *weak association*.
A value for Phi or Cramer's V which is close to one is considered as a *strong association*.

Values for Phi and Cramer's V can be obtained using SPSS (Figure 26.7). Click on **Statistics**, then on **Summarize**, then on **Crosstabs**. Click on **Statistics** at the bottom of the **Crosstabs** dialogue box. We are now in the **Crosstabs: Statistics** dialogue box. To calculate chi-square click on the box beside **Phi and Cramer's V**. Click on **Continue** and then **OK** when you return to the **Crosstabs** dialogue box to run the procedure.

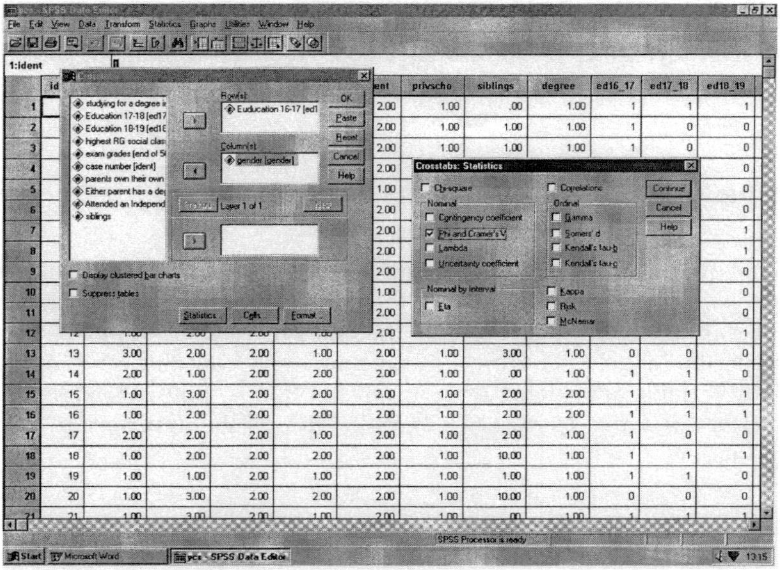

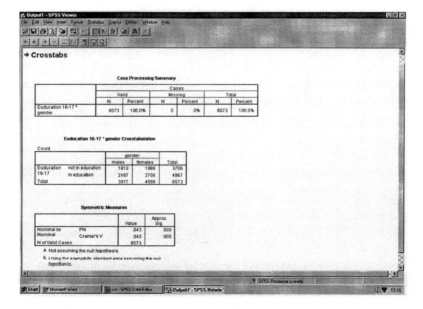

**FIGURE 26.7  Calculating Phi and Cramer's V using SPSS**

**FIGURE 26.8  Phi and Cramer's V for education by gender**

Phi equals .043 for our crosstabulation between gender and educational status age 16–17 (Figure 26.8).

Since .043 is close to zero we can conclude that there is a weak association between gender and educational status age 16–17.

## ASSOCIATIONS BETWEEN CONTINUOUS VARIABLES

If we want to find out if two continuous variables are related the most straightforward way is to plot them. This is possible in SPSS. Imagine that we wanted to explore the dynamics of young people's levels of pay. For example, we might wish to explore the relationship between how much a young person was paid in the first year after leaving compulsory education and how much a year later.

Open the data file ycs2.sav and click on **Graphs**, then on **Scatter** (Figure 26.9).

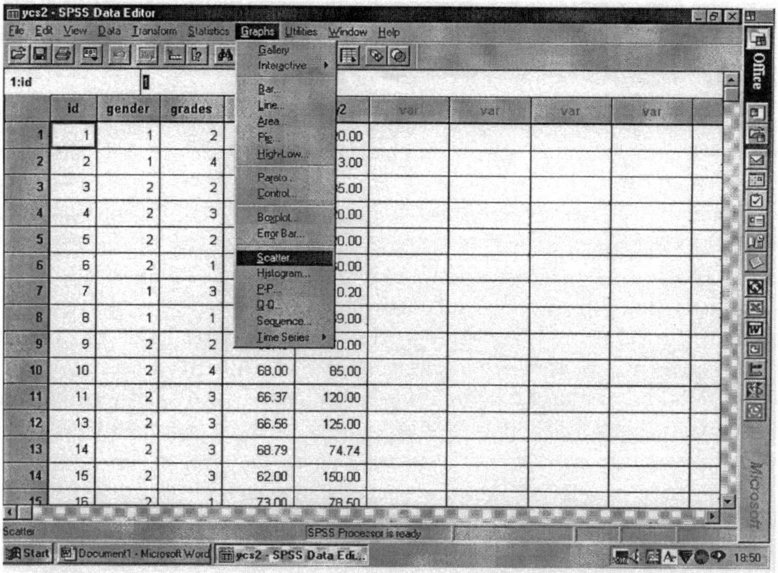

**FIGURE 26.9   Generating a scatter plot using SPSS**

Click on the box next to **Simple** and then on **Define** (Figure 26.9).

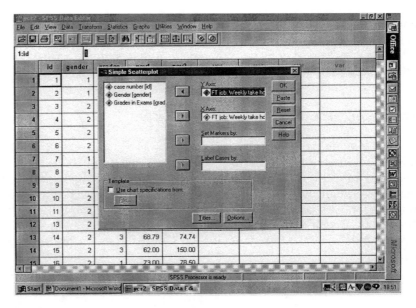

**FIGURE 26.10   Choosing variables for a scatter plot**

The Y variable is *FT job Weekly take home pay age 18–19*. Insert this variable into the **Y Axis** box.
The X variable is *FT job Weekly take home pay age 17–18*. Insert this variable into the **X Axis** box.
Click on **OK**.
You will see from the output that with large sets of data it is very difficult to interpret the relationship between the X and Y variables (Figure 26.11). What is required is a *measure of association* for continuous data.

   *Pearson's Product Moment Correlation Coefficient* is a test of association for two continuous variables. It is denoted by *r* and takes on values between +1 and −1.

Values close to 1 are *strong* and values close to 0 are *weak*. The sign, *positive* or *negative* indicates the direction of the relationship. Figure 26.12 shows a set of simple scatter plots to illustrate how *Pearson's r* can be interpreted.

   Scatter plot (a) shows a *strong positive* association. As the values of the *X variable* increase so do the values of the *Y variable*.

   Scatter plot (b) shows a *strong negative* association. As the values of the *X variable* increase the values of the *Y variable* decrease.

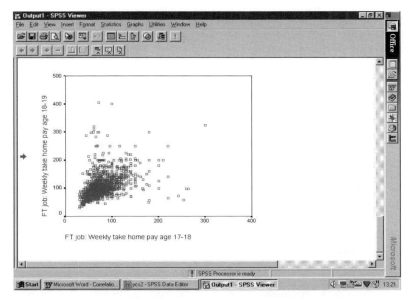

**FIGURE 26.11   Scatter plot of respondents weekly take-home pay at age 17–18 and 18–19**

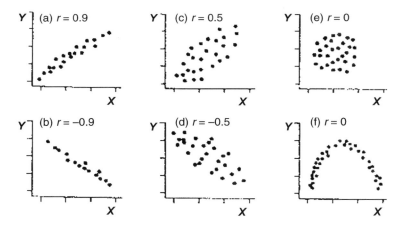

**FIGURE 26.12   Interpreting Pearson's r**

Scatter plot (c) shows a *weak positive* association. As the values of the X *variable* increase so do some, but not all, of the values of the Y *variable*. There is a positive relationship between the X *variable* and the Y *variable* but it is not strong.

Scatter plot (d) shows a *weak negative* association. As the values of the X *variable* increase some, but not all, of the values of the Y *variable* decrease. There is a negative relationship between the X *variable* and the Y *variable* but it is not strong. In scatter plots C and D the points are more dispersed than in A and B. This is why the correlation is lower even though the general trend in the data is similar.

Scatter plot (e) shows *no linear association* between the X *variable* and the Y *variable*. Neither a positive nor a negative relationship exists between the X *variable* and the Y *variable*.

Scatter plot (f) shows *no linear association* between the X *variable* and the Y *variable*. Neither a positive nor a negative relationship exists between the X *variable* and the Y *variable*. For small values of the X *variable* there appears to be a positive association with the Y *variable* and for large values of the X *variable* there is a negative association with the Y *variable*. Clearly there is *no linear association* between the X *variable* and the Y *variable* (i.e. a straight line could not be used to summarize the relationship between the X *variable* and the Y *variable*). However, in scatter plot (f) there is a strong curvilinear relationship.

SPSS computes Pearson's *r*.

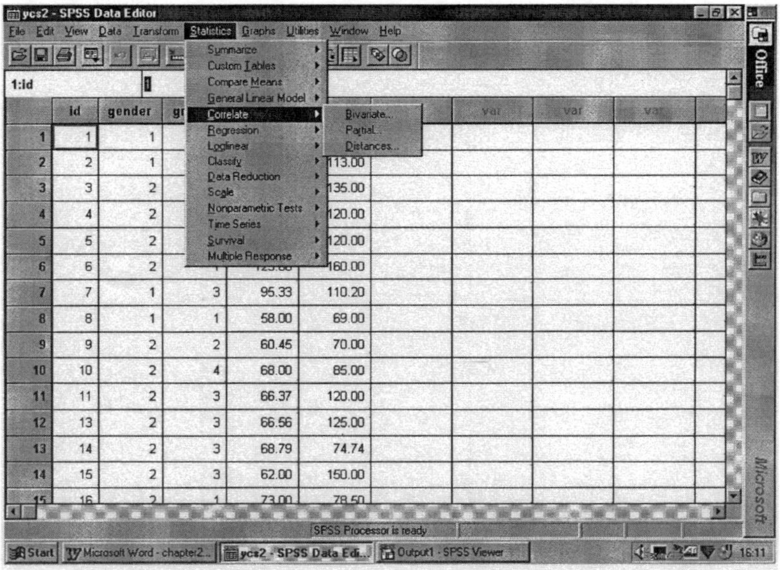

**FIGURE 26.13   Computing Pearson's r with SPSS**

Click on **Statistics**, then on **Correlate**, then on **Bivariate** (Figure 26.13). Move *FT job Weekly take home pay age 18–19* and *FT job Weekly take home pay age 17–18* into the **Variables:** box. Click on **Pearson** then click on **OK** (Figure 26.14).

From the table in Figure 26.15 we can see that the *Pearson Correlation* is .496 (i.e. *r*=.496).

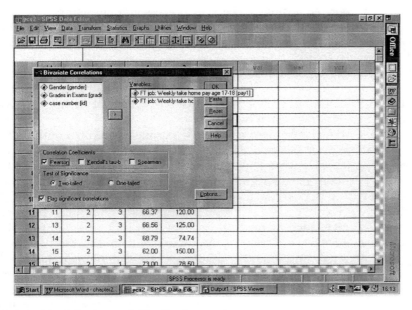

FIGURE 26.14   Selecting variables for Pearson's r

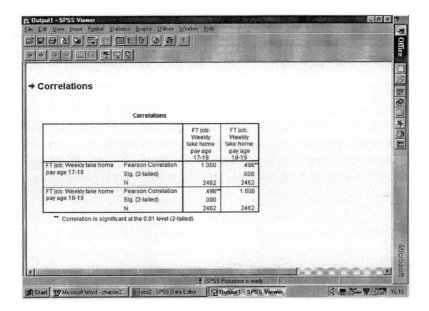

FIGURE 26.15   Correlation output in SPSS

A value of .496 is positive. There is no absolute measurement which decides whether or not an association is weak or strong. The strength of an association is usually decided by the substantive nature of the research and previous research in that area.

A correlation of .496 can be regarded as being fairly strong. The substantive conclusion which we can draw is that there is a fairly strong positive correlation between a young person's weekly take-home pay age 16–17 and their weekly take-home pay age 18–19.

Pearson's $r$ can also be used as a test of significance. In the output above the correlation .496** has two stars beside it. This is a conventional way of denoting significance. One * usually means significant at the $p < .05$ level and two ** usually means significant at the $p < .01$ level.

Using SPSS it is possible to get a *two-tailed* or a *one-tailed* result. For much survey research this distinction is unimportant but it can be important in other areas such as medical experiments. In a *one-tailed* test at the outset we predict the direction of the difference between the two groups which we are analysing. If on the other hand we cannot or do not need to be so specific we use a *two-tailed* test. If a *one-tailed* test is required click in the **Test of Significance** box next to **One-tailed** (Figure 26.15).

There are a number of other *tests of association*. These tests are interpreted in the same fashion as Pearson's $r$. The sign of the coefficient indicates the direction of the relationship, and its absolute value indicates the strength. Larger absolute values indicate stronger relationships.

*Spearman's Rank Order Correlation* is denoted by $r_s$ (or $\rho$ the Greek letter rho). Spearman's is similar to the Pearson correlation coefficient but is based on the ranks of the data rather than the actual values. It is an appropriate test for ordinal data. Values of the Spearman's Rank Order Correlation range from −1 to +1. This measure is often found in statistics textbooks but is seldom, if ever, reported in social science research.

This measure can be calculated in SPSS by clicking on **Spearman** in the **Correlation Coefficients** box.

**Kendall's tau b** is the measure of association for ordinal or ranked variables that takes ties into account. Possible values range from −1 to 1, but a value of −1 or +1 can only be obtained from square tables.

This measure is almost never reported in social science research.

This measure can be calculated by SPSS by clicking on **Kendall's tau-b** in the **Correlation Coefficients** box.

## ANALYSING THREE OR MORE VARIABLES

So far we have restricted our analysis to one (univariate) or two (bivariate) variables. In a great deal of social research we are interested in the relationship between three or more variables, which is termed as *multivariate analysis*.

There are a number of *statistical models* available in social science research. There is a huge statistical literature explaining the appropriate use of these models and how to interpret them. A range of these models is available in SPSS but a good number are very complex and require a great deal of skill and experience if they are to be used appropriately and interpreted correctly.

In most instances, in multivariate analysis, we are interested in the relationship between one Y variable and a series of X variables (Figure 26.16).

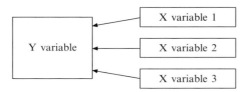

**FIGURE 26.16   Multivariate analysis**

If the Y variable is *nominal* and has two categories then the most popular statistical model that is used in social science research is the *logistic regression model*. Supposing we were interested in the effects of gender and parental education on young people remaining in education aged 16–17 (Figure 26.17).

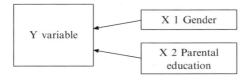

**FIGURE 26.17   Multivariate analysis in practice**

The logistic regression model is available in SPSS. Click on **Statistics**, then **Regression**, then **Logistic** (see Figure 26.18).

The dependent (Y variable) is *Education 16–17 [ed16_17]* move this to **Dependent:** variable box (Figure 26.19).

The independent (X variables) are known as *Covariates* in logistic regression. Move the *gender [gender]* variable to the **Covariates:** box. Move the *Either parent has a degree [pdeg]* variable to the **Covariates:** box (see Figure 26.20). Now click on **Categorical**. Since the gender variable and the parental education variable are categorical variables we must declare them as such. Move the *gender [gender]* variable to the **Categorical Covariates:** box. Move the *Either parent has a degree [pdeg]* variable to the **Categorical Covariates:** box (Figure 26.20).

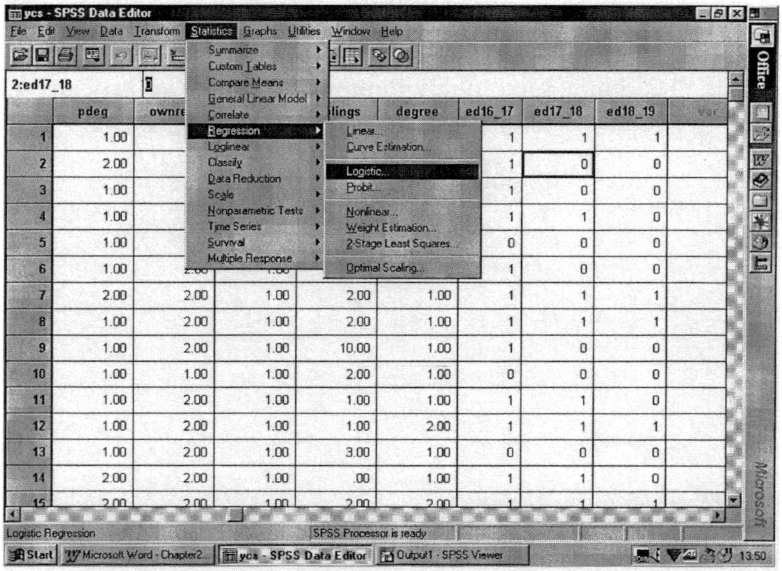

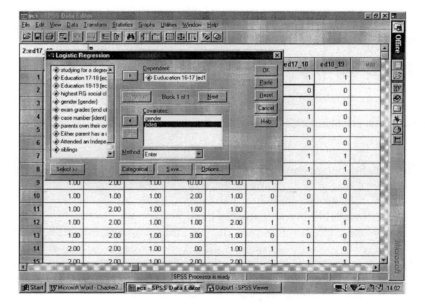

**FIGURE 26.18   Calculation logistic regression in SPSS**

**FIGURE 26.19   Choosing variables for logistic regression**

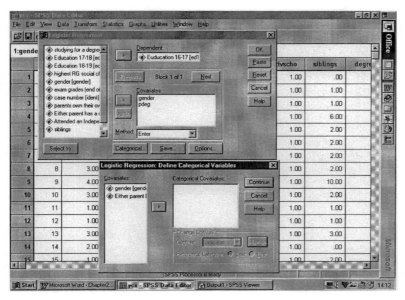

**FIGURE 26.20  Defining categorical variables**

There are a number of ways in which the logistic regression model can be constructed. The most common way in social science research is to compare categories of the X variable with its first category. However, this convention is not always followed by researchers. SPSS does not do this by default but has this facility. Hold down the shift key on the keyboard, and click on the *gender [gender]* variable and then on the *Either parent has a degree [pdeg]* variable. This should highlight both of the categorical covariates. Click on **First** in the **Change Contrast** dialogue box and then click on **Change** (Figure 26.21).

Now click on **Continue** and **OK** when you return to the **Logistic Regression** dialogue box.

In SPSS the logistic regression model produces a long output. The first portion of the output reports the number of *cases* which have been used in the analysis. In this example the number of *cases* is simply the number of young people in the data set (Figure 26.22).

The next portion of the output tell us how the variables have been coded for the analysis and tells us how many young people fall into each category of the X variables (Figure 26.23).

SPSS also tells us which codes have been used for the parameters.

The first statistic which is reported is the −2 **Log Likelihood** (11726.989), this is a measure of how well the model fits the data without any X variables (Figure 26.24). SPSS then reminds us which variables are entered into the logistic regression model. In advanced analyses there are a number of ways to enter variables into models. In the statistical literature

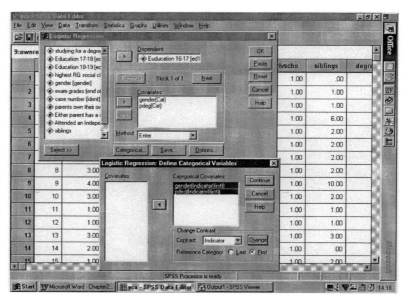

**FIGURE 26.21    Changing contrasts for categorical variables**

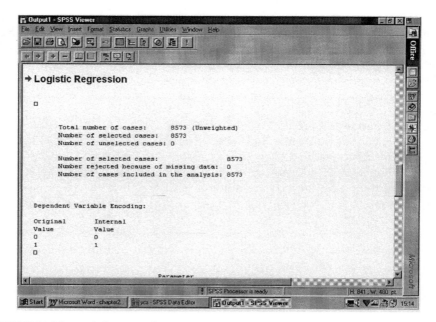

**FIGURE 26.22    Logistic regression output in SPSS**

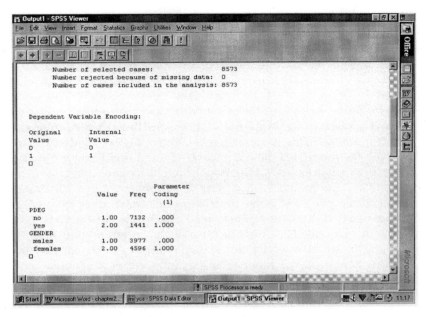

**FIGURE 26.23 Coding output for logistic regression**

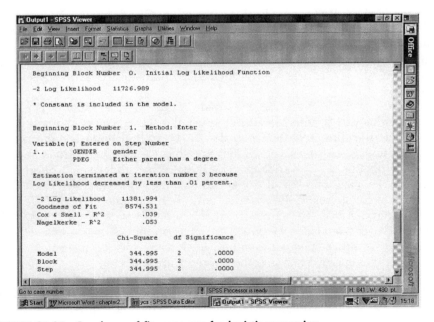

**FIGURE 26.24 Goodness of fit measures for logistic regression**

the pros and cons of these methods are hotly debated. The simplest method is called **Enter** and SPSS used this by default.

The logistic regression model is estimated in stages. These are called **iterations**. The estimation stops when the extra attempts at estimation are no longer helping to improve the accuracy of the model. SPSS tells us that the **Estimation terminated** at iteration number 3 because Log Likelihood decreased by less than .01 per cent (i.e. the accuracy of the model's estimates was not being improved by additional iterations).

The next statistic in the output is **−2 Log Likelihood** for the model with the two X variables. This is sometime called the *deviance* and is a measure of how well the model fits the data. Since **−2 Log Likelihood** for the model with the two X variables (11381.994) is much smaller than the **−2 Log Likelihood** for the model without any X variables we can conclude that including these two X variables improves our model.

Another way of looking at how well the model fits the data is the **Goodness of Fit** statistic. There is no obvious interpretation of this test statistic and in social research this statistic almost never reported. It is a measure of how well the model fits the data and is calculated by comparing the observed probabilities with those predicted by the model.

**Cox & Snell – R^2** is a measure of how well the X variables explain the Y variable. It takes on values between *zero* and *one*. A value close to 1 is a strong correlation and a value close to 0 is a weak correlation. This statistic is very seldom reported in social science research and has been criticized by statisticians as a measure of goodness of fit.

**Nagelkerke – R^2** is an adjusted form of the **Cox & Snell – R^2**. Within the statistical literature it has been suggested that it is difficult for **Cox & Snell – R^2** to achieve values close to 1. **Nagelkerke – R^2** makes an adjustment for this. Again this measure is very seldom reported in social science research and has been criticized by statisticians as a measure of goodness of fit.

The next table reports the chi-square value for the **Model**. This chi-square value can be interpreted in the usual fashion. The chi-square value 344.995 is the difference between the **−2 Log Likelihood** for the model without any X variables (11726.989) and the **−2 Log Likelihood** for the model with the two X variables (11381.994). The model has 2 degrees of freedom, i.e. (The number of categories in the gender variable − 1) + (The number of categories in the parental education variable − 1). At 2 degrees of freedom a chi-square value of 344.995 is highly significant *(p<.000)*. In some advanced analyses we add X variables in blocks or in steps so SPSS gives us two other chi-square values. In this analysis we have not added variables in steps or blocks so these values are the same.

In the final part of the output SPSS gives us a **Classification Table** for the Y variable (Figure 26.25). Another way to assess how well our model fits the data is to compare the outcomes which are predicted to the observed outcomes. In social research this method of assessing goodness of fit is almost never reported. Of the 3706 young people not in education

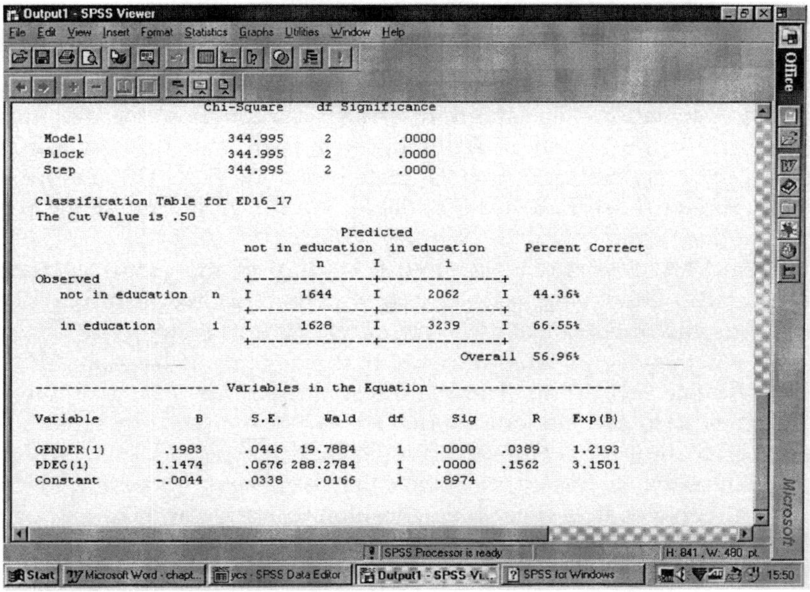

**FIGURE 26.25  Logistic regression output – variables in the equation**

the model correctly predicted 1644, i.e. 44.3 per cent of these cases were correctly predicted. Of the 4867 young people in education the model correctly predicted 3239, i.e. 66.55 per cent of these cases were correctly predicted. Overall our model predicted the correct outcome for 56.96 per cent of the case in our dataset.

SPSS also reports the **Cut Value**. By default this is .5 but for super advanced analyses SPSS allows us to determine the cut point for classifying cases. Cases with predicted values that exceed the classification **Cut Value** are classified as positive, while those with predicted values smaller than the **Cut Value** are classified as negative. The default value can be changed and the **Cut Value** can be varied between 0.01 and 0.99.

In terms of social science analyses the most important part of the output is **Variables in the Equation**.

```
- - - - - - - - - - - - - Variables in the Equation - - - - - - - - - - - -
Variable      B        S.E.      Wald       df     Sig      R       Exp (B)
GENDER(1)    .1983     .0446     19.7884     1    .0000    .0389    1.2193
PDEG(1)     1.1474     .0676    288.2784     1    .0000    .1562    3.1501
Constant    -.0044     .0338       .0166     1    .8974
```

The first column reports the names of the variables. The next column **B** is a little difficult to interpret. **B** is the estimate of the log odds ratios for the variables in the model. The column **B** reports the odds for the variables estimated on the **logarithmic scale**. This is notoriously hard to interpret but we will return to it later.

The next column **S.E.** reports the **standard error** of the log odds (**B**). The principal of standard errors is relatively easy to understand and is related to standard deviations. The **standard error** is a measure of the precision of the estimate of the log odds (**B**). A big standard error denotes a lack of precision. As a general rule if an estimate of the log odds (**B**) is more than twice its standard error then the variable will be significant at the $p < .05$ level.

The **Wald** test reported in the fourth column of the output is another version of the chi-square test. It tests whether or not including the X variable in the model makes a significant improvement. In the now familiar way there is a related measure of the **degrees of freedom (df)** and the **significance level (Sig)**. The Wald test is interpreted in the same way as the chi-square test. In our model we can see that both gender and parental education are significant ($p < .0000$).

**R** is a measure of linear association between the X variable and the Y variable. It behaves in a very similar fashion to *r* and can take on positive and negative values. This summary statistic does not often appear in social science research.

The final column of the output helps us to interpret the effects of the X variables. **Exp(B)** transforms the log odds into odds ratios. This is simply the **anti-log of B** and can be worked out with a scientific calculator.

The logistic regression model estimates the effects of each of the X variables by using **Odds**. **Odds** behave a little like probabilities. The probability of rolling a 3 on a normal unbiased die is 1/6. The **odds** of rolling a 3 on a normal unbiased die are **1 : 5**, i.e. there is one face of the die which is a 3 and 5 more faces which do not have a three on them. The odds of rolling a 3 are, therefore, 1 to 5. This is sometimes called a five to one chance. Expressed another way you are five times more likely to roll something other than a 3 than you are to roll a 3.

Let us first take the *gender* variable. Males are in category 0 and females in category 1. SPSS told us this at the start of the logistic regression output. Compared to males (all things being equal) females are 1.2193 times more likely to be in education at age 16–17.

The *Either parent having a degree* variable is classified as 0 if the answer is no and 1 if the answer is yes. Once again SPSS told us this at the start of the logistic regression output. Compared to young people who do not have a graduate parent (all things being equal) those with a graduate parent are 3.15 times more likely to be in education at age 16–17.

Overall, this is a simple analysis but begins to illustrate how statistical models can be built in SPSS and used to explore the relationships between more than two variables. Statistical modelling and multivariate analysis in general are advanced topics which require an increased understanding of statistical methodology. These techniques tend to be complicated and set snares for casual users. The knowledge which is required to use these techniques appropriately and correctly interpret the output of these procedures takes time to acquire.

In addition to the logistic regression model, within SPSS, a number of other models are available. The **Loglinear** model can also be fitted in SPSS. It is related to logistic regression and appropriate for a dependent variable with more than two categories. This is a popular model within social research because it is appropriate for categorical data and tabular data.

The most widely written about statistical modelling procedure is **Linear Regression**. This model is appropriate for continuous data and estimates the coefficients of the linear equation, involving one or more independent variables, that best predict the value of the dependent variable. Since many of the variables in social science research are not continuous this method is not as widely used as its popularity in statistical textbooks would indicate.

**Analysis of variance (ANOVA)**, is a model which can be used for analysing several group means by comparing the sample variance estimated from the group means to that estimated within the groups. ANOVA is extremely popular within the psychology community but is far less popular in other areas of social science.

GETTING STARTED

*Vernon Gayle*

As any experienced social researcher will tell you, inputting data is time consuming and labour intensive. If your aim is to analyse new empirical data it is important to get the process of coding and data entry right first time. Not doing so can be costly later.

*Coding*  SPSS works best with numerical codes, rather than alphabetic ones. You should work out your coding scheme in the design phase of your research and test it out after your pilot study.

*Labels*  While codes are necessary for statistical analysis they are, by their nature, cryptic. It is important to be able to comprehend output without looking up the variable descriptions and the codes elsewhere. So, while the data should be entered as codes for the benefit of the statistical analysis, it should be presented with labels, for the benefit of the user. SPSS addresses this need by allowing the user to assign labels to describe variables, **variable labels**, and labels describing specific values, **value labels**.

*Defining variables*  Each column in the data editor represents a variable of one type only: a number, text or perhaps a date. In addition, that type is qualified by attributes, such as the maximum number of digits, number of decimal places to display, etc. SPSS requires that you define your variables in those terms before entering any data into them.

Start up SPSS. Click next to **Type in data** then click on **OK** (Figure 27.1). The frontmost window which displays a grid is the **Data Editor** window. This is where data are entered or changed, and it is the window you will be using most during data entry (Figure 27.1). Each column of the grid represents a variable (typically a question) and each row, a case (a questionnaire). It is a good idea to save the data file very early on and as often as possible.

*Moving around the data entry window*  Before proceeding, experiment a little with moving and selecting cells. Click on a few individual cells one at a time. Notice how the cursor (the border around the cell) moves each time to the cell you clicked on. Click on a **column label**. This is the grey area immediately above the column (**var**). The whole column will be selected.

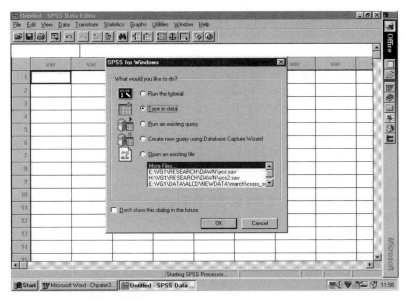

**FIGURE 27.1 Data editor window**

Drag across several column labels to select a range of columns. Click on a **row label**. This is the grey numbered area on the left of the row. The whole row will be selected. Drag across several row labels to select a range of rows.

*Defining variables*  The coding scheme should have been decided in the design phase of the research. Questions on a questionnaire sometimes require no coding. A numerical question (e.g. How old are you?) can be coded very easily. Others question responses are more complicated but should have a clear and consistent coding scheme. Some questions might collect responses which are not suitable for numerical codes to be applied. In SPSS such data can be entered as normal text, or a *string*, where it is considered to be *a string of characters*. Variables which are coded as strings do not lend themselves to statistical analysis.

*Variable names*  Some **variable names** will be obvious such as age and gender. The best policy is to use variable names which make substantive sense to the researcher(s) involved in the analysis. Variable names in SPSS must follow the following convention: they can be 1–8 characters long, the first character must be a letter, the remaining characters may be letters, digits or underscores (_).

*Identification*  The first variable in any data set should be an **identification variable** or **id number** as it is also known. This variable should ascribe a unique code by which each respondent can be identified. Being able to identify cases is especially important in large data sets.

*Defining a numerical variable*    A survey question on age or income will often, obviously, be a **numerical variable**. In the case of age measured in years a variable needs to be three digits wide, allowing for centenarians, and requires no numbers beyond the decimal point.

Position the cursor in the first column. Click on **Data** in the menu bar and choose **Define Variable**.

In the **Define Variable** dialogue box erase the provisional variable name VAR00001 and type the variable name instead (e.g. age).

Click on the **Type. . .** button in the **Define Variable Type:** dialogue box (Figure 27.2).

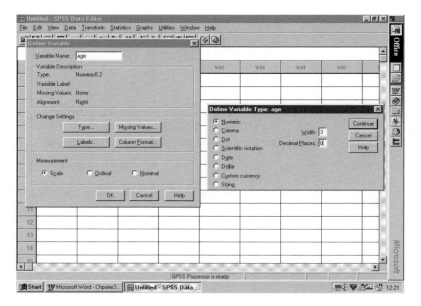

**FIGURE 27.2**   **Defining variables in SPSS**

Change the variable's **Width:** to 3 and the number of **Decimal Places** to 0, then click on **Continue** to return to the previous window. In the **Measurement** box we have three choices. By default SPSS expects the variable to be measured on a **Scale**. These are data values which are numeric values on an interval or ratio scale (e.g. age or income). Scale variables must be numeric (Figure 27.2).

Click on **OK** to return to the data editor.

The column width and label should change to the new settings. Make sure the cursor is in the first cell. To enter data we would now type the age of first respondent and press the **Return** key on the keyboard to enter it. The value will appear in the cell.

*Defining a categorical variable*   Gender questions on surveys are an obvious example of *categorical data* since a respondent can only be in one of two categories (i.e. male or female). To define a categorical variable place the cursor in the second column. Click on **Data** in the menu bar and choose **Define Variable**. Change the variable's name from VAR00001 to **gender**. Click on the **Type. . .** button in the **Define Variable Type:** dialogue box. Change the variable's **Width:** to 1 and the number of **Decimal Places** to 0, then click on **Continue** to return to the previous window (Figure 27.2).

Again, in the **Measurement** box we have three choices. By default SPSS expects the variable to be measured on a **Scale** by default. Change this to **Nominal**. Nominal data values represent categories with no intrinsic order (e.g. job category or company division). Nominal variables can be either *string* or *numeric* values that represent distinct categories (e.g. 1=male, 2=female).

Click on **OK** to return to the data editor.

*Measurement*   We have already encountered **Scale** and **Nominal** measurement. SPSS also allows us to specify **Ordinal** variables by clicking on **Ordinal** in the **Measurement** box. Ordinal data values represent categories with some intrinsic order (e.g. low, medium, high; strongly agree, agree, disagree, strongly disagree). Ordinal variables can be either *string* or *numeric* values that represent distinct categories (e.g. 1=low, 2=medium, 3=high).

*Defining a textual variable*   There are some questions on surveys for which we might want to record text. These can be defined as a text, or *string* variable. An example of this might be a respondent's job title. The only attribute that needs to be set for such variables is their width (maximum number of characters). To define a string variable place the cursor in the third column. Click on **Data** in the menu bar and choose **Define Variable**. Change the variable's name from VAR00001 to *job title*.

Click on **Type. . .** and change the variable type to **String**. Change its number of **Characters** to 20 and click on **Continue** to return to the previous window. Click on **OK** to return to the data editor (Figure 27.3).

*Labelling variables*   It is good practice to clearly label all of your variables. This will help you in your analysis and also help any researcher(s) undertaking secondary analysis of your data.

Click on the column of the variable which you wish to label. Click on **Data** in the menu bar and choose **Define Variable**. Click on the **Labels** button. Enter a meaningful label for your variable in the **Variable Label:** box. This label will be displayed within output generated by SPSS.

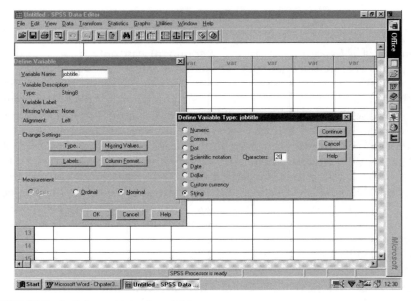

**FIGURE 27.3   Defining a textual variable**

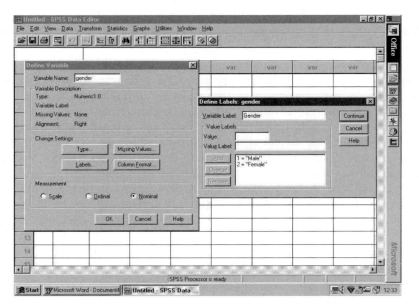

**FIGURE 27.4   Label variable**

Consider the example of a gender variable. To enter labels for specific values of the variable enter the value (or code) in the **Value:** box and the corresponding label for that value in the **Value Label:** box. Then click on the **Add** button. After all of the values for the variable are labelled click on **Continue** and then **OK** (Figure 27.4).

*Missing values*   There are a number of ways to treat missing values in SPSS. The user can define them by selecting the **Missing Values. . .** button in the **Define Variables** window. This allows the user to define **user-missing values**. These are values that you want to use to represent missing data. This function is not available for long string variables (string variables longer than 8 characters). A more practical way to treat missing values is to leave the cell blank. SPSS will treat this as a missing value and place a dot (.) in the cell.

The most important thing to remember when entering data is to save your work frequently.

At the end of the data entry process you are advised to check and double-check your data. It is advisable to run a frequency count on all of your variables in order to check if they have been correctly entered. It is also advisable to run some simple analysis such as a crosstabulation to check the values and labels which you have entered. Data entry can be a slow and labour-intensive process and good social researchers will spend a lot of time checking and cleaning their data before analysis begins.

# PART VIII

# FINISHING OFF: WRITING, PRESENTING AND PUBLISHING

Being able to write to a high standard is a core skill that research students need to acquire. Undertaking a PhD provides the opportunity for research students to explore different types of writing and practice and develop their writing skills. As a research student you will be required to use writing as a research tool by writing field notes, observations and constructing research instruments such as questionnaires and interview schedules. As your research progresses you will probably want to write seminar, conference or working papers. By the time you come to write the final draft of your thesis you should be a competent writer. Further development of your writing skills will enable you to write journal articles, chapters in edited books and perhaps write a book based on material contained in your thesis. For all of these reasons writing is an important skill to cultivate and hopefully the material contained in the following three chapters will help research students develop their writing and presentation skills.

In Chapter 28 Dawn Burton attempts to answer some of the questions which concern research students about writing a PhD thesis. For many students writing such a substantial piece of work can be daunting. Indeed for most academics their thesis will be the longest publication they will write during the course of their careers. The starting point in the chapter is comparing and contrasting writing undertaken on taught courses and writing a thesis, prior to considering ways in which a thesis might be structured. Other important issues discussed in the chapter include confidence and risk taking both as facilitators and as barriers to writing. Writing up on time and using a word processor are also considered. A key factor in successful writing is using your supervisor to the best effect. A range of factors which you might wish to discuss with your supervisor about your writing skills is addressed.

Writing and presenting conference and seminar papers are an integral part of academic life. It has not been unknown for a good conference presentation to make a major impact on someone's career progression. In Chapters 29 and 30 Doug Watts and Paul White provide guidance on writing and presenting conference and seminar papers which will hopefully help research students attain a good professional standard. The first part of Chapter 29 focuses on giving oral presentations and provides valuable tips about how to present conference papers, including ways to handle discussions and questions and coping with nerves. Since it is increasingly common for postgraduate conferences to require participants to give poster rather than oral presentations, the second part of this chapter is concerned with outlining the skills and techniques students need to be able to construct comprehensive and well-organized posters.

The theme of the final chapter is a subject which is very prominent in the minds of most academics – getting published. Publishing refereed journal articles is increasingly used as an important measure of quality for academics. Indeed in some disciplines the quality of a PhD is judged by the potential of the material it contains being published as refereed journal articles. It is also increasingly common when academics apply for research funding to provide details about how they are going to disseminate their findings to academic and non-academic audiences. Learning how to write in a variety of different styles is therefore an important skill for academics to acquire. In Chapter 30 Doug Watts and Paul White provide detailed and valuable advice about publication strategies. Issues covered include the process of planning for publication; choosing possible publication outlets; writing styles required by different types of journals; and the refereeing process. By way of a practical example they also supply publication outputs from one of their research projects which provides research students with an indication of the publication possibilities for their own research.

## SUPPLEMENTARY READING

Becker, H.S. (1986) *Writing for Social Scientists*. Chicago: University of Chicago Press.
Smedley, C.S. (1993) *Getting Your Book Published*. London: Sage.
Thyer, B.A. (1994) *Successful Publishing in Scholarly Journals*. London: Sage.
Wolcott, H.F. (1990) *Writing Up Qualitative Research*. London: Sage.

# 28 WRITING A THESIS

*Dawn Burton*

For many students the prospect of writing a PhD thesis can be daunting. Few individuals will have previously written such a substantial piece of work and for many academics it is the longest single publication written during the course of their careers. Furthermore, the skills required to write a thesis are not necessarily the same as those required for writing at undergraduate level. Torrance *et al.* (1993: 170) have drawn attention to this issue: 'Writing a thesis requires not only the ability to generate and organise considerably more content than is necessary for writing at an undergraduate level but also greater knowledge of the discourse and conventions of the academic community for whom the thesis is being written.' Despite the uniqueness of writing a PhD thesis, there are few texts which are entirely devoted to this issue. More typical of the type of literature available is Becker's (1986) *Writing for Social Scientists*, a general text about writing which also contains useful material about writing a thesis. Other sources are more general books about studying for a PhD, such as Phillip and Pugh's (1993) *How to Get a PhD* which has a small section on writing. The shortage of texts which focus on writing a thesis is further exacerbated by a lack of adequate training at the graduate level aimed at developing students' writing skills. Where such provision does exist, there is often a lack of consensus about which approaches work best (Torrance *et al.*, 1993).

The marginalization of writing skills as an important issue in studying for a research degree very often results in research students having to learn by trial and error and by word of mouth. Obviously this is not a satisfactory situation because difficulties with writing can have important repercussions, such as students producing poor quality text, not submitting on time, or in extreme cases failing to complete a thesis. In many cases it is also evident that the longer it takes students to complete a thesis, the greater the probability that factors external to the research will hinder progress such as entering employment and financial hardship (see Hockey, 1991 for an extended discussion).

The purpose of this chapter is to provide an insight into some of the issues that research students raise about writing a thesis and to suggest some ideas about how students can help themselves. A number of issues are addressed: the differences between writing assignments on taught courses and research-based writing; the defining qualities of a good thesis; structuring a thesis; confidence, risk and trust as important issues in

writing; using word processors in the writing process; and making appropriate timetabling plans.

## DIFFERENCES BETWEEN WRITING ON TAUGHT COURSES AND WRITING A THESIS

Many research students are concerned about what can often be the
daunting prospect of physically writing a PhD thesis. This is especially the
case for students who have previously not written a dissertation. In
attempting to get to grips with what is required it is often useful to
compare some of the characteristics of writing assignments on taught
courses and the writing required for a thesis (see Table 28.1). On taught
courses students are required to write fairly short assignments usually of
the order of 2,000 to 5,000 words. The writing length required at thesis
level is longer so, for example, thesis chapters are frequently between 5,000
and 8,000 words in length. Many journal articles in the social sciences are
of the order of 8,000 words long. The psychological challenge to write
more words on a particular issue can be eased by rethinking and critically
evaluating your own writing practices. It often helps to write short sections
of text of may be 1,000 or 2,000 words under specific headings or related
themes. Most research students will find writing such short pieces of text
manageable and something which they feel confident about attempting. At
some later date the various pieces of work will hopefully fit together rather
like a jigsaw, perhaps to construct a chapter. The focus on writing a couple
of thousand words at a time takes the pressure out of writing long pieces
of text.

   Another distinction between writing assignments on taught courses and
research work is the number of drafts which a student might be expected
to revise. On taught courses students can get away with writing few drafts
if any at all. Students are able to adopt this strategy because, by comparison to PhD work, the concepts used in assignments are reasonably
easy to grasp. The heightened importance of quality in PhD work and
because it takes place over three or more years means that many drafts are
usually required as the work needs updating to take into account the most
recent debates. As a result, research writing tends to be revised much
more than taught course assignments. The issue of getting it right first time
is rarely attained in good quality academic work. It is not usual for
academics to rewrite journal articles eight to ten times (Becker, 1986).
Research students have to acknowledge and accept that frequent revisions
are the norm throughout the life of a thesis. This said, it is not necessarily
good practice to spend time constantly revising a small number of words
and aiming for perfection. It is a far better strategy to get to the stage of
writing chapters that you are fairly happy with and then moving on to
write new material. Spending lots of time revising and re-revising early on
is something which is not advisable. A piece of text which seems perfect at

**TABLE 28.1** Some of the differences between writing on taught courses and writing a thesis

| Taught courses | Thesis |
|---|---|
| Short pieces of work | Chapters or papers |
| Few drafts (if any) | Many drafts |
| Can work out paper as you write | Ideas too complex to write out straight off |
| One-off assignments | Papers all related to build a thesis |
| Papers contain rather basic data | Papers contain a large amount of complex data |
| Writing schedules are imposed | Few (if any) writing schedules imposed |
| Writing focus is highly structured | Students impose own writing focus |
| Feedback minimal | Feedback should be considerable |
| Not always necessary to word process | Essential to word process |

one point in time might appear highly flawed some months later, partly because your writing skills will hopefully have improved and because debates have changed. Revisions will be required until the very day you hand your completed thesis in to be bound.

Another set of concerns for research students relates to the relatively unstructured nature of PhD work compared with highly organized taught course provision. As students on taught courses you are told what you should write about via lists of essay titles. Students are given reading lists to consult which indicate what material should be incorporated into the assignment. Deadlines provide an incentive to hand work in on time and a mark or grade for the assignment provides a clear indication of the quality of the work and provides a point of direct comparison with other students. Research work gives over the responsibility of the writing focus and schedule to the student. It is extremely important that research students take on this responsibility at an early stage. Supervisors should be available to provide guidance on many of these issues such as appropriate reading and how much work it is reasonable to expect in a specific period of time. However, at the end of the day the responsibility for writing the thesis lies with the research student. The feedback which supervisors should provide for their research students will hopefully be comprehensive and useful and therefore facilitate the writing process.

## STRUCTURING A THESIS

Getting to grips with writing such a large number of words can be facilitated by having a clear structure to work with. The most useful single activity research students can undertake to get a feel for how a thesis should be organized is to go and take a look at one, or preferably more than one completed thesis. If possible you should choose a recently completed thesis in your own subject area, since the form can vary over time and between disciplines. There is no one best way to write a thesis and having a look at a few will provide some ideas about the possibilities. Most students feel that taking the opportunity to read and physically hold a thesis gives them confidence that the production of such a substantial piece of work is in fact possible. Having indicated that a thesis can take a number of forms depending on the discipline and nature of the thesis, there are nevertheless several essential elements in an empirically based thesis (a theoretically based piece of work will obviously contain different elements). The way a thesis is organized usually conforms to the following structure:

- Introduction
- Literature review
- Methods section
- Results chapters
- Conclusion
- Bibliography

## Introduction

The purpose of the introduction is to provide an overview of the thesis, outlining what material is included in each chapter. To get an idea of what is needed, it is a good idea to read an introductory section to a book in which the author outlines the main themes of each of the chapters. The format for an introductory section is at its most obvious in an edited collection, because the editor has to make the whole thing hang together.

## Literature review

The literature review should provide a thorough analysis of all the relevant and up-to-date works concerning the research project. Although one might imagine that this is a clear objective it is not unknown for students to fail to understand what is required and interpret the concept of the literature review in different ways (Bruce, 1994). It is important to make sure you obtain very clear guidance from your supervisor(s) on this issue. The literature review should be developed thematically and must address theoretical debates. It should be a critical and analytical overview of the existing literature. By the end of the literature review the main debates to be addressed should have been identified, which in turn provides a framework for thesis. By way of a check list, Bruce (1994: 227–228) gives a list of questions which students should ask themselves from time to time about their literature review:

- What is the present state of my list of references? Is it up to date in my areas of present interest? Is it adequate?
- What literature searching have I done this fortnight? Are there any new areas in which I have become interested that I may need to search on?
- What have I read recently?

- What have I learned from the literature this fortnight? Have I changed, in any way, my understanding of the area in which I am working?
- Is what I have read going to influence my research in any way? Has it given me any ideas which I need to consider and incorporate?
- Have I been writing about what I have read? Do I need to reconsider how what I have been reading fits into my research?

## Methods section

Research students often underestimate the importance of the methods section, yet it is one of the most crucial chapters in the whole thesis. There is a tendency for students to give far more importance to advancing theoretical debates and analysing empirical data rather than spending time discussing methods and methodology. The methods section of a thesis should contain information about the methods used and why. It is important clearly to state why some methods have been used rather than others. In this discussion previous research and literature should be critically evaluated and cited as appropriate. If the research strategy is flawed and the methods used are inappropriate, the data and therefore the arguments in the thesis will be undermined. Being asked about the methods used is a favourite viva question. Students should have thoroughly thought through not only why they chose to use the method(s) contained in the thesis, but also why they discarded others.

## Results chapters

The results of the research will form the main body of the thesis. Chapters should take various aspects of your findings and integrate them with current theoretical debates and previous research findings. There should be a strong focus on argument and debate, not just listing results.

## Conclusion

The conclusion should provide an overall discussion of the research findings and how they have developed academic debate in the chosen area. Someone should be able to read a thesis conclusion and know what the thesis is about. If the research project has been of good quality, it should have raised issues for further research. These areas should be set out as possible future projects.

## Bibliography

By looking at a bibliography an expert will get a feel for the quality of work. Students need to make sure and double-sure that they have reviewed the literature very well indeed. Bibliographies can take a long time to compile if they are not constructed as the thesis progresses. The length of bibliographies varies enormously, depending on how much previous work has been written in the area and how competently literature searches have been conducted.

Once a structure for the thesis has been planned, the next issue which tends to concern students is the number of words which should be allocated to each of the sections. The number of words a thesis should contain is a point which has been much debated. There does appear to be a reduction in the length of a thesis in recent years, partly as a consequence of students having to undertake significant amounts of research training. O'Brien (1995: 11) describes a thesis as an artefact which is 'immediately recognizable as a word-processed script of some 80,000 to 100,000 words'. However, the reality is that there is no regulation word length which is applicable across all disciplines, even within the social sciences. The Economic and Social Research Council (ESRC) has indicated that a thesis which they are funding should contain 70–80,000 words. Many social science departments in British universities use the ESRC guidelines as the standard for all theses. This standard has also been adopted by many professional bodies. For example, the British Psychological Society has suggested that a PhD should be no longer than necessary, typically of around 75–80,000 words, with an absolute maximum of 100,000 words. It is important that research students write no more than absolutely necessary. It is far better to write 70,000 words that are informative and to the point than 100,000 words which contain a great deal of extra material which is surplus to requirements.

There is no definitive answer to the question of how many words should be allocated to each section since all theses are unique pieces of work in their own right. However, an example of a word count for a thesis might be:

| | |
|---|---|
| Introduction | 3,000 |
| Literature review | 10,000 |
| Methods | 5,000 |
| Results | 45,000 (5 chapters × 9,000 words) |
| Conclusion | 7,000 |
| Total | 70,000 + Bibliography |

The main considerations should be that the thesis is well balanced, with the findings taking up most of the words. The thesis should be coherent, have a clear structure and be well written.

**TABLE 28.2  Potential source of originality in a PhD thesis**

| Type of originality | Definition |
|---|---|
| Originality in tools, techniques and procedures | Selection, development and testing of specific procedures, tools and techniques could be the basis of originality |
| Originality in exploring the unknown | If the area of investigation has not previously been research, its exploration will meet the criteria of originality |
| Originality in exploring the unanticipated | While a particular area might have been researched previously along the way an opportunity may arise for investigation which was not planned but nevertheless is original |
| Originality in the use of data | Using data to develop a new theory or a verification or extension of an existing one |
| Originality in outcomes | Outcomes might not be original in absolute terms; they can be new to the situation, for example, applying tools, techniques and theories from one area of study to another |
| Originality in by-products | Research strategies may go so wrong that the research needs to be abandoned. Nevertheless, problems can be documented and used to reformulate or refocus research in a given area and in so doing generate original material |

Source: Adapted from Cryer, 1997.

## DEFINING CHARACTERISTICS OF A QUALITY THESIS

The unique defining characteristic of a good quality thesis is that it makes an original contribution to knowledge in a particular field of academic enquiry. However, the concept of originality can be operationalized in a number of different ways. Cryer (1997) identifies six main ways in which originality can be understood which are set out in Table 28.2 and include: originality in the use of tools, techniques and procedures; originality in exploring the unknown; originality in exploring the unanticipated; originality in the use of data; originality in outcomes; originality in by-products. What strategy is adopted to incorporate the concept of originality within a thesis will usually be generated from a thorough review of the relevant literature. If undertaken competently the literature review should indicate where 'gaps' exist. The next step will be to design a project to address those gaps and thus make an original contribution to knowledge. On completing your PhD you should know enough about your research area to be designated an expert (albeit that you are at an early stage in your academic career).

Another major issue involved in writing a thesis is quality. Meloy (1994) has provided some useful issues which might be useful for students to think about concerning the quality of their own thesis (see Table 28.3).

**TABLE 28.3   Criteria for judging quality research**

| Criteria | Questions to address |
|---|---|
| Verité | Does the work ring true? Is it consistent with accepted knowledge in the field? Or if it departs, does it address why? Does it fit within the context of the literature? Is it intellectually honest and authentic? |
| Integrity | Is the work structurally sound? Does it hang together? In a piece of research, is the design or research rationale logical, appropriate and identifiable within a paradigm? |
| Rigour | Is there sufficient depth of intellect, rather than superficial or simplistic reasoning? |
| Utility | Usefulness, professionally relevant. Does it make a contribution to the field? Does the piece have a clearly recognizable professional audience? |
| Vitality | Is it important, meaningful, non-trivial? Does it have a sense of vibrancy, intensity, excitement of discovery? Is the proper persona used for the researcher or author? Do metaphors, images or visuals communicate powerfully? |
| Aesthetics | Is it enriching, pleasing to anticipate and experience? Does it give me insight into some universal part of my educational self? Does it touch my spirit in some way? |

*Source:* Meloy, 1994: 44–45.

Some disciplines judge the quality of a thesis by the potential to publish the contents as articles in refereed journals. The British Psychological Society specifies that an acceptable thesis should have material which can be worked up into at least two good quality, refereed journal articles. Obviously if a student has had articles accepted by a refereed journal prior to submitting their thesis then, according to this requirement, they have achieved one of the elements of quality of a PhD. Other academics judge the quality of a PhD in terms of its potential in being published as a book (O'Brien, 1995). However, it does need to be recognized that the status of books, as opposed to articles, varies considerably across social science disciplines.

Part of the challenge of writing a PhD and an indicator of its quality is that it should be written in an academic style which is distinctive. Becker (1986) argues that one of the ways in which research students attain the goal of becoming a professional academic is through their writing. Writing plain English prose is not distinctive enough, for anyone can do that. Rather students should copy the style in which journal articles and books are written to signal that they are members of the academic 'club'. He acknowledges and articulates this issue, rather controversially one might add:

> Living as an intellectual or academic makes people want to appear smart, in the sense of clever or intelligent, to themselves and others. But not only smart. They want to appear knowledgeable or worldly or sophisticated or down-home or professional – all sorts of things, many of which they can hint at in the details of their writing. They hope that being taken for such a person will make what they say believable. We can explore what people mean when they talk or think about writing in a 'classy' way, or in any other way, through the idea of a *persona*. (Becker, 1986: 31–32)

Becker goes on to develop the idea of a persona further and argues that the adoption of a particular persona affects the very words that we use in our writing. So the 'classy' persona (which many academics adopt) 'leads us to use the fancy language, big words for little ones, esoteric words for commonplace ones, and elaborate sentences making subtle distinctions'. Supervisors are best placed to provide guidance on appropriate writing style and their views should be sought early on. This advice particularly applies to overseas students who are unfamiliar with Anglo-Celtic writing styles with their preference for linear structures, an emphasis on relevance and intolerance of digressions (Nightingale, 1991).

It does need to be acknowledged that the perception of writing quality is the outcome of highly subjective and political processes (see also Chapter 18 on writing up qualitative research). This issue is at its most obvious where research is funded by a sponsor who is also an end user. Lyon (1995: 536) has indicated that conflicts over the 'ownership' of research can lead to difficulties over 'problem definition, choice of research strategies and forms of writing up', with supervisors experiencing conflicts between 'the academic and the administrative mode of research and writing up'. One of the issues that is very often unexplored is the various conflicts between interested parties and the unequal distribution of power when it comes to enforcing one's views about ways in which research findings are presented. Research students who are involved in projects that are funded by a sponsor would be well advised to discuss the writing up of research as an issue with their supervisor(s) before they start the project.

## CONFIDENCE, RISK TAKING AND TRUST AS IMPORTANT ISSUES IN WRITING

The biggest barrier for many students in failing to write or to make progress in writing is lack of confidence. Writing and having someone evaluate your work is always a nerve-racking process and this is more so when studying for a high level qualification in a subject area which is very specific. You have to learn to have confidence in yourself and not doubt that you can write a PhD. If you are having difficulties, view them as a temporary setback which is there to be overcome. The most important thing is to be able to source appropriate help when you need it. Having your work open to scrutiny is part of academic life and the more you have your work evaluated, the more likely you are to progress. However, having your work evaluated by others is about risk taking. It is about risking whether someone in a superior position to yourself, such as your supervisor, will think your work is poor and not up to standard. This feeling of uncertainty is made all the worse because of the lack of direct peer comparison through being given a mark, percentage or grade. This sentiment and how to deal with it has been articulated by one academic at the beginning of their career:

As I write more and more, I begin to understand that it's not all or nothing. If I actually write something down, I'm liable to win a bit and lose a bit. For a long time I worked under the burden of thinking that it was an all or nothing proposition. What got written had to be priceless literary pearls or unmitigated garbage. Not so. It's just a bunch of stuff, more or less sorted into an argument. Some of it's good, some of it isn't. (cited in Becker 1986: 120)

All academics have had to go through the process of having their work critically assessed at some time in their careers. Indeed for most academics critical assessment is an ongoing process via the peer review of research proposals, articles and conference presentations (see Chapter 29), so as a research student you are likely to get a sympathetic hearing. If it helps, view the writing you undertake during the early stages of the thesis as drafts to be improved later. Writing 'draft' at the top of a paper signals to the reader that it is an example of work in progress and can be a good psychological strategy to take the pressure off. Starting with a piece of writing which you find quite easy or something in which you are very interested is also a good strategy. Writing chapter introductions is often quite difficult so it may be a good idea to leave them until the chapter is well under way, or indeed to the end when you know what it contains.

Trust can be an issue, particularly once you have collected all of your data and are writing up final versions. At that stage it is probably best to confine your work to a very close circle that is actively involved in your project. Should you wish to present your work to a wider audience, then you would be well advised to write it as a publication (working paper, seminar paper, journal article) that can be attributed to you and which you can copyright.

Your supervisor(s) will probably have a large number of publications to their credit. Many of them will have been involved in refereeing journal articles, research proposals and book outlines. Most will have supervised research students before and may have acted as internal or external PhD examiners. The vast majority of supervisors will therefore have a very advanced knowledge of styles of writing and different standards of writing competence. You must use your supervisors as much as possible; they will be willing to help you. But before they can help you with your writing you must first produce something for them to read. You should try to do this as soon and as often as possible. Once you have produced a piece of work you need to make the most of your supervision. There are various things you should know about the level of expertise of your writing upon which you should ask your supervisors to comment:

- Does the reader understand your account? Are you writing in a clear, uncomplicated manner?
- Are you addressing debates in a systematic way – as a method of structuring your work?
- Are you evaluating other work or merely stating findings?

- Are you reviewing the 'quality' literature?
- Is your account up to date?
- Is your account user friendly, e.g. can the reader find tables, figures and graphs and understand them without effort?
- What do you need to do to improve it?

Make sure you get feedback regularly, and if possible to an agreed time scale. It is good practice to have your work assessed, read the comments and then make an appointment to see your supervisor to go through some of the finer details.

## USING A WORD PROCESSOR FOR WRITING

Handwritten text is not acceptable when submitting a thesis; as a result you will have to word process your work at some stage. The key issue is when text should be word processed. Supervisors will usually insist that draft chapters are word processed from the start because it makes them easier to read. The development of word-processing skills is therefore something which research students should cultivate from the start of their research degree. How people interface with word processors is variable, but it is certainly the case that cultivating the skills required to compose straight onto a word processor could save you a lot of time in the long run, although time consuming and laborious in the short term. Composing direct onto a screen is liberating in the sense that text can be changed around and inappropriate text deleted at will. Other advantages are that 'it frees you from the discouragement of crossing out, discarding false starts and seeing a growing heap of crumpled bits of paper around the waste-paper basket' (Orna and Stevens, 1997: 173). The ability to spell check, replace words throughout the whole text and to reformat huge portions of text are also considerable advantages.

Despite the considerable advantages of composing direct onto a screen Fischer (1995) notes several risks that can be involved. The first is that authors tend to think in terms of notional pages and paragraph length. Problems arise because few computers actually show full pages of text. As a result researchers can fall into the trap of writing more briefly and in a coded manner. A solution to this problem is to print out text on a regular basis. A second issue relates to some of the negative consequences of being able to change and re-use text. Word processing allows text to be used again and again which raises the temptation for authors to re-use earlier text. Although this is a practice which saves time, it almost always leads to a decline in quality of the finished product. Third, the ability to import on-line information from a range of other sources is becoming increasingly common, especially given the huge amount of material on the Internet. There is clearly a case for critically evaluating whether such a practice is always a good strategy. A fourth issue relates to the reliability of the technology. It is always a good practice to have multiple back-up copies of files and also hard copies just in case the technology fails. Most researchers have tales to tell about losing text and having to recover it at some time or another. It is a good idea to be well prepared for this eventuality. Finally, there are physical hazards which arise as a result of using technology. Prolonged use of a computer combined with a poor ergonomic position can lead to serious strain injuries. Extensive use of computer monitors can also damage eyes since they emit small amounts of magnetic radiation.

Researchers need to be aware of the advantages and disadvantages which can arise as a result of composing straight onto a screen. That said, most academics who have cultivated the requisite skills would not work any other way. Students new to the process can help themselves by learning keyboarding skills. This should not be too difficult to organize since most universities provide appropriate courses. The aim should be to set modest targets at first by composing paragraphs and short sections which help to build up confidence. It will take some practice and though a slow process at first it is worth persevering.

## TIMETABLING THE WRITING OF A THESIS

There is some debate about when a thesis should be written up. The main division is whether writing up should be undertaken as the project progresses, or at the end when all the design, data collection and analyses have been undertaken. Phillip and Pugh (1993) suggest a schedule for writing up which is displayed in Figure 28.1.

It needs to be said that there is no right or wrong way about whether students should write up as they go along or at the end, as Phillip and Pugh suggest. Students who write up at the end usually prefer to do so because by that stage they have an overall picture of what the thesis contains, which helps to keep them focused during the writing up stage. A rather different perspective is advanced by Becker:

> If you start writing early in your research – before you have all your data, for instance – you can begin cleaning up your thinking sooner. Writing a draft without data makes clearer what you would like to discuss and, therefore, what data you will have to get. Writing can thus shape your research design. This differs from the more common notion that you do your research first and then 'write it up'. (Becker, 1986: 17–18)

Writing skills usually improve as students gain experience of writing. This is the reason why many supervisors encourage their students to start writing as soon as possible. It is sound advice to start writing early and writing often. Manageable targets should be set that you can reasonably attain. Setting demanding targets which push you too hard can be counter-productive and lead to depression and lack of confidence. Students need to

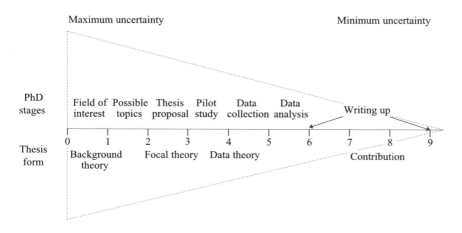

Maximum uncertainty                          Minimum uncertainty

PhD
stages

Field of  Possible  Thesis  Pilot    Data      Data
interest   topics   proposal  study  collection  analysis      Writing up

0       1        2       3       4      5        6       7       8       9

Thesis
form

Background          Focal theory    Data theory                Contribution
theory

Timescale in 'terms' (1 term = 4 months full time, 6 months part time)

**FIGURE 28.1   The PhD process as the progressive reduction of uncertainty (Phillip and Pugh, 1993)**

acknowledge that their 'rhythm of writing' can vary unpredictably (Creme and Lea, 1997). A huge amount of text might be written on one day, while on the next little might be achieved. Most of all students need to discover when are the best times in the day for them to write. Writing needs to be undertaken during periods of the day when an individual's thinking power is at optimum levels. By contrast, other parts of the day can be used for more mechanical sorting and checking jobs (Orna and Stevens, 1997).

Throughout the period of research it is important for students to keep copies of their writing. Even if these amount to a few pages of A4 on a particular topic or theme, keep them safe as they may form part of an interesting section later on. Old drafts also perform another function. They enable students to see that their writing skills, ideas and clarity of thought have developed. Students need continuous incentives when writing a PhD and having concrete evidence of improvement will help. This point is noted by Becker:

> You need to give the thoughts a physical embodiment, to put them down on paper. A thought written down (and not immediately thrown into the wastebasket) is stubborn, doesn't change its shape, can be compared with the other thoughts that come after it. You can only learn how few thoughts you really have if you write them all down, set them side by side and compare them. (Becker, 1986: 56)

Some students find it useful to keep an ideas book which they always have with them so if they come up with an interesting thought they can note it down.

Remember that drafts are being written up until the last few months when the final version is prepared for being assessed. It is at this point that major changes are likely to occur such as splitting one chapter into two, or deleting one or two chapters. The key to writing up on time is to write to a schedule. In planning a schedule leave extra time in case things go wrong, for example, illness or work and home commitments. Remember that time spent doing activities such as teaching and other forms of work will hinder writing progress. Pulling everything together at the end of the thesis always takes longer than students think. Leave plenty of time to polish up and collate a bibliography.

# 29 PRESENTATION SKILLS

## H. Doug Watts and Paul White

The dissemination and discussion of results is an important part of research activity and it is a common practice to present your preliminary findings at academic conferences. Research plans and very early results may also be presented at departmental or graduate school seminars. These seminars may be less formal than conference presentations but they do provide excellent opportunities to 'fine tune' presentation skills and to try out your ideas. In this chapter we introduce you to the nature of academic presentations and discuss two different forms of conference contributions: the oral presentation and the poster presentation.

## ACADEMIC CONFERENCES

Conferences provide opportunities for you to meet other researchers in your area (thus allowing you to begin building your own research network) and to present the findings of your own research. Information on forthcoming conferences of interest should be available from your supervisors. If they do not mention any, ask about them. Full-time students should watch departmental noticeboards or newsletters where circulars from conference organizers may be publicized. These 'calls for papers' are the starting point of most conferences. An example is shown in Box 29.1. If you belong to your subject association (such as the British Sociological Association, Political Studies Association, Royal Geographical Society, British Academy of Management) they will usually hold one or more meetings per year and will communicate with you direct.

Conference sessions may be a mix of oral presentations (in perhaps half-hour slots), poster presentations (displays of work in written/illustrated form) and informal workshops. A half-hour slot would usually be filled with a 20–25 minute presentation with some time for questions after the presentation. A number of conferences may offer only 15-minute time slots which often mean 10-minute presentations. Some conferences have slots especially designed for postgraduate presentations and most include some 'plenary sessions' often addressed by well-known figures in their field. Smaller conferences (perhaps 30–40 participants) usually run one series of presentations. Larger conferences (which can be of more than 1,000 participants) run a series of parallel sessions. You do not have to talk to

**Box 29.1   Example of a 'Call for Papers'**

### CALL FOR PAPERS

### URBAN GEOGRAPHY STUDY GROUP
### IBG 1996 STRATHCLYDE
### 3RD–6TH JANUARY

### GEOGRAPHY AND THE ENTREPRENEURIAL CITY:
**futures, strategies, perspectives**

It is commonly acknowledged that the government of urban areas has changed profoundly over the last fifteen years, with an increased reliance on 'entrepreneurial' modes of governance. Such entrepreneurial strategies have seen shifts in the nature of the public sector taking over roles once distinctive to the private sector; risk taking, inventiveness, promotion and profit motivation. These shifts have had profound impacts on urban lives at all levels producing an urban geography steeped in the ideals of economic growth rather than social justice. Geographers have begun to explore the nature of these impacts, and to contribute to debates surrounding the nature of our cities. This session will therefore provide an opportunity to consider how geography is responding to modern urban change and how debates surrounding the entrepreneurial city have changed the way in which geographers have interpreted 'the urban'. Papers are thus invited which relate to one or more of the following themes:

Urban planning and changing modes of urban governance
Culture, capital and the entrepreneurial city
Social justice and the new urban politics
Prospects for urban policy and practice
New urban geographies?

The aim of the session will thus be an assessment of where we stand within debates surrounding the entrepreneurial city, and a consideration of what lessons can be learnt for the city of the future.

In the first instance, please send an abstract of up to 300 words, to either Tim Hall, Department of Geography and Geology, Cheltenham and Gloucester College of Higher Education, Francis Close Hall, Swindon Road, Cheltenham, Gloucestershire, GL50 4AZ (01242 532971) or Phil Hubbard, Division of Geography, University of Coventry, Priory Street, Coventry, West Midlands, CV1 5FB (01203 838500).

1,000 people. The parallel sessions provide a small forum of 20–30 people to listen to any one paper. Larger sessions are often for 'keynote' papers by leading researchers. In your first year of research it is well worth attending your major subject conference to get an idea of the standards and to listen to the work of other researchers. It is much less nerve-racking if you have a 'feel' for a conference before you attend to present your own paper. You may be amazed at the low standard of some of the presentations.

Paper titles, abstracts or full papers are submitted to conference organizers for selection. Exactly what is required varies from conference to conference. The degree of formality in the selection procedures varies. In some cases there will be a full refereeing process (resulting in what are sometimes called 'refereed track papers'). For other conferences selection will be in relation to the conference topic/themes: occasionally everything submitted will be accepted (apart from the obviously bizarre). Where a refereeing process is involved the procedures are similar to those described for refereed papers in Chapter 30. Where the full refereeing process is followed you may be required to submit a full paper at least six months before the conference; other methods of selection often require only an abstract of a specified length. However, it is nevertheless useful to prepare a full copy of your paper and to take photocopies of this to the conference for distribution after your presentation. The reason for this timing is discussed later.

The output of a conference can take a number of forms. Most larger conferences now produce a volume or CR-Rom of abstracts. An example is provided in Box 29.2. This does not normally count as a publication in terms of your curriculum vitae. A volume of conference proceedings (unrefereed) may be produced as well as or instead of the abstracts. Although such proceedings are seen as a form of publication, they are not highly regarded. The most prestigious form of output that can emerge from a conference is a volume of refereed conference proceedings. This is a useful form of publication but generally of lesser 'status' in the English-speaking world than the refereed papers in international journals discussed in Chapter 30.

It is quite permissible to submit papers published in conference proceedings to academic journals. As will be argued below, conferences are good places to present early or preliminary results and the final paper submitted for publication will contain revisions arising from more detailed analysis and from points made in conference discussions.

## ORAL PRESENTATIONS

Although the focus here is on presenting a paper at a conference, much of the advice that follows can also be put into practice in any departmental seminar you present, right from the earliest stages of your research. Making an oral presentation can seem extremely daunting at first, but with a bit of thought it can be an extremely profitable and enjoyable experience. Here we consider the following issues:

- The paper
- Presentation skills
- Illustrative materials
- Foreign language presentations
- Handling discussion
- Coping with nerves

**Box 29.2  A typical page from a volume of abstracts (Association of American Geographers, Chicago meeting, 1995)**

set and a 1 value is a member of the set. Intermediate values 0.67 for example, represent a possibility of membership in the set. Using fuzzy sets as a mathematical base, geographic features such as hills, valleys, air pollution zones, and others, can be accurately represented and used in spatial analysis. Fuzzy set representation of geographic features requires fuzzy extensions to basic GIS operations such as spatial buffering, overlay, and boundary. This presentation examines several geographic features represented as fuzzy sets with the corresponding fuzzy GIS operations.

Keyword: representation, fuzzy sets, GIS

**Thomas R. Vale, Department of Geography, University of Wisconsin, Madison, WI 53706-1491. Historical Contingency and Sense of place in Yosemite National Park, California.**

The concept of national parks as unique places rather than generic natural space, a theme developed by Meyer, depends upon human history for the creation of park singularities. Various human activities contribute to the formulation of these differences, including the purposes of organizations, the goals of management, and the perceptions in literature. As in all matters historical, contingency plays a major role in the imagery of parks as places. A historical evaluation of Yosemite National Park (presented as a counter factual analysis) suggests the role of chance in park boundary, road system and recreational development. Given only slightly different circumstances in the human past, these characteristics likely would be vastly different today, thereby altering the imagery of the place we call Yosemite.

Recognition of the importance of place seems to encourage spatial differences but temporal continuity in park policy; acceptance of historical contingency accentuates variability in both perspectives.

Keyword: national parks, historical geography, Yosemite.

**Gill Valentine, Department of Geography, University of Sheffield, Winter Street, Sheffield, S10 2TN, UK. Parental Concerns for Children's Safety in Urban Neighbourhoods.**

Fear of crime is a social issue high on the public agenda. In particular, the sexual assault and murder of three children last summer contributed to a climate of concern about children's safety in urban neighbourhoods typified by newspaper articles such as 'Play Safe and Keep Your Child Free of a Monster' (Daily Express). This paper therefore aims to examine the nature and extent of parents' concerns for their children's safety. Consideration is given to how 'Stranger-Danger' fears are constructed, reproduced, mobilized and how parents attempt to restrict or control their children's use of space in city environments. The different roles of mothers and fathers in this process are explored and attention is paid to how parents' controls vary according to the gender of the child and the nature of the physical and social environment in which the 'family' live. The findings are based on a large scale questionnaire survey, in-depth interviews, and small group discussions which were carried out in Manchester, UK.

Keyword: children's safety, urban neighbourhoods, fears of crime, gender.

Manuel Valenzuela and Irasema Coronado, El Colegio de la Frontera Norte, 84020 Nogales, Sonora, Mexico. Binational Elites and New Forms of Transborder Linkages of Capital in the Sonora-Arizona Region.

Traditionally, in frontier areas, international laws have not been able to limit binational economic and political groups' activities even under conditions of national and protectionist policies. This has been the situation in the Sonora-Arizona region, and specifically in the twin cities of Nogales, Sonora and Nogales, Arizona where binational elite were able to gain economic profits on both sides of the border.

With the opening of Mexican economy in the middle of the last decade and specifically within the NAFTA framework, the space of the binational elites has widened. New forms of linkages of transborder capital have developed in order to capture emerging markets. This paper analyses the economic and political issues and tries to predict future effects on transborder relations.

Keyword: binational elite, transborder linkages, Sonora-Arizona border.

Herman van der Wusten, Virginie Mamadou, Nico Passchier, Department of Geography, University of Amsterdam, Amsterdam, NL 1018 VZ. Was 1994 a Critical Election in the Dutch Polity?

In terms of geographical voting patterns the history of Dutch electoral mass politics could so far be subdivided in three periods: the emergence of mass parties, 1888-1913; the predominance of polarization, 1918-1963; the re-emergence of multiple liberalism, 1967-1989. The analysis of electoral maps indicated definite shifts around WW1 and during the 1960's. These results were corroborated by significant changes in other aspects of the Dutch polity at these junctures. In 1994 the two liberal parties made new important gains in the national elections defeating christian democrats and social democrats. A new cabinet has been formed without christian democrat ministers for the first time since 1918. The major question to be answered is: do we see significant shifts on the electoral map indicating the onset of a fourth period in the history of Dutch electoral mass politics? The paper then speculates on the possible shape of a new pattern and its implications for the future of the Dutch polity. It tries to interpret and explain Dutch electoral dynamics by invoking Dutch electoral history as a distinctive experience among West European polities and the nature of current social pressures in the direction of postmodernity.

Keyword: electoral geography, the Netherlands.

Marina van Geenhuizen and Peter Nijkamp, Regional, Urban and Environmental Economics, Free University, NL-1081 HV Amsterdam, The Netherlands, Transborder Networking: Corporate Strategies and Regional Development in Eastern Europe.

Currently we are witnessing the disappearance of many man-made borders, exemplified by the opening up of the East European power block. At the same time, an increased international cooperation seems to prelude a gradual removal of unnecessary obstacles between the countries concerned. Whether this leads to an open society for the benefit of all actors remains, however, to be seen. In view of this, it is a fascinating research question – what the relationship is between political borders, barriers and regional development of Eastern Europe.

This paper will address the issue of cooperation in East European border regions from the perspective of West European companies based on a blend of applied studies. The paper contributes first to the conceptual discussion on borders and barriers (Section 2) and the influence of border barriers on regional development. Furthermore, the paper explores empirically trans-border cooperation in Eastern Europe (Section 3). The paper will proceed with a discussion of factors that cause a differentiation in regional development in border areas in Eastern Europe (Section 4). I will conclude with a number of scenarios for these border areas (Section 5).

Keyword: border barriers, Eastern Europe, investment scenario.

**George A.Van Otten and Megan K.Davis, Department of Geography and Planning, Northern Arizona University, Flagstaff, AZ 86011. Email:    mkd@alpine.for.nau.edu. Conflict Over Public Land Management in Rural Northeastern Arizona.**

Conflict between local communities in rural northeastern Arizona and various federal land management agencies is becoming increasingly volatile. Ranchers, loggers, as well as state and county leaders believe that the implementation of federal environmental legislation often threatens the free enterprise system in the western states and endangers the traditional customs and culture of the region. Many country and state leaders seek to significantly expand local control over the public land management process. For example, Arizona Governor Fife Symington recently proposed that the federal government relinquish management of land in Arizona that is now administered by the National Forest Service and the Bureau of Land Management to the state. The Governor believes that federal control of property in Arizona represents the antithesis of the essence of traditional American democracy and liberty. His philosophy is representative of many residents of rural northeastern Arizona who actively call for increased local control over public land management and in some cases, the transfer of public lands to the private sector. Local success in this endeavour would bring drastic and dramatic changes to the landscape of northeastern Arizona.

Keyword: conflict, control, public land.

Further discussion of some of these issues will be found in Elton (1983), Mathias (1991) and Hector-Taylor and Bonsall (1993). Much of the success of any conference depends on the preparation that has gone into the papers. The success of your paper will depend as much on what you do before as on how you present it on the day.

## The paper

Conference presentations can be of many different kinds. As a postgraduate student it is unlikely that you will be asked to give a position paper synthesizing research in a particular field, or to speak at a plenary session of a major gathering. It is much more likely that you will be expected (and will expect) to discuss your own research project to an audience of those interested in your topic, or in the research methods that you are using. The discussion which follows here is based on conference papers of this kind.

When your supervisor first suggests that you do a presentation at a conference, or you first see a notice asking for offers of papers for a meeting on your research field, your initial instinct will probably be to offer something that you are fully happy with and have finished – a section of the project that is complete. Think again! You can use the experience of giving a conference paper to further your work in a number of ways. A conference presentation should not just be about speaking to an audience, but should create a dialogue over your work. You can then benefit from the ideas, comments and reactions of your audience. If you present a completely finished piece of work one of two things might happen:

- The audience thinks it's interesting, but there's nothing they can really say other than that. You will come away with the glow that other people thought it was alright, but you haven't learned anything else.
- The audience think it's not good, that your research is flawed, or that the conclusions are trite. They tell you so, and you go away thinking you're back to square one with something that you thought you'd finished.

It is often much better, in giving one of the first conference papers from your project, to present incomplete work. In this way you can seek guidance from your audience and receive stimulus for thinking about the next stage in your work. The open-endedness of your work should lead to questions and to later discussion in the tearoom or the bar. In your paper you can direct that discussion towards particular issues on which you would like others' opinions by drawing attention to them. If you have a totally finished piece of work to offer you should be thinking about sending it off to a journal, not presenting it at a conference.

The title of your paper is obviously important: this will draw your audience to listen to you, particularly if there is no book of abstracts available to help their decisions on what to attend. Even if you have sent in an abstract for publication before the conference it is quite likely that few participants will have read what will often be a substantial volume of abstracts issued to them only at registration. While clever titles might look good on paper, it is better to go for a simple heading that accurately describes what you are going to talk about. As a beginner on the conference circuit you need to attract an audience through the potential interest of the subject matter that lies behind your title rather than through your existing reputation.

If you want your audience to remember your presentation as an interesting one you should emphasize your ideas, aims and conclusions. To do so is an exercise in getting to the heart of your topic and abstracting the main points. Unless you are specifically contributing to a session on methods you should only sketch these and not discuss them at length. You should avoid giving lots of detailed results: a paper that is heavy on such details is one that few will afterwards remember.

### Presentation skills

Give yourself plenty of time before the conference to prepare your paper. It is a good idea to have the paper written out in full (for potential distribution to the audience, see below), but you should also have a series of notes to talk from. Make sure these are legible and that you are totally familiar with the order in which you want to say things.

If you want your audience to go to sleep, read out the full text version you have prepared. There are few things more sleep-inducing for your audience (especially if you are giving the first paper after lunch) than for you to read directly the words you have written. Written language and spoken language use very different registers. Most people use much longer and more complex sentences when they write than when they speak. Use your notes or text as a guide, but talk to your audience in a more normal manner. Everyone accepts that the first time you attempt to talk like this from notes (rather than reading from a full text) you might be nervous. However, this is a presentation skill that needs to be learned if you are to become a skilled presenter. As we suggest below, the occasion on which you make your presentation at a conference should not be the first attempt at that presentation: it should have been practised first.

If you want your audience to leave, distribute the fully written out version of your paper at the start and then proceed to read from it word for word. Why should your audience stay? They can take your paper away and read it at their leisure. At many conferences you are asked to bring a number of copies of your paper for distribution. The best strategy for doing so is to say at the start of your presentation that copies of the full version of your paper will be available at the end if anyone wants to collect one from the front.

If you are distributing a paper, remember to add your full address to it, including your e-mail address if you have one, and some wording such as: *Not to be referred to without the permission of the author*. Also add the name of the conference at which you have made the presentation.

If your presentation will depend heavily on a few illustrations (tables, diagrams, graphs, etc.) it is a good idea to have copies of these for distribution to the audience at the outset of your talk. Such a procedure provides a cover for your presentation if there is a power failure involving the projection equipment: it also helps those who may not be able to see the screen clearly.

Ascertain from the conference organizer or the chair of your session well before the conference how long you will have for your presentation. Then plan accordingly and stick to it. To go beyond your time is ill-mannered to the audience and to the following speakers: you will also reduce the time available for discussion of your work, and therefore the benefit to yourself. Many chairs of sessions will indicate to speakers when there are only two minutes left – ask your chair if s/he will do that for you.

If you do find that you are running out of time, do not speed up. The best approach is normally to abort the presentation of your findings etc. and move straight to the conclusion. However, it is unlikely that you will mistime your paper if you practise it first. About two weeks before your paper ask a group of fellow postgraduates and your supervisor to listen to a rehearsal performance. Ask them to pay particular attention to the timing, to the logical flow of the paper and to the usefulness (and clarity) of any illustrative materials you are using (see also below). Ask them to be frank about what is needed. Get them to listen to the whole paper as you have prepared it – even if it is twice as long as it should be. Their comments will be invaluable in reducing it and you will then have sufficient time in which to do so. Ask them to fill in the sheet given as Box 29.3 and discuss it with you. This should aid the identification of weaknesses in your presentation style that you can then work on. Rehearsals sometimes show up presentations that last over an hour but which can then be cut down to 30 minutes, with no loss of clarity, through a series of simple adjustments.

Finally, when you get your rehearsal audience to listen to you, get them also to comment on visual distractions that you make. Think back through all the bad lectures you have been to and try not to emulate them. The list of things not to do is endless, but examples include:

- looking out of the window instead of at your audience;
- turning to face the overhead projector screen or blackboard and talking to it instead;
- crouching over the overhead projector and talking down at it;
- fiddling with part of your clothing (for example, a tie) or anatomy (for example, an earlobe);
- taking your glasses on and off;
- rattling jewellery;
- swaying to and fro, or from side to side.

### Illustrative material

It is a good idea to illustrate your talk in some way. Apart from anything else, this stops your audience from looking at you all the time. Illustrations can help you to get the main points across and can make the audience keep one set of information in mind (for example, concerning context) while you go on to talk about the next item.

**Box 29.3   Evaluation sheet for a trial presentation (Hector-Taylor and Bonsall, 1993)**

### STRUCTURE OF TALK

| | | | |
|---|---|---|---|
| Opening | Poor introduction, no outline | 1 2 3 4 5 | Good introduction and outline of presentation |
| Sequencing of material | Poor sequencing and linkage | 1 2 3 4 5 | Good sequencing – well linked |
| Coverage of material | Poor coverage of subject area. Main points not clearly 'signposted' | 1 2 3 4 5 | Subject area well covered. Clear 'signposting' of main points |
| Closing | Poor summary of content | 1 2 3 4 5 | Good summary of content |

### DELIVERY

| | | | |
|---|---|---|---|
| Appearance | Appears poorly prepared | 1 2 3 4 5 | Appears well prepared |
| Voice clarity | Monotonous and unclear | 1 2 3 4 5 | Varied speed and flow of speech, easy to understand |
| Stance/gestures | Appears nervous and uncomfortable, few gestures | 1 2 3 4 5 | Appears confident and comfortable, appropriate gestures |
| Eye contact with audience | Poor/inappropriate | 1 2 3 4 5 | Good/appropriate |
| Handling of audience | Talked up/down to audience | 1 2 3 4 5 | Appropriate level of speech for audience. Effective use of participation |
| Handling of visual aids | Poor/inappropriate | 1 2 3 4 5 | Effective/appropriate |
| Timing | Too long/short | 1 2 3 4 5 | Well timed to meet time limit |

### VISUAL AIDS

| | | | |
|---|---|---|---|
| Quality | Poorly prepared, hard to read | 1 2 3 4 5 | Well prepared, easy to read |
| Suitability | Do not fit well with talk | 1 2 3 4 5 | Fitted well with talk |

### QUESTION HANDLING

| | | | |
|---|---|---|---|
| Knowledge of subject | Poor knowledge of subject | 1 2 3 4 5 | Good knowledge of subject |
| Clarity and relevance of answers | Questions poorly answered | 1 2 3 4 5 | Questions well answered |
| GENERAL IMPRESSION | Very poor | 1 2 3 4 5 | Excellent |

COMMENTS

The range of illustrative materials that you might use is now very wide. Possibilities include:

- 35mm colour or black and white slides.
- The conventional overhead projector, for which you need material printed on special acetate sheets. You must be careful to use these special sheets, as ordinary 'write-on' acetates melt in photocopiers and then jam them. It is normal to print the materials you wish to use (whether in colour or black and white) onto paper and then photocopy them onto acetate. Some computer printers will successfully print direct onto acetates.
- The video overhead projector where your originals are videod and shown in real time on the screen. For this sort of projector you do not need acetates: material can be on ordinary sheets of paper. Small objects can also be displayed.
- Video.
- Audio illustration (e.g. from a cassette player or CD).
- Projection of a computer screen through some form of overhead or video projector. This might involve putting up ordinary screens from everyday programs, or the creation of special materials to support your presentation.

A number of presentations now use Powerpoint software. This is most frequently used to prepare conventional overhead transparencies. If you do follow this route be very careful in the use of some of the Powerpoint slide designs which can work well in colour but are sometimes less useful in black and white. Plain slides without decorative borders or geometric background material are often the most effective. Powerpoint can also be used direct from a PC. However, at the time of writing, only a small number of conference rooms have this facility available. You can, of course, take your own hardware. Powerpoint may be easier to use in your home institution where a LAN can provide a direct link from your Powerpoint files to the lecture theatre. Some very effective presentations can be made under these conditions.

We concentrate here on the first and second of these various media (i.e. 35mm slides and conventional overhead projector materials) since these are the ones most commonly used. You should ascertain from the conference organizers what illustrative infrastructure there will be in the room and plan your talk accordingly.

What might you use and how? Box 29.4 gives some detailed advice on this from a major American subject association.

The golden rule is not to use too much material. Cut out all items that are not relevant to your main purpose. This usually means that you will have to produce materials (particularly overhead transparencies) yourself, rather than using illustrations from already published works where some of what is shown is not relevant to you. It is difficult to find a bigger

**Box 29.4   Guidelines for effective visuals at professional meetings (*Newsletter of the Association of American Geographers*, July 1995, p. 5)**

**General Presentation**. Structure your presentation around graphics. A carefully prepared set of illustrations can serve as lecture text, notes, reminders, and as an aid to keeping the presentation on schedule.

Prepare your presentation beforehand. Hours of intellectual work can be ruined by transparencies out of order, upside-down slides or too many graphics for the time available. Rehearse and time yourself; make use of the speaker preparation room. Arrive for your session early enough to check the room size and the slide or overhead projector. Plan on a forward-only sequence; do not go backward – duplicate a slide you wish to refer back to and place the copies in sequence. Begin your presentation with a slide or transparency showing your paper title, name, affiliation, collaborators and acknowledgements. Follow this with an outline and finish with a visual summarising your conclusions.

Talk to your audience, not to your graphics. Whether shown by a slide or overhead projector, your graphics should be integrated into your presentation so well that you need only glance at them to verify that the correct graphic is on screen. If you wish to point to items on an illustration, use an overhead projector and face the audience as you identify specific elements of the graphic.

Ask yourself whether each graphic is really necessary. If a graphic is important enough to use, leave it on the screen long enough for the audience to read. Brief pauses for the audience to digest graphics may help comprehension. Do not remove the graphic and talk with a blank screen.

Colour adds interest and attracts attention. Check your local copy shop: colour transparencies and slides are not expensive, reduction and enlargement are easy, and copy quality is very high. Avoid garish colours, disappearing colours (yellow), and colours at opposite ends of the spectrum which 'jump' (for example, red on green). Also, be aware that a portion of the males in the audience may have red/green/brown colour blindness and that a colour combination such as a red dot on a green background may not be seen.

Graphics should not fill the whole display area. Leave gaps at the edges to allow for low screens and obstructed views. Never apologise for a graphic; if you constructed it well, you shouldn't have to.

**Text**. Text slides should have contrasting foreground and background. Use type no smaller than 16 points (there are 72 points to the inch), with no more than seven items or bullets per slide. Do not use more than two fonts or colours on a text slide. Use bold type, italics, underlining or colour to draw the audience's attention to ideas you want to highlight.

**Tables, Charts and Graphs**. Use only a few rows and columns and clearly label each. Include measurement units where necessary; metric units are preferred. Use colour, italics, underline or bold face to highlight numbers of importance. Keep tables and graphs simple and sparse; two simple ones are better than one that is complex. Use three-dimensional effects sparingly. Gaudy colours and fancy type fonts detract from the graphic.

Place no more than four simultaneous symbols, values, or lines on a graph or chart. Make each line or symbol clearly distinguishable from the rest and label it prominently. Make graph lines sufficiently bold to be visible from a distance. Use colour if possible. Avoid cross hatching and diagonal shading; little shading works better than too much shading.

*Prepared by the AAG Cartography Specialty Group*

turn-off for an audience than to put up a large table of statistics from a published volume and tell them that you only want them to look at two columns. Redraw such tables to make your points.

You may believe that your handwriting is legible and that you can therefore write overhead transparencies yourself, but these days there is no excuse for not using a word processor to produce professional looking materials. Remember, however, that a 12-point font size will almost certainly be illegible to anyone not sitting at the front. The minimum font size to use will depend on the room, but as a rule never use anything less than 16 point. It is better to have your font too big and use up more acetates than too small so that no one can read it (Figure 29.1).

---

- Word process a single sheet of paper with a variety of font sizes (10 point to 50 point) and styles.
- Make an acetate from it and display it in the largest lecture room you can find.
- What is the minimum size that you can read from the back of the lecture room?
- What is the optimum size and style for combining legibility with economy?

---

**FIGURE 29.1   Overhead transparencies**

If you intend to show colour slides use only the very best quality with high contrast: blackout facilities are often unsatisfactory and poor quality slides are then rendered invisible.

Make sure the notes for your presentation contain indications of when to use your illustrations and when to take them off. Have the illustrations themselves in the right order. A small number in the bottom right corner of overhead transparencies will help you keep track of them and if you drop them it is a quick exercise to re-sort. If you expect to use the same overhead more than once (for example, you may wish to remind listeners of the structure of your talk when you are halfway through and in your summing up) make extra copies. Too often speakers are to be seen fumbling in a file of overheads to find the one they want. Extra copies prevent this situation from arising. The loading of a slide cassette for a slide projector forces you to have your slides in the right order: again, if you want to use a slide twice have two copies of it rather than running in reverse through slides you have already shown.

While experienced presenters often use more than one source of illustrations in a talk, it is better to stick to one means of illustration if at all possible. You may feel that you want to use slides of people or places as well as text materials shown via an overhead projector, but you may find there are practical difficulties (for example, slides and overheads may have to share the same screen such that they cannot be used at the same time). Multimedia presentations are best kept for your own university (if you want to try them at all) where you can be confident of knowing the technical possibilities.

Work out in advance what you will do if the unthinkable happens and your visual aids fail (the bulb blows; the video won't work; there's a power cut; there's no black-out and you've based your talk on colour slides, etc.). If that happens you will get an instant wave of sympathy from the audience, but do not try to soldier on by saying 'if you could have seen the next transparency you would have seen in the top left-hand corner a value that seems out of line, etc.'. Instead move to those parts of your talk that do not need illustrating. Earlier in this chapter we suggested having paper copies of important diagrams and tables ready to distribute at the start if your talk is based around them.

Go to the lecture room well before the start of your session and make sure that you know where the relevant switches are and how to operate the equipment. Slide, video and overhead projectors vary widely in methods of operation. If there is a technician available ask her/him to run through what you should do. Pay very careful attention to the layout of the overhead projector and associated furniture. Is there somewhere to place your notes? Is there sufficient room to place the overheads you have used on a separate table? Does the slide projector have automatic or manual focusing and do you know how to operate it in the latter case? Can you speak into a microphone and use the overhead projector at the same time? Where should you stand to avoid hiding the screen on which images are projected? You will be amazed at how few well-designed lecture rooms there are in which such problems do not arise.

### Foreign language presentations

It is worth considering two issues here.

1   You may be asked to give a conference presentation in a language that is not your own. Your command of that language is certainly adequate, but you realize that sometimes you make less sense than you would wish.
2   You are scheduled to speak at a conference at which you know there will be a sizeable contingent of delegates whose first language is not the one in which the conference will take place.

Almost universally, those using second languages can follow written materials more easily than spoken materials. Therefore in both these cases you have a duty to your listeners and to yourself to facilitate communication by using both media – spoken and written. All headings, keywords and important points should be listed on overhead transparencies, which should be left up on the screen for as long as possible.

### Handling the discussion and questions

You have stood up and given the paper, talking naturally to the audience, who have listened respectfully, laughed at your attempts at jokes and have obviously followed the thread of your argument. Your illustrations have been clear and sensibly used. You glance at your watch and find that you have spoken for exactly the right length of time. Congratulations, but do not switch off yet. Keep the adrenaline flowing for a little longer.

Unless all discussion is being held for the end of a session, as soon as you finish your paper the chair will probably lead straight into discussion or questions. This is the time when you start to get the feedback and dialogue that you want on your paper. Sometimes a specific discussant will have been appointed to start the discussion on your paper. In such cases you will generally have been asked to provide a full copy of your paper to that individual (or via the conference organizers) before the meeting. Often there will be no such discussant, but questions will be invited from all present. Make notes of the points made and the questions as they are put to you. It is a good idea to get a friend in the audience to do the same and to make a note of your responses. You can then think over the issues raised later, at your leisure. If a question is difficult for the audience to hear (for example, because the questioner is sitting at the front and facing you) repeat it to the audience before you answer it. In answering all questions you should address the whole audience and not just the questioner.

Be brief in reply. Do not use question and discussion time to say all the things that you had to leave out of the main paper because time was short. If someone wants technical details on how you did something, or on some aspect of your analysis, offer to meet them after the session. This also means that you should not dash off immediately your session is finished. Almost certainly someone will want to have a word with you afterwards. Ask the chair or the convenor (who will probably know something about the topic, which is why they have those functions) if they have any observations or comments to offer you. You will often find that people who heard your paper will come up to you several hours (or even days) later to offer observations on your work. Such comments are usually extremely valuable because they are the product of reflection and not just of a quick reaction.

### Coping with nerves

Even the most experienced public speaker or lecturer gets nervous from time to time: this is a natural reaction that helps to stimulate the adrenaline which will speed up your reactions and result in a better presentation. The most important way of dealing with nerves is to practise the paper beforehand, as suggested above. A rehearsal with fellow students and your supervisor as the audience will enable you to develop confidence that the paper is pitched at the right level, that the illustrations are suitable and you know how to use them, that you will talk for the right length of time and that your presentation skills are effective. Your conference audience will be 'on your side' if it is clear that you have prepared for your presentation and thought hard about it in advance.

## POSTER PRESENTATIONS

In 1989 Smith argued that: 'Some people are born poster designers, some achieve great posters; but most of us have posters "thrust" upon us . . . accept the challenge. It need not be a daunting task.' In an academic context a poster is a self-contained summary of a research topic consisting of textual and graphic material fixed to a display board in a conference room. Some research students will have been involved in poster presentations at undergraduate level (Vulakovic, 1995). At graduate level the challenge in preparing a poster is to communicate your results effectively in a striking mix of text and graphics (e.g. graphs, charts, maps, pictures).

Many academic conferences have 'poster sessions' or 'poster presentations'. These are rarely refereed and the limits on the number of posters are usually the size of the room in which the posters are to be displayed. Poster presentations allow conference organizers to increase the number of 'presenters' without increasing the number of time slots. Cynics would argue that the system is a neat way of allowing as many people as possible to 'present' a paper without cluttering up the timetable. It also allows conference organizers to maximize attendance (and profit?) since many universities will only make a contribution to the conference expenses of participants who are presenting a paper.

There are two main ways in which posters may be presented at a conference. In the simplest format presenters are allocated an amount of space and asked to fix their poster in place by a specified time. This is often supplemented by a scheduled session when poster presenters are expected to stand by their posters to discuss their work. A more recent innovation is the 'illustrated paper' format. At the start of an illustrated paper session (lasting perhaps 90 minutes, with six to eight presenters) authors provide three- to five-minute overviews of their results indicating what was done, how it was done, what was learned and the implications of the findings. After these very short presentations authors stand by their posters to discuss their work with other conference participants. The posters will, of course, have been placed in position earlier.

### Guidelines for poster presentations

A poster may consist of a large piece of card of a specified size on which the text and illustrations may be pasted. It might also consist of a specified number of smaller cards/sheets to fit an allocated space. If you have an option to prepare your work on smaller pieces of card or paper it is advisable to take it up. They are far easier to carry to the conference than big cardboard sheets or cardboard tubes. These larger items can be particularly problematic for overseas conferences involving air travel.

Posters present an exciting academic challenge by asking you to express quite complex ideas in a simple form. Yet you must attempt to avoid trivialization. It is particularly important to keep in mind the level of expertise of your audience. The audience too will govern the style – cartoons may go down well in some informal conferences but may be less acceptable in the very formal conference room.

*Content*  This depends on the topic of your poster, but it may be appropriate to refer to some of the following: 'Problem', 'Previous situation', 'Aims', 'Results', 'Evaluation', 'Gains and losses', or other suitable headings. Begin with a title in large print. The title should be short, to the point and attract attention. Emphasize practical aspects which may be more generally applicable elsewhere. It is usually best to start from the general principle and illustrate with local detail rather than vice versa. In most cases, detailed accounts of the methodology are inappropriate. Also try to include some critical assessment and evaluation of the research. Poster presentations generally create fewer opportunities for interaction with an audience than do oral presentations, although where you are asked to be present to answer questions such opportunities to get feedback do exist. A poster therefore represents a chance to display more 'finished' work than an oral presentation. Remember to include your name, department and institution so that delegates know where they may obtain further information. It can be useful to record the poster title, your name and contact address on a set of small slips of paper fixed to a bottom corner of the poster. A treasury tag and drawing pin are useful for this. These slips may be particularly useful in sessions where you do not have an opportunity to stand by your poster. However, not all poster session organizers will permit a contact slip to be displayed.

*Text*  All material should be clearly legible at 1.5m and therefore much of the printed text will need to be enlarged above 12 point, the usual size in which much word-processed text is prepared. Avoid large sections of continuous text. Bullet points are an effective way of breaking up text into its key elements. Similarly, using different print sizes and styles can help. A mix of upper and lower case lettering is generally clearer than using only capitals.

*Illustrations*  Appropriate illustrations are not only useful to replace text but also provide a visual focus which breaks up what might otherwise be large written sections. Consider the possible use of photographs, diagrams, graphs, press cuttings, cartoons or maps. Colour can make a poster visually attractive, particularly where it is used to differentiate types/levels of material and provide links between similar types/levels of material. Graphic content tends to be high compared with traditional academic papers, but be careful not to overdo the graphics. Once you know you are going to prepare a poster, look out for striking visual material relevant to your topic (press cuttings, colour pictures, etc.). Many software packages provide professional standard output of charts and diagrams.

*Layout* The material should be clearly structured and links between different parts of the poster should be highlighted. Arrows and/or numbered boxes may be helpful so that readers are guided through the poster. Remember that it is not necessary to fill all the space.

These points are intended only to provide a guide, and should not stop you experimenting with novel ways of presenting your ideas. Above all, consider whether the methods of presentation make the material more interesting and help to communicate the points more clearly. Show a draft of your poster to other research students and your supervisor and ask them for a critical assessment.

In preparing the final material for display it may be useful to consult technical staff in your university or department who may be able to advise you on practical issues for preparing display boards, fixing laser printed sheets to a card base and similar matters.

### The poster session

As indicated above, conference organizers may require you to be available to discuss your poster at a particular time. You may be asked to bring your poster to a particular room 20 minutes before the poster session begins and be told that drawing pins and other fixing materials will be provided. Alert research students take their own fixing materials as organizers do not always live up to their promises.

Finally, do not forget to reclaim your poster. Your department may be happy to display it to illustrate the work undertaken by their research students. Alternatively it might adorn a research student common room or display space in a research student study area. Displayed in this way, it is likely that it will gain a further audience and elicit more questions and comments which can be of use in furthering your research project.

### CONCLUSION

Conferences are a very effective way of letting others know about your work and your research interests, and in getting your ideas discussed, both formally and informally. Enjoy the experience. Not only do you get to travel to different places, but you get to meet a wide range of people.

Many funding agencies will fund at least one conference outside the country of the university in which a research student is registered. The importance of the conference circuit for networking cannot be over-emphasized. Looking ahead, you may of course start making contacts and building a reputation which will help you into your first job if you wish to continue working in academia.

## ACKNOWLEDGEMENTS

The authors are indebted to Mick Healey who provided the original material upon which our guidelines for poster presentation are based.

# 30 GETTING PUBLISHED

## H. Doug Watts and Paul White

The publication of results is an important part of research activity and in this chapter we explore the processes involved in the publication of research. The chapter is in two parts. The first emphasizes the need to think through publication strategies very early on in a research project. The second part focuses specifically on publishing refereed papers in international journals. This latter form of output is the most highly regarded in the English-speaking world at the present time. New research students are sometimes surprised to learn that researchers receive no payment for papers published in these prestigious journals. A full discussion of publication in book form will be found in Smedley *et al.* (1993) while the issues surrounding publication in journals are reviewed in Thyer (1994).

Academic staff applying for research funding are always asked, as part of the application, to identify how the results of their research will be published. For example, the Economic and Social Research Council (ESRC) specifically requires consideration of 'the dissemination of findings to potential users and non-academic audiences, as well as to other research workers' (extract from ESRC research grant application form). Typical output from a three-year research project is shown in Box 30.1. This project involved a full-time, post-doctoral research assistant working under the guidance of two principal investigators, each of whom committed half a day a week to the project. Clearly, this project is somewhat larger than a typical PhD but the published outputs show how established researchers communicate their results through publication.

---

**Box 30.1  Publications from a three-year research project**

**New technologies, skills shortages and training strategies**

(ESRC grant: W105251010)

*Refereed Journals*

Foley, P.D., Watts, H.D. and Wilson, B. (1992) Local perspectives on new process technology and employment, *New Technology, Work and Employment*, 7, 125–135

---

Foley, P.D., Watts, H.D. and Wilson, B. (1992) Introducing new process technology: implications for local employment policies, *Geoforum*, 23, 61–72

Foley, P.D., Watts, H.D. and Wilson, B. (1993) External control, new process technology and training, *Regional Studies*, 27, 596–600

Foley, P.D. and Watts, H.D. (1994) Skills shortages and training a forgotten dimension in new technology, *R & D Management*, 24, 99–109

Foley, P.D. and Watts, H.D. (1996) Production site R & D in a mature industrial region, *Tijdschrift Voor Economische en Sociale Geographie*, 87, 136–145

Foley, P.D. and Watts, H.D. (1996) New process technology and the regeneration of the manufacturing sector of an urban economy, *Urban Studies*, 33, 445–457

Watts, H.D. and Foley, P.D. (1996) Organisations, recruitment and the local labour market: the case of the Sheffield metal sectors, *GeoJournal*, 40, 263–271

### Professional Journals

Foley, P.D and Watts, H.D (1990) New technologies, skills shortages and corporate training strategies, *Skills Bulletin*, 44, 20–21

Foley, P.D. and Watts, H.D. (1992) Skills shortages and training: a forgotten dimension in new technology adoption, *Employment Department Skills and Enterprise Briefing*, 10, February

### Book Chapters

Foley, P.D., Watts, H.D. and Wilson, B. (1993) New technologies, skills shortages and training strategies. In Swann, P. (ed.), *New Technology and the Firm*, London, Routledge, 131–152

### National Media

Staffing and training hampers technology, *Financial Times* (29 October 1991); Balancing skill of man and machine, *The Times* (29 October 1991); Engineers hit by skills shortage, *Daily Telegraph* (4 November 1991)

### Local Newspaper Reports

Firms coming unstuck on recruitment, *Sheffield Telegraph* (1 November 1991); High tech investors discover pitfalls, *Sheffield Star* (30 October 1991); High tech firms 'ignore' skills need, *Yorkshire Post* (30 October 1991)

## PUBLICATION STRATEGIES

In considering preparation for publication we need to discuss a number of general issues relating to the philosophy behind the publication of research results and the reasons why it is important to consider possible publishing strategies at an early stage in research design. These issues may be grouped under a number of headings: Why think about publishing at an early stage? Why should I publish at all? Where should I publish? What should I publish? How should I go about it? Although it is possible to identify a number of general guidelines in seeking to publish research, it is important to recognize that different strategies will be appropriate to different research projects. One key way of establishing what is most appropriate in your field is to think carefully about the sources of published information that you make use of in designing and carrying out your research. Reflecting on those will give an insight into publishing norms in your field.

## WHY THINK ABOUT PUBLISHING AT AN EARLY STAGE?

A strategy for the dissemination of research findings should normally be considered at a very early stage in a research project. Early consideration of a publishing strategy can influence the way in which you go about undertaking your research and how you decide to structure your thesis. We shall explore this issue further below. An early realization of the importance of disseminating your research findings will mean that you keep this in mind throughout the research process – looking out for suitable outlets, breaking your writing up into sections that might be suitable for publication, etc. Talk to your supervisor right from the start as to what s/he thinks might be the publication outcomes of your work.

## WHY PUBLISH AT ALL?

'My thesis will be deposited in a university library and will be available for consultation and borrowing from there. Why should I rewrite it to be published elsewhere?' Sad though it may seem, even the best thesis normally only gets borrowed on a limited number of occasions. Many of those borrowings probably result from someone having read another published work derived from the thesis. Reasons why research students should publish their work include:

- Because part of a responsible ethics of research should be to disseminate findings. Research should not be carried out solely for the personal satisfaction of the researcher: instead it is part of the responsibility of researchers to open up their conclusions to a wider community. Research adds to the store of human knowledge and understanding, shapes new ways of thinking and can have implications for the way people do things in the future. Without the dissemination of research findings none of those benefits can occur.
- Because through publication of your ideas and conclusions you may have the chance to influence policymakers. Those making decisions in the field that you have been researching often do not have the time to

reflect on their actions and the contexts in which they are taken. The researcher may have had the possibility to give these issues greater consideration. Particularly where policymakers have helped in your research, you owe it to them to tell them what you have found. In so doing you may be able to contribute to policy shifts in the future.

- Because publishing is a way to start building up a reputation as a person who has something useful to say in your field. It helps you to become known to a wider range of people.
- Because the vast majority of people find the successful publication of their ideas and conclusions carries with it a great deal of self-fulfilment.

However, although publishing is a way of starting to build up your reputation it does not guarantee you a job. If, when you finish your time as a registered research student you wish to get a job as a research officer or to work in a research and/or teaching position in higher education (such as a university lecturer), most employers will be more impressed by the person who has completed their PhD and got one or two good quality publications, than by the person with a longer list of publications but an incomplete thesis. The ideal is obviously to bring publishing within your research process, rather than diverting your attention to publishing as your first priority.

## WHERE SHOULD I PUBLISH?

The diversity of possible methods of publishing is immense and growing every year. University funding is partly dependent on the quality of research output and quality is partly measured according to perceptions of the publication forms it takes. This is, of course, highly subjective and there are some variations between different disciplines in the perception of the 'quality' of different outlets or types of outlets. Box 30.2 indicates the classification of publishing types used by the funding authorities at the time of the 1996 Research Assessment Exercise in UK higher education.

---

### Box 30.2 CVCP classification of publications

The CVCP classification of publications was used to group the publishing activities and publications of university staff members.

1  Books authored (singly or jointly)
2  Edited books
3  Books (short works)
4  Published conference contributions that have been refereed before publication

5   Other published conference contributions
6   Departmental working papers
7   Contributions to edited works
8   Journal editorships
9   Newsletter editorships
10  Letters to journals
11  Papers in academic journals
12  Papers in professional journals
13  Papers in popular journals
14  Official reports
15  Review articles in academic publications
16  Reviews of single academic books
17  Other research publications
18  Other research-equivalent publications
19  Output of research in other media
20  Output of research-equivalent materials in other media

You will see that there are many problems inherent in the use of this classification. In particular, it is often difficult for the reader to know whether the proceedings from a conference have been refereed or not (categories 4 and 5). The divisions between academic, professional and popular journals (categories 11, 12 and 13) are not always clear-cut. Categories 17 to 20 are rather unhelpful catch-alls.

In terms of publication outlets likely to be used by research students, a more helpful consideration of publishing possibilities might be as follows:

1   *Relatively popular monthly or quarterly journals* aimed generally at practitioners within your field. Such journals normally have relatively light refereeing by the editor or an editorial team. Examples include *Education* or *The Planner*. Accepted articles generally appear relatively quickly (within six months, often sooner).

2   *Academic journals*: the focus is firmly placed on these in the second part of this chapter. Articles submitted to such journals normally go through a stringent refereeing process and the time lag between manuscript submission and publication of the final article may be protracted – often well over one year.

    (It was noted above that the refereed academic journal article is normally held to be the 'highest' form of publishing in the social sciences in the English-speaking world. However, academic cultures vary from place to place and between disciplines. In the humanities the publication of a single-authored book is normally seen as most prestigious. In countries not of the English-speaking world, anonymous refereeing of articles submitted to important journals is not the norm. Papers are usually reviewed by an editorial board from whom the identity of the author is not hidden.)

3   *Conference paper*, given by a research student, where an invitation later comes from the conference organizer (or some other individual) to revise the contribution for publication in the conference proceedings or in an edited book based on a number of papers from the conference.

4   *Contributed book chapter* that has been commissioned by an editor.

5   *Monograph* in a series. Many academic departments and some learned societies have such series. A number of local or national government departments also produce them, as do various research institutes. The constraints on the length of material are often less than in the academic journal article (type 2 above).

6   *'Thesis-as-book'*: this consists of a revision of the whole (or a large part) of the thesis and its publication by a commercial publisher. It is rarer in the social sciences than in the humanities. There are a number of 'vanity publishers' who will undertake such publication, but there are also reputable firms involved.

7   *Newspaper articles* as an outlet for publishing material.

8   *Radio or television* as outlets. (Both items 7 and 8 in this list can be used as means of contacting possible research subjects: such uses are not considered further here, where the emphasis is on the dissemination of ideas and findings.)

9   *Electronic publishing* by making material available via the Internet or in some other electronic form. It should be noted that an increasing number of academic journals (type 2 above) appear in electronic form as well as in printed versions to go on library shelves. There are also certain electronic journals that are only available on the Internet and some of these involve refereeing processes. Other Internet materials involve no editorial controls.

The likelihood of a research student getting involved in each of these types of outlet varies markedly: for example, you are unlikely to be invited to contribute a chapter to an edited book until you have become known to the editor in some other way (for example, through a conference presentation). The likely first publishing outlets for most research students will be from categories 1, 2, 3 or 5.

In considering where you should aim to publish your work you should consider the following three major issues:

- speed;
- audience;
- degree of control.

### Speed

If it is important for you to get your ideas published quickly (for example, because you want to stimulate some feedback) you should consider the outlets that will allow that to happen, such as the popular or professional journal.

## Audience

Here you should consider both the number of those who will learn of your work and the characteristics of that audience. If you want to appeal to an academic audience you might consider outlets 2 to 6 above. However, you should also note the outcome of your own consideration of the outlets you have picked up on in your bibliography. If you want to appeal to practitioners you might consider trying to get your material into outlets 1 or 7. If you want to put your material before the general public you might consider trying outlets 7 and 8. Electronic publishing (type 9) is changing rapidly, and there is as yet insufficient knowledge of the market that it really commands.

You will generally want the widest possible audience of a given type for your work, but so do other researchers. Different journals and book publishers are normally seen as having a 'pecking order' or a place in a hierarchy. Some journals are more widely read than others.

## Control

Almost all forms of publishing involve commercial considerations. Even the most esoteric journal still has to print articles that will persuade its subscribers to continue paying year by year. The result is that all publishing is controlled by an editor in some form. The editor's controls work both against you and for you:

- *against you* where they prevent you disseminating material because they do not think it is of interest to anyone and thus not a commercial proposition;
- *for you* where the editors use quality control mechanisms (such as refereeing) to improve the quality of what finally appears.

The degrees of control vary markedly according to the type of publication outlet. They are at their greatest with popular media such as national newspapers, television or radio. With any of these you may have very little say in how your material is eventually used.

In choosing publication outlets there is a balance to be struck between speed, audience and control. You should discuss with your supervisor the relative merits of different outlets for your own work, given the objectives you have for publication. The ideal publishing strategy for a good thesis might involve a range of different publication types, to spread your findings as widely and as effectively as possible. You saw the outcome of such a strategy in Box 30.1, at the start of this chapter.

## WHAT SHOULD I PUBLISH?

Writing a thesis is an exercise in developing knowledge, but it also involves showing that you know how to go about acquiring that knowledge. Therefore a thesis is usually provided with an extensive scholarly apparatus to demonstrate that you have gone about things in a thoughtful, consistent and rigorous way. It will contain a lot of material designed to cover various eventualities and to show that you thought of alternative strategies, and considered potential criticisms. Methods used may be gone into in very great detail. In almost all cases, therefore, you cannot simply submit a chapter from your thesis as a prospective journal article. Even the thesis-as-book requires the thesis to be rewritten (researchers in the humanities often allow about two years for this process).

Apart from the problems of purpose already mentioned, thesis chapters very rarely stand alone. As part of the thesis they are set within an overall context: on their own they lack background and (generally) concluding discussion. The literature review material which a chapter draws on will generally have been developed separately elsewhere in the thesis. So, adjustments to thesis material are always needed before you can submit something for consideration for publication. In particular you need to assess whether all or some of the following need adding:

- statement of general context;
- brief review of relevant literature (only those aspects of the field referred to in the manuscript article/chapter, etc. need inclusion – not the full literature used to back up the whole thesis);
- brief statement on research methods (particularly if the material you wish to publish contains any empirical detail or research evidence);
- discussion relating the material presented to wider issues and concerns.

The adoption of certain thesis structures at the outset can help this process. Consider the following alternative structures for writing up two case studies over three characteristics shown in Figure 30.1.

Method 1 may be very suitable for a thesis, where the comparisons between the two case studies can be discussed at length in a separate, and later, chapter. However, it is less suitable for 'carving up' into papers for publication than Method 2, where the comparisons are contained within the individual chapters. It must be noted, however, that theses based on certain philosophical foundations are harder to divide up in this way than others.

What is often now regarded as the old-fashioned 'aspects of' thesis is much easier to divide into separate journal articles than the more 'realist-orientated' thesis which weaves a seamless web from structural context through mechanisms to event outcomes. Finally, the researcher about to publish the results of her/his work needs to think of the ethics of what is involved.

- If you are going to quote the case histories of individuals you should check with them that they do not mind. Do they want you to 'anonymize' them, or might they still be identifiable? Such considerations

| Method 1 | Chapter X | Case study $\alpha$ | Characteristic 1 |
|----------|-----------|---------------------|------------------|
|          |           |                     | Characteristic 2 |
|          |           |                     | Characteristic 3 |
|          | Chapter Y | Case study $\beta$  | Characteristic 1 |
|          |           |                     | Characteristic 2 |
|          |           |                     | Characteristic 3 |
| Method 2 | Chapter X | Case study $\alpha$ | Characteristic 1 |
|          |           | Case study $\beta$  | Characteristic 1 |
|          | Chapter Y | Case study $\alpha$ | Characteristic 2 |
|          |           | Case study $\beta$  | Characteristic 2 |
|          | Chapter Z | Case study $\alpha$ | Characteristic 3 |
|          |           | Case study $\beta$  | Characteristic 3 |

**FIGURE 30.1   Thesis structure for two case studies over three characteristics**

should occur before you start your collection of evidence, since your ideas on the publication of outcomes may influence what you say to respondents about how their testimony is to be used.

- Do not imagine that just because you are going to publish in a scholarly journal there will be less interest in the actual detail of your respondents.
- Think long and hard before identifying case studies to the media. Take advice from your supervisor or someone else with experience of media activities. Many universities have a press and public relations office: seek guidance from them. In particular, they can help you to frame a press release in the 'safest' manner.

## HOW SHOULD I GO ABOUT IT?

### Discuss your ideas on publication with your supervisor

If you are funded by the ESRC your supervisor must already have considerable publishing experience – otherwise they would not have got the grant with you. Why not suggest ideas for a joint paper (type 1 above, for a popular monthly or quarterly journal) early on in your research process? This could raise issues and present a brief case but with relatively little context and discussion. Joint publication with your supervisor is an excellent way to learn how publishing works through 'hands on' experience. However, you may be concerned that your supervisor might try to 'steal' your ideas and publish them as her/his own work (see also Chapter 28). Many departments and universities are developing policies on joint supervisor/research student publications (see Box 30.3). In recent Research Assessment Exercises carried out on all higher education departments, staff are allowed to include one item published by one of their research students as evidence of that staff member's involvement in research. Your supervisor does not need to have her/his name on your publication for it to 'count' for them.

### Box 30.3 Policy on joint supervisor/research student publications

The following is an extract from the final section of an agreed departmental policy on staff and postgraduate joint publications. Earlier sections dealt with postgraduate perspectives, academic staff perspectives, and with departmental perspectives, outlining benefits and problems in each case.

### Guidelines

In an issue such as this a few central points should be borne in mind:

1   Postgraduates have a right to expect their supervisor(s) to be sensitive to their longer term career aspirations even after the end of the studentship. They have a right to argue what they feel is *their* intellectual property and not to have it co-opted by a member of staff simply because that member of staff is the supervisor of the thesis.
2   Staff, particularly but not exclusively junior staff, have longer term career needs and they have a right to expect that if they put in major efforts (to define a project, secure funding, guide and/or assist in the execution of a thesis project) that these efforts should be recognized.
3   In an environment concerned with scholarship it is always to be hoped that such matters can be resolved by discussion and agreement rather than rules while recognizing the 'needs' of the institution (in this case the department) which makes all this possible.

The following guidelines may be helpful in such discussions:

1   In considering when, how and where to disseminate the results of the research, consideration must be given to points 1 and 2 above.
2   Where the supervisor's input is negligible or restricted to minor editorial comments, the postgraduate should be the sole author.
3   Where the supervisor makes a significant contribution to the paper, e.g. via intellectual input (either before or during the execution of the project) or extensive editing of the content, the publication should normally be jointly authored.
4   Where students gain the benefit of being part of a recognized research project, they can expect to name those academics involved in the project as authors on at least some of their work. Equally a student contributing significantly to a group project can be expected to be named on at least some of the work.
5   If a postgraduate does not publish from the research the supervisor may approach the former student regarding publication of a jointly authored paper largely written by the supervisor.
6   The order of authorship should depend on the intellectual contribution but where the paper is based largely or exclusively on work carried out by the postgraduate, the normal practice should be for the student to be the first named.

### Conference paper

Contribute a paper to a conference in your field and then revise it for publication in the light of comments received on it (see Chapter 29 on conference presentation).

### Oral examination

When you get to the oral examination on your thesis, ask your examiners if they have any advice to offer on where, and in what form, sections of your thesis might be published.

## PUBLISHING REFEREED PAPERS

We now examine in more detail the process of getting published in a refereed journal. In everyday terms we might talk of publishing an 'article' in a 'magazine', but in the academic world we talk of publishing *papers* in *journals*. We are considering a paper of 3–10,000 words in length, the norm for such journals. Guides relevant to specific disciplines are available, for example, for sociology (Coakley, 1994), and management (Day, 1997).

The process of publishing refereed papers involves a number of stages after you have identified a topic which you think is worthy of publication. You select the journal to which you wish to submit your paper and prepare the manuscript. The paper is then sent to the journal's editor who passes it to referees. The referees send back reports and, in the light of these reports, the editor makes a decision on your paper. There are various decisions which can be made ranging from acceptance of the paper as submitted to complete rejection. These various decisions are discussed fully later in the chapter. When the paper is finally in a form acceptable to the editor it moves into the publication stage and you may be asked to correct proofs. Increasingly journals require the final version of the paper on disk and do not expect the author to check the proofs. Do not expect rapid publication of your research. The delay between submission and the editor's decision can be lengthy (well over six months in some cases) and the delay between acceptance and publication, as has already been noted, can be even longer (exceptionally up to two years and often over a year).

## SELECTING A JOURNAL

It is helpful to select the journal for which you are writing before writing begins. As part of this process do consult your supervisors and others with experience of publishing in your research area. A useful starting point is to build up a list of potential outlets (journals) for your work from those you have identified and consulted as part of your research activity. Not all of these will necessarily be refereed journals. Increasingly journals indicate the refereeing process that they follow in their current issues. If you are unsure either ask your supervisors or contact the journal editor. For many journals this information may be available on the journal's web pages. Although international refereed journals are ranked highly as a publication outlet, some journals within the group are seen within individual disciplines as being the most prestigious. Again you should consult your supervisors and you may find that your department or discipline has a list identifying the top-ranked refereed journals in your field. Identifying the relative reputations of refereed journals can sometimes lead to lively and acrimonious debates among academics.

From your list of potential outlets for your work you will need to consider several issues in deciding upon the publication to which you wish to submit your paper. One key factor is a journal's aims. These are often specified on the cover or in preliminary or final material in each issue. It is worth noting that covers are often removed by librarians in the binding process: therefore always consult the current unbound issues on the library shelves. If your library does not subscribe to the journal, inter-library loan services will, if requested, lend you an original copy of one issue of a journal. Some journals will also send you specimen copies. As you gain experience in research activities and widen your reading you will get a 'feel' for the kind of material published in each journal. For example, some journals publish mainly empirical work, others theoretical, yet others are typified by highly mathematical or statistical approaches and others by qualitative work.

In practical terms it is worth seeking advice on a journal's reputation. Always submit to a high quality journal first if you and your supervisor think there is a chance of acceptance. If you get a rejection, the referees' comments will help you refine your arguments for submission to a second journal. As indicated earlier in this chapter, you should also consider speed of publication. Some journals report the average turnaround time on their papers, others record date of first submission and submission of the revised version which (if compared with publication date) give an insight into publication delays. If this information is not available your supervisor may be able to indicate those journals with reputations for rapid or slow publication.

Acceptance and rejection rates are worth some attention and are sometimes reported in the journals themselves. For example of 89 papers submitted to the geographical journal *Area* (a journal containing shorter topical articles of scholarly interest to geographers) over a 14-month period to the end of December 1998, 29 (33 per cent) had been accepted, 34 (38 per cent) were with authors for amendments and only 13 (15 per cent) had been rejected. The remaining papers were mainly still with referees. If it is assumed that most of the papers under revision are published we get an overall acceptance rate of about 70 per cent. In contrast, rejection rates as high as 70 per cent have been reported by leading journals in the field of management. Clearly, there are marked variations between journals and disciplines.

Finally, be wary of invitations to ask you to submit a paper to a particular journal. You may find that after your name has appeared in a set of conference abstracts you will be approached by the editor of a journal to submit your work. This will look like a personal letter (the word processor is a flexible friend) and you will feel flattered. You will usually discover that the letter has been sent to all conference delegates. Add the journal to your list of 'possibles' and review its potential as an outlet in the context of the points made above.

### Preparing a manuscript

All doctoral theses and some masters theses will have a number of potential papers within them. You should discuss possibilities with your supervisor and at the same time discover their views on the attribution of authorship. You could use the guidelines shown in Box 30.3 as a basis for discussion. Where several people are named as authors some supervisors will prefer alphabetical order, while others will insist that the principal author appears first in the list. Defining the principal author is not unproblematic. Is it the person who collected the data or the person who wrote the paper in its final form? An alphabetical listing avoids problems of author order although those with family names at the end of the alphabet can feel they never get full recognition for their contributions.

You will recall that in the first part of this chapter we emphasized that you must not simply select a chapter from your thesis and send it off. It is important that the paper can stand alone as a report on a specific part of your research. A chapter may be used as a basis for a paper but it will take time to build the material into something suitable for submission to a journal. We do not explore details of paper structure here. This can vary markedly according to philosophical approach and from discipline to discipline. Your best course of action is to model your paper on those appearing in recent issues of the journal to which it is to be submitted. One general point worth noting is that care needs to be taken in selecting material for citation, especially in the introductory sections of the paper. It may be possible to add some references to papers in the journal to which you are to submit your paper in order to flag the links between your work and the journal. Your reference list may be used by an editor to select a referee (editors will tend to deny this). It may be unwise to cite authorities who take a very different view or use very different methodologies, although failure to recognize key contributions may cause problems. Once the broad outline of the paper is complete it may be worth considering some of the issues below.

In selecting your material for publication and the journal pay particular attention to the length of paper required by the journal. A 6,000-word paper submitted to a journal with a normal word limit of 3,000 is a waste of your time and that of the journal editors. Such word limits are to be found in the notes on journal aims and publication processes referred to earlier in this chapter. These Notes for Contributors also give guidelines on the layout of the manuscript and referencing systems, and the methods for presenting tables and diagrams. You should follow these to the letter. This can be a time-consuming business, especially adjusting the punctuation and capitalization conventions which seem to vary markedly from journal to journal. With a word processor you can usually present a manuscript which looks very like a published paper, although many journals will require double or one-and-a-half line spacing to leave room for copy editors' marks at a later stage. Do not forget to number the pages. This makes the referees' job much easier as reference can be made readily to particular pages and paragraphs.

The title should reflect the contents and more importantly it should include at least some key terminology to ensure it is picked up in computer-based literature searches. However, a jargon-laden title is unhelpful. It is all a question of balance. Some journals can require you to provide a list of up to five key words. Again care needs to be taken in selecting these key words. Most journals also require an abstract of a specified length. This should communicate your key findings through a series of *substantive* statements (e.g. 'The paper shows that the elderly are significantly more likely to experience difficulty with hearing'). Avoid *procedural* statements (e.g. 'The paper examines the relationship between old age and hearing ability'). Like the title, an abstract should include key terms which will help computer-based literature searches to pick up your paper.

## SUBMISSION

This is perhaps the most straightforward and unproblematic stage of getting published. The number of copies required is usually specified in the Notes for Contributors. Most journals require three copies. Two copies are for referees and one is held by the editor for reference purposes. Do check the latest issue of the journal to ensure you have the correct name and address for the Editor. Keep the accompanying letter short: 'I enclose X copies of a paper which may be of interest to readers of your journal.' If it is a jointly authored paper it is worth making clear on the front of the manuscript (and in the letter) the name of the author to whom all correspondence should be sent. You should receive an acknowledgement of your submission within one month. If you do not receive an acknowledgement within this time you should send a follow-up letter to ensure that your material has been received.

If you are in a hurry to get your work published you may be tempted to send almost identical papers to different journals at the same time. This is not an acceptable practice and you must only submit a paper to one journal at a time. A number of journals will require you to confirm that the paper has not been sent elsewhere at the time of submission. Submitting the same paper to a variety of journals does have a major disadvantage. There is no chance to improve the paper in the light of referees' comments. If a paper is submitted to journal A and rejected it can be improved by taking on board the referees' comments before submitting to journal B.

## REFEREES

Quality in refereed journals is maintained by a system of peer review through which experts in the field are asked to provide their views on a paper to help an editor to decide whether or not it should be published. Peer review is used widely in academia both for reviewing applications for research grants and publications but it is not without its critics. It is criticized for encouraging research in fashionable areas and holding back innovative or unusual ideas which do not fit within the dominant paradigm of the time. Despite these criticisms it at least ensures papers are accepted or rejected on the basis of the views of more than one person. On receiving your paper the editor will send it out to referees. Some editors may read the paper to see whether it fits within the journal's aims. If the paper does not, it can be returned almost immediately but if you have followed the guidelines above you are very unlikely to meet this response. Referees are selected by the editor and some journals publish lists of referees consulted over the past year. There is usually a minimum of two referees but some journals use three in the hope that, if there is a difference of opinion among the referees, at least two will agree with each other. Some journals use 'blind' refereeing where the name of the author(s) is not known to the referee. In some cases you may even be required to omit self-citations from the list of references in an attempt to ensure anonymity. Others send the papers with the author(s) name(s), recognizing that for most referees it is not difficult to identify the author of a paper. The referees will be those whom the editor thinks have a knowledge of your field of interest and, as noted above, an editor may use a list of references as an aide-memoire of those knowledgeable in the field. If you acknowledge someone for commenting on a draft of the paper it is unlikely they will be used as a referee.

Referees are often asked to respond within a given time span (say, one month) but many do not do so. Just as authors do not receive payment for publication in international refereed journals, referees are not paid for their refereeing duties. You ought to receive a decision within six months. It is probably worth chasing up your paper after that time. Some delays are genuine; a referee may be ill or out of the country.

Editors ask referees to give an opinion as to whether a paper is suitable for publication in their journal. The referees provide a report and recommendations regarding publication. They are often given a check list of questions to which they should respond. In some cases referees provide a confidential report for the editor and a second report to be returned to the authors. In other instances the editor simply summarizes the referees' reports in communicating a decision on a paper. Some typical questions for a referee would include those listed below.

1   Is the subject matter suitable for publication in this journal?
2   Is there enough original material in the paper (new results, theories) to warrant its publication?
3   Are there any obvious faults in empirical basis, or theoretical reasoning?
4   Are interpretations and conclusions sound?
5   Are there any demonstrable errors in mathematics, calculations, units, etc.?
6   Are the terminology, nomenclature and units correct?
7   Is the order of presentation logical (allowing reasonable latitude for individual preferences)?
8   Are there any parts which should be expanded or condensed, and if so which?
9   Does the paper read well and is it clearly presented?
10  Does the title of this paper sufficiently/clearly reflect its contents?
11  Is the abstract adequate?
12  Are the figures and tables satisfactory and correctly labelled?
13  Are the figures and tables all necessary and acceptable?
14  Are the references appropriate and free from obvious omissions?

Until you submit a paper of your own it is unlikely that you will see referees' reports on particular papers. They can vary dramatically in detail and content. Some referees can be harsh and critical, others critical but broadly supportive. Most writers would agree that a paper published after amendments suggested by referees have been made is virtually always a better paper. Referees may tend to be particularly helpful to someone whom they think is just starting out on a research career. The flavour of referees' reports is provided by Boxes 30.4 and 30.5. The two reports relate to a short 3,000-word paper in the field of human geography. Inevitably the authors of these reports are anonymous.

---

**Box 30.4   Referee 1**

1   This is a well-written paper which attempts to draw some interesting contrasts between the decision-making characteristics of branch plant openings and closures. The strongest parts of the paper are the contextual sections at the beginning (pp.1–5) and the conclusions.

2   The results section entitled 'comparative perspectives', however, needs I feel some more work. At present it contrasts just two studies. The author rightly states some caveats about comparing the results of these two studies, but nevertheless goes on to suggest some significant differences. Without more evidence some of these contrasts may be misleading, while others would be strengthened by the inclusion of more supporting evidence. There are other studies of start-ups using a similar method-ology which could be used (e.g. DTI 1973). Although there are few com-parable studies of closures, some suggestions of the relative importance of different factors are available (e.g. Fothergill and Guy 1990; Watts 1991).

3   Two critical factors which affect any comparison made are the phrasing of the question asking about the factors influencing the decisions and the way the results are presented. This information is missing from the paper. In the case of Heron (1981, Appendix 1) the question was 'which of the following factors (i)–(xiv) played a major part, a minor part or no part at all in determining your choice of location?' The table in the paper combines the major and minor factors. The DTI (1973, 573) study asked a similar question, but the findings about the major and minor factors are presented separately. If the major factors only are examined the per-centages mentioning particular factors are markedly lower than in the Heron study and there are fewer breaks.

4   Without knowing the question used in the study of closures and whether any of the findings have been aggregated the reader cannot assess the comparisons. For example, on p.8 it is suggested that good accessibility to other corporate activities is far more important in the start-up than in the shut-down decision (40% compared with 25%). Yet if the DTI study is used the contrast is less clear (32% compared with 25%). Similarly the importance of site and property factors is much lower in the DTI study than in the Heron study (20% v 42%; 28% v 34% respectively). An advantage of comparing findings with the DTI study is that it covers all areas of the UK not just Assisted Areas as in the Heron study. Further discussion of the methodology of asking businessmen questions and interpreting the answers obtained is available in Healey (1991).

5   There are also spatial variations in the importance of factors which ought to be mentioned. For example, Fothergill and Guy (1990) show that property related factors influencing closures are more significant in the South of the country than in the North.

6   On p.5 it is suggested that two out of nine factors (limited room for expansion and high site values) are 'area' rather than 'site' factors yet the factor 'proximity of main plant' is considered a site factor. The distinctions seem unclear. None of the factors are truly attributes of the area, such as is the case with factors like labour availability and regional incentives.

7   Overall this is an interesting paper which could be markedly improved by taking account of the above points. By widening the comparisons, some of the contrasts may be less clear, but others can be strengthened. I suggest that the author is strongly encouraged to revise the paper. It is the kind of paper which ought to be published in XXXXX.

## Box 30.5   Referee 2

This is a worthwhile piece of work which would be well suited to XXXXX, without modification. The basic idea of the paper is clear, fresh and simple. The author makes clear what the limitations of the approach are, as applied in this particular case, and in my opinion they do not invalidate it.

The interpretations are reasonable, with one slight proviso. Could the author say how many plant closures his data relate to? (I should know how many openings Heron analysed, but don't). With 27 firms interviewed by the author, it could be that the percentage figures being compared are from smallish samples. With $n$ circa 30 in each sample, one standard error would be as much as $+/- 9\%$, so that the difference of 15 percentage points referred to on page 8 (40% versus 25%) could lie well within the realms of sampling variation. I imagine that the author will rapidly be able to assure the reader that all is well on that score by letting us know what $n$ is.

The conclusion is a little cumbersome. Could it say what it has to say more plainly?

It is on the basis of reports such as these that an editor makes a decision. The second report is succinct and to the point. Apart from one technical question the referee sees the paper as acceptable. The first referee is more critical but outlines ways in which the argument can be strengthened. Additional references are provided and the author is asked to think more carefully about the comparative data that have been used. There does not appear to be full agreement between the two referees. Referee 1 sees the conclusion as one of the strongest parts of the paper while referee 2 sees the conclusion as cumbersome.

## THE EDITOR'S DECISION

An editor may make a variety of decisions, as summarized below.

1   The paper be accepted for publication in its present form.
2   The paper be accepted for publication subject to minor amendments.
3   The paper be returned for revision and then resubmitted for publication.
4   The author be advised to withdraw the present paper and resubmit instead a much shorter paper, note or letter.
5   The author should be advised to seek publication elsewhere.
6   The paper should be rejected without qualification.

Acceptance with no changes at all is quite rare. Even in the best of papers there are often minor points which need clarification. Certainly well-written and high quality papers will come in categories 1 or 2 in the above list. If minor revisions are required, the author(s) should undertake them as rapidly as possible and get the final version back to the editor without delay.

Category 3 is a very common outcome and might be a reasonable expectation for a research student submitting a first paper to an international refereed journal. Resubmission sometimes necessitates further consideration by one or more of the referees; in other cases the editor may take the decision. The course of action to be taken will probably be made clear to you in the letter from the editor. The referees' criticisms may seem unfair (in some cases, they can make you very cross indeed), but do remember you are very close to your own work and may not be the best judge of its quality. The referees' comments can provide a useful critical appraisal of your work and they are often very helpful.

On receiving an editor's decision along the lines of category 2 or 3, along with the referees' reports, the author(s) should revise the paper in the light of what has been asked of them. At a recent meeting of editors organized by the British Academy of Management it was argued that many papers remain unpublished because authors do not bother to revise their work and resubmit. It would be very unwise to place yourself in this category. No matter how hurtful and unfair the comments seem on first reading, most points can usually be addressed with some careful thought, further analysis and a more rigorous development of the arguments. In some cases referees may be wrong, so you do not have to accept all their points. If you do think they are wrong, it is worth checking with your supervisors or other experts in the field. As you gain experience you will be able to judge for yourself whether or not to accept all the comments. Sometimes referees will have contrasting views and you will have to judge between them. Some referees' reports require authors to expand on certain points without indicating where cuts can be made to ensure the paper remains within the length requirements of the journal. Good editors may offer advice on these points.

When the paper is resubmitted it should be accompanied by a report telling the editor how you have responded to each comment. Such a report might begin as shown in Box 30.6.

---

### Box 30.6   Resubmission

*Referee 1*

*Table 1*. A line was inadvertently omitted from the table and this has been corrected

p10. Some extra text outlining the opposing point of view has been inserted

---

Rejection is, of course, the most disappointing outcome. It is even more of a disappointment if it is your first refereed paper. Your reaction will be one of shock and horror and a desire to hide the paper deep in your filing cabinet. The best reaction is that recommended by a leading academic with a record publication list: revise immediately and resubmit to another journal. A useful set of referees' comments from the journal which has rejected the paper will allow you to strengthen and develop your arguments in the new version. It may be necessary to modify the introduction and conclusion to fit the kinds of issues addressed by the new journal. It may be possible to add some references to papers in the new journal to flag the links between your work and material already published there. Redesign of the presentation to meet the requirements of the new journal is essential. You may spend more time revising the bibliographic conventions than in adjusting the substantive material. The aim should be to resubmit within one month, and remember that some very well-regarded papers were rejected by the initial 'quality' journals to which they were sent.

## PROOFS

As noted earlier, some publishers work direct from disk and do not require you to read proofs of your paper. However, proofs are still used by a number of publishers. Amendments to proofs are often required by return of post or within a week so it is important that if you are going to be away at any point you should advise the editor regarding arrangements for proof-reading. Prior to receiving proofs you may get queries from a copy editor. These might draw attention to inconsistencies in style, omitted references or references appearing in the reference list but not appearing in the text.

On receiving the proofs the author(s) should read them very carefully for errors. This is not a time to revise your paper. Follow standard proof-reading procedures; the journal may provide you with a list of symbols which are accepted in the publishing industry. Publishers rightly expect changes to be minimal and proofs should be returned within the deadlines set by the publisher.

## CONCLUSION

The publication of your research results marks the end of a research project. Indeed, such are the delays in the publication process that you may have moved forward to a new topic by the time your work appears in print. The overall time from start to finish may well be in the region of five or six years from your initial registration for a higher degree. We know of cases where the final paper from a thesis has appeared some ten years after initial registration, even though the thesis was submitted within four years of the initial registration. Inevitably publications from your thesis become intermingled with new research projects which you will have developed since submitting your thesis. It is vitally important to be thinking about new avenues you wish to explore while you are writing. A wish list of potential future projects is important to anyone completing their thesis. You must move on. You are now a trained researcher and exciting projects lie ahead. Good luck.

# REFERENCES

## CHAPTER 1

Bunge, M. (1991) 'A critical examination of the new sociology of science', Part 1, *Philosophy of the Social Sciences*, 21: 524–560.

Bunge, M. (1992) 'A critical examination of the new sociology of science', Part 2, *Philosophy of the Social Sciences*, 22: 46–76.

Chalmers, A.F. (1982) *What Is This Thing Called Science?*, 2nd edn. Milton Keynes: Open University Press.

Collins, H.M. (1985) *Changing Order: Replication and Induction in Scientific Practice.* London: Sage.

Collins, H.M. (1994) 'Yes, science is a social construct', *The Times Higher*, 30 September: 17–18.

Dawkins, R. (1994) 'The Moon is *not* a Calabash', *The Times Higher*, 30 September: 17–18.

Feyerabend, P. (1975) *Against Method.* London: New Left Books.

Friman, P.C., Allen, K.D., Kerwin, M.L.E. and R. Larzelere (1993) 'Changes in modern psychology: a citation analysis of the Kuhnian displacement thesis', *American Psychologist*, 48: 658–664.

Gholsen, B. and Barker, P. (1985) 'Kuhn, Lakatos and Laudan: applications in the history of physics and psychology', *American Psychologist*, 40: 755–769.

Grünbaum, A. (1979) 'Is Freudian psychoanalytic theory pseudo-scientific by Karl Popper's criterion of demaracation?', *American Philosophical Quarterly*, 16: 131–141.

Hacking, I. (ed.) (1981) *Scientific Revolutions.* Oxford: Oxford University Press.

Kuhn, T. (1962) *The Structure of Scientific Revolutions.* Chicago: University of Chicago Press.

Kuhn, T. (1970) *The Structure of Scientific Revolutions*, 2nd edn (with postscript). Chicago: University of Chicago Press.

Lakatos, I. (1970) 'Falsification and the methodology of scientific research programme', in I. Lakatos and A. Musgrave (eds), *Criticism and the Growth of Knowledge.* Cambridge: Cambridge University Press.

Lambie, J. (1991) 'The misuse of Kuhn in psychology', *The Psychologist*, 4 (1): 6–11.

Laudan, L. (1977) *Progress and it's Problems.* Berkeley: University of California Press.

Losee, J. (1980) *A Historical Introduction to the Philosophy of Science*, 2nd edn. Oxford: Oxford University Press.

Magee, B. (1982) *Popper*, 2nd edn. Glasgow: Fontana.

Masterman, M. (1970) 'The Nature of a Paradigm', in I. Lakatos and A. Musgrave (eds), *Criticism and the Growth of Knowledge.* Cambridge: Cambridge University Press. pp. 59–89.

Medawar, P. (1967) *The Art of the Soluble.* London: Methuen.

Medawar, P. (1969) *Induction and Intuition in Scientific Thought.* London: Methuen.

Pearson, K. (1892) *The Grammar of Science.* London: Methuen.

Peterson, G.L. (1981) 'Historical self-understanding in the social sciences: the use of Thomas Kuhn in psychology', *Journal Theory of Social Behaviour*, 11: 1–30.

Popper, K. (1945) *The Open Society and Its Enemies*. London: Routledge.

Popper, K. (1959) *The Logic of Scientific Discovery*. London: Hutchinson.

Popper, K. (1963) *Conjectures and Refutations*. London: Routledge and Kegan Paul.

Popper, K. (1976) *Unended Quest*. Oxford: Oxford University Press.

Popper, K. (1979) *Objective Knowledge: An Evolutionary Approach*, 2nd edn. Oxford: Oxford University Press.

Popper, K. (1986) Target article and commentaries, *The Behavioral and Brain Sciences*, 9 (2): 100–120.

Rowell, J.A. (1983) 'Equilibration: developing the hard core of the Piagetian research program', *Human Development*, 26: 61–71.

Watkins, J.W.N. (1970) 'Again "Normal Science"', in I. Lakatos and A. Musgrave (eds), *Criticism and the Growth of Knowledge*. Cambridge: Cambridge University Press. pp. 25–37.

## CHAPTER 2

Gadamer, H. (1974) *Truth and Method*. New York: Seabury Press.

Geertz, C. (1973) *The Interpretation of Cultures*. New York: Basic Books.

Giddens, A. (1984) *The Constitution of Society*. Cambridge: Polity Press.

Giddens, A. (1990) *The Consequences of Modernity*. Cambridge: Polity Press.

Heritage, J. (1984) *Garfinkel and Ethnomethodology*. Cambridge: Polity Press.

Habermas, J. (1990) 'Reconstructiotion and interpretation in the social sciences', in J. Habermas (ed.), *Moral Consciousness and Communicative Action*. Cambridge: Polity Press.

Ricoeur, P. (1981) *Hermeneutics and the Human Sciences*. Cambridge: Polity Press.

Said, E. (1993) *Culture and Imperialism*. London: Chatto and Windus.

Searle, J. (1969) *Speech Acts*. Cambridge: Cambridge University Press.

Soper, K. (1995) *What is Nature?* Oxford: Blackwell.

Taylor, C. (1985) 'Interpretation and the sciences of man', *Philosophical Papers*, vol. 2. Cambridge: Cambridge University Press.

Thompson, E.P. (1977) *Whigs and Hunters*. Harmondsworth: Penguin.

Wittgenstein, L. (1958) *Philosophical Investigations*. Oxford: Blackwell.

## CHAPTER 3

Abbott, A. and Wallace, C. (1990) *An Introduction to Sociology: Feminist Perspectives*. London: Routledge.

Barrett, M. (1987) 'The concept of "difference"', *Feminist Review*, 26: 29–41.

Becker, H. (1986) *Writing for Social Scientists: How to Start and Finish your Thesis, Book or Article*. Chicago: University of Chicago Press.

Bowles, G. and Klein, R. (eds) (1983) *Theories of Women's Studies*. London: Routledge and Kegan Paul.

Brah, A. and Minhas, R. (1985) 'Structural racism or cultural difference: schooling for Asian girls', in G. Weiner (ed.), *Just a Bunch of Girls: Feminist Approaches to Schooling*. Milton Keynes: Open University Press.

Carby, H. (1987) 'Black feminism and the boundaries of sisterhood', in M. Arnot and G. Weiner (eds), *Gender and the Politics of Schooling*. London: Unwin Hyman.

Collins, P.H. (1990) *Black Feminist Thought: Knowledge, Consciousness, and the Politics of Empowerment*. Boston: Unwin Hyman.

Currie, D. and Kazi, H. (1987) 'Academic feminism and the process of deradicalism: re-examining the "issues"', *Feminist Review*, 25: 77–98.

Denzin, N.K. (1997) *Interpretive Ethnography*. London: Sage.

Eichler, M. (1988) *Nonsexist Research Methods: A Practical Guide*. London: Allen and Unwin.

Feldberg, R.L. and Glenn, E.N. (1979) 'Male and female: job versus gender models in the sociology of work', *Social Problems*, 26 (5): 524–538.

Finch, J. (1984) '"It's great to have someone to talk to": the ethics and politics of interviewing women', in C. Bell and H. Roberts (eds), *Social Researching*. London: Routledge and Kegan Paul.

Finch, J. and Groves, D. (1982) *A Labour of Love: Women, Work and Caring*. London: Routledge and Kegan Paul.

Fine, M. (1994) 'Dis-stance and other stances: negotiations of power inside feminist research', in A. Gitlin (ed.), *Power and Method*. London: Routledge.

Grant, J. (1993) *Fundamental Feminism: Contesting the Core Concepts of Feminist Theory*. London: Routledge.

Habermas, J. (1972) *Knowledge and Human Interests*. London: Heinemann.

Hall, D. and Hall, I. (1996) *Practical Social Research: Project Work in the Community*. Basingstoke: Macmillan.

Haggis, J. (1990) 'The feminist research process – defining a topic', in L. Stanley (ed.), *Feminist Praxis*. London: Routledge.

Hammersley, M. (1992) 'On feminist methodology', *Sociology*, 26 (2): 187–206.

Haraway, D. (1988) 'Situated knowledges: the science question in feminism and the privilege of partial perspective', *Feminist Studies*, 14 (3): 575–597.

Harding, S. (1986) *The Science Question in Feminism*. Ithaca: New York Cornell University Press.

Harding, S. (ed.) (1987) *Feminism and Methodology*. Milton Keynes: Open University Press.

Hartsock, N.C.M. (1987) 'The feminist standpoint: developing the ground for a specifically feminist historical materialism', in S. Harding (ed.), *Feminism and Methodology*. Milton Keynes: Open University Press.

Kelly, L., Regan, L. and Burton, S. (1995) 'Defending the indefensible? Quantitative methods and feminist research', in J. Holland and M. Blair with S. Sheldon (eds), *Debates and Issues in Feminist Research and Pedagogy*. Clevedon: Multilingual Matters in association with Open University Press.

Kramarae, C. and Spender, S. (1993) *The Knowledge Explosion*. New York: Harvester Wheatsheaf.

Kuhn, T. (1970) *The Structure of Scientific Revolutions*. Chicago: University of Chicago Press.

Lather, P. (1991) *Getting Smart*. New York: Routledge.

Lather, P. (1994) 'Fertile obsession: validity after poststructuralism', in A. Gitlin (ed.), *Power and Method*. London: Routledge.

Layland, J. (1990) 'On the conflicts of doing feminist research into masculinity', in L. Stanley (ed.), *Feminist Praxis*. London: Routledge.

Lennon, K. and Whitford, M. (eds) (1994) *Knowing the Difference: Feminist Perspectives in Epistemology*. London: Routledge.

Lorber, J. (1975) 'Women and medical sociology: invisible professional and ubiquitous patients', in M.M. Millman and R.M. Kanter (eds), *Another Voice: Feminist Perspectives on Social Life and Social Science*. Garden City, NY: Anchor.

Lyotard, J.F. (1984) *The Postmodern Condition: A Report on Knowledge*. Manchester: Manchester University Press.

Maynard, M. (1994) 'Methods, practice and epistemology: the debate about feminism and research', in M. Maynard and J. Purvis (eds), *Researching Women's Lives from a Feminist Perspective*. London: Taylor and Francis.

Mies, M. (1983) 'Towards a methodology of feminist research', in G. Bowles and R.G. Klein (eds), *Theories of Women's Studies*. London: Routledge and Kegan Paul.

Millman, M. and Kanter, R.M. (1987) 'Introduction to another voice: feminist perspectives on social life and social science', in S. Harding (ed.), *Feminism and Methodology*. Milton Keynes: Open University Press.

Oakley, A. (1974) *The Sociology of Housework*. London: Martin Robinson.

Oakley, A. (1981) 'Interviewing women: a contradiction in terms', in H. Roberts (ed.), *Doing Feminist Research*. London: Routledge and Kegan Paul.

Olesen, V. (1994) 'Feminisms and models of qualitative research', in N.K. Denzin and Y.S. Lincoln (eds), *Handbook of Qualitative Research*. Thousand Oaks, CA: Sage.

Reinharz, S. (1983) 'Experiential analysis: a contribution to feminist research', in G. Bowles and R.G. Klein (eds), *Theories of Women's Studies*. London: Routledge and Kegan Paul.

Reinharz, S. (1992) *Feminist Methods in Social Research*. Oxford: Oxford University Press.

Ribbens, J. and Edwards, R. (1998) *Feminist Dilemmas in Qualitative Research*. London: Sage.

Robinson, L. (1989) 'What culture should be', *The Nation*, September: 319–321.

Smith, D.E. (1987) 'Women's perspective as a radical critique of sociology', in S. Harding (ed.), *Feminism and Methodology*. Milton Keynes: Open University Press.

Stacey, M. (1981) 'The division of labour revisited or overcoming the two Adams: the special problem of people work', in P. Abrams, R. Deem, J. Finch and P. Rock (eds), *Practice and Progress: British Sociology 1950–1980*. London: George Allen and Unwin.

Stacey, J. and Thorne, B. (1985) 'The missing feminist revolution in sociology', *Social Problems*, 32 (4): 301.

Stanley, L. (1990) '"A referral was made": behind the scenes during the creation of a social services department "elderly" statistic', in L. Stanley (ed.), *Feminist Praxis*. London: Routledge.

Stanley, L. (1993) 'The impact of feminism on sociology in the last 20 years', in C. Kramarae and S. Spender, *The Knowledge Explosion*. New York: Harvester Wheatsheaf.

Stanley, L. (1994) 'The knowing because experiencing subject: narratives, lives and autobiography', in K. Lennon and M. Whitford (eds), *Knowing the Difference: Feminist Perspectives in Epistemology*. London: Routledge.

Stanley, L. (1997) *Knowing Feminisms*. London: Sage.

Stanley, L. and Wise, S. (1990) 'Method, methodology and epistemology in feminist research processes', in L. Stanley (ed.), *Feminist Praxis*. London: Routledge.

Stanley, L. and Wise, S. (1993) *Breaking Out Again*. London: Routledge.

Trinh, T. M-ha (1991) *When the Moon Waxes Red: Representation, Gender and Cultural Politics*. New York: Routledge.

Webb, S. (1990) 'Counter-arguments: an ethnographic look at "women and class"', in L. Stanley (ed.), *Feminist Praxis*. London: Routledge.

Webb, S. (1991) 'Shop-work: an ethnography of a large department store'. Unpublished PhD thesis, University of Manchester.


**CHAPTER 4**


Anthias, F. and Yuval-Davis, N. (1993) *Racialized Boundaries*. London: Routledge.

Back, L. (1996) *New Ethnicities and Urban Culture*. London: UCL Press.

Blaut, J.M. (1992) 'The theory of cultural racism', *Antipode*, 24: 289–299.

Bourne, J. and Sivanandan, A. (1980) 'Cheerleaders and ombudsmen: the sociology of race relations', *Race and Class*, 21: 331–352.

Dyer, R. (1988) 'White', *Screen*, 29: 44–64.

Frankenberg, R. (1993) *White Woman, Race Matters: The Social Construction of Whiteness*. London: Routledge.

Gilroy, P. (1987) *There Ain't No Black in the Union Jack: The Cultural Politics of Race and Nation*. London: Hutchinson.

Gould, S.J. (1981) *The Mismeasure of Man*. New York: Norton.

Green, M. and Carter, B. (1988) '"Races" and "race-makers": the politics of racialization', *Sage Race Relations Abstracts*, 13: 4–30.

Hall, C. (1992) *White, Male and Middle Class: Essays in Feminism and History*. Cambridge: Cambridge University Press.

Hall, S. (1978) 'Racism and reaction', in Commission for Racial Equality, *Five Views of Multi-Racial Britain*. London: Commission for Racial Equality.

Hall, S. (1981) 'Teaching race', in A. James and R. Jeffcoate (eds), *The School in the Multicultural Society: A Reader*. London: Harper and Row.

Hall, S. (1992) 'New ethnicities', in J. Donald and A. Rattansi (eds), *'Race', Culture and Difference*. London: Sage.

Hartsock, N. (1987) 'Rethinking modernism: minority vs. majority theories', *Cultural Critique*, 7: 187–206.

Hernstein, R.J. and Murray, C. (1994) *The Bell Curve*. New York: Free Press.

hooks, b. (1990) *Yearning: Race, Gender, and Cultural Politics*. Toronto: Between the Lines Press.

Jackson, P. (ed.) (1987) *Race and Racism*. London: Allen and Unwin.

Jackson, P. (1992) *Maps of Meaning*. London: Routledge.

Jackson, P. and Penrose, J. (eds) (1993) *Constructions of Race, Place and Nation*. London: UCL Press.

Jeater, D. (1992) 'Roast beef and reggae music: the passing of whiteness', *New Formations*, 18: 107–121.

Lorimer, D.A. (1979) *Colour, Class and the Victorians: English attitudes to the Negro in the Mid-nineteenth Century*. Leicester: Leicester University Press.

McClintock, A. (1995) *Imperial Leather: Race, Gender and Sexuality in the Colonial Contest*. London: Routledge.

Miles, R. (1982) *Racism and Migrant Labour*. London: Routledge and Kegan Paul.

Miles, R. (1989) *Racism*. London: Routledge.

Miles, R. (1993) *Racism After 'Race Relations'*. London: Routledge.

Modood, T. (1988) '"Black", racial equality and Asian identity', *New Community*, 14: 397–404.

Morrison, T. (1992) *Playing in the Dark: Whiteness and the Literary Imagination.* London: Picador.

Sivanandan, A. (1983) 'Challenging racism: strategies for the '80s', *Race and Class,* 25: 1–11.

Solomos, J. (1993) *Race and Racism in Contemporary Britain.* London: Macmillan.


**CHAPTER 5**


Beauchamp, T. and Childress, J. (1994) *Principles of Biomedical Ethics,* 4th edn. Oxford: Oxford University Press.

Beecher, H. (1966) 'Ethics and clinical research', *New England Journal of Medicine,* 274: 1354–1360.


**CHAPTER 6**


Coser, L.A. and Rosenberg, B. (1967) *Sociological Theory: A Book of Readings,* 2nd edn. London: Collier-Macmillan.

Hobbs, D. (1989) *Doing the Business.* Buckingham: Open University Press.

Hullin, R. (1985) 'The Leeds truancy project', *Justice of the Peace,* 488–491.

Lock, S. (1993) 'Research misconduct: a resume of recent events', in S. Lock and F. Wells (eds), *Fraud and Misconduct in Medical Research.* London: British Medical Association, pp. 5–24.

Milgram, S. (1965) 'Some conditions of obedience and disobedience to authority', *Human Relations,* 18: 57–76.

Schacht, R. (1971) *Alienation.* London: George Allen and Unwin.


**CHAPTER 7**


Freedman, J. and Fraser, S. (1966) 'Compliance without pressure: the foot in the door technique', *Journal of Personality and Social Psychology,* 4: 195–202.

Kanouse, D. and Hayes-Roth, B. (1980) 'Cognitive considerations in the design of product warnings', in L. Morris, M. Mazzio and I. Barofsky (eds), *Banbury Report 6: Product Labelling and Health Risks.* Cold Spring Harbor: Cold Spring Harbor Laboratories.

Manne, S., Jacobsen, P. and Redd, W. (1992) 'Assessment of acute pediatric pain: do child self-report, parent ratings and nurse ratings measure the same phenomenon?', *Pain,* 48: 45–52.

Poulton, E., McCubbrey, H. and Munn, T. (1970) 'Ergonomics in journal design', *Applied Ergonomics,* 13: 207–209.

Silverman, W. (1989) 'The myth of informed consent: in daily practice and in clinical trials', *Journal of Medical Ethics,* 15: 6–11.

Snowdon, C., Garcia, J. and Elbourne, D. (1997) 'Making sense of randomization: responses of parents of critically ill babies to random allocation of treatment in a clinical trial', *Social Science and Medicine,* 45: 1337–1355.

Sutherland, H., Lockwood, G., Tritchler, D., Sem, F., Brooks, L. and Till, J. (1991)

'Communicating probabilistic information to cancer patients: is there noise of the line?', *Social Science and Medicine*, 32: 725–731.

Taub, H., Baker, M., Kline, G. and Sturr, J. (1987) 'Comprehension of informed consent information by young-old through old-old volunteers', *Experimental Aging Research*, 13: 173–178.

## CHAPTER 8

Adams, J.N. and Brownsword, R. (1999) *Understanding Law*. London: Sweet and Maxwell.

Beyleveld, D. and Brownsword, R. (1986) *Law as a Moral Judgement*. London: Sweet and Maxwell.

Dworkin, R. (1977) *Taking Rights Seriously*. London: Duckworth.

Gewirth, A. (1978) *Reason and Morality*. Chicago: Chicago University Press.

Hart, H.L.A. (1961) *The Concept of Law*. Oxford: Clarendon Press.

Hettinger, M.E. (1989) 'Justifying intellectual property', *Philosophy and Public Affairs*, 18: 31–52.

Kenny, A.J.P. (1980) *Aquinas*. Oxford: Oxford University Press.

Laslett, P. (ed.) (1964) *John Locke, Two Treaties of Government: A Critical Edition with an Introduction and Apparatus Criticus* Cambridge: Cambridge University Press.

Law Commission (1997) Consultation Paper 150, *Legislating the Criminal Code: Misuse of Trade Secrets*. London: HMSO.

Macpherson, C.B. (1978) *Property: Critical and Mainstream Positions*. Oxford: Blackwell.

Rawls, J. (1973) *A Theory of Justice*. Oxford: Oxford University Press.

Robson, J.M. (1965) *Collected Works of John Stuart Mill*. London: Routledge and Kegan Paul.

## CHAPTER 9

Barnes, J.A. (1967) 'Some ethical problems in modern field work', in D.G. Jongmans and P.C.W. Gutkind (eds), *Anthropologists in the Field*. Assen: Van Gorcum.

Berry, A.J., Capps, T., Cooper, D., Hopper, T. and Lowe, E.A. (1986) 'The ethics of research in a public enterprise', in F. Heller (ed.), *The Uses and Abuses of Social Research*. London: Sage.

Bulmer, M. (ed.) (1982) *Social Research Ethics*. London: Macmillan.

Gallagher, B., Creighton, S. and Gibbons, J. (1995) 'Ethical dilemmas in social research: no easy solutions', *British Journal of Social Work*, 25: 259–311.

Lee, R.M. (1993) *Doing Research on Sensitive Topics*. London: Sage.

Punch, M. (1986) *The Politics and Ethics of Fieldwork*. London: Sage.

Wenger, G.C. (ed.) (1987) *The Research Relationship: Practice and Politics in Social Policy Research*. London: Allen and Unwin.

Wilkins, L.T. (1986) 'Three projects involving prediction', in F. Heller (ed.), *The Uses and Abuses of Social Research*. London: Sage.

## CHAPTER 10

Copyright Designs and Patents Act 1988 (CDPA 1988)

Data Protection Act 1998 (DPA 1998)

Freedom of Information Bill 1999 (Freedom of Information Act 2000 by Summer 2000) (FoI Bill 1999)

Adams, J.N. and Brownsword, R. (1995) *Key Issues in Contract*. London: Butterworths.

Birkinshaw, P. (1990) *Government and Information: The Law Relating to Access, Disclosure, and Regulation*. London: Butterworths.

Birkinshaw, P. (1993) Argyle v. Argyle [1967] Ch 302. [1993] *Public Law* 557.

Carey, P.W. (1998) *Blackstone's Guide to the Data Protection Act 1998*. London: Blackstone Press.

Cornish, W.R. (1999) *Intellectual Property*, 4th edn. London: Sweet and Maxwell.

Dworkin, R. (1990) *A Bill of Rights for Britain*. London: Chatto and Windus.

Holyoak, J. and Torremans, P. (1998) *Intellectual Property Law*, 2nd edn. London: Butterworths.

Law Commission (1997) Consultation Paper 150, *Legislating the Criminal Code: Misuse of Trade Secrets*. London: TSO.

Phillips, J. and Firth, A. (1995) *Introduction to Intellectual Property Law*, 3rd edn. London: Butterworths.

Wadham, O. and Mountfield, H. (1999) *Blackstone's Guide to the Human Rights Act 1998*. London: Blackstone Press.

White Paper (1993) *Open Government*, Cmnd 2290. London: HMSO.

Winfield, S. and Jolowicz, R. (1994) *Winfield and Jolowicz on Tort*, 14th edn. London: Sweet and Maxwell.

Younger Committee (1978) *Younger Committee on Privacy*, Cmnd Paper 7341. London: HMSO.


## CHAPTER 11

Barry, C.A. (1997) 'Information skills for an electronic world: training doctoral research students', *Journal of Information Science*, 23 (3): 225–238.

Bell, J. (1996) *Doing your Research Project*. Buckingham: Open University Press.

Boynton, J., Glanville, J., McDaid, D. and Lefebvre, C. (1998) 'Identifying systematic reviews in MEDLINE: developing an objective approach to search strategy design', *Journal of Information Science*, 24 (3): 137–154.

Cooper, H. (1998) *Synthesizing Research*. London: Sage.

David, M. and Zeitlyn, D. (1996) 'What are they doing? Dilemmas in analyzing bibliographic searching: cultural and technical networks in academic life', *Sociological Research Online*, 1: 4, <http://www.socresonline.org.uk/socresonline/1/4/2.html>

Gash, S. (1989) *Effective Literature Searching for Students*. Aldershot: Gower.

Hodge, R. (1995) 'Monstrous knowledge: doing PhDs in the new humanities', *The Australian Universities' Review*, 38 (2): 33–36.

Johanson, G. (1997) 'Information, knowledge and research', *Journal of Information Science*, 23 (2): 103–109.

Newton, R., Sutton, A. and McConnell, M. (1998) 'Information skills for open learning: a public library initiative', *Library Review*, 47 (2): 1–9.

Orna, E. and Stevens, J. (1995) *Managing Information for Research*. Buckingham: Open University Press.

## CHAPTER 12

Atkinson, M. (1971) 'Societal reactions to suicide', in S. Cohen (ed.), *Images of Deviance*. Harmondsworth: Penguin.

Atkinson, M. (1979) *Discovering Suicide*. London: Macmillan.

Bulmer, M. (1984) *Introduction. In Social Research Methods*. Basingstoke: Macmillan.

Carrithers, M., Collins, S. and Lukes, S. (eds) (1985) *The Category of the Person: Anthropology, Philosophy, History*. Cambridge: Cambridge University Press.

Cicourel, A. (1964) *Method and Measurement in Sociology*. New York: Random House.

Douglas, J. (1967) *The Social Meanings of Suicide*. Princeton, NJ: Princeton University Press.

Douglas, J. (1971) *American Social Order: Social Rules in a Pluralistic Society*. New York: Random House.

Durkheim, E. (1952) *Suicide*. London: Routledge and Kegan Paul.

Durkheim, E. (1982) *The Rules of Sociological Method*. London: Macmillan.

Gelsthorpe, L. (1992). 'Response to Martin Hammersley's paper "On feminist methodology"', *Sociology*, 26 (2): 213–218.

Hammersley, M. (1992) 'On feminist methodology', *Sociology*, 26 (2): 187–206.

Hollis, M. (1977) *Models of Man*. Cambridge: Cambridge University Press.

Mead, G.H. (1934) *Mind, Self and Society*. Chicago: University of Chicago Press.

Meltzer, B.N., Petras, J.W. and Reynolds, L.T. (1975) *Symbolic Interactionism: Genesis, Varieties and Criticism*. London: Routledge and Kegan Paul.

Plummer, K. (1979) 'Misunderstanding labelling perspectives', in D. Downes and P. Rock (eds), *Deviant Interpretations*. London: Martin Robertson.

Rock, P. (1979) *The Making of Symbolic Interactionism*. London: Routledge and Kegan Paul.

Weber, M. (1949) *The Methodology of the Social Sciences*. New York: Stanford University Press.

Whyte, W.F. (1943) *Street Corner Society*. Chicago: University of Chicago Press.

## CHAPTER 13

Asante, M.K. (1995) 'Global perspectives on Afrocentricity'. Speech presented at the African Centred Research Conference, Sheffield University, October 1995, Sheffield.

Bernard, W.T. (1996) Participatory research, in D. Burton (ed.), *Qualitative Methods- Data Collection and Analysis*. University of Sheffield Distance Education Materials, pp. 15–37.

Black Learners Advisory Committee (1994) *Report on Education: Redressing Inequality – Empowering Black Learners*. Halifax: BLAC.

Collins, P.H. (1990) *Black Feminist Thought*. London: Routledge.

ESRC (1989) *Postgraduate Training Guidelines*. Swindon: London.

Freire, P. (1972) *Pedagogy of the Oppressed*. London: Sheed and Ward.

Guba, E. and Lincoln, V. (1981) *Fourth Generation Evaluation*. Newbury Park, CA: Sage.

Hall, B. (1993) 'Introduction', in P. Park, M. Brydon-Miller, B. Hall and T. Jackson (eds), *Voices of Change*. Toronto: Oise Press.

hooks, b. (1984) *Feminist Theory – From Margin to Centre*. Boston, MA: South End Press.

Krueger, R.A. (1988) *Focus Groups: A Practical Guide for Applied Research*. Newbury Park: Sage.

Lather, P. (1991) *Getting Smart: Feminist Research and Pedagogy with/in the Post Modern*. London: Routledge.

Lofland, J. and Lofland, L.H. (1984) *Analysing Social Settings*, 2nd edn. Belmont: Wadsworth.

Maguire, P. (1987) *Doing Participatory Research: A Feminist Approach*. Massachusetts: University of Massachusetts, Center for International Education.

Maguire, P. (1993) 'Challenges, contradictions and celebrations: attempting participatory research as a doctoral student', in P. Park, M. Brydon-Miller, B. Hall and T. Jackson (eds), *Voices of Change*. Toronto: Oise Press, pp. 157–176.

Marshall, C. and Rossman, G.B. (1989) *Designing Qualitative Research*. Newbury Park, CA: Sage.

Morgan, D.H.J. (1989 'Methodological perspective', in P. Park, M. Brydon-Miller, B. Hall and T. Jackson (eds), *Voices of Change*. Toronto: Oise Press, pp. 1–20.

Park, P. (1993) 'What is participatory research? A theoretical and methodological perspective', in P. Park, M. Brydon-Miller, B. Hall and T. Jackson (eds), *Voices of Change*. Toronto: Oise Press, pp. 1–20.

Park, P., Brydon-Miller, M., Hall, B. and Jackson, T. (1993) *Voices of Change*. Toronto: Oise Press.

Ralph, D. (1988) 'Researching from the bottom: lessons participatory research has for feminists', *Canadian Review of Social Policy*, 22: 36–40.

Reason, P. (1988a) 'The co-operative inquiry group', in P. Reason (ed.), *Human Inquiry in Action*. London: Sage, pp. 18–39.

Reason, P. (ed.) (1988b) *Human Inquiry in Action*. London: Sage.

Reason, P. (ed.) (1988c) *Reflections Research as Empowerment*. Toronto: Oxford University Press, pp. 65–77.

Reason, P. (1994) *Participation in Human Inquiry*. London: Sage.

Reason, P. and Rowan, J. (1981) *Human Inquiry: A Sourcebook of New Paradigm Research*. Chichester: Wiley.

Ristock, J. and Pennell, J. (1996) 'Power plays', in J. Ristock and J. Pennell (eds), *Community Research as Empowerment*. Toronto: Oxford University Press, pp. 65–77.

Strass, A.L. and Corbin, J. (1990) *Basics of Qualitative Research*. Newbury Park, CA: Sage.

Whitemore, E. (1994) 'To tell the truth: working with oppressed groups in participatory approaches to inquiry', in P. Reason (ed.), *Participation in Human Inquiry*. London: Sage, pp. 82–98.

**CHAPTER 14**

Basch, C. (1987) 'Focus group interview: an underutilized research technique for improving theory and practice in health education', *Health Education Quarterly*, 14: 411–448.

Buckingham, D. (1987) *Public Secrets. EastEnders and its Audience*. London: British Film Institute.

Catterall, M. and Maclaran, P. (1997) 'Focus group data and qualitative analysis programmes', *Sociological Research Online*, 2 (1): <http://www.socresonline.org.uk>

Faludi, S. (1991) *Backlash*. London: Chatto and Windus.

Frazer, E. (1992) 'Teenage girls reading *Jackie*', in P. Scannell, P. Schlesinger and C. Sparks (eds), *Culture and Power*. London: Sage.

Hermes, J. (1995) *Reading Women's Magazines*. Cambridge: Polity.

Holbrook, B. and Jackson, P. (1996) 'Shopping around: focus group research in north London', *Area*, 28: 136–142.

Jackson, P. and Holbrook, B. (1995) 'Multiple meanings: shopping and the cultural politics of identity', *Environment and Planning*, 27: 1913–1930.

Kitzinger, J. (1994) 'The methodology of focus groups: the importance of interaction between research participants', *Sociology of Health and Illness*, 16 (1): 103–121.

Knodel, J. (1993) 'The design and analysis of focus group studies', in D.L. Morgan (ed.), *Successful Focus Groups*. Newbury Park, CA: Sage.

Lunt, P. and Livingstone, S. (1996) 'Rethinking the focus group in media and communications research', *Journal of Communication*, 46 (20): 79–98.

Merton, R. and Kendall, P. (1955) 'The focused interview', in P. Lazarsfeld and M. Rosenberg (eds), *The Language of Social Research*. New York: Free Press.

Morgan, D.L. (1988) *Focus Groups as Qualitative Research*. Newbury Park, CA: Sage.

Morgan, D.L. (ed.) (1993) *Successful Focus Groups*. Newbury Park, CA: Sage.

Morley, D. (1980) *The Nationwide Audience*. London: British Film Institute.

Radway, J. (1987) *Reading the Romance*. London: Verso.

Schlesinger, P., Dobash, R.E., Dobash, R.P. and Weaver, C.K. (1992) *Women Viewing Violence*. London: British Film Institute.

Stewart, D.W. and Shamdasani, P.N. (1990) *Focus Groups. Theory and Practice*. Newbury Park, CA: Sage.

## CHAPTER 15

Baxter, J. and Eyles, J. (1997) 'Evaluating qualitative research in social geography: establishing "rigour" in interview analysis', *Transactions of the Institute of British Geographers*, 22: 505–525.

Blumer, H. (1966) 'Sociological implications of the thought of George Herbert Mead', *American Journal of Sociology*, 71 (5): 535–544.

Brannen, J. (ed.) (1992) *Mixing Methods: Qualitative and Quantitative Research*. Aldershot: Avebury.

Bryman, A. (1992) 'Quantitative and qualitative research: further reflections on their integration', in J. Brannen (ed.), *Mixing Methods: Qualitative and Quantitative Research*. Aldershot: Avebury, pp. 57–78.

Burgess, R. (1991) *In the Field: An Introduction to Field Research*. London: Routledge.

Cook, I. and Crang, M. (1995) *Doing Ethnographies*. London: Royal Geographical Society with the Institute of British Geographers.

Crang, M. (1997) 'Analyzing qualitative materials', in R. Flowerdew and D. Martin (eds), *Methods in Human Geography*. Harlow: Addison Wesley Longman, pp. 183–196.

Dey, I. (1993) *Qualitative Data Analysis: A User Friendly Guide for Social Scientists*. London: Routledge.

Eyles, J. (1989) 'Qualitative methods', in R. Johnston, D. Gregory and D. Smith (eds), *The Dictionary of Human Geography*. Oxford: Blackwell, pp. 380–382.

Eyles, J. and Smith, D. (1988) *Qualitative Methods in Human Geography*. Cambridge: Polity Press.

Fielding, N. (1993) 'Qualitative interviewing', in N. Gilbert (ed.), *Researching Social Life*. London: Sage, pp. 135–153.

Geertz, C. (1973) *The Interpretation of Cultures*. New York: Basic Books.

Glaser, B. and Strauss, A. (1967) *The Discovery of Grounded Theory: Strategies for Qualitative Research*. Chicago: Aldine .

Hammersley, M. (1992) 'Deconstructing the qualitative–quantitative divide', in J. Brannen (ed.), *Mixing Methods: Qualitative and Quantitative Research*. Aldershot: Avebury, pp. 39–51.

Hammersley, M. (1993) *Social Research: Philosophy, Politics and Practice*. London: Sage.

Löfstedt, R. (1995) 'Why are public perception studies on the environment ignored?', *Global Environmental Change: Human and Policy Dimensions*, 5: 83–85.

McDowell, L. (1991) 'Valid games? A response to Erica Schoenberger', *Professional Geographer*, 44 (2): 212–215.

Macnaghten, P. and Jacobs, M. (1997) 'Public identification with sustainable development: investigating cultural barriers to participation', *Global Environmental Change: Human and Policy Dimensions*, 7: 5–24.

Mitchell, J.C. (1983) 'Case and situation analysis', *The Sociological Review*, 31: 187–211.

Pile, S. (1990) *The Private Farmer: Transformation and Legitimation in Advanced Capitalist Agriculture*. Aldershot: Dartmouth.

Pile, S. (1991) 'Practising interpretative geography', *Transactions of the Institute of British Geographers*, 16: 458–469.

Pile, S. (1993) 'Human agency and human geography revisited: a critique of "new models" of the self', *Transactions of the Institute of British Geographers*, 18: 122–139.

Ryles, G. (1971) *Collected Papers Volume 2: Collected Essays 1929–1968*. London: Hutchinson.

Schoenberger, E. (1991) 'The corporate interview as a research method in economic geography', *Professional Geographer*, 43 (2): 180–189.

Schofield, J. (1993) 'Increasing the generalizability of qualitative research', in M. Hammersley (ed.), *Social Research: Philosophy, Politics and Practice*. London: Sage, pp. 200–225.

Smith, S. (1988) 'Constructing local knowledge: the analysis of self in everyday life', in J. Eyles and D. Smith (eds), *Qualitative Methods in Human Geography*. Cambridge: Polity Press, pp. 17–38.

Strauss, A. (1987) *Qualitative Analysis for Social Scientists*. Cambridge: Cambridge University Press.

Tesch, R. (1990) *Qualitative Research: Analysis Types and Software Tools*. Basingstoke: Science Press.

Valentine, G. (1997) 'Tell me about . . .: using interviews as a research methodology', in R. Flowerdew and D. Martin (eds), *Methods in Human Geography*. Harlow: Addison Wesley Longman, pp. 110–126.

Wallman, S. (1983) *Eight London Households*. London: Tavistock.

## CHAPTER 16

Becker, H.S. (1968) 'Observation: social observation and social case studies', in D.L. Sills (ed.), *International Encyclopaedia of the Social Sciences*, vol. 2. New York: Macmillan.

Burgess, R.G., Pole, C.J., Evans, K. and Priestley, C. (1994) 'Four studies from one or one study from four? Multi-site case study research', in A. Bryman and R.G. Burgess (eds), *Analyzing Qualitative Data*. London: Routledge.

Burgess, R.G. (1988) 'Conversations with a purpose: the ethnographic interview in educational research', in R.G. Burgess (ed.), *Studies in Qualitative Methodology*, vol. 1. London: JAI Press.

Burgess, R.G. (1991) 'Sponsors, gatekeepers, members, and friends', in W.B. Shaffir and R.A. Stebbins (eds), *Experiencing Fieldwork: An Inside View of Qualitative Research*. London: Sage.

Crompton, R. and Jones, G. (1988) 'Researching white collar organisations: why sociologists should not stop doing case studies', in A. Bryman (ed.), *Doing Research in Organizations*. London: Routledge.

Gurney, J.N. (1988) 'Female researchers in male-dominated settings', in W.B. Shaffir and R.A. Stebbins (eds), *Experiencing Fieldwork: An Inside View of Qualitative Research*. London: Sage.

Hakim, C. (1992) *Research Design*. London: Routledge.

Lijphart, A. (1971) 'Comparative politics and the comparative method', *American Political Science Review*, 65: 682–693.

Mitchell, J.C. (1983) 'Case and situational analysis', *Sociological Review*, 31 (2): 187–211.

Platt, J. (1988) 'What can case studies do?', in R.G. Burgess (ed.), *Studies in Qualitative Methodology*, vol. 1. London: JAI Press.

Ragin, C.C. (1992) 'Introduction: cases of what is a case?', in C.C. Ragin and H.S. Becker (eds), *What is a Case?*. Cambridge: Cambridge University Press.

Runyan, W.M. (1982) *Life Histories and Psychobiography*. Oxford: Oxford University Press.

Shaffir, W.B. (1991) 'Managing a convincing self-presentation', in W.B. Shaffir and R.A. Stebbins (eds), *Experiencing Fieldwork: An Inside View of Qualitative Research*. London: Sage.

Yin, R.K. (1994) *Case Study Research: Design and Methods*, 2nd edn. London: Sage.

## CHAPTER 17

Baxter, J. and Eyles, J. (1997) 'Evaluating qualitative research in social geography: establishing "rigour" in interview analysis', *Transactions of the Institute of British Geographers*, 22: 505–525.

Burgess, R. (1984) *In the Field: An Introduction to Field Research*. London: Routledge.

Cook, I. and Crang, M. (1995) *Doing Ethnographies. Concepts and Techniques in Modern Geography*. Norwich: Environmental Publications.

Crang, M. (1997) 'Analyzing qualitative materials', in R. Flowerdew and D. Martin (eds), *Methods in Human Geography*. Harlow: Addison Wesley Longman, pp. 183–196.

Dey, I. (1993) *Qualitative Data Analysis: A User Friendly Guide for Social Scientists*. London: Routledge.

Fielding, N. and Lee, R. (eds) (1991) *Using Computers in Qualitative Research*. London: Sage.

Gahan, C. and Hannibal, M. (1998) *Doing Qualitative Research using QSR NUD.IST*. London: Sage.

Gilbert, D. (1995) 'Between two cultures: geography, computing and the humanities', *Ecumene*, 2: 1–14.

Glaser, B. (1965) 'The constant comparative methods of qualitative analysis', *Social Problems*, 12: 436–445.

Glaser, B. and Strauss, A. (1967) *The Discovery of Grounded Theory: Strategies for Qualitative Research*. Chicago: Aldine.

Glesne, C. and Peshkin, A. (1992) *Becoming Qualitative Researchers*. New York: Longman.

Kelle, U. (ed.) (1995) *Computer-aided Qualitative Data Analysis: Theory, Methods and Practice*. London: Sage.

MacKenzie, D. and Wajcman, J. (eds) (1985) *The Social Shaping of Technology: How the Refrigerator Got its Hum*. Milton Keynes: Open University Press.

Miles, M. and Huberman, A. (1994) *Qualitative Data Analysis: A Source Book of New Methods*. London: Sage.

Miles, M. and Weitzman, E. (1994) 'Choosing computer programs for qualitative data analysis', in M. Miles and A. Huberman (eds), *Qualitative Data Analysis: A Source Book of New Methods*. London: Sage.

Pfaffenberger, B. (1988) *Microcomputer Applications in Qualitative Research*. London: Sage.

Reid, A. (1992) 'Computer management strategies for textual data', in B. Crabtree and W. Miller (eds), *Doing Qualitative Research*. London: Sage, pp. 125–145.

Richards, L. and Richards, T. (1991) 'The transformation of qualitative method: computational paradigms and research processes', in N. Fielding and R. Lee (eds), *Using Computers in Qualitative Research*. London: Sage, pp. 80–95.

Richards, L. and Richards, T. (1994) 'From filing cabinet to computer', in A. Bryman and R. Burgess (eds), *Analyzing Qualitative Data*. London: Routledge, pp. 146–172.

Richards, L. and Richards, T. (1995) 'Using hierarchical categories in qualitative methods', in U. Kelle (ed.), *Computer-aided Qualitative Data Analysis: Theory, Methods and Practice*. London: Sage, pp. 80–95.

Seidel, J. (1991) 'Methods and madness in the application of computer technology to qualitative data analysis', in N. Fielding and R. Lee (eds), *Using Computers in Qualitative Research*. London: Sage, pp. 107–116.

Strauss, A. (1987) *Qualitative Analysis for Social Scientists*. Cambridge: Cambridge University Press.

Strauss, A. and Corbin, J. (eds) (1990) *Grounded Theory in Practice I*. London: Sage.

Tesch, R. (1990) *Qualitative Research: Analysis and Software Types*. London: Falmer Press.

Weitzman, E. and Miles, M. (1995) *Computer Programs for Qualitative Data Analysis*. London: Sage.

**CHAPTER 18**

Chaney, D. (1994) *The Cultural Turn: Scene-setting Essays on Contemporary Cultural History*. London: Routledge.

Crang, P. (1992) 'The politics of polyphony: reconfigurations in geographical authority', *Environment and Planning D: Society and Space*, 10 (5): 527–549.

Geertz, C. (1973) *The Interpretation of Cultures*. New York: Basic Books.

Holbrook, B. and Jackson, P. (1996) 'Shopping around: focus group research in north London', *Area*, 28 (2): 136–142.

Keith, M. (1992) 'Angry writing: (re)presenting the unethical world of the ethnographer', *Environment and Planning D: Society and Space*, 10 (5): 551–568.

Marcus, G.E. and Fischer, M.M.J. (1986) *Anthropology as Cultural Critique: An Experimental Moment in the Human Sciences*. Chicago: University of Chicago Press.

Miller, D., Jackson, P., Thrift, N., Holbrook, B. and Rowlands, M. (1998) *Shopping, Place and Identity*. London: Routledge.

Okely, J. and Callaway, H. (eds) (1992) *Anthropology and Autobiography*. London: Routledge.

Orwell, G. (1946) 'Why I write', in G. Orwell (1968), *The Collected Essays, Journalism and Letters of George Orwell*. Harmondsworth: Penguin.

Pile, S. and Rose, G. (1992) 'All or nothing: politics and critique in the modernism–postmodernism debate', *Environment and Planning D: Society and Space*, 10 (2): 123–136.

Sayer, A. (1989) 'The "new" regional geography and problems of narrative', *Environment and Planning D: Society and Space*, 7 (3): 253–276.

Simpson, M. (1994) *Male Impersonators: Men Performing Masculinity*. London: Cassell.

Stanley, L. (1992) *The Auto/Biographical I: The Theory and Practice of Feminist Auto/Biography*. Manchester: University of Manchester Press.

Stanley, L. and Wise, S. (1993) *Breaking Out Again: Feminist Ontology and Epistemology*. London: Routledge.

Strauss, A.L. (1987) *Qualitative Analysis for Social Scientists*. Cambridge: Cambridge University Press.

Wolcott, H.F. (1990) *Writing Up Qualitative Research*. London: Sage.

## CHAPTER 19

Baxter, J. and Eyles, J. (1997) 'Evaluating qualitative research in social geography: establishing "rigour" in interview analysis', *Transactions of the Institute of British Geography*, 22: 505–525.

Cook, I. and Crang, M. (1995) *Doing Ethnographies*. London: Royal Geographical Society with the Institute of British Geographers.

Dey, I. (1993) *Qualitative Data Analysis: A User Friendly Guide for Social Scientists*. London: Routledge.

Fielding, N. and Lee, R. (eds) (1991) *Using Computers in Qualitative Research*. London: Sage.

Gahan, C. and Hannibal, M. (1998) *Doing Qualitative Research Using QSR NUD.IST*. London: Sage.

Miles, M. and Huberman, A. (1994) *Qualitative Data Analysis: A Source Book of New Methods*. London: Sage.

Richards, L. and Richards, T. (1991) 'The transformation of qualitative method: computational paradigms and research processes', in N. Fielding and R. Lee (eds), *Using Computers in Qualitative Research*. London: Sage, pp. 80–95.

Richards, L. and Richards, T. (1994) 'From filing cabinet to computer', in A. Bryman and R. Burgess (eds), *Analyzing Qualitative Data*. London: Routledge, pp. 146–172.

Richards, L. and Richards, T. (1995) 'Using hierarchical categories in qualitative methods', in U. Kelle (ed.), *Computer-aided Qualitative Data Analysis: Theories, Methods and Practice*. London: Sage, pp. 80–95.

Seidel, J. (1991) 'Methods and madness in the application of computer technology to qualitative data analysis', in N. Fielding and R. Lee (eds), *Using Computers in Qualitative Research*. London: Sage, pp. 107–116.

Tesch, R. (1990) *Qualitative Research: Analysis and Software Types*. London: Falmer Press.

## CHAPTER 20

Ackroyd, S. and Hughes, J. (1983) *Data Collection in Context*. London: Longman.

Babbie, E. (1989) *The Practice of Social Research*. California: Wadsworth.

Baudrillard, J. (1988) *Selected Writings*. Cambridge: Polity Press.

Bryman, A. (1993) *Quantity and Quality in Social Research*. London: Routledge.

Carley, M. (1981) *Social Measurement and Social Indicators*. London: George Allen and Unwin.

Cohen, L. and Manion, L. (1989) *Research Methods in Education*. London: Routledge.

De Vaus, D.A. (1996) *Surveys in Social Research*. London: UCL Press.

Easterby-Smith, M., Thorpe, R. and Lowe, A. (1995) *Management Research*. London: Sage.

Fielding, N.G. and Fielding, J.L. (1986) *Linking Data*. London: Sage.

Fink, A. (1995) *How to Design Surveys*. London: Sage.

Gephart, R.P. (1988) *Ethnostatistics: Qualitative Foundations for Quantitative Research*. London: Sage.

Hammersley, M. and Gomm, R. (1997) 'Bias in social research', *Sociological Research Online*, 2 (1) <http://www.socresonline.org.uk/socresonline/2/1/2.html>

Hughes, J.A. (1976) *Sociological Analysis: Methods of Discovery*. London: Thomas Nelson.

Lee, R.M. (1995) *Dangerous Fieldwork*. London: Sage.

McCrossan, L. (1991) *A Handbook for Interviewers*. London: HMSO.

May, T. (1993) *Social Research*. Buckingham: Open University Press.

Menard, S. (1991) *Longitudinal Research*. London: Sage.

Moore, P. (1996) 'Crown Street revisited', *Sociological Research Online*, 1 (3) <http://www.socresonline.org.uk/socresonline/1/3/2.html>

Payne, G., Payne, J. and Hyde, M. (1996) '"Refuse of all classes"? Social indicators and social deprivation', *Sociological Research Online*, 1 (1) <http://www.socresonline.org.uk/socresonline/1/1/3.html>

Prandy, K. (1990) 'The revised Cambridge scale of occupations', *Sociology*, 24 (4): 629–655.

Presser, S. (1994) 'Informed consent and confidentiality in survey research', *Public Opinion Quarterly*, 58: 446–459.

Rappert, B. (1997) 'Users and social science research: policy, problems and possibilities', *Sociological Research Online*, 2 (3) <http://www.socresonline.org.uk/socresonline/2/3/10.html>

Rose, D. (1995) Official social classifications in the UK, *Social Research Update*, 9 <http://www.soc.surrey.ac.uk/sru>

Sieber, J.E. (1992) *Planning Ethically Responsible Research*. London: Sage.

Singer, E., Vonthum, D. and Miller, E. (1995) 'Confidentiality assurances and response: a quantitative review of the experimental literature', *Public Opinion Quarterly*, 59: 66–77.

Singer, E., Vonthum, D. and Maher, M.P. (1998) 'Does the payment of incentives create expectation effects?', *Public Opinion Quarterly*, 62: 152–164.

Thomas, R. (1996) 'Statistics as organizational products', *Sociological Research Online*, 1 (3) <http://www.socresonline.org.uk/socresonline/1/3/5.html>

Willimack, D.K., Shuman, H., Pennell, B. and Lepkowski, J.M. (1995) 'Effects of a pre-paid non monetary incentive on response rates and response quality in a face-to-face survey', *Public Opinion Quarterly*, 59: 78–92.

## CHAPTER 21

Bryman, A. and Cramer, D. (1993) *Quantitative Data Analysis for Social Scientists*. London: Routledge.

Coomber, R. (1997) 'Using the Internet for survey research', *Sociological Research Online*, 2 (2) <http://www.socresonline.org.uk/socresonline/2/2/2.html>

De Vaus, D.A. (1996) *Surveys in Social Research*. London: UCL Press.

Elliott, C. and Ellingworth, D. (1997) 'Assessing the representativeness of the 1992 British crime survey: the impact of sampling error and response biases', *Sociological Research Online*, 2 (4) <http://www.socresonline.org.uk/socresonline/2/4/3.html>

Fowler, F.J. (1993) *Survey Research Methods*. London: Sage.

Hammersley, M. and Gomm, R. (1997) 'Bias in social research', *Sociological Research Online*, 2 (1) <http://www.socresonline.org.uk/socresonline/2/1/2.html>

Henry, G.T. (1990) *Practical Sampling*. London: Sage.

Kalton, G. (1983) *Introduction to Survey Sampling*. London: Sage.

Kent, R. (1993) *Marketing Research in Action*. London: Routledge.

Lee, R. (1993) *Doing Research on Sensitive Topics*. London: Sage.

Menard, S. (1991) *Longitudinal Research*. London: Sage.

Punch, M. (1986) *The Politics and Ethics of Fieldwork*. London: Sage.

Schillewaert, N., Langerak, F. and Duhamei, T. (1998) 'Non-probability sampling for WWW surveys: a comparison of methods', *Journal of the Market Research Society*, 40 (1): 307–321.

## CHAPTER 22

Abercrombie, N., Hill, S. and Turner, B.S. (1988) *The Penguin Dictionary of Sociology*. London: Penguin Books.

Ball, M.S. and Smith, G.W.H. (1992) *Analysing Visual Data*. London: Sage.

Bourque, L.S. and Fielder, E.P. (1995) *The Survey Kit-3: How to Conduct Self-administered and Mail Surveys*. London: Sage.

Coomber, R. (1997) 'Using the internet for survey research', *Sociological Research Online*, 2 (2) <http://www.socresonline.org.uk/socresonline/2/2/2.html>

de Leeuw, E. and Nicholls, W. (1996) 'Technological innovations in data collection: acceptance, data quality and costs', *Sociological Research Online*, 1 (4) <http://wwww.socresonline/1/4/leeuw.html>

Fowler, F.J. (1993) *Survey Methods*. London: Sage.

Frey, J.H. (1989) *Survey Research by Telephone*. London: Sage.

Frey, J.H. and Oishi, S.M. (1995) *How to Conduct Interviews by Telephone and in Person*. London: Sage.

Holstein, J.A. and Gubrium, J.F. (1995) *The Active Interview*. London: Sage.

Hunt, J.C. (1989) *Psychoanalytic Aspects of Fieldwork*. London: Sage.

Kleinman, S. and Copp, M.A. (1993) *Emotions and Fieldwork*. London: Sage.

Lavrakas, P.J. (1987) *Telephone Survey Methods*. London: Sage.

McCrossan, L. (1991) *A Handbook for Interviewers*. London: Sage.

McNeill, P. (1989) *Research Methods*. London: Routledge.

Martin, J. and Manners, T. (1995) 'Computer assisted survey interviewing in survey research', in R.M. Lee (ed.), *Information Technology for the Social Scientist*. London: UCL Press.

Schaefer, D.R. and Dillman, D.A. (1998) 'Development of a standard e-mail methodology', *Public Opinion Quarterly*, 62: 378–397.

Selwyn, N. and Robson, K. (1998) 'Using e-mail as a research tool', *Social Research Update*, 21 <http://www.soc.surrey.ac.uk/sru>

Thach, E. (1995) 'Using electronic mail to conduct survey research', *Educational Technology*, March–April: 27–31.

Thomas, R. and Purdon, S. (1995) 'Telephone methods for social surveys', *Social Research Update*, 8 <http://www.soc.surrey.ac.uk/sru>

Warren, C.A.B. (1988) *Gender Issues in Field Research*. London: Sage.

Wright, D.L., Aquilino, W.S. and Supple, A.J. (1998) 'A comparison of computer assisted and pencil-and-paper self-administered questionnaires in a survey on smoking, alcohol, and drug use', *Public Opinion Quarterly*, 62: 331–353.

## CHAPTER 23

Bell, J. (1993) *Doing Your Research Project*. Buckingham: Open University Press.

De Vaus, D.A. (1996) *Surveys in Social Research*. London: UCL Press.

DeVellis, R.F. (1991) *Scale Development*. London: Sage.

Fowler, F.J. (1993) *Survey Methods*. London: Sage.

Hague, P. (1993) *Questionnaire Design*. London: Kogan Page.

Hughes, J.A. (1976) *Sociological Analysis: Methods of Discovery*. London: Thomas Nelson.

Litwin, M.S. (1995) *How to Measure Survey Reliability and Validity*. London: Sage.

## CHAPTER 24

Bijleveld, C.C.J.H. and Van der Kamp, L.T. (1998) *Longitudinal Data Analysis*. London: Sage.

Bulmer, M. (1980) 'Why don't sociologists make more use of official statistics', *Sociology*, 14: 505–523.

Burton, D. (1996) 'Ethnicity and consumer financial behaviour: a case study of

British Asians and the pensions market', *International Journal of Bank Marketing*, 17 (7): 22–31.

Burton, D. (1997) 'Ethnicity and occupational welfare: a study of pension scheme membership in Britain', *Work, Employment and Society*, 11 (3): 505–518.

Czinkota, M.R. and Ronkainen, I.A. (1994) 'Market research for your export operations: Part I – using secondary sources of research', *International Trade Forum*, 3: 20–41.

Dale, A., Arber, S. and Proctor, M. (1988) *Doing Secondary Analysis*. London: Unwin Hyman.

Dex, S. (1991) *Life and Work History Analyses: Qualitative and Quantitative Developments*. London: Routledge.

Elliott, C. and Ellingworth, D. (1997) 'Assessing the representativeness of the 1992 British Crime Survey: the impact of sampling error and response biases', *Sociological Research Online*, 2 (4) <http://www.socresonline.org.uk/socresonline/2/4/3.html>

Elliott, C. and Ellingworth, D. (1998) 'The practical limitations of survey analysis: a brief response to Lynn', *Sociological Research Online*, 3 (2) <http://www.socresonline.org.uk/socresonline/3/2/9.html>

Fowler, F.J. (1993) *Survey Research Methods*. London: Sage.

Hakim, C. (1982) *Research Design*. London: Routledge.

Hakim, C. (1991) 'Cross national comparative research on the European Community: the EC labour force surveys', *Work, Employment and Society*, 5 (1): 101–117.

Hantrais, L. (1996) 'Comparative research methods', *Social Research Update*, 13 <http://www.soc.surrey.ac.uk/sru>

Hyman, H.H. (1972) *Secondary Analysis of Sample Surveys*. New York: Wiley.

Jarman, J., Blackburn, R.M., Brooks, B. and Dermott, E. (1999) 'Gender differences at work: international variations in occupational segregation', *Sociological Research Online*, 4 (1) <http://www.socresonline.org.uk/socresonline/4/1/jarman.html>

Kent, R. (1993) *Marketing Research in Action*. London: Routledge.

Lynn, P. (1998) 'The British Crime Survey sample: a response to Elliot and Ellingworth', *Sociological Research Online*, 3 (1) <http://www.socresonline.org.uk/socresonline/3/1/12.html>

Malhotra, N.K., Agarwal, J. and Peterson, M. (1996) 'Methodological issues in cross-cultural market research: a state of the art review', *International Marketing Review*, 13 (5): 25–45.

May, T. (1993) *Social Research*. Buckingham: Open University Press.

Moore, P. (1996) 'Crown Street revisited', *Sociological Research Online*, 1 (3) <http://www.socresonline.org.uk/socresonline/1/3/2.html>

O'Reilly, J. (1996) 'Theoretical considerations in cross-national employment research', *Sociological Research Online*, 1 (1) <http://www.socresonline.org.uk/socresonline/1/1/2.html>

Platt, J. (1996) 'Has funding made a difference to research methods?', *Sociological Research Online*, 1 (1) <http://www.socresonline.org.uk/socresonline/1/1/5.html>

Proctor, M. (1993) 'Analyzing other researchers' data', in N. Gilbert (ed.), *Researching Social Life*. London: Sage.

Sieber, J.E. (1992) *Planning Ethically Responsible Research*. London: Sage.

Stewart, D.W. (1984) *Secondary Research: Information Sources and Methods*. Beverly Hills, CA: Sage.

Thomas, R. (1996) 'Statistics as organizational products', *Sociological Research Online*, 1 (3) <http://www.socresonline.org.uk/socresonline/1/3/5.html>

Ward, C. and Dale, A. (1995) 'Statistical software packages', in R.M. Lee (ed.), *Information Technology for the Social Scientist*. London: UCL Press.


## CHAPTER 28


Becker, H.S. (1986) *Writing for Social Scientists*. Chicago: University of Chicago Press.

Bruce, C.S. (1994) 'Research students' early experiences of the dissertation literature review', *Studies in Higher Education*, 19 (2): 217–229.

Creme, P. and Lea, M.R. (1997) *Writing at University*. Buckingham: Open University Press.

Cryer, P. (1997) *Research Student's Guide to Success*. Buckinham: Open University Press.

Fischer, M.D. (1995) 'Desktop tools for the social scientist', in R.M. Lee (ed.), *Information Technology for the Social Scientist*. London: UCL Press.

Hockey, J. (1991) 'The social science PhD: a literature review', *Studies in Higher Education*, 16 (3): 319–330.

Lyon, E.S. (1995) 'Dilemmas of power in post-graduate practice: a comment on research training', *Sociology*, 29 (3): 531–540.

Meloy, J.M. (1994) *Writing the Qualitative Dissertation*. Hove: Lawrence Erlbaum.

Nightingale, P. (1991) 'Speaking of student writing', *Journal of Geography in Higher Education*, 15 (1): 3–13.

O'Brien, P.K. (1995) 'The reform of doctoral dissertations in humanities and social studies', *Higher Education Review*, 28 (1): 3–19.

Orna, E. and Stevens, G. (1997) *Managing Information For Research*. Buckingham: Open University Press.

Phillip, E.M. and Pugh, D.S. (1993) *How to Get a PhD*. Buckingham: Open University Press.

Torrance, M., Thomas, G.V. and Robinson, E.J. (1993) 'Training in thesis writing: an evaluation of three conceptual orientations', *British Journal of Educational Psychology*, 63: 170–184.


## CHAPTER 29


Elton, L. (1983) 'Conference: making a good time better?', *British Journal of Education Technology*, 14: 200–215.

Hector-Taylor, M. and Bonsall, M. (1993) 'Painless presentations', in M. Hector-Taylor and M. Bonsall, *Successful Study*. Sheffield: Hallamshire Press, pp. 85–95.

Mathias, H. (1991) 'Presentation and communication skills', in G. Allen and C. Skinner (eds), *Handbook for Research Students in the Social Sciences*. London: Falmer Press, pp. 107–116.

Smith, J. (1989) *The Art of Poster Making*. Gosport: Osmroid International.

Vulakovic, P. (1995) 'Making posters', *Journal of Geography in Higher Education*, 19: 251–256.

**CHAPTER 30**

Coakley, J.C. (1994) 'Producers guide to journal publishing', *Network*, 58: 4–5. (*Network* is the newsletter of the British Sociological Association.)

Day, A. (1997) 'How to publish management research' <http://www.mcb.co.uk/services/articles/literati/htpmr/htpmr.htm>

Smedley, C.S., Allen, M. and Briggs, H. (1993) *Getting Your Book Published*. London: Sage.

Thyer, B.A. (1994) *Successful Publishing in Scholarly Journals*. London: Sage.

# INDEX

Abbott, A., 35
academic community, 79
academic conferences, 437–9
access, 101–2, 189, 219
accountability, 71–3
Adams, J.N., 89
anonymity, 223, 301
anti-racism, 54
applied research, 76
autonomy, 63, 81

Babbie, E., 305
Barnes, J.A., 98
Barrett, M., 36
Barry, C.A., 137–40
Basch, C., 186
Baudrillard, J., 294
Beauchamp, T., 61
Becker, H.S., 33, 216, 423–4, 430, 432,
    434–5
Beecher, H., 66
Bell, J., 149, 346
beneficence, 63
Berry, A.J., 103
Beyleveld, D., 90
bibliographic skills, 138
Birkinshaw, P., 110, 112–3
bivariate statistics, 365
boolean operators, 4–5, 14
Bulmer, M., 105, 156, 347, 350
Bunge, M., 20
Burgess, R., 199–200, 202, 209–10,
    212–13, 217, 219, 227
Brannen, J., 203, 206
British Library, 141
British Psychological Society,
    72
British Sociological Association,
    72
Bruce, C.S., 426
Bryman, A., 203, 298–9, 311

Carey, P.W., 116
Carley, M., 293, 298–9
Carrithers, M., 165
Case, 215–16
case studies, 215–25
Catterall, M., 187
census, 307
Chalmers, A.F., 5
Chaney, D., 246
Chi-square, 392–7
Cicourel, A., 158
class, 7, 169
coding data, 211–12, 217, 226
Cohen, L., 298–9
Collins, H.M., 19–20
Collins, P.H., 43, 185
common sense, 157, 160, 162
communicative action, 28
Computer Assisted Personal
    Interviewing (CAPI), 323, 326–8
Computer Assisted Self-Interviewing
    (CASI), 323, 329–31
concepts, 293–5
conferences, 176, 437–9
confidence, 431–3
confidentiality, 65, 70, 125, 194, 223, 301
consent form, 84
consequentialist theory, 62, 72
content analysis, 333–4
contextual analysis, 221
control, 77
Cook, I., 196, 201, 203, 213
Cooper, H., 143
copyright, 121–4
Coser, L.A., 69
covert methods, 74–5
Cramer's V, 397–9
Crompton, R., 219–20
cross-national research, 349
cross-sectional research design, 296
cross-tabulation, 389–93

Crown Copyright, 78
Cryer, P., 429

Dale, A., 347–8, 350
data protection, 113–14
Data Protection Act 1984, 70; 1998, 114–16
data protection principles, 116–20
David, M., 138
Dawkins, R., 20
deduction, 37
defamation, 127
Denzin, N.K., 33
deontological theory, 62, 72
descriptive statistics, 363–84
De Leeuw, E., 326–7, 329
De Vaus, D.A., 293, 296, 305–6, 319, 340
Dey, I., 227–8, 231, 234–5, 238–40
Dex, S., 349
dissemination, 177
documentary sources, 221
Douglas, J., 161
Durkheim, E., 158–62
Dworkin, R., 91, 110
Dyer, R., 56

Economic and Social Research Council (ESRC), 5, 137, 244, 293, 351, 428, 456
Economic and Social Research Council Data Archive, 340, 352–4
Eichler, M., 38–40
elites, 76–7, 199, 225
Elliot, C., 309–11
e-mail, 329–31
empathy theory, 29
empowerment, 167, 184
end users, 306
environment, 55
epistemology, 36–7
ethical perspectives, 99–100
ethical principles, 51–67
ethics committees, 86
ethics in practice, 97–108, 299, 306
ethnicity, 32, 219, 354–9
ethnocentrism, 47
ethnography, 247
evaluation, 76
experimentation, 73–4, 296
Eyles, J., 197, 202–3, 210, 226–8

falsification, 17–18
Feldberg, R.L., 38
feminism, 33–48
Feyerabend, P., 19
fidelity, 65
Fielding, N., 210, 235, 299
financial constraints, 322
Finch, J., 38, 42
Fine, M., 33
Fink, A., 295
Fischer, M.D., 433
focus groups, 175, 186–95, 199, 247
Fowler, F.J., 319, 335–6, 340, 345, 351
fraud, 66, 70
Frankenberg, R., 57
Freedman, J., 83
freedom of information, 110
Freire, P., 168

Gadamer, H., 28–31
Gahan, C., 234, 254–5
Gallagher, B., 106
Gash, S., 138–9, 141–2
gatekeeping, 100–1, 220
Geertz, C., 26–7, 203, 246
Gelsthorpe, L., 157
gender, 55
generalization, 203, 225
Gewirth, A., 90
Giddens, A., 26–7
Gilbert, D., 237–8
Gilroy, P., 53
grounded theory, 187, 227
group dynamics, 193
group interview, 186
Gurney, J.N., 222

Habermas, J., 28–31, 34
Hacking, I., 5
Hague, P., 336
Hakim, C., 218, 347–8
Hall, B., 184
Hall, D., 35
Hall, S., 53, 55–6
Hammersley, M., 36, 157, 305, 318
Haraway, D., 33
Harding, S., 33, 36–7, 40, 42, 44–6
Hart, H.L.A., 89
Hartstock, N., 55
Harvard system, 149–52

Henry, G.T., 308–9, 312
hermeneutics, 21–32, 34
Hermes, J., 190
Hettinger, M.E., 93
Hobbs, D., 75
Hockey, J., 423
Holbrook, B., 247
Holstein, J.A., 324
Hollis, M., 156
hooks, B., 54
Hughes, J.A., 295, 305, 335
Hunt, J.C., 325
hypotheses, 386

incentives, 301–2
indicators, 293–5
induction, 37
inferential statistics, 203, 385–413
informed consent, 81–7
intellectual property, 121
Internet, 143, 236
interpretation, 21–32, 248
intersubjectivity, 25
interviewing, 130, 174, 217, 222, 323–6
interview schedule, 206–10

Jackson, P., 50, 52, 188
Jeater, D., 57
Johanson, G., 137, 139
jurisprudence, 88
justice, 64

Kanouse, D., 85
Keith, M., 246
Kelle, U., 235
Kelly, L., 43
Kenny, A.J.P., 90
Kent, R., 313–14, 352
key informants, 225
Kitzinger, J., 186–8, 192
Kleinman, S., 325
Kramarae, C., 34
Krueger, R.A., 175
Kuhn, T., 13–17, 19, 34

Lakatos, I., 17–19
Laslett, P., 92
Lather, P., 47, 182–3
Laudan, L., 19

law, 88–96
Law Commission, 94
Lee, R.M., 100, 302, 315
legal positivism, 89–90
Lennon, K., 36
librarians, 139
literature review, 426–7, 433
literature searches, 136, 152
Lock, S., 70
logistic regression, 407–13
Loose, J., 5–6
longitudinal research, 297
Lorimer, D.A., 51
Lunt, P., 187–8, 191
Lyon, E.S., 431
Lyotard, J.F., 34

MacPhearson, C.B., 92
Magee, B., 9
Maguire, P., 167–9, 180
Manne, S., 83
Marcus, G.E., 245
Marshall, C., 177
Martin, J., 326–7
May, T., 306, 350
McClintock, A., 51
McCrossan, L., 295, 300, 324–5
McDowell, L., 204
McNeill, P., 324
Mead, G.H., 162–5
measures of association, 397
Medawar, P., 9
Meloy, J.M., 429–30
Meltzer, B.N., 166
Menard, S., 297
Merton, R., 186
Mies, M., 41
Miles, M., 230, 235
Miles, R., 49–50
Milgram, S., 74
Millmann, M., 37
Mills, J.S., 91
Modood, T., 54
Moore, P., 302, 349
moral principles, 80
moral theory, 61–2
morality, 89–91
moral rights, 124–5
Morgan, D.L, 186–7, 194
Morley, D., 189

multivariate statistics, 363, 404–13
Musgrave, A., 16–17

natural law, 89–90
new ethnicities, 56
Newton, R., 139
Nightingale, P., 431
non-maleficence, 63, 67
normal distribution, 381–3 ·
note-taking, 145–9

Oakley, A., 42, 48
O'Brien, P.K., 430
official statistics, 350, 352
Olesen, V., 35
on-line searching, 142
originality, 137, 215, 314, 344, 429–30
oral history, 199
Orna, E., 140, 148, 435
overseas students, 148, 431

Park, P., 168, 178, 182
participatory research, 167–85
Payne, G., 295
Pearson, K., 8
peer review, 143
persona, 430–1
personal safety, 302–3
Pfanffenberger, B., 230, 236
Phi, 397–9
Phillip, E.M., 423, 434–5
philosophical anthropology, 156–7
philosophy of science, 5–20, 34
Pile, S., 203–4, 209
pilot studies, 222, 305, 343–5
plagiarism, 148
Platt, J., 216, 347
Plumber, K., 162
policy-orientated research, 105–6
Popper, K., 9–13, 17
positivism, 75, 89
posters, 452–4
post-modernism, 31–2, 34, 37, 44–5, 54, 140
Poulton, E., 86
power, 68–80, 168–9
power relations, 204
Prandy, K., 294
presenting, 219, 437–55
Presser, S., 299

privacy, 64–5
probability, 385–6
Proctor, M., 350
proofs, 475
property, 92–5
protection, 131–3
proxy consent, 83
publication, 132, 456–76
Public Records Act 1967, 111
Punch, M., 97, 107

qualitative data analysis, 226–43, 253–87
quantitative data analysis, 361–419
questionnaire design, 335–46
questionnaires, 157, 194, 197, 221
quotations, 224, 249

Race, 47, 49–58, 169, 354–59
racism, 49, 58, 184
race relations, 51
Radway, J., 188
Ragin, C.C., 215
Ralph, D., 168
Rappert, B., 306
Rawals, J., 91, 96
Reason, P., 168–9, 178, 182, 184
referencing, 145–7, 149–52
Reid, A., 232
Reinharz, S., 35–6, 47–8
reliability, 342–3
representativeness, 187, 224
research originators, 354
response rates, 222, 301, 322, 330, 353
revisions, 424–5, 436
Ribbens, J., 33, 36
Ricoeur, P., 27
Richards, L., 228–9, 231, 234–5, 238, 240
risk, 421
Ristock, J., 168
Rules, 64–5
Rock, P., 162
Roise, D., 293–4

Safety, 302–4
Said, E., 32
sampling, 201, 307–19, 353, 355–6
scaling, 338–40
scatter plots, 399–404
Schacht, R., 69

Searle, J., 25
secondary analysis, 347–60
Seidel, J., 231, 235, 240
self-administered questionnaires, 328–9
self-presentation, 219–20
sexism, 39, 47
sexuality, 55
Sayer, A., 246
sensitive issues, 179, 301, 329
Shaffir, W.B., 219
Sieber, J.E., 300
Silverman, W., 82
Singer, E., 301
Sivanandan, A., 51, 55
skills, 1
Smith, D.E., 41, 44
Snowdon, C., 82
Soper, K., 24
sponsorship, 219, 289, 299, 431
Stacey, J., 39
standard deviation, 381–3
standpoint theory, 40–4
Stanley, L., 34, 36, 47, 246, 250
statistical significance, 157
Strass, A.L., 177
Strauss, A., 210, 212, 226–7, 239
Stewart, D.W., 186–8, 190, 105
structuring a thesis, 424–6
supervisors, 138, 173, 421
survey designs, 295–7
surveys, 203, 247–360
Sutherland, H., 82
symbolic culture, 26–8
symbolic interaction, 162–4

tape recording, 193–4, 210, 224, 247
Taub, H., 86

Taylor, C., 22
telephone surveys, 331–3, 359–60
Tesch, R., 211–13, 227, 231, 236–8, 241
themes, 251
thesis, 130, 137–8
Thomas, R., 306, 331–3, 347, 352
Thompson, E.P., 23
Torrance, M., 423
triangulation, 156, 298

univariate statistics, 364

Valentine, G., 196–8
validity, 182–3, 203
variable, 27
veracity, 64
vignettes, 192
vivas, 219, 304
voluntariness, 83

Warren, C.A.B., 325
Webb, S., 38, 40, 47–8
Weber, M., 157
Wenger, G.C., 97, 105
Whitemore, E., 168, 177, 181–2
Whiteness, 56–7
Whyte, W.F., 165
Wilkins, L.T., 100
Wittingenstein, L., 26
writing, 245–52
writing a PhD, 423–36
writing skills, 423
Wolcott, H.F., 244
word processing, 231–2, 433–4

Yin, R.K., 216–8, 225